KITCHEN CREATIVITY

BOOKS BY KAREN PAGE AND ANDREW DORNENBURG

The Vegetarian Flavor Bible

The Food Lover's Guide to Wine

The Flavor Bible

What to Drink with What You Eat

Becoming a Chef

The New American Chef

Chef's Night Out

Dining Out

Culinary Artistry

KITCHEN CREATIVITY

Unlocking Culinary Genius—with Wisdom, Inspiration, and Ideas from the World's Most Creative Chefs

KAREN PAGE

PHOTOGRAPHS BY

ANDREW DORNENBURG

LITTLE, BROWN AND COMPANY
NEW YORK | BOSTON | LONDON

Little, Brown and Company
Hachette Book Group
1290 Avenue of the Americas, New York, NY 10104
littlebrown.com

First Edition: October 2017

Little, Brown and Company is a division of Hachette Book Group, Inc. The Little, Brown name and logo are trademarks of Hachette Book Group, Inc.

Cover design by Lucy Kim
Interior design by Tandem Books

ISBN 978-0-316-26780-9
LCCN 2017906789

10 9 8 7 6 5 4 3 2 1

QUAD

Printed in the United States of America

For the Creative Force in the universe—
which is known by many names,
including consciousness (neuroscience),
the Unified Field (physics), and God (religion). . . .
May everyone who buys and reads this book be blessed with
extraordinary creativity for good.

QUINCE

KITCHEN:
a room in which
food and drink
are prepared and
cooking is done

CREATIVITY:
the ability to
conceive ideas and/
or make things that are
original, meaningful,
and surprising

CONTENTS

> **Food is our common ground, a universal experience.**
>
> —JAMES BEARD

PREFACE
WHY CREATIVITY MATTERS

> Creativity is a central source of meaning in our lives...Most of the things that are interesting, important, and human are the results of creativity.
>
> —MIHALY CSIKSZENTMIHALYI, positive psychologist and bestselling author of *Creativity* and *Flow*

The only thing as fundamental as food to our lives—our pleasure as well as our survival—is creativity. We must eat to live, but our ingenuity in generating solutions is arguably the single most important ability human beings possess.

This is true not only personally but professionally. Creativity was cited by 60 percent of CEOs polled as the single most important leadership quality for success in business, ahead of even integrity (52 percent) and global thinking (35 percent), according to a study cited in *Fast Company*. Only one in four people believes they are living up to their creative potential, according to a 2012 Adobe study.

Beyond being a tool for survival and a source of meaning, the act of creation is a source of meaning that can bring us our greatest joys.

During graduate school, my then-boyfriend, Andrew, was working in the restaurant business—which I made the focus of my independent studies. I was fascinated by restaurants, and especially by professional chefs, whom I saw as unique hybrids of artists, entrepreneurs, and activists. By the late 1980s, I came to recognize the emerging cultural importance of chefs as among the most influential creative professionals of our time. This inspired me to radically change my life path to study chefs and their work in depth. My obsession was so all-encompassing, I even married one.

As I interacted with the world's leading chefs, I saw brilliance. I tasted genius. I sensed mystery. Among the most remarkable gifts of great chefs, I discovered, is exceptional sensory acuity—extraordinary senses of taste and smell, to be sure, but also finely honed senses of touch, sight, and hearing. New Orleans chef Susan Spicer shared:

I've really developed my eyes so that I can look at something three feet away and say "that needs rinsing off" or "that doesn't look fresh to me." I know when someone puts something in a sauté pan and it doesn't make a noise that the pan wasn't hot enough. I listen when someone is chopping an onion and it's going "crunch"—I know without looking that that person needs to sharpen their knife. I listen when I'm making a sauce in a blender, and I know if the sauce has broken by the sound.

But in addition to developing these powers of sensory perception, there seemed to be something more going on—something Andrew and I were at a bit of a loss to describe in our first book. We wrote in *Becoming a Chef* (1995):

An experienced chef's greatness is often evidenced by his or her development of a "sixth sense" when it comes to cooking, and many of the chefs we interviewed alluded to this ability in some regard. Over time, they have developed the ability to cook at a more intuitive level, for lack of a better description.

Besides the five senses and the central sense, Aristotle recognizes other faculties [including imagination] that later came to be grouped together as "inner senses."

—from the book *Ancient Philosophy*, edited by Brian Duignan

We referred to leading chefs' "extrasensory perception," which allowed them to "taste" with their other senses.

Even at that time, it was clear that there were forces at work beyond our full comprehension that resulted in leading chefs' extraordinary talents in the kitchen. Their experiences had honed not only their five *outer* senses. I came to believe the very best to be masters of their *inner* senses—their ability to see without actually seeing, to smell without actually smelling, to taste without actually tasting, and to bring an extraordinary breadth, depth, precision, immediacy, and intensity of perception to their cooking that I hadn't known was possible.

Philosophers, starting with Aristotle, have enumerated and characterized the inner senses differently. However, centuries later, the concept of "inner senses" serves as a metaphor for the interior capabilities that allow us to perceive that which is too subtle to be grasped by the outer senses. Simply put, they suggest direction for our creative attention, energy, and will.

Chefs may be the most perceptive professionals I have encountered. They can learn to harness their inner senses to fuel extraordinary creativity in the kitchen. This book shares the secrets of tapping those "inner senses"—as well as marshalling the power of finely honed "outer senses." This one-two punch can unlock your abilities as a cook to perform kitchen alchemy—turning common ingredients into something precious. Even now, knowing many chefs' secrets, it still strikes me as magical.

> Sense data alone do not produce insight or understanding of any kind. Ideas produce insight and understanding, and the world of ideas lies within us. . . . Inner individual authentic perception . . . is the only source of real knowledge.
>
> —**E.F. SCHUMACHER,** *A Guide for the Perplexed*

Andrew's photographs of chefs and their kitchens, creations, and inspirations are a necessary and most welcome collaboration for this book. Given that the genesis of creativity is preverbal—emerging as emotions, feelings, images, intuitions—sometimes concepts are more readily captured in pictures than in words, and I am awed by his gift for doing so.

This book is meant for you to dip into when seeking wisdom, ideas, and inspiration in the kitchen. It's presented in four primary sections. The first three address a triad of aspects of creativity: First comes **Mastery**, or the acquisition of knowledge and experience; followed by **Alchemy**, or the understanding of flavor synergy; which leads us to **Creativity**, which brings everything together. The **A-to-Z** section of the book can be flipped through whenever you're seeking ideas on a particular aspect of a dish or dessert or drink—or something to spur your next culinary creation.

I hope that this book will provide you with techniques, tools, and resources that you can put to work immediately at your own stove, not to mention wisdom from some of the world's best chefs and other experts that can help you be more creative in the kitchen—and beyond.

> **Learning to think creatively in one discipline opens the door to understanding creative thinking in all disciplines.**
>
> —**ROBERT AND MICHÈLE ROOT-BERNSTEIN,** *Sparks of Genius*

Creativity means not copying.

—JACQUES MAXIMIN, during the 1987 lecture (attended by Ferran Adrià) that changed the course of modern gastronomy

This simple sentence was what brought about a change in approach in our cooking, and was the cut-off point between "re-creation" and a firm decision to become involved in creativity.

—FERRAN ADRIÀ, whose elBulli was named number 1 on the 2002 World's 50 Best Restaurants list, and then again every year between 2006 and 2009, and held the title longer than any other

INTRODUCTION

The most extraordinary 30-year era of kitchen creativity the world has ever seen—with more new culinary concepts, techniques, and styles developed than at any other point in history—can be traced to a single moment: In 1987, when 25-year-old Spanish chef **Ferran Adrià** visited one of the most creative chefs in the world at the time, 39-year-old French chef **Jacques Maximin.**

Maximin had earned two Michelin stars for Le Chantecler at Nice's Negresco Hotel, where Jacques Torres then served as the pastry chef. After Ferran Adrià enjoyed a meal of lamb stomach and feet, pork belly, and asparagus ice cream, Maximin invited him to attend a chefs' conference he was hosting.

At the conference, Maximin was asked, **"What is creativity?"**

Maximin's reply: **"Not copying."**

Adrià returned to elBulli inspired to innovate. He experimented with countless new techniques, creating countless new dishes and flavors and textures. And the world of gastronomy has never been the same.

In 2002, elBulli came out on top of the World's 50 Best Restaurants list as the best restaurant in the world.

While Thomas Keller's Napa Valley–based French Laundry took the world's number 1 spot in 2003 and 2004, Adrià had created a stir. In 2003, *The New York*

Times Magazine ran a cover story, “How Spain Became the New France,” that sent shock waves through the world of gastronomy, which had long assumed France’s preeminence in all things culinary.

elBulli regained the number 1 title in 2006, and held it through 2009.

During elBulli’s heyday, until it closed in 2011, **Adrià was not only the most copied chef in the world, but the most inspirational**. His work encouraged others to develop their own creativity—adapting his ideas to their own cooking, innovating their own creations, or even rebelling against his style.

In 2010, the Copenhagen restaurant Noma, whose kitchen was helmed by René Redzepi—who first visited elBulli in 1998 and worked there in 1999—took the top spot. Noma held the title through 2012, and regained it in 2014, through Redzepi’s culinary philosophy:

For me cooking is something that is completely transparent and without pretense, that is honest and generous and has something true and original to it.

The number 1 restaurant of 2013 and 2015 was Spain’s El Celler de Can Roca, run by a triumvirate of brothers: sommelier Josep, pastry chef Jordi, and chef Joan. Joan had worked in elBulli’s kitchen in the late 1980s. While naming his mother as the chef he admires most, Joan has acknowledged that **“Ferran Adrià has influenced my cuisine and that of many of my peers.”**

José Andrés

Pastry Chef and Chocolatier Jacques Torres on Being in the Room Where It Happened

Jacques Maximin is one the most genius chefs I have ever known. We used to serve asparagus ice cream with candied asparagus on top, and it was actually good! In Maximin's [cook]book, a lot of dishes were inspired by pastry. We used to make a tart based on an apple tart, but it was a savory lamb tart.

He freed me to open my mind.

Watching the show *Mad Men*, you see them torturing themselves until they come up with an idea. That was Maximin. He would spend hours and hours and days and days to come up with his menu. Every item on the menu had to be innovative.

We were not allowed to say the word "impossible" or the phrase "I cannot do it." If you said that, he would kill you! He would just ask, "How do we accomplish this?"

Maximin was asked to give a demonstration in Cannes. I was his pastry chef, so he asked me to make the dessert. Jacques asked me to serve a dessert in the style of painter Giuseppe Arcimboldo, who created paintings of people with their faces created from food. He asked me to cut fruit and fill a mask then put a cake on it, so that when you unmolded the cake you'd see all the fruits for the eyes, cheeks, etc. and yet it is still a cake. It took a couple of tries, but I did it.

Maximin was always innovative. At the end of the demonstration in Cannes, someone with a very thick Spanish accent asked Maximin what innovation meant to him.

At the time, Maximin was the most innovative chef in the world. He asked, "Are you from Spain?" The reply was yes. So Maximin said to him, "If you make a paella, you will always be compared to someone else—someone's mother, or grandmother, or another restaurant that makes paella. Because you are going to be compared, there is always someone who is going to be better than you. However, if you do something that nobody else has ever done, that is yours 100 percent, you will be the best."

The man with the Spanish accent was **Ferran Adrià**.

Years later, I was having lunch at elBulli and Ferran came out with his brother [Albert, elBulli's pastry chef] and sat down and told me, "Maximin changed my life that day." Ferran said, "I was working here, doing Spanish food, and came back from that demo and said [to my kitchen team], "That is it—we are changing everything! From now on, we do only *our* things, *our* recipes."

That was the beginning of it all.

One of the chefs in elBulli's kitchen during the summer of 2000 was Italian-born chef Massimo Bottura, who has said of that experience:

It wasn't just about technique. . . . What changed me was the message of freedom that Ferran gave me, the freedom to feel my own fire, to look inside myself, and make my thoughts edible.

In June 2016, Bottura's Modena, Italy–based restaurant Osteria Francescana was named the Best Restaurant in the World.

• • •

So what is kitchen creativity? For now, let's think of it as "bringing into being something new and useful to eat or drink."

As Lidia Bastianich of Felidia in New York City has observed, "Today's innovation is tomorrow's tradition." Because we assimilate new ideas, they soon become old (passing) or classic (enduring). Part of the secret of being creative is keeping up with what's new—and combining old or classic elements in a new and useful way.

The goal of *Kitchen Creativity* is to do what Jacques Maximin did for Ferran Adrià in 1987: **inspire you to tap *your* uniqueness, and start cooking in a way that expresses who *you* are and allows you to connect with and please others through *your* food.**

It starts the same way it started for Maximin, Adrià, Redzepi, Roca, Bottura, and countless other culinary artists:

Decide *not* to copy. Decide to create your own food, your own way. Feel your own fire, look inside yourself, and make your own thoughts edible.

So, how does one get to be a great, creative cook—the kind who can walk into a kitchen without a recipe and create a dish from scratch and know exactly how to make it taste delicious?

First comes a period of receptivity—where the cook learns and absorbs expertise from those whose knowledge exceeds their own, whether in a classroom or through a stint in a restaurant kitchen. At this stage, the cook learns by **imitating** what s/he sees and tastes.

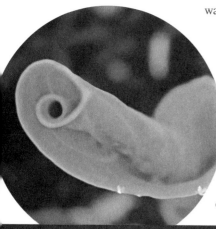

Ferran Adrià on Creativity

[My cuisine] searches for ways to **trigger emotions** through new techniques, concepts, and products. To me, cuisine is about the flavors, textures, visuals, and aromas that activate the senses when we eat—plus a sixth sense, which is the magic, the surprise, the culture.

I always try to ask myself the "why" of things, and never to do things just because they have always been done that way. Otherwise, we would never evolve.

I believe what we have achieved is to demonstrate that there are other ways, and other things, still to be created in cuisine. What really pleases us is that this is encouraging other chefs to look for new ways as well.

There is a generation of chefs that is looking for new things, and who, in short, will be the world's avant-garde.

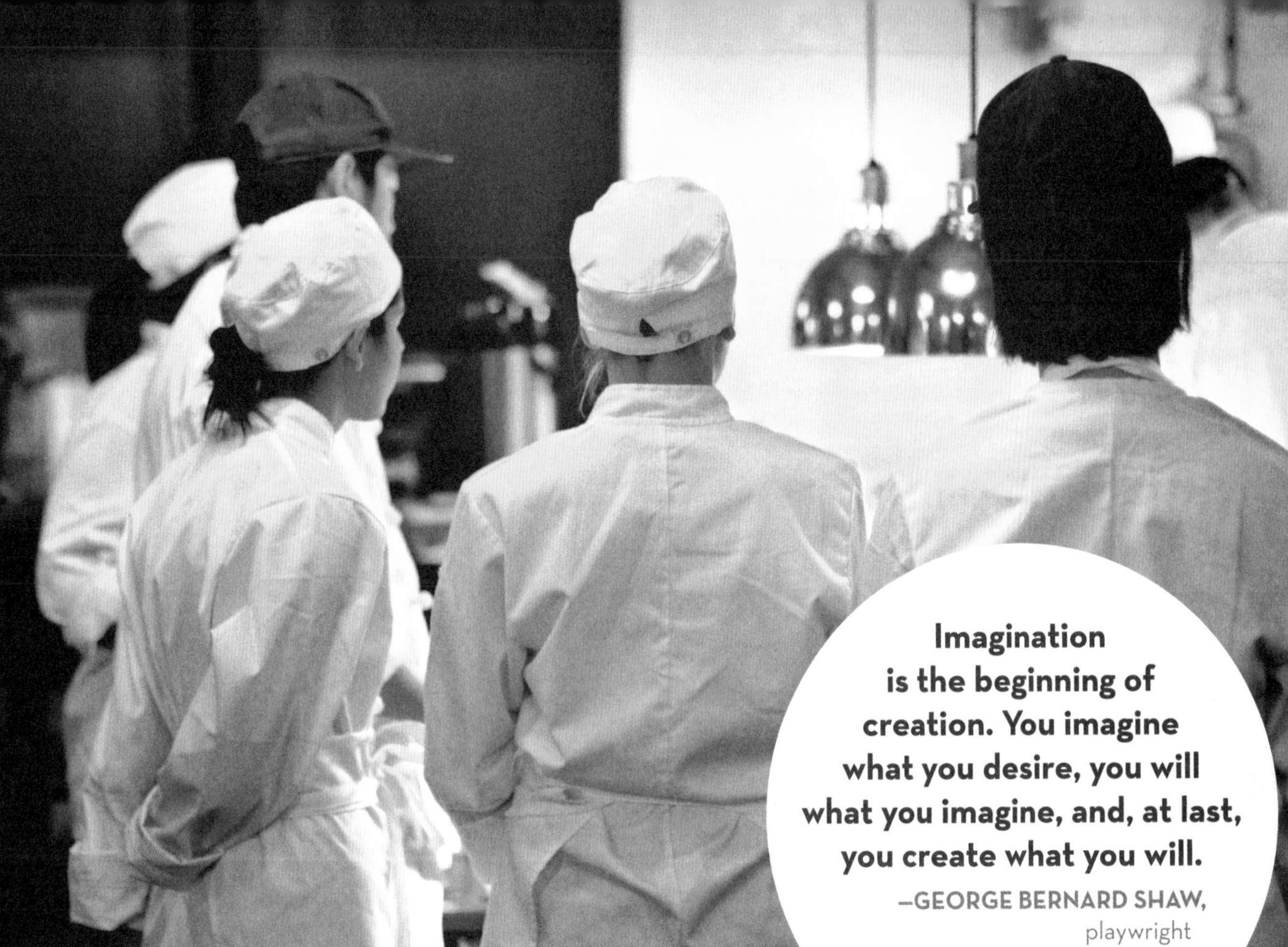

Imagination
is the beginning of
creation. You imagine
what you desire, you will
what you imagine, and, at last,
you create what you will.
—GEORGE BERNARD SHAW,
playwright

Yes, that's right—it's one of the paradoxes of creativity: The first stage of creativity (i.e., *not* copying) is copying.

In Stage 1 **(Mastery)**, a cook **copies** the masters—their dishes, their techniques, their seasoning—to develop a knowledge and skill base.

During Stage 2 **(Alchemy)**, new knowledge and experience are integrated and applied to the process of **converting** ingredients and classic dishes into something fresh.

By Stage 3 **(Creativity)**, one's own novel ideas are applied to the process of **connecting** and **combining** elements into a new creation.

And the ongoing cycle of copying, converting, and connecting and combining continues.

Three Tips for Using KITCHEN CREATIVITY

1. Keep a kitchen creativity journal. Whether it's a notebook or a dedicated file on your phone, have a designated place to store thoughts, feelings, daydreams, photos, and other ideas for reference later. Take your ideas seriously, and write them down. As *Getting Things Done* author David Allen says, "Your mind is for having ideas, not holding them."

2. Pay attention to what you pay attention to. Amid all the distractions we're faced with, certain things still grab your attention. Notice which chefs, restaurants, dishes, and other ideas captivate you (versus the countless others you skip over, unmoved). If you track them, you can analyze them to discover the patterns that unite them, and learn about what's important to you.

> You can't be creative if you don't *do* something.
>
> **—SIR KEN ROBINSON,** author of *Out of Our Minds: Learning to be Creative*

3. Finally, **take action on your best ideas, and make them a reality**. After you start using this book to help multiply the quantity and quality of the ideas you generate, never forget the end game is to create the future. Don't just write your best ideas down. Do the work. Make them happen! The world is waiting to taste what you create next.

> **There is never "no reason" that you are noticing what you notice. . . . Once you become aware of it, what you begin to notice is how much you know that you didn't know you knew.**
>
> **—LAURA DAY,** author of *Practical Intuition* and *The Circle*

KITCHEN CREATIVITY

PART I THE CREATIVE PROCESS IN THE KITCHEN

You need classic technique. You need to know everything, then forget everything.

—MASSIMO BOTTURA,
Osteria Francescana (Italy)

The difference between what is good, very good, and exceptional can be found in repetition. A chef must master the basics before he can create something that is truly exceptional, and the only way to master something is to repeat the process many times, honing your skills and making slight changes to your methods until you have reached your own version of perfection.

—ALEX ATALA, D.O.M.
(São Paulo)

Even an artist as creative as Picasso said, **"Learn the rules like a professional, so you can break them like an artist."** You can't break the rules if you don't know what they are to begin with.

To understand what's *new* and what's *useful,* you must first learn what's *old* and what *doesn't* work—which is the perspective you'll gain from getting grounded in culinary fundamentals. Expertise also enables efficiency: You'll stand on the shoulders of giants instead of having to rediscover that which others spent centuries figuring out.

"Kitchen creativity" is a relatively new concept in some regards if you consider that we've been cooking for two million years and yet it was just 200 years ago that the world's greatest chef's focus was systemization (that is, Auguste Escoffier's turn-of-the-19th-century codification of French cuisine). After decades of faithfully reproducing Escoffier's classic recipes, French chefs finally dared to depart from them, modifying and lightening their dishes in a movement that became known as *nouvelle cuisine.* As a result, there has been more creativity in food in the past 50 years than in any other period in world history.

Up until that point, classic dishes generally evolved from local ingredients in harmonious combinations that

THE *GAULT & MILLAU** TEN COMMANDMENTS OF NOUVELLE CUISINE (1973)

1. Avoid unnecessary complications.
2. Shorten cooking times.
3. Shop regularly at the market.
4. Shorten the menu.
5. Don't hang or marinate game.
6. Avoid too-rich sauces.
7. Return to regional cooking.
8. Investigate the latest techniques.
9. Consider diet and health.
10. Invent constantly.

*The influential restaurant guide founded in France in 1965.

caught the fancy of locals, achieving popularity and becoming part of the culinary canon. The role of restaurant critics was initially to judge whether a restaurant's version of a classic dish was authentic and well-executed or not.

American chefs—many of whom had served apprenticeships in France where they were exposed to these "new, radical" ideas—returned to the United States with these "commandments" in mind. The melting pot of America became a hotbed of culinary change. The boundaries of creativity expanded—including new combinations of ingredients (from the farthest reaches of the world, as well as untapped hyperlocal sources of foraged ingredients), new techniques (from sous-vide to spherification), and new presentations (from snacks to small plates to pre-desserts).

The culinary world saw innovations in codification (via Escoffier) at the turn of the century, and in the lightening of cuisine [via nouvelle cuisine] in the 1970s, and in the expansion of techniques and presentation (via Adrià, et al) since. Today, we're in the midst of an elevation of "goodness" in cuisine, as chefs strive to create the most delicious dishes with the best-available ingredients that do the least harm—to both sentient beings (e.g., healthful, unprocessed or minimally processed, non-GMO, humanely raised) and to the environment (e.g., local, sustainable, organic, biodynamic).

As our awareness of food and the myriad implications of growing it, cooking it, and consuming it continue to expand, our creativity with food is in turn continuing to expand.

We forget that during the "nouvelle cuisine" wave of 35 years ago, we never talked about produce. Creativity was the sole requirement. A chef as respected as Pierre Troisgros could not have cared less about knowing whether his salmon came from Scotland or Norway, or whether it was wild. Alain Chapel was a forerunner of the new movement because during the 1980s he was obsessed with the quality and freshness of the produce. Today we have 50 butters that are better than the best butters available 35 years ago. Each restaurateur has become an expert in dozens of products and can recognize the difference among varieties and the excellence of each.

—**ALAIN DUCASSE,** as quoted in the *Harvard Business Review*

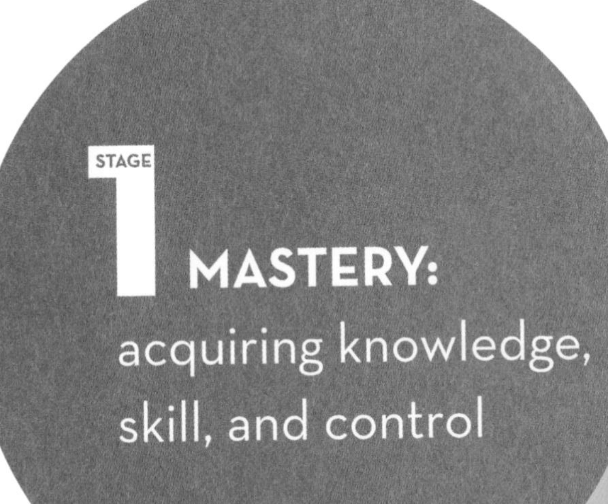

STAGE 1 MASTERY: acquiring knowledge, skill, and control

> **Great chefs don't ask "Why?" They ask "Why not?" They aren't afraid of a challenge and they aren't afraid to break the rules. But they also have the technical training necessary to play with recipes while intuitively knowing which crucial steps should not be sacrificed.**
>
> —**DANIEL BOULUD,** The Dinex Group (New York City)

If you're reading this book, you no doubt have a passion for food and drink, and likely have more than a passing interest in learning to prepare them more creatively.

But if you question whether you have any natural talent for it, take heart. Alain Ducasse, the first chef in the world to hold nine Michelin stars at his restaurants, estimates that **talent** is responsible for a mere 5 *percent* of great cooking.

Another 35 percent is **technique**, and fully 60 percent is the **quality of the raw materials.**

You can learn technique: in books (in addition to this one, see The Chef's Library on page 9), in the classroom, in a restaurant kitchen. And you should.

But the most important thing you can do to master cooking is to develop your palate and your ability to both 1) determine the excellence of your ingredients, and 2) make them taste delicious, even when they're imperfect.

Some believe that the process of mastery of any field demands a "10,000-hour" threshold of deliberate practice. In cooking, however, mastery involves gaining knowledge through not only the hands, but also the head and especially the palate—which involves a combination of practice (cooking), reading, and tasting

> **The whole movement that Ferran Adrià started in cuisine was possible because he knew classical cooking better than anyone. . . . How far you can take creativity is a function of the products you understand and techniques you've mastered.**
>
> —GABRIEL KREUTHER, Gabriel Kreuther (New York City)

(both while cooking and while shopping and dining). The Mastery section provides a broad-brush overview of some of the knowledge and skills to be mastered during this stage.

MASTERING THE FUNDAMENTALS

Learn foundational techniques and recipes.

Classical Western cuisine once required a foundation in French technique, just as classical Eastern cuisine did a foundation in Chinese technique. Both still provide a valuable foundation. However, you can also benefit from studying the classic ingredients, techniques, and dishes of many different cuisines. It's up to *you* what you feel most drawn to—whether learning to toast and temper and blend spices through studying Indian cuisine, or learning to toast hand-crafted marshmallows for perfect s'mores in the spirit of American campfire "cuisine."

If you learn the masters' recipes for building blocks, you can later build your own dishes from them. Mark Levy of Magdalena at the Ivy Hotel in Baltimore doesn't hesitate to acknowledge that he uses Alain Ducasse's gnocchi recipe. (Levy channels his creativity into his accompanying mushroom brodo, which he makes by deeply caramelizing mushrooms and deglazing them with a red wine syrup and adding a tiny hint of bird's eye chiles, which enhance the other flavors.) Nor does Levy hesitate to share that he uses the recipe for Dominique Ansel's Chocolate Pecan Cookies for the ones he serves with his own version of crème brûlée. "They're baked to order, and gluten-free," says Levy.

Be literate.

Read the gastronomic literature. It will be hard to talk your way convincingly into top chefs' kitchens if you've never even cracked the spine on their cookbooks. At the very least, make your way through some or all of the basic foundational texts.

THE CHEF'S LIBRARY

Top Books Recommended by Chefs

> Employ your time in improving yourself by others' writings, so that you shall gain easily what others have labored hard for.
>
> —SOCRATES

> No one who cooks, cooks alone. Even at her most solitary, a cook in the kitchen is surrounded by generations of cooks past, the advice and menus of cooks present, the wisdom of cookbook writers.
>
> —LAURIE COLWIN

> Cookbooks were my mentors.
>
> —BARBARA LYNCH, Menton (Boston)

ThinkFoodGroup

Top chefs and restaurants have long believed that food lovers shouldn't waste a moment *not* reading great books about food. Eric Ripert owns more than 1,000 cookbooks, including a 1907 first-edition of *Gastronomie Pratique,* which is also a beloved favorite cookbook of chefs Michel Richard and Jean-Georges Vongerichten. (Vongerichten has described Henri Babinski's imaginative yet technically precise book, written under the pseudonym of Ali-Bab, as "ahead of its time," and more interesting than Escoffier.) Ripert keeps many of them in a conference room under Le Bernardin in New York City. His sous chefs are required to review every single one.

Having interviewed leading professional chefs extensively about their most-loved and most-used food books, I'm very familiar with their top picks. They're listed chronologically. "Everybody knows that" the new generation sometimes scoffs about the contents of a decades-old book. Well, everybody *didn't* know that back *then*—and *these* are the books that *created* culinary "common sense."

A large cookbook collection allows you to research trusted sources regarding different ways to prepare a particular ingredient, apply a particular technique, or make a particular dish. When the approach you choose is informed by the wisdom of multiple experts that came before you, how can your version help but be better?

Read an inspiring book, then close it and really think about it—so its lessons become more intuitive.

—MICHAEL ANTHONY,
Gramercy Tavern and Untitled (New York City)

Leading Chefs' Top 20 Culinary Books

1. ***Le Guide Culinaire*** by Auguste Escoffier (1903) | codification of classical French cuisine that has won the admiration of chefs like Scott Conant, Jason Neroni, Rich Torrisi, and Ming Tsai
2. ***Encyclopedia of Practical Gastronomy*** by Ali-Bab (1907; first English edition in 1974) | classic treatise on gastronomy that is beloved by chefs like Daniel Boulud, David Kinch, Michel Richard, Eric Ripert, and Jean-Georges Vongerichten
3. ***Joy of Cooking*** by Irma S. Rombauer (1931) | codification of American cuisine; a favorite of chefs like Traci Des Jardins, Bobby Flay, Anita Lo, Emily Luchetti, and Christina Tosi
4. ***Larousse Gastronomique*** by Prosper Montagne (1938) | the A-to-Z French culinary encyclopedia that Daniel Boulud described as "the only [one] that is always up to date" and also counts as fans Dan Barber, Marcus Samuelsson, Mario Batali, Thomas Keller, Vitaly Paley, and Charlie Palmer
5. ***Mastering the Art of French Cooking*** by Julia Child, Louisette Bertholle, and Simone Beck (1961) | the classic that brought French cuisine to American kitchens; a favorite of Lidia Bastianich, Ris Lacoste, Emily Luchetti, Patrick O'Connell, Barton Seaver, and Nancy Silverton
6. ***Ma Gastronomie*** by Fernand Point (1969) | philosophy from the influential French restaurateur behind the long-time Michelin three-star La Pyramide, and a favorite of chefs like John Besh, Thomas Keller, Ludo Lefebvre, and Jasper White
7. ***Couscous and Other Good Food from Morocco*** (1973), ***The Cooking of Southwest France*** (1983), ***World of Food*** (1988), and other books by Paula Wolfert | a personal way with words, whether writing about rustic (and lighter) French cuisine or couscous, that has "mentored" chefs like Hugh Acheson, Jody Adams, David Lebovitz, Tony Maws, Nancy Silverton, and Susan Spicer
8. ***La Technique*** (1976) and ***La Methode*** (1979) by Jacques Pépin | illustrated guides to cooking fundamentals that are favorites of chefs like Andrew Carmellini, Roy Choi, Tom Colicchio, and Michel Nischan
9. ***On Food and Cooking: The Science and Lore of the Kitchen*** by Harold McGee (1984) Mark Levy | how-to on enhancing food through science from the Yale-educated PhD; taught readers like Dan Barber, Matt Dillon, Michael Laiskonis, Ivy Stark, and Paul Virant
10. **Chez Panisse cookbooks** (***Chez Panisse Desserts***, 1985; ***Chez Panisse Cooking***, 1994; ***Chez Panisse Menu Cookbook***, 1995; et al) by Alice Waters, Paul Bertolli and/or Lindsey Shere | local/regional/farm-to-table cookbooks that count chefs like Matt Dillon, Wylie Dufresne, Suzanne Goin, David Lebovitz, and Nancy Silverton as fans

Mark Levy

11. ***White Heat*** by Marco Pierre White (1990) | the bad-boy-chef-as-rock-star's first cookbook, with black and white photos of kitchen life juxtaposed with four-color photos of his vibrant food, that inspired chefs like Chris Cosentino, Paul Liebrandt, Michael Mina, and Rich Torrisi

12. ***Culinary Artistry*** by Andrew Dornenburg and Karen Page (1996) | insider guide to culinary composition and flavor pairings that is a favorite of Grant Achatz, Hugh Acheson, Timon Balloo, John Fraser, Will Goldfarb, Michael Laiskonis, Michael Mina, Jesse Schenker, Ivy Stark, and Ethan Stowell

13. ***The French Laundry Cookbook*** by Thomas Keller, Michael Ruhlman, and Susie Heller (1999) | California-style haute cuisine cookbook that influenced Justin Aprahamian, David Chang, and Marc Forgione, as well as notable alums like Grant Achatz

14. ***Le Grand Livre de Cuisine d'Alain Ducasse*** by Alain Ducasse (2001) | culinary encyclopedia created by one of France's greatest contemporary chefs and admired by chefs like Carrie Nahabedian, Alison Vines-Rushing, and Michael White

15. **River Cottage cookbooks (*The River Cottage Cookbook*, 2001, *The River Cottage Fish Book*, 2007, *The River Cottage Meat Book*, 2004, and *River Cottage Veg*, 2011)** by Hugh Fearnley-Whittingstall | authentic, locavore, sustainable cookbooks that have inspired chefs like Justin Aprahamian, Dan Barber, April Bloomfield, and Brad Farmerie

16. ***Essential Cuisine*** by Michel Bras (2002) | a visual-feast-inspiring presentation that is a favorite of David Chang, Dominique Crenn, Curtis Duffy, Daniel Humm, Gavin Kaysen, and David Kinch

17. ***Zuni Cafe Cookbook*** by Judy Rodgers (2002) | cooking philosophy from the late San Francisco chef, which Mike Anthony considers a foundational text that has inspired some of his own kitchen creations, and also counts as fans Anne Burrell, Suzanne Goin, Alex Guarnaschelli, Nigella Lawson, David Lebovitz, Bryant Ng, and Barton Seaver

18. ***Cooking by Hand*** by Paul Bertolli (2003) | cooking philosophy book by the former Chez Panisse chef that is a favorite of chefs like Justin Aprahamian, Jeremy Fox (who counts it as one of his two most-used books), Ben Ford, and Blaine Wetzel

19. ***The Flavor Bible*** by Karen Page and Andrew Dornenburg (2008) | A-to-Z guide to flavor pairings and affinities that counts as fans Nina Compton, Jared Gadbaw, Gunnar Gislason, Carla Hall, Josh Habiger, Timothy Hollingsworth, Hung Huynh, Matthew Kenney, and Michel Roux

20. **elBulli books** by Ferran Adrià (1994–2011) | books that expanded the boundaries of food through science and art, earned fans like Grant Achatz, José Andrés, David Chang, Eric Ripert, Damian Sansonetti, and Michael Voltaggio

Daniel Boulud, whose personal favorite books include **Le Repertorie de la Cuisine** *by Louis Saulnier (1914)*

Pick chefs and food worth copying—study the greats, and emulate their standards.

The ultimate way to learn from a master is to spend time in his or her kitchen. Not so many years ago, ambitious cooks looking to work in a restaurant kitchen might simply drop off their résumé at every four-star or three-star restaurant in town, as guided by the local newspaper's reviews. Today, the most ambitious cooks might be guided to work at restaurants that have been recognized on the World's 50 Best Restaurants list, or with chefs who have distinguished themselves via recognition through the James Beard Foundation Awards. (See the Appendix for listings of named restaurants, page 417, and JBF-recognized chefs, pastry chefs, and rising stars, page 416.)

Today, those restaurants are so diverse that you'll want to do your homework in advance. As a first pass, you can research restaurants online, reading about their cuisines and chefs, and seeing which dishes appeal to you and whose philosophies you're most drawn toward. As a next step, you could visit for a meal, or sit in the bar and order a drink and an appetizer or two to get a sense of the restaurant's vibe. Or you could attend a lecture or cooking class or volunteer at a charity event where you're able to taste the chef's food and interact with the chef.

Having a compelling reason to want to study with someone, and a sense that there's already a fit between the restaurant's style and your own interests, can help you land a stint in a coveted professional kitchen.

Somebody once said to me that you have to be as excited about mashed potatoes or a PB&J sandwich as you are about a dish with truffles. And I think it's true. If you look at it and think, "Eh, it's just mashed potatoes...," then it is just going to be mashed potatoes. But if you look at it and think, "I'm going to make the best mashed potatoes I possibly can," and you get it down to the type of potato you're going to use, and down to the gram how you're going to season them perfectly, then it changes your approach. And you can approach everything that way.

—MICHAEL VOLTAGGIO, ink (Los Angeles)

Cooking at Melisse with [chef-owner] **Josiah Citrin** is where I learned so many fundamentals—like making sauces, and making smooth pureed soups, and roasting mushrooms. Working the meat station at Melisse, we'd have eight different jus on hand—including chicken jus seasoned with dried orange zest, duck jus finished with caramelized sugar and star anise, and beef jus finished with herb butter. Josiah and [chef de cuisine] **Ken Takayama** were constantly creating new dishes, inspired by their visits to the market.

—**KATIANNA HONG**, The Charter Oak (Napa Valley)

Jon Shook and Vinny Dotolo on Changing Influences

Cooking was different when we started cooking together in the late 1990s: Chefs were all about "the best" ingredients [and flying them in from wherever they were sourced, whether Thailand, North Dakota, or South Africa]. That was the mentality. When we moved to California in the early 2000s, we really adapted a lot of its philosophies, stemming from **Alice Waters,** obviously, and it became about "hyper-local." We didn't want to fall into that mix of just California-based cuisine, but we wanted to respect it.

We worked in Miami for **Michelle Bernstein,** which is where we first started cooking together. You still had to use your imagination then. Like, a cook would go to New York and bring back copies of the menus of the restaurants they ate at, and you had to use your imagination to figure out what these dishes were actually like. Now, there's Instagram, so you feel like you've already been to all these restaurants in your mindspace.

A year or two ago, we wanted to hire some culinary students, so we had a questionnaire, and one of the questions we asked was "What's your favorite cookbook?" And 90 percent of the people cited a website (e.g., Epicurious.com). Shocking. The irony was that we were doing the interviews in a library. We went to school at the beginning of the end. Now, some [culinary students] don't even know guys that were key to American cooking. If you walked down the line and asked, "Who was **Charlie Trotter**? Who was **Jean-Louis Palladin**?," they'd be scared. Everybody knows **René Redzepi**, but that's it.

Vinny Dotolo and Jon Shook

Remember that there's also much to be learned from those who have studied under great chefs and soaked up their lessons, but whose own still-rising star status may make their kitchens more accessible to mere mortals. You'll read about a few of them in this book, and the lessons they've been able to absorb during their time in top kitchens across the country.

LEARNING TO TASTE

Just as there is more to a song than its sheet music, there is more to a dish than its recipe. Chefs' know-how with regard to seasoning and flavoring gives them the power to make crucial creative decisions in the moment regarding a dish-in-progress.

> **Flavor is more important than technique.**
>
> —**GAVIN KAYSEN,** Spoon and Stable (Minneapolis)

You can follow a recipe perfectly, yet still end up with a dull, listless dish. Why? Recipes can't account for every possible variable—in ingredients (the age of your spices, the strength of your herbs, the ripeness of your fruit; not to mention that the same six-ounce fillet can be thick or thin), in equipment (an oven running hot or cold), in weather (that day's humidity), and so on. Luckily, you can develop the ability to taste and to adjust a dish's flavor as you go—which is the fundamental skill for anyone looking to master cooking.

In music, there's such a thing as perfect pitch—or you can simply use a pitch pipe to tune your own instrument to the same musical scale as every other musician. However, in food, we haven't yet invented a "flavor pipe" to be able to tune our own dishes to perfection. That's why "Taste, taste, taste" has become the mantra great chefs teach their cooks—and why learning to imitate an expert's palate via cooking classes or stints in professional restaurant kitchens can be invaluable. You'll learn how to make each carefully chosen ingredient through perfect cooking and seasoning reach its peak of perfection—something the French refer to as *à point*. While in time you can and should develop your own individual palate, you'll want to learn to season with a master whose palate and seasoning techniques you can imitate. And you'll learn that the quality of the dish you're creating will never be better than the quality of the ingredients you put into it—so you'll learn to shop where the best chefs shop, and to patronize the same producers the best chefs do (see Set Your Standards: Choosing the Highest Quality Ingredients, page 21).

When I first opened Public [in 2003], food was more about whiz-bang technology—circulators, sous-vide, bendable solids, liquid nitrogen. But now that's gone into the background. Today, it is much more about ingredients and flavor.

—BRAD FARMERIE,
Saxon + Parole (New York City)

Having a trained palate allows you to take any ingredient and know how to enhance its flavor—or when to leave it alone. It also serves as the foundation of creating a dish from start to finish—or of rescuing one that's falling flat.

Cooking begins with getting to know your ingredients every single time you use them—that is, tasting them at the very *beginning*, and *during* the entire cooking process, all through to the very *end*.

You have to have an attention to detail and a knowledge of what is good and what is possible. You have to know how to work with textures, or what salt or lemon will do to your food. You have to understand balance.

—JEREMY FOX, Rustic Canyon (Los Angeles),
on the necessary foundation for creativity

STRIKING A BALANCE

Everything changes; everything stays the same.
—BUDDHA

Balance is one of the central tenets of great food, and one of the most frequently cited characteristics of great cooking among the best chefs we've interviewed over the years.

Understanding when a dish is in balance is one of the most essential aspects of mastering flavor. A feeling of completeness is achieved by the embrace of opposites within a dish—whether hot *and* cold (e.g., hot chocolate with whipped cream), crunchy *and* soft (e.g., nachos with melted cheese), or spicy *and* sweet (e.g., Thai sweet potato curry).

Balance is fundamental to creative *individuals* as well. Dr. Scott Barry Kaufman, scientific director of the Imagination Institute at the University of Pennsylvania, sees two opposing super-factors in the personalities of creative individuals: *divergence* and *convergence*. Divergence is non-conformity and out-of-the-box thinking related to impulsivity. Convergence is the ability to be practical, and to bring ideas into reality. Given the definition of creativity as the ability to make new things that are both novel and useful, it's clear how creative types need both.

According to psychologist Mihaly Csikszentmihalyi, creative individuals also have a predisposition *to psychological androgyny*: "Creative and talented girls are more dominant and tough than other girls, and creative boys are more sensitive and less aggressive than their male peers."

So the most creative people tend to be "both/and" people: paradoxically, both masculine *and* feminine, extroverted *and* introverted, imaginative *and* realistic, playful *and* disciplined, humble *and* proud.

The chef's profession is a messy set of contradictions that fits right in: Chefs at the highest levels of the profession have taken their rightful place among so-called right-brain conceptually driven (culinary) artists, even as they must think like left-brain analytically driven managers or entrepreneurs who must keep an eye on costs in order to be profitable and to keep their doors open.

It's crucial to taste as you go. Analyze what's going on in your dish, and what the objective is. Start by identifying the dominant taste: sweet? salty? sour? bitter? savory? Is it appropriately balanced? If not, you'll be able to work with the other tastes to find a better balance.

Think about the context of what it is you're tasting. What is its intended final format? A hot soup that will be garnished with other ingredients? A room-temperature dipping sauce for something more neutral-flavored? Imagine it in that context, and at that temperature, and adjust appropriately. Take what you know or can intuit about your guests' palates into account.

And if wine is part of the equation at the meal, try to taste the sauce alongside the wine the dish will be served with.

Cooking at Charlie Trotter's, I learned to taste things over and over again. Even though you tasted it at 2 pm when you made it, this afternoon it changed—and at 7 pm it's different, and at 9 pm it's different from what it was at 7 pm. Oxygen affects it, reduction affects it, time affects it—all these things affect it. So you've got to taste it, and fix it, and make it right again.

—**CURTIS DUFFY**, Grace (Chicago)

LEARNING TO SEASON

One of the most important things you'll learn as you imitate the masters is how to season a dish to deliciousness. Embedded in classic recipes is information about recommended proportions of various ingredients. While you'll develop your own palate so that you can "season to taste," you'll have to learn to taste first—and there's no better place to start than by having a benchmark in your taste memory of some of the best versions of particular dishes. Eating at the best restaurants—as a guest, while cooking in their kitchens—is an invaluable part of this process.

In the kitchen at Coi, it struck me how much we tasted the food. You tasted what every other person there was working on. You only had two dishes, and every day you brought them to the chef to taste for consistency. You would taste it five or six times and talk about it every day for 20 minutes. Daniel [Patterson, the chef] would tell you, "You need two drops of this or two grams of that"...But you learn to trust certain people's palates. Every night [at Natalie's], we will hand each other a spoon and ask, "What do you think?" At Coi, there was an acceptable range of salt or acid, and we could just look at each other and know.

—**SHELBY STEVENS,** Natalie's at the Camden Harbour Inn (Maine)

Seasoning makes an ingredient taste like more of itself. An asparagus spear will still taste first and foremost of asparagus, for example, once it's been sprinkled with just the right amount of salt. Strawberries will taste more like strawberries, once they've been hit with just the right amount of sugar.

Salt is the single most important flavor enhancer for savory foods, and sugar the single most important for sweet foods such as fruit. Acidic ingredients—such as citrus juice, or vinegar—are the second-most-important flavor enhancers. And while a pinch of sugar in a savory dish can serve the role of balancing flavors as a flavor enhancer, once that sweetness is noticeable, it's wrong. The dish should taste *better,* but *not* salty or sweet.

Seasoning and spicing is the first thing a young cook needs to learn, and it's the hardest thing to teach. There's no miracle recipe to follow.

—DANIEL BOULUD,
The Dinex Group (New York City)

The most important thing for a chef to know? Seasoning. . . . How to use salt. . . . Salt really is what enhances flavor.

—THOMAS KELLER,
The French Laundry (Yountville, California) and Per Se (New York City)

Seasoning Savory Dishes

Saltiness is the first place to start in any savory dish, as it's the most important taste. You'll want to taste your ingredient(s) first, and determine whether a bit of salt might add value as a flavor enhancer. The key is to learn to add just enough to enhance the flavor of the ingredient without being detectable—and no more. Salt slowly and gradually.

Once you've reached an optimal level of saltiness, check to see whether adding a hint of **acidity**—e.g., a squeeze of lemon or lime, or a dash of vinegar—would enhance the dish's flavor further. A bit of brightness can make a dish that's flat or heavy start to sparkle. You're looking to bring out the dish's flavors—not to mask them with acidity.

This is the point at which experienced chefs can learn to finesse even further. Perhaps you're making a tomato sauce that's now beautifully balanced in saltiness and acidity, but would still benefit from a rounder flavor. You might consider adding a bit of **sweetness** through a pinch of sugar. Or perhaps you want to heighten those flavors even further—in which case you might add **piquancy** through a pinch of cayenne instead.

Flavor enhancement can also take place through adding an ingredient rich in **umami** to a dish. However, this is a bit more complex, given that many ingredients that add umami also simultaneously add another taste, such as salt (as in miso paste or Parmesan cheese); this will be addressed further during Stage 2.

It's easier to add more than to remove seasoning. Don't believe you must season the whole pot of soup at once—remove a cup for your seasoning experiment, and once you achieve your desired flavor, season the entire pot that way. From time to time as you taste and adjust a dish, be aware that you will want to cleanse your palate (e.g., with a sip of water, or a bite of bread or cracker—Eric Ripert tastes bites of cheese between spoonfuls during his daily sauce tasting).

Don't hesitate to seek another opinion to counterbalance your own. Married chefs de cuisine Katianna Hong of the Charter Oak and John Hong of The

It's mandatory that cooks bring every [element on their stations] for me to taste, every day. It's not so I can judge it, but because it makes *them* taste it. I hardly ever corrected anyone near the end [of her term as chef de cuisine at Manresa]. If something needed correcting, I'd ask, **"Did you try this?"** Then they'd go back and taste it and fix it, and if they brought it back and it still wasn't correct, we'd work together to fix it.

—**JESSICA LARGEY,** Simone (Los Angeles)

Seasoning is like tuning: You taste and adjust your ingredients to get them perfect. If you oversalt something, you can't redo it. With too much acidity, you can add sweetness to bring down the acid.

—**EDDY LEROUX,** chef de cuisine, Daniel (New York City)

Restaurant at Meadowood go to each other first to taste each other's dishes. (Katianna says she'll ask, "Am I crazy, [or does this need something]?") Of the couple and their executive chef Christopher Kostow, Katianna characterizes Kostow as having the strongest preference for acidity in food, herself as having the strongest preference for pungency and stronger flavors, and her husband as having the strongest preference for restraint and subtlety. "We balance each other well," says Katianna. "John will keep me from adding too much, and I'll keep him from being boring."

Meg Galus, pastry chef of Chicago's Boka, notes that it's important to get feedback, because when you taste dishes too many times you lose any kind of objectivity. "Lee [Wolen, Boka's chef] is a more *collaborative* chef, so we'll taste together," she says. "I like a hint of salt in desserts, while Lee likes acid in desserts. Citrus is my go-to, and I'll also use fruit vinegars and 'drinking vinegars,' either to macerate berries or straight on the plate. I try to make every component in a dessert as light as it can be."

Seasoning Sweet Dishes

Sweetness is the first place to start in any sweet dish. If your strawberries are perfectly ripe and sweet, there's no need to add sugar. In fact, following a recipe blindly and adding sugar to strawberries when it's *not* needed can *destroy* a dish.

Sugar enhances flavor—up to a point. Too much sugar dulls flavor.

—**EMILY LUCHETTI,** chief pastry officer of The Cavalier, Marlowe, and Park Tavern (San Francisco)

After a dish's sweetness is optimized, see whether some **acidity** might enhance the flavor further—just as with a savory dish.

This is the point at which experienced chefs can finesse even further. Perhaps you're making a lemon sauce for a dessert that's beautifully balanced between its sweetness and acidity, but would still benefit from a rounder flavor. That's the time you might consider adding a bit of **salt** through a pinch of salt or another salty ingredient.

Jean-François Bruel on Seasoning to Taste

You can't season if you don't know how to taste.

You learn the most when you're a young cook and, early on, it's hard to learn to control salt. Once you add too much, it's too late!

[Bruel shares the expert tip of using **two**, **three**, or **four** fingers to grab a pinch of salt, in order to deliver a consistently **small**, **medium**, or **large** pinch of salt, respectively, as needed.]

We only use two kinds of salt, which we never, ever change. We use classic French sea salt [*sel de mer*] from La Baleine for cooking, and *fleur de sel* for finishing a dish when we want a bit of crunch.

You have to **think about the dish, and understand what it is you're seasoning.** You'll want to season a tiny accent of coulis very differently from an entire bowl of soup. A few drops of coulis should be tart and spicy so it makes an impact—but if you're eating an entire bowl of soup, it should be flavorful with enough acidity and salt without being overpowering (and wearing out the palate).

You taste, and taste, and taste—and add what's missing, adjusting the flavor. You'll want to make sure the spice and seasoning and acidity are all in balance. Acidity adds a nice pop to a dish, and can cut the fat. Bitterness often needs a bit of sweetness to balance it out.

You want to think about where the **kick** is in your dishes—in the spice? in the acid? in the sauce? Or in a pureed vegetable on the side?

Even traditional French dishes like a velouté sauce will have a dash of Tabasco or cayenne pepper to push the other flavors forward. **Michel Guérard would say, "It's the ingredients you can't see that boost the other ingredients." Things like cayenne, espelette, mustard, and vinegars all serve this function.** Even in France, chefs will add a dash of soy sauce to enrich a consommé. Orange zest will be added to braised veal—and while you won't see it in the dish, its flavor makes a big difference.

ENHANCING FLAVOR VS. ADDING FLAVOR

The minute the taste of salt or sugar or acid or anything else is apparent on the palate, that's not enhancing flavor, that's **adding flavor.** Key sources of added flavors are herbs, spices, and other flavorings (such as garlic).

Certain ingredients play different roles at different times. Capsicum-dominant ingredients (e.g., chile peppers) are so strongly flavored that their heat is typically thought of as an added flavor. But cayenne pepper can be used in miniscule amounts such that it's not noticeable by itself, yet it quietly boosts the flavor of the other ingredients. In those cases, it is a flavor enhancer.

A spice is anything and everything I can use to flavor food. In my spice blends, I use everything I can dry, embracing the notion "Reuse before Recycle." And that goes for herbs, peppers, and citrus. I'll grate a whole dried lemon. If I have leftover herbs, I'll dry them—dried herbs serve a different function than fresh. Fresh, a tomato is a vegetable—but dried, it is a seasoning. Tomato powder, cheese powder, bonito flakes—I think of them all as spices.

—LIOR LEV SERCARZ, La Boîte (New York City)

Lior Lev Sercarz

When Andrew cooked in the kitchen of Lydia Shire in Boston, her motto was, "Don't spare the fat, dear." "Fat equals flavor" was pounded into many cooks' heads. And when fat—such as butter and cream—were added in judicious amounts, their richness could indeed enhance mouthfeel and thus flavor. When cooks went overboard and the presence of butter and cream became dominant, the balance—and the flavor of what should have been the "star" ingredient—was lost. When you're making cream of tomato soup, you want to be able to taste the *tomato* and its acidity and other properties.

When you actually want to *add flavor* to a dish, there's another huge world of possibilities available to you. Understanding what herbs, spices (and spice blends), and other flavorings (from garlic to zest) best enhance a particular ingredient can give you a huge advantage in the kitchen.

Jessica Largey of Simone on Seasoning and Adding Flavor

You want to have your salt, acid, and sugar ready in order to balance flavors. At Manresa [where Largey served as chef de cuisine under chef-owner David Kinch], I think both David and I saw acid as equal in importance to salt when seasoning food. **LEMON JUICE IS MY GO-TO ACID**—one of my friends says my middle name is "Lemon Juice" because whenever I'm asked to taste a dish, I almost invariably say it needs lemon juice. I love citrus in general, but I especially love lemon juice for the acidity and brightness it gives. When I dress salads, I'll be asked what kind of salad dressing I used, and I'll say, "None—just lemon juice and olive oil." Not everyone loves all the other citrus fruits, but virtually everyone loves lemon.

I have an entire selection of vinegars. **Champagne vinegar is the lemon juice of the vinegar world.** It has higher acidity [typically 7 percent] versus other vinegars, like cider vinegar [typically 5 percent]. White balsamic vinegar is one of the most neutral types, so it marries well with flavors like fennel or herbs. I love making my own infused vinegars, especially at Manresa with produce from the farm....

When something is too salty, you can sometimes fix it with acid or with sugar. You don't want to add enough sugar to make it sweet—you just want to add it until the dish's flavor hits equilibrium without its sweetness being noticeable. If it's a hot dish and the sugar will melt easily, you can use granulated sugar—otherwise, if it's a cold dish [or iced tea], you can add simple syrup. But the syrup contains water, so it's diluted—and you don't want to risk diluting flavor.

When I was in China, I visited a Szechuan cooking school that was training cooks not to use MSG, and to use sugar instead. Apparently MSG breaks down into sweetness, so sugar can serve the same function.

If I were making an onion sauce and wanted more sweetness, I might substitute shallots—which are naturally sweeter—in order to increase the sauce's sugar content.

Jessica Largey

SET YOUR STANDARDS: CHOOSING THE HIGHEST QUALITY INGREDIENTS

Do you know the resource sections that typically appear at the end of leading chefs' cookbooks, listing their suppliers of the specialty ingredients mentioned in their recipes? These compilations are too often overlooked, but they're pure gold: a database of where the best chefs source the best ingredients. Use them to stock your own pantry, realizing that no dish can ever be any better than the ingredients you put into it.

While many produce suppliers are local farmers and greenmarkets, others ship cross-country and beyond. The trusted food sources listed below provide high-quality ingredients to some of America's best restaurants.

AmadeusVanillaBeans.com for vanilla beans

Amoretti.com for flavor sprays, nut flours

AnsonMills.com for beans, Carolina Gold rice, fine-ground polenta, grits, heritage grains

Asiachi.com for bitter almonds (aka apricot seed)

AsianFoodGrocer.com for dried bonito flakes, kombu, yuzu

AUISwiss.com for chocolate, rose petals

BaldorFood.com for finger limes, hearts of palm

BellaVado.com for avocado oil

BlisGourmet.com for barrel-aged products (e.g., fish sauce), maple syrup, sherry vinegar

BobsRedMill.com for flours (e.g., almond, hazelnut, semolina), grains, other ingredients (e.g., dried sour cherries)

BoiledPeanuts.com for green peanuts

BoironFreres.com for cherry puree

BourbonBarrelFoods.com for Bluegrass soy sauce, bourbon-smoked black pepper, bourbon-smoked paprika, aged vanilla extract

BulkFoods.com for apple pectin powder

BuonItalia.com for Italian foods (e.g., dried pastas, olive oils, truffle oil, truffle paste, white truffles)

ChefRubber.com for cocoa butters, Pop Rocks (aka pastry rocks)

ChefShop.com for French olive oils

Chefs-Garden.com for baby herbs, baby turnips, edible flowers, micro-greens

ChefsWarehouse.com for Banyuls vinegar, brik dough, flavored olive oils, Korean dried chili threads, liliput capers, pastry cream powder, pistachio paste, strawberry puree, Valrhona chocolate, white balsamic vinegar

CookingDistrict.com for Huilerie Beaujolais vinegars, Melfor vinegar, Orleans mustard, pistachio oil, walnut oil

Dartagnan.com for dried and fresh mushrooms, Perigord truffles, truffle juice

DeanDeluca.com for honey, pastas, salts, vinegarsDespanaNYC.com for aged sherry vinegar, pimentón, piquillo peppers

Our suppliers also supply inspiration. . . . For two years, we've been working with Daniel Leiber, a CIA graduate who has StarDust Farm in Pennsylvania....And we get Castle Valley Bloody Butcher Red Grits, which comes in a fine flour and a coarser grain. For the best texture, I combine both with mascarpone and butcher-cut black pepper into a creamy polenta-like dish. It's a very pinky color, and I'll pair them with nettles and asparagus.

—**EDDY LEROUX,** chef de cuisine, Daniel (New York City)

KALUSTYAN'S in New York City is frequented by countless chefs and culinarians including Padma Lakshmi and Martha Stewart, and even actor Richard Thomas, who turned us on to its medjool dates during one visit.

Eataly.com for pastas

FarmersDaughterBrand.com for pickles, preserves

Freddyguys.com for hazelnuts

Guittard.com for bittersweet chocolate, cocoa powder

Gustiamo.com for artisanal, authentic Italian products (e.g., olive oils, Sicilian pistachios)

HaydenFlourMills.com for durum flour, farro flour, polenta, semolina

Huilerie-Beaujolaise.com for Huilerie Beaujolaise nut oils

ImportFood.com for betel leaves, coconut cream, coconut milk, fresh Thai chiles, makrut limes and lime leaves, Pandan leaves, pad thai noodles, tempura flour

Kalustyans.com for spices and other flavorings from more than 75 different countries, including Aleppo pepper, argan oil, bitters, black garlic, chile pastes, dried apricots, dried chiles, five-spice powder, ghost peppers, Hawaiian sea salt, lemon confit, Madras curry powder, orange blossom water, peperoncino, pimenton, pomegranate molasses, spices, Thai tamarind concentrate, umeboshi vinegar, vandouvan curry spice, vinegar powders

Katagiri.com for kombu, shiro dashi, white miso paste

KingArthurFlour.com for flours

KingOfMushrooms.com for dried mushrooms (e.g., candy cap)

KLWines.com for Boker's baked apple bitters

KodaFarms.com for sweet rice flour

KoppertCress.com for purple shiso

LaBoiteNY.com for Lior Lev Sercarz's spices and spice blends

LaTourangelle.com for pistachio oil, truffle oil

LEpicerie.com for Banyuls vinegar, bitter almond extract, chestnut honey, cocoa butter, edible gold dust and leaf, egg white powder, frozen fruit purees, La Baleine salts, pink salt, Valrhona chocolate, violet mustard [*moutarde violette*]

Le-Sanctuaire.com for carnaroli rice, Szechuan peppercorns, spices

LeVillage.com for Edmond Fallot mustards, Le Puy lentils

LocalHarvest.org for honeys (e.g., acacia, lavender)

Manicaretti.com for black olive paste, pastas

McEvoyRanch.com for extra virgin organic olive oil, olio nuovo

Melissas.com for Brussels sprouts on the stalk, cherimoya, dragon fruit, finger limes, mangosteens, morels, passion fruit, Ruby Gold potatoes, starfruit, truffles (black, burgundy, white)

MikuniWildHarvest.com for vinegars

Minus8Vinegar.com for 8 Brix red and white verjus, ice wine vinegar, rice wine vinegar

MELISSA'S in Los Angeles provides hard-to-find produce for James Beard House and Foundation events such as Chefs and Champagne (in the Hamptons) and Taste America (chefs on tour).

Mitsuwa.com for bonito flakes, kombu, ponzu, shiro dashi, soy sauce, wakame seaweed, yuzu, yuzu juice, yuzu kosho

ModernistPantry.com for agar-agar, xantham gum

MurraysCheese.com for cheese, Marcona almonds

Mycological.com for chanterelles, morels, Oregon truffles, porcini

NielsenMassey.com for vanilla extract, vanilla paste

OliverFarm.com for benne oil

Pastaworks.com for pastas

PerfectPuree.com for apricot puree

PollenRanch.com for fennel pollen

RanchoGordo.com for heirloom beans, posole

RareSeeds.com for seeds

RockRidgeMarketHall.com for Espelette and piquillo peppers, pink salt, verjus, walnut oil

RoveySeed.com for dried corn, pickling lime

Saffron.com for saffron, vanilla beans

SaltTraders.com for Viking sea saltSaltWorks.us for espresso salt, Maldon smoked sea salt, Murray River sea salt

SantaBarbaraPistachios.com for pistachio flour, pistachio oil

Seaweed.net for bladderwrack, dulse seaweed

SeedSavers.org for seeds

SpanishTable.com for Spanish foods (e.g., chickpeas, smoked paprika, white beans)

Starwest-Botanicals.com for fennel extract, orange blossom water

TempleOfThai.com for galangal, fresh Thai chiles

TennesseeTruffle.com for Tennessee truffles

TerraSpiceCompany.com for beet powder, chicory root granules, dried chiles, freeze-dried fruits and vegetables, piment d'espelette, roasted barley powder, seaweed powder, tonka beans, yogurt powder

TheSpiceHouse.com for adobo seasoning, aleppo pepper, black garlic, Ceylon True cinnamon, fennel pollen, grains of paradise, habanero powder, Indonesian cassia cinnamon sticks, maple sugar, molecular gastronomy ingredients, Saigon bark, spices, star anise, toasted sesame seeds, Vadouvan curry powder, vanilla beans, za'atar

Tienda.com for Spanish products (e.g., Calasparra rice, capers, piquillo peppers, saffron)

TrueFoodsMarket.com for almond flour

Truffe-Plantin.com for black truffles, truffle juice, white truffles

Urbani.com for truffle juice, truffles

Valrhona-Chocolate.com for chocolate, cocoa nibs

Verjus.com for red verjus, white verjus

Zingermans.com for olive oils, vinegars

If angels sprinkled a spice from their wings, this would be it.

– **PEGGY KNICKERBOCKER** in *Saveur*, on the fennel pollen at Chicago's **SPICE HOUSE**, the store Julia Child called "a national treasure"

La Boite

The heart of good food is to start with the most delicious ingredients you can find.

—MICHAEL ANTHONY, Gramercy Tavern and Untitled (New York City)

TRAINING YOUR PALATE: ONLY THE BEST WILL DO

You can follow chefs' recipes or advice on compatible pairings (e.g., sherry vinegar + walnut oil), but *your* version will never taste as good as *theirs* unless you're willing to invest in the same high-quality ingredients.

Train your palate to be able to taste the quality differences between various ingredients. Once you've done your homework and tasted some of the benchmark versions, if you still prefer a different producer of course you should go with your own favorite. But never settle for less until you've tasted some of the *best* versions out there of various ingredients, which may be versions from a specific region or specific brands.

Below, you'll find a list of chefs' recommended ingredients, which you can track down to use as a flavor benchmark against locally available or other versions:

Adobo paste: Doña Maria

Almonds, Marcona: Murray's Cheese (New York City)

Anchovies: Agostino Recca, Scalia

Beans, heirloom: Rancho Gordo

Butter: Beurre Echiré (84%+ butterfat), Jonathan White's Bobolink Dairy butter, Diane St. Clair's Animal Farm in Vermont (87% butterfat); David Kinch's housemade butter at Manresa in California (local cream broken in a Mennonite churn); Norman butter, Plugrá (82% butterfat)

Capers: Pantelleria

Cheese, feta: Pastures of Eden

Cheese, Parmesan: Di Palo (New York City)

Cherries, preserved: Fabbri (Amarena/sugar syrup), Luxardo (Maraschino/liqueur)

Chickpeas: Matiz Navarro, Rosara

Chiles, Calabrian: Tutto

Chili flakes: Hatch (New Mexico)

Chocolate: Amedei, Cacao Barry, Callebaut, Chocolates El Rey, Felchlin, Grenada Chocolate Factory, Guittard Chocolate Company, Kellari, Luker, Scharffen Berger, TCHO, Valrhona

Chocolate, white: Cacao Barry, Guittard, Valrhona (Ivoire)

Cocoa powder: deZaan, Valrhona

Fennel seeds: Lucknow (region of India)

Fish sauce: BliS barrel-aged Red Boat fish sauce (Vietnamese, via Michigan); Delfino Colatura di Alici di Cetara (Italian); Red Boat 40°N or 50°N (Vietnamese)

Flour: King Arthur

Flour, chestnut: Allen Creek Farm

Grits: Anson Mills, Geechie Boy Mill

Hot sauce: Crystal, Texas Pete

Lentils, French green: Du Puy

Maple syrup, Indiana: Burton's Maplewood Farm

Maple syrup, Michigan: American Spoon, barrel-aged BliS

Maple syrup, New Hampshire: Fadden's

Maple syrup, Ohio: Pappy & Company (barrel-aged Bissell's)

Maple syrup, Quebec, Canada: Remonte-Pente Sirop d'Erable

Maple syrup, Vermont: Hartshorn Farm

Mustard, Dijon: Fallot, Maille

Mustard, spicy brown: Gulden's

Mustard, whole-grain: Tin (Brooklyn)

Nut oils: Hammons Products (Missouri: black walnut), Huilerie Beaujolaise (France: almond, hazelnut, pecan, pistachio, walnut)

Olive oil, extra-virgin, California: Arbequina, **California Olive Ranch, DaVero,** McEvoy Ranch Organic

Olive oil, extra-virgin, Greece: Naturally Greek

Olive oil, extra-virgin, Italy: Agrumato (lemon-pressed), Capezzana, Castello di Ama, Fontodi, Frantoio, Laudemio

Olive oil, extra-virgin, Spain: Miguel & Valentino, Valderrama

Paprika, smoked, Spain: La Chinata

Pasta, dried, Italy: Afeltra, **De Cecco, Latini Senatore Cappelli**, Martelli, **Rustichella d'Abruzzo,** Setaro (e.g., porcini)

Pasta, dried, New York: Sfoglini (Brooklyn)

Peanut butter: Koeze's Cream-Nut and Koeze's Sweet Ella's Organic (Michigan)

Peppercorns, black: Tellicherry (India)

Rice, carnaroli (for risotto): Acquerello

Rice, short-grain: Koshihikari

Rose water: Cortas, Mymoun

Salt, kosher: Diamond Crystal

Salt, local (U.S./Mid-Atlantic): J.Q. Dickinson Salt-Works

Salt, local (U.S./Pacific Northwest): Jacobsen Salt Co.

Salt, pink (Australia): Murray River Gourmet

Salt, sea: La Baleine, Maldon

Salt, smoked: Danish Viking, Maldon

Sorghum: Muddy Pond Sorghum Mill

Soy sauce, China: Koon Chun Sauce Factory Thin

Soy sauce, Indonesia: Conimex

Soy sauce, Japan: Kamebishi

> The 40°N [fish sauce] is perfect for everyday use; the 50°N is wonderful for last-minute seasoning. Think of 40 as extra-virgin olive oil and 50 as cold-press extra-virgin olive oil, or fleur de sel: just a light sprinkling to finish a dish will do.
>
> —**CORINNE TRANG**, author of *Essentials of Asian Cooking*

We have a scallop dish on the menu with a squash brandade, fried Brussels sprouts, pomegranate seeds, and spiced pecans. The dish has been on the menu for three years and we have adjusted the brandade every time. This year, we did a blind taste test of nine different SQUASHES from our farmer, because everybody typically gets the same butternut squash or pumpkin. When we tasted them, we found that the butternut squash and the pumpkin were the least flavorful. Pumpkin doesn't taste like anything! So this year we are making the dish with delicata squash, which is fantastic. We are also using these huge banana squashes, which were my second favorite. This was a squash I had never seen before and did not know where else to get them, so we asked our farmer to only sell them to us so we can use them all year.

—STEPHANIE IZARD, Girl & the Goat (Chicago)

Soy sauce, thick: Koon Chun

Soy sauce, thin: Wan Ja Shan (aged)

Soy sauce, U.S.: Bluegrass (Kentucky)

Spices, whole: Kalustyan's (New York City), La Boîte (New York City), Spice House (Chicago, Milwaukee)

Tahini: al wadi (Lebanon), El-Karawan (Middle East), Soom (Philadelphia)

Tomatoes, canned, California: Bianco DiNapoli (from Chef Chris Bianco), Muir Glen

Tomatoes, canned, San Marzano (whole): La Bella San Marzano, La Valle

Tomatoes, preserved: Mount Vesuvius, Mutti, Pomi, San Marzano

Tomato paste: Muir Glen, Mutti

Truffles, black: Plantin (which also makes black truffle products, like mustards)

Truffles, white: Urbani

Vanilla and **vanilla extract**: Nielsen-Massey

Verjus: Fusion Napa Valley, Minus 8 Brix

Vinegar, artisanal: Jean-Marc Montegattaro (e.g., honey, quince)

Vinegar, balsamic: Aceto Manadori; Giusti's Aceto Tradizionale, La Vecchia Dispenza, Villa Manodori

Vinegar, drinking: Pok Pok

Vinegar, flavored: Jean-Marc Montegottero (e.g., honey, lemon), Pok Pok (e.g., black pepper, pomegranate)

Vinegar, ice wine: Minus 8

Vinegar, sherry: BLiS barrel-aged 9-year-old, BLiS Extra Old Fine Solera Aged Sherry Vinegar, Noble XO refined finishing vinegar

Yeast, fresh: Red Star

Yuzu juice: Yakami Orchard

Stephanie Izard

Just because two components are amazing doesn't mean that combining them will work. I have learned this lesson over and over.

—**DANIEL PATTERSON,** Coi (San Francisco) and LocoL (Oakland and Watts)

FLAVOR COMPATIBILITY (e.g., X + Y + Z)

Beyond choosing the highest-quality **ingredients** available to you, you'll want to cook with those that have a natural **affinity** for one another.

When you combine different ingredients, sometimes 1 + 1 does not equal 2—but it equals 3 or more. Think of the magic of tasting the first **basil + tomatoes** of summer—or the first **beets + cheese + walnuts** of winter. You can achieve these synergies between food and wine as well, as in the case of **oysters + Sancerre**, or **mushrooms + pinot noir**, or **Roquefort + Sauternes.**

Once you understand time-tested **flavor pairings** (two ingredients that are a match made in heaven) and **flavor affinities** (groups of three or more ingredients that harmonize well), you can use them as the building blocks to creating new dishes, new cocktails, and more.

Dominique Ansel [Boulud's former pastry chef] approached classic American flavors with the naive curiosity of a student in his first cooking class: WHY do the combinations of peanut butter and chocolate—or Key lime and graham cracker—get people so excited?

—**DANIEL BOULUD,** The Dinex Group (New York City)

Each gin is as different as a different cut of steak or type of fish. Plymouth Gin is soft and delicate, so I'd never pair it with a bold flavor like ginger or chartreuse, but it would work well with Lillet. Tanqueray is a big, bold gin, on the other hand, so it could stand up to ginger or chartreuse. Beefeater has the largest array of botanicals, which pair well with citrus, like lemon and orange. Just as in food, you want to keep everything in balance and MAKE SURE YOUR INGREDIENTS DANCE WELL TOGETHER.

—**AUDREY SAUNDERS,** mixologist and owner, Pegu Club (New York City)

But how on earth can you possibly know what flavors go well together? Isn't that a lifetime's worth of work to discover?

It used to be. Rocco DiSpirito wrote in his book *Flavor* that he remembers begging his instructors at the CIA for insights into what ingredients go well together before discovering our 1996 book, *Culinary Artistry*, our first book to chronicle classic flavor pairings.

Later, we expanded our exploration of food and drink synergies in our 2006 book, *What to Drink with What You Eat*, and then modern flavor synergies in 2008 with *The Flavor Bible*, and in 2014 with *The Vegetarian Flavor Bible*. Today, some of the world's best chefs and cooks and sommeliers and mixologists turn to them to leverage centuries of historic wisdom in order to make better choices.

STUDYING THE PAST

How do new dishes come into being?

I remember reading an interview with rising star chef Jeremiah Langhorne of the Dabney in Washington, D.C., on his "aha" moment of first realizing that kitchens could be a place of creativity. Having previously cooked only at McDonald's, his job at a modest Italian pizza place was the first time he'd seen guys in the kitchen coming up with a dish. "I don't know why, but it shocked me that you could actually create new dishes," he'd told *Washington Life*'s Laura Wainman. **"I literally thought that all dishes were just recipes that already existed,** and the idea of making something new was mind-blowing to me at the time."

Every great and iconic American dish has a STORY TO TELL.

—**MICHAEL LOMONACO,** Porter House (New York City)

Given our culture's overwhelming focus on published recipes, with little attention paid to the process of creating them or of cooking without them, this made perfect sense to me.

Some dishes are so ever-present in our culture that they seem to take on a life of their own, making it hard to imagine a time when they didn't exist. It's too easy to forget that each of them began with a human being (or team of them) and a spark of inspiration—inevitably a desire or need (which is simply desire in a pressure cooker).

Through the examples that follow, you'll see that some of the dishes you might take for granted each started with a spark of inspiration. Some of the most common sparks include pressure, product placement, pleasure, even providence—though they are by no means mutually exclusive.

Pressure

Italian native Caesar Cardini found himself at the end of an especially busy July 4th weekend at his restaurant Caesar's at the Hotel Caesar in Tijuana, Mexico, where he was able to escape the restrictions of the Prohibition era. His kitchen was caught short on ingredients, and with VIPs in the house (including the entourage of the Prince of Wales, according to folklore), the pressure was on. So he threw together a salad based on what he had on hand, including **Romaine lettuce + grated Parmesan cheese + coddled egg + garlic croutons + olive oil + vinegar + mustard + Worcestershire sauce,** finished tableside with a dramatic flourish. Cardini's customers loved the show and the salad so much that, since that day in 1924, word has continued to spread about his Caesar salad.

Product Placement

Girl Scouts have been selling cookies to finance troop activities for the past century. In the 1930s, the Camp Fire Girls were looking for something they, too, could sell to raise funds. Kellogg's home economist Mildred Day and her coworker Malitta Jensen were inspired by the popularity of popcorn balls held together with honey, maple, or molasses, the first recipe for which appeared in the 1860s. Day and Jensen substituted **Rice Krispies** (which Kellogg's debuted in 1928) for popcorn, and concocted a melted **marshmallow + butter + vanilla** mixture as the edible "glue" to hold it together, pressing it into buttered sheet plans so it could be cut into squares when cool. The treat proved so popular that the recipe was printed on the sides of Rice Krispies boxes starting in 1941.

Pleasure

Michelin three-star chef Michel Bras loves to run, something he counts as a source of endless inspiration to his cuisine. He was running in the French countryside one particularly fragrant and flower-filled day in June 1978 when he was inspired to re-create the beauty of the moment on a plate. The result was an ever-changing signature dish he called a *gargouillou* [gar-goo-YOO] of young vegetables, which features a colorful array of as many as 80 different raw and cooked vegetables, flowers, fruits, herbs, leaves, sprouts, and seeds showcasing the local seasonal terroir and accented by spices (and a dry-cured slice of country ham), arranged on the plate in a way that suggests movement. His salad-as-seasonal-mosaic has since become one of the most imitated dishes in the world, inspiring

Long runs in open space bring an amazing sense of well-being and fluidity. Aubrac is inhabited by silence and saturated with light, a perfect setting to feel the ever-changing cycle of nature. Sounds, colors, fragrances fill each moment with wonder, and every run takes me on an "inner trip."

—**MICHEL BRAS,** Bras (Laguiole en Aubrac, France)

customized offerings in Denmark (at René Redzepi's Noma), Spain (at Andoni Luis Aduriz's Mugaritz), and the United States (including at David Kinch's Manresa).

Providence

Sure, maybe there are even examples of dishes that were created when the hand of God intervened. There's no telling whether all of these examples might have had a touch or more of providence behind them. But remember that each of these creations started with a human being—just like you—with a wish to create something new and delicious.

While the creative process can seem obscure or mysterious, it's also very human—people like you, dealing with everyday life, including sparse refrigerators coupled with hungry guests. So don't sell yourself short. You never know what you'll be able to create until you try.

YESTERDAY'S AVANT GARDE, TODAY'S TRADITION

Today's classic dishes were the cutting-edge of creativity at another point in history—so they're worth studying. It can be surprising to realize how long some dishes and techniques have been around—and how relatively new others are. Many origin stories of dishes are unknown or contested. Precious few are crystal clear. But all of them can provide food for thought when creating your next dish. The proof of flavor affinities is in the tasting.

The avant garde of today will be tomorrow's tradition.

—ALBERT ADRIÀ, Tickets (Barcelona)

The culinary world learned a lot before—and since—the nouvelle cuisine revolution of the 1960s and 1970s and the molecular gastronomy movement of the turn of the 21st century, and we shouldn't let the lessons of centuries of trial-and-error go unheeded. If we're smart enough to learn from our ancestors' mistakes, we can free ourselves to make new ones!

And most importantly, you'll want to internalize the principles of—and **be on the lookout for—the patterns of creation**, including necessity (which can indeed be the mother of invention, as exemplified through the origins of many classic dishes, from Buffalo wings to nachos), accidents (like chimichangas, which were thought to be the result of knocking a burrito into a deep-fat fryer), and mere happenstance.

THE CLASSICS

You don't have to reinvent the wheel when it comes to certain aspects of cooking. Someone's already figured out the basics of sauces and stocks, and pancakes and ramen, and a lot of other dishes. So, learn how to make the classics—not because you'll want to always serve them in their original form, but to be able to apply the knowledge embedded in them.

For example, to make a classic **Eggs Benedict**, you're not just learning a single dish—you're learning about baking (English muffin), classic sauce-making (hollandaise), poaching (eggs), sautéing (Canadian bacon), seasoning, plating, garnishing, and more. You can apply that knowledge to countless other dishes (including **Eggs Florentine**, asparagus hollandaise, ramen with a poached egg, etc.).

Classic dishes did something right to have withstood the test of time. Eventually, rather than copying them blindly based on nostalgia, we can turn a critical eye toward them, asking the question, **What can we learn?** This information about ingredients and techniques will serve your creativity.

Some of the wisdom they contain has to do with pleasing combinations of ingredients. Other lessons may have to do with flexible platforms or appealing presentations of dishes. Think about what made them successful in the first place, and what aspects—if any—are worth keeping.

Those lessons can be learned via **deconstruction**: breaking down a dish into its component elements and concepts and ideas, which we'll explore in greater depth in Stage 2.

> In cuisine as well as in design, architecture, and art, what survives is timeless. You can't define it in the moment—it must be defined later, in time.... In the same way, you don't decide what is your signature dish—your guests decide.
>
> **—GABRIEL KREUTHER,** Gabriel Kreuther (New York City)

> **Sometimes you don't want too much creativity. Steak frites are steak frites. Quenelles—fish pudding with lobster sauce—have a spongy texture that's soothing and comforting and delicious. It doesn't need a crunchy element. I love cooking to satisfy people; I never wanted to be a scientist.**
>
> **—DANIEL BOULUD,** The Dinex Group (New York City)

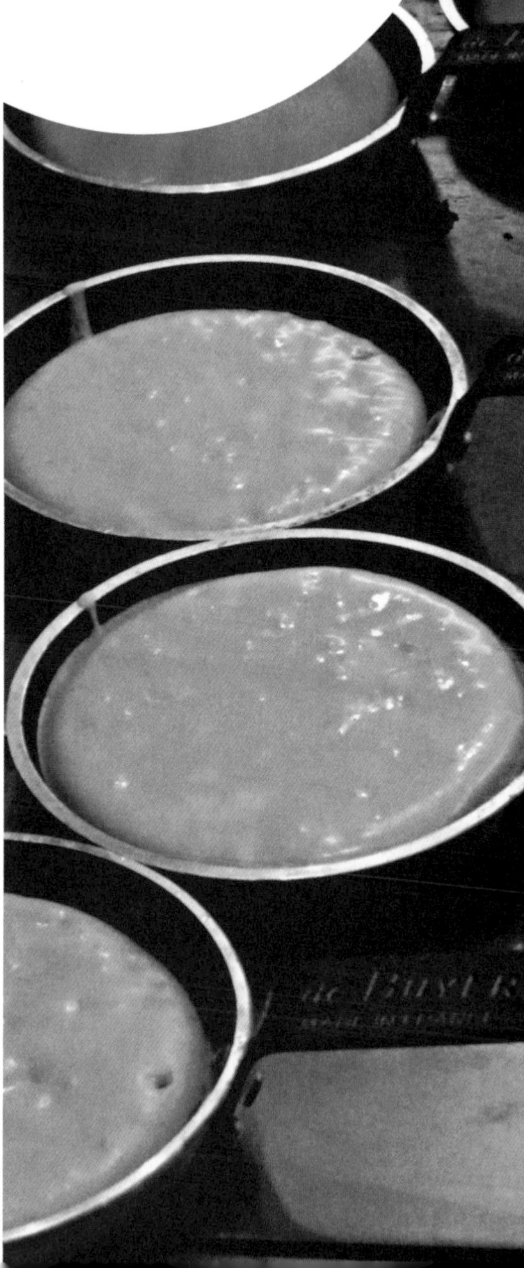

FLAVOR AFFINITIES OF CLASSIC DISHES THROUGH TIME

There are lots of history books detailing the stories behind how various classic dishes came to be. This isn't one of them.

Rather, you'll find just enough information to give you a general sense of when and where and how and through whom various dishes likely made their earliest appearances—although as previously mentioned, there are often conflicting claims of authorship made. You'll also learn the underlying flavor affinities that helped turn them into classics.

[KEY = Origin / City or Region / Creator / Circa]

BC

BAKLAVA [Assyrian/ 8th century BC]
(ground) nuts + phyllo dough + syrup (or honey)

10 AD

MOCK ANCHOVIES [Apicius]
Part of a long tradition of dishes that pretend to be other foods.
fish (sprats) + bay leaves + lemon peel + salt + sugar

100s

FRENCH TOAST
bread + eggs + milk + *fried*

200s

CHEESECAKE [Greek / Aegimus / c. 230 AD]
The Greek physician wrote the first known cheesecake recipe.
cheese + honey + sesame + wheat flour

300s

DOLMAS
Part of a very long tradition of stuffed dishes.
grape leaves + rice + *stuffed*

1200s

MOUSSAKA [Arabic]
béchamel sauce + eggplant + lamb + tomatoes + *baked*

1300s

WAFFLES [Dutch]
batter + *waffle-ironed*

1400s

PESTO [Italian / Rome]
Though created in the 1400s, pesto didn't hit the American mainstream until the 1980s.
basil + cheese + garlic + olive oil + pine nuts + *mortar & pestle*

1500s

GUACAMOLE [Aztec]
avocado + (fresh) chiles + cilantro + lime juice + onions + salt + tomatoes

ZABAGLIONE [Italy / Bartolomeo Scappi / c. 1570]
Found in *The Works of Bartolomeo Scappi*
cinnamon + egg yolks + spirits/wine (Malmsey, marsala) + sugar

1600s

TIRAMISU [Italian / Treviso / Le Beccherie]
Carminantonio Iannaccone credited with later version in the early 1970s.
(shaved dark) chocolate + coffee/espresso + ladyfingers/sponge cake + (sweet) Marsala wine + mascarpone + sugar + *chilled*

INDIAN PUDDING [American / New England]
Thought to be an adaptation of England's hasty pudding, which is made with milk (or water) + wheat flour.
cornmeal + milk + molasses

PUMPKIN PIE [Europe / c. Medieval times]
Today an icon of American Thanksgiving tables, a crustless pumpkin pie was eaten in 1621 at Plymouth Plantation.
Amelia Simmons includes a recipe for a pumpkin pie baked in a crust in her 1796 *American Cookery*: **cream + pumpkin + spices (allspice + cinnamon + cloves + ginger + nutmeg) + sugar + *baked in pie crust***

Credit for innovation in American cuisine must be given to PRESIDENT THOMAS JEFFERSON (1801–1809), who appointed a French chef to cook at the White House to teach French techniques to African-American cooks. He also introduced the WAFFLE IRON from Holland and the pasta maker from Italy.

1700s

NEW ENGLAND CLAM CHOWDER [American / New England]
Served at Boston's Union Oyster House since 1826.
clam juice + clams + potatoes + roux + salt pork

FRENCH ONION SOUP [French]
Gallic lore suggests that French onion soup was created when King Louis XV (1710–1774) found himself at a hunting lodge late one night when there was nothing in the pantry but butter + Champagne + onions. A version with croutons and melted cheese became popular in the United States starting in the 1960s.
(melted) cheese + croutons + (cooked) onions + stock

GAZPACHO [Spanish]
First recipe appeared in Juan de la Mata's *Arte de reposteria (The Art of Pastry)* in 1747, although the dish may date back to the Middle Ages.
anchovies + bread + garlic + oil + vinegar + "vegetables of the Royal Salad"

Evolves into **bell peppers + bread + cucumbers + garlic + olive oil + salt + (raw) tomatoes + (sherry) vinegar**

Or simply: **garlic + sherry vinegar + tomatoes**

MACARONS [Italian / Venice / monastery / c. 1700s]
The almond-flavored meringues are believed to have been brought to France by Caterina de Medici in the 1500s, and popularized by nuns in the 1790s. It wasn't until the 1830s that macarons were sandwiched around jams and other fillings.
almond flour + egg whites + sugar

flavored with:
lychee + raspberry + rose (called *Ispahan*, after the Iranian city), macaron + milk chocolate + passion fruit (called *Mogador*, after the Moroccan city), olive oil + vanilla

Parisian patissier Pierre Hermé credits his contemporary success with MACARONS to "constant experimentation," starting his process with a drawing inspired by something he has tasted, read, or seen.

After Hermé's three attempts to create a chestnut + pear macaron were unsuccessful (as the flavors of each were not distinct), he instead decided to create two separate macarons which he then sold together.

APPLE PIE [American]
First recipe appears in Amelia Simmons's 1796 *American Cookery*, which forged indigenous American ingredients with European cooking techniques.
allspice + apples + cinnamon + dough + nutmeg + sugar

1800s

STRAWBERRIES ROMANOFF [English / Carlton Hotel / Auguste Escoffier—who called the dessert "Strawberries Americaine Style," before a similar dessert was popularized at Romanoff's in Hollywood]
cream + orange + strawberries

CHERRY CLAFOUTIS [French / Limousin]
black cherries + flan batter + powdered sugar

BEEF STROGANOFF [Russian]
Named for 19th-century Russian diplomat Count Pavel Stroganov.
beef + mushrooms + onions + sour cream

While BEEF STROGANOFF is traditionally served with crispy straw potatoes in Russia, when it came to the United States in the 1940s, Stroganoff was served on egg noodles.

SOUFFLÉ [French / Antoine Carême / c. early 1820s]
Carême invented the classic soufflé by taking advantage of the advent of new (non-coal) ovens heated by air drafts.
egg whites + *baked*

SACHER TORTE [Austrian / Franz Sacher, while working for Prince Metternich / c. 1832]
apricot jam + chocolate cake + chocolate icing

PAELLA, VALENCIAN [Spanish / Valencia / c. 1840 (its first appearance in a newspaper)]
butter beans + olive oil + paprika + (short-grain) rice + saffron + snails + tomatoes + *cooked in paella pan*

DOUGHNUT HOLES AND **RING DOUGHNUTS** [American / New England / Elizabeth Gregory and her son Hanson Gregory / c. mid-1800s]
In response to their wish to eliminate the uncooked center of fried doughnuts.

KEY LIME PIE [American / Florida / c. mid-1800s]
(whipped) cream + eggs + graham cracker crust + Key lime juice + sweetened condensed milk + *chilled*

STRAWBERRY SHORTCAKE [American / c. mid-1800s]
biscuits + (whipped) cream + strawberries + sugar

BOSTON CREAM PIE [American / Boston / Parker House Hotel / c. 1850s]
cake + chocolate + custard

WELSH RAREBIT [British]
First recipe appeared in Charles Elme Francatelli's *A Plain Cookery Book for the Working Classes* in 1852.
(toasted) bread + butter + cheese + mustard

BAKED ALASKA [American / New York City / Delmonico's / Charles Ranhofer / c. 1876]
Following Alaska's admission to the Union in 1867.
ice cream (frozen hard) + cream or meringue + *baked or flambéed (to brown)*

SHEPHERD'S PIE [English / c. 1870s]
(minced) meat + (mashed) potatoes + vegetables + *baked*

CHILI [American / c. late 1800s]
Inspired many regional variations, and many regional chili cook-offs.
beans + chili powder + cumin + garlic + ground meat + onions + tomatoes

TARTE TATIN [French / Lamotte-Beuvron / Hotel Tatin / Stephanie Tatin / c. 1880s or 1890s]
Created after the chef was either slammed, distracted by flirting, or resourceful when faced with a broken oven—in any case, she created this legendary tarte accidentally.
apples + butter + pastry crust + sugar + *caramelized*

In music, as in life, there are no mistakes—just chances to improvise.

—**MILES DAVIS** to Herbie Hancock

Joanne Chang soaks her cake for BOSTON CREAM PIE in coffee syrup, and lightens her custard with whipped cream at Flour Bakery + Café in Boston.

In 1894, chef Charles Ranhofer published his 1,100-plus-page cookbook, *The Epicurean*, which caused an uproar among his fellow professional chefs for sharing secrets behind popular dishes like BAKED ALASKA and Eggs Benedict.

HOT DOG [American / New York / c. late 1800s]
bun + hot dog + mustard (+ sauerkraut)

LOBSTER NEWBERG [American / New York / Delmonico's / Charles Ranhofer / c. 1876]
Captain Ben Wenberg is said to have brought in the recipe from his travels and given it to the restaurant, which reproduced it and added it to the menu as Lobster Wenberg—but after Ranhofer and Wenberg had a falling out, it was renamed "Lobster Newberg."
butter + cayenne + cognac + cream + lobster + sherry

RAMOS GIN FIZZ [American / New Orleans / Imperial Cabinet Saloon / Henry C. Ramos / c. 1888]
The drink's proper execution originally called for 12 to 15 minutes of shaking to achieve its creamy richness.
cream + egg white + gin + lemon juice + lime juice + orange flower water + simple syrup + soda water

PIZZA ALLA MARGHERITA [Italian / Naples / Pizzeria Brandi / Raffaele Esposito / c. 1889]
Inspired by the colors of the Italian flag upon a visit by Queen Margherita of Savoy.
(green) basil + (baked) dough + (white) mozzarella + (red) tomato sauce

The original OYSTERS ROCKEFELLER, on which many interpretations have been based, did not feature spinach; the recipe remains a family secret.

OYSTERS ROCKEFELLER [American / New Orleans / Antoine's / Jules Alciatore / c. 1889]
In honor of John D. Rockefeller, then the richest man in the world: The dish was billed as the richest dish in the world.
butter (and/or cream) + greens + oysters

Many interpretations contain: **breadcrumbs + butter + oysters + spinach**

EGGS BENEDICT [American / New York City / Charles Ranhofer of Delmonico's or Oscar Tschirky of the Waldorf-Astoria Hotel / c. 1890s]
In both versions of the story, a hangover spurred the dish's creation.
(poached) eggs + English muffin + ham/Canadian bacon + hollandaise sauce

WALDORF SALAD [American / New York City / Waldorf-Astoria Hotel / Oscar Tschirky (formerly of Delmonico's) / c. 1890s]
Created for the hotel's inaugural dinner.
apples + celery + mayonnaise (+ walnuts were added in the early 1900s; other later additions have included citrus juice and/or rind + grapes + raisins)

CRACKER JACK [American / Chicago's World Fair / Frederick William Rueckheim / c. 1893]
caramel/molasses + peanuts + popcorn

Eggs Benedict

Waldorf Salad

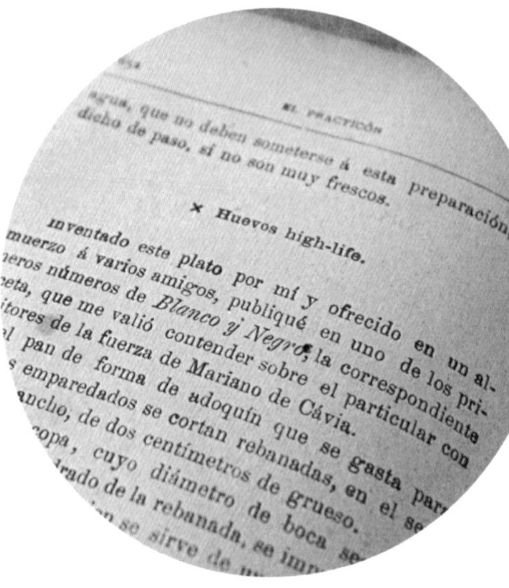

EL PRACTICÓN

agua, que no deben someterse á esta preparación,
dicho de paso, si no son muy frescos.

× Huevos high-life.

Inventado este plato por mí y ofrecido en un al-
muerzo á varios amigos, publiqué en uno de los pri-
meros números de *Blanco y Negro*, la correspondiente
receta, que me valió contender sobre el particular con
tores de la fuerza de Mariano de Cávia.
pan de forma de adoquín que se gasta par
emparedados se cortan rebanadas, en el se
ancho, de dos centímetros de grueso.
copa, cuyo diámetro de boca se
rado de la rebanada, se imp

EGG-IN-A-HOLE (AKA HUEVOS HIGH-LIFE) [Spanish]
The first known recipe of the classic dish with an egg fried in a yolk-size hole in the middle of a slice of bread was published in the 1894 cookbook *El Practicon* by Angel Muro.
bread + butter + eggs + *fried*

HOT FUDGE SUNDAE [American / c. 1880s–1890s]
Folklore attributes the creation to the so-called Blue Laws of the time restricting certain behavior (ranging from fornicating to selling ice cream sodas) on Sundays.
hot fudge + vanilla ice cream

PEACH MELBA [England / London / Savoy Hotel / Auguste Escoffier / c. 1890s]
Inspired by hearing Dame Nellie Melba sing at Covent Garden in 1892 or 1893.
(poached and halved) peaches + raspberry sauce + vanilla ice cream

CREPES SUZETTE [Monte Carlo / Café de Paris / Henri Charpentier / January 31, 1896]
Created for Prince of Wales Edward VII and named after his female companion.
butter + crepes + Grand Marnier + orange juice + *flambéed*

CHERRIES JUBILEE [English / London / Auguste Escoffier / c. 1897]
Created in honor of Queen Victoria's diamond jubilee celebration.
cherries + cherry brandy or Kirsch + vanilla ice cream + *flambéed*

Early 1900s

BLACK FOREST CAKE [German]
cherries + chocolate + whipped cream

EGG CREAM [American / Brooklyn]
chocolate syrup + milk + seltzer

REUBEN SANDWICH [American / New York / c. early 1900s, although the exact origins are contested]
corned beef + Russian dressing + rye bread + sauerkraut + Swiss cheese

HAMBURGER [American / New Haven, CT / Louis' Lunch / c. 1900]
Created when a customer in a rush requested something he could eat on the run.
bun + burger patty (+ optional cheese + onion + tomato at Louis' Lunch)

PB&J (PEANUT BUTTER AND JELLY SANDWICH) [American / c. 1901]
The first reference appeared on the heels of a St. Louis doctor's making peanut butter in 1890.
bread + (grape) jelly + peanut butter

ICE CREAM CONE [American / St. Louis World's Fair / Ernest Hamwi / c. 1904]
The Syrian entrepreneur sold crisp waffled pastries next to an ice cream vendor; one day, Hamwi rolled some of the pastries into cones to help the ice cream vendor when he unexpectedly ran out of bowls.
ice cream + waffled pastry

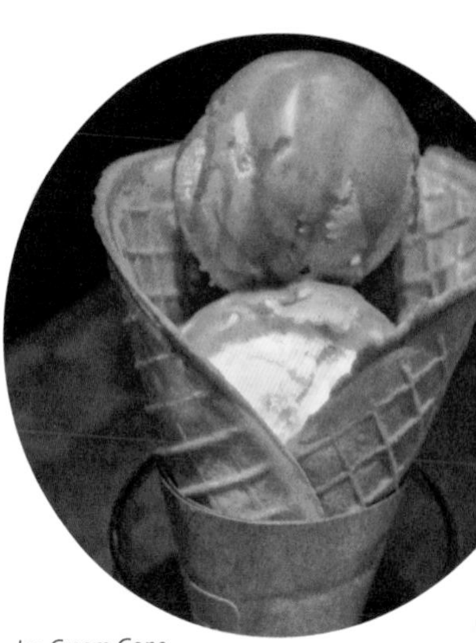

Ice Cream Cone

PIZZA, AMERICAN [American / New York City / Lombardi's / Naples native Gennaro Lombardi / c. 1905]
cheese + dough + tomato sauce + *baked in a coal-fired oven*

CANDY APPLE [American / New Jersey / William Kolb / c. 1908]
The confectioner experimented by dipping apples into a melted red cinnamon candy syrup.
apples + cinnamon + sugar syrup

FETTUCCINE ALFREDO [Italian / Rome / Trattoria Alfredo / Alfredo Di Lelio / c. 1910s–1920s]
Created for his wife who had just given birth and had fussy food cravings, but popularized by Hollywood celebrities like Mary Pickford and Douglas Fairbanks, who loved Fettuccine Alfredo so much they dubbed Alfredo "King of the Noodles."
butter + fettuccine + Parmesan cheese

The celery stick stirrer used in a BLOODY MARY is believed to have gained popularity in the 1960s.

BLOODY MARY [France / Paris / Harry's New York Bar / Fernand "Pete" Petiot / c. 1920, or 1940s after the bartender moved to the St. Regis Hotel's King Cole Bar in New York City]
(canned) tomato juice + (Russian) vodka (+ various seasonings, e.g., horseradish + lemon + salt + Tabasco sauce + Worcestershire sauce)

Whatever the origins, the FRENCH DIP SANDWICH was not thought to be the case of a chef proactively thinking, "How can I make this sandwich even better?" It happened either by accident, or by listening to a request. So, pay attention to your accidents—as well as to your guests' special requests!

FRENCH DIP SANDWICH [American / California / Philippe's or Cole's, both of which opened in 1908 / c. 1910s–1920s]
The legends of this sandwich's origins vary, but include 1) a sandwich accidentally fell into some jus; 2) a customer requested that a sandwich be dipped in jus (either due to receiving a stale roll, or simply seeing the juice at the bottom of the pan of meat); or 3) a customer with sore gums requested that a sandwich be dipped in jus.
(thinly sliced) beef + *jus* + roll

VICHYSSOISE [American / New York / Ritz-Carlton / Louis Diat / c. 1912]
(chopped) chives + cream + potatoes + stock

CROQUE MONSIEUR [c. 1915]
First known recipe by E. Defouck in *The Belgian Cookbook* by Mrs. Brian Luck.
bread + butter + egg (beaten) + Gruyère cheese + ham + *fried*

Variations include: **Croque Madame (+ fried egg) and Croque Provencal (+ tomatoes)**

TURTLES [American / DeMet's Candy Co. / c. 1918]
caramel + chocolate + pecans

NEGRONI [Italian / Florence / Caffè Casoni / c. 1919]
Created by a bartender after a suggestion by Count Camillo Negroni to fortify his Americano cocktail.
bitters + gin + vermouth

OMELETTE ARNOLD BENNETT [England / London / Savoy / c. 1920s]
Named after the writer and critic staying at the hotel while writing his novel *Imperial Palace.*
eggs + hollandaise sauce + smoked haddock

PAVLOVA [Australia or New Zealand / c. 1920s]
Inspired by Russian ballerina Anna Pavlova (1881–1931), the meringue and fruit dessert was said to be "light as Pavlova."
fruit (e.g., kiwi, passion fruit, strawberries) + meringue (egg whites + superfine sugar)

Pavlova

CHIMICHANGAS [American / Tucson, Arizona / El Charro Café / Monica Flin / c. 1922]
As the story goes, the chef-owner accidentally knocked a burrito into the deep-fat fryer.
beans + cheese + tortillas + *fried*

GREEN GODDESS SALAD DRESSING [American / San Francisco / Palace Hotel / Chef Philip Roemer / c. 1923]
In honor of actor George Arliss, who starred in the play *The Green Goddess.*
anchovies + chives/scallions + parsley + mayonnaise + sour cream + lemon juice + white wine vinegar

CAESAR SALAD [Mexican / Tijuana / Hotel Caesar restaurant / Caesar Cardini / c. 1924]
Cardini's brother Alex has his own claims to the salad, and is sometimes credited for the addition of anchovies.
(anchovies) + croutons + (coddled) eggs + garlic + lemon juice + olive oil + Parmesan cheese + Romaine + Worcestershire sauce

MIMOSA [France / Paris / Hôtel Ritz Paris / Frank Meier / c. 1925]
Champagne + orange juice

COBB SALAD [American / Hollywood/ Brown Derby / Bob Cobb / c. 1926]
Created as a late-night snack for himself to use up leftovers, and worked on before adding to the menu in 1929.
chicken + Romaine lettuce + *chopped* (1926 version)

evolved into 1929 version:

avocado + bacon + blue cheese + chicken + chicory + chives + French dressing + hard-boiled eggs + iceberg lettuce + Romaine + tomatoes + watercress + *chopped*

S'MORES [American / Girl Scouts / c. 1927]
Possibly inspired by the commercially produced Mallomars of 1913 or Moon Pies of 1917 featuring the same flavor affinities.
chocolate + Graham cracker + (toasted) marshmallow

ROCKY ROAD ICE CREAM [American / Dreyer's and Edy's Ice Cream / William Dreyer and Joseph Edy / c. 1929]
The ice cream maker and confectioner who teamed up to form Dreyer's and Edy's claim to have invented this popular ice cream flavor.
almonds + chocolate ice cream + marshmallow

RED VELVET CAKE (aka Hundred-Dollar Cake or Waldorf-Astoria Cake) [American / New York City / Waldorf-Astoria Hotel / c. early to mid-1900s, or possibly 1959]
buttermilk + cocoa + flour + sugar + vanilla + vinegar

Red Velvet Cake

Maine Congressman Cleveland Sleeper introduced legislation in the late 1930s that would "make it an illegal as well as a culinary offense to introduce tomatoes to CLAM CHOWDER." Eleanor Early wrote in her *New England Sampler* cookbook that "Tomatoes and clams have no more affinity than ice cream and horse radish. It is sacrilege to wed bivalves with bay leaves, and only a degraded cook would do such a thing."

After Andrew's former boss Lydia Shire took over Locke-Ober in 2001, her version of LOBSTER SAVANNAH replaced the pimientos with red bell peppers and lightened the sauce.

The Texas State Fair version of CORN DOGS was popularized as "Fletcher's Original State Fair Corny Dogs," while those introduced at the Minnesota State Fair were called "Pronto Pups."

1930s

RATATOUILLE [French / Provence / c. 1930]
The first citation to describe this particular dish was in 1930, although the term had been around years longer to refer to stews.
bell peppers + eggplant + garlic + herbes de Provence + olive oil + onions + (stewed) tomatoes + zucchini

PHILLY CHEESESTEAK [American / Philadelphia]
(sliced) beef + onions + roll

Later add-ons: **cheese (Cheez-Whiz, American, or Provolone) + ketchup + mushrooms + sweet peppers**

MANHATTAN CLAM CHOWDER (aka Coney Island Clam Chowder and Fulton Market Clam Chowder) [American / New York / c. 1930s]
This version, which was popularized by New York chefs, was inspired by the huge rise in popularity of tomatoes in the mid-1800s.
clams + tomatoes

RUM RAISIN ICE CREAM [American]
cream + raisins + rum + sugar + vanilla + *frozen*

TOASTED RAVIOLI [American / St. Louis / Angelo Oldani's]
A German staff member named Fritz is said to have thrown fresh ravioli into the deep fryer by accident—and it was discovered that guests loved them.
ravioli + *deep-fried*

SHIRLEY TEMPLE [American / Hollywood/ Brown Derby or Chasen's restaurant]
The famed mocktail was created so the child star could drink alongside her adult peers.
ginger ale + grenadine + maraschino cherry

LOBSTER SAVANNAH [American / Boston / Locke-Ober restaurant]
béchamel sauce + lobster + mushrooms + Parmesan + pimientos + sherry + *baked in lobster shell*

BELLINI [Italian / Venice / Harry's Bar / c. 1934–1948]
peach puree + prosecco

RICE KRISPIES TREATS [American / Kellogg's / home economist Mildred Day and her coworker Malitta Jensen / c. 1939]
butter + marshmallows + Rice Krispies

1940s

CORN DOGS [American / Minnesota or Texas State Fair]
cornbread batter + hot dog + *deep-fried*

MAI TAI [American / California / Trader Vic's or Don the Beachcomber]
Curaçao + lime juice + rum

PAD THAI [Thai]
Prime Minister Phibun mandated the creation of a Thai national dish to inspire national pride.
bean sprouts + chiles + egg + fish sauce + lime + palm sugar + (chopped) peanuts + (fried) shrimp + rice noodles + tamarind + tofu + *stir-fried*

KENTUCKY FRIED CHICKEN [American / Colonel Harland Sanders / c. 1940]
The Colonel built his popular fried chicken business on a recipe made in a fast-cooking pressure fryer with "11 secret herbs and spices" which are thought to include flour combined with:
basil + black pepper + celery salt + garlic salt + ginger + mustard powder + oregano + paprika + salt + thyme + white pepper

CHICAGO-STYLE DEEP-DISH PIZZA (WITH BISCUIT-LIKE CRUST) [American / Chicago / Pizzeria Uno / Rudy Malnati / c. 1943]
cheese + (thick) pizza crust + tomato sauce + toppings

NACHOS [Mexican / Piedras Negras / Victory Club / Ignacio "Nacho" Anaya / c. 1943]
Created by the Club's maître d' who threw them together as canapés for a group of wives of military officers when he couldn't locate the chef; the dish was a hit and Nacho was named the Club's chef.
Cheddar cheese + jalapeño peppers + tortilla chips + ***melted***

BLACK BEAN SOUP WITH MADEIRA [American / New York City / Coach House / c. 1949–93]
black beans + hard-boiled eggs + Madeira

1950s

CARAMEL APPLES [American / Kraft Foods / Dan Walker]
The Kraft employee experimented with surplus caramels post-Halloween and invented it in time for the holidays.
(raw) apple + caramel [+ (chopped) peanuts, when they're often called "taffy apples"]

Pad Thai

SANDWICHES: WHAT'S IN A NAME?

Two centuries after avid gambler Earl of Sandwich—wishing to have a meal brought to him at the gaming table—asked in 1762 for a thin slice of meat between two slices of buttered bread, which was named the first "sandwich," American regions name their own:

1952: po' boy (New Orleans)

1954: grinder (New England)

1955: submarine (Connecticut)

1955: hero (New York City)

1956: hoagie (New Jersey and Pennsylvania)

WEDGE SALAD [American]
bacon + blue cheese dressing + iceberg lettuce (+ scallions) + tomato

CARPACCIO [Italian / Venice / Harry's Bar / c. 1950]
Created while artist Vittore Carpaccio's exhibit was in town in response to a guest who said she'd been advised by her doctor not to eat cooked meat; the dish was said to be named for the artist's paintings' characteristic red and white colors.
(raw, sliced) beef + mayonnaise sauce

BANANAS FOSTER [American / New Orleans / Brennan's Restaurant / Chef Paul Blangé / c. 1951]
Owen Brennan challenged his chef to include bananas in a new dish, which he then named after Richard Foster, a regular customer.
banana + banana liqueur + brown sugar + butter + cinnamon + rum + vanilla ice cream *flambéed*

GERMAN CHOCOLATE CAKE [American / Texas / c. 1957]
The cake is *not* German; the name comes from that of chocolate maker Samuel German, who developed Baker's sweet chocolate for Baker's Chocolate Company; 1957 was the first publication of a recipe in a Texas newspaper.
(Baker's German's Sweet) chocolate + coconut + pecans

POUTINE [Canadian / Warwick / Quebec / Café Ideal / c. 1957]
Truck driver and patron Eddy Lainesse suggested that owners Fernand Lachance and Germaine Lachance mix their fries with cheese curds.
cheese curds + French fries + gravy (the original gravy was brown sugar + ketchup + Worcestershire sauce)

White House Chef Cristeta Comerford served her own elegant take on POUTINE—smoked duck and cheese curds with a red wine gravy served on wafer fries—as a canapé at a White House State Dinner in honor of Canada's Prime Minister Justin Trudeau and his wife in March 2016.

CHOCOLATE VELVET CAKE [American / New York City / Four Seasons / Albert Kumin / c. late 1950s]
amaretto + chocolate + heath bars + rum

SPAGHETTI ALLA CARBONARA [Italian / c. 1950s–1960s]
black pepper + cream + (Parmesan and/or Pecorino) cheese + (raw) egg + pancetta (or guanciale) + spaghetti

1960s

NEGIMAKI ROLLS [American/Japanese / New York / Restaurant Nippon / Nobuyoshi Kuraoka / c. 1963]
Created after *New York Times* restaurant critic Craig Claiborne wrote that a Japanese restaurant based in New York *must* serve beef.
beef + scallions + soy sauce

BUFFALO WINGS [American / Buffalo, New York / Anchor Bar / Teressa Bellissimo / c. 1964]
Created out of leftovers she had on hand for her hungry sons and his friends after a late-night movie.
chicken wings + garlic + hot sauce (e.g., cayenne / red peppers + salt + vinegar)

***later accompanied by:* blue cheese + celery**

POP-TARTS [American / Kellogg's / c. September 1964]
The original flavors were apple + currant, blueberry, brown sugar + cinnamon, and strawberry.
filling + pastry + *toasted*

CALIFORNIA ROLL [American / Los Angeles / Tokyo Kaikan restaurant / chef Manashita Ichiro and his assistant Mashita Ichiro / c. late 1960s]
Created the "inside out" roll to hide the nori on the inside and subbed avocado for raw tuna.
avocado + crab + cucumber + nori + sushi rice

Don't underestimate the power of a catchy name, such as POP-TARTS, in the success of a new product. Post actually beat Kellogg's to market with toaster pastries in February 1964, but had the misfortune of naming theirs "Country Squares."

1970s

ALMOND TORTE [American / Berkeley, California / Chez Panisse / Lindsey Shere]
almond paste + butter + flour + sugar + vanilla

STICKY TOFFEE PUDDING [England / Sharrow Bay hotel]
custard or ice cream + sponge cake + toffee sauce

ORANGE BEEF [American / New York City / Shun Lee Palace / Michael Tong / 1971]
beef + (bittersweet preserved) orange

CHICAGO-STYLE STUFFED PIZZA (WITH FLAKIER CRUST) [American / Chicago / Giordano's or Nancy's / c. 1974]

SPAGHETTI ALLA PRIMAVERA (AKA SPRINGTIME PASTA) [American (Italian) / New York / Le Cirque / Sirio Maccioni, c. 1975]
Created with ingredients in the refrigerator while visiting Prince Edward Island and served to *New York Times* critic Craig Claiborne.
cream + Parmesan + spaghetti + spring vegetables (e.g., asparagus + broccoli + mushrooms + peas + zucchini) + toasted pine nuts

CHICAGO-STYLE STUFFED PIZZA is said to be based on traditional Italian Easter pies called *scarciedda*, which were made in Turin and featured cheese, meat, and other ingredients—but no tomato sauce.

GARGOUILLOU [France / Laguiole / Michel Bras / c. 1978]
flowers + fruits + herbs + sprouts + vegetables

BAGEL, EVERYTHING [American / New York / c. 1970s–1980]
bagel + caraway seeds + garlic + onions + poppy seeds + salt + sesame seeds

1980s

BEGGAR'S PURSES [American / New York / Quilted Giraffe / Barry Wine]
Said to have been inspired by *un aumoniere* served by Chef François Clerc of La Vieille Fontaine in Maisons-Laffitte, France.
(melted) butter + caviar + chive (for tying the crepe into a bundle) + crème fraîche + crepe + gold leaf

PUT YOUR HANDS BEHIND YOUR BACK, LEAN FORWARD, AND SCOOP IT UP IN ONE BITE.

—**BARRY WINE'S STAFF**'s instructions to guests at the Quilted Giraffe, for eating **BEGGAR'S PURSES** off the candlesticks or candelabras upon which they were served; some guests were handcuffed to their chairs for the $50-a-pop experience.

SALADE GOURMANDE [French / Eugénie-les-Bains / Les Prés d'Eugénie / Michel Guérard]
black truffles + chervil + chives + foie gras + green beans (haricots verts) + lettuce + vinaigrette

RED MULLET WITH ZUCCHINI "SCALES" [Swiss / Frédy Girardet]
herbs + olive oil + red mullet + zucchini

RED MULLET WITH POTATO "SCALES" [French / Paul Bocuse]
red mullet + potato

LOBSTER CLUB [American / New York City / Arcadia / Anne Rosenzweig]
bacon + brioche + lobster + mayonnaise

MACARONI AND CHEESE WITH COUNTRY HAM AND SHAVED BLACK TRUFFLES [American / Virginia / The Inn at Little Washington / Patrick O'Connell / c. 1980s]
black truffles + cheeses + ham + macaroni

PENNE ALLA VODKA [American / c. early 1980s]
cream + penne + tomato + vodka

BAKED GOAT CHEESE WITH GARDEN LETTUCES [American / Berkeley, CA / Chez Panisse / Alice Waters / c. 1981]
breadcrumbs + garden lettuces + (baked) goat cheese

COULANT AU CHOCOLAT [French / Laguiole / Bras / Michel Bras / c. 1981]
chocolate [biscuit dough + frozen ganache + *baked*]
We still remember our first life-changing bites of **Jean-Georges Vongerichen**'s own version of this molten-centered cake at Manhattan's Jojo shortly after we were married in 1990—which, under various names including "Chocolate Lava Cake" and "Chocolate Truffle Cake," went on to inspire other versions from coast to coast and around the world (see page 273).

GRILLED PIZZA [American / Providence, RI / Al Forno / George Germon and Johanne Killeen / c. 1981]
The chef-couple misheard of a technique being used in Italy, which inspired them to start cooking their pizza doughs directly over an open grill.
cheese + pizza dough + scallions + tomato sauce + *grilled*

BLACKENED REDFISH [American / New Orleans / K-Paul's Louisiana Kitchen / Paul Prudhomme / c. 1982]
Said to have been created because Prudhomme didn't have a grill, so he had to crisp his fish in a large black skillet instead.
butter + redfish + spices (cayenne + onion powder + oregano + paprika + salt + thyme) + *blackened*

Inspired: Other "blackened" dishes, including other fish (e.g., salmon), shrimp, chicken, steak

If the original **Spago** had never run out of bread in 1982, who knows how long it might have taken for the kitchen at **Wolfgang Puck's** and **Barbara Lazaroff's** Los Angeles restaurant to think of serving chilled smoked salmon and two caviars (milder black, and stronger red salmon) with crème fraîche, dill, and sweet red onion (not to mention a squeeze of lemon juice to counterbalance the salmon's richness, plus a sprinkle of chives) on hot baked *pizza dough* instead? Time, by the way, is also a key ingredient of this dish (as it is of many): The pizza must be served quickly so the crust stays hot while the salmon and caviar stay cold, achieving that all-important balance of opposites.

SMOKED SALMON PIZZA [American / Los Angeles / Spago / Wolfgang Puck / c. 1982]
caviar + crème fraîche + pizza dough + smoked salmon

***RISO ORO E ZAFFERANO* (SAFFRON RISOTTO WITH GOLD LEAF)** [Italian / Gualtiero Marchesi / c. 1984]
gold leaf + risotto + saffron

GUALTIERO MARCHESI was the first Italian chef (and non-Frenchman) to receive three Michelin stars.

BEETS AND LEEKS [American / Thomas Keller / c. 1980s (at Rakel) and c. 1990s (at the French Laundry)]
Inspired by a combination Keller had tasted at Jean-Louis at the Watergate.
beets + leeks (+ lobster + potatoes)

CHICKEN FOR TWO ROASTED IN THE BRICK OVEN [American / San Francisco / Zuni Café / Judy Rodgers / c. 1987]
(salted) chicken + panzanella (bread salad) + *wood-fire roasted*

MAINE SEA SCALLOPS "IN BLACK TIE" [American / New York / Le Cirque / Daniel Boulud / c. mid-1980s]
Inspired by his first New Year's Eve dinner at the restaurant.
(alternating layers of) black truffles + scallops + *wrapped in spinach*

1990s and beyond

BACON ON A CLOTHESLINE [American/ Chicago / Alinea / Grant Achatz]
apple + bacon + butterscotch + thyme

BEEF CHEEK RAVIOLI [American / New York / Babbo / Mario Batali]
beef cheeks + ravioli

BLACK COD WITH MISO [American / New York / Nobu / Nobu Matsuhisa / c. 1994]
black cod + (sweet saikyo) miso

BOUQUET OF ROSES [French / Paris / L'Arpège / Alain Passard]
apple + berlingot + puff pastry + sugar

CANARD APICIUS [French / Paris / Lucas-Carton / Alain Senderens]
A remake of an earlier version made in 1970, inspired by Apicius's original version published in the world's oldest cookbook, *De re Coquinaria.*
apple + dates + duck + honey + caraway + coriander + mint + oregano + pepper + saffron + vinegar

CAPPUCCINO OF WHITE BEANS WITH GRATED TRUFFLES [English / London / Gordon Ramsay]
cream + truffles + white beans (e.g., canellini) + wild mushrooms

CAULIFLOWER IN A CAST-IRON POT [American / Napa Valley / Ubuntu / Jeremy Fox]
brown butter + cauliflower + cilantro + citrus + curry

CRACK PIE [American / New York City / wd-50 / Christina Tosi]
Inspired by *Joy of Cooking* to create a rich and buttery filling for an oatmeal cookie crust for family meal that became one of her signature dishes.
butter + oats + sugar

CRISP PAUPIETTES OF SEA BASS IN BAROLO SAUCE [American / New York City / Daniel / Daniel Boulud]
Boulud says the dish was inspired by Paul Bocuse's and Frédy Girardet's red-mullet-with vegetable-scales dishes—and which has inspired other dishes in Daniel's kitchen starring those ingredients.
leeks + potatoes + sea bass + thyme + (red) wine (e.g., Barolo)

Crispy Crepe, being spread with scallion jam

CRISPY CREPE [American / Lummi Island, Washington / The Willows Inn / Blaine Wentzel / c. 2013]
crepe + (grilled) scallions + (preserved) smelt

CURRIED TUNA TARTARE [American / New York City / Le Cirque / Daniel Boulud] Came about after the sushi craze opened Americans' minds to eating raw fish.
curry + tuna + *raw* + *chopped*

DB BURGER [American / New York City / db bistro moderne / Daniel Boulud]
beef + bun + foie gras + short ribs

EGG CAVIAR [American / New York City / Jean-Georges Vongerichten]
caviar + (scrambled) eggs + vodka + whipped cream

THE FOREST [French / Menton / Mirazar / Mauro Colagreco / c. 2011]
mushrooms + parsley ("moss") + quinoa (risotto)

WHO CAN BE CREATIVE WITH FOOD? EVERYBODY!

Maize (which we now call **corn**) is believed to have existed for 7,000 to 10,000 years. The technique of **deep-frying** is thought to have existed for nearly that long, with the Egyptians deep-frying in 5000 BC.

But it took until 1992 for a janitor named **Richard Montañez** to propose to Frito-Lay's president (after receiving his video memo encouraging all employees to "think like owners") coating Cheetos in chili powder, which eventually became Flamin' Hot Cheetos, one of Frito-Lay's bestselling snack items—and led to his new career as the company's executive vice president.

How did some of these popular snack foods first come into being?

late 1920s / early 1930s: Mexican native **Gustavo Olguin** sells deep-fried extruded masa called *fritos* ("little fried things").

1932: San Antonio confectioner **Charles Elmer Doolin** seeks a new treat to diversify out of the ice cream business, and hopes to find a corn snack that won't go stale like tortillas. He discovers Olguin's fried corn chips, and buys the original recipe plus a converted potato ricer and 19 retail accounts for $100. He starts to make **Fritos** corn chips in his mother's kitchen, and he and his family experiment with other uses for Fritos as well as other snack foods.

1947: Doolin expands into other snack foods, including roasted peanuts, peanut butter crackers, potato chips, and fried pork skins.

1948: Through ongoing kitchen experiments, Doolin creates **Cheetos**, a cheese-flavored puffed snack:
cheese powder + cornmeal + *deep-fried*

1949: Doolin's mother, **Daisy Dean Doolin,** is said to have poured some leftover chili onto Fritos, creating the original **Frito Pie.** The recipe appears in a 1950s-era cookbook:
(grated) cheese + chili + Fritos + onion + *baked*

1966: Doritos tortilla chips are introduced.

1969: Fun-Yuns onion-flavored rings are introduced.

1977: Tostitos tortilla chips are introduced.

1992: Richard Montañez, a janitor at the Rancha Cucamonga plant in California, comes up with the idea of adding chili powder to Cheetos—creating **Flamin' Hot Cheetos**:
cheese powder + chili powder + cornmeal + *deep-fried*

2002: The introduction of **Flamin' Hot Cheetos con Limon:**
cheese powder + chili powder + cornmeal + lime + *deep-fried*

2000s: Frito Pie is such a ubiquitous dish in the South that leading chefs such as **Dean Fearing** and **Emeril Lagasse** share their own recipes for the dish. **Daniel Boulud** ushers in 2012 with his first taste of Frito Pie at a tailgate at MetLife Stadium, telling FoodRepublic.com: "That was my first **Frito Pie** experience ever. You talk about technique. You just rip open the bag and pour the chili right on top with sour cream and jalapeño. It is something. The chili was fantastic."

Jasper Hill Farm Cheesecake

"FOURPLAYS" [American / New York City / Jean Georges / Johnny Iuzzini]
Four miniature desserts served on one plate, each representing a different take on the same theme.

GEORGES V CAKE [American / New York City / François Payard]
caramel + (dark) chocolate + (roasted) peanuts + vanilla

JASPER HILL FARM CHEESECAKE [Spanish / Barcelona / Tickets / Albert Adria / c. 2015]
cheese + cookie + hazelnut + white chocolate

"LE KIT CAT" [American / Washington, D.C. / Central / Michel Richard]
corn flakes + milk chocolate + peanut butter + semisweet chocolate

MUSCOVY DUCK [American / New York City / Eleven Madison Park / Daniel Humm]
duck + figs + honey + lavender + turnips

OYSTERS & PEARLS [American / California / French Laundry / Thomas Keller]
caviar + oysters + tapioca

PHEASANT + SHALLOTS + CIDER GEL + BURNING OAK LEAVES [American / Chicago /Alinea / Grant Achatz]
burning oak leaves + cider gel + pheasant + shallots

POTATO PULP [American / Los Angeles / Trois Mec / Ludo Lefebvre]
bonito flakes + browned butter powder + (grated) cheese + potato puree + (riced) potatoes

ROAST BONE MARROW WITH PARSLEY SALAD [British / Smithfield / St. John / Fergus Henderson / c. 1994]
Inspiration: Henderson watched 1973's *La Grande Bouffe*, which he called "the greatest food film ever," and saw a character played by Marcello Mastroianni suck the marrow from bones.
bone marrow + parsley

SAFFRON PANNA COTTA [American / New York City / Babbo / Gina DePalma]
cream + eggs + saffron + sugar

SALMON CORNETS [American / California / French Laundry / Thomas Keller]
(chopped and seasoned) salmon + tiny crispy cones

SAVORY RICE BOWL [American / Los Angeles / Sqirl / Jessica Koslow]
brown rice + (poached) egg + (creamy) feta + (fermented) hot sauce + sorrel pesto

SEA SCALLOPS WITH CARAMELIZED CAULIFLOWER AND CAPER–RAISIN EMULSION [American / New York City / Jean-Georges Vongerichten]
capers + cauliflower + raisins + scallops

SOUFFLÉ SUISSESSE [British / Roux Brothers / Le Gavroche restaurant]
butter + cream + eggs + flour + milk+ cheese (Gruyere or Emmental) + baked

Kyle Connaughton of Single Thread on Being Inspired by Tradition

Everyone organizes their creativity in a particular way. Having principles that guide your creativity is the most important part.

I had an awareness of this and observed a lot in the kitchens I was in, from the **Fat Duck** [in England] to **Michael Bras** [in Japan] to the **elBulli Lab** [in Spain]. I watched everyone's creative process and how they went about it.

In the kitchens in Japan, it was not so much about creativity as about living within that moment: Here is what nature is giving us, and what are we going to do with it? But there was so much less discussion in Japan about "What should we do?" The sense was that "This is here, and this is obvious." Every year, you come back to the same dishes where you improve or slightly modify them. The cuisine is from the 1500s, and the wheels of change turn much more slowly in that environment.

In the Western world, chefs are under a lot of pressure. It is all about what's new, what's never been done, who is the best new chef, and what is the best new restaurant? That is rewarded, and there is nothing wrong with that.

The tension between the two extremes is good. If all we did was copy, we would still be eating Escoffier.

Here at Single Thread, creativity is calculated. Nature dictates things to us, and we have to react to nature. Some people think creativity is blue-sky thinking, and sometimes it is and we let our minds go. But creativity is boxes: We have natural rules, aesthetic rules, and even the products we use dictate their own rules. While these may seem to be constrictions on our creativity, they are actually what guides us—what we do, when we do it, and how we do it.

Kyle Connaughton

Cuisine and culture went through a period that was just "go for it," starting in the late 1990s with fusion cuisine, followed by the Modernist movement, which I was a big part of [as an editor and contributor to the ***Modernist Cuisine*** series]. A lot of great things came out of that, and a lot of bad stuff and bad food as well. **What came out of it, ultimately, was a better understanding and reverence for cuisine** from around the world: a better understanding of ingredients, of cooking techniques, and of the underlying science of cooking.

What we are trying to do here [at Single Thread] is respect all the things we know. Once you know something, you can't un-know it, and you can't ignore it. You understand how things work, and the connectivity of nature, cuisine, farming, and floral arrangement. We have all these opportunities to be creative.

We are so lucky to have this incredible platform that drives and dictates what we do. Since we are not beholden to anything, anyone, or any cuisine or culture in particular, we have ultimate freedom to do anything we want.

You need the avant-garde who push boundaries and explore things. What we do here is very slow and incremental progressions.

But you need the **Heston Blumenthals**, **Ferran Adriàs**, and **Wylie Dufresnes** who say, "I am going to put a flagpole over here."

If someone didn't do that in art, fashion, architecture, or food—with people willing to go way out on a limb to try something—you wouldn't have big moments of progress.

LEARNING BY COPYING

Copying (or even just studying) classic dishes also teaches us what ingredients pair well together. That Pizza Margherita we enjoy with **basil + mozzarella + tomatoes** shows that those ingredients have an amazing affinity for one another. And the magic is that when ingredients work well together in one context (e.g., as a pizza), they'll also work together in other contexts or **flavor platforms** (e.g., in casseroles, omelets, pastas, risottos, salads, sandwiches, soups, stews—possibly even cocktails and desserts).

Learning and memorizing classic **flavor pairings** (that is, two ingredients that represent a match made in heaven, such as **basil + tomatoes** or **mushrooms + Pinot Noir** or **peanut butter + jelly**) and classic **flavor affinities** (that is, three or more ingredients that work beautifully in concert, such as **garlic + Parmesan cheese + Romaine** or **garlic + ginger + soy sauce**), will give you a leg up in the next stages when you're improvising a new dish on the fly, whether in your home kitchen, at your restaurant, or on the set of a televised cooking reality show racing to create a dish against the clock with a handful of oddball ingredients.

CREATIVITY UNFOLDS

Jacques Torres was the pastry chef at the Hotel Negresco who created the asparagus ice cream that was served to Ferran Adrià in 1987. In his days as pastry chef at New York City's Le Cirque (1989–2000), his whimsical chocolate stove dessert (which featured a cake served inside an edible chocolate oven, with tiny stovetop pots of mango and raspberry sauces meant to be poured on top of the cake) was legendary. But he recalls that his creativity manifested on a daily basis, sometimes based on practical considerations. "We used to serve chocolate-covered almonds as *petit fours,* and one day we unexpectedly ran out of almonds," the native Frenchman recalls. "I came across a box of corn flakes, and asked someone, 'What's this?' I tasted it, and liked the texture. So I covered corn flakes with chocolate, and found that our guests loved it."

Jacques and Hasty Torres

> **A "Kellogg's paella" consisted of puffed Rice Krispies, to which the waiter added an intense seafood reduction; on the side was a small, flash-fried shrimp, a piece of shrimp sashimi, and an ampule containing a thick brown extract of shrimp heads that you were instructed to squeeze into your mouth.**
>
> —**ARTHUR LUBOW,** *New York Times,* on Ferran Adrià's dish at elBulli

Patrick O'Connell on Creativity: Yesterday, Today, and Tomorrow

In the old days, a French chef like François Haeringer would say, "You are in my kitchen, and you will do it my way . . ." . . . "There is my way, and the highway . . ." . . ."There are seven doors in my restaurant, and you can go out any one of them . . ." . . ."Young man, if my restaurant burns down and you open a restaurant, and I have to come and work in *your* restaurant, I will do it *your* way. But right now you are in *my* kitchen and you will do it *my* way."

We've gone a complete circle from how the French originally taught us to think about kitchen creativity. They were indoctrinated with the formula, the recipe, the rigid way to do everything. But they were also constricted in their creativity by the rules. So when bright Americans entered the field and began rethinking some of the rules, or looking at them through a different lens, with a different perspective, everything changed. Now, we sometimes miss that training that [the French] may have had, but many of them couldn't free themselves from it.

As Charlie Trotter seemed to extract [from his experiences in France], the universal idea was **excellence**—and that, in a word, is the theme. **I think American chefs proved that excellence doesn't have to be rigid.** And then what we began to discover is that **guests were feeling the energy coming from the newness and the freshness of the creative spirit.** And so you'd sometimes go to a restaurant and be exhilarated by the imagination and the energy, and that became as powerful as a perfectly concocted *coq au vin.* Now, we've gone so far to the other extreme that now instead of "more imagination," we crave the soulful, perfectly made French classic specialty that nobody bothers with anymore. **It's a pendulum swing.**

Later, when Torres was running his own retail stores, a woman came in with a crying toddler. "I saw her give something to the child that made the cries stop immediately," Torres remembers. "I was so impressed that I asked her what it was, and she told me: Cheerios." This is how Torres came to cover Cheerios with chocolate. "When I saw how much people loved it, I knew we had our next new product." Chocolate-covered Cheerios have been on offer ever since.

Since that time, pastry chef Christina Tosi, who was named the James Beard Foundation's Rising Star in 2012 and Outstanding Pastry Chef in 2015, put herself on the map in part through celebrating her own—not to mention the influential millennial generation's—love of breakfast cereals. She's offered "cereal milk" as a flavor for panna cotta, ice cream, and ice cream pie at Momofuku in New York City, made from a base of toasted cereal that's been steeped in milk.

From asparagus ice cream to cereal milk ice cream, creativity in the kitchen keeps unfolding in new and unexpected ways—fueled by individual chefs' understanding of history and drive to re-create and re-interpret it, which is explored further in Stage 2.

2 STAGE ALCHEMY: converting the common into the precious

> **I learned to cook in order to get away from recipes.**
>
> —TOM COLICCHIO, Riverpark (New York City)

> **A recipe is not meant to be followed exactly—it is a canvas on which you can embroider.**
>
> —ROGER VERGÉ

Alchemy is the stage at which you begin to impose your own will on ingredients, dishes, even cuisines.

First, we'll take a look at how chefs today are revisiting classic dishes. Then, we'll explore the subject of flavor—including flavor chords, flavor platforms, and enhancing and adding flavor—in greater depth, which is the secret to defeating an over-reliance on recipes and being able to cook more improvisationally in the kitchen.

After mastering cooking knowledge and skills, you'll know how that expertise can be applied to converting any ingredient or dish into a newer, better version of itself.

Alchemy is also the stage during which you develop your own style. Not every answer to every cooking question can be found in the pages of a book, so it's up to chefs to improvise.

When Aaron Bludorn was named the chef at Café Boulud in New York, he realized he was stepping into some very big shoes. "Like [previous chefs] Daniel Boulud, Andrew Carmellini, Bertrand Chemel, and Gavin Kaysen, I want to be able to leave my own mark on the restaurant, the way that each of these chefs did," he says. "Yet we're all doing the same thing: interpreting and reinterpreting the idea of classic peasant dishes, elevated to a fine dining level."

No two carrots taste the same. So you really can't follow a recipe, because there's no way to predict the amount of salt or acid you're going to need. You've got to taste your ingredients, and taste throughout the cooking process so that you can create a consistent end product even though your ingredients taste different every time.

—**JESSICA LARGEY,** Simone (Los Angeles)

Bludorn inherited a restaurant menu with "four muses": *tradition* (classic French cuisine), *potager* (the vegetable garden), *saison* (seasonal delicacies), and *voyage* (flavors of world cuisines). "I'm able to play around within the boundaries of the muses—and there are literally endless possibilities," he says. "With the voyage menu, we can go anywhere in the world without leaving the kitchen—just by cooking. We have a new general manager, Cherif Mbodji, who's from Senegal and who helped to inspire me to take on a Senegalese menu," a daring challenge for an elegant French restaurant.

After grounding himself in the cuisine's primary flavors—"We ate in Little Senegal on 116th Street between Frederick Douglass and Adam Clayton Powell Boulevards to taste some classic Senegalese dishes"—Bludorn then trusted his own sense of what would work best with the restaurant's style and clientele. The effort was so successful it spurred a menu kick-off dinner with Pierre Thiam (author of *Senegal,* and the first English-language book on Senegalese cooking, *Yolele!*), who cooked with the team.

A recipe is like when you buy an Ikea closet with maddening instructions. You need to bring common sense to it. Cooking is about being aware, tasting constantly. We have recipes because we need to give the kitchen staff guidelines, we need to give direction, but ultimately, it is the chef cooking that makes the magic.

—**RENÉ REDZEPI,** Noma (Copenhagen)

Crosstown from Café Boulud, at Boulud Sud, colleague Travis Swikard faces similar challenges. "There are two sides to creativity: sort of an emotional creativity that is inspired by what's going on around you, and a next-level creativity that is rooted in a mastery of techniques—which allow you to properly respect an ingredient and get out of its way—plus palate, flavor pairings, and the season," says Swikard. "My creativity is focused on telling a story with our food. My goal in this [Mediterranean-inspired] restaurant is that a Moroccan grandmother in our dining room, who might not recognize a dish influenced by Moroccan flavors, will still feel the soul in our food. I don't act on every single opinion of those

Amanda Cohen of Dirty Candy on Vegetable-Based Dishes, Drinks, and Desserts

Amanda Cohen

I want to be in the box—and then outside the box. It helps me be creative. By being in the box, I mean choosing an ingredient, and focusing on how to bring out its flavors. That's something as chefs we have to do. But then I'm interested in the question, **"What *can* I do?"** Being outside the box is asking myself, "How can I push it in different directions?" I'll play with different textures and shapes—why shouldn't peppers look like Froot Loops? **Breaking the rules is the fun part of what we do.** When we're in the box creating our **Corn Boil**, we stew and pickle corn to make it as delicious as we can possibly make it, serving corn smoked and grilled and as tempura. Then we go outside the box, giving everyone lobster bibs when we serve it, and give them fava beans to crack open like crawfish.

Umami

At our [meatless] restaurant, we don't have the inherent umami of meat. So I'm always adding fermented black bean paste to dishes for umami. In our stocks, I'll use sun-dried tomatoes for umami. Or olives. I'll also use a lot of sea weeds, like dulse and kombu, and dashi stocks to add umami.

The X Factor

Veggie burgers are getting a lot of attention. There's a new wave vegetable revolution, and now vegetable-driven food is being seen as worthwhile. While lots of veggie burgers are the same in terms of mimicking the texture of meat, our **[Carrot Sliders on Carrot Buns]** uses a vegetable you sink your teeth into with our play on Big Mac sauce—which together prove you can have the flavor of a burger without the texture. A veggie hot dog won't have the same texture as a hot dog, but can it have everything else? The popularity of our **Broccoli Dog** seems to suggest the answer is yes.

Quiet vs. Loud Flavors

Most guests today don't have an attention span beyond 25 bites. So you have to go BIG to get people's attention, which results in the trend toward big, heavy flavors. Subtle dishes like my signature **Portobello Mousse** pale in comparison. If guests have a bolder dish first, we'll change out their plates and silverware for that course.

The Flavors in the Glass

We're in the process of switching all our cocktails to vegetable-based cocktails. I love our **Smoked Tomato Margarita** made with tomato water that is smoked, which is rimmed with tomato powder and salt. Our **Zucchini Tini** tastes just like zucchini, made from juice with either gin or vodka and a tiny bit of sweet vermouth.

Ending on a Sweet Note

Serving vegetable-driven desserts vs. entrées is harder, because you don't want to overwhelm with the flavor of the vegetable. Carrots, corn, and onions are easy, because they're sweet. But we had to add chocolate to our **Onion Chocolate Tart with Smoked Almond Ice Cream** to get guests to order it. Celery is not so easy—no one likes celery, and lots of guests hate celery and its bitterness. But once they try our **Celery Cheesecake Roll with Celeriac Ice Cream**, many are surprised by how much they like it. Eggplant doesn't really taste like anything—it's very subtle. But we found that juiced eggplant tastes like banana, and blueberry and eggplant tastes like a banana smoothie.

PASTRY CHEF GHAYA OLIVEIRA OF DANIEL REINTERPRETS CLASSIC DESSERTS

In the 1600s, ***kugelhopf***, a sponge cake studded with raisins and baked in a fluted pan, is said to originate in Lemberg, Poland.

In the 1700s, the king of Poland, Stanislas Leszczyński, finds his *kugelhopf* dry, providing the inspiration to pour rum over it. The king loves it so much he names it after the hero of the popular tale *1001 Nights*: Ali Baba. It becomes known as ***baba au rhum***. (*Baba* is the French word for *babka*.) Polish pastry chef Nicolas Stohrer introduces it to France when he accompanies the king's daughter Marie to Versailles as her pâtissier (following her marriage to King Louis XV), and later through his own pâtisserie in Paris.

Kugelhopf

In the 1800s, a French pastry chef leaves the raisins out of *baba au rhum* and is so proud of the results he names his version after his own hero: Brillat-Savarin—or ***savarin***, as the dessert is more commonly known.

So, *savarin* wouldn't exist without *baba au rhum*—which itself wouldn't exist without *kugelhopf.* Each owes a debt of gratitude to the creations that preceded them.

Ghaya Oliveira, executive pastry chef of New York City's Daniel, continues the tradition. Each month, she takes on another classic dessert and reinterprets it through a contemporary, cosmopolitan lens. In her hands, *baba au rhum* becomes a cubic baba with Jamaican rum, exotic fruit, and coconut Chantilly.

Her starting point might be a French classic like tarte Tatin, or Escoffier's own peach Melba (**Chantilly cream + peaches + raspberries**), or even a classic dessert from elsewhere—whether Italian tiramisu or American key lime pie. "But there's always a big twist," she explains.

Oliveira begins her process by researching each dish's history, going deep inside the story of the dessert. "I learned that tiramisu was originally based on **ladyfingers + mascarpone**—and that the coffee flavor only came later," she said. "That freed me to leave coffee out of my version," a fruity interpretation that was instead flavored with **apricots + fresh almonds + lemon verbena powder.**

A favorite project was coming up with her spin on Black Forest cake—which, in the end, didn't even turn out to be a cake: "I created a chocolate tube that was filled with the traditional flavors: **cherry + chocolate + cream.**"

Something that proved to be a challenge was cherry clafoutis, which is typically a homier, more rustic-style dessert that doesn't immediately suggest haute cuisine. Oliveira got around it by creating a custard flavored with kirsch (cherry brandy), served with bing cherries and a lemon-vanilla Chantilly. "I can really do anything here, as long as it's exceptionally elegant, with exceptional technique," she says. "Of course, it's best if it is done in more of a French style—and I like it best when it is also a reflection of me."

Here are her takes on other classic desserts:

Mont-Blanc (Italian, c. late 15th century /French, c. 1620) **chestnut paste vermicelli + meringue + whipped cream**

Ghaya Oliveira

Oliveira's interpretation: A coconut meringue covering a tiered slice of dacquoise, mandarin gelée, and chestnut-cognac vermicelli

Lemon Meringue Pie (American / Philadelphia / Elizabeth Coane Goodfellow / c. late 17th century) **lemon curd + meringue + pie crust**

Oliveira's interpretation: Tahitian vanilla sablé, light lemon cream, Italian meringue

Key Lime Pie (American / Key West, FL / late 1800s: William Curry's cook, known as Aunt Sally, who used the sweetened condensed milk Curry brought to the islands, where fresh milk and cream were not available.) **Key limes + sweetened condensed milk**

Oliveira's interpretation: Light key lime cream, graham cracker sablé, Italian meringue

Paris-Brest (French / Maison Laffitte / Louis Durand / c. 1910, in commemoration of the Paris-Brest bicycle race) **choux pastry + cream + pralines**

Oliveira's interpretation: Crispy choux pastry with gianduja mousse and hazelnut praline coulant

I don't cook Indian food. I cook *my* food, inspired by Indian flavors.

—**LIOR LEV SERCARZ,** La Boîte (New York City)

who come into our restaurant, but I will listen with my ears wide open to that Moroccan grandmother. We are sincere in learning about the cooking that's being done in the Mediterranean and paying homage to tradition, while adding our own interpretation."

You won't become a good chef by following a recipe.

—**DAVID BOULEY,** Bouley (New York City)

THE EVOLUTION OF CLASSICS

Tastes evolve, and chefs reinvent existing dishes to match those new tastes.

Ice cream (**cream + sugar + *freezing***) is believed to have been around since 3,000 BC, and baklava (**ground nuts + pastry + sweet syrup**) is believed to have been around since the 8th century BC. (Baklava is made differently in different regions: Greeks tend to favor it with **walnuts + phyllo + honey**, while Arabs prefer **cashews (or pine nuts or pistachios) + orange blossom water + simple syrup**.) Yet our first taste of baklava ice cream didn't occur until a 2010 visit to José Andrés's restaurant Zaytinya in Washington, D.C.

We're happy that a classic hotel like New York City's Waldorf-Astoria hasn't been content to rest on its laurels but instead is moving into yet another new century with grace. When we stopped by to taste the **Eggs Benedict** circa 2016, we were impressed to find the eggs perfectly poached, and the hollandaise light and frothy. The **Red Velvet Cake** uses four ½-inch layers of very moist cake layered between creamy and sweet-but-not-too-sweet white icing, with a decidedly modern garnish of a dehydrated beet chip alongside a more classic tuile. The **Waldorf Salad** wasn't at all as Karen had remembered it from a few decades ago. Instead, matchstick-cut sweet and tart apples (i.e., Granny Smith and Gala) and celery root were accented with a few red grapes and spiced candied walnuts. The mayonnaise had been 86ed, substituted with a much lighter and more contemporary yogurt-and-crème-fraîche dressing seasoned with lemon juice, white pepper, walnut oil, and—if you're lucky—a hint of earthy, aromatic black truffle.

If the venerable Waldorf-Astoria can update the ingredients, techniques, and presentations of its legendary dishes, so can you. Learn to deconstruct the essential elements of the dishes you're making. Think about reasonable substitutions—whether of ingredients, techniques, or presentation, or some combination of the three. There is nothing stopping *you* from converting a dish into something more to *your* liking.

CONVERTING THE CLASSICS

Dishes inspire other dishes. Louisiana jambalayas (both red Creole, made *with* tomatoes, and brown Cajun, made *without*) were inspired by Spanish paella. Chicken-fried steak was inspired by Austrian and German wiener schnitzel. San Francisco cioppino was inspired by French bouillabaisse. Ground corn inspired American classics like corn pone, hush puppies, johnnycakes, and more. What new version will *your* experimentation inspire?

These are a few examples of other classics that have been converted and updated:

BAKED ALASKA

ice cream + meringue + *bruléed*

INSPIRED:

Baked Alaska for Two: pistachio and vanilla ice cream, raspberry sorbet, fresh meringue flambéed with kirsch

—DBGB Kitchen and Bar (New York City)

Baked Alaska for Two: strawberry and crème fraîche ice cream, graham cracker biscuit, meringue flambéed with vanilla-infused vodka

—DBGB Kitchen and Bar (New York City)

And if it worked for the 49th state, why not the 50th? **Ravi Kapur** of the Liholiho Yacht Club in San Francisco is wowing diners with his native Hawaiian cuisine, and whimsical desserts like his beehive-shaped **Baked Hawaii**, the caramelized pineapple ice cream and toasted meringue dessert inspired by **Baked Alaska**.

BAKLAVA

(ground) nuts + phyllo dough + syrup (or honey)

INSPIRED:

Baklava Croissant

—Travis Lett, Gjelina (Los Angeles)

Baklava Ice Cream

—José Andrés, Zaytinya (Washington, D.C.)

BEEF WELLINGTON

beef + Madeira + mushrooms + pastry crust + truffles

INSPIRED:

Carrots Wellington

—John Fraser, Narcissa (New York City)

Mushroom Wellington: vegetarian roasted mushroom, truffled mushroom duxelles, crisp puff pastry, vegetarian bordelaise

—Brad Steelman, River Café (New York City)

BREAD AND BUTTER

bread + butter

INSPIRED:

Flavored rolls with paired flavor butters, e.g., black sesame and roasted garlic **rolls** with Worcestershire sauce **butter**

Country ham fat **bread** with coffee butter

Duck fat and poppy seed **rolls** with truffle salted **butter**

Garlic and black sesame **rolls** with Worcestershire sauce **butter**

Miso rolls with sweet soy **butter**

Molasses-cumin **bread** with orange and sorghum **butter**

—Mark Levy, Magdalena at The Ivy Hotel (Baltimore)

CHEESECAKE

cream cheese + graham cracker crust + sugar

INSPIRED:

Coconut Pineapple Cheesecake: vanilla cheesecake, coconut-lime sorbet, roasted pineapple, passion fruit sauce

—Taiesha Martin, pastry chef, Glenmere Mansion (Chester, New York)

When I was making a cheesecake, I asked myself what was in season, and ended up with a **pineapple coconut cheesecake**. The **graham cracker** crust is classic, and the sour cream topping gives it a glossy finish. The **coconut powder** garnish sprinkled on the plate gives it an element of surprise, and a bit of **basil + mint** foam adds color and an earthy, minty note that plays well off the pineapple.

—**TAIESHA MARTIN**, pastry chef, Glenmere Mansion (Chester, New York)

Cheesecake-Flavored Macarons (e.g., Matcha, Mixed Berry, Pumpkin)

—Marc Aumont, pastry chef, Gabriel Kreuther (New York City)

Marc Aumont

After running my family pastry shop in France since I was a teenager, I moved to America, where the first thing I had to learn was how to work with Philadelphia cream cheese. **Americans love cheesecake**, and I studied dozens of different recipes. Cheesecake is sweet and rich, and that sweetness and fattiness needs to be cut. Acidity does both. I'll often accompany it with an acidic sorbet. I've learned to adjust my cheesecake style depending on where I'm making it, as different regions call for different products. For example:

Chicago-style cheesecake: sour cream
French-style cheesecake: Neufchâtel
German-style cheesecake: quark
Greek-style cheesecake: myzithra cheese
Italian-style cheesecake: ricotta or mascarpone
New York–style cheesecake: cream cheese + graham cracker crust.

—**MARC AUMONT**, pastry chef, Gabriel Kreuther (New York City)

CARPACCIO

Carpaccio is the most popular dish served at Venice's Harry's Bar. It is named for Vittore Carpaccio, the Venetian Renaissance painter known for his use of brilliant reds and whites. My father invented this dish in 1950, the year of the great Carpaccio exhibition in Venice.

—from *The Harry's Bar Cookbook*, by Arrigo Cipriani (1991)

While the same cookbook advocates the garnishing of the thinnest-possible slices of beef with shaved cheese or an olive-oil dressing, it emphasizes the "genius" of the dish as "the light, cream-colored sauce that is drizzled [on top] in a cross-hatch pattern."

Since the 1950 advent of carpaccio, spins abound. In the 1990s, we remember first tasting **Patrick O'Connell**'s popular Carpaccio of Herb-Crusted Baby Lamb Loin with Caesar Salad Ice Cream at the Inn at Little Washington, which has since become a classic.

Beet often subs for beef in meatless versions, as it did in the version on which **Nancy Silverton** collaborated with Los Angeles' Osteria Mozza executive chef **Elizabeth Hong** made with roasted unpeeled beets. Other vegetable and even fruit versions are gaining traction, including those made from eggplant, mushrooms, persimmon, and both summer and winter squashes.

Imagine: What else could you use your mandolin to slice paper thin and turn into "carpaccio"?

In a place that has been ongoing for a period of time, there's an opportunity to refine and build on a foundation or a dish. A regular **lamb carpaccio** went on the menu around 1982, and it was served with tabbouleh—no one knew what it was at that time. Every night you had to explain it. Now, it's in every grocery store. You had to evolve the dish further, and give it a different dimension—and yet it had to work. For me, it's something that really works, and has universal appeal, and that's what you strive for. It may be weird, in that it's something that people may never have experienced before, but they have to love it. So often what I'm seeing in trendy restaurants are dishes that are intriguing, but that you never want to eat them a second time. There are people who come here once a year, and they have to have the lamb carpaccio. And that is living proof that the dish has passed a test.

—Patrick O'Connell, The Inn at Little Washington (Washington, Virginia)

Grilled King Oyster MUSHROOM CARPACCIO finished with Hijiki Seaweed Vinaigrette, Cara Cara Oranges and Marcona Almonds

—**JOHN FRASER,** Dovetail (New York City)

DELICATA SQUASH CARPACCIO, with honey agrodolce, pink peppercorns, crème fraîche, chopped parsley, and pepitas

—**MARIO CARBONE** and **RICH TORRISI**, Santina (New York City)

SUMMER SQUASH CARPACCIO, with garden oregano, hazelnut, caper, and Kootenay Alpindon Cheese

—**WARREN BARR,** The Pointe at Wickaninnish Inn (Vancouver Island, Canada)

CHERRIES JUBILEE

brandy + cherries + *flambéed*

INSPIRED:

Flaming Saganaki (brandy + cheese + lemon juice + *flambé*)
—The Parthenon (Chicago), c. 1968

The Parthenon made its debut in 1968; one of the owners, **Christos Liakouras, said that it was the popularity of continental cuisine and dishes such as steak Diane [beef + cognac + flambéed] and cherries jubilee that inspired him to put flame and brandy to a plate of fried cheese.** As fast as you could say "Opaa!" a legend was born.

—**PHIL VETTEL,** *Chicago Tribune* (September 8, 2016)

COCONUT CAKE

cake + coconut + marshmallow frosting

Popular at ladies' teas in the 1920s, President Truman boosted the popularity of coconut cake with marshmallow icing further after he developed a fondness for it on a 1950s visit to Key West.

INSPIRED:

Coconut Cake: Coconut Cream Cheese Frosting, Yellow Cake, Toasted Coconut, Chantilly
—Taiesha Martin, Glenmere Mansion (Chester, New York)

The coconut layer cake was already on the menu [at Glenmere Mansion] when I arrived, one year after the [Relais & Châteaux] property was restored and opened in 2010. There were already lots of regulars who loved what they loved—including this cake. Glenmere's owners [**Dan DeSimone and Alan Stenberg**] are very knowledgeable about food history and had ideas for me, but in the end they said, "Let's see what you can do." The Supper Room provides a modern spin on classic ideas, so the style of the cake had to give a nod to the classic versions [the owners] grew up with. I ended up deciding to keep the same three-layer format—however, the rest is different. I don't use the same cake recipe, or the same coconut frosting. For the filling, I use cream cheese and shredded coconut and cream of coconut, and for the icing, **butter + confectioner's sugar + cream of coconut + cream cheese.** The cakes are soaked in coconut syrup. I toast the coconut, so that it cuts through the sweetness, and provides a touch of bitterness along with the textural and color contrast, as it matches the colors and textures of the oaky room.

Taiesha Martin

—**TAIESHA MARTIN,** pastry chef, Glenmere Mansion (Chester, New York)

CRACKER JACK

caramel/molasses + peanuts + popcorn

INSPIRED:

Cracker Jack Éclair: filled with popcorn pastry cream and topped with peanut butter glaze and caramel brittle

—Scott Cioe, The Back Room at The Park Hyatt (New York City), c. mid-2010s

Cracker Jack Sundae: made with popcorn ice cream, caramel sauce, peanut brittle and caramel popcorn

—Tara Glick, American Cut (New York City)

Herbed Cider Sorbet with Pine Nut Cracker Jack

—Dana Cree, Poppy (Seattle)

S&S Cracker Jack: light peanut butter mousse balanced with salty popcorn sherbet and crisp caramel corn

—Meg Galus, Swift & Sons (Chicago)

EVERYTHING BAGEL

bagel + caraway seeds + garlic + onions + poppy seeds + salt + sesame seeds

Ash, Mustard, and Everything Bagel Macarons with Murray's Cheese Selection

—Jesse Schenker, The Gander (New York City)

Everything Bagel Ice Cream (shaped like a bagel), accompanied by threads of smoked salmon and crispy cream cheese

—Wylie Dufresne, wd-50 (New York City)

The Everything Doughnut, with cream cheese glaze topped with sesame seeds, pepitas, sea salt, and garlic

—Troy Neal, The Doughnut Project (New York City)

Cucumber Salad with Smoked Salmon, Lemon, Everything Bagel Crumble, Garden Radish, Dill

—Gunnar Thompson, Glenmere Mansion (Chester, New York)

Taiesha Martin's Coconut Layer Cake at Glenmere Mansion

FLUFFERNUTTER SANDWICH (C. 1961)

marshmallow fluff + peanut butter + white bread

INSPIRED:

Roasted Banana Parfait: Swiss meringue folded into roasted bananas and finished with whipped cream, with candied peanuts, hazelnut sponge cake, caramel sauce, and a toasted sesame gelato

—Taiesha Martin, Glenmere Mansion (Chester, New York)

I was inspired to create an adult dessert based on the Fluffernutter marshmallow and peanut butter sandwiches I used to see kids coming to school with—a dessert that combined banana + chocolate + marshmallow + peanuts. We always have bananas on hand, and often they go bad before you can use them, so I often have bananas to use up. When bananas are super-ripe, their flavor is strong, and the contrast of Armagnac will brighten them up. Then again, I'd put booze in everything if I could!

—**TAIESHA MARTIN,** Glenmere Mansion (Chester, New York)

FONDUE, CHEESE

(cubed) bread + (melted) cheese + white wine + *dipping*

Originated in Switzerland c. 1800s as a way to use up leftover cheese.

INSPIRED:

Bourguignon Fondue, substituting hot oil for the cheese and beef cubes for the bread cubes. **beef + hot oil + *dipping***

—Konrad Egli, Chalet Suisse (New York City) c. 1950s

Chocolate Fondue, substituting melted chocolate for the melted cheese and cubes of cake and fruit (a twist that became so popular it made its way back to Switzerland!) **cake + chocolate + fruit + *dipping***

—Konrad Egli, Chalet Suisse (New York City), July 4, 1964

Katianna Hong

FRENCH TOAST

bread + eggs + milk + *frying*

INSPIRED:

Contemporary versions made with babka, brioche, and even carrot cake, and with toppings from custard to pineapple + rum—not to mention without eggs (e.g., subbing Just Scramble vegan egg substitute) or dairy (e.g., subbing almond milk).

(Eggless) French Toast, made with Just Scramble

—Ben Roche, pastry chef, Hampton Creek (California)

Babka Bread Pudding French Toast with Preserved Apples, Spicebush Syrup, and Whipped Cream

—Katianna Hong, The Charter Oak (Napa Valley)

We made babka at Meadowood to serve a single square of it toasted in brown butter at the end of a meal, along with some [flavored] nougat, a dot of cultured cream, and a tempered sheet of chocolate. So we sometimes had some scraps of babka left over that we'd turn into bread pudding for staff meal. Christopher [Kostow, The Restaurant at Meadowood's executive chef] suggested a bread pudding French toast, and I thought of the babka for it, which led to the **babka bread pudding French toast**. Meadowood's preservationist Cameron [Cole Rahtz] had jars of tons of apples—and they were so soft that they wouldn't hold their form well, making them better suited for the Charter Oak. We used sweet potato starch, which is neutral with no need to boil it and which sets clear like cornstarch, but thickens without the gumminess you sometimes get with cornstarch. Spicebush was popping up right before we came out to Chicago, so we flavored the maple syrup with spicebush syrup, which is light with a melon-y flavor, so that lightened the maple syrup. And the whipped cream was 100 percent unsweetened, so it was more of a cleansing accent instead of yet another sweet note.

—**KATIANNA HONG,** The Charter Oak (Napa Valley)

GAZPACHO

garlic + sherry vinegar + tomatoes + *raw*

INSPIRED:

Carrot-Orange Gazpacho

—Wolfgang Puck, Spago (Beverly Hills), who served it as shooters at the Governors Ball following the 2014 Oscars

Chilled Heirloom Carrot Gazpacho, made with buttermilk espuma, caraway, cilantro

—Travis Swikard, Boulud Sud (New York City)

Crab Salad with Chilled Gazpacho Sauce

—Eric Ripert, Le Bernardin (New York City)

Peach Gazpacho with Toasted Almonds

—Daniel Humm, Eleven Madison Park (New York City)

Strawberry Gazpacho (balsamic vinegar bell pepper + cucumber + garlic + olive oil + strawberries)

—Jeremy Fox, then of Manresa (Los Gatos, California)

Watermelon Gazpacho with Crab Meat

—Donald Link, Herbsaint (New Orleans)

White Gazpacho (almond milk + breadcrumbs + cucumbers + garlic + pink peppercorns)

—Terrance Brennan, Picholine (New York City)

White Gazpacho with Shishito Peppers, Fluke, and Almonds

—Marcus Samuelsson, Red Rooster (New York City), served at the 2012 JBF Chefs & Champagne event

White Gazpacho with Strawberries and Almonds

—Lee Wolen, Boka (Chicago)

It was eye-opening to discover that I could replace one ingredient [tomatoes] with another acidic and fruity ingredient [strawberries], and that the dish could still work.

—**JEREMY FOX,** then of Manresa (Los Gatos)

GUACAMOLE

avocado + (fresh) chiles + cilantro + lime juice + onions + salt + tomatoes

INSPIRED:

Spicy Ginger Guacamole: Michoacán avocados, habanero chile, ginger, orange, jicama, cucumber, cilantro

—Richard James, Frontera Grill (Chicago)

Mango-Morita Guacamole: Michoacán avocados, honey Manila mango, morita chile, grilled red onion, lime, cincho cheese

—Richard James, Frontera Grill (Chicago)

We're highly motivated by seasonality here and Manila mangoes are in season, so I made them part of this guacamole. In Mexico, they put chile, lime, and cheese on fruit, so I just took all of those ingredients and put them in the guacamole.

—**RICHARD JAMES,** Frontera Grill (Chicago)

Spring Pea Guacamole: avocado + cilantro + lime + onions + spring peas + sunflower seeds

—Jean-Georges Vongerichten, ABC Cocina (New York City)

HOT DOG

bun + hot dog (+ mustard + sauerkraut)

INSPIRED:

Broccoli Dog

—Amanda Cohen, Dirt Candy (New York City)

Hokkaido (Scallop) Dog with caramelized onion, house-smoked mustard, and chives

—Michael Cimarusti, Connie & Ted's (Los Angeles)

The restaurant that inspires me most is usually the last one I ate at. I went to Connie & Ted's the other night—they take scallops and turn them into a mousseline sausage that was either lightly smoked or roasted so it had a smokiness to it and put it on a bun and serve it like a hot dog. It's basically a Hokkaido scallop dog with smoked mustard on top on a piece of brioche—but it's delicious. My girlfriend doesn't eat meat, but she eats seafood, so it was fun for her to be able to have a "hot dog" and that nostalgic memory from when she did eat meat.

—**MICHAEL VOLTAGGIO,** ink (Los Angeles)

LEMON MERINGUE PIE

egg whites + lemon curd (butter + eggs + lemon juice + lemon zest + sugar) + pie crust + sugar

INSPIRED:

Dan's Lemon Meringue Cake: Three-Layer Lemon Cake, Lemon Filling, Toasted Meringue Frosting

—Daniel DeSimone, co-owner, Glenmere Mansion (Chester, New York)

Meyer Lemon Meringue Pie with salted caramel sauce

—Colby and Megan Garrelts, Rye (Leawood, Kansas)

Lemon Meringue Pie Ice Cream: lemon ice cream studded with bits of lemon curd, burnt meringue, and graham cracker crumbs

—Sam Mason, OddFellows Ice Cream Co. (New York City)

Lemon Meringue Tart (described as "the marriage of a classic French tart and a Southern icebox pie")

—Dolester Miles, Highlands Bar and Grill (Birmingham, Alabama)

Lemon Egg-ceptional (a trompe l'oeil dessert consisting of a white chocolate eggshell containing a lemon meringue "yolk")

—Michel Richard, Citronelle (Washington, D.C.)

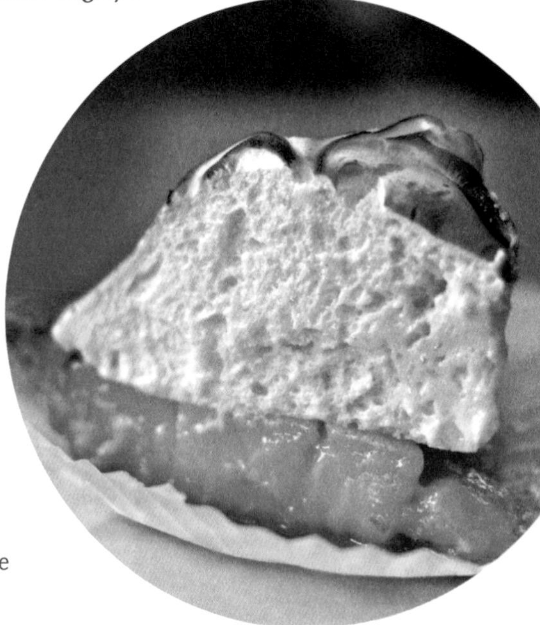

Lemon Meringue Pie

LOX AND CREAM CHEESE

cream cheese + lox

INSPIRED:

Jann's Bagel: Everything Bagel, Almond Cream Cheese, Smoked Heirloom Carrot Lox, Shaved Red Onions, Capers

—Tal Ronnen and Scot Jones, Crossroads (Los Angeles)

Smoked Steelhead Roe with Maple Cream and Pumpernickel

—Jon Shook and Vinny Dotolo, Son of a Gun (Los Angeles)

My favorite dish was smoked steelhead roe with dots of maple-flavored cream and razor-thin shards of pumpernickel toast, which tasted like an extreme deconstruction of **lox and cream cheese**.

—**JONATHAN GOLD,** *LA Weekly* (2011), review of Son of a Gun

MEATLOAF

chewy + *loaf-shaped* + *sliced* (+ often accompanied by tomato sauce and mashed potatoes)

INSPIRED:

Meatloaf with mashed potatoes and green beans (on Mondays)

—Ris Lacoste, RIS (Washington, D.C.)

WHICH INSPIRED:

Morel "Meatloaf," which substitutes morels + oats for ground meat

—Patrick O'Connell, The Inn at Little Washington (Washington, Virginia)

In 1979, there was a bumper crop of morels, so they were abundant and cheap. We had no idea how rare they were, so we used them to make **meatloaf** for the staff meal—which was deeply satisfying yet very light. I love Ris Lacoste's meatloaf downtown [which inspired "Meatloaf Mondays" at Ris, in Washington, DC], which is based on her mother's recipe using rolled oats [as a binder]. This year [in 2016], we added rolled oats to ours, too. It has an airy lightness to it. Our new [meatless] morel "meatloaf" is made with sautéed morels and egg, wrapped like a sausage and sous-vide, then finished in the oven. Ketchup was the inspiration for the sauce, which gets its sweetness from white balsamic vinegar and a touch of heat from jalapeños.

—**PATRICK O'CONNELL,** The Inn at Little Washington (Washington, Virginia)

The Inn at Little Washington's Morel Mushroom "Meatloaf"

MILKSHAKE

Milk + Ice Cream (American / Walgreen's /Ivar "Pop" Coulson / c. 1922)

+ Soft-Serve Ice Cream (American / Carvel's and Dairy Queen / c. 1930s)

INSPIRED:
Frosty

—Wendy's E.M. "Bill" Barker (who invented it c. 1969 at the request of Wendy's founder Dave Thomas, as a cross between a milkshake and soft-serve ice cream)

WHICH INSPIRED:
French Fries and Frosties

—Phillip Foss, EL Ideas (Chicago)

French Fries and Frosties [the latter served in a fountain-style milkshake glass, with a long spoon] has become one of our signature dishes, and it was inspired by my kid, whose babysitter taught her to dip her French fries in ice cream. I tried it, and found the combinations of hot + cold and sweet + salty fun. The next day, **I spoke with my chefs, and more than half of them said that they had dipped their French fries in a Wendy's Frosty.** So even though this is a fine dining restaurant, we gave it a shot—and found that we were able to transport them. Any time you connect with nostalgia and connect with guests based on taste, you create a memory that will last. It's a dish that breaks up the monotony of the assault of flavors from the other dishes, and gives the palate a break with something that is sweet and fun. And the interaction of pouring the vanilla ice cream [chilled by liquid nitrogen] over the [potato-leek] soup [which emits clouds of vapor] from table to table, makes me look like a mad chemist. It creates the kind of jump-out-of-your-seat moment we want all our guests to have.

—**PHILLIP FOSS,** EL Ideas (Chicago)

PEACH MELBA

(poached and halved) peaches + raspberry sauce + vanilla ice cream

INSPIRED:
Pêche Melba (interpretation): Poached Peaches, Berry Coulis, Meringue, Mauritius Vanilla Chantilly

—Ghaya Oliveira, Daniel (New York City)

Pêche Melba: Created by the famous French chef, Auguste Escoffier, the Peach Melba is named in honor of legendary Australian opera singer Nellie Melba. Escoffier often cooked for Melba at the Savoy Hotel in London where he was the chef in the late 1890s and the two became good friends. One evening, Melba presented Escoffier with tickets to the production of the opera *Lohengrin,* which featured a swan-shaped boat. To express his appreciation, both for the tickets and her performance, Escoffier crafted a dessert he called "Peach with a Swan" made of vanilla ice cream and fresh peaches inside a sculpted ice swan. As chef at the Ritz Carlton, he later added raspberry and dubbed it Peach Melba in her honor.

—**FROM THE MENU AT DANIEL** (New York City)

POP-TARTS

filling + (rectangular) pastry + *toasting*

INSPIRED:

Pop-Tarts have inspired leading pastry chefs including **Joanne Chang** at Flour (with a five-spice glaze), **Hedy Goldsmith** at Michael's Genuine's (mango and passion fruit, strawberry), and **Della Gossett** at Spago (baked apple).

POUTINE

cheese curds + French fries + gravy

INSPIRED:

Curry Fries: Homemade Fries with Fresh Paneer and Curry

—Amanda Cohen (a native of Canada), Dirt Candy (New York City)

Poutine, Oxtail Gravy, Cheddar

—Jon Shook and Vinny Dotolo, Animal (Los Angeles)

SOUFFLÉ + TWICE-BAKED POTATO

INSPIRED:

Twice-Baked Roquefort Soufflé

—Mark Levy, Magdalena at The Ivy Hotel (Baltimore), photo below

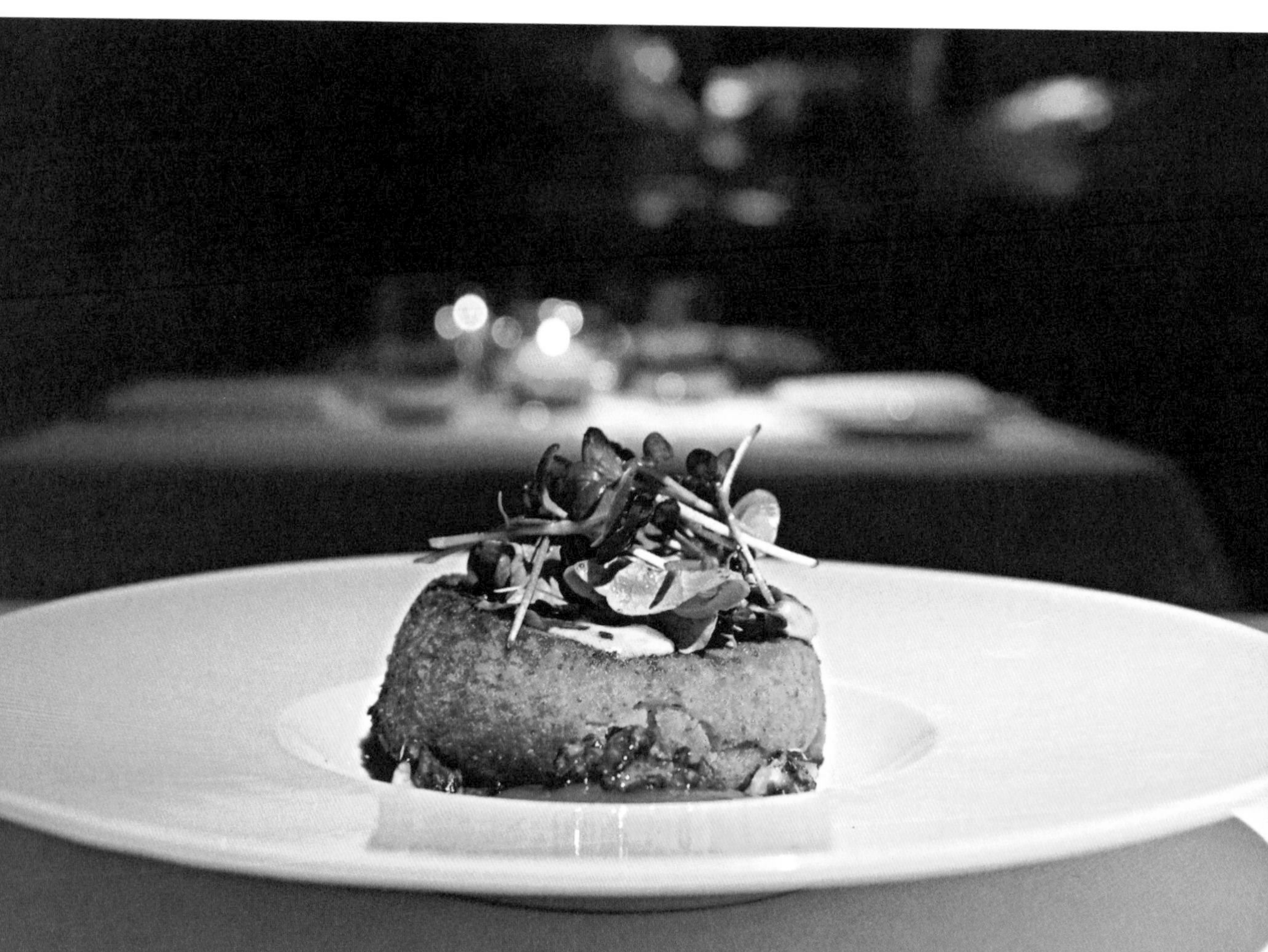

Twice-baked soufflés were a pub thing in England; I think I first saw a recipe for them in the late 1990s, for Cheddar soufflé with rutabaga puree. You'd grind toasted nuts—hazelnuts, pecans, or walnuts—into panko breadcrumbs with some butter, and line ramekins with the mixture. For the soufflé, I'd substitute blue cheese for the Cheddar—and if I were using Roquefort, which is wetter, I'd cut down on the milk, or else I'd use Stilton, which is drier. I'd [bake] the ramekins in a bain-marie until they were poofed and cooked, then I'd run a knife around the edges and cook them for [another] eight minutes at 400 degrees, which lifts them up and browns the crusts. With this dish, I never mess with garnishes too much—I just keep it in season, and all it needs is a green salad and some fruit. Blackberries or wild blueberries are nice with goat cheese soufflés, and I'll serve Gruyère soufflés with black truffles, and a pear and walnut salad.

—**MARK LEVY,** Magdalena at The Ivy Hotel (Baltimore)

SOUP DUMPLINGS

dumpling wrappers + *filled with frozen soup, which turns to liquid when cooked*

INSPIRED:

Foie Gras Soup Dumplings, with a Chinese black vinegar reduction

—Anita Lo, Annisa (New York City)

Signature dishes are created by the media—it's not necessarily what you think of as your own crowning achievement. And the media attached themselves to my **foie gras soup dumpling**s, which I put on Annisa's opening menu in 1999, before the soup dumpling craze and before they appeared in any other mainstream restaurant. My dad was from Shanghai, so I'd eaten soup dumplings before, and always loved them. We worked with a lot of foie at Chanterelle. Balsamic reductions were in back then, so when I was eating soup dumplings with Chinese black vinegar, which is kind of like balsamic, I thought, "Hmm . . . foie gras works well with acidity." I ended up using one of my mom's recipes [for a red-cooked broth, with soy sauce and cinnamon, star anise and dried mushrooms] to create a Chinese black vinegar reduction for the plate.

—**ANITA LO,** Annisa (New York City)

STEAK TARTARE

beef + chopped + *raw*

INSPIRED:

Curried Tuna Tartare

—Daniel Boulud, Le Cirque (New York City)

Potato Tartare: small cubes of pinkish-purple potatoes lightly encased in cream [with the appearance of tuna tartare, it paired beautifully with red wines]

—Gunnar Thompson, Glenmere Mansion (Chester, New York)

TARTE TATIN

apples + butter + pastry crust + sugar + *caramelized*

INSPIRED:

Peach Tarte Tatin, scented with Lemon Verbena and Bergamot, Salad of Mâche, Kohlrabi and Meadow Flowers, Raspberry Vinaigrette

—Carrie Nahabedian, Brindille (Chicago)

Shallot Tarte Tatin (substituting shallots for apples, and minimizing the sugar)

—David Mawhinney, Haven's Kitchen (New York City)

"Tarte Tatin" of Red Blush Apricots, Caramelized Onion and Fennel with a Salad of Arugula, "Frosted" Interlaken Grapes and Cracked Hazelnuts, Lambrusco, and Apple Balsamic

—Carrie Nahabedian, Naha (Chicago)

Tarte Tatin (interpretation): Slow-Roasted Honeycrisp Apples Sit Upon a Delicate "Feuilletage," Tahitian Vanilla Crème Fraîche

—Ghaya Oliveira, Daniel (New York City)

Shallot Tarte Tatin

TIRAMISU

cocoa + coffee + eggs + ladyfingers + mascarpone + sugar

INSPIRED:

Rosemary and Eggplant Tiramisu, with rosemary and eggplant cotton candy

—Amanda Cohen, Dirt Candy (New York City)

Tiramisu: Orgeat Poached Apricot, Light Verbena Mascarpone Mousse, Lime Gelée, Ladyfingers (interpretation without coffee, after Oliveira learned it wasn't in the original dessert)

—Ghaya Oliveira, Daniel (New York City)

TWICE-BAKED POTATOES

(bacon +) cheese + (baked) potato + scallions + sour cream + *mashed* + *stuffed*

INSPIRED:

Baked Idaho Potato filled with Black-Truffled Mashed Potatoes

—Stephanie Abrams & Francisco Blanco, Rotisserie Georgette (New York City)

Stuffed and Crisped Baked Idaho Potato filled with Gruyère Mashed Potatoes

—Stephanie Abrams & Francisco Blanco, Rotisserie Georgette (New York City)

Twice-Baked Potato

and a number of the best bread courses we tasted in 2016, including:

- At **Aaron Silverman**'s restaurant Rose's Luxury (Washington, D.C.), **hot potato bread** is served with whipped **butter + chives + dried fried potato skin crumbs** (which sub for bacon bits in appearance and flavor)
- **John Fraser** at Nix in New York City serves **Yukon potato fry bread** with **broccoli + Cheddar cheese + radishes + scallions + sour cream**
- **Beverly Kim** and **Johnny Clark** of Parachute in Chicago serve **crispy potato + Cheddar + scallion "bing bread" + sour cream butter**

TAL RONNEN AND SCOT JONES OF CROSSROADS IN LOS ANGELES: A FISH(LESS) TALE

> [The food at **Crossroads**] will surprise you: I indulge in oysters, Bolognese sauce, and a well-curated cheese plate. I eat fried calamari, caviar, fresh salads, and hearty pastas, and even desserts. . . .The dishes are thoughtful, playful, nourishing, satisfying, and yes, they happen to be vegan.
>
> —MICHAEL VOLTAGGIO, ink (Los Angeles)

Tal Ronnen and Scot Jones

Vegan Everything Bagel and "Lox"

Scot Jones: I got a call early one morning, and all Tal said was, "Jones, what about **a seafood tower?**" And I said, "Oh my God." Then we started riffing on the phone.

Tal Ronnen: We decided we could do some things that weren't traditionally on a raw tower, but that were still very seafood-esque. Normally, you see mostly cold preparations, on ice, on a tower, but ours has one level that's cold preparations and one level that's hot preparations. The hot level has "baked oysters" and "baked clams," which are shiitake mushrooms poached in olive oil and kombu, which really changes the texture of the mushroom, and then we season them with nori. An artichoke leaf stands in for the clam or oyster shell, in which we put the poached mushroom before treating it like a **Rockefeller [breadcrumbs + spinach]** or **Casino [breadcrumbs + smoked shallots** instead of bacon].

The "fried calamari" is fresh hearts of palm we hollow out—we get them from a farm in Costa Rica that makes them the only sustainable way I know, letting the shoot grow three different ways, and cutting only one shoot at a time, so they never cut the tree down. We use the bottoms of the palms for crabcakes, and hollow out the tops of the palms for rings of calamari. When you walk in the kitchen when we're cooking lobster mushrooms, you think you're smelling seafood. On the bottom, we have our take on a **Crab Louis** salad, an oyster shooter, and smoked carrot **"lox" with crème fraîche and [kelp] caviar.**

Scot was smoking these baby heirloom carrots for a dish last winter, and I ate one and I was like, "Wow—that smoke is incredible!" For me, I'm such a visual person that I saw it automatically: I saw that the rings of the carrot, when sliced horizontally, almost looked like the fat in salmon. So it triggered something in me. Then that morning, we were doing a shoot for our latest cookbook [***Crossroads***] and I brought in bagels from the only respectable bagel place in town for the crew. We'd just released this Kite Hill [the vegan cheese company in which Ronnen is a partner] almond cream cheese. So I took these carrots that we'd smoked and sliced them on a mandolin, and [put it out with the bagels and cream cheese], and those guys were like, "Whoa!" And I thought, "This is kinda cool."

But we're always improving things, so we took nori [seaweed] ground in a coffee grinder and baked the carrots in it so that it soaks it up and almost looks like a pepper-crusted salmon. And just to drive everyone else nuts, I said, "Now we have to make our own bagels." I have a very good friend whose mom showed me how to make New York–style bagels. So I showed the guys, and they were really into it—and every Sunday, they come in to make this beautiful proofed dough that they cut and boil and bake it.

Scot: But then you really get the experience of this hot bagel, and the cream cheese, and the lox, and the capers. We just did a pasta dish on the menu that's our version of **bagels and lox.** It's fettuccine, and instead of the cream cheese we make a prosecco cream sauce, with kelp caviar, smoked carrots, lox, and capers. It's definitely one of my favorite pastas.

Vikram Sunderam of Rasika on Inspiration and Adaptation

Whether you're looking through Indian cookbooks, or cookbooks by American chefs, it's always a matter of how to adapt a particular idea to *your* cuisine. But if you're eating it here, the guest shouldn't think that it is *not* Indian. So, if I decide to make a lamb burger, and I put onions and mustard and pepper in it, how do I make it Indian? I might add garam masala powder, mint, cilantro, green chiles, and mince everything together, and that would give more Indian flavors to it.

We've never offered a burger here [at Washington's Rasika], but we offer brunch now. *Pao* is like an unsweetened Parker House roll, and you might find a *keema pao* [made with lamb and onion] as Indian street food. We cut the *pao* in half and grill it on the skillet with some butter, and put minced lamb seasoned with green chiles and ginger between it: It becomes a **Sloppy Joe**. . . .

In Indian cuisine, it's very popular for appetizers and snacks to be fried, but traditional Indian batters can be very heavy. In creating my *palak chaat* [his signature fried spinach appetizer described as "iconic" by D.C. media in 2010], I wanted something fried but light to begin the meal. Pakora in a graham flour batter is a classic example. Spinach fries very quickly, so it's important not to use too much batter and to use a very thin batter to hold the spinach together so it doesn't crumble. Ours is made with baby spinach, besan [chickpea] flour, spices, and water—no egg. It's also important to fry it in oil at the right temperature, which is very hot. I use canola oil, given all the allergies to peanut oil....New Orleans chef **Alon Shaya** [of Domenica and Shaya, the latter of which was named the 2016 James Beard Best New Restaurant] tasted the dish here a few years ago, then adapted it as fried kale [in a garbanzo bean batter, tossed with pine nuts, shallots, scallions, cherry tomatoes, date vinegar, and lemon juice, and topped with grated Parmesan].

Domenica's kale was inspired by [New Orleans chef **Alon] Shaya**'s own mind-blowing vegetable experience. "My wife and I ate at an Indian restaurant in Washington, DC, [Rasika] that had a fried spinach dish that was just amazing," he said. "It had yogurt and tamarind and a lemon vinaigrette with it. I remember the flavors hitting all parts of my mouth at one time." Back at his own restaurant, Shaya played with the concept. The garbanzo-bean batter gives his kale a crispy, webby texture; a scattering of pine nuts and cherry tomatoes, shaved Parmesan and a drizzle of date vinegar and lemon juice make it feel substantial enough for a meat-less main.

—SUSAN LANGENHENNIG, *The Times-Picayune*

Vikram Sunderam

CONVERTING FOOD THROUGH FLAVOR

The best chefs develop their own methods to impose their will on their ingredients.

"Working with vegetables allows me to be more creative as a chef. I think of the vegetable first, and what its flavor is when you eat it raw, or blanched, or roasted—because only then can you balance its flavors," says Boulud Sud's Travis Swikard. "It used to be natural to blanch vegetables before throwing them in the oven, but I don't blanch them anymore because now I know you lose flavor. More often, I use a plancha with a lid on top so vegetables like artichokes can steam in their own natural moisture and retain more of their natural flavor."

"**Any way you manipulate an ingredient will either add flavor or take flavor away.** I want my artichokes to taste more like artichokes, not less. I'm always picking up techniques—and inspired by books like [Judy Rodgers's] *Zuni Cafe Cookbook,* where she writes about not putting peeled artichokes in lemon water because then they taste like lemons instead of artichokes," he says.

Swikard says he thinks of creating dishes "like a mathematical puzzle, where certain ingredients are a plus and others a minus." **A perfect Greek salad** comes to his mind as one of the best examples of a perfectly balanced dish: "It offers bites that are sweet from the tomato, salty from the feta, bitter from the greens, acidic from the vinegar, fat from the oil—you can have a perfect bite," he says. "I think of it as a 'treasure pot'—it may look simple, but it's exciting to get a bite with an amazing boom of salt from the kalamata olive, and the amazing freshness and herbaceousness of whole leaves of raw parsley."

Know your star ingredient, and don't add any sauces, garnishes, or other ingredients that detract from its flavor. If you combine coconut with blackberries and mango, it doesn't stand a chance. But coconut works well with caramel, or chocolate, or coffee.

—EMILY LUCHETTI,
chief pastry officer, The Cavalier, Marlowe, and Park Tavern (San Francisco)

ADAPTING A NEW DISH

The Evolution of Baked Goods—A Few Variations

Since croissants and doughnuts have both been around for centuries, why did it take until 2013 for the cronut craze to make its appearance? The potential was there—as when the experimentation process led another baker to cross baked goods a few years earlier: But City Bakery's Maury Rubin's subjects were croissants and pretzels instead, for which fans of his own popular pretzel croissant are grateful.

Ancient Rome: sweet dough was known to be fried in oil

600s: pretzels in the twisted knot shape

1400s: doughnuts

1610: bagels

1686: early Austrian croissants (dough made in crescent shape)

mid-1800s: ring doughnuts and doughnut holes

1900s: French croissants (crescent-shaped, but made from lighter puff-pastry-like dough)

1980s: pretzel bread

2007: pretzel croissant (croissant + rock salt + sesame seeds) from Maury Rubin, City Bakery (New York City)

May 10, 2013: cronuts from Dominique Ansel Bakery (New York City)

Ferran Adrià has argued that all innovation in cooking happens first in PASTRY. . . Pastry chefs are the only ones in the kitchen who are alchemists by necessity.

—ADAM GOPNIK,
The New Yorker

The Evolution of Eggs—A Few Variations

Eggs have been around as long as chickens, and inventive cooks have been playing with eggs ever since, both showcased as themselves in some dishes, as well as used for their binding and leavening properties in others. While muffins didn't become popular until the 18th century, anyone could have baked a muffin with a hard-boiled egg inside it at any point since. But it took until this decade for an intern to "screw that up," soft-boiling it instead—and a San Francisco baker to realize the delicious appeal of that "mistake."

1st century: French toast, omelets

1300s: scrambled eggs

1400s: stracciatella (egg-drop soup)

1500s: quiche (crust + eggs + seasonings + cheese/veggies/meats

1760: egg nog

1782: soufflé

1786: deviled eggs

1893: High-Life Eggs (egg fried in bread with hole cut out) appears in Angel Muro's Spanish cookbook, which is essentially the same concept as...

1896: Egg with a Hat appears in Fannie Farmer's *Boston Cooking-School Cookbook*; also known as Egg in a Hole, Egg in a Basket, Egg in a Frame, Eggs in Toast, Eggy in a Bready, Eggy in the Basket, Gashouse Eggs, Hobo Eggs, Moonstruck Eggs, One-Eyed Egyptian, One-Eyed Monster, and Toad in the Hole.

1893–1894: Eggs Benedict (egg + English muffin + ham + hollandaise) is served at Delmonico's and the Waldorf-Astoria in New York City.

1990s: Hot-Cold Egg from Alain Passard of L'Arpège in Paris: egg + crème fraîche + maple syrup + sherry vinegar, where the warm egg yolk contrasts with the cool crème fraîche served inside a topless egg shell. Chefs paying homage to the dish on their own menus include California chef... David Kinch at Manresa in Los Gatos and Mark Best of Marque in Sydney, Australia.

2010s: The Rebel Within from William Werner, Craftsman and Wolves (San Francisco): The soft-poached egg-in-a-muffin was created accidentally when an intern undercooked what were intended to be hard-boiled eggs; the muffin celebrates **egg + Asiago cheese + sausage + green onions**.

The Evolution of Ice Cream—A Few Variations

The evolution of ice cream–making partly reflects the evolution of the freezing process. Natural blocks of ice were first shaved and flavored, thousands of years before the advent of refrigeration and freezers. By the time cryogenic technology was invented, liquid nitrogen presented a new opportunity for chefs to freeze foods—including turning custards into ice creams. And ice cream's presentations have even been influenced by legislation, including the 1890 blue laws of Evanston, Illinois, precluding the service of ice cream sodas on Sunday, which led to the creation of soda-free "sundaes."

3,000 BC: The Chinese are believed to make the first flavored ices, which evolve into ice creams.

17th century: The style of ice cream we eat today is said to have originated in Italy. As ice cream spreads, it sees variations, including French style (with egg yolks).

1670: Café Procope opens in Paris, bringing ice cream and sorbet to the public.

1768: First reference in print to chocolate ice cream; before this, the most common flavorings were fruit.

1792: The first recipe for ice cream appears in the United States in *The New Art of Cookery* by Richard Briggs.

1780s: Thomas Jefferson's ice cream recipes/references

1802: fried ice cream

1807: ice cream cones

1824: oyster ice cream

1860s: Baked Alaska (ice cream + meringue + sponge cake): Said to have been created in celebration of the U.S.'s purchase of Alaska

1869: parfaits (layered, molded ice cream treats with fruits, liqueurs, and sauces)

1870s: Neapolitan ice cream (slices of vanilla, chocolate, and strawberry)

1887: malt powder exists, followed by malts

1890s: ice cream sundaes (ice cream + nuts + sauce + whipped cream)

1893: *à la mode* dishes with ice cream

Baked Alaska

1900: ice cream sandwiches

1904: banana splits (banana + ice cream + syrups + whipped cream)

1917: Black Cow (vanilla ice cream + root beer or chocolate soda)

1920s: Rocky Road (chocolate + ice cream + marshmallow + nuts)

1930s: Rum Raisin (ice cream + raisins + rum)

1948: Howard Johnson's "28 Flavors" (The slogan refers to its broad array of ice cream flavors, most of which were single-flavors.)

1953: Baskin-Robbins Ice Cream (founded in 1945) advertises "31 Flavors," more of which were combination flavors. Original flavors included Banana Nut Fudge (banana + chocolate + nuts), Black Walnut, Burgundy Cherry, Butterscotch

Ribbon, Cherry Macaroon, Chocolate, Chocolate Almond, Chocolate Chip, Chocolate Fudge, Chocolate Mint, Chocolate Ribbon, Coffee, Coffee Candy, Date Nut, Egg Nog, French Vanilla, Green Mint Stick, Lemon Crisp, Lemon Custard, Lemon Sherbet, Maple Nut, Orange Sherbet, Peach, Peppermint Fudge Ribbon, Peppermint Stick, Pineapple Sherbet, Raspberry Sherbet, Rocky Road, Strawberry, Vanilla, and Vanilla Burnt Almond, which went on to spur the development of 1,300+ new ice cream flavor combinations.

> Not everyone likes all our flavors, but each flavor is someone's favorite.
> —IRV ROBBINS, co-founder, Baskin-Robbins

1968: So-called "astronaut" (i.e., freeze-dried) ice cream becomes a fad.

1987: Microbiologist Curt Jones applies a method used to freeze livestock feed with liquid nitrogen to freeze ice cream into small beads. He founds a company in his parents' garage that becomes Dippin' Dots.

2007: Robyn Sue Fisher founds, and subsequently takes out four patents on her liquid nitrogen ice-cream maker used at her California-based chain Smitten Ice Cream.

The Evolution of Pizza—A Few Variations

Too late—you can't invent pizza. But that doesn't mean you can't make a great thing even better, as has been proven time and again in the years since the first pizzeria opened in 1830. In fact, only later in the 1800s did mozzarella even become a now-classic topping. In 1889, Raffaele Esposito of Pizzeria di Pietro in Naples made the first **basil + mozzarella + tomato** pizza, featuring the colors of the Italian flag in honor of the visit of Queen Margherita. Pizza changed as it came to the U.S., where Lombardi's opened the first pizzeria in 1905: cow's milk vs. buffalo mozzarella was used, and local marjoram was initially substituted for Italian oregano. Others have since converted the platform of pizza through their own versions, with a variety of takes on the dough and its toppings alike.

1830: Naples thin-crust pizza (dough + tomato)

later 1800s: (dough + mozzarella + tomato)

1889: pizza Margherita (dough + mozzarella + tomato + basil)

1943: deep-dish pizza (thick-crust pizza)

1974: stuffed pizza: a 4-inch biscuit-crust pizza stuffed with ingredients, and topped with a second crust—stuffed spinach pizza a specialty. This was inspired by an Italian Easter cake called *scarciedda*, according to Nancy's in Chicago.

1981: grilled pizza (dough + cheese + scallions + tomato + *grilling*) from George Germon and Johanne Killeen, Al Forno (Providence, Rhode Island)

1980s: smoked salmon pizza from Wolfgang Puck, Spago (Los Angeles)

2010s: In Ricotta da Vegan pizza (featuring almond ricotta + meatless fennel sausage) from Paul Giannone, Paulie Gee's (Brooklyn)

PLAYING WITH CHORDS

The French folk song "Ah, vous dirai-je, maman," first published in 1761, inspired Mozart's "Twelve Variations" (circa 1780s). The tune is so catchy and versatile that it later became the basis of multiple English nursery rhymes, which you'll recognize immediately if you're familiar with the three-chord (C, F, G7) "Alphabet Song," "Baa Baa Black Sheep," or "Twinkle Twinkle Little Star."

More recently, the Australian comedy rock band Axis of Awesome created a YouTube hit with their videos of "The 4-Chord Song," which features 40 songs you can play with the same four chords (C, G, Am, F), starting with the opening riff of Journey's "Don't Stop Believin'" and continuing that four-chord progression as they sing lines from dozens of songs that fit the same structure, including U2's "With or Without You," Maroon 5's "She Will Be Loved," Marcy Playground's "Sex & Candy," Toto's "Africa," Lady Gaga's "Poker Face," and the Fray's "You Found Me." (Want to test it out? Pull up the GarageBand app on your iPhone—or pull your guitar out of the closet—and play away.)

CHORD: a harmonious group of (usually 3+) notes played simultaneously

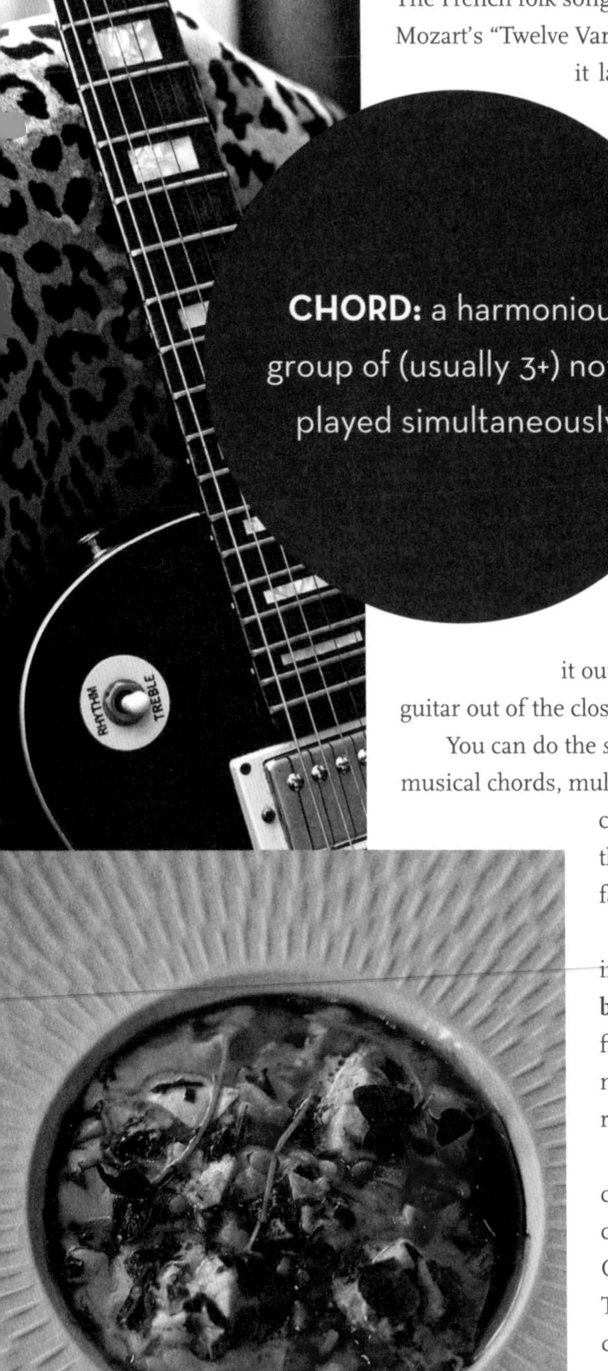

Travis Swikard's Acquerello Risotto "Caprese" at Boulud Sud

You can do the *same* with flavors. Just as multiple notes played together form musical chords, multiple flavors tasted together form **flavor chords.** These chords can start you humming a dish or an entire cuisine, and provide the jumping-off point for coming up with a riff on one of your favorites.

For example, *anyone* who's ever enjoyed a Caprese salad in the summertime knows the powerful three-note chord of **basil + mozzarella cheese + tomato.** It's the same chord you'll find in a classic eggplant Parmesan, and pizza Margherita, and mozzarella cheese omelet with tomato and basil, and mozzarella panini with tomato-basil soup.

How could you choose to tweak the combination? You could serve the basil raw or cooked (e.g., fried), whole or chopped, and the tomatoes raw, cooked, even sun-dried. Or, you could substitute another cheese for the mozzarella: Tomato and watermelon salads with basil can work with feta cheese; Bobby Flay has taken the combination to the Southwest with Grilled Quesadillas with Black Olive Tapenade, Goat Cheese, and Tomato-Basil Relish.

Taking *another* example, the combination of **basil + olive oil + Parmesan + pine nuts** is a four-note chord better known as **pesto.** And you can use that same fabulous foursome of flavors in dishes ranging from pastas to pizzas to sandwiches to soups. Or, you could deconstruct the foursome into a savory "sundae" comprised of, say, basil ice cream with a warm olive oil sauce, Parmesan foam, and toasted pine nuts. Once you know what notes work together, you can reconstruct them in any way you like.

Other chord examples:

- **chervil + chives + parsley + tarragon** is better known as **fines herbes**
- **anchovies + garlic + lemon zest + parsley** is better known as **gremolata**
- **cinnamon + cloves + fagara + fennel + star anise** is better known as **Chinese five-spice powder**
- **almonds + garlic + parsley + saffron** is better known as **Spanish picada**
- **cinnamon + cloves + grains of paradise + nutmeg + pepper** is better known as **Tunisian five-spice mix**
- **garlic + onions + peppers + tomatoes** is better known as a (Latin) **sofrito**
- **aji dulce + cilantro + culantro** will take you to **Cuba**
- **chiles + cilantro + lime** will take you to **Mexico**
- **chiles + coconut + mint** will take you to **Thailand.**
- **(red) chiles + garlic + ginger + oil + shallots + turmeric** will take you to **Burma**
- **fish flakes + kelp** will take you to **Japan**
- **garlic + ginger + soy sauce** will take you to **Asia**
- **garlic + lemon + oregano** will take you to the **Mediterranean**
- **sour cream + beets + dill** will take you to **Russia**
- **sour cream + paprika** will take you to **Hungary**
- **blue cheese + celery + hot sauce** will take you to **Buffalo chicken wings**
- **cucumbers + garlic + peppers + tomatoes** will give you a **Spanish gazpacho**
- **miso + scallions + tofu + wakame seaweed** will give you **Japanese miso soup**
- **almonds + maple syrup + oats** will (usually) take you to **breakfast**
- **chocolate + nuts + vanilla** will (usually) take you to **dessert**

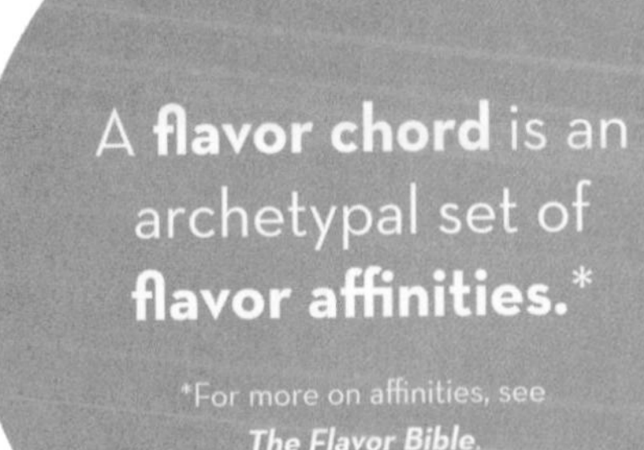

A **flavor chord** is an archetypal set of **flavor affinities.***
*For more on affinities, see *The Flavor Bible*.

Once you master a flavor platform, you can convert it by employing different flavor chords. "Coming up with new dishes often starts with the season, and what vegetables we want to create dishes around," says Stephanie Izard of Chicago's Girl & the Goat, who uses her signature chickpea fritters as a flavor platform for different seasonal flavor chords.

"I have been making chickpea fritters since my first restaurant. I had read about them in one of Mario Batali's books [2005's *Molto Italiano* features a recipe for Sicilian Chickpea Fritters] and realized they are a classic Italian thing made of fried chickpea flour. So I created my own recipe. Now, we always keep a chickpea fritter dish on the menu for vegetarians, and we change it seasonally. Our summer version had heirloom **tomato + red onion + feta cheese** with a **masala + yogurt + rosemary** dressing."

Other versions over the years have included Crispy Chickpea Fritters with:

- basil/parsley sauce + feta
- chile paste + honey + mint + olives + Parmesan + preserved lemon
- garam masala + roasted vegetables + yogurt
- goat feta + hazelnut hummus + romesco + sesame
- Green Goddess + MontAmore cheese + tomatillo-tomato jam
- mushroom aioli + okra-tomato relish + Prairie Fruits Farm chévre + royal trumpet mushrooms
- Prairie Fruits Farm chèvre + stewed winter greens

Not knowing what month in 2016 the Charter Oak would open in Napa Valley, former Meadowood chef de cuisine Katianna Hong and her kitchen team focused on devising some simple, elemental **flavor platforms** that would allow them to plug in seasonal flavors—including gnudi, a gnocchi-like pasta that typically substitutes ricotta cheese for potato. "We often play with fresh curds for bar dishes, and have made gnudi with them. The gnudi at Meadowood are more perfectly formed, while they're a bit looser for the Charter Oak. For example, we'll make a cheesy gnudi [with the fresh curd] served in a ham bone broth with pea leaf pesto and a hint of horseradish. We aged some ham bones and made a broth from them, which is not heavy but has an amazing depth of flavor from the aged bones. **Ham + peas** is an obvious combination. At a different time of year, we'd serve the same gnudi with squash blossoms and squash leaves. When they're raw, squash leaves can be a bit thistly like borage, but they're great when they're braised like hearty greens."

THE FLAVOR EQUATION

FLAVOR = Taste + Mouthfeel + Aroma + The X Factor

Corollary Equations

TASTE = Salty + Sour (Acidity) + Sweet + Bitter + Umami (Savory)

MOUTHFEEL = Temperature + Texture + Piquancy + Astringency

AROMA = Aromatics + Pungency + Chemethesis

THE X FACTOR = Other Physical, Emotional, Mental, and Spiritual Factors

Every single opportunity you have to create deliciousness in any dish is reflected in THE FLAVOR EQUATION and its corollary equations—so make them your friends.

If you commit these to memory, you can use them as mental checklists every time you're creating or seasoning a dish to try to identify what might be missing from it and added to enhance it.

FLAVOR DYNAMICS

Another level of knowledge can be extrapolated after mastering *how* to prepare classic dishes: the principle of *why* a dish works. For instance, through the example of a Caesar salad, we know that **croutons + Parmesan + Romaine** work well together.

But why? Croutons are typically relatively neutral in flavor—their primary contribution is their toasted crunch, which adds texture and contrast to the salad. The Parmesan cheese primarily adds its saltiness and umami, and whether it's grated or shaved, it also adds texture. Romaine is a slightly bitter green, and it's typically dressed with olive oil and a raw egg with acidity from the lemon juice. Sometimes raw garlic is used to rub the wooden bowl a Caesar salad is served in or from, contributing pungency.

We can extract the principle of what can make a great salad great from the beloved Caesar salad:

- crisp, bitter greens
- balanced by the **richness** of the dressing (e.g., olive oil, egg yolk) and the **saltiness** of the cheese (and anchovy, when it is used, which also contributes **umami**), which are in turn balanced by the **acidity** of the lemon juice, and perhaps the **pungency** of garlic
- accented by the **crunchy** texture of the croutons

> **All of us—sensory scientists, anesthetists, chefs alike—experience TASTE as if it's coming from the mouth, but in fact ALL the other SENSES are involved. Our brain's just sort of doing it all together and telling us it's there in your mouth.**
>
> —CHARLES SPENCE, professor at University of Oxford

We can keep these lessons with us when we're making a salad of any kind: Have we balanced its flavors and textures appealingly? Learning to recognize and apply flavor principles will help us to maximize the flavor and enjoyment of dishes of all kinds.

Deconstructing Flavor Principles

Build your own memory bank of flavor principles—examples of your favorite combinations of tastes, mouthfeels, and aromas. Take note of the dishes and drinks that meld flavors well, and deconstruct them to discover the flavor principles that made them work. You can then use those principles as idea-starters when you are looking for ideas for working with flavors that are astringent, bitter, cold, "cool," fat, hot, piquant, pungent, salty, sour, sweet, and/or savory.

For example, if you enjoy the flavor principle of **salty + smoky + sweet**, you'll understand that it doesn't only work in a classic pairing such as **bacon + (caramelized) onions + potatoes**—and that it can also take the form of **smoked feta + watermelon**, or a number of other combinations limited only by your imagination.

Understanding how to make any ingredient or dish taste better starts with understanding the components of flavor, which we spell out in the Flavor Equation, which we first introduced in *The Flavor Bible:*

THE FLAVOR EQUATION

FLAVOR = Taste + Mouthfeel + Aroma + The X Factor

Each element of the Flavor Equation offers opportunities for enhancing and adding to the flavor of a dish.

The Flavor Equation emphasizes that **"flavor" and "taste" are *not* the same,** with taste a mere subsegment of flavor, along with mouthfeel, aroma, and other factors. While many use the words synonymously, they're quite different, as we'll see below.

There are four corollary equations to the Flavor Equation, which we will also discuss in this section:

TASTE = Salty + Sour (Acidity) + Sweet + Bitter + Umami (Savory)
MOUTHFEEL = Temperature + Texture + Piquancy + Astringency
AROMA = Aromatics + Pungency + Chemethesis
THE X FACTOR = Other Physical, Emotional, Mental, and Spiritual Factors

TASTE = SALTY + SOUR (ACIDIC) + SWEET + BITTER + UMAMI (SAVORY)

The first element of the Flavor Equation is *Taste*. Every delicious bite you've ever tasted has been a result of these five elements coming together on your taste buds. We taste them as individual notes as well as in concert. Each taste affects the other. Different tastes affect us in different ways: Saltiness stimulates the appetite, while sweetness satiates it. As you explore the five basic tastes—Salty, Sour, Sweet, Bitter, and Umami—you'll discover that they're often influenced by factors such as freshness and ripeness, helping to fuel the trend toward local cuisine.

Balancing these tastes is the key to making food taste delicious. This process can be incredibly nuanced and complex, but we'll try to simplify it somewhat, starting with a suggested order for adjusting flavor elements:

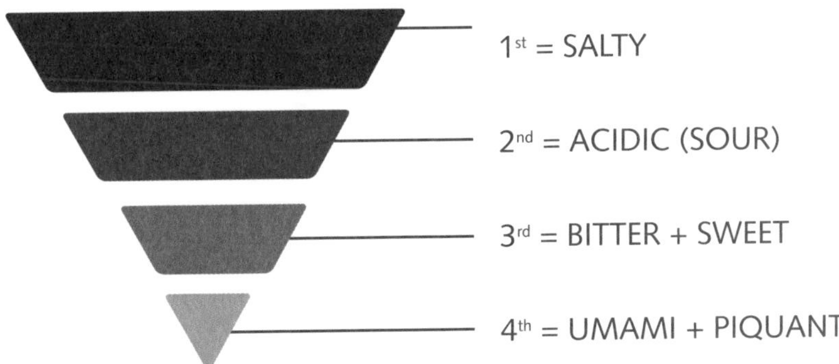

Michael Scelfo on the Inspiration of Memory

Pickled Verrill Farm Corn Pancake

For me, most dishes come from a sentimental place of memory, an emotional muscle memory of something my mom or grandmother did.

When I was growing up, my mom made delicious corn pancakes out of canned corn. My corn pancake [at Alden & Harlow], Pickled Verrill Farm Corn Pancake, made with buttermilk, maple, shishito peppers, and popcorn] is my nod to her dish. A lot of ingredients and dishes are very subtle nods to things I grew up on. I'm not heavy-handed about it—I don't call it "My Mom's" on the menu; it is more personal to me.

I am very big on **texture,** so everything that comes out of the kitchen has to have some kind of contrasting texture....I find when there is a little crunch on the plate, it keeps you interested and keeps you eating.

The same thing with **acidity**—it keeps you coming back to the plate when you are eating. The pickled corn in the pancake dish is my way of getting acidity on the plate to play against the richness.

We added fried shishito peppers to the dish [for the mildest hint of **piquancy**] because they go with corn—because I went through *Culinary Artistry,* like I still do to this day, and see **corn + peppers** is the most natural combination there is.

Charred Broccoli with Butternut Hummus & Smoked Cashew Crumble

We were one of the first restaurants to do a dish like this in the area. One of the things my mom would make several nights a week was slowly cooked broccoli. She would chop a lot of broccoli, then start with olive oil, garlic, butter, red pepper flakes in a cast iron pot with the garlic and olive oil melting together. Then she threw in the broccoli and cooked it down to mush for a couple of hours—it would end up with a pesto-like texture. Then she would boil some pasta and toss it in with a ton of pecorino Romano. We lived on that.

Charred Broccoli

I love the flavor of it and my kids have grown up with it as their baby food. I still make it a couple of times a week. So for my charred broccoli dish, I wanted to play off the [style of] broccoli that I love so much. I char the heck out of it, throwing it on the grill raw with no blanching, so it has crunch and bitterness on the outside. My favorite nut is cashew and I had never had a smoked one before, so I smoked some and made a tahini out of them.

We also had surplus squash bulbs left from being spiralized on another dish and the staff could not look at it any more at staff meal. So we made a squash hummus with cashew tahini, urfa [pepper], Szechuan peppercorn, honey, orange, lemon juice, and salt and pepper.

So one night my cooks were looking at me like I was crazy as I grilled off some broccoli and I honestly did not know where I was going with this. I just thought, "This will be a fun small plate."

I took some raw cashew and pulsed it down to a meal consistency, mixed it with bianco sardo, grilled off the broccoli, and tossed it with honey, olive oil, gremolata and served it on this pool of squash hummus—and we have never looked back since. It is the bestselling dish along with our pancake and kale salad since day one. We will sell 75 to 80 orders a night.

Vegetables as Inspiration

We do simple vegetable-focused cooking. I liked the challenge of vegetable cooking at first because I wanted to move the vegetable to the center of the plate and use meat sparingly as a condiment, the way you would use a vegetable traditionally for basically eternity. Then it just became natural.

We would see the first spring onions and parsnips and it is just obvious that this is what we want to feature on the plate. I want to feature the eggplant coming out of the ground in the center of the plate verses crowbar it onto a meat dish because that is what we have always supposed to have been doing with a starch.

Getting away from that is liberating and fun. It opens up your mind to possibilities. What if broccoli, celery root, or pumpkin is the center of my plate now? How can I maximize these flavors? How can I make a dish that is memorable versus forgettable?

Corn Pancake

SALTINESS

As acknowledged in Stage 1, **mastering salt is the Holy Grail of seasoning**—so much so that it is often the first thing taught in restaurant kitchens. Salt is nature's flavor enhancer, and the single most important taste for making savory food taste delicious. Beyond salt, regionally appropriate salty ingredients also play an important role in enhancing savory dishes, such as Parmesan or pecorino with dishes like pastas and pizzas, and soy sauce or tamari with dishes like Asian dumplings and stir-fries. Depending on what you typically cook, you'll likely want to have several alternatives on hand, from salt itself to tamari and aged Parmesan cheese. Even different salts—including different sources (sea, earth), different terroirs (e.g., England, France, West Virginia), different brands, and different grain sizes (fine, medium, coarse)—have different degrees of saltiness, so it's vital to know *your* salt and *your* salty ingredients. Taste, taste, taste.

Remember that whenever you add salty ingredients to a dish, you'll want to cut down on the amount of actual salt you use to season that dish, lest your dish end up oversalted.

We wanted to serve gnocchi [potato-based pasta] that was different. So, we asked ourselves, "What do you put on potato chips?" SALT. Our version [made from potatoes + seaweed] features four different "salts": cheese, fish sauce, miso, and ham hock broth—but no actual salt. This makes it a fun dish for us.

—**CHRIS LONG** and **SHELBY STEVENS,**
Natalie's at the Camden Harbour Inn
(Camden, ME)

> **Christopher [Kostow, executive chef at the Restaurant at Meadowood, where Hong was previously chef de cuisine] won't just say, "You should add salt." He'll suggest a very specific ingredient: "You should add some reduced oyster liqueur" or "You should add a pickled lime."**
>
> —**KATIANNA HONG,** The Charter Oak (Napa Valley)

SALTY INGREDIENTS

anchovies or anchovy paste (salt + umami)

artichokes (which are high in natural sodium)

bacon (salt + fat)

black salt (for snack foods in northern India)

bottarga (salt + umami)

Bragg liquid aminos

butter, salted (salt + fat)

capers

celery (which is high in natural sodium) and celery salt

cheese, aged, hard, and/or salty (e.g., blue, feta, Parmesan, pecorino) (salt + fat)

clam juice

cured meats (salt + fat)

feta cheese liquid

fish sauce (salt + umami)

flake salts (fine-crystaled, low in minerals salt, e.g., Maldon salt) for baked goods (e.g., cookies, dinner rolls, pie crusts, pretzels), for lighter foods, and for raw or steamed vegetables

fleur de sel (finishing salt) for (scrambled) eggs, fish, mozzarella, pork, vegetables

Himalayan salt, e.g., kala namak (salt + astringent)

kosher salt

Maldon sea salt (finishing salt) e.g., for fish

meats, cured (e.g., bacon, ham) (salt + fat)

miso (salt + umami)

mojama (salt-cured Spanish tuna) (salt + umami)

nuts, salted (salt + fat)

olive brine and olives

oyster liquor

pickled vegetables (salt + acidity)

pink salt, Hawaiian, for corn on the cob, fruits

pink salt, Peruvian, for raw tomatoes

salted plums (e.g., umeboshi)

seafood (fish and shellfish, which contain natural salinity)

sea salt (inexpensive) for brines, pasta water

seaweed/sea vegetables (e.g., dulse, Irish moss, wakame)

sel de mer from La Baleine

sel gris (coarse salt used for loud-flavored ingredients) for meats, roasts, root vegetables

shio [Japanese] salts for quiet dishes, e.g., delicate broths and sauces, steamed vegetables

smoked salt (salt + smoke)

soy sauce and white soy sauce (salt + umami)

tamari (salt + umami)

truffle salt (salt + umami)

Salt Techniques

brining (both *dry-brining* and *wet-brining*)

salt-baking

Preferred Salts

Every chef has their own preference of salts for various purposes, e.g., cooking vs. finishing dishes. Salts range from fine (which dissolves quickly) to coarse (which retains crunch longer), with different implications for flavor, so it's important to choose your salt carefully given your aim. For example:

Daniel Boulud prefers *sel de mer* from La Baleine.

Thomas Keller offers his own Ad Hoc Salt Cellar featuring *fleur de sel* for vegetables, Maldon sea salt for fish, and *sel gris* (gray salt) for meat.

Spike Gjerde is so devoted to using only local ingredients at his Baltimore restaurant Woodberry Kitchen that he only uses J.Q. Dickinson heirloom salt from Malden, West Virginia, which has a hint of iron with a clean, crunchy finish.

Salt Dynamics

Salt can reduce perceived acidity and bitterness in a dish. Salt high—sprinkling 12 inches or higher above the food—so that the crystals are more evenly spread out on whatever you're salting. Salt before (e.g., mirepoix), during (e.g., stock), *and* after (e.g., stew) cooking—yet err on the side of less vs. more, as you can't remove salt once it's added. If a dish is oversalted, you can try to balance it with acidity, sweetness, and/or fat, or simply by adding more of the non-salted ingredients, if possible.

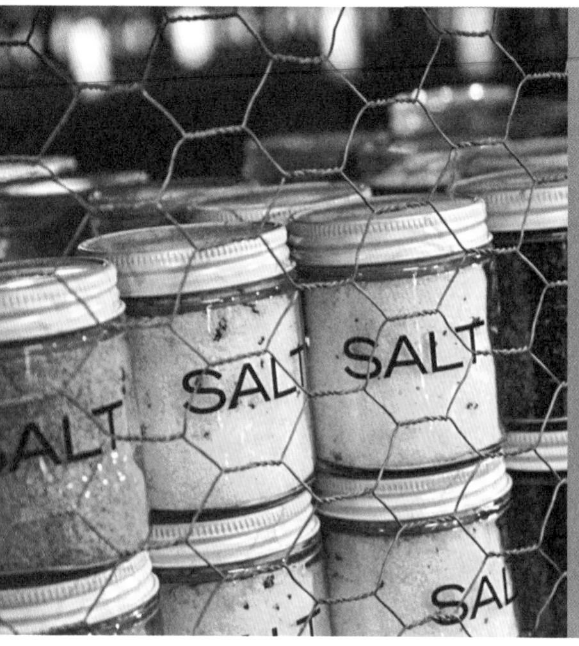

You must always consider portion size when seasoning, especially with sauces, soups, and bouillons. Too often, chefs will taste one bite, but it's different to season for one bite versus an entire plate of food. There is a French phrase, *trop corse* ["too concentrated"], which could describe something like a soup that is seasoned for a small demitasse, but if served as a large bowl, the layers of salt add up and are too strong.

—GABRIEL KREUTHER,
Gabriel Kreuther (New York City)

Using Salt

Consider using **sea salt** with seafood (fish and shellfish) and sea vegetables (kombu, nori, wakame), and "salt of the earth" (that is, mined from the earth, like kosher salt) with foods from the earth.

Salty + Umami: Chefs love the depth of flavor that **anchovies** can add to sauces and other dishes in addition to their saltiness.

Salty + Umami: It's impossible to count the number of chefs who extol the virtues of **fish sauce** as a way of adding both salt + umami to dishes (perhaps especially those containing garlic). Chefs add fish sauce to vegetables and salads (including Caesar) as well as dipping sauces, hastening to point out that using it judiciously contributes to a "roundness" of flavor while *not* adding "fishiness."

Salty + Umami: Don't overlook the power of using a great quality **Parmigiano-Reggiano** cheese, which chefs remind us adds so much flavor to everything you add it to—whether pastas or salads, or soups or stocks (both of which can be made using Parmesan rinds).

Salty + Umami: Chefs appreciate cooking with **seaweed**, which does double-duty as a flavor enhancer and as a source of umami.

Salty + Umami: A number of chefs keep not only **soy sauce** but also dehydrated **soy sauce crystals** on hand as a way to give a pinch of meaty flavor to dishes, or to even add a hit of umami to mustard vinaigrettes. Lee Wolen finds he uses more **white soy sauce** (e.g., Oregon's Yamasa), in dishes ranging from sauces to vinaigrettes, observing, "It's a bit lighter."

Salt Principles

Salty + Smoky + Sweet
bacon + (caramelized) onions + potatoes
smoked feta + watermelon

Salty + Sour
salt + cucumber + vinegar —> pickles
salt + potato (e.g., chips, French fries) + vinegar

Salty + Sour + Sweet + Umami
salt + vinegar + sugar + tomatoes —> barbecue sauce

Salty + Sweet
blue cheese + honey
caramel + corn + cheese popcorn (*à la* Garrett's Mix)
pretzels + (milk) chocolate
prosciutto + melon
nuts + sugar
Parmesan cheese + honey
peanut butter + jelly
feta cheese + watermelon

Salty + Umami
bacon + tomato
ham + potato
salt + tomatoes

Salt can enhance chocolate, bring up the flavor of pie crusts, and make pecans taste even more pecan-y.

—**EMILY LUCHETTI,** chief pastry officer, The Cavalier, Marlowe, and Park Tavern (San Francisco)

We keep a variety of VINEGARS at our disposal. We had an abundance of strawberries in our garden but didn't have them on the menu, so we made a strawberry vinegar from them.

—**KATIANNA HONG,** The Charter Oak (Napa Valley)

ACIDITY lifts and brightens flavor.

—**BRAD FARMERIE,** Saxon + Parole (New York City)

SOURNESS (AKA ACIDITY)

The mouth-puckering taste of **sourness** is the result of acidity, leading professional chefs to often refer to it as simply that. Sour is second only to salt in savory food and sugar in sweet food in its importance as a flavor enhancer. Sour notes—whether a squeeze of lemon or lime, or a drizzle of vinegar—add sparkle and brightness to a dish. Selecting the best option for adding acidity to a particular dish—whether lime juice to guacamole or sherry vinegar to gazpacho—can enhance the dish even further. Balancing a dish's acidity with its other tastes is critical to its success.

SOUR INGREDIENTS

agrodolce (honey + red wine vinegar) (sweet + sour)

beer

berries (e.g., blackberries, raspberries)

buttermilk

carob molasses (sour + sweet)

cheese, sour (e.g., chèvre, cream, goat) (sour + fat)

cherries, sour

chocolate (sour + bitter)

citric acid powder

citrus juices (grapefruit, lemon, lime, mandarin, orange, tangerine, yuzu)

cornichons

cranberries (sour + astringent)

crème fraîche (sour + fat)

cultured foods (buttermilk, cheese, kombucha, yogurt)

currants, fresh

fermented foods (e.g., kimchee, sauerkraut)

fruits, sour/unripe (e.g., green apples, green grapes, green strawberries)

SOUR INGREDIENTS (CONT.)

grapefruit
kefir
kiwi
kumquats
lemon, Meyer
lemon, preserved
lemongrass
lemon juice
lemon thyme
lemon verbena
lime juice
makrut lime, dried and fresh
milk, goat
passion fruit (sour + sweet)
pickles and pickled foods, esp. vegetables (e.g., cucumbers, onions, peppers)
plums (esp. unripe)
pomegranate molasses (sour + sweet)
ponzu
quince
rhubarb
sabas, grape (sour + sweet)
sauerkraut
sorrel
sour cream (sour + fat)
sumac
tamarind
tamarind paste
tomatillos
tomatoes (e.g., green, red, yellow) (sour + umami)
tomato essence (sour + umami)
tomato paste (sour + umami)
tomato powder (sour + umami)
verjus
vin cotto (sour + sweet)
vinegar, aged white wine
vinegar, apple cider
vinegar, balsamic and white balsamic (sour + sweet)
vinegar, Banyuls
vinegar, beer
vinegar, cane
vinegar, Champagne
vinegar, Chinese black
vinegar, coconut
vinegar, malt
vinegar, Moscatel
vinegar, red wine (e.g., Cabernet)
vinegar, rice or rice wine
vinegar, sherry
vinegar, sugar cane
vinegar, sushi and sushinoko
vinegar, Swiss
vinegar, tomato
vinegar, umeboshi plum
vinegar, white wine
whey
wine, dry (e.g., red, white, esp. in western European cuisines) (sour + complexity)
yogurt (sour + fat)

Chocolate actually has a lot of ACIDITY—which is why I don't think it pairs well with raspberries, as the combination is too acidic and there's no bridge between them. I think [lower-acidity] white chocolate makes a much better pairing with raspberries, or with passion fruit.

—**EMILY LUCHETTI,** chief pastry officer, The Cavalier, Marlowe, and Park Tavern (San Francisco)

David [Bouley] and Rocco [DiSpirito] both had a lot of raw, ice-cold TOMATO WATER in the kitchen that would go in after a dish came off the heat—it was more brilliant than a verjus, with all this acidity yet really natural and really clean. It adds a dimension and depth that took a dish to another level, but yet was undefinable by someone who didn't know it was there.

—QUINN AND KAREN HATFIELD,
Odys + Penelope and Sycamore Kitchen
(Los Angeles)

VINEGARS BY ACIDITY

Not all acids are alike. Among vinegars alone, their acidity can range from a low of 4.5 percent (as in Swiss vinegar, whose acidity is strictly regulated by law) to a high of 8 percent (for sherry vinegar).

8%	Sherry vinegar
7%	Champagne vinegar
6.5–7%	White wine vinegar / flavored white wine vinegar (e.g., garlic, raspberry)
6–7%	Red wine vinegar / Cabernet vinegar
6%	Aged white wine vinegar
6%	Balsamic / white balsamic vinegar
6%	Moscatel vinegar
6%	Tomato vinegar
5%	Apple cider vinegar
5%	Distilled white vinegar
5%	Malt vinegar
4.5–5%	Cane vinegar
4.5%	Swiss vinegar

Sour Techniques

macerating (i.e., fruit)

marinating (i.e., other ingredients)

spritzing (e.g., lemon juice from a spray bottle)

Sour Dynamics

Sourness (acidity) balances saltiness, sweetness, and even piquancy. Choose your acidic ingredients as carefully as you choose your salt: Citrus tends to pair best with fruits, vegetables, and seafood, while vinegars have a greater range of applications. Not all vinegars are interchangeable, as they vary significantly in acidity, sweetness, aroma, etc. Wine, in addition to adding acidity, can add complexity. If a dish is too acidic, consider balancing with salt, sweet, bitter, or fatty ingredients.

Using Sour

When to opt for which acid? Daniel's Jean-François Bruel turns to **citrus** when working with **vegetables** (noting that it depends on the vegetable) and **seafood** (when he often turns specifically to lemon, although his citrus repertoire also includes limes, finger limes, makrut lime, and yuzu). He mostly turns to **vinegars** (often sherry vinegar, but sometimes also balsamic vinegar or berry-flavored vinegars) when working with **mushrooms** and **meats.**

Citric acid counts chefs, pastry chefs, and mixologists as fans. It's used in very small amounts to enhance the flavor of fruit in jams, mousses, and cocktails as it adds acidity without diluting other flavors. It can be used to make a quick buttermilk or ricotta by adding it to milk. It will also prevent fruits and vegetables from oxidizing (turning brown). Chefs combine it with salt to make their own "sour salt."

Many chefs, including Brad Farmerie, count **citrus** as their go-to flavor enhancers. Farmerie attests, "I love my vinegars, but I also love lemons, orange, yuzu, and preserved lemons," the last of which occupy their own shelf in Public's walk-in, while other chefs swear by the complexity of the Japanese citrus fruits *calamansi and sudachi.*

Mark Levy loves the flavor of *combava*—"**dried makrut lime,** grated on a Microplane"—which he discovered to be "great with chocolate."

OTHER ACIDIC INGREDIENTS

Acidic substances are <7.0 on the pH scale. The lower the pH, the more acidic a substance is.

- **Lime juice** averages a pH level of 2.0 to 2.35, and is therefore often more acidic than lemon juice, which is typically 2.2 to 2.3 on the pH scale.
- **Vinegar** averages about 2.9 on the pH scale, is therefore often less acidic than lemon or lime juice.

Food	% Sugar	pH Level
lime juice	1.7%	**2.0–2.35**
lemon juice	2.4%	**2.2–2.6**
cranberry juice (canned)	12.0%	**2.3–2.52**
distilled white vinegar	0.0%	**2.4**
vinegars, in general	-	**2.4–3.4**
balsamic vinegar, traditional	15.0%	**<2.8**
balsamic vinegar, Modena	-	**>2.8**
wine, dry red	0.0%	**2.8–3.8**
red wine vinegar	0.0%	**~2.9**
plums, raw	9.9%	**2.9**
pomegranate	14%	**2.93–3.20**
cider vinegar	0.4%	**3.1**
grapefruit, raw white	9.1%	**3.1**
apple, raw	10.4%	**3.1**
rhubarb, raw	1.1%	**3.2**
cherries, raw sour	8.5%	**[3.2–4.5 all cherries]**
apricots, raw	9.2%	**3.3**
blackberries, raw	4.9%	**3.3**
pineapple juice	10.0%	**3.3–3.6**
orange juice	8.0%	**3.3–4.2**
apple juice	10.0%	**3.35–4.0**
strawberries, raw	4.9%	**3.4**
peaches, raw	8.4%	**3.5**
raspberries, raw	4.4%	**3.6**
sauerkraut	1.8%	**3.6**
orange juice	8.4%	**3.7**
blueberries, raw	10.0%	**3.7**
cherries, raw sweet	12.8%	**3.8**
pears, raw	9.8%	**3.9**
honey	82.1%	**3.9**
whey, acid	-	**4.3–5.1**
chocolate, non-alkalized ("natural")	-	**5.1–6.2**
chocolate, alkalized ("Dutch-processed")	-	**6.0–7.8**

Underripe, very firm, and very, very tart, **green strawberries** have been gaining in popularity for several years. Curtis Duffy pickles them to add to the green strawberry jam served with squab at Chicago's Grace. Ducks Eatery's Will Horowitz sells them at Harry & Ida's in Manhattan.

Chefs love **lemon juice** for its ability to make ingredients "taste more like themselves" without adding the flavor of lemon. Emily Luchetti says, "Lemon juice makes the flavor of berries—like blueberries and raspberries—pop. Vinegar can work, too, but **strawberries + balsamic vinegar** is a very distinct thing. If you're looking for something more subtle, stick with lemon juice."

The team at the French Laundry consider fragrant, low-acid **Meyer lemons** to be one of the most versatile ingredients in their kitchen; they preserve them in jars with salt and sugar for use throughout the year. They'll use the juice in panna cottas and soufflés as well as to season sea bass tartare, and will mix the zest with salt to cure king salmon.

Sherry vinegar is used by chefs to spark up beans, rice, salad dressings, stews, and much more. José Andrés has his own **PX sherry vinegar**, which is aged in oak barrels—and Gabriel Kreuther especially loves **aged XO (extra-old) sherry vinegar.**
Sumac is a spice prized for adding both lemon notes and depth to dishes ranging from soups to starchy foods (including beans, breads, hummus, popcorn, potatoes, and rice) to yogurt sauces.

Matthias Merges [of Chicago's Yusho, and then chef de cuisine] at Charlie Trotter's opened me up to using gastriques and vinegars and other acids in desserts. He didn't want desserts that were very sweet at the end of the meal, so he'd help me balance them with acid or spice. He also encouraged my use of olive oil, such as in olive oil ice cream, which was pretty cutting-edge back then.

—DELLA GOSSETT, pastry chef, Spago (Beverly Hills)

Verjus has its fans among chefs who love it for its versatility in salad dressings and sauces, not to mention its relative wine-friendliness. Spike Gjerde's commitment to local cuisine led to his wish to eliminate citrus at Woodberry Kitchen and his other Midlantic restaurants, so he approached an area winery about making verjus for them.

Vinegars might be the single most popular "secret ingredient" among chefs—who often keep several at hand, such as apple cider vinegar (for its lower acidity), balsamic vinegar (for avocado toast, fruit tarts), red wine vinegar (for vinaigrettes), rice wine vinegar (for pickling vegetables, salad dressings, and tomato sauce), white wine vinegar, and sherry vinegar (for cream sauces, desserts, marinating red onions, hearty salads, and dressings, such as shallots + olive/walnut oil + Dijon mustard +/or thyme, or even with meats). Pastry chefs even love vinegar for giving depth of flavor to caramels, fruit tarts, ice creams, sauces, and stewed fruits.

Vinegar powders (e.g., apple cider, balsamic, malt, red wine, rice wine, and white wine) add acidity without dilution. Heston Blumenthal uses *sushinoko,* sushi vinegar powder, to season other dishes with its characteristic salty, sweet, bitter, and umami notes. Gunnar Gíslason heightens the acidity of the butter for Agern's bread with cider vinegar powder and buttermilk.

Sour + Sweet: Michael Solomonov has turned other chefs on to **carob molasses** (aka *dibs el kharrub*), which he uses with everything from creamy desserts to root vegetables to lamb. Carob molasses is sweet and sour, with notes of chocolate, fruit, and molasses. *Tip:* Love the pairing of **chocolate + peanut butter?** Try the Arab version: **carob molasses + tahini!**

Sour + Sweet: Katianna Hong shares that the Restaurant at Meadowood and the Charter Oak use a variety of **grape sabas** (including both red and white). Also known as *vin cotto,* it's an ancient condiment made from reducing grape musts; it is somewhat comparable to balsamic vinegar in its sour + sweet combination.

Sour + Sweet: Pastry chefs have a soft spot for **passion fruit**, which they love for its acidity as well as its bright color and exotic flavor, which works with everything from chocolate to macarons.

Sour + Sweet: Chefs like Sam Kass love **pomegranate molasses** for its delicious fresh and sweet flavor, and use it to balance salad dressings or complement meat and poultry dishes.

Sour + Umami: Even the best Japanese chefs such as Yoshihiro Narisawa are impressed with the umami qualities of tomatoes, and use **tomato essence** in dishes for its umami. Likewise, other chefs are using **tomato paste** to add umami to sauces and stews and other dishes. Alon Shaya of Shaya in New Orleans pan-roasts it with garlic, olive oil, parsley, and salt to slather on goat cheese–topped toast. **Tomato powder** is used by some chefs (even Italian chefs!) to add greater depth and intensity to their tomato sauces.

Sour Principles

Sour + Fat

blackberries + cream
sorrel + cream

Sour + Fat + Sweet

sour cream + cream cheese + sugar —> cheesecake

Sour + Sweet

vinegar + sweet corn —> corn salsa
lemon + sugar —> lemonade

Sour + Sweet + Umami

lime juice + cilantro + fish sauce + mint + sugar

If something is too sweet, you can balance it with either more acidity or more bitterness. For [the latter], I'd use ingredients like citrus zest or bitter herbs. I might pour a sauce over fresh rosemary long enough for it to pick up some of the bitter resin, but not long enough for it to infuse it with rosemary flavor.

—JESSICA LARGEY, Simone (Los Angeles)

SWEETNESS

Among the basic tastes, **sweetness** requires the greatest amount to register on the tongue. However, we can appreciate the balance and "roundness" (an almost textural effect that's created, versus the taste itself) that even otherwise imperceptible sweetness adds to savory dishes. Sweetness can work with bitterness, sourness—even saltiness. Whether delivered via honey, maple syrup, molasses, or sugar itself, sweetness can also bring out the flavors of certain foods, such as fruits and certain vegetables (e.g., tomatoes) and grains (e.g., oats).

SWEET INGREDIENTS

agave nectar

apples (sweet + sour)

barley malt syrup

birch syrup

brown rice syrup

brown sugar

butter (sweet + fat)

cane juice

caramel

caramelized ingredients, e.g., garlic, onions, shallots

carrots (esp. cooked)

chocolate (sweet + bitter)

cinnamon (e.g., cassia [louder] or Sri Lankan [quieter])

coconut palm sugar

date sugar and dates

fennel pollen (sweet + bitter)

fructose

fruit, dried (e.g., dates, raisins)

fruit, fresh (e.g., apples, berries)

fruit jams and preserves

SWEET INGREDIENTS (CONT.)

fruit juices (e.g., apple, grape)
fruit purees (e.g., applesauce)
garlic, caramelized
granulated sugar
honey
jaggery
maple sugar
maple syrup
mirin
molasses
muscovado (unrefined brown sugar)
nutmeg
onions (esp. caramelized, Vidalia)
palm sugar
raisins
rice syrup
shallots (esp. caramelized)
simple syrup
sorghum
stevia
sweetened condensed milk
sweet liqueurs or wines
sweet vegetables (e.g., carrots, corn, fennel, pumpkin, sweet potatoes, tomatoes, winter squash)
turbinado sugar
vanilla

Sweet Techniques

candying (cooking in simple syrup, e.g., citrus rinds)

caramelizing (cooking sugar or ingredients containing sugar until they brown, e.g., bananas, Brussels sprouts, carrots, cauliflower, endive, onions, shallots)

macerating (which is to fruit what marinating is to other ingredients) in sweet ingredients

roasting (e.g., beets, carrots, eggplant, garlic, meats, onions, root vegetables), which brings out a nutty, slightly sweet flavor in ingredients

toasting (e.g., nuts and seeds), which brings out their sweetness in addition to their bitterness

Sweet Dynamics

Sweetness can balance sourness (acidity), bitterness, and saltiness. Through the alchemy of cooking, some herbs and spices have the power to emphasize sweetness in a dish, like herbs (basil, bay leaves, and tarragon) and spices (cinnamon). If a dish is too sweet, try cutting it with an acidic, bitter, or piquant ingredient.

Using Sweet

Fructose can enhance the sweetness of fresh fruit, as Heston Blumenthal does by macerating fruit in fructose before incorporating it into desserts.

Spike Gjerde's dedication to cooking locally has him turning to a variety of sweeteners other than sugar, including **honey**, **maple**, and **sorghum**. Other chefs specifically recommend Quebec's 70 brix **maple syrup**, which has even more

HOW SWEET IT IS

Comparing Apples and Oranges and Other Foods

(per 100-gram serving)

[* Note: The lower the pH, the more sour it tastes.]

Food	% Sugar	pH Level*
granulated sugar	**99.9%**	-
brown sugar	**97.0%**	-
honey	**82.1%**	3.9
medjool dates	**66.5%**	6.3
maple syrup	**59.5%**	4.6-5.5
molasses	**55.5%**	4.9–5.4
nutmeg	**28.5%**	-
balsamic vinegar	**15.0%**	-
mango, raw	**14.8%**	5.8–6.0
cherries, raw sweet	**12.8%**	3.8
vanilla extract	**12.7%**	-
apple juice	**10.7%**	-
apples, raw	**10.4%**	3.1
blueberries, raw	**10.0%**	3.7
plums, raw	**9.9%**	2.9
tangerines, raw	**9.9%**	-
pears, raw	**9.8%**	3.9
apricots, raw	**9.2%**	3.3
clementines, raw	**9.2%**	-
grapefruit, raw white	**9.1%**	3.1
cherries, raw sour	**8.5%**	[3.2–4.5 all cherries]
orange juice	**8.4%**	3.7
peaches, raw	**8.4%**	3.5
beets, raw	**6.8%**	5.3
milk, whole	**5.3%**	6.6
blackberries, raw	**4.9%**	3.3
strawberries, raw	**4.9%**	3.4
carrots, raw	**4.7%**	5.0
raspberries, raw	**4.4%**	3.6
sweet potatoes	**4.2%**	5.4
corn, raw sweet white	**3.2%**	6.3
chocolate, non-alkalized ("natural")	-	5.1–6.2
chocolate, alkalized ("Dutch-processed")	-	6.0–7.8

concentrated sweetness than the 66 brix industry standard. Remonte-Pente maple syrup has been used in the kitchens of Betony, Daniel, and Del Posto in New York City, and of Quince in San Francisco.

Palm sugar is favored by some chefs (often in combination with butter) for basting meats near the end of the roasting process, as well as for its flavor in desserts.

Simple syrup (equal parts sugar + water, simmered) is the secret ingredient used judiciously to add "roundness" (but not necessarily sweetness) to flavors in some of America's top restaurant kitchens.

In Japan, they cut sweetness with bitterness. During a kaiseki dinner one November, I was served a very sweet chestnut paste. They accompanied it with a bowl of whipped warm matcha tea to drink with it, which offset it perfectly.

—MARC AUMONT, pastry chef, Gabriel Kreuther (New York City)

Sweet Principles

Sweet + Astringent
bananas + walnuts
caramel + walnuts
maple syrup + walnuts

Sweet + Fat
corn + butter
dates + cream cheese
sweet plantains + *fried*

Sweet + Fat + Salty
melon + prosciutto

Sweet + Piquant
corn + chiles
honey + mustard

Sweet + Salty
caramel + salted peanuts
chocolate + sea salt
dates + Parmesan cheese
watermelon + feta cheese

Sweet + Sour
beets + goat cheese
beets + sour cream → borscht
papaya + lime
pineapple + lime
pineapple + vinegar → sweet + sour sauce
strawberries + balsamic vinegar
strawberries + rhubarb

Sweet + Umami
applesauce + pork chops

BITTERNESS

Human beings are most sensitive to **bitterness** of all the basic tastes, and we recognize it even in tiny amounts. Bitterness balances sweetness and can also play a vital role in cutting richness in a dish.

> **I would infuse milk with burnt oats to add a balancing BITTER note to a flan. And I might crust venison with ground cocoa or coffee to add a balancing bitter note.**
>
> —TRAVIS SWIKARD, Boulud Sud (New York City)

For example, the bitterness of walnuts balances the sweetness of a beet salad while cutting the richness of the goat cheese that often accompanies it. Chocolate's bitterness is an innate counterbalance in rich desserts. Fueled in part by the cocktail movement and the popularity of bitters and other bitter ingredients, bitterness has been growing in popularity among guests in both savory dishes as well as desserts, while chefs continue to see it as an indispensable "cleansing" taste—one that makes you want to take the next bite, and the next.

BITTER INGREDIENTS

absinthe

alcohol (e.g., bitters, spirits, wine)

anise

arugula

basil

bay leaves

beer (esp. hoppy, like bitter ale)

bell peppers, green

bitter gourd

bitter orange

bitters

broccoli and broccoli rabe

Brussels sprouts

burned foods (e.g., sugar, toast)

butter, brown (bitter + fat)

cabbage, green

caffeine

Campari

caraway seeds

celery leaves

chard

chicory

chiles and chili powder (bitter + heat)

chocolate, dark

cilantro stems

cinnamon (bitter + sweet)

citrus pith and zest (grapefruit, lemon, lime)

citrus pith and zest powder

cocoa powder

coffee (esp. dark-roasted)

coriander

cranberries (bitter + sour)

cumin

eggplant

endive

BITTER INGREDIENTS (CONT.)

escarole

espresso and espresso powder

fenugreek

frisée

galangal

greens, bitter (e.g., dandelion)

green vegetables (e.g., broccoli)

herbs, bitter

horseradish (bitter + pungent)

juniper berries

kale

lemon, preserved (bitter + sour)

lemon confit (bitter + sour)

lemon zest and lemon zest powder

lettuces

licorice root

lime, preserved (bitter + sour)

melon, bitter

mustard (bitter + pungent + sour)

nettles

nutmeg

nut oils, toasted

nuts, well-toasted

olive oil

olives

orange zest and orange zest powder

parsley

pastis

peppercorns (bitter + hot)

radicchio

Romaine

smoked foods (e.g., cheeses, fruits [esp. dried], nuts, meats, seafood)

spinach

sugar, burned (e.g., palm) (bitter + sweet)

tea, tannic black or green

toast (well-done or burned)

tobacco

tonic water

turmeric

walnuts, black

wasabi (bitter + pungent)

watercress

wine, tannic red (e.g., Cabernet Sauvignon, Tannat)

zest, citrus

Bitter Techniques

charring

grilling

smoking (e.g., with walnut)

toasting (e.g., bread, nuts, seeds)

There are only three BITTERS that really matter: Angostura, Pisco, and orange. I prefer tinctures [aka extracts, or infusions of ingredients such as cardamom, cinnamon, or star anise into a neutral spirit, such as vodka], which I use like a liquid spice rack.

—AUDREY SAUNDERS, Pegu Club (New York City)

Bitter Dynamics

Bitterness suppresses sweetness, and can cut richness. Bitter ingredients can also counterbalance strong flavors, e.g., **parsley + garlic**, or **endive + blue cheese**. If a dish is too bitter, consider counter balancing it with saltiness, sourness, sweetness, or richness.

Using Bitter

Pastry chef Taiesha Martin loves the way **bourbon** plays off other ingredients in her desserts. She says, "I don't think I could cook without bourbon. I make a hard cider apple crisp with bourbon and caramel swirl ice cream that our guests love."

Lydia Shire loves the light yet earthy flavor that deep-fried and salted individual **Brussels sprouts** leaves add to dishes such as fish.

Caffeine is prized by chefs for more than just keeping them awake during service. Emily Luchetti notes, "A very creamy dessert should have its intensity cut. You want a contrast in flavor, such as the bitterness of **coffee or espresso.**" Whether you're making chocolate mousse or a salad dressing, **espresso powder** can add a mysterious note—and, in the right amount, whatever you're making *won't* taste like coffee.

Lemon zest is the secret ingredient in a number of Anita Lo's dishes at Manhattan's Annisa.

Bitter + Sour: Lemon confit is a frequent addition to a number of Eric Ripert's dishes, including broiled fish and pork and beans—but he allows that it's fine to substitute jarred Moroccan **preserved lemons.**

Bitter + Sour: David Bouley grinds dehydrated orange rinds into **orange powder,** which he'll use to season steamed vegetables, or roasted or grilled fish or poultry.

Bitter + Sweet: Chefs enjoy the mild yet irreplaceable flavor that fresh **bay leaves** can bring out in soups, stews, and stocks; Emeril Lagasse uses leaves from the bay laurel tree in his yard. In addition to roasting meats with them, some chefs use them with root vegetables and infuse them into purees.

Bitter + Salty + Sour + Sweet + Umami: Vietnamese caramel fish sauce (aka *nuoc mau)*—a combination of **bitter burned palm sugar + fish sauce + lemon juice**—*is prized for its combination of the five major tastes, which works its magic with vegetables (e.g., carrots, corn, lentils), tofu, seafood, and meats alike.*

Tip: The **Bitter + Fat** combination has broad applicability. Remember this combination, and you'll know how welcome tucking broccoli or another bitter green into your next lasagna, cheese fondue, or macaroni and cheese can be.

Bitter Principles

Bitter + Cold + Hot

chocolate + ice cream + jalapeño

Bitter + Fat

arugula + Parmesan cheese
asparagus + hollandaise sauce
broccoli + Cheddar cheese → soup, twice-baked potato
broccoli rabe + olive oil
Brussels sprouts + bacon
chocolate + walnuts
coffee + cream
collard greens + ham hocks
endive + walnuts
red cabbage + walnuts
Romaine + Parmesan cheese

Bitter + Fat + Salty
basil + olive oil + Parmesan cheese → pesto
broccoli + peanut oil + soy sauce

Bitter + Fat + Salty + Sour
salad greens + olive oil + salty cheese + vinegar

Bitter + Fat + Salty + Sweet
chocolate + pretzels → chocolate-covered pretzels

Bitter + Fat + Sour + Sweet
burnt honey + orange + sesame

Bitter + Fat + Sweet
coffee + cream + sugar
coffee + crème fraîche + carrots

Bitter + Salty
bok choy + soy sauce
collard greens + ham
salad greens + salty cheese (e.g., feta, Parmesan)

Bitter + Salty + Sour
spinach + bacon + vinegar

Bitter + Salty + Sweet
caramel + salt

Bitter + Sour
salad greens + vinaigrette
tea + lemon

Bitter + Sour + Sweet
cranberries + orange + sugar → cranberry sauce
tea + lemon + sugar

Bitter + Sweet
dark chocolate + sugar

I might hide anchovies in very small amounts in dishes, as they can provide a strong umami flavor without tasting of anchovy. It gives more of an Italian rather than an Asian flavor. I'll also use Parmesan rinds to add UMAMI to dishes—I'll create a reduced, creamy sauce that's mounted with butter, and use that as a concentrated base for Parmesan dumplings, peas, and pistachios with a green garlic confit.

—**JESSICA LARGEY,** Simone (Los Angeles)

UMAMI (AKA SAVORINESS)

The taste of umami is imparted by glutamate, a type of amino acid discovered in 1908 by Dr. Kikunae Ikeda of Tokyo Imperial University. In studying kombu (kelp), Ikeda managed to isolate glutamate as its own compound, giving it the name of *umami,* which translates as "savoriness." Thus, 5,000 years after the discovery of salt, and 4,000 years after the discovery of sugar, and 3,500 years after the discovery of sour (vinegar), umami is a relatively new taste concept. Japanese cooks had been using umami-rich ingredients intuitively for centuries, long before their scientific properties were discovered to enhance flavor.

While we first mentioned *umami* in our 1996 book *Culinary Artistry,* it did not begin to gain more widespread acceptance until after 2000 when glutamate receptors were discovered on the tongue. The main sources of umami are those deriving from 1) the amino acid **glutamate** (found in, e.g., kelp); and those deriving from 2) so-called "nucleotides"—such as a) **adenylate** (aka AMP, which is found primarily in fish and shellfish), b) **guanylate** (aka GMP, which is found primarily in plants and fungi, e.g., shiitake mushrooms, esp. dried), and c) **inosinate** (aka IMP, which is found primarily in meat and fish, e.g., bonito flakes).

The big umami magic happens when one or more nucleotides are combined with glutamate, as there is a synergistic affect—resulting in umami with as much as *eight times* the potency.

UMAMI INGREDIENTS

anchovies and anchovy paste (glutamate)

asparagus (glutamate)

beer

black garlic

bonito flakes (glutamate + inosinate)

bottarga

Bragg liquid aminos

brewed foods (e.g., beer, soy sauce)

broth (e.g., meat, mushroom)

cabbage, Chinese

carrots

cheese, aged (e.g., Parmesan)

cheese, blue (glutamate)

cheese, Cabrales (glutamate)

cheese, Emmental (glutamate)

cheese, Parmesan (glutamate)

chicken (glutamate)

crab (glutamate + adenylate + guanylate)

dashi broth (i.e., kelp + bonito flakes) (inosinate + glutamate)

doenjang (Korean fermented soybean paste)

egg yolks, chicken (glutamate)

fermented foods (e.g., bean paste, fish sauce, garlic, kimchi, miso, pickles, sauerkraut, soy sauce, soybeans, XO sauce)

fish paste

fish roe

fish sauce (glutamate)

ham, dry-cured (glutamate)

hoisin sauce

huitlacoche

kelp (glutamate)

ketchup (glutamate)

kombu (glutamate)

marmite (glutamate)

meats (e.g., cured) (inosinate)

mirin

miso (glutamate)

mojama (salt-cured Spanish tuna)

MSG

mushrooms, dried and powdered

mushrooms, enoki (guanylate)

mushrooms, morel

mushrooms, porcini (guanylate)

mushrooms, shiitake (guanylate, the level of which triples when the shiitakes are dried)

mussels

natto

nori (glutamate + inosinate)

nutritional yeast

olives (glutamate)

onions (glutamate)

oysters

oyster sauce

potatoes, cooked (glutamate + guanylate)

prosciutto (glutamate)

sake

I use lots of MISO. It adds a more complex umami + salty flavor versus just salt. I like to mix with it honey or orange. Miso + lobster is one of my favorite combinations. Throw it on a grill with that char, and oh-my-God.

—**CHRIS LONG,** Natalie's at the Camden Harbour Inn (Camden, ME)

UMAMI INGREDIENTS (CONT.)

sardines and dried sardines (glutamate + inosinate)

sauerkraut

scallops (adenylate)

sea urchin (glutamate + guanylate + inosinate)

seafood (inosinate)

sea vegetables (e.g., kelp, nori, wakame)

shrimp (adenylate + inosinate)

soy beans, fermented

soy sauce (glutamate)

squid (glutamate)

stock (e.g., meat, mushroom)

sweet potatoes

tamari

tea, green

tomatoes, tomato paste, and tomato sauce (glutamate)

tomatoes, sun-dried (glutamate)

truffles (glutamate + guanylate + inosinate, a rare trifecta making them a global delicacy)

umeboshi paste and umeboshi plums

vinegar (e.g., balsamic, umeboshi)

wakame (glutamate)

wakame chazuke furikake (a dried seaweed and crisped rice seasoning)

walnuts (glutamate)

wine

Worcestershire sauce

XO sauce

yeast extract

Umami Techniques

browning

caramelizing

dehydrating/drying (e.g., anchovies, egg yolks, mushrooms, seaweed, shrimp, tomatoes)

fermenting (e.g., vegetables)

grilling

marinating (e.g., in soy sauce)

roasting (e.g., root vegetables)

rubbing (e.g., with miso)

Umami Dynamics

Umami can enhance a bland dish's appeal with mouth-filling savoriness. Umami can also enhance a dish's perceived sweetness, while tempering its perceived bitterness. If you find yourself with too much of a good thing when it comes to umami, try balancing with salty, sweet, bitter, acidic, or piquant ingredients.

Umami is a taste that tends to linger on the palate—something referred to as a "long finish" in the wine world. Because it contributes to the qualities of deliciousness and satiation, umami is especially prized as a taste in dishes and menus.

Note: Certain herbs and spices can also emphasize a dish's **savory** aspects, such as bay leaf, cumin, oregano, paprika, sage, and thyme.

Using Umami

Chefs praise **black garlic** (aka fermented garlic) for its ability to add depth and earthiness to dishes ranging from vegetables to meats.

If you doubt umami's importance as one of the five primary tastes, consider the fact that leading chefs like Michael Anthony, Eric Ripert, and Jean-Georges Vongerichten believe **dashi** to be a key component of their cooking. Some chefs use it to replace liquids in countless preparations, from brines to broths to salad dressings.

Chefs have rising enthusiasm for all manner of **fermented ingredients** (e.g., fermented soybeans, fish sauce, kimchi, miso, pickles, sauerkraut, XO sauce), which bring umami to dishes including vegetables.

The corn smut known as **huitlacoche** is prized as a Mexican delicacy, not only by chefs cooking in the vernacular like Rick Bayless, but also mainstream chefs who find themselves using it in quesadillas, soups, and tacos. Sean Brock declares it "insanely delicious and luxurious, like black truffles."

Kombu (aka kelp, the sea vegetable) is prized for its umami by Yoshihiro Narisawa.

Brad Farmerie is fanatical about **miso**, which allows him to achieve a rich mouthfeel without butter or cream. Miso is an integral part of Farmerie's roasted chile caramel Brussels sprouts, which involve caramelizing sugar (sweet) before adding chiles (hot), cilantro stems (bitter), lime juice (sour), fish sauce (salt/umami), and miso (richness). He adds miso to **sweet potatoes + brown butter + rosemary** to create another dish he's not able to take off the menu. Other chefs will add misos (e.g., white) to salad dressings or soups for an umami boost.

From his time in Japan, Michael Anthony picked up a love of "**sea weeds** and **pickles.**"

Thomas Henkelmann describes rich, flavorful **stocks** as "essential" for cooking in every season.

Umeboshi paste is prized by chefs, including Isa Chandra Moskowitz of Omaha's and Brooklyn's Modern Love, for its umami quality. Moskowitz adds it to her Caesar salad dressing for its anchovy flavor.

Even native Brits like Mark Levy fall prey to the charms of **white truffles**, which he prizes for their mysterious aroma and short availability.

Tip: Many chefs' "secret weapon" for enhancing umami is to serve a well-paired **wine** (esp. red) with every dish whenever possible—guided by the recommendations in *What to Drink with What You Eat*.

Umami Principles

Umami + Umami

grilled cheese + tomato soup

mushrooms + Parmesan + risotto

MOUTHFEEL = TEMPERATURE + TEXTURE + PIQUANCY + ASTRINGENCY

The second element of the Flavor Equation is *Mouthfeel.* In addition to our sense of taste, our sense of touch contributes to the flavor we experience. Our tongues and mouths are our secondmost sensitive receptors after our fingers and hands. We call the way touch contributes to flavor **mouthfeel.**

TEMPERATURE + TEXTURE

The **temperature**(s) of what we're eating, as well as its **texture**(s), play an important role in how we experience its flavor—and can unlock its enjoyment (e.g., through welcome creaminess and/or crunchiness) or ensure disappointment (e.g., through unintended mushiness).

A room-temperature pie can work with whipped cream, but a pie served à la mode should be warm, so that the two work together....Salted caramel ice cream finished with [a salty crunch of] Maldon sea salt makes sense. But when ice cream has salt emulsified into it, that doesn't make sense.

—**EMILY LUCHETTI,** chief pastry officer of The Cavalier, Marlowe, and Park Tavern (San Francisco)

TEMPERATURE

Serving the same ingredient at different **temperatures** can make a world of difference. Imagine the texture of spinach raw in a salad, versus wilted after being tossed with a hot vinaigrette, versus steamed and pureed for *spanakopita.*

The combination of multiple temperatures in a single dish provides another source of contrast and interest, explaining the popularity of such foods as warm apple pie *à la mode,* hot borscht with sour cream, and hot chocolate with whipped cream—let alone a cult favorite like French fries dipped in a Frosty (see page 69).

I think there has to be some amount of homeyness and familiarity in a dessert. **Claudia Fleming** was very influential on me and my cooking style. There are very few recipes of hers that I use today, but it was more applying her approach of using the same main ingredient in multiple ways in a dessert. If we did a peach dessert, it might have roasted peach and a peach puree and a little brunoise of fresh marinated peach and a peach granita. That still makes sense, and is something that I still do today. Also seasonality, texturing, layering—I'm always looking for many different contrasting flavors—the creamy, the crunchy, the richness, the acidity, and different temperatures.

—**KAREN HATFIELD,** pastry chef, Odys + Penelope and Sycamore Kitchen (Los Angeles)

> **Appealing texture is not just about crunch. Sometimes it's a tackiness on the teeth, from an al dente pasta or from cheese that's at the perfect melting temperature. Or it's in a rich sauce that coats the tongue and lingers on the palate, as opposed to fading quickly.**
>
> —JESSICA LARGEY, Simone (Los Angeles)

TEXTURE

A food's **texture** is central to its ability to captivate and please. We value pureed and/or creamy foods (such as soup and mashed potatoes) as "comfort" foods, and crunchy and crispy foods (such as caramel corn and nachos) as "fun" foods. We enjoy texture as it activates our other senses, including touch, sight, and sound.

Texture is so appealing that Michelin three-star chef Massimo Bottura named a signature dish after what we all crave: The Crunchy Part of the Lasagne. Crunchiness and crispiness are fun textures. The chewiness of whole grains can be alternately meditative and stick-to-the-ribs satisfying—or bordering on exhausting. The creaminess of comfort foods adds to their appeal when we're sick (or homesick). Our appreciation for textures varies culturally—Japanese love chewy (e.g., mochi) and more textural variations in general. Texture is a well-known reason for food rejection. Auditory texture: crispy, crunchy—differ for wet (e.g., fruits, vegs) and dry (e.g., chips, cookies, crackers) foods. Every ingredient (salt, fruit, vegetables, grains, etc.) has its own texture (soft, chewy, crisp, crunchy) in its raw state and in its cooked states, affected by one's selection of a cooking process. In the case of pasta, while a standard of "al dente" is widely accepted, each specific shape has its own textural implications that suggest various pasta sauces and add-ins.

The shape of an ingredient influences its texture, as well as its aroma, and thus its flavor. Dicing versus slicing a carrot can make a notable difference in a dish, with smoother edges perceived to be more flavorful. Texture is the reason chefs go to the trouble to use an old-fashioned mortar-and-pestle vs. an electric food processor.

TEXTURE

The texture of food varies with both moisture and density:

Moisture Content

Dry:	chips, crackers
Moist:	cake, chicken
Juicy:	mangoes, peaches, watermelon
Wet:	juices, smoothies, soups

Density

Airy:	foams, meringues, soufflés, whipped cream
Tender:	cakes, clotted cream, ice creams, quiches
Firm:	brownies, frittatas
Hard:	biscotti, shortbread

Lighter, airier dishes tend to correlate with lower-perceived flavor intensity (i.e., quietness), while denser, harder dishes tend to correlate with higher-perceived flavor intensity (i.e., loudness).

Brandade, a creamy mash of salt cod with potatoes and a barely poached egg, is a small essay on the virtues of soft food.

—**JONATHAN GOLD,** *LA Weekly,* in his rave review of Jon Shook and Vinny Dotolo's Son of a Gun

A salad with too many walnuts or a sauce with too many capers is like a Sunday with too many free hours—you stop appreciating the pleasure they provide. I think about that when I cook. Put just enough sweet cubes of carrots in a soup, and you won't have to search too hard to find one—but when you do, it'll still give you a little thrill.

—**APRIL BLOOMFIELD,** The Spotted Pig (New York City)

Michael Voltaggio on Cooking Techniques He Couldn't Live Without

Out of all the cooks that have come through the show, **Michael** is the most talented—both from a sensibility and technical standpoint. He has the chops to pull off what he's trying to do.

—TOM COLICCHIO, *Top Chef* judge, on Season 6 winner Voltaggio, who went on to open ink, ink.sack, and ink.well in Los Angeles

Sous-vide cooking is the one thing that survived through all the gastronomic trends. We couldn't stop cooking under vacuum [at ink, his restaurant in Los Angeles]. It's another consistent way of cooking that allows you to control the results from start to finish—and also to pass off to your cooks and not have to trust them so much to not mess it up. It's a technique that's allowed us to put the focus on refining our dishes, rather than constantly having to produce them.

Pressure cooking is something else we couldn't give up. There are usually eight pressure cookers on the stove every single day during prep time.

Dehydrating: We have four to six dehydrators in operation, 24 hours a day. We use them to make the cauliflower chips, which are sliced thin and cooked in a starch syrup, then we shingle them on top of each other and dehydrate them, and then fry them. We also evaporate a lot of liquids in there. We'll take orange juice and mix it with sugar or glucose, and dehydrate it to get the water out of the juice and just be left with the concentrated flavor. We'll do that with things like soy sauce, too. A lot of vegetables—like carrots—get dehydrated. We'll cook them, take all the water out of them, then glaze that back in a syrup made out of carrot juice. It creates a chewy kind of texture. Concentrating flavors is a big thing—and **making things taste more like themselves is something we put a lot of focus on.**

Deep-frying: When I was first learning how to deep-fry as a cook, I was throwing anything and everything into the deep-fryer [to learn what would happen]. We quarter heads of cauliflower, and fry them until they're dark brown, and then throw them right into the Vitamix while they're piping hot to blend them. You end up with a vegan cauliflower puree or pudding that tastes like it has cream and everything else in it, but it's really just deep-fried cauliflower and a little bit of salt.

Michael Voltaggio

THE FLAVOR OF WATER

A Key Secret of America's Best Restaurants?

Does water have flavor?

Imagine the importance of water to so many aspects of what you eat and drink—from the drinking water that is a constant presence on the table with your food (and which affects the flavor of everything you eat and drink alongside it), to coffee and tea, to stocks and soups, even to house-made bread. What impact is water having on the flavor of your cooking? You might well be shocked to discover the flavor difference the water you're using can make.

That difference is so significant that most of the world's best restaurants are thinking about this seriously—and that might be one of their biggest secrets to flavor. "Our water is the secret weapon of this place," acknowledges Mark Levy of Baltimore's Magdalena at the Ivy Hotel.

Levy had a Nordaq Fresh in-house water filtration system installed after tasting the difference it made in the cuisine and beverages served in other restaurants that have used it, which include Daniel Boulud's Daniel; Thomas Keller's Bouchon, French Laundry, and Per Se; and Eric Ripert's Le Bernardin. (Other restaurants like Daniel Humm's NoMad in New York City have used other water filtration systems, such as Vero.)

Filtration systems like those of Natura, Nordaq Fresh, and Vivreau allow restaurants to purify and bottle local tap water. Similar systems are available for home use; we just acquired an AquaTru filter. First and foremost, it's about taste, but it also reduces carbon footprint, eliminating shipping costs and bottle disposal for bottled water.

Serving quality filtered water can positively affect the perceived flavor of food, wine, and other beverages. Le Bernardin's Aldo Sohm, named the world's best sommelier in 2007, selected Nordaq Fresh in a blind tasting as the best water to enhance food and wine.

"Wine is probably the biggest difference maker when tasted against iced tap water. For years we have all sipped tap water to save a few bucks at dinner to maybe afford a slightly nicer wine to no avail. Great water makes cheap wine taste fab!" says Levy. "As far as food is concerned, the bread is the biggest guzzler of Nordaq water in the kitchen. I cannot imagine not making our bread without it now. . . . I would love to make all the stocks from it, but I would need a much bigger valve to cope with the demand. We have tried it on smaller-scale stock and have had great results."

FAT

Referred to by researchers as *oleogustus* (a mash-up of Latin words for "oil" and "taste"), some advocates argue that **fat** is actually a taste. However, there is more universal agreement that fat is a *texture* (and therefore a component of mouthfeel), often described as richness. Butter and oils are virtually 100 percent fat, but other high-fat ingredients can affect mouthfeel (by adding richness, viscosity, and/or moistness to a dish). If its creaminess you're after, there are other ways to achieve that without cream (see Richness Without Fat, page 117). Fat also affects the *length* of a flavor, e.g., its aftertaste and the amount of time it lingers on the palate.

> When I cooked at Charlie Trotter's, the kitchen didn't use a lot of butter or cream, so many of our dishes were vegan. We served a lot of vegetable-based dishes emulsified with canola oil.
>
> —**CHRIS LONG,** Natalie's at the Camden Harbour Inn (Camden, ME)

FAT INGREDIENTS

almonds (72% fat*)

avocado (77% fat)

bacon (70% fat) and bacon fat (100% fat) (fat + smoke)

butter (97% fat)

butter, brown (~100% fat)

cashews (66% fat)

cheese, Cheddar (74% fat)

cheese, cream (88% fat)

chocolate, dark (65% fat)

coconut (88% fat), coconut cream and coconut milk (% fat varies)

cream, heavy (94% fat)

duck fat (~100% fat)

eggs (61% fat)

fats, animal-based (e.g., bacon fat, clarified butter, duck fat, ghee, lard) (100% fat)

fats, plant-based (e.g., nuts and nut oils, seeds and seed oils) (100% fat)

ghee (~100% fat)

lard (100% fat)

mayonnaise (% fat varies)

meat (% fat varies)

nuts and nut butters (67 to 87% fat)

oils (100% fat): acorn squash seed, almond, argan, avocado, camelina seed, canola, chili, coconut, extra-virgin olive (louder in flavor), flaxseed, garlic, grapeseed (quiet in flavor), hazelnut, hemp, lemon, olive, peanut, pine nut, pistachio, pumpkin seed, red palm, safflower, sesame, sunflower, truffle, vegetable, walnut (louder in flavor)

olives (88% fat)

peanuts (73% fat)

pecans (87% fat)

pistachios (67% fat)

seeds, pumpkin (71% fat)

seeds, sesame (73% fat)

seeds, sunflower (74% fat)

sesame paste (73% fat)

sour cream (90% fat)

tahini (73% fat)

walnuts (83% fat)

yogurt and Greek yogurt (% fat varies)

**All percentages are based on fat as a percentage of total calories—not volume.*

Karen: Quinn likes to cook raw vegetables all the way through in butter, whether via braising or pan-roasting.

Quinn: There was a wave of big-pot blanching that got really popular, and I felt like you were just washing flavor away. So I developed my [approach] to cooking vegetables raw in butter, which essentially glazes them with their own juices.... With our cauliflower [dish], you're sort of sweating this grated, raw cauliflower in butter—and what you end up with is all of the liquid that came out is reduced back around it, so you end up with this really creamy, intensely flavored cauliflower. Millet works really well with the cauliflower. There's zero cream in this really creamy dish (Creamy Cauliflower and Millet with Walnut Pesto)—just a little ricotta, in addition to the butter.

—**KAREN** and **QUINN HATFIELD**, Odys + Penelope and Sycamore Kitchen (Los Angeles)

Fat Techniques

without heat:
- *larding*
- *marinating*

with heat:
- *deep-frying*
- *frying*
- *glazing*
- *larding*
- *saucing*
- *sautéing*

Fat Dynamics

Fat has a well-known ability to serve as a vehicle for flavor. Choose your fat as wisely as you choose your other ingredients. There's an imaginary dividing line across France separating the butter-loving north from the olive oil–loving south but, more generally speaking, you may find butter a better match for cooked ingredients and hot dishes, and olive oil a better match for raw ingredients and cold dishes. If a dish is too rich, consider balancing with acidity or bitterness.

Using Fat

Many chefs praise the luxurious richness of French salted **butter** as the perfect way to finish sauces, especially for seafood.

Whether you're making winter soups, Thai curries, or dairy-free ice creams, **coconut milk** comes in handy. (Some chefs will mix coconut milk with sautéed garlic to turn into sauce, e.g., for Asian noodles, or even a salad dressing.)

David Bouley uses **garlic oil** for everything from basting fish to intensifying the flavor of gazpacho and pesto.

Gabriel Kreuther finds he uses a lot of **grapeseed oil**, "because it is literally tasteless."

Chefs swear by a variety of flavorful **oils** (e.g., grapeseed, hazelnut, olive, walnut) as a means of adding flavor and/or richness. Christopher Kostow has cited olive oil as his favorite ingredient.

Tahini is prized for adding richness to dishes—from cookie dough to lamb to salad dressings to sauces—without the need for dairy, and for being the secret to a "lighter, less pasty" hummus when blended with **chickpeas + cumin + garlic + lemon + salt**, according to Zahav's Michael Solomonov.

Fat Principles

Fat + Astringent
- blue cheese + walnuts
- chocolate + walnuts
- ricotta + walnuts

Fat + Bitter
- ghee + turmeric

Fat + Bitter + Sour
- bacon + lettuce + tomato

Fat + Bitter + Sweet
- butter + cocoa + sugar

Fat + Piquant
- sausage + hot mustard

Fat + Piquant + Sour
- sausage + hot mustard + sauerkraut

Fat + Salt
- mayonnaise + French fries + salt
- Marcona almonds + olive oil + salt
- onion rings + salt
- peanuts + salt
- potato chips + salt
- tortilla chips + salt

Fat + Salt + Sour
- avocado + lime + salt

Fat + Sour
- cream cheese + strawberries —> strawberry cheesecake
- oil + vinegar —> salad dressing
- walnuts + citrus —> salad add-ins
- white chocolate + raspberries

Fat + Sour + Sweet
- peanut butter + grape jelly —> PB&J
- peanuts + pomegranate seeds —> salad add-ins
- cream + strawberries + sugar —> strawberry shortcake

Fat + Sweet
- butter + flour + sugar —> shortbread

RICHNESS WITHOUT FAT

- Some chefs reach for **kuzu** (root starch) to thicken soups or to gel liquids (ranging from pineapple juice to tomato water). Faux "creaminess" in sauces can also come from adding starchy liquids, such as **pasta water** or **cornstarch**.
- Pureeing sauces or soups with **an immersion blender** makes them creamier.
- **Pureed overcooked rice** adds richness to dishes like sauces and creamless creamy soups.
- **Pureed roasted onions** add richness to dishes like pastas, risottos, sauces, and soups without the need for cream.
- **Other pureed vegetables** (e.g., cauliflower, celery root, potatoes) or **legumes** (e.g., chickpeas, white beans) can add thickness and richness to dishes and sauces in lieu of butter or cream.

PIQUANCY + ASTRINGENCY

Piquancy and astringency are other aspects of mouthfeel, which affects our experience of flavor.

Piquancy is the "heat" we perceive ourselves as experiencing via the capsicum of chile peppers, but what we might term "hotness" is actually more of a sharpness or spiciness. **Astringency** is the mouth-drying sensation caused by tannins, alcohol, and other substances. Each is described further below.

PIQUANCY

In addition to adding flavor through its distinctive aroma, the **piquancy** of chiles or peppercorns adds mouthfeel—a "heat" that every person eating the dish experiences in his or her own way: Some love their food hotter than hot, while others prefer milder dishes. The "hotness" of chiles, which is the result of capsaicin, is known to stimulate their characteristic burning sensation via our touch nerves, which we experience via our tongues, mouths, throats, and skin.

Korean chili paste is great [for adding piquancy] because it simultaneously adds umami—which is something that you don't find with other chili products. It contributes base notes, so especially if you are doing vegetarian cooking, it provides a flavor that might otherwise be missing or lacking....I had eliminated black pepper from all my cooking except for mignonette. However, Lior [Lev Sercarz, owner of the spice store La Boîte] has a pepper blend of about nine different varieties of pepper that has made me and others believers. It does not just smell like spicy dust—it has a high note and a fruity, fresh flavor that is completely different from any other pepper.

—**BRAD FARMERIE,** Saxon + Parole (New York City)

Piquancy and pungency (see page 133) are both "loud" aspects of flavor, and are often confused. **Piquancy** is more often applied to the type of persistent "false heat" experienced in the mouth when consuming ingredients that contain *capsaicin* (e.g., chiles, chili paste, chili pepper flakes, chili powder, Sriracha, Tabasco, etc.) or *piperine* (e.g., peppercorns, long pepper). Pungency, on the other hand, more often refers to the type of brief "false heat" that mostly affects the nose when consuming ingredients containing isothiocyanates (e.g., horseradish, mustard, radishes, wasabi) or other chemical irritants (e.g., clove, garlic, ginger).

Mexican cuisine most famously celebrates chiles' piquancy, although other cuisines—from Indian and Thai (in which chiles are frequently showcased in curries) to Italian (in which you'll commonly find garlicky broccoli rabe accented with a shake of chili pepper flakes)—do, too.

PIQUANT INGREDIENTS

chile peppers (habaneros, jalapeños, poblanos, etc.)

chili paste, pepper flakes, and powder

curry powder, Madras

gochujang, aka Korean chili paste (piquant + umami)

harissa

kirmizi biber (Turkish pepper)

nam prik pao sauce

paprika, Hungarian

paprika, Hungarian bittersweet (aka *édes* [sweet], *félédes* [semisweet], and *rózsa* [mildly pungent rose])

paprika, Hungarian hot (aka *eros*)

paprika, Hungarian sweet

paprika, Spanish smoked (available in both hot and sweet styles)

parsley and parsley water

peperoncini

peperoncino (Calabrian pepper)

peperone (Italian pepper powder)

pepper, Aleppo

pepper, black

pepper, cayenne

pepper, Espelette

pepper, Maras (Turkish pepper + often sour +/or salty) (piquant + sour +/or salty)

pepper, Szechuan or Sichuan

pepper, urfa (Turkish pepper + often salt) (piquant + salt + bitter + sweet)

peppers, fish

piment d'Espelette (Basque pepper powder)

pimentón, smoked: *agridulce* (bittersweet), *dulce* (sweet), *pimentón*, smoked, *picante* (hot) *pimentón*, unsmoked

pimentón de la Vera (Spanish smoked paprika) (heat + smoke)

pimiento

piri piri peppers and powder (aka some of the hottest peppers available) (piquant or piquant + sour)

seven-spice powder, Japanese

Sriracha sauce

Tabasco sauce

urfa biber

Worcestershire sauce (piquant + salty + sour + sweet + umami)

Piquant Technique
marinating (e.g., in dry BBQ rubs or BBQ sauces)

Piquant Dynamics

We measure piquancy (i.e., false heat) on our palates with the **Scoville scale**, which provides a sense of the range of piquancy that exists in various peppers. Sweet bell peppers are close to zero on the scale, while very mild **shishito peppers** have 50 to 200 units and mild **Anaheim chiles** might have anywhere from 500 to 2,000 units. Average **jalapeño chiles** have 3,500 to 8,000 units, hot **habaneros** have 200,000 to 350,000, and uber-hot **ghost peppers** have 855,000 to 2,200,000—a reminder that not all peppers are alike!

In small doses (e.g., a pinch of cayenne), piquancy's "heat" can be a flavor enhancer, especially in salty or sour dishes. Preferred piquancy levels vary from person to person, but whenever things get too hot, be careful what you reach for to cool them down: Alcohol exacerbates piquancy, while dairy can cool things down—helping to explain the popularity of sour cream as an accent on Mexican dishes, and yogurt-based raitas with Indian curries.

Piquant Examples

Many leading chefs are enamored with the mild-yet-smoky **Aleppo pepper**, which can be used during the cooking process as well as just before serving. Gabriel Kreuther says he loves it "even more than cayenne," finding that it has a little acidity, along with "an elegant flair that lingers on the palate." Brad Farmerie calls it his "go-to pepper. It's warm with mild heat, and has almost a sundried-tomato-y sweetness."

Black pepper takes a starring role in some of baker Melissa Weller's bagel doughs and laminated doughs at Sadelle's in New York City. Weller favors an extra-coarse "butcher's cut" black pepper.

Just a pinch of **cayenne pepper** "turbo-charges" the flavors in one four-star chef's dishes—you'll virtually never taste it, but you'll be left wondering why they're so delicious.

Chefs love the way that **chile peppers** can make other flavors on their menu sing—but don't always mention it in the menu descriptions for fear of turning off customers who are wary of chiles' heat. Even Jean-Georges Vongerichten has cited them as his favorite ingredient, saying, "Anything that gives dishes a good kick is in my pantry," from Thai chiles to serranos.

Many chefs swear by **gochujang**, the fermented Korean chile paste (containing glutinous rice, fermented soybeans, red chiles, and salt), when they need to add layers of flavors beyond mere piquancy.

A good-quality **harissa** is worth having on hand to add a piquant note to dishes, either as marinade, as a seasoning, or as a sauce.

Nam prik pao sauce is Thai chili sauce used by chefs to enliven dishes from noodle dishes to soups to stir-fries.

Daniel Boulud's favorite pepper blend is said to be La Boîte's **Pierre Poivre**, which is a mix of eight different peppers.

Daniel Boulud and Thomas Keller both sing the praises of the aromatic yet elegant ***piment d'Espelette***, a powder made from a very-flavorful-yet-not-very-hot pepper from the Basque area of France, which can be used to season scrambled eggs and seafood. (Its heat level is beyond that of paprika, though not quite as loud as cayenne.) Boulud notes that it can protect or even enhance the taste of a great wine.

Szechuan peppercorns—especially uber-strong green peppercorns from China—are popular among chefs for their "numbing" quality that can be frightening to newcomers testing their potency. Some chefs credit Danny Bowien for their love of green Szechuan peppercorns, which make the tongue tingle.

Chefs love the deep flavor of **smoked paprika** and, similarly, smoked Spanish salt to give dishes a touch of smokiness. Some use smoked paprika as a substitute for the smokiness of pork when they want to keep a dish vegetarian.

Sriracha adds more than heat—some use it to add flavor to everything from aioli to Asian noodle dishes, to cocktails (e.g., Bloody Marys) to crabcakes to eggs to soups.

You might be very surprised to learn which restaurants, including high-end French restaurants, regularly use a tiny dash of **Tabasco sauce** in their dishes—while you'll never taste it, its presence turbocharges the other ingredients.

Keep an eye out for **urfa biber**, a medium-spicy Turkish pepper with sweet, salty, and sour notes of coffee, raisins, and smoke that's increasingly popular among chefs who season dishes ranging from produce (e.g., eggplant, peppers) to cheese (feta, halloumi) to seafood (shrimp) and meats (lamb) to desserts. Jerry Traunfeld–trained protégé Matt Bumpas even pairs it with a burnt-honey ice cream.

Piquant + Salty + Sour: Spike Gjerde of Baltimore's locavore Woodberry Kitchen created his own hot sauce, called **snake oil**, to serve as a local replacement for Tabasco sauce, explaining, "Michael Twitty [a culinary historian] wrote about fish peppers, a hot pepper growing on the Chesapeake—and that was catnip to me." This led to his developing snake oil, his version made from **fish peppers + salt + vinegar** that's not as hot or acidic as Tabasco, with more fruitiness and body.

Piquant + Salty + Sour + Umami: Turn to **Worcestershire sauce** for a "cooked" saltiness that can be added to egg dishes (e.g., scrambled), salad dressings (e.g., Caesar), or soups (e.g., chowders).

Worcestershire sauce = distilled white vinegar + molasses + sugar + water + salt + onions + anchovies + garlic + cloves + tamarind extract + natural flavorings + chili pepper extract

Piquant Principles

Piquant + Cooling
salsa + sour cream

Piquant + Pungent + Salt + Umami
chiles + anchovies + garlic + spaghetti

Piquant + Sour
chiles + vinegar → salsa

Piquant + Sour + Salt
aged red pepper + distilled vinegar + salt → Tabasco
(red) chiles + garlic + salt + vinegar → Sriracha

ASTRINGENCY

Many bitter-tasting, and some sour-tasting, foods are also **astringent**. While taste is gustatory (experienced primarily on the tongue), astringency is characterized by a drying, puckering sensation experienced in the entire mouth, often prompted by the presence of tannins (e.g., in strong tea or red wine), alcohol (e.g., gin), or astringent ingredients such as cranberries, unripe persimmons, and walnuts. The astringency of cranberries is often a welcome addition to sweeter apple and pear desserts such as pies or crisps, while a handful of astringent pomegranate seeds can add a refreshing counterbalance when sprinkled atop rich Mexican moles or Persian walnut sauces.

ASTRINGENT INGREDIENTS

acorns
apples (esp. green)
apricots
bananas, green
beans (esp. dried and/or red)
beer (esp. ales)
blueberries
cacao (tannin)
cauliflower
chickpeas
chocolate (esp. dark)
cinnamon (tannin)
coffee
cranberries
fruits, many
grapes (esp. skins)
hazelnuts
legumes (esp. dried and/or red beans)
nuts
olives
parsley
pears, some
pecans
persimmons (esp. unripe)
pistachios
plums
pomegranates
popcorn
potatoes
quince
rye
strawberries
tea (esp. strong) (tannin)
turmeric
vanilla (tannin)
walnuts (tannin)
wine (esp. red) (tannin)

Astringent Dynamics

Astringent notes of, say, cranberry or tea in cocktails, mocktails, or other drinks may need "rounding off," e.g., with a hint of simple syrup or other sweetener, or with the acidity provided by a squeeze of lemon or other citrus or even high-acid berries. (Grapes or grape juice could provide sour and sweet flavors simultaneously.)

Balance astringency with sourness, sweetness, or fattiness.

Astringent Principles

Astringent + Fat

celery + blue cheese
coffee + cream
red wine + well-marbled steak

Astringent + Sour

cranberry + orange
lentils + sherry vinegar
plums + orange
tea + lemon

Astringent + Sweet

cranberry + sugar
tea + honey

Astringent + Sour + Sweet

tea + lemon + honey

AROMA = AROMATICS + PUNGENCY + CHEMETHESIS

The third component of the Flavor Equation is *Aroma*. Considering the aspects of flavor we experience via our tongues, mouths, and noses, the vast majority—80 to 90 percent or more—are via our noses as **aroma**. While there are only five basic tastes, the nose can discern more than 10,000 different aromatic compounds (e.g., alliums, citrus, herbs, spices), which actually comprise most of what we refer to as flavor. Most aromas can be characterized as either sweet or savory.

Am I getting spice, sweet, acid, salt, bitter, crunch? Am I hitting all the notes to hit a home-run dish for you? The best dishes activate all your senses, and all of your palate—and aroma is a big part of that, too.

—**MICHAEL SCELFO,** Alden & Harlow (Cambridge, Massachusetts)

Sweet notes are largely associated with sweeteners, fruits, and certain vegetables (e.g., sweet potatoes), herbs (e.g., basil), and spices (e.g., cinnamon). **Savory** notes are typically associated with "meatiness" almost as much as with alliums such as garlic and onions, even across different cultures. Other savory notes can include *cheesiness, smokiness,* and *spiciness*. Cheesiness can even be found in vegan (i.e., dairyless and eggless) cuisine, such as in nutritional yeast or in vegan cheeses (which are often based on nuts and/or seeds). Smokiness can be imparted via cooking techniques (e.g., grilling, hot or cold smoking; many chefs favor the Smoking Gun handheld food smoker) and/or ingredients (e.g., liquid smoke, smoked paprika). And spiciness can reflect flavor chords that are regionally specific combinations of flavors (e.g., garlic + ginger + soy sauce = Asia; garlic + lemon + oregano = Mediterranean).

You want to experience a cocktail both on your tongue and in your gullet. . . . I think about the notes in my cocktails the way I learned to think about notes in perfume. There are top notes, middle notes, and base notes. The top notes are the "Welcome Wagon" to your cocktail—such as the fragrance citrus provides. The middle notes come afterward, floral and rich. The base notes are deeper, richer foundational notes that warm the base of your cocktail, such as frankincense, oak moss, or patchouli.

—**AUDREY SAUNDERS,** Pegu Club (New York City)

We actually perceive aroma in two different ways: via nose-smelling and mouth-smelling. When the food we're smelling is outside our mouths, it's called nose-smelling (or orthonasal olfaction). When the food we're smelling is already inside our mouths, the aromas that flow from our mouths to our noses are considered mouth-smelling (or retronasal olfaction). In both instances, the aromas are processed by the nose.

Chefs skewer foods onto everything from rosemary branches to vanilla beans in order to treat diners to a whiff of their scent before eating. Indeed, there is no limit to your means of enhancing aroma within a dining experience, as proven by avant-garde chefs like Grant Achatz of Chicago's Alinea, who has served pheasant alongside burning oak leaves and bison alongside smoking cinnamon sticks. He served a tomato dish atop an inflatable "pillow" that had been filled with the aroma of grass, and punctured the pillow with a few pinpricks before serving so that it would release the aroma as the diner ate it.

Some qualities are perceived through both taste and smell, including **pungency** and **chemethesis** (see below).

AROMATICS

Aroma comprises the vast majority of the flavor we experience via our noses and mouths. Anyone looking to heighten a dish's flavor is wise to consider a dish's aromatics—that is, ingredients that emit strong and distinctive aromas, which can be associated with savoriness (e.g., cumin, onions) or sweetness (e.g., cinnamon, vanilla). Such ingredients include the entire **allium** family (chives, garlic, garlic scapes, leeks, onions, ramps, scallions, shallots), **citrus** fruits (grapefruits, lemons, limes, oranges, yuzu), edible **flowers** (chamomile, geranium, lavender, rose), **herbs** (especially hard-stemmed, like bay leaves, lovage, marjoram, oregano, rosemary, sage, savory, tarragon, thyme), and **spices** from sweet to savory to hot (anise, black pepper, cinnamon, cloves, cumin, nutmeg). Adding a final aromatic note to a finished dish (e.g., a sprinkling of fresh, chopped herbs at the last moment) can enhance aroma, and thus flavor, enormously.

> Back in 2005, when we opened, it was all about the quarter-ounce [1½ teaspoons]—the idea that just that small of an amount of an ingredient could make a dramatic difference. Today, it's all about ⅛ of a teaspoon of an ingredient. We'll be in a bar meeting, and will taste drinks made with and without ⅛ of a teaspoon of an ingredient, and we'll all agree, "Wow—that makes a huge difference." That ingredient [e.g., cinnamon, hot sauce] might not necessarily be there for its flavor, but rather as something under threshold that adds complexity and does its magic.
>
> —**AUDREY SAUNDERS,** Pegu Club (New York City)

AROMATIC INGREDIENTS

allspice
angelica
basil
bay leaves
berbere
bergamot
cardamom
carrots (e.g., as in mirepoix)
cassia
celery (e.g., as in mirepoix)
chamomile
chives
chocolate
cilantro
cinnamon
citrus zest (aroma + bitter + freshness, without acidity)
cloves
cocoa
coffee, roasted

AROMATIC INGREDIENTS (CONT.)

coriander
cumin
dill
fennel (leaves, seeds)
fenugreek
galangal
garlic
geraniums
ginger
grapefruit
herbs, dried and fresh
hops
Japanese 7-spice powder (aromatic + piquant)
jasmine
juniper berries
lavender
leeks
lemon
lemon balm
lemongrass
lemon thyme
lemon verbena
lemon zest (aroma + bitter + freshness, *without* acidity)
licorice
limes
lovage
mace
marjoram
mint
nasturtiums
nutmeg
onions (e.g., as in mirepoix)
orange
orange, blood
orange, mandarin
orange blossoms
oregano
parsley
peppercorns (e.g., black, esp. freshly ground)
pomelo
ramps
rose (e.g., water)
rosemary
saffron
sage
sassafras
savory
scallions
shallots
shiso
spearmint
spirits, aromatic (e.g., Cognac)
tangerines
tarragon
tea (e.g., green)
thyme
truffles (esp. white)
vanilla
vermouth
violets
wines, aromatic (e.g., Gewurztraminer, Muscat)
yuzu

Aromatic Techniques

heating (releases the aromatics of spices and certain other aromatics)

sous-vide (can help to retain aromas that might otherwise evaporate during the cooking process. Part of the popularity of the sous-vide technique is to capture all-important aromas.)

spritzing (Adding a spritz of lemon juice from a spray bottle just before serving to impart more aroma, freshness, and acidity to a dish or a cocktail.)

Aromatic Dynamics

Certain aromas (e.g., sourness) can suppress our perception of certain tastes (e.g., sweetness).

Most of the flavor essences of various cuisines are based on characteristic combinations of aromatic vegetables and/or herbs:

- French (carrots + celery + onions)
- Indian (chiles + garlic + ginger + onions)
- Indonesian (chiles + garlic)
- Italian (fennel + garlic + onions)
- Mexican (chiles + garlic + onions + tomatoes)
- Spanish (garlic + onions [+ peppers])
- Thai (chiles + makrut lime leaves + lemongrass + shallots)

Using Aromatics

Brooks Headley loves the Ethiopian spice blend ***berbere***, which he uses liberally to make berbere-flavored dishes, or in tiny pinches to add a mysterious note to dishes featuring caramel or tomatoes.

berbere: allspice + black pepper + chiles + cinnamon + coriander + fenugreek + garlic + ginger + red pepper

Cardamom is praised for its versatility in both savory and sweet dishes. Chefs will pair cardamom + lime + seafood, or cardamom + chocolate + coffee.

Substitute **cilantro** (or mint) for basil in pesto and other pasta sauces to add a twist to pasta.

Not just the not-so-secret flavor enhancer for many fruit desserts, **cinnamon** also works its magic in savory dishes, adding complexity to sauces (e.g., moles) and stews.

Coriander wins raves for its versatility in seasoning curries, soups, stews, and more—plus you can find lemon notes in Indian coriander, and orange notes in French coriander.

Dried herbs (e.g., rosemary, sage, savory, and/or thyme) can be ground into an intense powder used to flavor salt, according to Daniel Boulud.

Many chefs count **fresh herbs** (e.g., anise hyssop, dill, lovage, parsley) as must-have ingredients for the complexity they add to dishes.

The **Japanese 7-spice powder** (made from black sesame seeds + crushed red pepper + dried orange peel + dried seaweed + ginger + Japanese pepper + poppy seeds) known as *shichimi togarashi* seasons the ramen at Michelin-starred Kokage, Kajitsu's informal restaurant in New York City, and Masaharu Morimoto is a fan of it as well. Other uses range from noodle dishes to rice dishes to soups, to fried foods such as tempura, even to fruit salads.

Some leading chefs—including Daniel Boulud, Eric Ripert, Michael Solomonov, and Ana Sortun—swear by **La Boîte à Epice spice blends** created by Daniel alum Lior Lev Sercarz, with whom they've collaborated on spice blends for everything from cocktails to fish to desserts. "The range of exotic tastes is endless, but we constantly strive for the ideal equilibrium that defines my idea of French cuisine," notes Boulud.

You can use a few grains of **Madras curry powder** to add another level of toasted flavor to dishes from salads to curries, even desserts.

Don't overlook the importance of flat-leaf **parsley**, an herb some chefs will never let themselves be without. David Bouley keeps **parsley water** on hand for pastas (+ grated cheese + olive oil + pasta + pine nuts) and salad dressings (+ lime juice + olive oil).

Aromatic Principles

When you're blending aromatic ingredients, you'll want to pay as much attention to harmonizing their aromas as to their taste components. This is a listing of flavor pairings and flavor affinities based on aromatic ingredients.

allspice + cinnamon + cloves + vanilla

basil + garlic

cardamom + chocolate + coffee

cardamom + cinnamon

cardamom + coffee

cardamom + ginger + lemon + mint

cardamom + rose water + saffron

carrots + celery + onions (French mirepoix)

carrots + cumin + lime

carrots + ginger + oranges

chamomile + lemon

chocolate + cinnamon

chocolate + coffee + orange

chocolate + mint

chocolate + vanilla

cilantro + lime

cilantro + mint + Thai basil

cinnamon + cloves + cumin + onions + oranges

cinnamon + cloves + oranges + vanilla

citrus (e.g., orange) + shallots + vermouth

coffee + orange

coriander + citrus (e.g., grapefruit, lemon, pomelo)

garlic + ginger

garlic + ginger + scallions

garlic + rosemary

garlic + saffron

lemon + oregano

lemon + rosemary

lemon + tarragon

lime + parsley

parsley + pine nuts + olive oil

THE APPEAL OF EDIBLE FLOWERS

Edible flowers can add beauty, color, and emotion (they're symbols of love, after all) to your dish or drink—all aspects of flavor represented by the X Factor—as most are limited in how much they contribute to flavor via taste, aroma, or texture. Josiah Citrin grows edible flowers on the roof of his restaurant Mélisse in Santa Monica, and notes that pollen gives most their "sweet, individual flavors." Damon Baehrel harvests flowers (including day lilies, vegetable flowers, and wild violets) from his 12-acre property in Earlton, New York, which he uses on a variety of dishes. Edible flowers can be used as flavorful garnishes for both savory and sweet cocktails, desserts, and salads, as with **dill flowers + cucumbers** or **squash blossoms + tomatoes** or **thyme flowers + mushrooms.**

Below you'll find a list of edible flowers, along with their typical colors, flavor notes, and culinary uses. [Note: "Edible" should mean both non-poisonous *and* grown without pesticides. Don't take chances if you're not sure.]

Flowers are one of the most intimate, seductive things that exist. You get the beauty of the color, but you also get the aroma and the bouquet of that flower.

—**FARMER LEE JONES** of the Chef's Garden in Ohio, which grows 65 varieties of edible flowers, including violas, whose flavor he describes as "Necco wafer-like"

angelica (blue, purple, rose): notes of celery and/or licorice *(candied; fish dishes, teas)*

anise hyssop (purple): sweet, with notes of anise, licorice, and/or root beer *(Chinese dishes, salads)*

basil flowers (pink, purple, white): notes of basil, lemon, and/or mint, but louder *(pastas, salads)*

begonias (pink, red): sour, with notes of citrus, e.g., lemony *(garnishes, salads)*

borage (blue): loud, sweet, with notes of cucumber and/or honey *(cocktails, cold soups, mocktails, roasts, salads, sorbets)*

calendulas (aka marigolds; gold, orange): aromatic, bitter (quiet, moderate), and/or sour; notes of citrus, grass, pepper, and/or spices, esp. saffron *(butters, pastas, rice, salads, scrambled eggs, soups)*

chamomile (white-and-yellow): quiet, sweet *(cocktails, teas)*

chervil blossoms (white): notes of anise *(salads)*

chive blossoms (purple): quiet to moderate, with notes of onions and/or spices *(oysters, salads, soups)*

chrysanthemums (orange, red, white, yellow): bitter and/or sour *(salads, stir-fries, vinegars)*

dill flowers (yellow): loud, with notes of dill *(salads, seafood)*

elderflowers (white): sweet, with notes of flowers, fruit, and/or honey *(spirits, syrups, teas)*

fennel flowers (yellow): notes of licorice *(salad dressings, salads, sauces, soups, teas)*

garlic chives (lavender, pink, white): notes of garlic *(salads)*

hibiscus (orange, red): notes of citrus and/or cranberries *(cocktails, salads, teas)*

honeysuckle (pink, red, white, yellow): sweet, with notes of honey *(desserts)*

jasmine (white): very aromatic *(cocktails, teas)*

lavender (purple): aromatic, sweet, with notes of citrus, esp. lemon and/or herbs *(desserts, e.g., custards, ice creams, sorbets; savory dishes; teas)*

lemon verbena flowers (white): notes of citrus, e.g., lemon *(desserts, e.g., custards; teas)*

lilacs (purple): very aromatic, with notes of lemon *(candied; salads)*

marigold, citrus (orange, yellow): bitter and/or sour, with notes of citrus, e.g., lemon and/or orange, and/or flowers *(salads; sauces, e.g., beurre blanc)*

nasturtiums: loud, with notes of flowers, honey, pepper, and/or spices *(burrata; pizzas; salads, e.g., tomato; soups)*

orange blossoms (white): notes of citrus, e.g., orange *(cocktails; pastries, esp. Middle Eastern)*

pansies (pink, white, yellow): sweet, with notes of mint *(flavored butters)*

radish blossoms (yellow): quiet, with notes of pepper *(salads, vegetables)*

rose petals (various colors, esp. pink, yellow): sour or sweet, notes of apples, mint, spice, and/or strawberries *(candied; desserts, esp. ice cream; honey, jams, esp. with strawberries; salads; teas)*

sage flowers (blue, violet, white): notes of citrus *(corn, leeks, mushrooms)*

squash blossoms (yellow): quiet, with notes of squash *(fried; stuffed, e.g., with cheese; pastas)*

sunflower petals (yellow): bitter, sweet, with notes of grass *(baked goods, salads)*

thyme flowers (purple, white): notes of thyme, but louder *(butters, salads, soups)*

violets (purple): sweet *(candied; desserts, e.g., ice creams, sorbets, syrups)*

Karen and Quinn Hatfield on Chefs as Inspiration

Quinn and Karen Hatfield

Quinn: Rocco [DiSpirito, at Union Pacific] was of the envelope-pushing generation before chefs decided that they were going to use chemicals—he was still cooking like a cook.

Karen: Squab with cocoa! Mustard oil with raw scallops! It was appropriate.

Quinn: Jean-Georges [Vongerichten] had a huge impact on me as well that was just as profound....But my last year as a cook I worked with **David Bouley,** and I always say that I learned more in that year than I learned in the ten years before that. He was the best cook you ever met—he was amazing. I based everything about how I wanted to be as a chef in the kitchen on how I saw him in the kitchen. He was always really good at combining elements. He was not afraid to be wrong. If he was making something for a regular and trying to do something they hadn't seen before, if it failed, he was OK with throwing it away. The only thing that ever mattered to him was what was in the pan, and what was going on the plate. And I kind of loved that.

I learned layering of flavors. He worked with a palette of purees that he would add to dishes.

Karen: In our era, everyone was coming out of a few kitchens: **Jean Georges, Daniel,** and **Bouley.** You could tell who was coming out of Bouley's kitchen, because there are a few takeaways that are just so brilliant that you can't *not* use them once you learned them.

Quinn: You're basically working with a few purees—onion, garlic, fennel, and parsnip (for earthy sweetness) purees—that were background players in his dishes. They allowed him to manipulate what was in the pan to a totally different level that was unpredictable, not obvious, and just brilliant.

At Hatfield's, our cooks all called it GOP—garlic, onion, and parsnip purees, which all looked similar, but were always in that order, from top to bottom, or from left to right. Some dishes got more G than others, and other dishes got more P, but they were always there in line with salt, pepper, garlic, onion, parsnip, butter.

The ratio was typically 50 percent onion, to 15 to 20 percent garlic, and 30 to 35 percent parsnip. Garlic was always the least, because you could ruin a dish with too much garlic. The parsnip's wild, sweet earthiness worked better with certain dishes than others....One dish we did was a lamb dish I was well known for with roasted root vegetables, like carrots that were cooked in butter from their raw state until they were done; and glazed with liquid and whole butter and a little GOP and parsley.

Karen: The GOP was used to round out soups, potato purees, glazed green beans. We made *quarts* of GOP every day.

Quinn: [David Bouley's] **ocean herbal broth** had an insane number of ingredients—including celery water, celery puree, parsnip, onion, garlic—and you had to make it to order, every time.

Karen [his wife and the restaurants' pastry chef] is a huge creative force at our restaurants. She's better at immersing herself in the process.

—**QUINN HATFIELD,** Odys + Penelope and Sycamore Kitchen (Los Angeles)

My inspiration for desserts are Quinn's [her husband and the restaurants' chef] savory dishes.

—**KAREN HATFIELD,** Odys + Penelope and Sycamore Kitchen (Los Angeles)

PUNGENCY + CHEMESTHESIS

Additional concepts can help us to understand other aspects of flavor that is processed by our noses: **Pungency** refers to the taste *and* aroma of such ingredients as horseradish, mustard, and wasabi that are as irritating (albeit often pleasantly) to the nose as they are to the palate. **Chemesthesis** is certain chemicals' ability to create sensations that tickle (e.g., the tingle of carbonated beverages) or play tricks on our gustatory senses (e.g., the false perception of "heat" from chile peppers, which are covered under Piquancy, page 118, or "cold" from peppermint).

PUNGENCY

Just as astringency and bitterness are often confused (and indeed often overlap), it's just as common to see pungency conflated with piquancy. **Pungency** refers to a type of brief "false heat" that mostly affects *the nose* when consuming ingredients containing isothiocynates (such as horseradish, mustard, radishes, wasabi) or other chemical irritants (such as cloves, garlic, ginger, peppercorns). **Piquancy** is more often applied to a type of persistent "false heat" experienced in *the mouth* when consuming ingredients that contain *capsaicin* (such as chiles, chili paste, chili pepper flakes, chili powder, Sriracha, etc.) or *piperine* (such as peppercorns, long pepper).

PUNGENT INGREDIENTS

- arugula
- asafoetida (aka hing)
- buckwheat
- cardamom
- cloves
- coriander
- cumin
- fennel
- garlic
- ginger
- greens, mustard
- horseradish
- kohlrabi
- lemongrass
- mustard and mustard seeds
- onions
- piquant foods (e.g., chiles, peppercorns), see page 118
- radishes
- sage
- spelt
- spinach, raw
- thyme
- turmeric
- turnips
- wasabi

Joshua Skenes of Saison on Flavor-Based Creativity

We had heard that San Francisco's ***Saison*** *had gotten its start as a weekly pop-up. It had since earned three Michelin stars, and four stars from the* San Francisco Chronicle. *The World's 50 Best Restaurants list had designated it in 2014 as "One to Watch," before its first appearance on that list at number twenty-seven.*

Still, our dinner there in 2017 literally took our breath away.

Just a few courses into the evening's tasting menu, we became convinced that we were in the midst of one of the most extraordinary meals of our lives. It was so unexpectedly...moving. So much was communicated wordlessly through the array of dishes we were served that we knew it to be the result of a singular vision.

It turned out that chef ***Joshua Skenes****, co-owner with wine director* ***Mark Bright****, wasn't even in the kitchen that night.*

Finding it intolerable to be unable to ask Skenes about all we'd noticed and experienced, we'd offered to drive back to the city from wine country for as brief a conversation as he'd be willing to have in person. Our wide-ranging conversation with Skenes a few days later lasted hours.

You'll find his thoughts throughout Kitchen Creativity*—including on such disparate topics as* ***balancing flavors*** *(page 256),* ***fire*** *(page 299),* ***knowing yourself*** *(page 320),* ***nutrient density*** *(page 342),* ***quality*** *(page 355–356),* ***texture*** *(page 389), and* ***time as an ingredient*** *(page 391). And we fully expect you'll be reading more about Skenes, from us and from others, in the years to come. He seems to be regarding food on a whole new wavelength.*

Just about every course is touched by fire. Because many dishes are delicate, precise, and refined, and the smoky elements are always subtle, it's a guessing game as to where the flames come in.

—MICHAEL BAUER,
San Francisco Chronicle,
in awarding Saison four stars

I get my inspiration from the products. A lot of our cooking is not planned. I have always come more from the intuitive side of things. I will pick up something and taste it, and my mind will wander in some direction.

There is creativity to what I do. It is not blatant, in-your-face [creativity]; it is based around flavor. When you smell a peach you have to say, "That is an incredible peach," and then ask, "What do we do with it?" That is where the thought process begins. What is the best taste, texture, temperature, timing? Those are the considerations for creativity. From there, we create a dish and continue to tweak it. If we miss the season, we miss it.

We taste day-to-day. A product that was good yesterday may not be good today. The best peach of your life that you got on Tuesday may not be that peach on Wednesday. You have to reassess and go from there.

When I was seventeen until I went to culinary school, one of the unexpected benefits of eating only plants [as a vegetarian] was the ability to enjoy an orange off a tree. Your sensitivity increases so much that your ability to taste is something that people who eat junk food will never experience. The wool is lifted, and you get to experience a whole new sense of taste that you didn't before.

You need to be able to dissect fundamental flavors in your head because in the end, it makes a big difference.

Joshua Skenes

Pungent Techniques

Those who like their pungent flavors "loud" often enjoy them "straight up," i.e., raw. But pungency's sometimes overwhelming "loudness" is often neutralized, such as by *sautéing* or even *caramelizing* garlic or onions, which reduces pungency and increases sweetness.

Pungent Dynamics

Pungent ingredients are typically used judiciously as accent flavors in a dish in proportions allowing them to stand up to moderate-to-loud flavored—and often rich—food (like **horseradish + salmon**, or **mustard + pastrami**). In other instances, they are paired with relatively neutral ingredients (as with **hot mustard + pretzel + salt**, or **radishes + butter + salt**).

Pungent Examples

Black pepper is finally coming to be seen by leading chefs as a flavoring in its own right, rather than just salt's sidekick to add to taste.

Mustard is appreciated for its ability to bring up the flavor of salad dressings and sauces. Katianna Hong reveals that spicy Asian **mustard seed oil** is a secret ingredient in many dishes at Meadowood and at Charter Oak. "You can use it to season sauces, dressings, vegetables (e.g., cabbage), cheese—even ice cream," she says.

Principles

Pungent + Cold
wasabi + raw fish

Pungent + "Cool"
horseradish + cucumber

Pungent + Fat
hot mustard + pastrami

Pungent + Fat + Sour
horseradish + sour cream

Pungent + Umami
black pepper + Parmesan cheese → caccio e pepe (pasta)
scallions + fermented bean paste
mustard oil + scallops + uni
onions + tomato paste + wine

Nancy Silverton on Creativity for the "Uncreative"

I don't think of myself as creative. I think of creative chefs as those who come up with something original, although there are very few of them. I think of myself as someone who sucks up things that inspire me [that are then transformed in original ways]. I feel like I'm able to pick out those things that are crowd-pleasers, whether it's a good loaf of bread, or our kind of pizza. I don't pretend to create.

I tasted a celery root remoulade at [**Ludo Lefebvre**'s] Petit Mec that came with almonds and a generous grating of horseradish, which transformed it. What did Ludo do? You can picture him looking at those two gnarly vegetables together and deciding to try to combine them. I'd never seen that combination before. But after I tasted it, I walked across the street [to **Osteria Mozza**], and came up with my own version.

I don't make popcorn at home in L.A., but I make it when I go to Italy. I don't have a garden there because I'm not there year-round, but when I arrive at Panicale, I plant herbs in pots. I love savory popcorn, which I used to make with sage, rosemary, bay leaf, and other herbs from my pots. Then I had this popcorn in Santa Barbara that was amazing. I hate when someone does something better than me—it drives me crazy! It was essentially seasoned with pastrami spices [e.g., coriander, mustard seeds, peppercorns]. And I came up with my own version, finished with an orange butter and a ton of chopped, fresh dill. So while I feel like I'm not creative, I feel like I know flavor and I know what's good!

Sometimes young cooks put six ingredients too many in their dishes. I think I started out with restraint. I'm really happy I grew up under the influence of the **Alice Waters** of the world, and other chefs who cooked with restraint—people like **Jonathan Waxman** and **Jeremiah Tower** and **Mark Miller** and **Wolfgang Puck.** Cooking today is mixed up with mechanics—so now it's harder to taste the soul in a dish. Chefs like **Anne Rosenzweig** just cooked. Now, there's more ego involved, versus taste and memory and celebration and all the reasons people enjoy food.

Michael Cimarusti is a great example of an L.A. chef who is more cutting edge, yet he's so grounded and knowledgeable that he can make it work.

The Importance of Flavor Synergies—Even on a Buffet Table

When I think of entertaining for 20, I always think outdoors. Everything is served at room temperature, nothing is plated, and everything is what you expect on an antipasti table. I love cooking for large groups of people, and I love food that's served at room temperature, for a number of reasons. If you're an entertainer, you as a host won't be in the kitchen the entire time—sweating and swearing and all the things that can make entertaining miserable.

The other thing that I really hate is the potluck. If I'm having a party and you say, "What can I bring?" I will only say, "Wine." The reason is that I'm really a stickler when it comes to things that are on the table together. There's always the person who brings the strawberry ambrosia that ruins the plate. I like to approach it that if you take all the items that are on the table and you put them on the plate, and if you stir them all up, they'd all taste good. **Flavor compatibility isn't only important within a dish, but throughout what's on the table.**

I'm also very particular about the vessel that dishes are served in. I don't want someone bringing a Styrofoam bowl or something disposable. There's a right vehicle and a wrong vehicle—whether it's shallow and wide, or deep, and the right amount [of the right food] has to fit in it.

Nancy Silverton, at Ludo Lefebvre's Petit Trois, which she describes as her favorite restaurant in Los Angeles other than her own

I tend to make a protein, such as something I'm roasting or grilling, then I choose the contorni [vegetables] that go with it, with the idea that I could stir everything up and it would all taste great together. Everything I picked is just as good just-made or in two hours—so there are no arugula salads, but rather all sturdy lettuces, like escarole and Romaine and bok choy—greens that are hearty and won't wilt. Or I'll serve chicories—especially radicchio—because I actually like when they're dressed and they sit for a half-hour or longer; I like when they break down. They're more palatable, and the brightness of the radicchio transforms into a more beautiful sort of color, the way the purpley-ness comes out. . . .One of my favorite things is a Niçoise Deconstructed—which doesn't necessarily have anything to do with a Niçoise salad per se, but there are all these dishes that [set out together] will remind you of it: soft lettuces with herbs, poached tuna, deviled eggs or egg salad with bagna cauda toasts, a wax bean salad with a mustard dressing and chiles and almonds, potatoes, onions that are roasted with anchovies—all the components of a Niçoise.

THE X FACTOR = OTHER PHYSICAL, EMOTIONAL, MENTAL, AND SPIRITUAL FACTORS

Aspects of flavor that are sometimes difficult to quantify are categorized under **the X Factor**, which sums up the collective importance of everything else we perceive physically, emotionally, mentally, and spiritually.

An endless range of factors can play a role in how we perceive the flavor of a dish.

Some of these are external factors—that is, a function of something outside ourselves, whether some aspect of the dish itself, or the environment in which it is served.

To me, food is as much about the moment, the occasion, the location, and the company as it is about the taste. It is the only thing we do that involves all the senses. It has the ability to generate so much emotion and so much memory. It has endless possibilities. It is one of those subjects where the more you learn about it, the more you realize you don't know.

—HESTON BLUMENTHAL,
The Fat Duck (England)

An array of internal factors can also come into play here—including our own ability to perceive flavor over time. As we age, we tend to experience a decline in our sense of smell. Half of those over the age of 65, and 80 percent of those over 80, have a decreased sense of smell—and thus a lessened capacity to perceive flavor.

Our personal preferences, learned associations, and emotional reactions are no less important. During a once-in-a-lifetime meal at Damon Baehrel in Earlton, New York, the pleasures of the exquisite flavors we enjoyed were magnified by their origin on the 12 surrounding acres of property—from sipping the sap of sycamore trees to eating bread that had been baked from the flour ground from acorns that grew just yards away. The fact that the final fruit ice course reminded Andrew of childhood was a personal experience that no one could have anticipated.

"When I was working with Alain Senderens at Lucas Carton, every Wednesday we'd sit down and plan for the week, and talk about ideas behind dishes, even classics like **lobster + vanilla.** We'd try some of them ten or fifteen times before they met with the approval of chef and his wife," recalls Daniel's Eddy Leroux. "She didn't like cinnamon, so we learned not to add it to dishes. In the same way, Daniel [Boulud] doesn't like bananas or piquillo peppers, so we learned not to use them."

A dish's visual appearance, which is a matter of execution and presentation, has a noticeable impact on how its flavor is perceived.

Influenced by Michel Bras's much-imitated *gargouillou,* plating has become an art unto itself, with colors and arrangement of ingredients able to provoke contemplation, or even whimsy.

Likewise, the provision of eating utensils—or lack thereof—will affect the experience of flavor. At a book party hosted for us at in Beverly Hills, former Spago Las Vegas chef Eric Klein served a passed appetizer in white Chinese takeout cartons with wooden chopsticks, which added to the party's fun vibe as well as guests' enjoyment.

The environment in which we're tasting a dish is critical—whether a four-star dining room hung with works of art, or a picnic blanket lit by the setting sun in the middle of Central Park. Even sound can affect our perception of flavor, with flavor sometimes masked by ambient sound. In *The Flavor Bible* (page 217), we used high-pitched notes as a metaphor for sour tastes, and indeed subsequent research at Oxford has since documented that certain tastes are associated with certain pitches (e.g., sweet + sour = high notes; bitter + umami = low notes), and that ambient sound can influence the perception of sweetness.

In a fine-dining temple like Daniel, it's whimsical to find a pirate's treasure chest brought to your table and unlocked to reveal a selection of rums for the Pirate's Booty cocktail, which is then made tableside. Various dishes, including Poireaux: Wood Fire Grilled Leeks with Matsutake-Pine Nut Vinaigrette, Tarragon Oil, and Mustard Salad, are presented and carved tableside for their aroma as well as the entertainment value.

Phillip Foss asks guests at his Michelin-starred EL Ideas in Chicago to pick up their plates and lick them during the first course. During our dinner there, one of our favorite dessert courses was a delicious "chocolate cake batter" served to us with spatulas to lick, which made the course all the more memorable.

Chefs on Plating

An essential aspect of music is silence. An essential aspect of paintings is **white space.** An essential aspect of a dish can be the white space on the plate, or the **neutrality** in flavor that allows another flavor to shine. Chefs have their own aesthetic preferences when it comes to the subject of plating their food, which can be thought of as the "frame" given to their culinary artistry:

> I am big on having some **neutrality** on the plate. A "matte" flavor works as a unifying baseline, and as a counterpoint for other, sharper flavors. A neutral flavor could be a nut puree, crema, squash hummus, yogurt, dried fruit puree—there are a lot of things that can tie other things together.
>
> —MICHAEL SCELFO, Alden & Harlow (Cambridge, Massachusetts)

> [Presentation-wise,] I don't like things that are very symmetrical. I like things that are odd-numbered. I try to show my team visually that I like things a little off-balance. It may be Asian aesthetics—that a little imbalance and imperfection aids perfection. I'll tell them I'd like things trailing off the plate a little bit.
>
> —DELLA GOSSETT, pastry chef, Spago (Beverly Hills), on her art training's influence on her desserts

Brad Farmerie

> At Charlie Trotter's, if you were serving a table of eight, Charlie would encourage you to do eight different presentations. If eight people ordered beef, it would be eight different beef presentations.... Charlie loved jazz. The notes are one aspect of the music, but how you interpret the notes is a very different thing. **It is like art: It is not the painting, but what you get from the painting.** To me, flavor is everything, and presentation is the last five seconds, so that is where I learned my à la minute fun with plating.
>
> —CHRIS LONG, Natalie's at the Camden Harbour Inn (Camden, Maine)

> One of the things I picked up from Michael [Cimarusti] at Providence was the importance of thinking about how someone was going to be eating a dish. You want to **plate it intentionally** so that it has an obvious perfect first bite that everyone will go to first when they see the plate. You can't leave it to chance—you want to design the plating so that the guest eats it the way you want it to be eaten, whether that's eating the elements separately or layering them together. Michael would hold plates at eye level to look closely at the presentation to make sure it achieved what he wanted it to.... Sometimes I like to hide things in my plating to provide an element of surprise to the guest. In my burrata salad, I will stud it with some very crispy croutons that aren't visible, so that when the guest discovers them, it's a happy surprise.
>
> —JESSICA LARGEY, Simone (Los Angeles)

Quinn: If you set a plate in front of someone, are they going to get that bite that I wanted them to have? We do a lamb lettuce cup here—as a buddy said, "It's a taco!" It's a cup, you pick it up, and you bite it. **Wolfgang Puck** [their former boss at Spago, where the couple met] did a dish forever that was a radicchio cup with ground lamb inside it, that was intended to be picked up and eaten. But when you look over and see someone eating the ground lamb out of the cup with a fork, and leaving the cup . . .

Karen: We hate to tell people how to eat a dish, so it should be plated in a way so that it's very clear.

—QUINN and KAREN HATFIELD, Odys + Penelope and Sycamore Kitchen (Los Angeles)

In plating these days, everyone seems to be taking an asymmetric approach, but I just don't do it. We have a tomato cake on the menu, and it's meant to look like a tart. There are no cake crumbles or shards of fruit leather. Why not let a dish look like what it is?

—AMANDA COHEN, Dirt Candy (New York City)

Natalie's at the Camden Harbour Inn

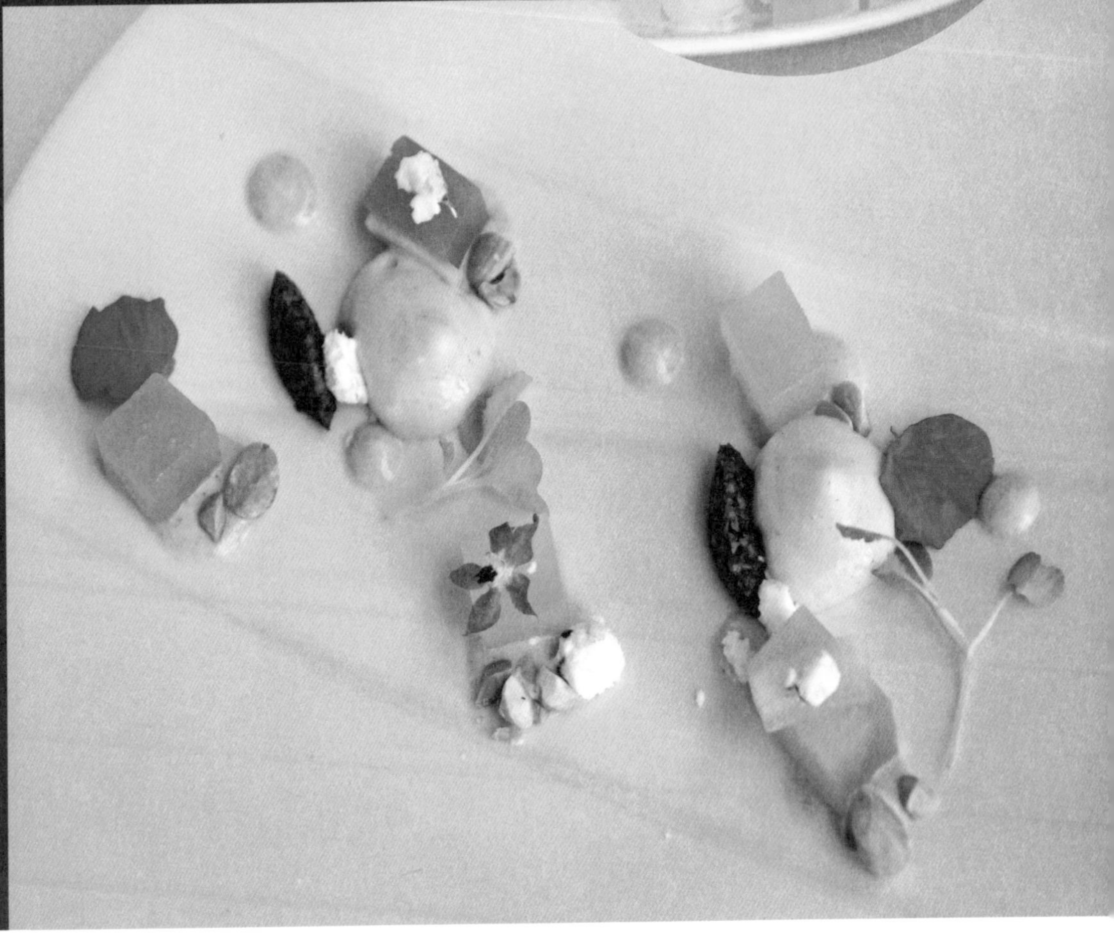

COOKING WITH SOUL AND SOULFULNESS

In our conversations, chef after chef brought up the subject of "soulfulness" in food—that elusive quality that one can sense more easily than one can put into words. The best chefs know it's not only real (and a critical component of the Flavor Equation, represented as the X Factor), but that it is the secret to cooking alchemy. "When soulfulness is missing from food, you can taste it and know it," San Francisco pastry chef Emily Luchetti told us. "You can tell cooks about this, but some can't get it. But it's the reason you can give the same ingredients to different chefs to make the same dish, and it will come out differently. I can look at eight desserts, and tell you everything about the people who made them—how precise and anal they are, or how free-flowing, humorous, warm, or soulful they are. You'd think I'm psychic. Once you actually taste it, it's possible to know if they're cooking with their heads or their hearts."

A recipe has no soul. You, as the cook, must bring the soul to the recipe.

—**THOMAS KELLER,** The French Laundry (Yountville, CA) and Per Se (New York City)

Luchetti often finds herself critiquing other pastry chefs' desserts in her current position, where she finds it easy to tell them which desserts she likes and which she doesn't like, and why. "Often, I'll say, 'This is pretty, and looks like something that could appear in *Art Culinaire* or *Saveur,* in that it's current and trendy and technically fine—but I don't taste *you* in it,'" she says.

Emily Luchetti, with a cacao pod

Certain ingredients take desserts into more intellectual vs. soulful directions. Ingredients like traditional baking spices (e.g., cinnamon, nutmeg) and nuts are more soulful. I think the use of herbs in desserts is more intellectual. Chiles can be soulful, depending on how they're used.

—**EMILY LUCHETTI,** chief pastry officer of The Cavalier, Marlowe, and Park Tavern (San Francisco)

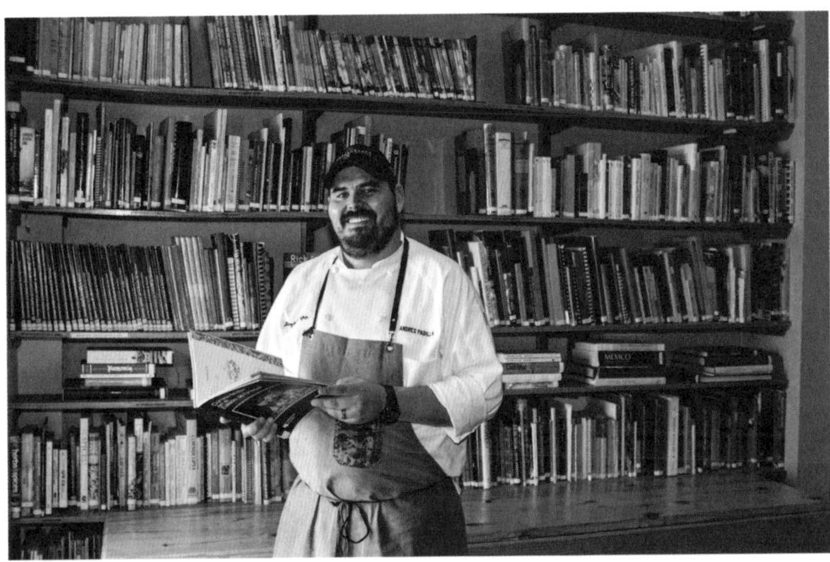

Andres Padilla

Part of the process of moving through the three stages of cooking includes becoming a more soulful cook, which happens through a combination of factors. "Learning about the various regions of Mexico here at the restaurant is great—but it's only through travel that you're able to connect the dots," says Topolobampo executive chef Andres Padilla. "Going to Mexico and being able to taste dishes at their source is mind-blowing—it's literally like an explosion in your brain. You're able to understand a dish on a much more intimate level."

Padilla shares the evolution of his experience making a particular dish: "I remember making a *sopa de pan*—a bread soup—from a very old recipe from Chiapas, the poorest state in the country [which calls for toasted bread slices, chicken broth, vegetables, hard-boiled eggs, and cinnamon, oregano, and pepper]. I made the dish, but deconstructed it even more, and when Rick [Bayless] tasted it, he said, 'It's not the dish.' Rick told me, 'Go to a recipe book that's 40 years old and make it like that!'

"So I referenced all the regional books in our extensive library here, and made another version with reduced chicken stock and using the traditional lard instead of the olive oil I'd substituted, and a lot more sweet spices, and it was so much better.

"Then Rick and Deann [Bayless] took me on a trip to Chiapas, and I ate the dish there—which brought me full circle in terms of truly understanding the dish. After that, I was able to create a truly delicious version," concludes Padilla. "There's a point at which the dish says, 'I'm home,' and strikes the same chord."

Bringing soulfulness to your cooking will allow you to conjure memories for some, and create memories for others. As Emily Luchetti observes, "Soulfulness is what allows flavor to linger on the palate in our memories for decades."

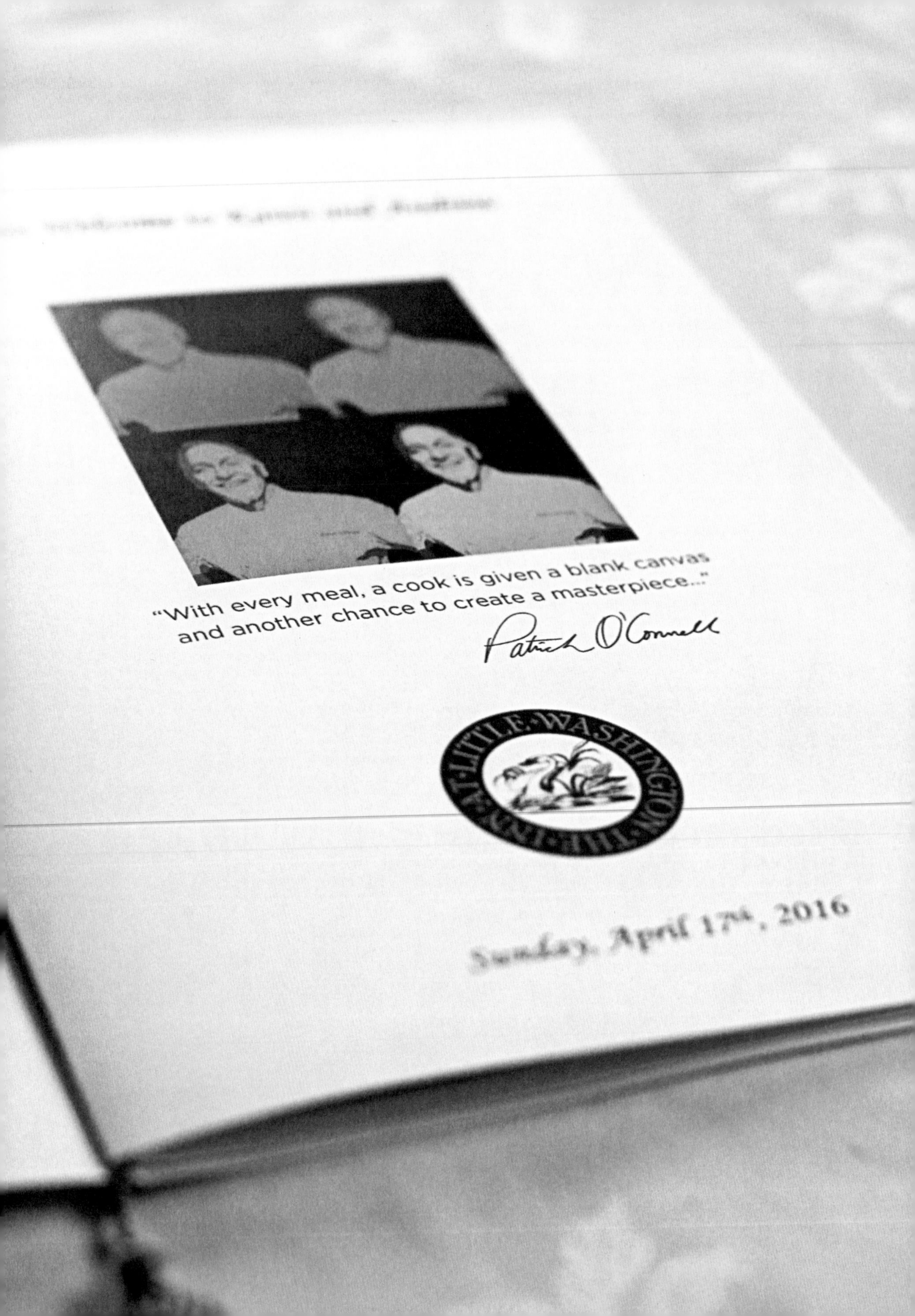

"With every meal, a cook is given a blank canvas and another chance to create a masterpiece..."

Sunday, April 17th, 2016

STAGE

3 CREATIVITY: making something new and valuable

A jazz musician can improvise based on his knowledge of music. He understands how things go together. For a chef, once you have that basis, that's when cuisine is truly exciting.

—CHARLIE TROTTER

You've now **copied** dishes. You've also **converted** dishes.

Now you're called to move on to the process of **creating** unique dishes of your own.

Your eagerness to push the limits of creativity might be tempered by awe for all you've learned—not to mention anxiety over whether it's even possible that, in a country with more than 100,000 chefs and head cooks, you could ever have a chance of coming up with something unique.

That's when it's important to remember something: **you *are unique*.** *No one* else in the world has had the same upbringing and education and experiences that you have had, and no one else has filtered theirs through *your* unique perspective.

The secret to creating something unique is to turn *inward*. Your **inner senses** are unique to you, and only you. You already know everything you need to know to be a creative cook.

Think about it: You've been eating an average of three times a day for decades now, and you've built up a palate that knows what it likes and doesn't like.

Knowing your own palate is key. So, think for a moment about five to ten favorite dishes you *loved* as a child. Seriously—write them down, right here, right now. Andrew and I will do this with you.

> **Some wardrobe consultants can look in your closet and combine things into outfits you never would have thought to put together yourself. Some people look at the same ingredients and think differently about how to combine them.**
>
> —**EMILY LUCHETTI,** chief pastry officer of The Cavalier, Marlowe, and Park Tavern (San Francisco)

Our lists include: caramel apples, bean with bacon soup, turtle sundaes, cheesecake, peanut butter-and-chocolate Rice Krispie "sandwiches," peanut butter and honey on toast, lasagna, split pea soup with ham, tacos, and cheeseburgers.

Now think about *what* you loved about each of the dishes you named. Jot down a few notes about each dish. Again, we're right here with you, reminiscing about the 1970s:

Caramel apples: Karen loved the fun of eating an apple on a stick, plus the sweet and salty flavors together, and all the great textures: biting into the crisp, juicy apple and the crunch of the peanuts against the chewiness of the caramel. **Bean with bacon soup:** She loved that soup could taste like bacon, then one of her five favorite foods and something she typically only had for breakfast on weekends. **Turtle sundaes:** She never sacrificed when she ordered a turtle sundae—it had it all: hot fudge AND caramel sauce (versus one or the other) AND crunchy toasted pecans and, it was fun to experience hot and cold in a single bite. **Cheesecake:** She loved the creamy richness of cheesecake, especially against the crunchy graham cracker crust. **Peanut-butter-and-chocolate Rice Krispie "sandwiches":** She loved being able to enjoy not just two but *three* of her favorite ingredients (**chocolate + peanut butter + Rice Krispies**) in a single treat, which somehow made them all taste even better together (i.e., 1+1+1=4).

Peanut butter and honey on toast: Andrew loved the combination of salty and sweet and crunchy at the same time. **Lasagna:** His mother's lasagna was all about its softness and ooziness. **Split pea soup:** He loved the smooth texture of split pea soup and the fact that it didn't taste like vegetables (which he hated back then) but rather like ham (which he loved back then). **Tacos:** He loved the crunchiness of taco shells, and the punch of flavor that sprinkling the magic packet of taco seasoning brought to the ground beef. **Cheeseburger:** He loved how everything melted together in a cheeseburger to create one great flavor and texture.

Lots of memories come up about flavors and textures and juxtapositions of both, once you stop to think about it.

Now, think about what you learned about what flavors go together, based on your own favorite childhood dishes. Here's what we learned from ours:

apples + caramel + peanuts

bacon + beans + tomatoes

caramel + chocolate + pecans

cream cheese + graham crackers + sugar

chocolate + peanut butter + Rice Krispies

bread + honey + peanut butter

cheese + pasta + tomato

ham + split peas

(ground) beef + cheese + seasoning mix + tortillas

bun + burger + cheese

The trick as an adult who cooks is to realize that you can do more with these beloved flavor combinations besides re-creating the dish that made you fall in love with them.

Take **apples + caramel + peanuts.** What else could you do with them besides dip a raw apple into melted caramel and roll the top in crushed peanuts to make a caramel apple?

- You could make a crepe, fill it with **caramel**ized **apples**, and serve it with a **peanut** sauce.
- You could make **peanut** butter cookies studded with bits of dried **apple** and **caramel.**
- You could make **caramel-apple** muffins, topped with chopped **peanuts** baked into the muffin tops.
- You could make an elegant **apple** pie, garnished with a **peanut** foam on the side along with a few pieces of **caramel** corn.
- You could make a green salad with slices of fresh **apple,** and toss it with a **caramel** vinaigrette and toasted **peanuts.**
- You could make an **apple** martini, which you could pour into a martini glass whose rim had been rolled in melted **caramel** and then crushed **peanuts.**
- You could make a **peanut** butter sandwich, and eat it with a glass of **apple** juice, followed by a single **caramel** for dessert.

> **An idea is nothing more or less than a new combination of old elements.**
>
> —VILFREDO PARETO, Italian philosopher

So, what did we just learn from this exercise?

One of the best-kept secrets of kitchen creativity is mastering **flavor pairings** (two ingredients that harmonize well together), and **flavor affinities** (three or more ingredients that harmonize well together): tried-and-true

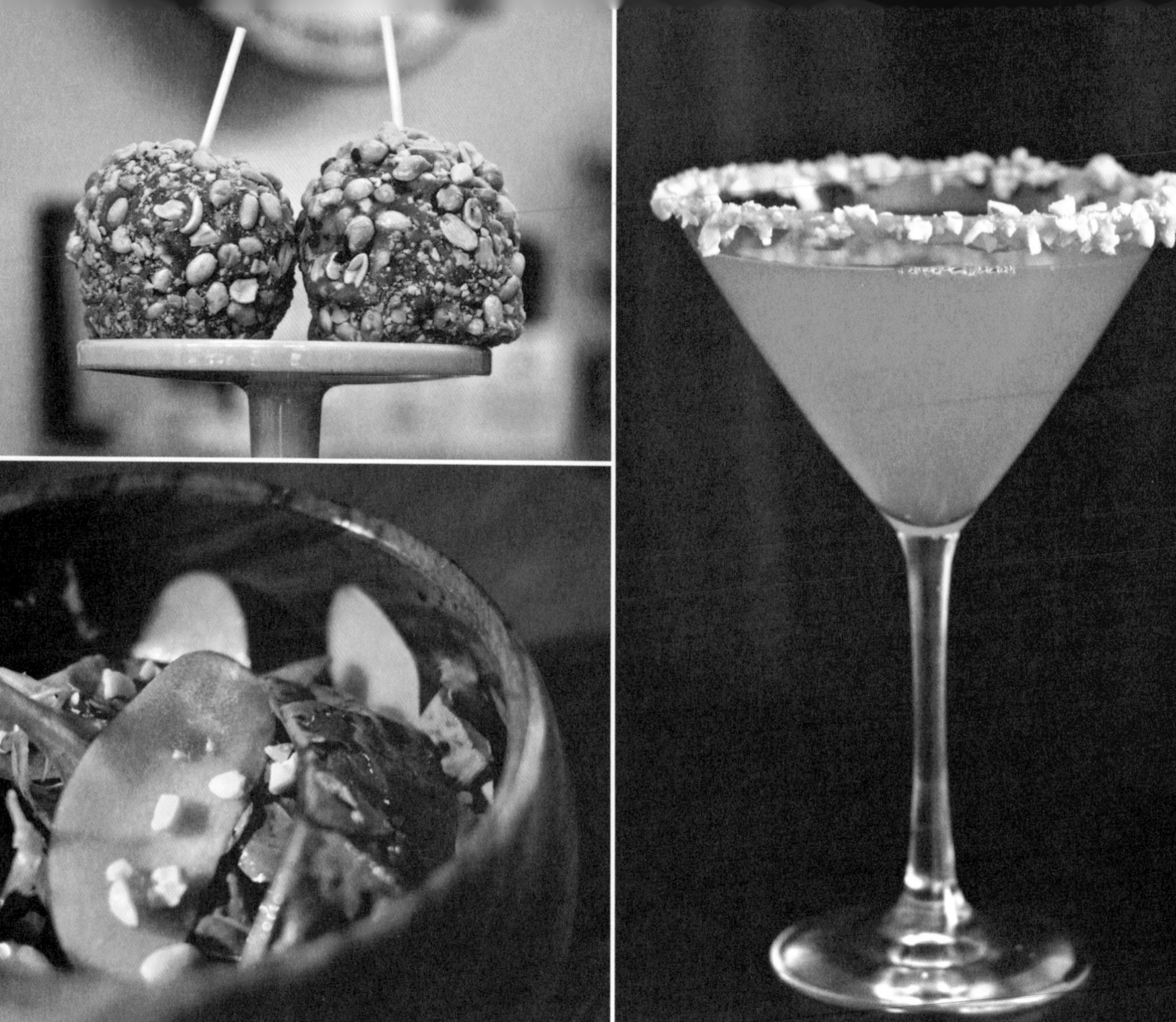

combinations of flavors that you can simply apply to create new dishes, drinks, and menus. These are some of the most extraordinary shortcuts available to creative cooks—and the intuitive starting point of most professional chefs.

Once you know which flavors combine well together, and why, you can take those flavors in different directions, confident in the knowledge that both these exact flavors and similar flavor principles are very likely to work together in other contexts.

It's easy to see how **apples + caramel + peanuts** would work together in other sweet dishes, such as baked goods, breakfast/brunch items, and desserts. It only takes a bit more thought to consider how these flavors might work together in a savory setting. What savory dishes might feature apples? Salads, for one—clearly a Waldorf salad (which is typically based on **apple + walnuts**), but other green salads often feature sliced raw **apples.** And crunchy **peanuts** can easily stand in for the crunch of croutons in a salad. The challenge then becomes to add **caramel** flavor without adding too much sweetness—which makes adding a hint of caramel (bitter + sweet) to the vinaigrette (acidity + fat) a workable solution.

And if you can make a plated savory *dish* with **apples + caramel + peanuts,** where else could you take those flavors? How about to a *glass?* Yes, you can create a Caramel Apple Martini.

And because those flavors work so well together, you don't even have to have them all in the same glass or on the same plate to enjoy them: If they all show up at the same simple *menu,* it can provide a unifying theme to your sandwich, juice, and candy.

Let's return to the question of *why* you like what you like.

Karen loves **sweet + salty** tastes together, and—come to think of it—that caramel had some nice bitterness to it. The apple brought acidity to the party. So apples + caramel + peanuts may have come to her in a sweet treat, but the **taste** was *more* than just sweet: it was **sweet + salty + bitter + sour,** all at once.

The caramel was chewy, the apple crisp, and the peanuts crunchy—together, a great combination of **textures: chewy + crisp + crunchy.**

And while the apple was raw, the caramel was cooked, so there was also a contrast of **states** at play: **raw + cooked.**

And finally, food on a stick is **fun**—the X Factor.

So, let's re-cap: We know that certain flavors go well together (e.g., **apples + caramel + peanuts**), and we know that flavors that pair well together in one context can pair well together in other contexts. We know that a balance of different **tastes** can be synergistic—as can the combination of different **textures** and even **states.** And we know that you can't underestimate the **fun** factor.

What else can we take away from **apples + caramel + peanuts?** What is similar to apples? Pears. Would **pears + caramel + peanuts** work? I'd bet money on it. What's similar to caramel? Butterscotch (which is made from brown sugar, versus caramel's white sugar). How about **apples + butterscotch + peanuts?** Definitely worth a shot! And what other nuts might work with apples + caramel? Wouldn't **apples + caramel + pecans** be worth a try?

And finally, how far can this envelope be pushed? What about **pears + butterscotch + pecans?**

All of this from the love of a simple caramel apple . . . once we start to think about it.

Now, imagine how much *you* must know based on *your* favorite childhood dish! Now, multiply that knowledge by every dish you've ever loved, and you'll understand how much information is already rattling around in that brain of yours. Being able to readily access this information is a creative goldmine—something you'll be able to tap by developing your inner senses.

CREATING DISHES, WITHOUT RECIPES

How do you evolve from simply following recipes to creating your own dishes? You don't have to be as brilliant as Einstein to be able to take advantage of his insight into **the secret of creativity: playing with combinations**.

> **Cooking is like painting or writing a song. Just as there are only so many colors or notes, there are only so many flavors. It's how you combine them that sets you apart.**
>
> —WOLFGANG PUCK, Spago (Beverly Hills)

There are endless combinations you can play with in the kitchen, including combinations of flavors, platforms, presentations, states, techniques, temperatures, and textures—and every imaginable combination of *those*. But when it comes to kitchen creativity, flavor is paramount.

So the essential question is: If combining flavors is one of the most important aspects of kitchen creativity, yet if two flavors you love won't necessarily combine well together (as Daniel Patterson points out), then what is the secret to understanding flavor compatibility?

We were hoping you'd ask.

TAKE A SHORT CUT: FLAVOR AFFINITIES

Becoming familiar with lots of **flavor pairings** and **flavor affinities** will help your creativity in the kitchen dramatically and give you the ability to walk into a kitchen and know how to throw together ingredients that will harmonize.

How can you get familiar with them? You could think about all the combinations you've enjoyed in the past, and pay closer attention to the dishes you eat from this day forward, compiling them into your own personal flavor database. You could also add your favorite combinations mentioned in Stages 1 and 2.

Or, you could stand on the shoulders of culinary giants, and learn about some of the best classic and modern flavor pairings and flavor affinities in our books *The Flavor Bible* and *The Vegetarian Flavor Bible*, which have been called "treasure troves" of this information.

Or, you could do all of the above. Countless culinary students have shown us their annotated copies of *The Flavor Bible* and/or *Culinary Artistry* featuring their personal favorite pairings in the margins after we've recommended that they track new favorites they run across.

Once you're familiar with flavor affinities, you'll have ready-and-waiting ideas to combine, based on groups of ingredients that are already famously well-paired, such as:

almonds + cinnamon + oats

bacon + baked potato + sour cream

balsamic vinegar + figs + goat cheese

basil + mozzarella + tomatoes

beans + rice + sour cream

beets + dill + sour cream

blue cheese + endive + walnuts

blueberries + lemon + ricotta

blueberries + maple syrup + orange

bread + jelly + peanut butter

broccoli + chiles + garlic

coconut + pineapple + rum

cranberries + ginger + orange

cream cheese + lox + scallions

garlic + olive oil + tomatoes

garlic + Parmesan + Romaine

maple syrup + pecans + sweet potatoes

Then, all you have to do is pick a group of affinities, and start to play with them!

I love the combination of blueberry + orange, and I created a brioche bread pudding that showcased both of those flavors—although blueberries are the star and are shown in a variety of ways including the sauce and the crystalized dehydrated blueberries. To create a brunchy theme, I used maple syrup, and to freshen and brighten up the plate I added a lemon ricotta frozen yogurt.

—**TAIESHA MARTIN**, pastry chef, Glenmere Mansion (Chester, New York)

Combinatory play seems to be the essential feature in productive thought.

—**ALBERT EINSTEIN**

Let's think about **broccoli + chiles + garlic.**

You could obviously sauté the **broccoli + garlic** in olive oil, and add a shake of **chile** pepper flakes. That would work as a side dish—or you could add some stock to turn it into a sauce for pasta and, if you wanted to take it in an **Italian** direction, garnish it with Parmesan.

If you were craving **Asian** flavors, you could wok-fry your **broccoli + garlic** with Thai **chiles,** serving it with rice and a ginger-soy sauce.

But we're getting ahead of ourselves—so let's take a step back and consider the hardest part of creating something new: figuring out where to start.

STARTING FROM SCRATCH

1. Start **where you are:** There's a **reason** behind your desire to create a dish in the first place (e.g., cravings, availability, a special occasion). And there are certain **resources** (e.g., ingredients, equipment) and/or **constraints** (e.g., budget, time) you might have. These constraints are advantages, because they help narrow your focus. Work with them as reference points.

   What's your **starting point?** For example:

   A. an ingredient (whether in-season local produce or an exotic condiment)
   B. a tool (like your shiny new backyard grill, spiralizer, or takoyaki pans)
   C. wine (such as a bottle—or two—you were gifted)

2. Your starting point will either be or suggest a **primary ingredient.**

3. Choose a compatible **secondary ingredient.**

4. Then, consider a compatible **tertiary ingredient** that will harmonize with your first two ingredients flavorwise, and contribute something of its own to the combination. (If you're feeling ambitious, feel free to add a quaternary, quinary, senary, septenary, octonary, nonary, or denary ingredient as well, taking Grant Achatz's rule on page 156 into consideration.)

Many leading chefs will stop at three major ingredients, and focus on showcasing the flavors of these three, but you can always feel free to add more—as long as the flavor of each is compatible with all of the ingredients to which you're already committed. (And bear in mind that trying to feature too many ingredients is a common pitfall, especially among less-experienced cooks.) Let's run through a handful of examples—keeping things simple for the sake of those less experienced (as more experienced or intuitive chefs can simply jump ahead if they wish):

EXAMPLE A

Start with an Ingredient

Let's say you picked up some beautiful eggplants at the market today. But now you're looking to figure out what to do with them for dinner tonight.

1. & 2. Starting point: **eggplant**

Think about all your favorite eggplant dishes. What other flavors did they feature? The ingredients that come to mind for us first are **garlic + olive oil + tomato.**

But if you were having a hard time thinking of ingredients, you could look in ***The Flavor Bible*** for recommended pairings for eggplant, and you'd find ingredients like **basil, bell peppers, bread crumbs, CHEESE, chile peppers, cilantro, cinnamon, GARLIC, ginger, LEMON, miso, OLIVE OIL, olives, ONIONS, PARSLEY, rosemary, sesame, soy sauce, tahini, thyme, TOMATOES, VINEGAR, yogurt,** and **zucchini.** (The pairings in capitals are especially popular.)

As you scan the list, imagine each of the flavors with your eggplant—and notice which one(s) make your mouth water. That's your body's wisdom at work, telling you what it wants. All of these flavors may have made your mouth water when combined with eggplant on various occasions, but on any particular day, one flavor will do it for you more than another. It may be based on what you know you have in the refrigerator. It may be based on what you had for dinner last night, and your desire for diversity. It may be based on your having just read an article on garlic and ginger as superfoods, and wanting to take advantage of their super-healthful properties sooner rather than later.

Let's say you choose **eggplant + garlic** as your starting point.

3. Secondary ingredient: **garlic**

Because those are widely used ingredients, there are any number of directions you could take them next. In our home, we often ask ourselves, "What **country** do we want to be in tonight?" That means, are we in the mood for the flavors of **Asia,** for example, or for the flavors of the **Mediterranean?**

If the answer is Asia, press yourself to be more specific: **China** or **India** or **Japan** or **Thailand?** Although there are regional commonalities, each country would take you to a more specific set of flavor affinities.

If the answer is the Mediterranean, are you craving the flavors of southern **Europe** (**France**, **Greece**, **Italy**, or **Spain**)? Or of north Africa (e.g., **Morocco**)? Or the **Middle East** (maybe **Lebanon, Turkey**)? Again, each would suggest a more specific set of flavor affinities.

It turns out that you're actually craving curry.

4. Tertiary ingredient: **curry**

   And so it becomes **eggplant + garlic + curry**. Now, are you craving Indian curry, or Thai curry?

   It turns out the idea of **Thai** curry is what makes your mouth water most—so that takes you in the direction of **jasmine rice** (versus the basmati rice that an Indian curry would have suggested). Luckily, you have a can of Thai curry paste and some coconut milk on hand. [It's a weeknight at home when you're pressed for time, so you're using a shortcut—although if you had more time, or you're cooking at a restaurant, you might decide to pull out one of David Thompson's cookbooks and make a curry paste from scratch instead.]

   So your dish becomes: **eggplant + garlic + curry paste** (turned into a sauce with **coconut milk**), which you decide to serve over **jasmine rice.**

   Your mouth is salivating again.

EXAMPLE B

Start with a Tool

So you just got a shiny new backyard grill. (We group-gifted one to a family member, so know firsthand the beauty of a moment when Boy—or Girl!—Meets Grill!)

1. Starting point: **new grill**

   But what would you like to grill on yours?

   All the wonderful things you've ever grilled—or heard about grilling—start to come to mind. You might have a childhood memory of grilling burgers in your backyard with relatives that is so vivid you'd swear you could smell the smoke rising from the burning embers. Then you might start to picture some of the less obvious ones . . . like the Halloumi cheese you've only heard about—a white cheese that is so firm and that doesn't melt, so you can actually *grill* it. Cool! Let's start there.

2. Primary ingredient: **Halloumi cheese**

   But as you've never had it before, what if you aren't sure of what else goes with the cheese? That's when a reference like ***The Vegetarian Flavor Bible*** can come in handy. If you look up **CHEESE, HALLOUMI,** you'll find a description of its flavor ("salty/sour, with notes of feta cheese and sometimes mint, and a firm, chewy, almost meaty texture that can even stand up to grilling without melting"), flavor volume ("quiet"), what it is ("Greek cheese made from sheep's or, sometimes, goat's milk"), and recommended cooking techniques ("bake, **GRILL**, sauté, sear—or serve fresh"), along with a list of dozens of

compatible ingredients, which include bell peppers, bread, **capers, lemons, mint, olive oil, parsley,** and **tomatoes.** There's also a mention of the flavor affinity of **Halloumi cheese + capers + lemon.**

Seeing the mention of Halloumi as a Greek cheese just prompted a memory of how much you enjoy the flaming saganaki at Greek restaurants, and the play of the tangy fresh-squeezed lemon juice that helps to douse the flames against the richness of the cheese.

3. Secondary ingredient: **lemon**

   You decide to go with **Halloumi cheese + lemon.**

   While you don't have any capers, you like the idea of something green on the dish to balance the whiteness of the cheese—so you opt for parsley, which will lend a fresh, bitter note to help balance the richness of the cheese:

4. Tertiary ingredient: **parsley**

   This is how your dish becomes **Halloumi cheese + lemon + parsley,** which you realize you'll either need to serve with a knife and fork and/or with a pusher like bread. Given the cheese's Cyprian/Greek associations, you're thinking warm pita would be nice, alongside that new bottle of olive oil you just picked up. Come to think of it, this would be nice with a salad, which you decide to dress with lemon juice instead of vinegar, so that everything on the plate works together: **lemon juice + lettuce + olive oil + oregano + tomatoes.**

EXAMPLE C

Start with Wine

The other day, your neighbors gave you two bottles of **Pinot Noir** that they brought back from their visit to Oregon's Willamette Valley as a thank-you for picking up their mail. You were hoping to be able to try the wine tonight, if only you could figure out what to serve alongside it.

1. Starting point: **Pinot Noir**

What goes with Pinot Noir anyway? You could think about all the dishes you've previously enjoyed with Pinot Noir, of course. Or you can turn to a reference book such as ***What to Drink with What You Eat***, which lists ideas for the dishes that would best accompany any bottle of wine (or any other beverage) under the sun. (By the way, it also does vice versa, listing wine, beer, spirit, cocktail, mocktail, and more ideas for every food and dish you can think of.)

Look up Pinot Noir in *What to Drink with What You Eat*,* and you'll find suggestions of basil, **beets**, cheese, **duck, eggplant, game birds, ginger, lamb, mushrooms and mushroom sauces**, onions, pesto, pork, **salmon, smoked meats and other food (but not fish)**, **soy sauce**, thyme, **tomatoes and tomato sauces, tuna**, and "vegetables, in general, but esp. root," among many others.

[*There's also a *What to Drink with What You Eat* app available via iTunes, which is handy during visits to wine stores or restaurants.]

FLAVOR BOUNCING

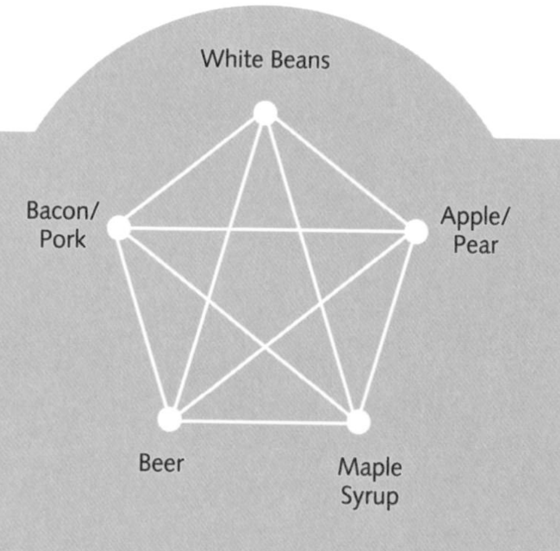

Creating a new dish can begin with choosing an ingredient you'd like to work with, then determining other ingredients that go well with that ingredient, "bouncing" around your choices to come up with a list of flavor affinities you'd like to base your dish on.

Alinea's **Grant Achatz** called this process ***flavor bouncing*** in an October 2010 lecture he gave at Harvard University. Achatz gives the best three-minute example available via YouTube (search for "flavor bouncing") on how to use the information featured in *Culinary Artistry*, *The Flavor Bible*, and *The Vegetarian Flavor Bible* to create a dish based on compatible flavors (such as, in his example, one based on **white beans + bacon/pork + apple/pear + maple syrup + beer**).

As Achatz underscores, "The only rule to this is that—starting with the focal ingredient—**whatever supporting component that you put in the puzzle has to go with every other one**."

Gabriel Kreuther on Triggers and Inspiration

When someone pushes you in the corner a little, it challenges you—and **triggers** can bring out the best in you. When we opened at the Modern [at Manhattan's Museum of Modern Art], I was asked by a guest why I, as an Alsatian chef, didn't have a dish with sauerkraut on the menu. So I started trying things out, which led to my signature dish of smoked sturgeon and sauerkraut tart....

Thinking of my childhood in Alsace can serve as a trigger. A particular wine can serve as a trigger. The start of a new season can serve as a trigger. A craving you have can serve as a trigger. The initial trigger serves as the beginning of a conversation with yourself, where you push yourself: "What about this? What about that?" And it's often a conversation between two or more people who are into food and love what they do, who throw ideas into the air together.

We create two or three new dishes a week to add to the menu, so it is always rotating. In the spring, we look forward to cooking with ramps and morels and rhubarb and strawberries. It's exciting to have new flavors in the kitchen. We talk about new dishes in our daily lineup, which takes place at 11:30 am and 4:30 pm, and which will spark ideas that feed off each other. I'm open to anything that feels in the spirit of the house. While we have offered a lot of pasta dishes [e.g., gnocchi], Alsace is never very far away, and many dishes feature onions or vinegar or Riesling and are reminiscent of my heritage.

Gabriel Kreuther

As you're observing Meatless Monday tonight, you're thinking of a vegetarian main course—maybe something with beets or mushrooms. You decide on mushrooms, for no particular reason, and find some beautiful cremini mushrooms in the market.

2. Primary ingredient: **cremini mushrooms**

   That has you thinking of Italy, which leads you to:

3. Secondary ingredient: **risotto**

   Risotto is a neutral flavor platform that allows you to showcase the mushroom flavor, and let the mushrooms and the Pinot Noir play off one another unfettered. As you have two bottles of the Pinot Noir, and know that the best way to build a bridge between the food on your plate and the wine in your glass is to add a splash of the same wine to the dish during the cooking process, you decide you'll add some to the risotto before the veg stock.

   Believing the dish could use another pop of flavor, you revisit the list of compatible ingredients with Pinot Noir and spy pesto. You've got a jar of your favorite pesto in the refrigerator, and while it's actually *multiple* ingredients—**basil + pine nuts + olive oil + Parmesan**—it functions like one in this case. You decide to stir some into the risotto at the last minute.

4. Tertiary ingredient: **pesto**

   Your doorbell rings just as you're about to sit down to dinner. Surprise: It's your nice neighbors, this time wanting to drop off yet another souvenir from their trip that they'd just unpacked. You invite them in to have a glass of wine, along with a taste of what you created from their Pinot Noir—and silently thank yourself for choosing mushrooms instead of beets, remembering that neither of them is crazy about beets. You have so much fun at this impromptu get-together that you pull the cork on the second bottle of wine.

   Yes, the creative process *can* be this simple. And it can also be a whole lot more complex. So, read on . . .

COOKING WITH *ALL* YOUR SENSES

As we go deeper into the subject of kitchen creativity, it seems like the right time to make good on our promise to introduce the concept of using the **inner senses,** which has enhanced the creativity of many of the best chefs we've ever known.

In addition to their *outer senses* (taste, smell, touch, sight, and hearing), the most creative chefs also make use of their five *inner senses* (instinct, intuition, insight, imagination, and inspiration) to inform their cooking.

The door to Phillip Foss's walk-in refrigerator at EL Ideas (Chicago)

The good news is that you already know how to use them, too. How do we know? Because you just used all of them as you read the previous examples:

- You used your **instinct** to determine which flavors made your mouth water. Your salivary glands know what you crave before you're even conscious of your mental or emotional choice. Instinct is a gut manifestation of the body's wisdom. When it's hot out, it's instinctive to reach for a cold glass of water as opposed to a hot cup of tea.

- When you opted for mushrooms instead of beets, you had no idea that your beet-averse neighbors who gave you the Pinot Noir would be stopping by. Yet your **intuition** to go with mushrooms proved useful. Intuition has been described as "facts hidden in the brain" by Nobel laureate James Watson. Sometimes you somehow know more than you know you know. You know? *That's* intuition.

- As you'd only read about Halloumi cheese and had never tasted it before, you might have initially envisioned it as akin to another cheese you've tasted, perhaps Cheddar or mozzarella. Then, when you scanned the list to discover that it was common to Greek cuisine, your mind made a connection between Halloumi and the cheese used in the flaming Greek cheese dish saganaki (often a hard yellow cheese, e.g., *graviera, kefalograviera, kefalotyri*), which led to pairing it with lemon. Making an analogy between Halloumi and saganaki involved **insight**—having an idea about the true nature of something.

- When you pictured grilling Halloumi cheese, which you'd never seen before and didn't have in front of you yet, you had to use your mind—specifically, your **imagination.** That's how you can conjure the sight and sound and smell of cheese sizzling on a grill, and can imagine it landing hot and chewy on your palate, with a bright hint of lemon juice cutting through its richness—even if you've never experienced it before.

- In every case, you had a desire to learn about the process of creating a new dish, which taps your **inspiration.** Sometimes, we're inspired by something we lack (e.g., time!) or something we do have (e.g., thyme!), but invariably inspiration's root is *desire.* We're inspired by our awareness of something we want—whether that's recreating a memory, or creating something that's never existed before.

The ability to perceive or think differently is more important than the knowledge gained.

—DAVID BOHM,
quantum physicist

We don't just passively perceive the world; we actively generate it. The world we experience comes as much from the inside-out as the outside-in.

—ANIL SETH,
cognitive scientist, in his TED talk

DEVELOPING YOUR INNER SENSES

Our reality is exactly what we *perceive* it to be.

Creativity is enhanced by using our five primary inner senses: **instinct**, **intuition**, **insight**, **imagination**, and **inspiration.** Think of each of our inner senses as tending to process the information it receives from our outer senses in a particular manner:

> **Creativity is best when it comes from an organic place. . . . Find out who you are and what makes you tick. . . . Our minds are blocked and clogged and need to be opened.**
>
> —**PHILLIP FOSS,** EL Ideas (Chicago)

- Our gut will *unify* that information, providing us with greater *immediacy* of perception through **instinct**.
- Our heart will *sift* through that information, providing us with greater *depth* of perception through **intuition**.
- Our mind will *clarify* that information, providing us with greater *precision* of perception through **insight**.
- Our merged inner and outer senses will *retain* that information, providing us with greater *breadth* of perception through **imagination**.
- And our spirit will *energize* that information, providing us with greater *intensity* of perception through **inspiration**.

Our five inner senses are our means of perceiving the world beyond that perceived by our five outer senses—a non-physical world that can be just as real, if not more so.

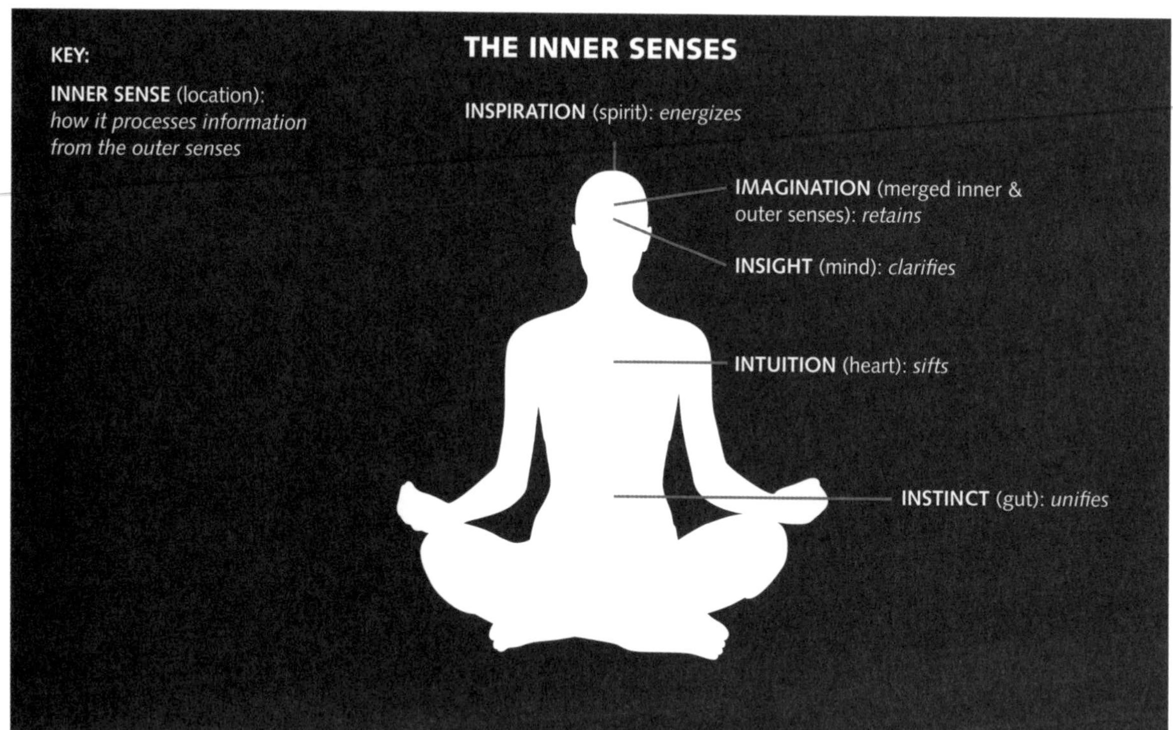

Just as our outer senses allow us to perceive the outer world, our inner senses allow us to perceive our inner world, and its desires and imaginings. These shape the way we perceive the outer world, often subconsciously or unconsciously, and the more we make that awareness conscious, the more we can bring to our creative efforts.

If you believe that something is real only if you can perceive it with your outer senses, consider: What about the symphonies that Beethoven could hear in his head before he ever sat down at a piano to play them? What about the images that Picasso was driven to paint? What about a dish we dreamed about that was so real we could still taste it on our lips when we awoke?

Who looks outside, dreams; who looks inside, awakes.

—CARL JUNG

While strolling through the greenmarket on a crisp autumn day in search of ideas for something to cook (**inspiration**), your eyes set upon the first-picked apples of the season, and you notice your mouth watering and feel a flutter of excitement (**instinct**). You walk over to the apples and smell them, and their aroma makes you think of your visit to an apple cider mill, and how much the person you visited with would enjoy it if you turned the apples into a dessert for them (**intuition**). You remember the smells there of apple cider doughnuts being fried, and caramel apples dipped in chopped peanuts, and from out of nowhere an image surfaces of a caramelized apple tarte Tatin you'd read about in a novel (**imagination**). Suddenly, you make the connection between the **apples + caramel** of a caramel apple on a stick and the same flavors in a tarte Tatin, and realize the flavor of **peanuts** is complementary with both (**insight**). You start to imagine ways to incorporate peanuts into your dessert, whether through serving your warm sautéed apple "doughnut pudding" (bread pudding made from day-old doughnuts) with a scoop of peanut ice cream, or with a peanut sauce, or with an accent of candied peanuts, or even a dusting of peanut powder (back to **imagination**).

INSTINCT

Marcel Boulestin (1878–1943), a French chef described in *The Guardian* as the most imaginative and liberating food writer of his time, observed that "Cooking is not chemistry. It is an art. It requires **instinct** and taste rather than exact measurements."

INSTINCT: an innate, typically fixed pattern of behavior in response to certain stimuli

Instinct is the body's gut-level wisdom, which is based on a subconscious knowledge of all our experiences, of all we've ever learned and felt.

We had stopped following our natural INSTINCTS and trusting that our memories are valuable enough to shape our daily lives at the restaurant.

—RENÉ REDZEPI, Noma (Copenhagen), on burnout

Our instincts are biological or physiological impulses that do not involve conscious thought. Neuroscientists have found that there are actually three "brains" in the body: in the head, in the heart (our cardiac nervous system),

Creativity is an art form. It might be something you can't teach. You can teach the skills, and you can practice them, but there's also an INSTINCTIVE nature to it.

—AMANDA COHEN, Dirt Candy (New York City)

and in the gut (our enteric nervous system). Instinct correlates most closely with so-called "gut intelligence."

One of the functions of instinct is to unify the information we take in from our outer senses, which could otherwise be too overwhelming to process sequentially. This can be thought of as a single "common sense" that allows us to take immediate action, especially in the face of challenges to our safety and security.

Every animal has instincts, such as the maternal instinct often exhibited toward one's offspring, or the "fight or flight" response to a perceived threat. When it comes to food, human beings have an instinctive attraction to sweetness (e.g., the taste of breast milk) and aversion to bitterness (a taste often found in poisons). Many cooks have lost touch with their natural instincts, given the now-widespread availability of ingredients from around the world year-round—including asparagus in December and tomatoes in February. The movement toward seasonal and local cooking is one powerful way that chefs are reconnecting with their instincts.

Instincts can arise in response to challenges, but you can also access them proactively: Scan your body for information—whether sweaty palms, goosebumps, "butterflies" in your stomach, flushed cheeks, or a salivating palate, all of which can guide you to the wisdom of your instincts.

One particular challenge of instinct is that some of these signals can be misread by our primitive, "reptilian" brains as fear—leading to inappropriately hostile or otherwise heated reactions. However, many are simply signs of the body's readiness to take action; as we mature, we develop our ability to choose to *respond* versus *react* to any stimulus.

INTUITION

The author of the *New York Times* bestseller *Practical Intuition,* Laura Day distinguishes between **intuition** and instinct. "On some level, instinct is based on your experience and knowledge, whereas intuition is really those out-of-the-blue flashes that direct you to a need that hasn't occurred yet or one that isn't apparent."

INTUITION: a natural ability or power that makes it possible to know something without any proof or evidence

If instinct is believed to be based in the gut, intuition is thought to be based in the heart, or in the connection between the gut, the heart, and the head. Intuition is a balancing system that has the power to alert cooks to risks and opportunities alike.

Cooking is about interacting with ingredients. If you TALK TO YOUR INGREDIENTS, they will always tell you a story.

—JOSÉ ANDRÉS, ThinkFoodGroup (Washington, D.C.)

There's a part of you that's much smarter than you are, and the smartest people learn to consult that part of themselves. . . .The number-one thing you can do [to enhance your creativity] is be in tune with and guided by your INTUITION.

—**MICHAEL GELB,** author of *How to Think Like Leonardo da Vinci*

You need intuition that's trained like an Olympic athlete. That's one of the strongest forces that we have in our cooking.

—**RENÉ REDZEPI,** Noma (Copenhagen)

Laura Day explains, "What an artist experiences and wants to put into the world is a spark. But sometimes chefs, like other artists, fall short in paying too much attention to that internal experience and not using those same senses to experience what someone else needs and wants, and what will be experienced by the guest consuming a dish. The most successful chefs seem to use that same exquisite attention to what they're creating to extend that perception to what the guest consuming it needs to receive and how it needs to be presented to have that effect."

The best chefs use intuition to gain a deeper understanding of their guests **and** their ingredients. How? Patrick O'Connell of the Inn at Little Washington says, "It's simple: **Be the guest. Get into their minds and heads.** Eat the whole dish. Eat the whole meal."

All great achievements of science must start from INTUITIVE knowledge. I believe in intuition and inspiration. . . .

At times I feel certain I am right while not knowing the reason.

—**ALBERT EINSTEIN**

Lars Williams, who formerly cooked at Copenhagen's Noma, uses his intuition to let the natural taste of ingredients guide him to how to "slowly twist and shape them into something else." The same intuitive approach leads chefs like José Andrés and Ghaya Oliveira and many others to talk to—and listen to—their ingredients.

INSIGHT

While **insight** is most associated with transformative thoughts, it paradoxically often results from *not* thinking. It's that "Aha!" moment when you realize two seemingly unconnected things are connected. It occurs when you observe a pattern that you didn't notice before—such as my own realization that all my favorite salmon dishes involved a "warming" ingredient such as horseradish or mustard, plus a "cooling" element such as cucumber or dill.

During insight meditation [aka vipassana, a form of Buddhist meditation that focuses on mind/body sensations through the mindfulness of each moment], I get INSIGHTS.

—**RICK BAYLESS,** Topolobampo (Chicago), who has regularly practiced yoga for two decades

Practical Intuition author Laura Day distinguishes insight from intuition: "While intuition will give you that first word of a sentence, **insight almost puts a period at the end of your sentence, so you can work on the next sentence.**"

INSIGHT: the power or act of seeing into a situation; self-generated realization

Creative insights can be spurred by recalling similar situations to address novel ones, or by the use of the mental tool of analogies. For example, Roundhouse chef Terrance Brennan realized that the luxurious mouthfeel of the broth for his pork ramen was largely a function of its pork fat. So when his vegetarian "kohlramen" (made with spiralized kohlrabi "noodles") was clearly missing something, he realized that he needed to add a high-fat ingredient or two, discovering that a combination of white miso and cooked pureed cashews, which he emulsifies right before serving, gives it a similar richness.

Rather than pursue it relentlessly, you must occasionally take a break from whatever you're working to create. Go for a run. Take a shower. Listen to classical music. Go to sleep. During these activities, while your brain is doing "nothing," it can do some of its most important work of all: "incubating," or processing, all the inputs it's taken in. Eureka—new connections are made, resulting in insights which drive creative ideas.

I might dream about tomatoes, but even in my sleep my mind will sense whether they are ripe August tomatoes or whether they are high-acid, low-sugar June tomatoes, which aren't at their best with basil and are better with tarragon.

—**TRAVIS SWIKARD,** Boulud Sud (New York City)

"I'll do silent walking meditations," Rick Bayless told us. "If I have a problem, I'll go for a walk and come back with a solution."

To think creatively is first to feel. The desire to understand must be whipped together with sensual and emotional feelings and blended with intellect to yield imaginative INSIGHT.

—ROBERT AND MICHÈLE ROOT-BERNSTEIN, *Sparks of Genius*

To achieve your peak creativity, it's important to meditate or do tai chi or another practice daily, in order to give yourself time for incubation on a daily basis.

—MICHAEL GELB, author of *How to Think Like Leonardo da Vinci*

Amanda Cohen of Dirt Candy in New York City shares, **"I'll get some of my best ideas during those quiet moments like lying in bed, or on my walk to work.** While I'd work on a dish at the restaurant, I'd go home and discover that that's a part of the process, too. I'll be lying in bed after reading a novel, and after I turn off the lights but before I fall asleep, an image will come into my mind of a new way of doing something. The next day I'll come in with a new approach."

She's not alone in her discovery of the power surrounding bedtime. Researchers note that insights can come during REM sleep (the time of our most vivid dreaming, which connects brain regions that are unconnected during conscious states), when the brain continues to be very active in the regions that are key to attaining insights and creative thinking. To be more creative, in addition to making sure you get enough sleep, use your sleep time productively: **Set an intention before falling asleep** that will help you access information for your dish, your menu, or the solution to another kitchen creativity challenge. When you awaken, write down whatever comes to mind—images, words, remnants of a dream. If the answer you were seeking isn't obvious, look for the connection between whatever comes to mind and the intention you set.

If you had no **imagination**, it would be impossible to create anything new. Imagination is where information from our outer and inner senses is retained and merged with fantasy.

IMAGINATION: the ability to experience in your mind something you have not seen or experienced; the ability to think of new things

In creative work, **imagination** is more important than knowledge. For knowledge is limited to all we now know and understand, while imagination embraces the entire world, and all there ever will be to know and understand.

—ALBERT EINSTEIN

As James Beard wrote in *Delights and Prejudices*: **"The ability to recall a taste sensation**, which I think of as 'taste memory,' is a God-given talent, akin to perfect pitch, which **makes your life richer if you possess it."** The same is true of fantasy. Momofuku Milk Bar pastry chef Christina Tosi credits her love of cooking to "the combination of an unhealthy relationship with cookie dough and the love of wandering through the creative space in my mind/imagination."

Pablo Picasso's dictum that "Art is a lie that makes us realize the truth" came to mind during our visit with José Andrés's creative team—including Rick Billings and Joe Raffa—when we witnessed the complete deconstruction and then reconstruction of a single cauliflower floret (see page 168). Thanks to ThinkFoodGroup's imaginative undertaking, we've never looked at a cauliflower floret the same way again.

Creativity is applied imagination.

—SIR KEN ROBINSON, author of *Out of Our Minds: Learning to Be Creative*

One of the functions of imagination is to retain (via memory) the information taken in from the outer senses, which it can transform into new images and creations. In this way, imagination serves as the key conduit between our outer and inner worlds. Our imagination is what allows us to have inner experiences of our outer senses—that is, to see without using our eyes, to hear without using our ears, to taste without using our tongues, to smell without using our noses, to touch without using our hands.

Chefs can come up with some of their most creative ideas away from the kitchen—sometimes with the taste of a sea breeze on their lips. José Andrés recalls, **"I was sitting on a beach in southern Spain when I came up with the idea for my salt-air margarita**. I never liked my margarita with salt on the rim. So I came up with the idea to make a sea water foam on the surface of the margarita, making it the most delicious margarita ever [blending **kosher salt + lime + water + Sucro,** the powdered emulsifier, or soy lecithin]. It is now our most popular drink."

IMAGINATION and originality are the most important aspects of cooking.

—DOMINIQUE CRENN,
Atelier Crenn (San Francisco)

. . . Imagination, that capacity to link mind and body, intellect and intuition.

—ROBERT AND MICHÈLE ROOT-BERNSTEIN, *Sparks of Genius*

Chefs' experiences with imagination are often the result of combining dissimilar subjects (the culinary world blended with aspects of other interests, ranging from dance to jewelry design to linguistics) or thinking paradoxically. Chefs create new ideas for dishes and for the restaurant experience as they explore not only what *is,* but what *can be*. They imagine it in all its perfection, brainstorming possibilities that might raise additional questions or challenges.

Sometimes the world is simply ready for a particular idea. Rick Bayless shares, "Elizabeth Gilbert [author of *Eat Pray Love* and *Big Magic*] has put forth the idea that **ideas are out there looking for people to grab hold of them**—and I really believe this is the case. There are certain ideas whose time has come, with many people thinking about them simultaneously. When the time is right, they happen. There are chefs in Mexico reinventing classic dishes in the same way. And I think the zeitgeist is such that when our culture is ready for an idea, it finds a way to manifest."

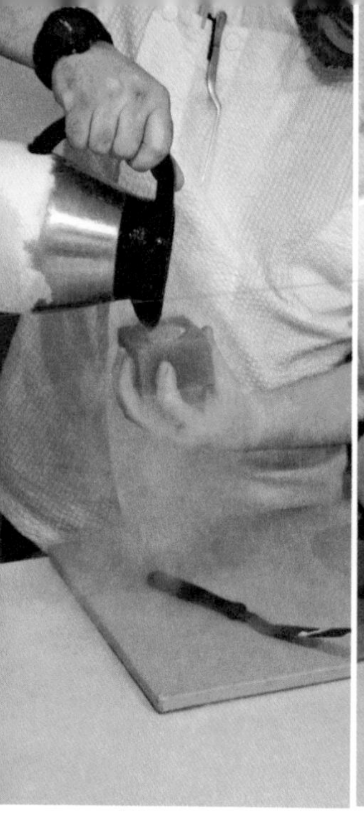

Rick Billings of ThinkFoodGroup creates a cauliflower floret

INSPIRATION

It's easy to do nothing. But to do something, to take action, requires a motive. Every creative act is set into motion by an intention. That's **inspiration.**

INSPIRATION: the process of feeling spurred to take action—especially to create something

Even chefs who cook from loftier inspirations at work will other times cook from sheer need. **"Cooking at home is like an Iron Chef challenge,"** confesses Animal's Vinny Dotolo. "Against the clock—here we go! Nobody shopped, and it's 4:30 pm and the kid's got to leave by 5:30 pm, so it starts with opening the cabinets and seeing what's there."

I always say I could find inspiration in a gas station in Gary, Indiana. It is all about how you open your mind.

—CARRIE NAHABEDIAN, Naha and Brindille (Chicago)

Inspiration can evolve over time. Ink's Michael Voltaggio witnessed his own motivation shift from extrinsic (trophies) to intrinsic (the challenge of making vegetables taste delicious) over the course of many years, starting in childhood. "I was the pickiest eater growing up—I ate nothing," he recalls. "My brother [Bryan] had all these sports trophies, so Mom had to bribe me with a trophy: If I ate my dinner every night for a month, I'd get a 'Champion Eater' trophy.

"[Cooking professionally] forced me to start tasting things that I didn't like, but I had to cook for people who did like them," he recalls. "I didn't like any vegetables—broccoli, cauliflower, any of them—so if I could make them in a way that

I liked it, then people who actually liked them would love them. So **I learned to challenge myself by cooking things I didn't personally like.** My first attempt was to try to make it not taste like itself. Then, I started to try to make it taste more like itself. When you overcook broccoli, it gets mushy and that weird green color, and that's what I had been turned off by. But if you shave the green parts off a floret, cook it very quickly, emulsifying just a little bit of cream into it as a puree, it was like tasting broccoli for the first time. I finally learned that it wasn't the vegetable I didn't like, but the [preparation] that I hadn't liked."

Without passion, all the skill in the world won't lift you above craft. Without skill, all the passion in the world will leave you eager but floundering. Combining the two is the essence of the creative life.

—**TWYLA THARP,** choreographer and author of *The Creative Habit*

[In general], mindfulness is the most important part of finding INSPIRATION. Being aware of smells, light, and memories.

—**HESTON BLUMENTHAL,** The Fat Duck (England)

David Levi of Vinland in Portland, Maine, sources 100 percent of his hyper-local menu from New England, if not Maine itself, including clams, lobsters, maple syrup, and sea vegetables (e.g., dulse, Irish moss, nori, wakame)—eschewing olive oil, citrus fruits, cane sugar, and even chocolate. Anyone who would imagine his inspirations to be limited would be mistaken. "Having a 100-percent local restaurant has been incredibly liberating," says Levi. "Because we have such a strict form, we can take our **inspiration** from wherever we want."

Chefs' inspirations can come from the environment they're cooking in—down to aspects of their own kitchen. In the case of Curtis Duffy's kitchen at Chicago's Grace, that much-photographed kitchen includes a wall full of colorful jarred spices. "My spice rack was never intended to be an aesthetic thing," Duffy admits. "If I have to open a cabinet, and I have to look behind all these things to find what I'm looking for, that's inefficient. If I see everything that's there as a palette, then I might get inspired to use something other than what I was reaching for. **Everything in view has the ability to inspire you.** Maybe you're reaching for the coriander seed and think, 'You know what—this black cardamom would be awesome in this dish.' So it kind of takes you out of your usual pattern."

Curtis Duffy

The word *inspiration* comes from the idea of "breathing in" life, that which makes us feel alive (love). As the 14th-century Persian poet Hafez advised,

> **I am inspired by travel. . . . When I get an idea, I write it down on whatever piece of paper I have nearby.**
>
> **When I fly, I seem to have the most inspiration. . . . [At home], I carve out a spot conducive to creativity—calm, quiet, and clutter-free. I look at my list and see what the menu needs.**
>
> —ERIC RIPERT, Le Bernardin (New York City)

"Stay close to everything that makes you glad you are alive." We do this by acting on our inspirations.

Our inspirations can be as simple as wanting to showcase a particular ingredient, technique, or bottle of wine. Among professional chefs and mixologists, inspirations range widely.

"I have described myself as an eccentric person," admits Ghaya Oliveira, executive pastry chef at Daniel. **"I am a former ballerina, so everywhere I go, I see choreography in my head.** . . . I'll notice the choreography of people arriving for work, and how it changes during service. I find noticing movement inspiring."

Oliveira's desserts have been inspired by a wide range of influences. **"It could be seeing a dress on a beautifully made-up woman on the street,** or smelling a perfume. It could be seeing colors, shapes, textures, fashion, art, architecture, or even nature," she says. "I like watching the fashion shows [e.g., on YouTube] of Hermès and Yves Saint Laurent and Dior and Chanel, which might make me wonder, 'How can I put a veil on a dessert?'

Ghaya Oliveira

I love watching movies, and was influenced by *Moulin Rouge* to create a Coupe Glacé with the flavors of **absinthe + blood orange + coffee**. The plate was covered with tuile that was wavy like the dresses, and a gelée that was [reminiscent of] can-can dresses."

Oliveira loves the inspiration that comes from discovering new ingredients. "I'm very inspired by chocolate from Madagascar, Africa, and South America, so I explored chocolate in Vietnam, which is quite different. I ended up smoking sandalwood chips, and adding the chocolate. When I smelled it, it took me immediately back to my grandmother's house, when I was young, and opening her closet with her jewelry and perfume—it smelled like the velvet in there. It was such a familiar smell to me.

"I like to go back to my childhood memories. Growing up, I ate a lot of strawberries, which we would eat warm from the sun, with cool whipped cream and drops of geranium water, when we had it, or orange blossom water.

"I'll search the Internet, and visit perfume websites, like CreedBoutique.com [which lists the Top Notes, Middle Notes, and Base Notes for its various perfumes]. I'll study [seventh-generation perfumer Erwin Creed's] components, which often include flowers—as I love floral notes, such as jasmine, geranium, and orange blossom, in desserts," she says.

Q: What is creativity?

A: The relationship between a human being and the mysteries of inspiration.

—**ELIZABETH GILBERT,** *Big Magic*

INSPIRATION = IDEAS. So until this world is devoid of inspiration, there will never be a shortage of ideas or passion or enthusiasm from Milk Bar.

—CHRISTINA TOSI, Milk Bar (New York City)

Chef Ana Sortun and Farmer Chris Kurth on Keeping Farm-to-Table "All in the Family"

Ana Sortun [on how being married to a farmer changed her perspective]: As a chef [at Cambridge's **Oleana**], my orientation was toward the whim of wanting to cook something. Now, I focus more on the ingredients. My creativity is more seasonal, too. I'll be inspired by what's growing on the farm at that time. It's been a learning curve for me.

The farm teaches us responsibility for seasonality, freshness, quality, standards. Once you've had [farm-fresh] strawberries, you're not going to want grocery store strawberries anymore. You get spoiled. It goes from being a curiosity to being a necessity, as you're introduced to something you learn you can't live without.

The produce teaches you. Just cutting into a watermelon, you learn so much from sound, sight, and smell. There's an "unzipping" sound a ripe watermelon makes as you slice through it. The flavor of fresh-dug potatoes is like nothing else. **Once you know what fresh produce *should* be, you have a better sense of what it *can* be—which affects creativity.**

Teaching quality to my cooks is easy. You can set down a croissant from Au Bon Pain next to a croissant from the best bakery in Paris, and they'll be able to taste the difference for themselves. They figure it out.

Receiving a CSA box is stressful for many of our members. It represents work—food that they need to cut and store and find a way to use. Some tell us it's so beautiful they just want to keep it on the counter and look at it. But then they're tasting the difference.

When customers buy our produce at the farmers' market, what gets them there in the first place is usually their desire to eat better, or to support local farmers—because they've been told that "fresh" and "local" are better. But what *keeps* them there? Flavor.

I've enjoyed learning more of **the nuances of flavor**—like the way garlic evolves from green garlic to garlic scapes to fresh garlic. They **give you more to work with, and open up new levels of creativity.**

Chris Kurth: Seeing our [**Siena Farms**] produce handled by professional chefs and home cooks inspires us to try to reach new levels of quality.

I remember participating in a Chardonnay festival in Westport, Massachusetts, and getting our mesclun mix ready for the salad for Saturday night's dinner. I remember being especially proud of the beautiful colors and textures in the mix I'd put together. But Ana helped me realize that the proportion of mustard greens I'd included made the mix particularly mustardy/spicy—a proportion I realized only in hindsight would have been better if the greens were going to be used wilted instead of fresh. That was eye-opening.

The two most important aspects of what we do are growing produce and marketing produce. I used to be predominantly focused on the first aspect—issues of soil fertility, seeding, cultivation, and irrigation—until I came to realize that the second aspect is 51 percent of the equation. I used to think "marketing" was a bad word, but I learned that we had to focus on the customer experience, including customer service, just as much as, or more than, the "product" itself.

Ana: I couldn't do what I do if the farm didn't exist, just as Chris feels he couldn't do what he does if the restaurants didn't exist.

Beyond the emphasis on the industry problem of food waste and the hunger issue, I've come to realize how this stuff is precious. Every item represents an investment of time and resources, so I want to use every part of it.

The farm definitely drives our specials. I like getting a sense of what's going to be in season for a month, versus what's going to be in season for a week. That issue is still a learning curve for chefs, who still don't fully understand what goes on in the fields. If it doesn't rain, broccoli isn't going to be as available. And our chefs are at the point that if they can't get *our* broccoli, they don't want just *any* broccoli instead. And if you think it's hot because the air-conditioner isn't working right and it's in the low 70s, imagine a farmer in 95-degree weather, with no shade, bending over and picking things in the dirt.

Chris: We have an intern who's just graduating from Johnson & Wales, starting here versus in a restaurant kitchen. I think that's a good sign that chefs are starting to realize that flavor begins at the farm.

We lost our tomatoes two years ago to a blight...

Ana:...and our customers were complaining, "Why are there no tomatoes on the menu?" That challenged our creativity. We would pick green, unripe tomatoes, and find ways to use them. We'd pickle them, or bread and fry them. We'd make green tomato velouté, or green tomato and nectarine salads, or breaded-and-baked green tomato Parmesan with a green tomato sauce. At our restaurants [inspired by the Mediterranean and the Middle East], we call anything that's stuffed "dolmas," and we'd stuff baked green tomatoes to serve as "dolmas."

Chris [on what he wishes all chefs knew about working with farmers]: Look for the silver linings in the challenges of working closely with farmers.

Expect there to be gaps in the harvest, and don't get stumbled by the challenges.

There will be surprises and spontaneity. Moments come and go quickly, so stay light on your feet to capture them.

We sold some baby turnips to one "farm-to-table" restaurant, and they ordered more the following week—but then sent them all back to us because the turnips were bigger. Well, *yeah*—those turnips were *a week* bigger! Turnips grow.

Ana [on what she wishes all chefs knew about working with farmers]: Know that the quality is worth it. In that instance, that restaurant could have cut the turnips in half!

Ana Sortun and Chris Kurth

THE WHOWHATWHENWHEREWHY&HOW OF CREATING A DISH

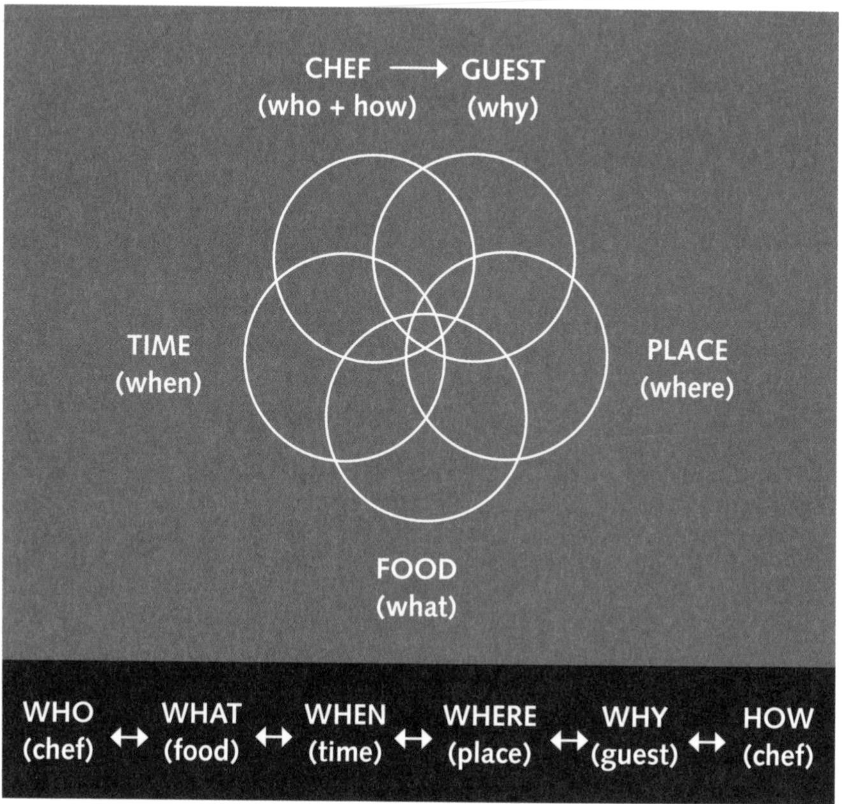

> **There is no such thing as creating food for the sake of being creative. Guests have to understand it and be able to relate to it. It might taste good, but the guest has to connect to it in order to like it.**
>
> —PATRICK O'CONNELL, The Inn at Little Washington (Washington, Virginia)

A great dish, or a great meal, is most often the result of a dance between the **chef,** his or her **guest,** and the **food** itself—set to the tempo of a particular **time** and **place.** But it all begins, and ends, with the chef.

Culinary artists bring their individual expertise to their medium of expression: food. But chefs don't create in a vacuum. Because food is ingested, the guest's preferences and aversions become paramount. And the food itself plays a role, as ingredients' locality, seasonality, and maturity are subject to their own life rhythms.

Beyond this, there is an integrative role the chef can play, of pulling all the elements of the dish and the moment together. The late Judy Rodgers of San Francisco's beloved Zuni Café told us that she tried to encourage her cooks to develop and use their own intuition when cooking, leaving them instructions like "Do this, this, and this for the soup, and when you get it this far, look out the window and see what the weather is and decide what the soup wants to be."

Every dish starts with a goal: Why are you making this dish? What is it you hope to achieve? Any dish you're creating will benefit by thinking through its context: the who, what, when, where, why, and how.

WHO

Who is doing the *cooking*? Consider the chef: you. What are your available resources? What are your constraints, such as budget or time? What are your capabilities, your weaknesses, your preferences, your aversions, your needs and desires?

Rustic Canyon's Jeremy Fox says, "If you've only worked for one chef, you only know one chef's version of creativity—and when you've only worked in fine dining, you only know about certain foods and don't know anything about others. For example, I don't know how to make stuffing. I don't know how to make 'regular' food entirely well, but my wife can and she is an excellent cook. I can make fancy things, but I don't really know simple, honest food."

As Patrick O'Connell of the Inn at Little Washington has observed, "A dish represents the distillation of a chef's entire being." The better you know yourself, the more of yourself you'll be able to bring to your cooking.

My creativity is a function of who I am. Your creativity is a function of *your* past and *your* present and how *you* see tomorrow.

—**MARC AUMONT,** pastry chef, Gabriel Kreuther (New York City)

Cook the food *you* truly believe in.

—**GAVIN KAYSEN,** Spoon & Stable (Minneapolis)

Patrick O'Connell on Role Playing

There's a big difference between a youthful palate and a mature palate. The tragedy is that you have to be young enough to withstand the physical rigors of being in the kitchen for 13 hours a day slamming pans—but [at that age] you can't easily get into the heads of a 50- or 60-year-old clientele who's not coming because they're starving, and don't regard generosity as how much you can fit onto a plate. So, the cooks' palates and the clients' palates are at odds very often, and they can't find the bridge.

So, I am the client. I am [my cooks'] worst nightmare of a client, and they have to watch me eat the food, too. A client has to look good while they're eating it. The first curse of any cook under 28 is putting too much food on a plate, and the second is making food that's awkward to eat—julienned vegetables that are cut four inches long on a mandoline, that hang out of a client's mouth when they take a forkful.

Right now, young cooks are into pork. And smoke. And the minute you introduce smoke into a dish in the assertive manner in which they're introducing it, you destroy the palate for [wine or] anything else. It isn't something you can clear your palate of quickly. So that isn't taken into consideration with their love for smoking—so they want to smoke everything. And I fight them on that.

Every day in my kitchen, I have to get the blindfold out. And they'll bring me a dish that they're working on. They're all working on something, which is as it should be. We used to say, "What do you think this is—a school?" Of course it's a school. Their newness keeps them learning, and keeps me learning.

[One cook] has Paul Bocuse's cookbook, and every night he cooks me a dish from the book for my dinner. And every night I say, "This isn't the recipe." And he'll admit, "Well, no, I kind of changed it." In one instance, [he] had never cooked a rabbit before. We had rabbit on our menu in 1978. Then you realize how little [young cooks today] know—and that you take for granted everything that you've seen. So I critique the rabbit, and suddenly I'm right back there as a youth, through his eyes, and experience seeing it for the first time, and making the correction.

Whenever a cook gives me something shitty, which is about twice a week, I'll say, "I want a little country club salad, 1964." And sometimes I put a price on it: "$12.95." Or I say, "Italian restaurant. $12.95." In other words, don't make it fancy. Don't try to go to France through Asia.

WHAT (FOOD)

What food shall be served? What ingredients and other resources are available to work with?

Even the food has a "say" in the process of its own preparation. It is available and edible and ripe, or it's not. It has its own intrinsic characteristics that will suggest other ingredients or techniques to bring it to its zenith.

"Cooking with **David [Kinch**, at Manresa] allowed me to get in touch with more creativity," says Rustic Canyon's Jeremy Fox. "It was local and organic—but to an extreme, because we were growing the vegetables as well. As [Manresa's] chef de cuisine, it was my responsibility to use these things. Given this approach to creativity, it was much less about planning dishes conceptually in advance. We would not know what was going to arrive. David would simply unload the car, and that was what we had and we had to use it. It definitely makes you work harder.

With every meal, a cook is given a blank canvas and another chance to create a masterpiece.

—PATRICK O'CONNELL,
The Inn at Little Washington
(Washington, Virginia)

"The first year of the garden, the yield was pretty low. So if we got a handful of leeks, in David's mind these were '$600 leeks,' so we'd better use every part of them, whether they were perfect or not; and these were '$7,000 squashes,' so let's do them right.

"With David, it was a matter of tapping into creativity—creativity I did not know I had. Some people say, 'You can't teach creativity,' but going through this process repeatedly made me feel maybe you could. It is like exercising; if you use [that muscle], it gets easier and things happen more easily.

If I think of apples, I know all of the ways I've seen them in the past—such as a compote, sliced, in a tarte Tatin. So I'll ask myself, "What's different?" I'll put an apple on a piece of parchment in the middle of the table, and HAVE A CONVERSATION WITH IT: "Let's do something together!" We'll push each other to go to a new place together.

—GHAYA OLIVEIRA,
pastry chef, Daniel (New York City)

"It was my job to cook for the vegetarians, and we had these big plates and I would do 30 different vegetables on the plate. It was called a Rock Out, because I was just rocking out. When I cook vegetables, it is not about health food. After being obsessed with cooking meat, that informed me on how to cook vegetables. I am trying to use every part of the vegetable and achieve a lot of flavors. These are not light dishes because I try to get as much fat into them as any other dish. From meat cooking, I applied roasting techniques, and I also tried to run the gamut of using all the textures, from crunchy to creamy."

BE THE INGREDIENT. How would you like to be treated if you were fennel, or whatever you're cooking? Think about it: What does this ingredient want me to do? The ingredients are children, you're their parent, and how you raise them will dictate how happy they'll be. It's emotional, mental, and spiritual.

—**PHILLIP FOSS,** EL Ideas (Chicago)

In dining, what's in the glass is often as important as what's on the plate, especially when you're a chef who also happens to be a sommelier—and respecting the creativity already in the bottle. "I like to learn and grow, which is why I did the Master Sommelier program," says FLX Table's Christopher Bates, who is one of 147 master sommeliers in the United States—and perhaps the only one who is also a gifted professional chef. "The ability to cook and make wine [as he does at Element Winery] at the same time is great for me. Loic [Leperlier, chef at the Point resort] and I wanted to offer two different menus while we were cooking together at the Hotel Fauchère [a Relais & Châteaux property in Milford, Pennsylvania, 90 minutes outside New York City]: a culinary menu and a wine menu. The wine menu would be all about the wine, with the stupidest, simplest dish cooked for it. If it were Champagne, it would be bread soup with mushrooms. No fancy dots of garnish, capers, or hibiscus. Here is a bottle of Chardonnay with a lobster with butter....By the way, thinking about what tastes great in wine will give you ideas for [what will pair well in] food. 'Olive, pepper, smoke, bacon, and meat is what Syrah tastes like. Strawberry, blood, and lavender is what Châteauneuf-du-Pape tastes like."

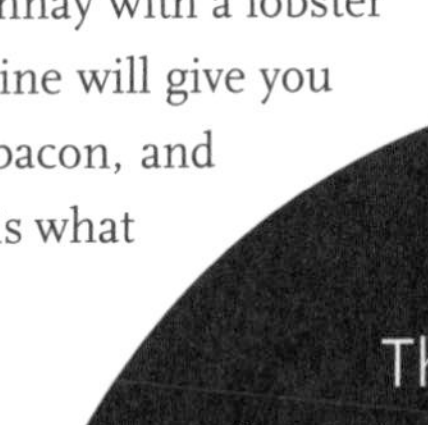

Christopher Bates

WHEN (TIME)

When is the food being served? Seasonality drives great cooking, but the best chefs take into consideration not only the time of year but also the time of day, and the particularities of that particular day and time—whether an unseasonably cool summer night, or an unseasonably warm winter morning.

"A Japanese meal is a communion with nature," award-winning author Hiroko Shimbo told us. From his travels and particularly through his time in Japan, Michael Anthony developed his own sensibility about the almost sacred importance of expressing time (When) and place (Where) through food, which he sees as inextricably linked.

The Japanese attention to nature can be found in our inspiration from the changing of the seasons....Natural ingredients and flavors can have a spectacular place on the plate. It's courageous to allow the natural flavors to be comfortable.

—**MICHAEL ANTHONY,** Gramercy Tavern and Untitled (New York City)

"Because of the stark design of this restaurant [Untitled], some might see it as intimidating, so we want to give a feeling of warmth in our welcome. Now [one year in], we've got flowers growing outside, which is a visual warm hug. This place was built to capture light and manage sound, and some might find the minimalism cold. But our restaurant has the same goal as the design of the space: to provide **a unique expression of this time and place,**" Anthony says. "Because of the minimalistic approach, we probably under-manipulate our food versus other restaurants. We want guests to recognize the ingredients, and to provide immediate approachability. When we design dishes, it's as a flavor experience."

My creative process always starts with THE SEASON.

—**LEE WOLEN**, Boka (Chicago)

Some chefs have fun breaking with convention regarding the serving of particular dishes at certain times of day. Jon Shook and Vinny Dotolo serve a signature breakfast pizza at Jon & Vinny's in Los Angeles, which features **egg + olive oil + Parmesan + red onion + rosemary + Yukon Gold potatoes.** At the Inn at Little Washington, Patrick O'Connell serves a signature breakfast *soufflé*, which combines currants + oatmeal + warm maple syrup.

WHERE (PLACE)

Where is the food being served? Cooking local has become a mantra of chefs who seek to reflect a sense of place in their food. But will it be served on a white-table-clothed table by candlelight, or outside at a picnic table in broad daylight? The setting of a meal—whether a region, a neighborhood, or a specific restaurant—has intrinsic implications that should be reflected in the menu's creation.

Florida fusion cuisine pioneer Norman Van Aken opened Florida's 1921 by Norman Van Aken in 2016. "Like many of my fine dining contemporaries, I would say that [20 years ago] I brought in the most faraway, exotic, hyper-unique foods to give me the fullest cache of firepower I could use to both understand all I could about a tremendously broad spectrum of foods *and* how I could engage my guests in doing that," he recalls. "But as the consciousness of our planet's fragility seeped in more—and I exhausted the needs of those earlier artistic penchants—I began in the last period of 'this 20' [years] circling back to the roots more of Florida and to where we live."

It's easy to cook well in Los Angeles, because it has the best produce available anywhere. In the mountains [during catering gigs], we have to cook differently. Produce doesn't travel well. There, you're masking flavors—you end up using a lot more spices, and longer-cooking techniques, to basically hide the quality of something like a tomato.

—**JON SHOOK,** Animal (Los Angeles)

The implications? Van Aken says, "The really long tasting menus went away." (He still offers them, but "more concisely.") "The fish flown in from wherever, along with meats, herbs, etc., were deemed something that we no longer wished to do, realizing how much we had 'in our own backyard.'... Faulkner could express global human nature within a very small county. It looks like that is what I am trying to do in my own way, even more than I was 20 years ago."

Michael Anthony finds that a cosmopolitan area offers great flexibility. "While living and working in New York, we can really tell our story in any way that we decide. I have found that it is the most powerful when we tell it through the lens of the ingredients that are grown close to home. So that's been the backbone of the menu at Gramercy Tavern and our source of inspiration," he says. "In my search trying to find distinctive ingredients, I went back to the garden that [growing up] I had hated weeding and working in, and realized that my father and uncles and great-uncles had never purchased seeds—they only saved seeds from year to year. When I asked my great-uncle if I could use the family's garlic to propagate through a professional grower in upstate New York, he said fine. Now eight years later, we buy 900 pounds of that garlic."

I hate overly sweet desserts, but I do adjust the sweetness level of my desserts based on the restaurant and its clientele. My desserts at [steakhouse] Swift & Sons are sweeter and simpler. At [fine dining] Boka, they are less sweet and more creative. Momotaro is a Japanese restaurant—it doesn't need 12 dessert items; it needs four really good ones that won't change that often.

—**MEG GALUS,** pastry chef, Boka, Momotaro, and Swift & Sons (Chicago)

"Our creativity comes into play when creating a restaurant, and thinking about what the neighborhood needs," Los Angeles chefs Jon Shook and Vinny Dotolo told us. "Jon & Vinny's [a casual spot serving breakfast, lunch, and dinner] is our sixth place. At Trois Familia [in Silver Lake], it's only breakfast and lunch. [Dinner-only, meat-centric] Animal started as a bare-bones restaurant. Son of a Gun was based on a lakehouse restaurant or shack. Trois Mec has an open kitchen, and Petit Trois is a bar [both in partnership with chef Ludo Lefebvre]. Each of our restaurants attract a different clientele. Son of a Gun is more neighborhood-y, more female, more pescatarians [which that menu reflects]. Jon & Vinny's attracts more Persians, Armenians, and vegetarians/vegans, so all of our extruded pastas there are egg-free."

New York City chef Marcus Samuelsson migrated three-and-a-half miles from Midtown Manhattan to Harlem, which he found to be a world apart from his longtime home at Aquavit. "I would consider myself slow in terms of figuring out what mattered to me in my life," he

My creative process when I start at a new restaurant [Thompson was previously chef at Erna's Elderberry House in California] starts with getting out and surveying the area first. I'll go to farmers' markets and talk to farmers to find out what's available to me, and I'll even forage in the area. Then I determine what fits the property, based on what the clientele wants . . . [creating] A SENSE OF PLACE wherever I am.

—**GUNNAR THOMPSON,** Glenmere Mansion (Chester, New York)

acknowledges. "Thinking through modern Scandinavian food took me a very long time, if you don't measure it through the success of a review or having a job. I felt I graduated after 20 years of thinking about it. When I wrote the *Aquavit* cookbook, it was like writing a PhD dissertation, saying, 'Here—this is yours' to the world. It was a turning point to be able to move on to the next thing after having taken it as far as I could at that point. As far as Scandinavian cuisine is concerned, whether it is Noma or what is going on here, others have taken it further and crushed it—which is fantastic!

"I wanted to discover Africa and, after that, this moment makes more sense. Because I am in this moment now. I have opened two restaurants in 12 years. I spent a lot of time on the research...and in this day and age, that is slow, not fast! Red Rooster and Streetbird speak to one another through the migration of Harlem and the food from the South coming up, and the immigrants in this community. When you think of Africa and the African-American diaspora, Harlem makes complete sense—it is a review of what it was, of what it can be."

Harlem, Samuelsson discovered, is more than a place. "Harlem is an idea that spans the globe," he told us. "When you think about Harlem, it is bigger than the 40 streets of the village itself. I always grew up with a strong gratitude of place. I didn't grow up in Harlem, so I did not feel like I had the license to open a restaurant here. The guy across the street [from Streetbird] cooks chicken, pizza, and burgers, and I don't even know how he does that. He is clearly not of a place; he is about opportunity, and there is nothing wrong with that.

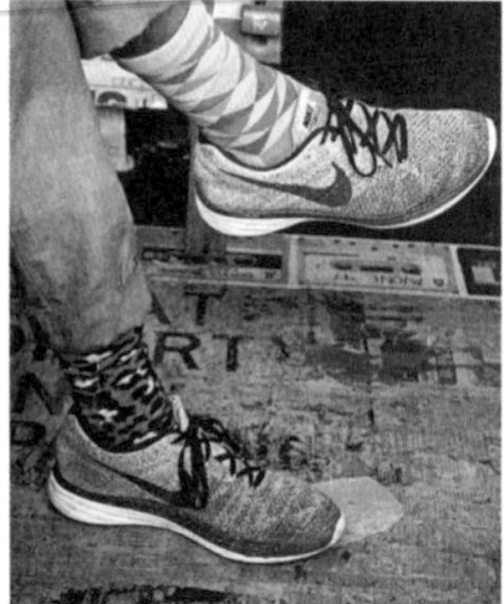

Marcus Samuelsson

"I can't create a business like that," Samuelsson says. "For me, it was about learning this place and being willing to go on a seven- or eight-year journey to do it. I learned a lot, and met incredible people. Through that and through those interactions, you learn and reshape what you thought it was when it turns out to be something else. Streetbird used to be a crack house, which is something I learned from my doorman. So as bad as that is, it is also a great place to reshape that image, create jobs, and have kids coming in with their moms eating after school. That—for me—is success. This restaurant [Streetbird] is based on creativity, but it is reshaped and formed by the community."

WORLD-CLASS CREATIVITY AT THE POINT

Formerly the Rockefeller family summer home on Lake Saranac, the Point is now one of the nation's most exclusive luxury resorts. The Relais & Châteaux-affiliated remote resort property consists of 11 rooms and a few others scattered about the property with no televisions, cell service, or Internet.

Dinner is served every night with all guests seated around one or two tables, preceded by cocktails. (A note is slipped under your door with the location of that night's cocktail hour, which could be in the main dining room or at the pool hall or elsewhere.) Dinner is hosted by general manager **Cameron Karger** or one of his colleagues (e.g., **Jake Kipping** or **Joe Maiurano**). Occasionally guests may choose to dine in their rooms in front of their fireplace, where dinner is served not by a waiter but by one of the members of the kitchen team. There also is a "chefs table" in the kitchen, which is actually the same table where all the prep work is done during the day.

While breakfast is often served in the main dining room, lunch is very much another story. Lunch can be served anywhere on the property: a private island (with guests dropped off and picked up by boat), a lean-to overlooking the lake, on a boat ride, or countless other places limited only by the imagination.

Loic Leperlier, Executive Chef, on the Wow Factor in Menu Planning

"The Point does have an herb and flower garden, and there is a farmers' market in Saranac Lake, but the season is very short. I have found local feta cheese and goat's milk caramels from Asgaard Farm, which is a local dairy about an hour south of here.

"Up here it is difficult to find a ricotta cheese purveyor to use for my ricotta gnocchi with crème fraîche and the heirloom tomatoes from our garden. So, I make my own ricotta to make sure I can control the flavor.

"During the growing season, one thing we do have is lots of tomatoes. I like to take advantage of that and I will even smoke them for a tomato sorbet appetizer. If I do a tomato tasting I will do it from appetizer to dessert. I might start with tomato chutney with tempura, tomato sorbet, or cake.

"I love to be as seasonal as possible, but up here during the winter, there are only potatoes!

"I have to be very aware of what is available during the season as I write my menu for the week and that includes the tradition of the Saturday barbecue [which has guests united outside around a picnic table, come sun or snow].

"The Point has a global clientele. Since I began here, I have not repeated a single dish. I have created more than 200 different appetizers just for dinner alone. Since guests are staying and dining only here, I cannot serve the same dish to them.

Loic Leperlier

Planning a Menu

"For every menu I will talk to **Cameron [Karger],** the Point's general manager, who also chooses the wine pairings for the night.

"A menu will start with **soup**, especially in the winter. After that, we might serve a **light pasta,** followed by **fish or shellfish.** After a **sorbet** course, there would typically be a **meat** course, followed by **cheese,** and finally **dessert.**

Saturday Barbecue at The Point

"Other things I have to consider is that the lunch menu has to be able to travel. If the guests are eating on the island, I can't serve risotto because by the time it gets there it will be a solid block. In some cases, the food has to stand up to the waves on the lake and must be able to travel in Tupperware.

"For any dish, there has to be a lot of built-in flavor, as well as a "Wow!" factor in both flavor and presentation.

"Everything can be incorporated into fine dining. I love using turmeric because it enhances other flavors like curry. I like to work with cumin, coriander, chiles, and rubs for barbecue and Mexican dishes.

"I went to cooking school and had a background in fine dining, at Lucas Carton. I started out there as a commis and finished as a saucier. [Chef-owner] Alain Senderens would have a dream and tell the chef Frédéric [Robert] about the dish. There would then be 15 to 20 versions tested—and sometimes zero would work out, or they wouldn't be able to find a wine to work with the dish so it would not be used. Senderens also had the boldness to serve only one thing on a plate."

D'Anthony Foster

D'Anthony Foster, Pastry Chef, on Comfort in Desserts

"Loic sees a global picture. He understands that guests like simple things here because they can go around the world and get foie gras [or other luxury ingredients]. We have guests from France to Singapore, but sometimes what they want is oatmeal, or chocolate chip cookies. I want to give them something comforting. I enjoy the thought process and trying new things and in the end want to create something I enjoy eating.

"I might want to re-create a candy turtle. I will deconstruct its ingredients of **caramel + chocolate + pecans,** then I will use the best chocolate by Valrhona, making a chocolate mousse, candied pecans, and caramel sauce. I will add some crunch under the mousse to keep it from sliding off the plate.

"[Because no dishes are repeated], you need to master basic elements and be efficient. You also have to be able to change things around. If I have a chocolate sorbet on the menu, it may be in another dish the next day but you would never recognize it.

"A macaron has two elements: something crunchy and something soft. So, you have to play with the smoothness and the crunch, and then add something unexpected. I will add a **sweet + salty + sour** flavor that will be balanced to make it interesting.

"Cameron once told me he wanted a **s'mores** dessert, so I came up with **graham cracker tuile + marshmallow fluff filling + chocolate ganache.**"

Cameron Karger, General Manager, on Excellence in Service

"We strive to give guests anything they wish for. A visit to the Point is about the whole experience.

"I love to go to other properties to see what they do better than we do. The Inn at Little Washington in Virginia has the best housekeepers—there is not a speck of dust anywhere! I never want to plateau, because we are the Point.

"Here, we hire on drive, passion, character, and charisma because you can't transform those. We actually prefer to hire people who are green. We want people who forget they are working. If we train properly, they have a level of excellence that is the norm. For us, excellence is what we do—it is the bare minimum.

"**Loic** and **D'Anthony** are passionate about the service here. I think Loic is one of the most talented chefs I have worked with and it took me three years to get him up here. **Food tastes better when you have excellent service.** That is why we try so much harder with our room service. We know we are under a microscope, so we will pull a cook off the line to deliver room service, not just pull a dishwasher. We take it very seriously."

Cameron Karger

Spike Gjerde on Local Sourcing and Maximizing Ingredients

[Local dishes, **Woodberry Kitchen**–style include VA Full Salt Clams & Egg Noodles; Cape May, New Jersey, Dayboat Scallops; and Fried Scrapple Chopped Salad (with Cheddar, chipped ham, spicy Ranch, and onion)—if you're Baltimore's Spike Gjerde.]

With Woodberry Kitchen, we did not start with a concept. **We started with a question: "Can we feed ourselves, and can ingredients supplied by local farmers support a restaurant?"** The first year we opened with that question in mind, the answer was not clear—to put it mildly.

When we opened, we had a five-page list of things we would order from our outside purveyors. Now that list is less than a half-page long—just things like baking powder or cocoa powder.

What got me focused on sourcing locally were the consequences of large-scale farming, processing, and transportation. Now, other things support that, [like the fact that] I want to eat less-processed foods.

We canned 30,000 pounds of tomatoes last year. If you eat a tomato at one of our restaurants, it is a tomato grown by a local farmer, at a price that the farmer set and that sustains the farmer. If you eat that tomato in the wintertime in one of our restaurants, we canned it and put it up. We have a full-time canner. We have five tomato products—whole, crushed, juice, paste, and jam—that are also sold retail. We are participating in the economy to the maximum extent that we have figured out how to right now, and we are going to figure out how to do even more in the future.

Spike Gjerde, at Artifact Coffee (Baltimore)

I like Tabasco sauce and spice in general. I would look at the Tabasco sauce on our shelf and think, "We can do better—we can find a local pepper and do it ourselves." The DIY aspect is just as important as finding a local source. I became aware of the fish pepper from **Michael Twitty,** who is a local food anthropologist, especially [focused on] the African-American community in the Mid-Atlantic. **Hearing about a hot pepper grown on the Chesapeake was like catnip to me.** It turns out there was a guy who wanted to work with us and heard I was looking for fish peppers. He planted a quarter of an acre of fish peppers right here in the city and when we ran into each other at an event, he asked me if I wanted them. Next thing you know, we are in the car to go check them out.

We made a commitment to get rid of citrus [which isn't grown locally]. I approached Black Ankle Vineyards about making *verjus* for us. A couple of months later, he came in with baggies full of hard, green grapes, and we just smashed them and tasted the juice, and I said, "This is amazing!" It was tart, fruity, and had malic acid that we did not have in the kitchen. It is now a mainstay for us. I know exactly where the product comes from. We help bottle it, and the money goes right back to the farmer.

A local chef once said to me, "We could never do what you do . . ." But the truth is, yes, you can.

Maximizing Your Ingredients = Maximizing Value

Our mission drives us in a direction that is resourceful and creative in the service of the economics of the food system that also results in something delicious on the plate or in the bowl. It is really driven by the fact that we have to figure out how to make this work for us so that it can work for the farmer.

Part of the equation—and the challenge—is getting all the value you can out of an animal. Duck is rare and expensive for us, and we get everything of one we can—down to the wing tips....We cure the breasts lightly and cook them to order. We separate the drumsticks from the thighs and braise the drumsticks and confit the thighs, which will each get used in separate dishes. A thigh will be paired with duck livers in dirty rice and sold as a small plate. The drumstick meat is turned into a rillette that is breaded and fried and served with the four-ounce breast. The rillette helps the entrée feel complete. So instead of a single breast sliced, which is a lot of duck breast to eat, we get four main dishes out of a single animal, which is huge for us. We still go a little farther. Part of the wings get used as snacks, plus we use the frames and wing tips for stock to make a really beautiful soup, and we make agnolotti with some of the drumstick meat that did not go into the rillette.

I think it is unfortunate that chefs, myself included, generally are unaware of and unfocused on the health implications of what we do. I do not have a deep understanding of nutrition.

All of this does not happen on its own. It happens with a great deal of focus with our staff as well, through repetition and everyone questioning "What is this?" and "What is in this?"

When all is said and done, people will say, **"This happened in Baltimore."**

WHY (GUEST)

Why is the guest at your table? Any food is as much about the person who will be eating it as it is the person creating it. Are they simply hungry for a quick bite of lunch after a tough morning before returning to work—or are they looking for a romantic dinner over which to celebrate their 25th wedding anniversary?

Understanding and communicating the reason a guest is at your table is key. Patrick O'Connell of the Inn at Little Washington says, "The hope is that they feel it. When you see this moment of personal connection, **it's almost mystical. It's being present for them. It's an exchange of consciousness that can happen in seconds.**"

"You don't have to have a long, long discussion with them. But usually they'll key you

You can learn technique. And you can educate your palate. But one of the most important aspects of food is its "AURA"—the empathy or connection it sparks. It's like a lightning bolt that flows from the chef through the food to the person eating it. And I don't know how to describe it, but it's real. . . . There needs to be a LINK between the FOOD and the GUEST—and that link is LOVE.

—**EMILY LUCHETTI,** chief pastry officer, The Cavalier, Marlowe, and Park Tavern (San Francisco)

> **When I talk to other chefs my age, we are experiencing very similar things. I spoke to Marco Canora [of Hearth in Manhattan] and Carla Hall [of Carla Hall's Southern Kitchen in Brooklyn] and we shared that when you are young, you have so much to prove: You push yourself to explore and find new boundaries and then to cross those boundaries. As you get older, it gets back to the pure essence of hospitality. You want that immediate recognition, that smile—and it is no longer contemplative food that you have to go home and think about. It is about a gut reaction and taking someone back to your childhood or their childhood or a magical moment in their life.**
>
> —**BRAD FARMERIE,**
> Saxon + Parole (New York City)

in—they'll reveal who they are, and where they're coming from, and what their consciousness is," says O'Connell. "And you're trading—because they're usually imparting information to you, too. In the early days, our guests taught us everything, the well-traveled ones. We either couldn't afford, or couldn't get out of here, to see what was going on."

When the chef is in the kitchen, the primary means of communication is through the food itself. As Curtis Duffy of Grace points out, "When you want to create a dish that's familiar to guests, you'll primarily achieve that through **flavor profiles, texture,** and **temperature.** You lose the connection with your guest if you don't give them *something* they're familiar with. I don't want it to be so far out there that you can't connect with it."

But increasingly, the starting point is guests' individual needs, preferences, aversions, or allergies. Loic Leperlier of the Point says, "Forty percent of my clientele orders gluten-free, vegetarian, vegan, or dairy-free dishes. I have to be flexible."

Michael Voltaggio of Los Angeles' ink says, **"We're not about being everything for everyone, but we believe in hospitality.** We have some vegan regulars in the restaurant. As much as it would be easier to say, 'You know—we just don't do that here,' you have to think about the other people at the table, too. If it's a couple, and only one is a vegetarian or vegan, they wouldn't get to experience the restaurant together. It goes back to understanding who your guests are and what it is that they need....There are certain things you should know how to do before you open up a restaurant and are trusted with the safety of employees and guests alike. Learning about food takes time—and continues every single day."

Stephanie Izard of Chicago's Girl & the Goat reflects on the effect of guests' needs on her creative process. "Sometimes when I am creating a dish, I get bummed because I have to think about this or that allergy: 'Let's not put nuts in this dish, or let's make this gluten-free,' " she admits. "But now, it has just become about regular menu set-up. We have a gluten-free menu, a dairy-free menu, and a vegan menu. It makes the guest feel more comfortable to see we put a lot of thought into this. It also helps the servers because even though they know the menu well, they don't have to feel so nervous at the table. We have made adjustments in the kitchen like shifting from soy sauce to gluten-free tamari. I use fish sauce like it is going out of style because I love it so much. We recently switched to Red Boat fish sauce that is gluten-free."...

"A lot of times if you are vegan and you go into a non-vegan restaurant, they just throw together some random dish and send it out to you. Guests seek us out because they know we have multiple menus that can cater to them," she says.

There's a limit to Izard's compassion, however. "On the other hand, I was hosting a pork dinner at which a guest informed me [at the last minute] that they were vegetarian," she recalls. "Not to be rude, but the star of the night is something you don't eat. Why are you here? I have nothing to serve you."

UNDERSTANDING YOUR GUEST

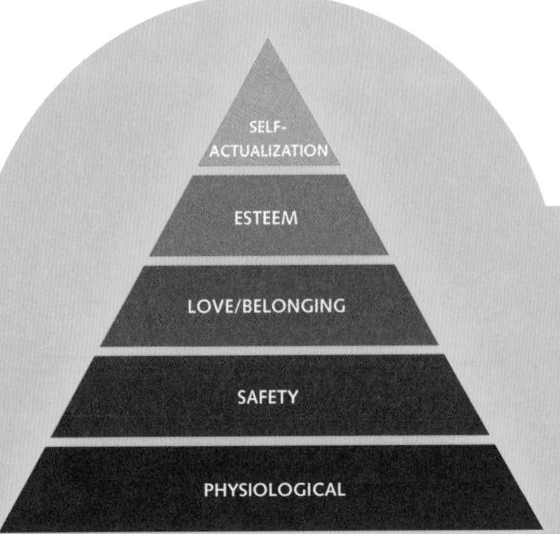

Maslow's Hierarchy of Needs

While different individuals may need or wish for different things, all guests share the same human needs, as identified through Abraham Maslow's famed Hierarchy of Needs. Keep them in mind throughout your creative process.

How can you meet guests' needs for the following through the food you serve?

1. **Physiological / Safety** = air, water, food, temperature, sleep, safety/security **[physical]**

   e.g., serving healthful, nutritious dishes that comply with dietary restrictions (e.g., dairy-free, gluten-free, peanut-free), non-GMO, organic, sustainable

2. **Love / Belonging** = connection / intimate relationships / friends **[emotional]**

   e.g., serving classic dishes, a communal menu, ethnic dishes (of one's own heritage), signature dishes

3. **Esteem** = accomplishment / prestige **[mental]**

   e.g., showcasing prestige ingredients (e.g., gold leaf, truffles), serving intellectually stimulating dishes

4. **Self-Actualization** = achieving one's full potential, including **creativity [spiritual]**

   e.g., one-of-a-kind experiential meals (e.g., serving dishes made entirely from food waste, as at wastED; serving dishes from ingredients sourced exclusively from a 12-acre property)

Michael Scelfo on How an Interdependent Kitchen = A Creative Kitchen

I will write many drafts of a menu [for **Alden and Harlow** and for **Waypoint**, both in Cambridge Massachusetts], and I am very much a writer when it comes to creating my food:

1. If it sounds good in my head, I am confident it will taste good on the plate—but it has to sound good in my head first.
2. I won't bother testing an idea or dish until I am really certain how it looks on paper. I am on draft seven of the menu for our new restaurant [Waypoint]. Sometimes I will put the draft menu away and not look at it for days or a week. If I have a great meal out or something else inspires me, I will go back and revisit it. Then I tweak it. Once I get the first good thing on paper, everything else flows from there, and I can't stop at that point. That is how it is when I am writing about food. I have stream-of-consciousness writing, and cannot stop writing dishes into my phone.

Michael Scelfo

I use **Evernote,** which is great because it allows me to share notes with the whole kitchen. I have the entire restaurant broken down into folders. I will write out a "mood board" of what I want the food to be, the beverages, the physical design, the uniform, the menu—none of it is final, and it will change three or four more times.

At Alden and Harlow, we change the menu every Friday and every menu change for the last year-and-a-half I keep in a folder. When I make a menu change, I share a note with my sous chefs, and will get a response of "Heard, Chef," which means they got it.

[Every month, Scelfo challenges everyone on his kitchen team to develop a dish around a different seasonal ingredient, such as apples, carrots, eggplant, or tomatoes.]

I can see how the cooks have evolved over the year we've been doing this challenge. They know "Chef" is going to be looking for crunch on the plate. I will ask what is missing, and they will know. When doing the bluefish challenge, I said, "The first rule out of the gate is 'no smoking' and no 'pâté' [the most common preparations of bluefish in New England]—now you have to be creative.

For the last challenge, we did crabapples—which was tough. The best dishes end up on the menu as specials, and one of the last dishes from the crabapple challenge even went onto the fall brunch menu: It was a homemade sausage with a crabapple hash and crabapple butter. Our brunch items are a little crazy and we have fun with them—we don't do "eggs any style."

It is a great way to keep everyone involved, thinking about food, and invested. I even discovered my pastry chef through the challenges: He was one of my line cooks, and every time we did a challenge, he would bake something for a dessert. When we got to eggplant, he made an eggplant and bitter chocolate cake-like dessert that was very creative. Before that, I don't know that I would have ever sat him down and asked, "What are you looking to do?" But by doing this challenge, it became obvious [that he was interested in baking]. Now, we bake all our breads in house.

[In December 2015, we joined members of Scelfo's kitchen team (Al, David, Justin, Keith, Kenny, Manya, Nick, and Ray) as they presented to Scelfo the dishes they'd created around sunchokes for his comments and critique.]

Michael Scelfo: I try to be positive, yet honest, with my feedback. I'll comment on their seasoning, execution, texture, acid balance, presentation, and portion size.

The entire team brings a lot of excitement to this exercise, and a certain comfort level exists with it. While the front of the house still asks, "Who won?" afterward, [among the kitchen team] there's more of an aversion to cooking competitively—food is meant to be shared. Everyone is evolving in a positive way, and there's a balance of both the positive and the negative, as well as making it clear why there was a criticism so they can always learn from it.

The cooks are learning to focus to **enhance the key ingredient,** and not just to put bacon or foie gras or bone marrow on a plate [for its own sake]. And they're breaking away from the notion of heavy fats on the plate—I love pureed sunchoke for the richness it adds to a plate. It's clear that some are already focused on **the importance of putting complementary flavors at the center of the plate.**

[He is presented with a dish of Confit Sunchoke with Foie Nugget, Shredded Phyllo, Parsley, and Preserved Lemon Aioli.] Really beautiful. Love the presentation. The dumpling is a little heavy, and the foie gets a little lost, but it's super-creative and I love the idea.

[Another dish prompts Scelfo.] Awesome. There's one thing that doesn't need to be on this plate, and you wouldn't miss it—so you could strip it back by one component. **Once you hit five or seven components, it's time to start stripping back.** You've got a great vegetarian plate here—it doesn't need the bone marrow.

[The next dish prompts praise.] This is something I would do. I might like a little more acid. It's "sunchoke-forward," so it's a great example of a sunchoke dish. I really like it.

[A sunchoke timbale prompts more.] The greens are awesome, but I'm finding myself wanting acid—it's really sweet....It was baked at 350 degrees, which is high, so it scrambled a little. Maybe next time try 275 or 300 degrees in a water bath for two hours.

[A cook presents Roasted Sunchoke Gnocchi, made from peeled and dry-roasted sunchokes instead of potatoes, with pickles and hazelnuts.] The flavors are really great—and this is the first dish with orange, and **sunchoke + orange** is my favorite flavor combination. The **hazelnut** is awesome with them. Sunchokes have a higher moisture content [than potatoes], so they got a bit water-logged. Maybe try gnudi [similar to gnocchi, but made with ricotta instead of potatoes] instead. I would happily serve this dish.

[The cooks reflect on the experience.]

Justin: As a line cook, I'm paid to execute the kitchen's food and maintain [the restaurant's vision], so this is a great exercise. It's a great way to pick up ideas, because we all have different backgrounds. I was raised Italian-American, and my mom cooked pasta. Ray comes from a French fine-dining experience.

Al: We're all pushing each other, and being in the kitchen with everyone else is exciting. It forces me to think, "What am I going for?" with this ingredient as the main focus, and to personalize it, within the style of the restaurant. Next time, I'll take more time, and set myself up better in advance.

Keith: As the sous chef, I came in on my one day off to do this exercise. It's absolutely a chance to push the envelope for myself, and to bring my take to something new and to experiment with a new technique. It's also a great way to learn about myself and the other cooks.

Manya: I look forward to these challenges and, with time, **we're learning to think more outside the box and to "be ourselves" on the plate.** I never worked with sunchokes before, so I did a few test batches, some of which failed miserably. But it was a great opportunity to do something I don't normally do.

Ray: This is definitely a great exercise—I learn to push myself to the limits, and to try something new every time. When work is fun, it doesn't feel like a job or a burden. These exercises are competitive, but they also **allow us to help each other.**

David: This exercise definitely helps my creativity, and **helps me learn how to focus dishes** to get flavor on the plate the way I want it.

Kenny: I started here as a line cook, and did desserts and pastries during these monthly challenges, and have since become the pastry chef. It definitely enhances creativity to be able to bounce ideas off others. **I know the chef is looking at our plating, and wants to see something pop on the plate, because that's the first sensation it delivers.** Then, it should have a sweet/salty balance with good texture.

Nick: I've been here less than three weeks, but it's been a cool opportunity to see what everyone's all about. It's interesting to see how you have to push to make space to work on your dishes, and how the chef grades for flavor and plating styles. It was really fun—and **I've never worked anywhere else where they've done this. Sure, everyone encourages creativity, but here they really mean it. It's a very positive, team-building exercise.**

[The chef gets the last word.]

Michael: I'm surprised no one did a dessert version, or that they didn't take even more chances with their dishes. **I hope they'll push even farther next time.**

It's nice to see they all have different perspectives, and it's been great getting to know them as cooks and what they're really thinking. It's fun to watch them develop, and sometimes I learn as much as they do. We look back fondly on these challenges.

When we first started doing this, it was all about "Who won? What's the best dish?" But we've realized we're more interested in where everyone's coming from. It's important to take the opportunity to cook for yourself, and to do your own thing." [This comment prompted lots of head nodding among his cooks.] It's not about "What's Chef going to like?" I spent ten years cooking someone else's idea of what food should be. **Take this opportunity to push *yourselves* creatively.**

HOW (CHEF)

The final question of **how** to execute a dish brings the process back full circle to the chef. Taking into consideration all of the previous questions of who, what, when, where, and why, the chef channels the best answers to all into the solution of *how* to create a dish for the guest.

How food that "fits the bill" will be prepared by the chef is a function of your talents, values, and imagination. Also, how will you influence how the food will be remembered by the guest? Are there takeaways, e.g., custom-printed menus? Photographs suitable for framing or social media? It's in every chef's power to create a memory.

"Some courses are about the shock factor," Phillip Foss of EL Ideas acknowledges. "Making people lick their plates [which Foss does early during a meal at his Michelin-starred restaurant] is childish, but it works well to break people out of the mindset of stuffiness. We do it during the most expensive course of the night [one featuring osetra caviar]."

I want to bring the subject of our food system to the table. It's one thing to serve great, organic, nutritious food. LOCAL means it's FRESHER. But being creative with food also means using it to creatively solve problems. And while I use creativity to make delicious food for our guests, at the end of the day, I also use it to create a broader conception of what good food is.

—**SPIKE GJERDE,**
Woodberry Kitchen (Baltimore)

It's never just about the dish—it's about the DISH and the STORY behind it. You want to create a CONNECTION with the guest beyond the food on the plate. If you can create an emotional connection, you can enjoy a meal on a deeper level. HOSPITALITY is all about making connections and creating an experience for guests that will make them choose this place again over all others.

—**PHILLIP FOSS,**
EL Ideas (Chicago)

When serving food to Japanese guests, I ask my cooks to season it about five percent less. I've found the Japanese appreciate the natural flavors on the plate. It's not about the layering of flavors; it's more about the melding of flavors....In French kitchens, you might make stocks that will last for a few days, with daily readjustments. But in Japanese kitchens—and in my kitchens at Gramercy Tavern and Untitled—you start with dashi, which is made fresh every day. Dashi is the building block of the cuisine. It allows the melding of delicate flavors.

—**MICHAEL ANTHONY,** Gramercy Tavern and Untitled (New York City)

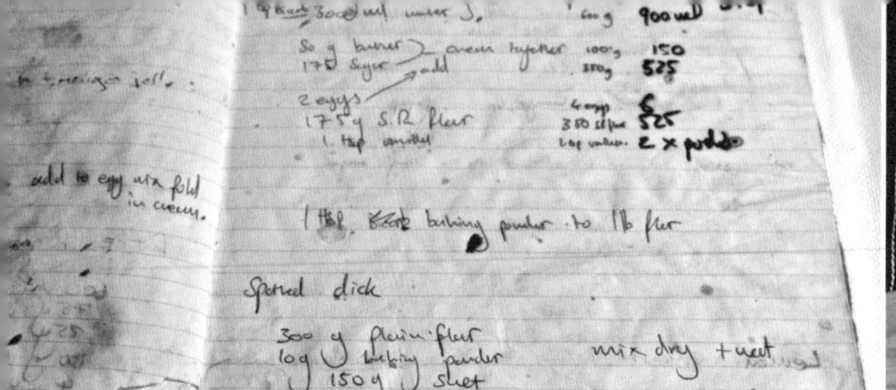

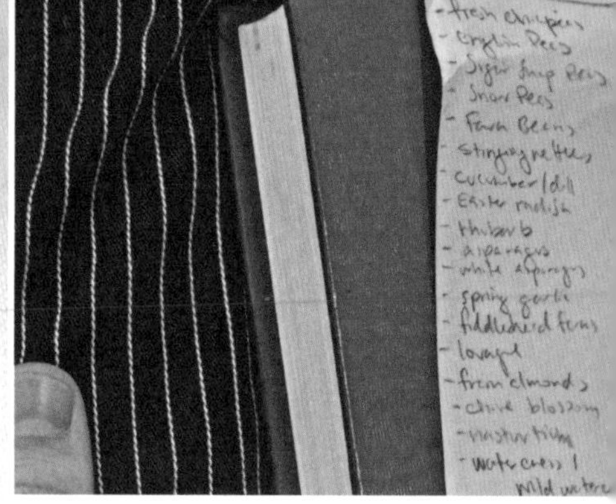

CREATIVE CHEFS' MASTER CHECKLISTS

What is most important for you to reflect and express through your food? Creative chefs think long and hard about what they want to convey through theirs.

When Andrew first started cooking professionally in the 1980s, he found it helpful to make a checklist of what more experienced chefs told him about what was important to have on the plate, from making sure everything was not only edible (e.g., *no* rosemary branches) but delicious (e.g., only *dressed* greens). Beyond that, he developed his sensibility about what great food had in common, whether abundance, aroma, balance, flavor, freshness, harmony, healthfulness, quality, regionality, ripeness, seasonality, and/or variety. Today, other considerations among chefs include a dish's social media–readiness.

Be inspired by these chefs' thought processes to undertake your own, which can help drive your creations in the kitchen:

Michael Anthony

MICHAEL ANTHONY, Gramercy Tavern and Untitled (New York City)

"Creating dishes that are pristine versus boring is a fine line in an aesthetic. There's less prep work—our success hinges on execution. And because there's nothing to hide behind, mistakes can be catastrophic. So we have to get it right—or it sucks. . . . In the creation of dishes, there always has to be three things: 1) **simplicity**, 2) **refinement**, and 3) a **hook**—something that grabs the guest's attention that they can remember and share. And if you do it right, and offer it to guests at a value, people will come back. It provides a true sense of connection, maybe even over a lifetime."

AMANDA COHEN, Dirt Candy (New York City)

"Creating dishes for [our new, larger location] was easier. We already knew what we were doing, and had our frameworks and techniques in place. We knew our narrative: that we took one vegetable and had a team of brains to celebrate it in all kinds of ways. We'd go through a testing process for each dish—what was the **dish**? What **story** was it trying to tell? It was not always an instinctive process—sometimes it involved trial and error. The development of a dish from idea to menu can take as long as three months, not including pre-thinking/mulling time. In three months, sometimes you're past the season, and have to rejigger the idea with a new vegetable.

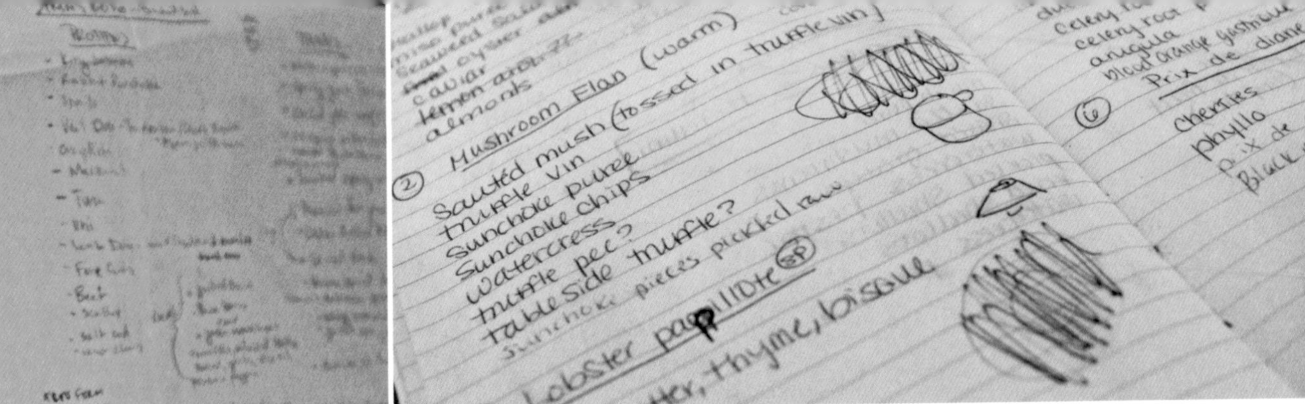

"We will add new dishes to the menu once or twice a month. When we come up with a new dish, we ask ourselves how it is uniquely Dirt Candy. Our carrot dish [Carrot Buns] is a perfect Dirt Candy dish: It's delicious, it's pretty cute, it's visually fascinating, and it's funny with a sense of humor. We love to make people laugh or giggle or smile. . . .

"**What's the point of doing any of this if you're not pushing boundaries and trying to change the conversation?** If you're in the business of making food and asking for attention for it, there ought to be a really good reason behind your dishes."

CURTIS DUFFY, Grace (Chicago)

"We sit down almost every day with books and notes, talking about our dishes. **But for me, it always starts with the ingredients**, and especially that main ingredient that we pair with different flavor profiles. Yesterday was the first day white asparagus was on the spring menu—which started with the white asparagus itself. Then we think about what direction we want to go with it in terms of **cooking technique.** And then it's really just the **flavor profiles**—what do we want to do with it this year? We haven't used it in a few years, because I don't use the same ingredients every spring. I haven't used morels in probably six years. Everybody uses them when they come into season, and I don't want to be that trend guy. . . . **I'm always trying to think outside the box** rather than, 'Well, that's the way we always cook it.' If we like tempura-frying asparagus, maybe the next time we'll serve part of the dish that way and then [juxtapose] that with asparagus cooked another way. . . . As a younger chef, putting more ingredients on the plate was the more intriguing thing. But I also couldn't be the guy with just three things on a dish, because that was *too* simple. My dishes have three, maybe four, flavor profiles—and I stick to that strictly, because it's easy to get lost and confused with too many things going on."

BRAD FARMERIE, Saxon + Parole (New York City)

"Our dishes [at Public] feature fewer ingredients [now than they did upon the restaurant's opening in 2003]. **There are just three 'heroes' on each plate.** My checklist when creating a new dish is 1) **richness,** which typically comes from the main hero on a plate, which might be the protein; 2) **acidity,** to balance out the richness; 3) **color,** which should be harmonious, 4) **texture,** which often involves a bit of crunch, and 5) **complementary flavors.** And, in this day and age, there's also a question of whether it **photographs well.** I'll ask my cooks, 'How would someone describe this dish the next day to a friend?' or 'If a journalist ate it, what would they write about it?'

"Our cooks always ask themselves:

- Is the dish on brand? How does it fit into the overall menu?
- Is the dish feasible—based on available equipment, space in kitchen, time to prepare and serve?
- Does it fit into our food cost matrix?
- What makes it memorable?
- What part will people talk about?
- Would people order it again?
- What makes it press worthy?
- Does it photograph well?"

In our restaurant, we question everything, all the time. Forward motion and endless reinvention are part of our DNA.

—**DANIEL HUMM,** Eleven Madison Park (New York City)

DANIEL HUMM OF ELEVEN MADISON PARK (NEW YORK CITY)

In a presentation delivered at a Relais & Châteaux event, Daniel Humm mentioned that he used to think a dish always needed something more—perhaps a crispy element, a sauce or puree, or three more techniques.

Today, Humm says, he realizes that a dish needs to meet only four criteria:

1. **Delicious:** This is something a guest will recognize instantly.
2. **Beautiful:** It should appear effortless.
3. **Creative:** A new dish will "move forward"—with new techniques or unusual ingredient combinations, in order to surprise guests.
4. **Purpose:** Perhaps most importantly, a dish needs to make sense—such as a dish that features ingredients grown next to each other, or one that references an historic dish.

JESSICA LARGEY, SIMONE (LOS ANGELES)

"I tend to think of the **vegetable first**, and then the **sauce and garnish,** and only think of the **protein last,** fitting it into the whole dish. But there's no formula to it—it's a more organic process than that. I'll taste the ingredients, and wonder, 'How far can I strip it down?' I'll often add different forms of the same ingredient (e.g., raw, pickled, cooked different ways) because I don't want to add new flavors to the dish—I want to *intensify* the flavors that are *already* there. At Manresa, we really liked to showcase ingredients, so that the dish tasted of that ingredient."

TAIESHA MARTIN, GLENMERE MANSION (CHESTER, NEW YORK)

"My process for creating desserts from scratch starts with asking myself, "What's in the **walk-in?** What's in **season?** What's **trending?** What will our **guests** like? **What haven't I done?**" And I'll ask myself these questions, and think about the answers, every single day....After Easter, we had a lot of mixed berries left over, which I turned into my triple-berry and Champagne sorbet. The bar had some extra blood orange juice, which was very intense in flavor, so I turned it into blood orange spritz sorbet with some Champagne, seltzer, and simple syrup."

GHAYA OLIVEIRA OF RESTAURANT DANIEL (NEW YORK CITY)

"What do I look for in a dessert? Four things:

1. Every plate must have an element of **sourness or acidity**, which is a flavor that wakes you up—it's refreshing and brightening.
2. There should be a **super-sweet** element as well.
3. There should also be an element that is **a clear flavor**—whether that's **fruit, or nuts, or chocolate, or something else.**
4. And from the very first bite, a dessert should have some **freshness**, some **texture**, some **smoothness**, and some **creaminess**—and some **magic**!

"I like to introduce certain ingredients into a dessert as secret ingredients—ones you don't necessarily taste, but that make you ask, 'What's that flavor?' I'll use things like orange blossoms, geraniums, and jasmine gelées. I love showing chocolate from different origins and regions, so you can learn about the different chocolates and come to respect the cacao. And this is an important aspect of our job: to bring the world to you on one plate."

JOAN ROCA, EL CELLER DE CAN ROCA (SPAIN)

Everything served at El Celler de Can Roca, ranked number one on the 2013 and 2015 World's 50 Best Restaurant lists, and number two on its 2016 list, is intended to touch on one or more of the following influences, shared by chef-owner Joan Roca during a 2014 lecture at Harvard University: 1) **tradition**, e.g., Catalan cuisine; 2) **memory**, e.g., childhood; 3) **academia**, e.g., what was learned in culinary school or inspired by it; 4) **product**, e.g., high-quality; 5) **region**; 6) **landscape**; 7) **wine**; 8) **sweet**; 9) **chromatism**, e.g., color; 10) **transversal creation**, which he has described as "free creative interplay around a humanistic conception of culinary phenomena. It is a fluent dialogue whose leitmotifs are passion, enjoyment and rigor"; 11) **perfume**; 12) **freedom**; 13) **innovation**, e.g., adapting or inventing new techniques; 14) **poetry**; 15) **boldness**; 16), **magic**; and 17) **sense of humor.**

CHRISTINA TOSI, MILK BAR (NEW YORK CITY)

Christina Tosi has described her perfect dessert as having five characteristics: 1) **balance**, 2) **depth of flavor**, 3) **point of view**, 4) **texture**, and 5) **a point of inspiration.**

The creation of something new is not accomplished by the intellect but by the play instinct acting from inner necessity. The creative mind plays with the objects it loves.

—CARL JUNG

THE FIVE-STEP CREATIVE PROCESS

Creativity is unpredictable. Breakthroughs can occur spontaneously, or progress can be made through a deliberate, step-by-step process. Mozart famously had entire symphonies "come to him," which he would then simply write down.

In between Mozart-like visits from the muses, you can make progress by proactively pursuing the five steps of the creative process. Don't expect the steps to be perfectly chronological: they can overlap and circle back into one another. But the process generally involves four or **five key steps,** as enumerated by writers since Graham Wallas (1920s: preparation, incubation, illumination, verification) and Alex Osborn (1950s: orientation, preparation, analysis and ideation, incubation, and evaluation). In his 2014 book, *Creativity on Demand,* Michael Gelb uses the terms *preparation, generation, incubation, evaluation,* and *implementation,* which I loved intuitively before being surprised and delighted to discover that they happened to coincide beautifully with the five inner senses:

1. **Preparation / *Inspiration:* Name your desire.** What's the problem or challenge you're facing that is the impetus for your wish to create something? Do your homework, gather your facts (e.g., see the 5Ws + 1H on page 174), and focus on articulating it carefully, so that you can formulate the best solution.
2. **Generation / *Imagination*: Brainstorm *lots* of ideas** as potential solutions to your problem or challenge. As Nobelist Linus Pauling asserted, "The best way to have a *good* idea is to have a *lot* of ideas." Brainstorm on your own at first, and then ideally as part of a team with whom you can debate the best—great advice from Gelb himself, who consults on creativity with Fortune 500 companies.
3. **Incubation / *Insight:* Give it a rest—literally.** Let your idea incubate by taking a break, meditating, going for a walk in nature or for a drive; taking a nap, a shower, or a bath, and letting the subconscious go to work on the problem and possible solutions. People don't often get their best ideas at work—they more often occur when you're out of your habitual mindset, and in a relaxed, receptive state. That's when your "aha" moments of insight—into a problem, or its solution, or an opportunity—will likely hit.

What you can do, or dream you can do, begin it! Boldness has genius, power, and magic in it.

—JOHANN WOLFGANG VON GOETHE, German poet

4. **Evaluation / *Intuition:*** Based on your best insight-driven imaginings, **evaluate your alternatives,** and their strengths and weaknesses, and decide on the best course of action to solve the problem at the current time. On what will you base your judgments? Look to your intuition to sift the best wisdom from your head, heart, and gut.
5. **Implementation / *Instinct:*** Follow your instincts to **take action** to implement the solution (e.g., create your dish!), and complete the process of bringing your idea into physical reality.

The entire creative process—not just the moments of deep insight—involves states of euphoria and inspiration as well as states of calm, rational focus.

—SCOTT BARRY KAUFMAN, in the *Harvard Business Review*

THE CREATIVE BALANCE: STIMULATION AND STILLNESS

The creative process alternates between two extremes: what might be considered "euphoric inspiration" on one hand (or what we call ***stimulation***), and "calm focus" on the other (which we refer to as ***stillness***).

Some chefs know their creativity is heightened at certain times or in certain places, such as when they're surrounded by lots of stimuli and/or in high-energy environments. José Andrés acknowledges that he needs an environment that "keeps all these ideas coming and coming, and keeps me alive."

Openness to experience—the drive for cognitive exploration of one's inner and outer worlds—is the single strongest and most consistent personality trait that predicts creative achievement.

—SCOTT BARRY KAUFMAN and CAROLYN GREGOIRE, coauthors of *Wired to Create*, as quoted in *Scientific American*

Creativity is about far more than generating new ideas. It's about opening to your full life energy, which then circulates the passion and gusto that give your life meaning and sparkle.

—MICHAEL GELB, author of *Creativity on Demand*

STIMULATION: ENGAGING WITH THE OUTER WORLD

Stimulation comes naturally to chefs—much of it food-related. Reading cookbooks. Shopping. Cooking. Eating. Watching food porn. Reading restaurant reviews. Dining out. Traveling. Sampling new cuisines and flavors. There's a never-ending variety of stimuli available. Food's diversity means there's always another new cuisine to explore, or new ingredient or technique to discover.

"I love to travel," says Carrie Nahabedian of Chicago's Naha. "It is important to have experiences you can bring to your guests. I was in Morocco and came back with amazing Tunisian couscous. I also brought back amazing argan oil. I had two guests going to Tunisia and told them exactly where to get the oil and to bring some back for me."

Carrie Nahabedian

"**I like to visit another country every year,**" she adds. "I was in and out of India in one week to cook with other Michelin-starred women chefs at the Leela Palace New Delhi. It was an event organized by the Creative Support Services Group, which was created to help women in India without prospects get into the creative culinary arts."

Nahabedian remembers being on the plane to Delhi not knowing what she was going to be making. "I had no idea of the scope of the event. I only knew we were going to do a series of dinners and demos, work with the kids, go to farms, and make a difference," she remembers. "But the cooks in Delhi when I was there were very open with me because I was so open with them, and they taught me all sorts of tricks."

"After I returned home to Chicago, I did a dish for an event at Embeya restaurant based on that trip," she says. "I explained to [Embeya chef] Mike Sheerin that they prepare a fish in a light batter, tossed in a tamarind glaze and served with kiwi, papaya, and lemon. I had no recipe—all I had was the memory of the flavor of what I'd tasted, and it took me all day working with the tamarind."

While food-related exploration is a given, travel often offers chefs a welcome break in their routines to explore the world beyond. "I love visiting the Met[ropolitan Museum of Art] in Manhattan—even just being on the outside looking in and realizing everything you *could* learn, and that is just waiting to be discovered," says pastry chef Emily Luchetti, who compares it to the anticipation of eating a really good dessert. "I think it adds to your creative process, to go to a museum and see people doing different works of art, whether it's painting or sculpture....You learn more about the creative process, and the different styles of art. **It exposes you to different ideas, which you keep in the back of your mind, and it all kind of synthesizes in the cement mixer in your head, and comes out in a new way.**"

Dining out is one of the most educational experiences a chef can have. "[Our former chef] Michelle Bernstein advised us to **spend all of our extra money on eating out**, and it's **the best advice we ever received,**" swear Animal's Jon Shook

> **Since creativity is so important for individual well-being and societal innovation, it's important that we systematically pull the right triggers. A crucial trigger is the experience of unusual and unexpected events….If you want to get into a creative mindset, do your normal routine in a completely different way. Write with your other hand….Eat something new for lunch. Smile at strangers. Be weird.**
>
> —SCOTT BARRY KAUFMAN, author of *Wired to Create*

and Vinny Dotolo. "We've been to Noma [in Copenhagen] twice. Some ideas don't translate well to the U.S., where we've seen the overuse of flowers and nasturtium leaves. And we've learned the difference between being inspired by something versus straight copying."

Boka's Lee Wolen muses about how much of an inspiration dining out has been to him and his pastry chef, Meg Galus. "We're inspired by eating out—and Alinea was my best meal ever," he remembers. "There was nothing that wasn't perfect. It's inspiring to see that. We might take things one degree past where others take them, but Grant [Achatz] takes them 25 degrees past that."

Galus agrees. "There is a lot of derivative food out there, especially given the popularity of social media," she says. "But Alinea is totally original."

The tuition doesn't have to be as high as the price of a tasting menu at a temple of gastronomy, either. "We're very influenced by the food we eat. But when

Meg Galus and Lee Wolen

Great works of art, music, and architecture . . . can transport us temporarily to higher levels of consciousness and are universally recognized as inspirational and timeless.

—DAVID R. HAWKINS, MD, PhD, *Power vs. Force*

we lived in Florida [where they met at culinary school], our outside influences were mainly Cuban," Jon Shook and Vinny Dotolo remember. "However, L.A. is deeply ethnic, with influences that are Japanese, Chinese, Korean, Mexican, and Central American, and we're influenced by these flavors."

Fellow Los Angeleno Michael Voltaggio of ink is influenced by them, too. "When I lived in New York, we would go eat at Jean Georges and Daniel. But in L.A., the places to go and get inspired were these small, ethnic restaurants. It was what we were eating, and where we went to do our research. If we went to Thaitown, even the first time you'd taste a green papaya salad, you'd think, 'Whoa, **chiles + dried shrimp + peanuts + lime juice + green papaya**—I can do something with this.' We opened this restaurant with a similar dish. Then we tried the same flavors with watermelon rind [instead of green papaya]. A lot of the creative process starts with that."

Curtis Duffy of Chicago's Grace told us, "I love the flavor profiles of Japan, Thailand, Malaysia, and Vietnam, which I find clean and subtle, so you can taste what you're eating. On my days off, if I'm not cooking at home, I always gravitate to those kinds of restaurants. In San Francisco, I love the Slanted Door, where I had the best papaya salad I've ever had. Its flavor haunts me—I'd want to eat it every day. But I wouldn't serve a green papaya salad here. We realized squash was in season, so we shave raw **butternut squash** the same way, and serve it with **caramelized shallots + garlic + ginger + red jalapeño threads**, with a similar dressing made with **cilantro + fish sauce + garlic + lime juice + palm sugar**."

Even without in-person visits, restaurants can still be a source of inspiration to chefs. "The Internet has changed the field," observes Marcus Samuelsson. "It has brought us closer together because you can search even further [afield]. For me, I don't want to go online to be creative. I want to have my idea in my head first; then, I will go online to find a better ingredient. However, I don't want to discover the original idea online. I don't want to use the Internet as a creative tool—I want to use it as a tool of information. Otherwise, I think you are cheating as a chef. I would never *start* my process there."

Norman Van Aken of Florida's 1921 by Norman Van Aken agrees. "The world of young cooks has been changed dramatically by the Internet," he says. "What in many ways should be an environment for a *wide* cosmos of food inspiration has ironically seemed to create a *narrowing* one. I think the very slow process of matriculation that I took—e.g., reading one cookbook at a time (due in part to the fact that was really all I could afford)—was a steadier firmament and also one that gave me a chance to pay closer attention to the many lessons within those great books. To teach them about flavor and the creative process we really have to

unplug them from the 'machinery' routinely and get them into the grassroots of truly tasting the food."

"Instagram is a good tool but like any tool it must be used in just the right way," he continues. "I think that many young cooks are too busy looking at the plates and presentations at the very point they need to understand the power of taste. I don't think James Beard, Edna Lewis, or Elizabeth David suffered for not having all of the *flood* of information young cooks have now. And it's my belief that is the way those three culinary gods (and other culinary gods) got down (and still can get down) to the essence of what is vital to flavor and creativity."

The best chefs see their education as a never-ending process. Chicago pastry chef Meg Galus was nominated for the James Beard Foundation's Outstanding Pastry Chef award in 2016, yet doesn't consider her education complete. "I stay inspired by learning all the time," she says. "Two months ago, I staged with my friend Sandra Holl at Floriole Café & Bakery in Chicago. I hung out for a day, shaping baguettes—which is not like riding a bike—and making crusty breads and sourdough breads."

Gavin Kaysen employs a different strategy at Minneapolis's Spoon and Stable than he did when he was cooking in Manhattan. "In New York City, virtually every cook talked about spending time in the kitchen at Eleven Madison Park, Gramercy Tavern, Momofuku, or Per Se—it was always the same four restaurants. In Minneapolis, I found the cooks weren't talking about cookbooks or the World's 50 Best Restaurants list," he says.

"So I started a continuing education program where every month, everyone in our front- and back-of-the-house will read a book—one month we read the book *Creativity, Inc.* [by Ed Catmull and Amy Wallace]—or attend a program, and then on Fridays at 2 pm we'd spend 45 minutes discussing it," Kaysen says. "I started our Synergy Series to bring chefs like Daniel Boulud and Michael Anthony and April Bloomfield into our kitchen so our team can meet them and cook with them and learn from them. None of them will ever forget the two hours they spent making pasta with Michael White."

Restaurant chefs often ask potential hires about their interests outside the kitchen—believing that if the only thing a cook is interested in is, say, watching TV or playing video games, s/he might not bring much inspiration to the rest of the cooks in the kitchen. In addition, they recognize that sports and other athletics are a great way to stay in shape for the physical demands of being on your feet all day—and great recovery to avoid burnout. Through interacting with diverse colleagues with varied interests, the way chefs think about their cooking changes, either directly or indirectly.

Rick Bayless likes to ask prospective cooks about the last thing they cooked at home. If they cooked a special meal for their girlfriend a month ago, that's not the same level of engagement of someone who made something delicious last night.

I try to not always think about food.

—AMANDA COHEN, Dirt Candy (New York City)

Bayless wants to work with people like him—those who can't *not* think about food. And people who have an outside passion—other hobbies that inspire them as much as cooking does. Those people, he finds, can bring more to the kitchen in terms of experience and can inspire others.

Given their portability, books are arguably chefs' favorite sources of both stimulation *and* stillness. As Le Bernardin's Eric Ripert has mused, "The importance of reading, to me, is that it allows you to dream." British chef Heston Blumenthal counts an 1865 first edition of *Alice in Wonderland* as one of his favorite sources of inspiration, noting that "it's full of fantastic ideas."

"I read more about agriculture than cookbooks," admits Woodberry Kitchen's Spike Gjerde. "I read Wendell Berry and got my mind blown—start with *Bringing It to the Table*, then *The Unsettling of America*, and *Sex, Economy, Freedom & Community*. After Woodberry Kitchen had opened, I found these books and finally understood what we were doing. He's informed me."

I'll judge a meal two months later, asking myself, "What do I remember?"

—RICK BAYLESS, Topolobampo (Chicago)

Pastry chef Emily Luchetti says she's always loved books. "Talk about creativity and opening people's minds—you read a book, and you're opened up to a whole new world," she enthuses. "I love reading not just to get new ideas, but to be inspired. I loved Jacques Pépin's memoir [*The Apprentice: My Life in the Kitchen*], which I found very soulful. I loved Marcus Samuelsson's memoir [*Yes, Chef*]—he's an amazing human being who's living an authentic human life. It was very heartfelt. I also loved the memoirs of Katharine Graham and Madeleine Albright. I'm inspired to learn how people choose to live their lives, and when they take the time to look inward."

New ingredients are as important to creativity metaphorically as they are literally. Research shows that the more we diverge from our regular routines, the greater the stimulation to our creativity. At the 2016 annual Cherry Bombe Jubilee in New York City, keynote speaker Martha Stewart mentioned that she never takes the same route to get where she's going, staying on constant lookout for new ideas and inspirations. The best chefs know to push themselves to experience new influences, which they use as fodder for their creative efforts—whether it's looking at art, or traveling somewhere new every year.

When we "temporarily" started to eat vegetarian for research purposes for the first time in our lives in 2012 while writing and photographing *The Vegetarian Flavor Bible*, it was a revelation to discover that this shake-up in our eating routine inadvertently prompted us to think about food and flavor in entirely new and more creative ways. We encourage everyone to experiment with changing their diet in some way periodically—or at least to experiment by actively seeking out dishes you'd never imagined you might enjoy—simply for the shift of perspective it brings.

Shifting perspective can be powerful indeed. Author David R. Hawkins celebrated the universally inspirational and timeless effect of (to cite just a few examples) the art of Rembrandt, the music of Robert Gass, Arvo Pärt, and Johann Pachelbel, and the architecture of great cathedrals and temples, such as St. Peter's Basilica, the Taj Mahal, Notre-Dame, and Westminster Abbey, which he argued have the power to elevate one's level of consciousness, albeit temporarily.

STILLNESS: ENGAGING WITH YOUR INNER WORLD

The most creative chefs build rituals around not only gaining stimulation but also making time for stillness. The former fuels their energy and ideas, while the latter allows them to access the goldmine of material available to them through their inner senses. As René Redzepi learned, it's vital to make the time and effort to listen to yourself.

> **Stillness is where creativity and solutions to problems are found.**
>
> —**ECKHART TOLLE,** author of *The Power of Now*

Activities that provide an opportunity for stillness may slow your brain waves—but they don't necessarily slow your body.

Stephanie Izard of Chicago's Girl and the Goat gets up at 5:30 every morning to go to the gym. "I am on a masters swim team, which is my release," she told us. "You have to do something, and I think more chefs realize exercise is better than going out drinking. I feel better and happier. I am still stressed, but swimming takes away at least 25 percent of the stress.

"Then I go to work at 8:30 am, and split my time between the restaurants and meetings. I only work until 8:30 or 9:00 pm—only twelve hours," she says. "Then I go home and hang out with my dog and husband, who will cook us a late dinner so I have some sense of normalcy."

Other chefs are as committed to other sports. Eleven Madison Park's Daniel Humm used to be on a Swiss mountain bike team until he was forced to choose between cycling and cooking. After he opted for the latter, he picked up marathon running to fill the gap, running the New York City Marathon in less than three hours. "Running relaxes and inspires me," he says.

Humm's enthusiasm for sports has been infectious. The NoMad's chef James Kent told us, "I lost 50 pounds over the past two years [after being challenged by chef Daniel Humm to start biking and running], and I'm part of the 'Made Nice' team and ran the New York City Marathon."

> **It's no accident that the best idea I've ever had in my life—perhaps maybe the best one I'll ever have in my life—came to me on vacation. When I picked up Ron Chernow's biography [of Alexander Hamilton], I was at a resort in Mexico on my first vacation from *In The Heights*, which I had been working seven years to bring to Broadway. The moment my brain got a moment's rest, *HAMILTON* walked into it.**
>
> —**LIN-MANUEL MIRANDA,** playwright and star of *Hamilton*, as quoted in *GQ*

He discusses how this affected his cooking: "Over time, your palate changes. I still love delicious, incredible, and healthy food, but I'm not so into cream and butter anymore. In the past, I would add cream and mount foie gras into everything. Now, I want to take you to the same place and create the same feelings with different ingredients," says Kent. "Daniel Humm is a competitive athlete, and doesn't do classic French cuisine—his sauces are lighter, and his food is more delicate. Our food has more simplicity. There's more focus on serving perfect ingredients....These days, I use more nuts, healthy fats like avocados, oils, acidity like citrus, including finger limes, orange juice, and grapefruit juice....At EMP, we focused on making vegetables special, and learned how to add flavor and depth without fat and dairy, such as with dashi."

Other times, chefs slow both their bodies and their minds. "I'm a very physical person, so I like the physicality of yoga—but I also like that it's so meditative. My yoga practice is my meditation," says Rick Bayless. **"Meditation is a way to put my mind in neutral, and to allow creativity.** During my yoga practice, ideas often pop up in my mind. I'll be tempted to stop and write them down, or I'll hope to remember them and not leave my yoga state."

Rick Bayless

"I will run, bike, or do jujitsu. I love the power of martial arts and the sense of being stronger inside," says Chris Long of Natalie's at the Camden Harbour Inn. "It helps me find my breath and be more peaceful."

Other chefs will take the time for stillness whenever they can make it. Emily Luchetti told us, "**I value silence.** I'm always trying to stop and clear out my head."

Eddy Leroux, the chef de cuisine at Daniel in New York City, is religious about carving out time for himself. "Every day at 1:30 pm, I'll go to Table 63 [in the corner of Daniel], and have an hour of **quiet time** to work on the projects in my files, like new dishes and dishes for special upcoming events....In addition to **keeping a notebook** in my top pocket, I also use the app **Paper by FiftyThree** on my iPad when I'm conceptualizing new dishes. I love how technology can make it so much easier

Eddy Leroux, and his iPad (right)

I wasn't listening enough to myself.

—RENÉ REDZEPI,
on the insight that led to Noma's original breakthrough

to do this. I use a stylus to make rough sketches of the dish [the app turns hand-drawn circles and squares into perfect shapes], and the program can even color in the food. Then I'll email the sketches and description to my team."

Dirt Candy's Amanda Cohen agrees about the need to carve out time just to think. **"If you don't think new thoughts, it's harder to come up with new ideas,"** she says. "We did an event in Philadelphia this week, and Johnny [the restaurant's bread baker] drove. I wanted to sit in the backseat so I could look out the window, daydreaming or thinking."

Jeremy Fox of Rustic Canyon in Los Angeles says he doesn't really know how he creates anything. "But usually it is on the hour drive in to work," he says. "I stop at my Shell gas station and grab my $1.99 coffee with the pump creamer and get that coffee jolt. Then **not being able to do anything else for the next hour is when I will think of things,** and when dishes come together."

Jeremy Fox

While the time on the ground can provide nonstop stimulation, traveling by plane can offer its own time for stillness. Marcus Samuelsson says, "When I travel, it is a way to escape and be in other places and really apply myself in a good way. I have always been a writer. On a trip to Sweden, I will write for two hours, catch up on a podcast or a film I need to see, and then sleep for two hours. It is a seven-hour flight so it is two, two, and two, and a very productive use of time. More than anything, **finding this kind of 'alone space' is the key.**"

Running is a huge part of turning my mind off. . . . On a great run, you can start with one idea, chew it through, change your mind in the middle, and land someplace entirely different.

—MARCUS SAMUELSSON,
Red Rooster, Ginny's Supper Club, and Streetbird (Harlem)

Patrick O'Connell on Stillness and Imagination

The first thing I do every morning: I have a little balcony [at his house, which is across the street from the Inn at Little Washington's main property], and I go out and assess the day and the light. And it affects everything about how I feel. . . .

The only place that moves me in the same way is Paris—because it's picking out certain details that you wouldn't see otherwise. So on a gray, drizzly day in Paris, you'll walk outside and it's like Washington [D.C.]: just gray. And then the light will hit—and it will be as though theater lighting has picked out all the details, and you're just drawn to all of them. You wouldn't think that you could have that same feeling of excitement here, because you live here—but you do. And you can see it in people that they're just excited to be out and seeing it differently.

I'll commune. My eyes can see the flaws. **But they can also imagine what it's going to look like here 20 years from now—when the trees grow bigger, when a certain eyesore may be obliterated. So, it's exhilarating.** . . .There are cold, damp days, of course, and on those days, food is your salvation. On one of those days, I'll walk into the kitchen and I feel wonderful—because it smells great, it's warm everywhere, but it's a nourishing kind of deep, comforting warm. And you think, "I'll get through it."

I think the reason I'm here is to prove that you can turn all your liabilities into assets, little by little. Everything that is a curse also has a flip side. So if you're only seeing what's wrong, treat it as a gift. Be a flaw corrector. Make money off it! If you can't get anything right [elsewhere], *make* it right for others.

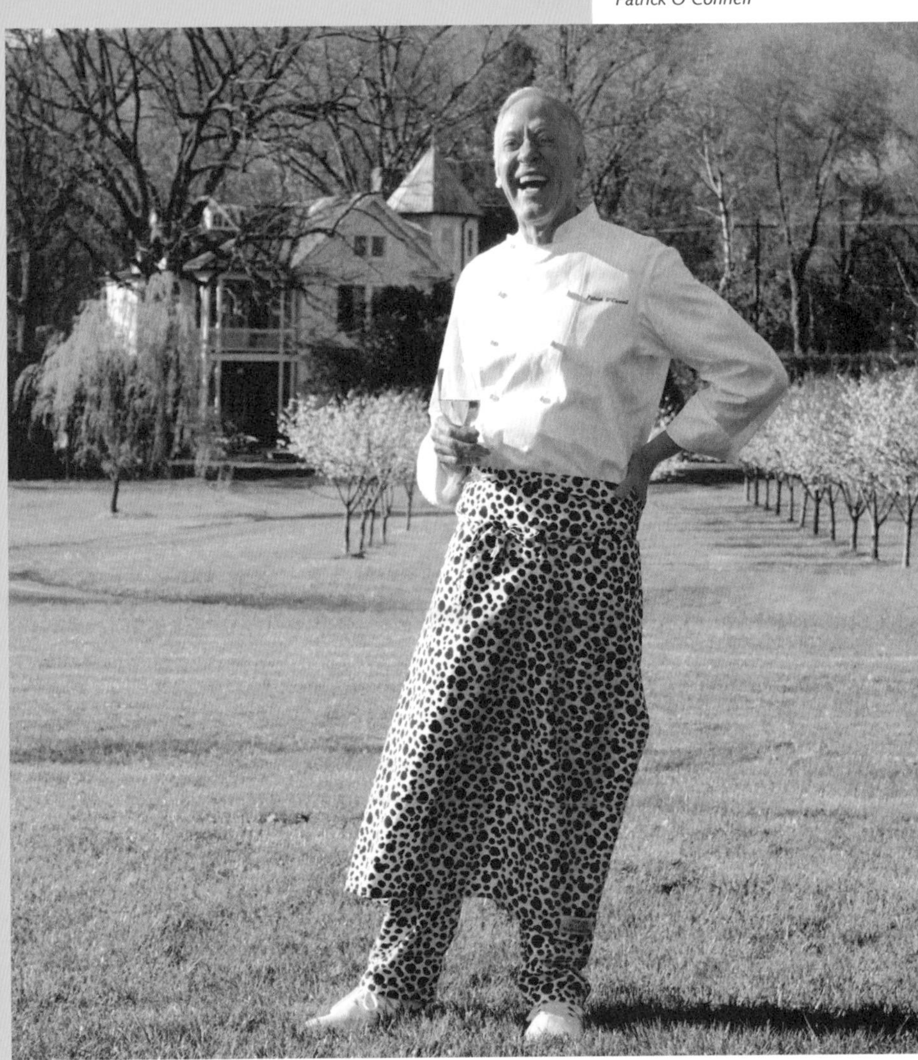
Patrick O'Connell

RIDING THE WAVES OF CREATIVITY: OUR BRAIN WAVE STATES AND THEIR SENSORY FOCUS

When you're seeking to access and enhance your inner senses in order to boost your creativity, it can be helpful to realize that different senses correlate to different brain wave states.

Brain waves are measured in cycles per second, called Hertz (Hz). Our normal waking state for working is called **Beta,** in which we're primarily focused on our outer senses (such as sight, hearing, touch).

In order to tap more of our inner senses (including intuition, insight, imagination), we need to practice ways of relaxing in order to slow our brain wave state down to **Alpha** or even **Theta.**

See tips for slowing your brain waves in **How to Get Your Creativity Flowing** (pages 210–211).

State (Hertz)	Consciousness	Activities	Primary Sensory Focus	Primary Inner Senses Enhanced	Best For
Beta (12–40 Hz)	Conscious	Awake / alert	OUTER	Instinct	Working: concentrating, linear thinking, problem-solving; reasoning
Alpha (7–12 Hz)	Conscious / Subconscious	Relaxed	Outer & Inner	Imagination & Intuition	Focused concentration and creative readiness ("flow"); daydreaming (with eyes open); meditating; peak athletic performance; superlearning
Theta* (4–7 Hz)	Subconscious	Deeply relaxed / dreaming	INNER & Outer	Imagination & Insight & Intuition	Deep meditating, dreaming, about to fall asleep or just waking up; being hypnotized
Delta (0–4 Hz)	Unconscious	Asleep	INNER	[all]	Deep, dreamless sleep (as well as sleepwalking and sleep talking); healing

*The sudden insight experience often starts in **Theta** and sometimes produces a spike in **Gamma** (40–130+ Hz) waves, which represents a very rare state of elevated consciousness (achieved by very experienced meditators), one accompanied by heightened awareness, perception, and concentration, not to mention inspiration, compassion, and creativity.

Resources: While it's possible to reach all the brain wave states above unassisted, there are audio programs designed to help access various states, including those created by field pioneers Bill Harris of Centerpointe (Holosync) and Monroe Products (Hemi-Sync), as well as Jeffrey Thompson's Brainwave Suite, and John Dupuy and Pam Parsons Dupuy's iAwake Technologies. There is a growing industry of companies that work with clients to train their brain wave states to boost creativity and performance, for instance 40 Years of Zen and the Biocybernaut Institute.

The difference between a noncreative person and a highly creative person is the ability to turn on Alpha waves at will.

—**DR. JAMES HARDT** of the Biocybernaut Institute, whose Stanford Research Institute scientist subjects experienced a 50 percent increase in creativity after being trained to reach high Alpha states

WANT TO TRIPLE YOUR CREATIVITY? CHOOSE TO BE HAPPY

Harvard professor Shawn Achor, who wrote the bestselling book *The Happiness Advantage*, underscores the fact that **"scientifically, happiness is a choice.** It is a choice about where your single processor brain will devote its finite resources as you process the world."

The book *The How of Happiness* by Stanford PhD Sonja Lyubomirsky backs this up. She's written that one's genetic set point determines just 50 percent of happiness, while 10 percent is attributed to differences in one's life circumstances [e.g., wealth, health, marital status]. **Fully 40 percent of our capacity for happiness is within our power to change—via our intentional activity [i.e., attitudes and actions].**

Lyubomirsky has detailed the seven things the research shows the world's happiest people do every day: 1. **nurture and enjoy relationships** with family and friends; 2. **express gratitude;** 3. **offer help** to others; 4. **practice optimism** when imagining their futures; 5. **savor life's pleasures** and try to **live in the present** moment; 6. **exercise** weekly or even daily; and 7. **hold deep commitments** to lifelong goals and ambitions. She adds that while the happiest people have their share of stresses and crises, **"their secret weapon is the poise and strength they show in coping in the face of challenge."**

Achor suggests applying five research-tested ways to focus on enhancing your happiness *every day for 21 consecutive days,* which is how long it takes to reprogram the neuropathways in your brain to create a new habit:

1. Write down **three new things you are grateful for.**
2. Write for two minutes, describing **one positive experience you had over the past 24 hours.**
3. **Exercise for ten minutes.**
4. **Meditate for two minutes,** focusing on your breath going in and out.
5. Write **one quick email first thing in the morning, thanking or praising someone** in your social support network (e.g., a relative, friend, former teacher).

Life is difficult. This is a great truth, one of the greatest truths. It is a great truth because once we truly see this truth, we transcend it. Once we truly know that life is difficult—once we truly understand and accept it—then life is no longer difficult. Because once it is accepted, the fact that life is difficult no longer matters.

—M. SCOTT PECK, *The Road Less Traveled*

Increases in positive mood broaden attention and allow us to see more possible solutions to creative problems.

—DR. SHELLEY CARSON, *Your Creative Brain*

Happy employees have, on average, 31 percent higher productivity, their sales are 37 percent higher; their creativity is three times higher.

—*HARVARD BUSINESS REVIEW Guide to Managing Stress at Work*

HOW TO GET YOUR CREATIVITY FLOWING

- **Change** whatever it was you were doing at the moment you discovered your creativity *wasn't* flowing and that you felt stuck. Shift your physiology. If you were seated, stand up—and if you were standing, take a seat. Go to another room, or outside.
- **Be in the moment.** Dwelling in the past (e.g., regret) or future (e.g., anxiety) is a major cause of stress. **Focusing on the present** will help to reduce your fear (i.e., anxiety about the future) and increase your joy (i.e., appreciation for the present moment). When you are stressed, your thought processes are under the control of your emotions, so your creativity is challenged. When you are relaxed, your ability to come up with a greater number of ideas and to make novel combinations is enhanced.
- **"Slow down."** When we slow our brain waves, we move more deeply into our "inner" world. Faster brain waves typically correlate with our conscious mind, and slower brain waves with our subconscious/unconscious mind.
  - **Move your body.** The Alpha brain state is a peak performance state for many professional or Olympic athletes—and indeed running, biking, or swimming, or even taking a walk or a yoga class, can help to bring your brain waves to an Alpha state.
  - **Close your eyes.** As fully 80 percent of our sensory inputs come from our sense of sight, the first thing you can do to take yourself from Beta to the more creative state of Alpha is to close your eyes! This alone will help you to be more aware of your inner senses.
- **Meditate.** Many leading chefs espouse the benefits of regular meditation, including **Mario Batali**, **Rick Bayless**, **Eric Ripert**, and **Christina Tosi**. Batali says he meditates twice a day for 20 minutes using TM (Transcendental Meditation), after being turned onto it by comedian Jerry Seinfeld and his wife Jessica, and recommends the David Lynch Foundation (created by the celebrated film director, who also wrote the book *Catching the Big Fish: Meditation, Consciousness, and Creativity*) as a resource for learning more: davidlynchfoundation.org.
  - **Keep it fresh.** Experiment with following a "guided" (i.e., recorded) meditation if you typically meditate in silence—or vice versa.
  - **Breathe deeply.** Slow your brain waves by **focusing on your breath.** As your breath slows (and deepens), so, too, do your brain waves. Jessica Dibb reminds us that the archaic definition of the word "inspiration" is "to breathe into," and that our deep inhale breathes in inspiration while our deep exhale releases resistance.
  - **Quiet your "monkey mind."** Most of us recycle the same thoughts over and over (e.g., fear-based negative self-talk), so that there's little room in our heads for new, original thoughts. Thinking too much destroys creativity—it keeps your mind focused on the outer rather than **the inner world, where ideas are created**.

My brain is only a receiver. In the universe there is a core from which we obtain knowledge, strength, and inspiration. I have not penetrated into the secrets of this core, but I know that it exists.

—**NIKOLA TESLA,** inventor

Creativity is the most important aspect of our lives—the one that makes us bigger than we are . . . Our creative thoughts are right there in our minds, just waiting to be noticed . . . To increase our creativity, all we need to do is give what's already there a chance to be discovered...by slowing our breath to slow our minds.

—**JESSICA DIBB,** breathwork expert

Meditation is one of the best antidotes for overthinking. Eliminating thinking through meditating can take us to the deeply relaxed Theta state.

- **Listen to music.** If you're looking to quickly **lower your brainwaves into a more relaxed Alpha state**, turn on slower-tempo **Baroque** music (e.g., compositions by Bach, Handel, Mozart, Vivaldi). Alternatively, listen to specific hemi-sync recordings that are designed to use binaural beats via headphones to change brain waves (see suggestions on page 208).
- **Let go of a grudge.** Neurofeedback equipment is being used to prove that **practicing forgiveness**—of anyone in your life you perceive as having wronged or angered you—is possibly the single best way to spike Alpha brain waves.
- **Sleep on it:** To get the most out of the deeply creative Theta state (in which "aha" moments occur) and the healing Delta state (in which our body receives vital R&R, allowing its self-healing mechanisms to function), write down your intention (e.g., awakening with ideas for your next sunchoke dish or anniversary menu) before you go to sleep. Keep a notebook by your bed, and write down anything that comes to mind before falling asleep or upon waking, including your dreams. While this process may not yield an exact word-for-word recipe, it may very well be possible to connect the dots between whatever ideas come up and the dish or menu you're working on.
- **Write "Morning Pages":** Following *The Artist's Way* author Julia Cameron's practice of starting every morning with three longhand pages of stream-of-consciousness journaling frees the mind for your creative endeavors.

Everything is the result of our thoughts . . . [yet] eighty percent of our thoughts are [typically] negative . . . [The solution lies in] the act of catching ourselves.

—**ANTHONY RUDOLF,** cofounder of The Welcome Conference

Dreams can be creative indeed—having provided the inspiration for Albert Einstein's theory of relativity, Elias Howe's sewing machine, Paul McCartney's "Yesterday," Dmitri Mendeleev's periodic table, Stephanie Meyer's *Twilight*, Larry Page's Google, Mary Shelley's *Frankenstein*, and Dr. James Watson's double-helix structure of DNA.

Your perceived sense of well-being is enhanced by any type of meditation. There are two main types of meditation:
1. focused attention, such as the repetition of a mantra; and
2. open monitoring of whatever comes into your attention based on whatever is present. . . . The key is to spend 20 minutes sitting upright, paying attention to your breathing, and repeating one word or phrase ("om," "one," "love," etc.). In addition to enhancing your sense of well-being, there's more and more evidence that meditation allows you to generate more ideas in less time and to make better decisions.

—**MICHAEL GELB,** author of *How to Think Like Leonardo da Vinci*

Eric Ripert on Enhancing Creativity Through Meditation

It is impossible to be creative if you are stressed out. . . .Meditation can help your creativity, no doubt—it helps you go deep with concentration.

Because I am Buddhist, I combine the theory of emptiness in Buddhism with the secular approach of the scientist through quantum mechanics—and it all comes together for me.

For me, Buddhism is a way to become a better person. I try not to bring it back to the restaurant in a religious way or to impose anything on the team. If I do bring something in, I try to bring it in a secular universal message that doesn't attach itself to a religion.

I have my meditation time for myself, as well as my meditation room at home. Everyone—even the cats—knows not to come into the room.

I practice two types of meditation: **samatha** [also known as calming or one-pointed meditation] and **vipassana** [also known as insight meditation].

Samatha Meditation

If you are not in control of your brain, your brain is in control of you. Our brains are typically very analytical and distracted. They have a tendency to go into the future or into the past, but they're very rarely in the present.

Samatha is single-pointed meditation, which means basically that you decide you are going to "shut down the engine" and bring your brain to the present. The most classic technique, which I don't use

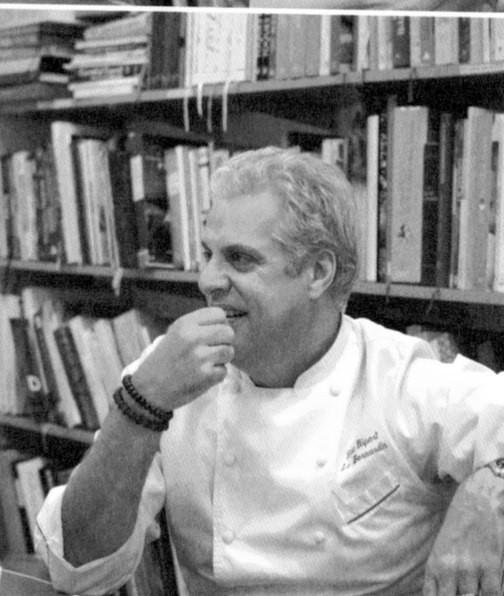

Eric Ripert

necessarily, is to focus on your breathing: You focus on the process of inhaling, and then focus on the process of exhaling. You do that with no distractions, only focusing on that—and it is very difficult.

For myself, I focus on the energy going through my chakras [see CHAKRAS, page 270] and other energy points. When I inhale, I focus on my energy going up [from the root chakra at the base of the spine to the crown chakra at the top of the head], and when I exhale, I focus on my energy coming back down to my root chakra. I just observe the energy going up and the energy coming down without any judgment.

Concentration is the king that rules the mind. When stabilized, it sits like a mountain; when directed, it can enter every creative sphere. It leads to every physical and mental joy.

—Lama Tsongkhapa

That is my way of meditating in samatha. . . . I do a short version of this on a daily basis.

The difficulty a lot of the time—no matter what technique you practice—is that your mind has so many thoughts passing through it. So you observe, acknowledge the thought, and let it go. If you look up and see one cloud in the sky, you'd say, "One cloud," and let it go. Then, you go back to your state of mind that is very peaceful.

I don't count the minutes. Focusing on time is a big mistake for beginners, because that then becomes a stress on your mind. It is better to meditate for three minutes that are amazing rather than to meditate for a half-hour and having 57 thoughts arise.

This is the way you train your mind to concentrate. It is helpful because it also relaxes your mind. That way, when you research a subject, you can go extremely deep into your investigation of it.

Vipassana Meditation

I also do vipassana, which is basically a Buddhist guided meditation. Every morning I do the Seven Leaf meditation from the Tibetan master Lama Tsongkhapa, who was an expert at defining what emptiness means.

I do both [samatha and vipassana] because if you want more concentration in the guided meditation, it is good to do a little samatha first to calm the mind and create an environment that is almost like a soil for the good seeds for yourself.

I sometimes do other meditations that may not be Buddhist, including one on compassion. The idea is to prepare your mind to have compassion for everyone.

THE EVOLUTION OF CREATIVITY IN COOKING

Cooking has been evolving along with society itself.

As we evolved beyond being hunter-gatherers dependent on kill-or-be-killed for our **survival**, cooking has helped to exert a civilizing influence on society through its own evolution into a professional **trade.**

Those bringing great care and skill to cooking elevated it into artisanship or **craft.** And the huge influx of talent into the profession in the 1970s and 1980s introduced a new level of love and imagination in the field, demonstrating that it was even being raised to an **art**, as we argued in 1996 in *Culinary Artistry*.

Since then, some chefs have increasingly elevated the intention behind their creativity to the level of compassion, through embracing **mission**-driven projects (e.g., those referenced on page 224), not to mention offering even more compassionate cuisine (e.g., allergen-free, plant-based, minimal carbon footprint, sustainable, zero-waste) at multiple price points expanding accessibility (from fine dining to fast-casual). The world of food has since been experiencing unprecedented creativity—within each category, between categories, and extending beyond them.

One can expand one's power—including creative power—by elevating one's level of consciousness and dominant emotional state.

Imagine: What might be possible in the future of food as creativity continues to rise to new levels?

Chefs have an opportunity—and perhaps the responsibility—to use their cooking to shape culture, to manifest what's possible, and, in doing so, to inspire a new ethic of eating.

—**DAN BARBER,** Blue Hill at Stone Barns (Pocantico Hills, New York)

To me, everything is sacred. . . . I pray for the life of the animals. . . . I think when you regard every ingredient as something sacred, and as a life, you approach it and transform it in a very different way.

—**ERIC RIPERT,** Le Bernardin (New York City)

[It] changed the dynamic about what it means to be a great restaurant. . . . That model was always based on an ego-driven concept. The new standard is about having a social mission.

—**ROY CHOI,** on his and Daniel Patterson's LocoL winning the *Los Angeles Times* 2017 Restaurant of the Year award

	PRE-CHEF	TYPES OF CHEFS			
	Survival	**Trade**	**Craft**	**Art**	**Mission**
Category	"Hunter-Gatherers"	"Burger Flippers"	"Accomplished Chefs"	"Culinary Artists"	"Culinary Missionaries"
Customer Goal	True Survival	Survival	Enjoyment	Entertainment	Nourishment
Chef's Intention		Fill / Feed	Satisfy / Please	Transcend / Transport	Compassion / Consciousness
Price of Lunch	Life, if necessary	Movie ticket	Off-Broadway theater ticket	Broadway orchestra ticket	Tiered pricing (accommodating all)
Who Determines Meal	Force / Fate	Customer ("Have it your way")	Customer / Chef	Chef (Tasting Menu)	Customer Needs / Chef Mission Statement
Chef's Primary Repertoire	—	Burgers	Classic dishes	Chef's own dishes	Inspired, nourishing dishes
Number of Senses Used	—	5 (outer)	5 (outer)	6 (5 outer + "sixth")	10 (5 outer, 5 inner)
Customers Leave Saying	"What's next?"	"I'm full."	"That was delicious."	"Life is wonderful."	"We are all one."
Consciousness / Emotional State	Fear / Anxiety	Courage / Affirmation	Willingness / Optimism	Love / Reverence	Universal Love / Peace

THE CREATIVE PINNACLES: INDIVIDUATION AND INTERDEPENDENCE

Individuation is Carl Jung's way of describing self-actualization, or the process of living authentically while expanding the boundaries of what we allow ourselves to perceive and experience. Through using both our outer and inner senses, we are able to tap more deeply the realm of unlimited creative possibility.

Mark Levy of Magdalena at the Ivy Hotel in Baltimore recalls, "From my first day as a cook until I turned 30, everything I cooked was inspired by others. Grant Achatz's book [*Alinea*] came out, and I'd try making mozzarella using a CO_2 canister and chasing down different spices. Then I started asking myself, 'What *is* this chemical?' and then, 'Do I really want *that* in my food?'"

"**Finally, I started asking myself, 'What do *I* like?'**" he says. "Since that time, I've been trusting and cooking what I like. As a cook, a lot of times you get beaten down, or you turn into a robot—and no one ever develops your confidence in what you're doing. So to really start believing in what I know or what I feel is right—it was probably the most important thing I had to learn. Now, I will buy books by people with similar views, or who know something I specifically want to learn about."

Finger Lakes chef-restaurateur-master sommelier Christopher Bates of FLX Wienery and FLX Table has long kept a close eye on what is trending in food, so much so that his former dining room at the Hotel Fauchère in tiny Milford, Pennsylvania, was serving foraged foods on slate even before some Manhattan restaurants started doing likewise. "Food is so good and pretty now—everyone wants to eat off a broken barn door now, and it is hard not to want that," he acknowledges. "But **at some point you have to resist [the trends] and come up with your own ideas and walk your own path**. Today, I have to look away from everyone else....I see the Nordic plating and it is so cool and beautiful, but I need to do my own thing and not try to keep up with the Joneses. **I'd rather come up with what is next versus [imitating] what is happening now.**"

"Culinary inspiration is funny," Bates continues. "Loic [Leperlier, of the Point resort in Saranac Lake, New York] and I were talking about it, and he explained that he didn't look at cook-

—ERIC RIPERT,
Le Bernardin (New York City)

Think carefully about what makes you special and different from everyone else.

—**MICHAEL ANTHONY,**
Gramercy Tavern and Untitled (New York City)

In the forest, you can't see the individual trees. . . . It's important to ask yourself the question: How are you unique and different? . . . Being creative reflects an evolution of who you are as a person. . . .The door is currently wide open to different expressions.

—**EMILY LUCHETTI,** chief pastry officer, The Cavalier, Marlowe, and Park Tavern (San Francisco)

books as much anymore. I try not to keep up with stuff anymore, either, so I got what he was saying. These were things I was thinking five years ago. Today, **I want my inspiration to come from *my* life and *my* interests.**" Those personal inspirations seem to be resonating with others; FLX Table was named the country's best new restaurant in a 2017 *USA Today* 10Best Readers' Choice poll.

Curtis Duffy of Chicago's Grace recognizes the difference in his cooking. "We can do a lot of crazy things, but it has to fit the big picture of what I'm trying to achieve," he says. "It has to fit the identity. As a young cook, I could pick out Charlie Trotter's dishes or Thomas Keller's dishes anywhere. So I always wanted to have that kind of identity, too," he says. "People who know me personally would describe my cuisine as a personality cuisine. **It's foods that I enjoy cooking with and eating when they're in season—it's foods that make me happy.** I would never put shrimp or green bell peppers on my menu, because these are things that I don't eat—I'm allergic to shrimp, and I don't like the flavor of green peppers. I veer away from heat [i.e., capsicum] altogether. I can appreciate it, but I don't cook with it."

As a pastry chef, I am very focused on who I am and what I want to do. I pay attention to trends, but I'm not a copycat. I JUST DO ME.

—**TAIESHA MARTIN,** pastry chef, Glenmere Mansion (Chester, New York)

San Francisco's Emily Luchetti shares that her MBTI (Myers-Briggs Type Indicator, a leading personality test) type is ESTJ (Extroverted, Sensing, Thinking, Judging), which means she likes "rules and making decisions...."But there's no recipe for an ideal pastry chef," she acknowledges. "Why can some people cook? Why can some people be creative? You can learn technique, and to train your palate, but I don't think you can teach creativity. **You just have to take it all in—all you study, all you read, all you taste—and then it starts churning inside you. And, if you're lucky, it comes out—as a replication, or as an adaptation, or as something completely original.**"

Animal's Jon Shook and Vinny Dotolo recall that at Bastide, Ludo Lefebvre, their partner in Trois Mec was "doing elBulli stuff....Now, he's cooking over an open fire. He really brings all of it together," they told us. **"That's what you do as a chef: You're telling your story."**

"We're telling a story through all of our restaurants—all of our life experiences, all of the things we learned about food," they continued. "Chefs used to do it through a tasting menu, and now I think they're doing it through multiple restaurants. Many chefs now have five restaurants—once they hit something, they're trying to find that other thing where they can have that creative outlet. You can

You have to write your own story. Everyone else's is taken. . . . Have something to say? Go for it. REMAIN TRUE TO YOURSELF.

—LIOR LEV SERCARZ,
La Boîte (New York City)

only stuff so much into one place. We couldn't pack a seafood concept, an Italian concept, and Animal into one thing. You need a release."

Patrick O'Connell believes every chef can carve out his or her own niche. "I think the creative process and that energy can be exhibited in anything, anywhere. I like the Blue Ocean idea [as explained in the bestselling book *Blue Ocean Strategy* by W. Chan Kim and Renée Mauborgne] that if you differentiate yourself clearly in every possible way, you won't be chasing after the same goals that everyone else is—you will carve out a [niche for yourself].

"It's an intriguing book," he continues. "We had a speaker talk about it at one of our international Relais & Châteaux meetings. **The idea is that you don't go after what your competition is going after. You go after what is totally authentic to you. And ultimately there won't be any competition—because we're all unique in who we are."**

José Andrés at Beefsteak (top), holding the glass vases he blew with artist Dale Chihuly (middle), and planting tomatoes in his garden (bottom)

José Andrés on Creativity

Creativity to me is anything that allows you to solve a problem. It doesn't matter how big or small—but it solves a need, challenge, or dilemma in a successful way. So you could argue that behind every creative process there needs to be a question or a challenge. It could even be one you invent, like, "I want to create a cauliflower [that] is frozen on the outside and creamy on the inside!" (See page 168.)

Despite coming up with the idea for my salt-air margarita there, in general, it is hard to be creative on a beach. **Creativity can happen at any time**—and I think creativity happens in the most unexpected ways in daily life. But it's more likely that I'll be working, not on the beach in the Caribbean.

You need to be aware of who you are and how you relate to ingredients. For inspiration, you can go to your main sources and look for new ingredients or equipment. Sometimes you might get inspired by the farmers' market or fishermen.

True creators are challenged by moving away from their comfort zones. Sometimes I need to move away from my normal forms of inspiration to be inspired. Working with Dale Chihuly blowing glass served as a source of inspiration for the first-ever caramelized olive oil, based on how Dale works with glass....The caramelized olive oil started out as one bite then became part of a salad that developed into the **Dale Chihuly, *Garden* and *Glass Salad*** [in which the olive oil looks like it has been dipped in glass]. This was my homage to him.

Knowledge alone is just a doorway to creativity. Knowledge alone does not make a creative person, system, or organization. You need to have the right knowledge to apply to improve something. Creating something new is what makes your creative process powerful.

What I am saying is that **you have to move away from your comfort zone to discover the true potential of your creativity and the creative process.**

We use creativity on my team to create new amazing techniques and [figure out ways of] applying them. We do something new with techniques that has not been done before, and will use them in our restaurants to push the envelope.

Our office is filled with sofas to make everyone comfortable and not waste time. We use everything from text messages, Evernote, email—or I will tweet or post something on Instagram. I don't post things as To Do's for my team—I post them for inspiration. I want them to get excited because they see [what I'm thinking about], and what I see as worth getting inspired about. I want to create the desire to experiment and learn.

Creativity = knowledge + organization + desire + experimentation + learning

To people who complain about "too much" creativity, I say, "Who are you to judge?" **Without Galileo [who has been called the father of science], where would humanity be?**

You always need creativity and creative people to move humanity forward. You need those who push and those who follow. It is OK to make good paella or a good crepe. That is also part of my life. More important than creativity is truly good execution. If I were to make the best soup dumpling ever, I would not consider it creative—I would simply consider it a great dish.

Creativity is that top layer of people pushing, and society has always evolved from those efforts.

At the end of the day, **CREATIVITY IS WHAT MAKES HUMANITY GREAT.**

THE X FACTOR AT THE INN AT LITTLE WASHINGTON

The Inn at Little Washington in Virginia constantly delights through thoughtfully considered touches that leverage the X Factor—from shaving truffles tableside onto popcorn in old-fashioned red-and-white-striped movie popcorn boxes emblazoned with the Inn's logo, to wheeling their cheeses through their elegant dining room on a mooing cow named Faira.

The Inn at Little Washington

DAMON BAEHREL TAKES CREATIVE CONTROL—TO AN EXTREME

Chefs love having control, but **Damon Baehrel** lives for it—and with it. He does not wait for produce deliveries, hope his line cook or dishwasher shows up, or worry that his ingredients are at their peak. Instead, he harvests virtually everything (with the exception of meat and fish) on his 12-acre property himself, prepares everything himself, cooks everything himself, serves everything himself, and even cleans up afterward at his tiny 20-seat eponymous restaurant in Earlton, New York, which the *New Yorker* referred to as the Most Exclusive Restaurant in America.

Damon Baehrel

Two years, four months, and 14 days after our first inquiry about a reservation, we were able to experience Damon Baehrel—the man and the restaurant—for ourselves. Our departure following our first visits to other extraordinary properties had moved us to tears (e.g., the Inn at Little Washington, the Point). However, our departure from Damon Baehrel prompted pure, stunned silence: If the extraordinary, handcrafted meal we'd experienced hadn't been a mirage, was it a miracle?

Disliking the metallic flavors imparted by cooking in pots and pans, Baehrel says he cooks on stones for more of a mineral flavor. After noticing deer eating tree bark for just a few weeks in the early spring, he tasted it and found it salty—and started using it as a salt substitute in preparations. Baehrel discovered acorn oil—which he uses in lieu of butter, thanks to its buttery flavor—by accident. After paving his driveway because of the New York State code, he kept noticing oil spots on his driveway. One day he happened to notice that the car tires were crushing the acorns and creating the oil spots. He then started harvesting the acorns for oil. On his cheese plate, each individual cheese had its own garnish, from a single celery leaf to a half-inch of fennel frond.

That's not to say there are no hints of luxury. However, the flavor of truffles comes not from truffles themselves but—surprise!—from dried, powdered, and reconstituted Louisiana Greens, an heirloom variety of green-skinned eggplant that Baehrel discovered happens to have a flavor reminiscent of them, when it's not cooked out or canceled out by dairy. And we were also served tiny savory acorn flour cones, reminiscent of Thomas Keller's salmon cornets, presented in a hole in an oak log, which Baehrel says he's been making for catering events since 1986.

In his cookbook *Native Harvest,* he details how he even makes or cures his own:

- **acidifiers:** using unripened green strawberries, or sumac berries brined in sumac powder
- **breads:** from scratch from homemade flours and yeast from local wild grapes on the property, and baked on bluestone slabs; served on black walnut log "plates"
- **broths:** from branches, e.g., ironwood, maple wood, eparch wood
- **cheeses** (aged): dozens of varieties, including blue cheese made from cow's milk, one made from a mix of sheep and goat milk curdled with fresh stinging nettles; as well as a cow's and sheep milk cheese (which used fermented cauliflower juice to curdle it)

- **coffee:** fermented mashed acorn and hickory nut "coffee," sweetened with stevia
- **flours:** made from acorns, beech nut, cattail, cedar (which is naturally bitter, so it takes an entire year to rinse sufficiently to eliminate the bitterness and make it palatable), clover, dandelion, goldenrod, pine tree bark, wild clover
- **flowers:** marigolds, pine flowers, wild sweet clover flowers; thickened with wild violet leaves and stems
- **greens:** lambs quarters, which many consider a weed, are used as greens in multiple dishes (The ones he sent us home with got tossed into pasta in lieu of spinach.)
- **mushrooms:** wild oyster mushrooms; wild honey mushrooms; wood ear (birch polypore); his property has 140 to 150 different varieties of mushrooms, about half of which he says are edible and half of those delicious; some must be slow-cooked for 55 hours to soften. (He has been working land for over 30 years and seeds logs for mushroom harvesting.)
- **oils:** acorn oil (with a toasty, buttery flavor), butternut oils, hickory nut oil, grape seed oil, hemlock needle oil
- **pepper:** apple bark "pepper," hickory shag bark "pepper"
- **pungents:** a green powder that turned out to be lichen that had been soaked in water and baked, which tasted onion-y; wild onion powder; garlic scape powder; chopped wild onions
- **saps:** sycamore (incredibly fresh-tasting water, as if you'd cupped your hands for a sip from a pristine stream)
- **seasonings:** pickled baby maple leaf powder (mildly spicy); Black Krim tomato powder; wild fennel powder; caraway and marjoram powder, beechnut powder, flax, cedar berries, spruce and pine shoots; (truffle-like) green eggplant powder
- **slushes/ices:** wild grapes sweetened with unripened grape syrup filled with a tiny cluster of wild maple seeds cooked in homemade maple sap "sugar"
- **sweeteners:** stevia; unripened wild grape syrup made from seven different types of wild grapes
- **vegetables:** baked wild black burdock root, tiny wild carrots, sliced daylily tubers (rather like potatoes), kohlrabi (kohlrabi cooked in a homemade "saffron" broth made from smoked wild bergamot flowers, and a sauce made from wild brassica roots cooked in the soil they were with, giving a smoky briny effect; wild crispy baked sunflower roots completed the dish
- **vinegars:** green strawberry vinegar; onion vinegar, chard root vinegar and aged tomato vinegar; makes four or five dozen different vinegars

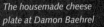

The housemade cheese plate at Damon Baehrel

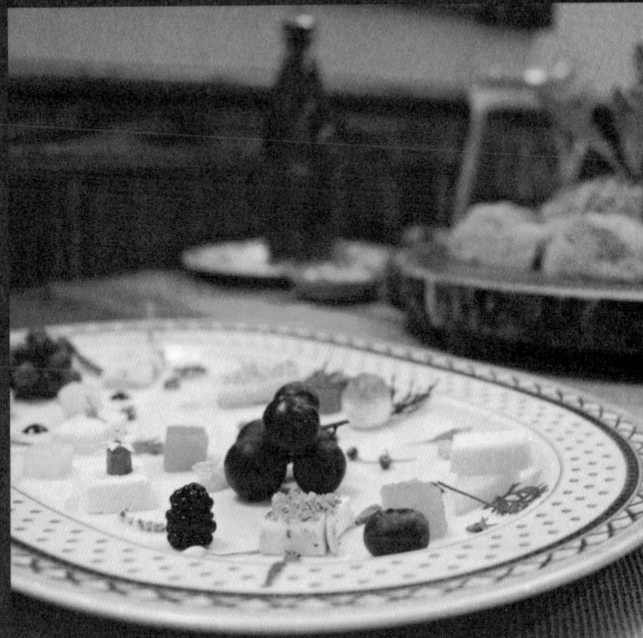

EVOLVING FROM DEPENDENCE TO INDEPENDENCE TO *INTERDEPENDENCE*

The best technique for brainstorming is to first work alone to generate ideas, then to pool ideas with others and debate them.

—**MICHAEL GELB,** author of *How to Think Like Leonardo da Vinci*

We've already learned that creativity is enhanced by happiness. Happiness, in turn, is enhanced by perceived social support, such as being part of a team.

The image of the solo creative genius—like a solitary Michelangelo on his back painting the ceiling of the Sistine Chapel over four years—is becoming rarer, as the realization of the power of collaboration grows.

Through self-mastery, you grow and evolve from dependence to independence as a cook. But moving from independence to *inter*dependence has taken many of the most creative restaurant kitchens in America to creativity of an even higher order (see sidebar on pages 214–215) by leveraging the power of teamwork. Witness all the ways leading chefs have been coming together to address social problems, whether it's José Andrés's World Central Kitchen; Dan Barber's wastED (which showcased how discarded food could be transformed into exquisite cuisine); Rick Bayless's Frontera Farmer Foundation; Daniel Boulud's co-leadership of Citymeals on Wheels; Ann Cooper's Chef Ann Foundation; Michel Nischan's Wholesome Wave; Daniel Patterson and Roy Choi's LocoL; Jessamyn Rodriguez's Harlem-based Hot Bread Kitchen; Michael Solomonov's Rooster Soup; Bill Telepan's Wellness in the Schools; or Marc Vetri's Vetri Community Partnership—to name just a few.

If you give a good idea to a mediocre team, they will screw it up. If you give a mediocre idea to a brilliant team, they will either fix it or throw it away and come up with something better. . . . Find, develop, and support good people, and they in turn will find, develop, and own good ideas."

—**ED CATMULL,** cofounder of Pixar, in his book, *Creativity, Inc.*

On a daily basis in their kitchens, chefs are learning and then teaching the power of collaborative creativity. "We have quite the following for our family meal [the kitchen staff's meal before dinner service]," says Jeremy Fox of Rustic Canyon. "Everyone [in the kitchen] makes it one day a week and they have a budget and they get a lot of recognition for it. I will post pictures of it on Instagram and sometimes it seems like the only thing I post that people care about."

He continues, "Every other day, the cooks have to cook what I want them to cook—but this is the day they can cook anything they want to cook, and can order what they want. Since they know what day they are cooking, they can space it out by making a marinade or braising their meat a day or two in advance.

"Our signature dish of posole [Clam Pozole Verde: **beans + cilantro + clams +**

Early on in my career, some days I was more creative than others, and I just sort of accepted that fact—the same way that I accepted the fact that some people were more creative than others. But I started to really challenge that. . . . Now, I believe that creativity can be systemized.

—DANIEL HUMM, Eleven Madison Park (New York City)

clam liquid + garlic + hominy + jalapeño + olive oil + poblano peppers + radishes + tortillas + vinegar] came about as a conceptual dish that I didn't know how I was going to execute before we opened. Then one day, one of our sous chefs made a green sauce for family meal. I threw it into the cooking liquid for the clams, and there you go.

"When I started here, I didn't want to serve dishes I had served in the past," he says. I felt some had gotten too contrived. I wanted the food to be good products cooked simply, put on the plate with care but without being so focused on what they looked like.

"I think Instagram was an important part of [developing] my food. I can see looking at the pictures since we opened that it helped me define what my style is. What my food is now is probably the first time I've ever been happy with it acknowledges Fox."

James Kent recalls his days as chef de cuisine at Eleven Madison Park and the rigorous development process every dish on the menu went through. "We never put it on the menu unless we loved it," he recalls. "**Daniel Humm** was definitely the creative driving force at EMP at the beginning, but **we learned that the results were even better if we all contributed.** So we'd have weekly meetings to discuss the food—Daniel, Bryce Shuman [now of New York City's Betony], Angela Pinkerton [then the pastry chef], and I would meet to talk about ideas. We'd throw ideas out during brainstorming, or pick a theme—like **scallops + tomatoes**—and work around that. We do the same thing here [at the NoMad]. I've worked at restaurants where as a young cook I couldn't be creative, and those were places where I learned to cook, picking up techniques and recipes and how to weigh ingredients and a strong work ethic—but I left with limitations. I want to teach my cooks not to be my drones, but how to think about food for themselves. **Cooks are problem solvers—we must know how to adapt.** Every time, the lamb is different.

I'll mentor my cooks who want to create new dishes. They'll present me with dishes they're working on, asking me, "What do you think?" I'll taste them, and ask, "What is missing?" That alone pushes them in their thinking. If they can figure it out themselves, great—and if not, we have a conversation until we get there.

—**GABRIEL KREUTHER,**
Gabriel Kreuther (New York Ci ty)

CHANGE THE WORLD THROUGH THE POWER OF FOOD.

—THINKFOODGROUP'S corporate mission statement

A CASE STUDY IN CREATIVE COLLABORATION: JOSÉ ANDRÉS'S THINKFOODGROUP

We spent a few hours at Chef **José Andrés**'s ThinkFoodGroup in Washington, D.C., with his team—including executive chef **Joe Raffa,** pastry chef **Rick Billings,** and head of R&D **Ruben Garcia**—who are charged with infusing creativity into the company and making it systematic. The tour of the office spotlighted vision boards dedicated to new restaurant concepts and other projects, complete with white board notations and lots of photos, as well as a test kitchen and a room lined with couches for brainstorming sessions.

Rick Billings, pastry chef: Ideas are cheap. Our motto here is: "It's not about ideas—**it's about making ideas happen."**

It's true that creativity can't be forced. Sometimes it just happens. However, **we wanted to create an incubator so creativity happens more often.**

Chefs are good at creating, but we're not always the most linear people, so it's especially important to find a way to stay focused and organized. We're forever changing our formats and templates. Each restaurant we're working on has two boards: 1) a pre-concept board which is the genesis of the starting point, along with a digital folder on the computer; and 2) a conceptual board. We have a lot of different restaurants, but we never take a cookie cutter approach to them. **José loves when food tells a story.**

Our sources of inspiration definitely include books, because **we must always know the reference point for a dish.** Tasting good and being pretty isn't enough of a reason for the existence of a dish here, even if it is at other places. **Dishes are too often missing that third element, whether it's being whimsical, historical, or having some other context.**... We'll never serve dishes simply for the sake of technique. If there's a guava sphere on a dish, why? But if there's an olive sphere in a dirty martini, it isn't forced—you get it.

José is huge on photos, including on Instagram and Twitter. **We need to learn to think like him.**

José isn't in the kitchen cooking, but he's always watching everything. So you never want him to be the first to see mistakes. It's the sous chefs' jobs to find the mistakes before the chefs do.

Ruben Garcia, director of R&D: I read between the lines, so I know what José wants before he says it out loud. A dish has to have three things: good product, good technique, and context. And a team has to be better than me, which makes my life easier—to make the team proactive, I need a system.

Joe Raffa, executive chef: We learned through one trip to Spain that it's severely ineffective to "wing it." So **all our research trips are planned out extensively.** We went to China with 11 people six years ago when we were researching the concept for China Chicano, and hit three or four restaurants a day where we'd order the entire menu. We learned to organize trips by day and location, and by restaurants and dishes. We'll name all the photos at the end of the day, and collect menus from the restaurants, making as many contacts as possible with chefs, farmers, winemakers, and mixologists, and organize

Rick Billings (left) and Joe Raffa (right)

all their contact information. We'll also pull together all the photos and a master list of all the business cards and menus, so nothing is lost.

When we finally start cooking, we're always sharing information. **This is a collaborative, not a competitive, process.** When testing recipes, we document each dish with photos, timing, temperature, and weight. Through repeated testing, we see the menu start to come to life. Then we'll ask ourselves, "What's missing?" This process gives form to the menu, and when we finally have José taste the dishes we've developed, it gives additional direction to our efforts. Without this system, each of us is too much in our individual heads—but with it, it allows us to go from concept origination to operation as a team. And we treat the process just like we treat the food here: It's a continual evolution.

We strive to be creative, but it's still a business and we still need to make money. We do that by raising the experience level. Where do we spend our money? **We invest in high-impact details.** Do we have to get our chocolate, grasshoppers, and Mezcal from Mexico [for Oyamel]? No—but we do. And we pay to have experts like Diana Kennedy and Carmen "Tita" Ramirez [Degollado] come into the kitchen for ten days at a time to cook with our team at Oyamel, and Aglaia Kremezi to do the same with our team at Zaytinya. We need to hone our palates to make sure we're doing the right thing, since what we do isn't always traditional from a cultural standpoint. The flavor has to be right. And the return comes later down the line.

It's never just about recipes—it's about how you **present** them, and how you **serve** them.

José changed the hierarchy in the company. He laid the [organizational chart] on the floor so that it's flat—meaning that everyone here talks to everyone else. This way, egos don't dominate. Blatant egos can't make it here. You have to be able to contribute, and you have to not always have to win. **We allow everyone—from José to an intern—to give feedback.**

I'm inspired by Eddy [Leroux, of Daniel], who's always bringing in new ingredients and researching their origins and usage and applying his French technique to them. He's always pushing himself outside his comfort zone and educating himself, yet everything he makes is perfect and refined. That's an inspiration.

—**AARON BLUDORN,** Café Boulud (New York City)

Every time, the leeks are different. You've got to learn to think on the fly and evolve."

Kent applies the creative approach he learned at EMP to his kitchen at the NoMad. "At EMP we'd have 'Food Battles,' where everyone in the kitchen would have to make a canapé, and we'd taste each other's dishes. Or we'd do Battle Broccoli, and the next Wednesday everyone would make a broccoli dish. Even the pastry team was charged with coming up with savory ideas. We had a Flatbread Battle here [at the NoMad], and the winner was a flatbread with mozzarella and tomatoes and peaches. We'll work on R&D every Friday, and will document and photograph dishes and email them to the whole team. While the [executive team] focuses on the summer menu, the line cooks will focus on fall food—they'll draw dishes and write out the recipes for 50 or 60 dishes that would make sense on our menu (e.g., no sushi). We'll pick five or six concepts for the cooks to make, present, and have tasted, and occasionally we'll end up tweaking one or two that will make it onto the menu, often in a very different form. The goal is to have everyone contribute—the process is as much about team-building as it is about creativity. We want them to be proud of where they work, and to talk about the restaurant as 'we,' instead of 'they,' which shows they're really invested in the restaurant."

Daniel Humm has observed that at Eleven Madison Park, "It is unbelievable what we have learned from cooks who have only worked with us for six months or a year. Then we do the same on a higher level, where the sous chefs [go through this process as well]. In the end, it doesn't matter if the dish ends up on the menu [because] it's amazing what a collaborative environment creates....[During this process the dining room is also involved] because even if you are not a chef you can have a great idea about food or how it is served."

In the end, the most important lesson Humm has learned from the process is reflected at left.

EVERYONE IS CREATIVE. I've seen people who thought they weren't creative become some of the most creative. There is no excuse. If you create an environment where everyone thinks creatively and collaboratively, it's like a muscle that you train.

—**DANIEL HUMM,** Eleven Madison Park (New York City)

I found that there was a [70 percent] correlation between perceived SOCIAL SUPPORT and HAPPINESS. This is higher than the connection between smoking and cancer.

—**SHAWN ACHOR,** author of *The Happiness Advantage*

Daniel Boulud with Eddy Leroux, Travis Swikard, Ghaya Oliveira, Jean-Francois Bruel, and Aaron Bludorn

While Daniel Boulud is often singled out for his culinary prowess, he insists, **"There's no great chef without a great team."**

Boulud has selected and trained a great team indeed, one whose members inspire others' creativity as much as they are inspired by Boulud himself.

[Pastry chef] Ghaya Oliveira's Grapefruit Givré [a dessert made from a frozen hollowed grapefruit filled with grapefruit sorbet, grapefruit jam, sesame crumble, sesame foam, and rosewater loukoum, topped with halva "hair"] is the latest classic [dessert]. The year before we opened, I took a trip to Turkey and I was eating all this crazy stuff—loukoum [aka Turkish delight, candies made from a gel of starch + sugar], rosewater, halvah [a fudge-like confection made from sesame paste]—a lot of things with sesame. Ghaya is Tunisian, so this was a little voyage toward the eastern Mediterranean where she grew up. The beginning of the idea was the loukoum and the sesame. Then we added the citrus, and that's how the dish developed a little bit more and eventually became the Givré.

—**DANIEL BOULUD,** The Dinex Group, which includes Manhattan's Daniel, Café Boulud, Boulud Sud, Bar Boulud, db bistro moderne, DBGB Restaurant and Bar, and other restaurants globally

Chris Long (left) with Bart van der Velden

A CASE STUDY IN CREATIVE COLLABORATION: NATALIE'S AT THE CAMDEN HARBOUR INN IN MAINE

Camden, Maine, is one of the last places on earth we ever expected to discover a restaurant that is a beacon of culinary excellence in America. Yet on each of multiple visits to Natalie's at the Relais & Châteaux–affiliated Camden Harbour Inn, we found wildly impressive cooking by 30-something married co-chefs **Shelby Stevens** and **Chris Long,** graciously and flawlessly served by an expertly trained staff.

The credit for Shelby and Chris's captivating cuisine resides no doubt in the training they absorbed both separately and together via working under some of America's best chefs, including Daniel Boulud (at New York's Daniel), Daniel Patterson (at San Francisco's Coi), Ana Sortun (at Cambridge's Oleana), and the late Charlie Trotter (at Chicago's Charlie Trotter's).

But the excellence of the entire dining experience also seems to be the result of the chefs' creative process paired with an exceptionally thorough process of vetting each new dish, then sharing it with and seeking feedback from the front-of-the-house staff through not one but two team tastings during each change of the menu, which happens every six to eight weeks.

Chefs Shelby Stevens and Chris Long on the Team Approach

"For our first eight menus, we pulled out *Culinary Artistry* to see what was in season each time. Now, we have our own notebook tracking what is in season here [in northern Maine] and we pull that out. We go through it to see what sounds fun and what we want to work with that's in season first.

"We also look to see what will challenge us, from terrines to tableside smoke. [Chris] saw the smoke dish when [he] spent a week at Alinea staging before moving here from Chicago. At Alinea, the quality of ingredients is spectacular but the amount of people was double that working at Trotter's. You had people who were only focusing on half a dish.

"We will talk about the ingredients at home. We like working on this at home because, well, we are sitting and eating and no one is interrupting us, versus at work. At home, the only one who needs anything is our dog—and he can wait.

"We will look at the whole menu and all of a sudden realize, 'Oh, crap—there is no sauce on this dish.' So what is the sauce or the puree? What is the crunch, the acid? We then run through the tastes and the textures together.

"We love changing up an ingredient on the same plate, so you might see charred leeks, leek ash, and fried leeks together. We will do potato puree with a potato chip, or carrot puree with a carrot pickle. Celery root puree, celery root leaves, celery root chips and ribbons, and now you have four elements of celery root. The flavors complement each other *and* it is good for food cost—no waste.

"We have worked with cooks who would say, 'We need something red in this dish.' But 'red' is not a flavor. You can say a dish needs more color, and work to find that flavor and a bright note."

We don't end our creative process until we know the dish can be set down in front of a guest exactly the way we want it to be.

—**SHELBY STEVENS and CHRIS LONG,** co-chefs, Natalie's at Camden Harbour Inn

- **First-Draft Menu**

  "We write the menu and email it to everyone, then two weeks later we do the formal tasting for them. It turns out to be about 20 or more dishes. We get input from everyone and make the adjustments.

  "We have never had a dish not work on the menu because it gets tasted so many times. You have Raymond [Brunyanszki, the co-owner], who has eaten everywhere; Bart [van der Velden, the GM], who has a great palate; and Micah [Wells, the sommelier], who knows his wines. We go through them—the heavy hitters—first, and then two days later, we do a second-round tasting for the entire crew."

- **Tableside Service**

  "When [Shelby] worked at Daniel, [she doesn't] think a single sauce ever went on a plate. They did not sauce in the kitchen. If a guest steps in the way or a server misses a step, there goes the dish.

  "With a soup being served tableside, you can see all the different garnishes before the soup gets poured in. You would not see all that work if we portioned it in the kitchen. With a soup, we also control how much gets poured—not too much or too little.

"It is fun for the guest because it engages them and wakes them back up. If they are sitting for seven courses you want to bring them back in again.

"With tableside saucing, we will show the server exactly where to pour the sauce and how much, because one tablespoon too much might make the dish too salty. The presentation is very exact. It also engages the staff to be more present. It brings them all closer."

- **First Tasting**

The inn's well-traveled co-owner **Raymond Brunyanszki** sits down with a few key members of the staff—including general manager **Bart van der Velden,** restaurant manager **Timothy O'Neill,** wine director **Micah Wells**, and mixologist **Trevin Hutchins** (of both Natalie's and sister property the Danforth Inn in Portland)—and together they taste and discuss every one of Shelby and Chris's proposed new dishes and pastry chef **Brian Song**'s desserts. It's a thoughtful session focusing on how to elevate its flavor even further or enhance its tableside presentation or wine-friendliness, and at the end of it, Shelby and Chris are provided with detailed feedback on each dish. Following are bits and pieces of their conversation:

Bart: There's never too much cheese in a dish for me—but that was *a lot* of blue cheese.

Raymond: I'm not sure about the portion size. Is it an appetizer, or an entrée? If it's an appetizer, maybe it needs to be slightly smaller with more acidity.

Trevin: To my palate, a lot of the elements on this plate read sweet.

Micah: I've got a big, fruit-forward, old-viney wine to pair with this.

- **Second Tasting**

A couple of days later, there is a second tasting of revamped dishes for members of the kitchen and front-of-the-house staffs, led by general manager **Bart van der Velden.**

Everyone is provided with detailed descriptions of each dish on a **"cheat sheet"** that they are expected to memorize, and on which they're later quizzed ("Which dishes are gluten-free?" "All our dishes can be made dairy-free except which dishes?" "What silverware should be served with this dish?"). Everyone pulls out an iPhone to photograph each dish and takes notes on how each is to be served. After it's shot, they pull out forks to take a bite of each dish, and have a firsthand experience of it. Micah describes his recommended wine pairing for each dish, and the rationale behind each pairing, giving the key characteristics of the dish enhanced by certain characteristics in the wine. He underscores that a regular pour is 6 ounces, while a pairing pour is just 3 ounces.

Wait staff are cold-called to describe each dish, based on the ingredients and techniques mentioned on the cheat sheet. Bart coaches them, "Use terms like 'on top of' and 'on the side with.'" As certain ingredients are mentioned, more pop quizzes take place: "What's a Meyer lemon?" "What's a persimmon?" When the Maine lobster dish is brought out, it's emphasized that this is one of the signature local dishes on the menu. Micah describes a Pommery Brut Royal Champagne that has been branded for the Relais & Châteaux organization, which consists of Chardonnay, Pinot Noir, and Pinot Meunier grapes in nearly equal amounts. The restaurant's lobster tasting menu is described, along with the selling points of the restaurant's most expensive menu: It features four luxury ingredients—truffles, caviar, foie gras, and local Maine lobster—and the staff is reminded that Chef Chris Long was named Maine's 2013 Lobster Chef of the Year. The lobster roll has been re-plated on a platter, replacing the previous paper dish version which was deemed "too cute" for the winter months.

Chefs Shelby Stevens and Chris Long Reflect on the Process

"Raymond has an amazing palate. He eats out everywhere, so his palate is also always on trend. There are certain ingredients he just doesn't like—like bell peppers, and pineapple—so we don't use them.

"While it hurts at first to be critiqued, sometimes important improvements result. . . . The pasta dish really improved between the first and second tastings. We made sure to use smaller pieces of blue cheese, and to use more chestnut, which we also roasted a bit longer in brown butter.

"Our inspiration for our oyster velouté dish came from our dinner at Eleven Madison Park with Raymond. They did it very differently there, but we talked about how we could do something similar."

Shelby Stevens (right), with Raymond Brunyanszki and Trevin Hutchins

Raymond Brunyanszki Reflects from an Owner's Perspective

"Chris and Shelby are very open-minded, and want the best for our guests. I came up with the idea of having staff tastings of the new menu and having the cooks involved in the tasting of the menus, so they get some sense of participation in the creation of the menu. And I sat down with the kitchen team to understand the thought process behind the new menu.

"It's not just tasting a dish—it's thinking through the presentation, and the way a guest puts their fork into it and takes a bite and the layers of flavor they get on each forkful. Do you get a balanced flavor profile on each bite?

"So it's not just, How does it taste? It's also, Is it seasonal? Is it from our gardens, or sourced locally? How does it look? For me, it's also very important to have 'safe spots' on the menu for guests—e.g., halibut, beef, a vegetarian option—who are not used to fine dining so they still see some dishes they recognize and feel comfortable coming into the restaurant.

"While the final menu runs for six to eight weeks, we pay especially close attention to feedback from our regulars, so we can take their opinions into account, too."

Dan Barber of Blue Hill on Creativity

Dan Barber credits much of his creativity as stemming from his ten years of research for his book, ***The Third Plate,*** which argues that the move from commercially produced food (Plate #1) to farm-to-table cuisine (Plate #2) isn't sufficient, but that culinary evolution must also reflect a shift toward a more plant-driven cuisine that supports the underlying farm economy (Plate #3).

Dan Barber

The Third Plate

When I started my book project, I thought it was simply about farm to table, and celebrating connections with a very inspiring group of farmers, artisans, scientists, and breeders.

But then I went to write about wheat and my wheat guy, Klaas Martens. I found myself standing in the middle of a 2,000-acre field and there was no wheat, but there were soil-building crops and all these things that were going to build the soil so the wheat would be delicious. But I saw the wheat was a very small percentage of the success of the farm ecologically—and was relying on a bunch of other crops, like buckwheat and Austrian winter peas, that no one was buying or talking about at the time. I had the insight that if I was going to celebrate the wheat, I had to celebrate everything that goes *into* the wheat.

That's when I realized that farm to table doesn't work—and that I was a farm-to-table chef without any clothes. I was advocating for something that didn't change the landscape, and didn't promote a different type of food system that would become a more sustainable way to eat in the future.

That was a seminal moment when I realized I had it all wrong—and my farm-to-table book evolved into *The Third Plate.*

No Printed Menus

At Blue Hill at Stone Barns, I have to figure out a cuisine that supports the whole system, the "nose-to-tail" of the farm. That forces creativity because you are restrained in your pantry. **Restraints always kickstart creativity. The more restrained, the easier it is.** The most frustrating time is July through October, because there are so many ingredients available, and they are all just singing.

I think true gastronomy comes through the transmutation of food into something else. To cook a steak is to heat a piece of protein, but to make oxtail taste good is transformative. That's where cooking and creativity really is. The gastronomic side is so important for the agricultural side. You have to eat the whole animal—that's an easy one. But you also have to eat the whole vegetable—stalk and leaves, too. What supports the [economic] system supports the rest of the flora and fauna.

You need to dial back to the seed—that is the blueprint. Once you have selected the seed, the cake is baked. The captain will interview the table after the guests sit down, and will profile the table for the kitchen [where the menu and number of courses then gets determined for each individual table]. Fewer than 10 percent of guests might be "people who could care less about the farm and are drinking big Chardonnay!" We love those people because they will get the steak from the cow that we don't want to serve someone else who has waited months to eat here and doesn't just want a steak they could get someplace else.

But more than 90 percent of our guests are open to experiencing what we do and more unusual courses. We have worked very hard for that. When we opened, 90 percent of our guests wanted steak, and we needed to survive in order to stay open.

wastED

WastED [Blue Hill's month-long pop-up serving 100 percent recycled ingredients] came about in part from the wheat experience. There was not a market for all that was grown—so it either got plowed back into the ground or fed to pigs. Forty percent of what is produced ends up in the trash, either before or post-consumer, which is a pretty staggering number.

So it got us thinking: What if we ate those grains directly? What if we thought about a meal not just as a delicious celebratory experience but as an educational one as well—one that connects you to a more meta-level thinking about the table as a place of connection to a lot of different things? And what if we used that time to connect guests to larger issues—issues that affect the world, and connect guests with something bigger?

Nothing is bigger than food, which is something we all know.

Evolving Creativity

Some creativity is a kind of reading the winds of culture. I don't do any of that. I get my ideas from the ecological agriculture space, 100 percent. **A lot of inspiration is how you connect the pieces.**

There are ways to be supercreative in a quiet, almost imperceptible way that is conscious and incremental over ten years....I can now be fearless and bold because I have the tools to do it.

wastED veggie burger (made from juice pulp) featured at Shake Shack

The KITCHEN CREATIVITY 50

A list to spur ideas when you need it.

1. Be inspired. Choose a song, a book, a movie, a painting, or another creative work in another medium, and capture it in a dish. **2. Celebrate the past.** Classic dishes are classic for a reason—celebrate that reason. **3. Connect the seemingly unconnected.** If you look, you'll inevitably find one—because *everything* is connected. Claudia Fleming combined sautéed plums and tomatoes in a dessert showcasing the fruits' tart sweetness. **4. Constrain it.** Embrace your constraints (e.g., lack of equipment, ingredients, time), and find a way to work around them. **5. Cross-breed.** Combine two different ideas into a single concept, e.g., a croissant with a donut (the cronut). **6. Deconstruct.** Break a well-known dish into its component parts, and serve them separately. **7. Describe it whimsically.** Instead of an oyster topped with granite, call it an "oyster Slurpee." At the Inn at Little Washington, dishes are also sometimes "nestled" or served in a figurative "wreath." **8. Don't fake it.** Don't pretend to be something else (i.e., "mock")—celebrate another alternative that works instead of the usual, e.g., tomato gazpacho → carrot gazpacho, or Buffalo chicken wings → Buffalo fried cauliflower with blue cheese and celery. **9. Embrace the opposite.** As the popular Black and White Cookie proved, opposites can indeed attract, e.g., high/low (e.g., caviar beggars' purses), vegan/carnivore (e.g., carrot tartare, cauliflower steak), and other dichotomies. **10. Feed your ingredient something different.** You are what you eat—and what what you eat eats. At Blue Hill, Dan Barber fed us two eggs from two different chickens in the same dish—and the one fed only red peppers had a yolk that was distinctly reddish, making an unforgettable impression. **11. Ingredient-shift.** Instead of apples, substitute pears. Instead of peanuts, try pecans. **12. Interactivate it.** Serve it with a knife for guests to cut themselves, e.g., sprouts off a kalette branch, à la Dan Barber at Blue Hill. **13. Localize.** Make it from ingredients procured within a 100-mile or ten-acre radius (or closer!). **14. Make a look-alike.** Make it appear to be something familiar (e.g., a fried egg) with unfamiliar ingredients (e.g., cattails and tree bark), à la Damon Baehrel. **15. Mimic nature.** Be inspired by the outdoors (e.g., dew, smoke, snow) and bring these elements magically indoors. **16. Miniaturize it.** Make it much smaller than usual (e.g., hamburger → slider, cake → cupcake). **17. Minimalize it.** Eliminate one more ingredient up to the point that risks losing the essence of the dish. **18. Mock it.** Make your apple pie with Ritz crackers instead of apples. Make your gyro with seasoned seitan instead of lamb or beef. **19. Pair with a beverage.** Create a presentation of those oysters with an accompaniment of Chablis, Sancerre, or a stout. **20. Pair with its soulmate.** The Inn at Little Washington has served an amuse-bouche of a grilled cheese sandwich the size of a silver dollar, accompanied by a shot of tomato soup. **21. Pay homage.** Create a tribute to a famed, or favorite, version of a dish—whether Escoffier's or your grandmother's. **22. Perspective-shift.** Imagine the dish from another point of view, e.g., that of a child, a Martian, or the main ingredient itself. **23. Plate it.** Beautify the elements via inventive plating, e.g., truffled popcorn served in a red-and-white-striped movie popcorn box. **24. Platform-shift.** Serve expected flavors in an unexpected way, e.g., Caesar salad ice cream or soup. **25. Play with words.** Pair lamb with lamb's lettuce, as we first saw Lydia Shire do at Biba. **26. Portable-ize it.** Make a handheld version—e.g., as a push-up, on a stick, in a wrap. **27. Present whimsically.** When the Inn at Little Washington serves a single gougère on a pedestal, it elevates the single bite both literally and figuratively. **28. Reconstruct it.** Take the component parts of a well-known dish and reassemble them in a new way (e.g., clam chowder as potato and chive gnocchi with clam sauce). **29. Reinterpret it.** Use a classic dish as your inspiration, and give it your own spin. **30. Reverse it.** Lydia Shire's version of vitello tonnato (veal with tuna sauce) flipped the dish into tuna with veal sauce. **31. Revisit a childhood memory.** This allows the brain connections between your memory cells and stored "lessons learned" to gain strength and speed. **32. Satirize it.** Serve a meal in a TV dinner tray circa 1970s. **33. Sauce it.** Add an irresistible sauce. José Andrés served us a dish with a romesco so delicious that anything that accompanied it would have been a knockout. **34. *Senza* it.** Create a *something*-free version, e.g., *senza* gluten (GF chickpea pasta). **35. Serve it tableside.** A flair for the dramatic can enhance the experience of your dish, such as tableside carving (e.g., of a roast, whether meat or vegetable) or flambéing. **36. Shape-shift.** Change the usual shape—e.g., serve a round sandwich, instead of a square. **37. Solve a unique problem.** Think big: "How to reduce America's 40 percent rate of food waste?" Dan Barber's veggie burgers made from leftover juice pulp was one of the best we've ever tasted. **38. Stuff it.** Slip a soft-cooked egg inside the muffin you're baking, à la Craftsmen & Wolves' The Rebel Within, or the "gnocchi" you're making, à la Michael Voltaggio's at ink. **39. Super-size it.** Make it much larger than usual—e.g., the TKOs (Thomas Keller Oreos) at Bouchon Bakery, which are elegant, gigantic chocolate shortbread cookies sandwiched around a creamy white chocolate filling. **40. Sustainable-ize it.** Substitute biodynamic and/or organic ingredients from your local farmer. **41. Taste-shift.** Serve a savory version of a typically sweet dish (e.g., babka)—or vice versa. **42. Technique-shift.** Prepare a dish that's typically cooked one way in another way. Instead of grilling it, try wok-frying it. **43. Temperature-shift.** Serve a cold version of something that's typically served hot, e.g., frozen hot chocolate. **44. Theme it.** Patrick O'Connell serves a dessert plate inspired by the seven deadly sins. **45. Time-shift.** Imagine what a version of this dish will look like 50 years into the future. **46. Treat vegetables like meat.** Confit vegetables, grill them, grind them (e.g., in a meat grinder attached to the table, à la Eleven Madison Park), roast them, serve them as steaks. **47. Vary it.** Serve the same ingredient multiple ways on the same plate—e.g., ashed, cold, cooked, crunchy, dehydrated, fermented, foamed, frozen (e.g., sorbet), hot, juiced, moussed, raw, reconstituted, savory, soft, sweet, tartared, tempura-fried. **48. Veg-ify it.** Create a meatless option with the same flavor and allure, e.g., Tal Ronnen and Scot Jones's "lox" made from sous-vide smoked carrots. **49. Waffle it.** Just kidding. Or not—Daniel Shumski turned this idea into his bestselling first book, *Will It Waffle?*, detailing everything you can waffle besides waffle batter, from mac-n-cheese to oatmeal chocolate chip cookies. Find a new, unexpected use for a piece of equipment, a technique, or an ingredient. **50. Waste not.** Use carrot tops in your pesto, and create banana cupcakes with those black bananas.

Otherwise, to be creative in the kitchen, try finding a way to apply any concept from another field to food and drink. For example,

- In **music, variation** is a formal technique through which material is repeated, albeit in a different form (e.g., through counterpoint, harmony, melody, orchestration, rhythm, timbre, or some combination thereof). *Imagine:* How could you create a variation on the dish or drink you're working on? How could you provide it with a counterpoint? What new ingredient would harmonize beautifully with all its existing ingredients?
- In **literary criticism, deconstruction** (whose Greek root itself means to break up, or to loosen) is a form of analysis of the relationship between text and meaning. *Imagine:* What are each of the elements that make a dish that dish? Think about each individually. How could you (re)present each separately? How could they be recombined in a new way?
- Apply analogies from other fields and disciplines in the **arts** (beauty), **sciences** (truth), and **ethics** (goodness).

CONCLUSION

If another restaurant had been named number-one on the World's 50 Best Restaurants list in 2017, it might have chosen to celebrate by setting the cruise control and coasting on all the hard work that led to the accolade.

But Eleven Madison Park (often affectionately referred to as "EMP") isn't just any restaurant. The site of two of our peak dining experiences of recent memory didn't get that way by resting on its laurels.

After reading and reflecting on EMP's first review in 2006 from Moira Hodgson in the *New York Observer*, manager Will Guidara and chef Daniel Humm decided to make some changes. "We realized we weren't inventing anything . . . we were just playing copycat," Guidara told the audience at the 2017 Welcome Conference, citing examples of picking out top-of-the-line china and furnishings. "But invention is a matter of being open to so much change!"

[Moira Hodgson's review of Eleven Madison Park, saying she wished the restaurant had a bit "more Miles Davis"] was the best gift we could ever hope to receive. . . . We were fired up, and got to work.

—**WILL GUIDARA** and **DANIEL HUMM,** at the 2017 Welcome Conference

The partners famously took Moira Hodgson's suggestion to heart, brainstorming the eleven words most often used to describe Miles Davis, which included terms like ***adventurous, cool, collaborative, endless reinvention, forward-moving, fresh, innovative, inspired, light, spontaneous,*** and ***vibrant***.

Guidara and Humm "got to work," investing in their cocktail program, changing their menu format, and "creating a four-star restaurant we'd feel comfortable going to. EMP is a genuine expression of the two of us. As we change, it has to change with us."

They acknowledged that the process of reinvention is "very, very personal": "You can't focus on the risks. You have to live in your hopes and not your fears."

This led to their decision to do the unthinkable: At the height of their restaurant's global distinction, they announced plans to close it to work yet again at reinvention: "We know we need to change in order to stay the same—and that we must change with authenticity."

What would you attempt to do if you knew you could not fail?

—**WILL GUIDARA,** Eleven Madison Park, on the most important question his restaurateur father, Frank Guidara, used to ask him

Contemplating the creative process that he and Guidara had already undertaken, and that which still lies ahead, appeared to give Daniel Humm pause. "Closing and rebuilding EMP is beyond exciting," he said, before the two acknowledged: "We're genuinely scared."

But fear has never seemed to stop Humm or Guidara, nor the inspiration behind their restaurant's re-creation, Miles Davis, who famously said, ***"Do not fear mistakes—there are none."***

PART II A WORLD OF INFINITE CULINARY POSSIBILITIES: THE LISTS (A-Z)

[Inspiration] is really about filling ourselves with interesting knowledge that's within our trade."

—RENÉ REDZEPI, Noma (Copenhagen)

I view trends in food like haute couture. From wild, wonderful, and wacky come changes, growth, and evolution.

—SHERRY YARD, 2002 James Beard Foundation Outstanding Pastry Chef

GRAND CENTRAL
TERMINAL

As you develop as a creative cook, the world will continue to change. People will change. *You* will change. Pay attention to these changes, and you'll find new sources of inspiration.

- The world of **edibles** will change—as ingredients from the corners of the earth (or the forest a few miles away) make their way to your kitchen, with heirloom varietals restored and new hybrids created.
- The world of **eaters** will change—as new preferences and aversions are shaped by new options and new information about extrinsic (e.g., the environment, trends) or intrinsic (e.g., aging, health) factors.
- The world of **cooks** will change—as chefs form new insights and develop new techniques to allow new ways of preparing edibles for eaters.

This chapter features reminders of the changing world around us, which presents ideas and opportunities that may have been unimaginable just a few years ago. In addition to offering a grounding in ideas containing timeless wisdom, it reflects some of the most eye-opening changes and best practices we've witnessed while researching, writing, and photographing this book.

Where to begin? Why not just start where you are—for instance, with the season, as you'll find comprehensive seasonality listings. You can also flip through until you find a word or phrase that catches your attention. Highlights include ideas for creative jumping-off points, as well as occasional inspirational quotes and exercises to help you bring new life into your own cooking immediately.

AFRICAN AND AFRICAN-AMERICAN CUISINES

The idea that black folks cooking are only making soul food is frightening. What we have to say is much bigger than that. It's our job to expand the conversation.

—ALEXANDER SMALLS, The Cecil (Harlem), as quoted in the *New York Times*

Interest in **African cuisines and flavors** was reported to be up 20 percent for 2016, placing it among the fastest-rising cuisines of interest in the U.S. Credit goes to a new generation of African-American chefs and food writers educating others about traditional African cuisines and the African-American cuisine that has emerged from them—and that is continuing to evolve through new ingredients, techniques, and restaurants such as the **Cecil** and **Minton's** in Harlem. The flavors of *berbere, dukkah, harissa, ras el hanout,* and *tsire* are becoming more familiar to Americans.

Culinary scholar **Michael Twitty** has been characterized by Noma chef René Redzepi as "the voice of our generation" leading "to a much more serious scholarship around African-American foodways." Twitty has prepared educational dinners showcasing dishes from pre-colonial Africa, such as black-eyed pea fritters, African yams sliced and fried in palm oil, and spicy Ghanaian fish stew served with yams boiled and pounded into *fufu.*

Education results from looking forward as well as back. Hoping to stem the rate of obesity and related health problems among African-Americans, in 2015 the nonprofit Oldways Preservation Trust hosted a series of cooking classes teaching more nutritious ways to prepare traditional foods, such as collard greens sautéed with olive oil, caramelized onions, and Dijon mustard, which is lower in fat and preserves more nutrients than traditional methods (e.g., braising with ham hocks).

Some offerings from chef Joseph "JJ" Johnson at Harlem's the Cecil and Minton's:

- "The Carrot": Carrot Puree, Roasted Heirloom Carrots, Tops, Coriander Dressing
- charred okra with red beans
- Collard Green Salad: Adzuki Red Beans, Candied Cashew, Coconut Dressing
- grits + edamame
- West African peanut lentil stew + Asian pear

For further reference:

The Jemima Code: Two Centuries of African-American Cookbooks by Toni Tipton-Marton

The Cooking Gene: A Journey Through African-American Culinary History in the Old South by Michael W. Twitty

AGING (SEE ALSO **FRESH**)

The Japanese have long aged ingredients (e.g., miso, sake, tea, tofu) to intensify their flavors.

Today, the restaurants of **Daniel Boulud, Alain Ducasse, Thomas Keller,** and **Marc Vetri** use **Acquerello carnaroli rice,** which has been aged for more than a year, in their risottos, resulting in a complex, nutty flavor and toothy texture. **Mark Levy**'s version at Magdalena at the Ivy in Baltimore is one of the best Acquerello risottos we've ever tasted.

Joshua Skenes of Saison in San Francisco **accidentally aged turnips** from the restaurant's garden in the walk-in, which he discovered had become "a concentrated version of themselves."

Mixologists like **Jeffrey Morgenthaler** have turned **barrel-aged cocktails** (e.g., Manhattans, Negroni) into a thing—and Tippleman's is **aging flavored syrups** (e.g., cola, maple) to add to cocktails, using bourbon barrels to create more complex flavors. Brewmasters are barrel-aging beers as well.

We recently blind-tasted a wonderful sweet wine with

caramel notes that we simply couldn't identify. It was a 30-year-old **aged Vietti Moscato d'Asti**—which upended the common belief that Moscato d'Asti must be served "young and fresh."

Point: What foods or drinks have not traditionally been aged that might benefit from the aging process?

Counterpoint: What foods or drinks might benefit from being served hyper-fresh?

AGRARIAN CUISINE, PROGRESSIVE

"What would you do if the environment was the most important consideration?" asked Mission Street Food founders **Anthony Myint** and **Karen Leibowitz** when opening the Perennial in San Francisco in 2016. The restaurant champions "progressive farming" and features **"progressive agrarian cuisine"** based on their mission of fixing the food system. The farm-to-table restaurant optimizes energy efficiency, features reclaimed materials, and uses table waste as fertilizer and fish food.

Sample offerings from the Perennial:

- Pisco Sherbet cocktail, using leftover juice from the bar to create a sherbet that is topped with California-made pisco and corn nuts
- Kernza bread, made from a perennial wheatgrass developed to reduce the release of carbon into the atmosphere via its deep root system
- Pumpkin Seed Bisque with crisp sunchoke, cardamom, lemon oil

ALICE IN WONDERLAND

While I was at the British Library, they let me see Lewis Carroll's original manuscript of *Alice's Adventures in Wonderland*. It was the most exciting moment of my life. It was lying there on a cushion, with all his original drawings, written in his amazingly legible hand—no crossing out . . .

—**HESTON BLUMENTHAL,** as quoted in *The Telegraph*; the chef has served dishes inspired by the Mad Hatter's Tea Party at the Fat Duck

Moscow's White Rabbit restaurant, which opened in 2011, was inspired by Lewis Carroll's best-selling novel that takes readers on a mind-bending journey through his subconscious. In 2016 the restaurant shot to number 18 on the World's 50 Best Restaurants list. Russia's most influential chef, **Vladimir Mukhin,** is the Mad Hatter behind the experience, which is said to start with a "Drink me" bottle and to continue through fairy tale–like dishes such as "drunk starfish" (massandra covered with sand) served with "fish milk," a ceremonial "brains-carried-out" concoction, "gipnopops with spaghetti and whine," and shrimp doughnuts with smoked teapuccino.

While *Alice's Adventures in Wonderland* is one of the most beloved books of all time, with more than 100 million copies estimated to have been sold s ince its first publication in 1865, it still seems to have disproportionately inspired chefs and restaurateurs all around the globe to create new dishes, tasting menus, and even restaurants and bakeries.

Imagine: What was your favorite book as a child? How could it inspire your cooking?

ALLERGIES AND AVERSIONS, SEE FOOD ALLERGIES, SENSITIVITIES, AND AVERSIONS

ALTITUDE (SEE ALSO PLACE)

Tallos extremos [meaning "extreme stems"—his signature dish inspired by a man who fermented wild Andean yams in river water before cooking them underground on hot stones]

—**VIRGILIO MARTÍNEZ VÉLIZ,** Central (Lima, Peru)

At Central Restaurante in Lima, which ranked number 4 on the 2016 World's 50 Best Restaurants list, chef **Virgilio Martínez Véliz** celebrates Peru's biodiversity by serving indigenous ingredients from various altitudes (e.g., from an elevation of 4,100 meters in the mountains to 20 meters below sea level), with the dishes listed on his restaurant menu by elevation.

AMISH CUISINE

A former sous chef at Charlie Trotter's, **Matthew Secich** left behind his high-end restaurant career to move with his wife Crystal and their children to join an Amish community in rural Maine, opening an artisanal deli called Charcuterie that offers handmade smoked cheeses and meats. Based on Amish beliefs, Secich uses a manually operated slicer and gas smoker.

Point: What would happen to the flavor of a dish if you slowed it down, making it without electricity?

Counterpoint: How could electricity and modern technology improve the flavor of a dish?

APERITIFS (SEE ALSO DIGESTIFS AND DRINKS, ALCOHOLIC)

What could be a chef's best friend more than a light, refreshing, typically dry, low-alcohol beverage designed to spur the appetite before a meal? No wonder **aperitifs** (from the Latin *aperire,* "to open") like white Lillet and vermouth are starting to gain in popularity in the U.S. after being popular offerings in Europe for ages. Little bites of food are the best accompaniments, such as crostini or toasts, or nuts, olives, or pickles.

Aperol
balanced cocktails, i.e., between bitter/sweet
bubbly cocktails
Campari
Champagne
Dubonnet
Lillet
lower-alcohol spirit-based cocktails
sparkling wine cocktails
spritzes, e.g., Aperol
Suze
vermouth
wine, dry white
wine, sparkling (e.g., cava, Champagne, prosecco, Sekt)

Aperol + orange (slice) + prosecco + sparkling water
Campari + fennel + sparkling wine
Lillet + orange

The aperitif course that has long been a part of European culture has also been gaining in popularity stateside. Seattle chef **Holly Smith** of Cafe Juanita has been ahead of the trend for years, pairing aperitifs with small bites in an Apertivi section on her restaurant's menu. A sampling:

- Dolin Blanc vermouth, orange twist, with Castelvetrano olives, fennel seed, citrus
- Bisson Glera Prosecco, with 30-month-aged Parmigiano-Reggiano
- LeLarge Pugeot, Champagne Brut 1er Cru, NV, with cured salmon roe, herb butter, hearth bread
- Quartecello "Neromaestri" Lambrusco, with fried rabbit liver
- Uncle Val: Uncle Val's Botanical gin, tonic, Dolin Blanc with radish hearth bread

APPLES

The University of Minnesota created the Honeycrisp **apple** in 1991, after which it rose quickly to popular acclaim. However, now that the varietal's flavor has been found to be inconsistent with finicky growth, new varieties of hybrid apples are bring developed, such as Opal, RubyFrost, and Cosmic Crisp, a cross of Honeycrisp and Enterprise.

Try to match the right apple to the right use. Given the surge of interest in heirloom varietals for their greater complexity of flavor and aroma, there are many heirloom and hybrid options available. Pastry chef **Dominique Ansel** uses Granny Smiths in juices and sorbets, while opting for Honeycrisp apples in his tarte Tatin. One he skips? Red Delicious, which he finds "kind of grainy" and which falls apart during baking.

Apple Ceviche
—Gastón Acurio and chef Diego Muñoz's signature dish at Astrid y Gastón (Peru)

Apple Edible Helium Balloon (tied with a "string" made of dehydrated Granny Smith apple)
—Grant Achatz, Alinea (Chicago)

Apple Fritters with Salted Caramel Ice Cream
—Annie Wayte, White Hart Inn (Salisbury, Connecticut)

APRIL, SEE SPRING

ARCHITECTURE

The Fine Arts are five in number: Painting, Music, Poetry, Sculpture, and Architecture—of which the principal branch is Confectionery.

—MARIE-ANTOINE CARÊME

There's a long-standing connection between the pastry arts and **architecture**, and modern pastry chefs continue that thread.

Pastry chef **Pierre Hermé** spoke at Harvard University on "The Architecture of Taste" and his design process:

> I have what I call a scenario of taste—I imagine this in a sequence as you bite into the cake . . . what happens first, what happens second, what may provide a surprise in the middle.

The 2016 James Beard Foundation Outstanding Pastry

Chef finalist, Lafayette pastry chef **Jennifer Yee**, attended Le Cordon Bleu in London *and* studied interior architecture before becoming a pastry chef. Her study of painting and color influences how she combines colors and flavors on a plate. Yee loves meringue—crispy and dry, or soft and fluffy (e.g., floating island)—as well as fruit desserts (e.g., apple tart) and mochi stuffed with sweet red bean paste.

Architecture—whether the lines of a building or the detail of its facade—can inspire anyone creating a dessert with regard to its shape and structure.

ART AND DESIGN

Art is the queen of all sciences communicating knowledge to all the generations of the world.

—LEONARDO DA VINCI

The visual aspect of food can play a role in inspiring a new dish. Colors, lines, and shapes are all mentioned as part of the conceptual stage, with chefs turning to actual or virtual (e.g., Paper by FiftyThree on the iPad) sketchbooks to draw dishes. Sometimes appreciating art in a museum, gallery, restaurant, or home can provide inspiration—as can simply appreciating fashion while walking along a city street.

ART AND FOOD

Andy Warhol was inspired to paint pictures of Campbell's soup can labels. Was that creative?

Is it creative if a chef intentionally replicates other living chefs' food? That's how the French Laundry's former chef **Corey Lee** conceived his new restaurant in the San Francisco Museum of Modern Art, called In Situ, where he serves a rotating menu of signature dishes of other chefs, including **Wylie Dufresne** and **René Redzepi**. Think of it as akin to an "art installation," albeit one where not only touching but eating the exhibits are actively encouraged. Lee has described his mission as:

> . . . An extension of the museum's larger mission—to present great works worldwide and make them accessible for greater public engagement. In Situ will build appreciation for culinary traditions and hopefully encourage dialogue about our relationships with food, not unlike the way SFMOMA curates and exhibits important works of art.

Boston's Café ArtScience was opened by inventor and Harvard professor **David Edwards** as a way to showcase his conceptual dishes to adventurous guests seeking new experiences in form and texture—and those open to explore literally "inhaling" their beverages.

Rick Bayless periodically has his kitchen team in Chicago come up with new dishes based on different paintings.

Imagine: Think of a work of art you love—a painting, a sculpture, a piece of music. Use it as your inspiration to capture its essence in a new dish.

ATTENTION

My experience is what I agree to attend to. . . . Only those items which I notice shape my mind.

—WILLIAM JAMES

In addition to this truism from the American philosopher and psychologist, we also know that our energy goes wherever our attention flows. And we know that **Attention + Energy = Creation**.

Are you paying attention to what you most want to create?

By avoiding originality, In Situ is the most original new restaurant in the country.

—**PETE WELLS**, *New York Times*

ATTITUDE

Everything can be taken from a man but one thing: the last of the human freedoms—to choose one's attitude in any given set of circumstances, to choose one's own way.

—**VICTOR FRANKL,** Holocaust survivor and author of *Man's Search for Meaning*

About 10 percent of your life is what happens to you. The other 90 percent is created by how you choose to react to it.

Choose wisely.

AUGUST, SEE SUMMER

AUTHENTICITY

There's been increasing interest in "**authentic ethnic cuisine**"—which was up 14 percent in the one-year period of 2015 to 2016—as distinct from creative spins on ethnic cuisines, such as fusion takes.

Point: What could you do to research the authenticity of a dish you'd like to make?

Counterpoint: How far could you push a dish in the opposite direction, yet still have aspects of it be identifiable?

SEASONAL INGREDIENTS KEY

Flavors mentioned in regular type are seasonal ingredients suggested by at least one expert.

Bold marks those recommended by a number of experts.

BOLD CAPITALS mark those very highly recommended by the greatest number of experts.

Italics mark either specific dishes or cuisines that make use of seasonal ingredients.

A

AUTUMN

Weather: typically cool/warm
Needs: staying warm, storing energy

Autumn Ingredients

acorns
allspice (peak: autumn/winter)
almonds (peak: October)
APPLES and **APPLE CIDER** (peak: September–November)
artichokes (peaks: autumn, spring)
artichokes, Jerusalem (peak: autumn/winter)
arugula
basil (peak: September)
beans, e.g., **green** (peak: summer/autumn)
beans, shelling (peak: August–October)
beets
bell peppers (peak: September)
bok choy (peak: summer/autumn)
broccoli
broccoli rabe
Brussels sprouts (peak: November–February)
burdock (peak: summer/autumn)
cabbage, e.g., green, red, savoy (peak: autumn/winter)
cakes, esp. served warm
Calvados
caramel
cardamom
cardoons (peak: October)
carrots
cauliflower
celery
celery root (peak: October–November)
chard (peak: June–December)
cheeses, autumn (see page 251)
chestnuts (peak: October–November)
chicories, e.g., endive, escarole, frisée, radicchio
chiles (peak: summer/autumn)
cinnamon
citron, Buddha's hand (peak: October–January)
coconuts (peak: October–November)
corn (peak: September)
CRANBERRIES (peak: October–November)
crosnes (Chinese artichokes)
cucumbers (peak: September)
daikon (peak: autumn/winter)
dates (peak: autumn/winter)
dragon fruit (peak: August–November)
eggplant (peak: August–November)
eggplant, Japanese
endive, Belgian
escarole (peak: summer/autumn)
feijoas (peak: November–December)
fennel (peak: autumn/winter)
fennel seeds, wild
FIGS (peak: September–October)
foraged foods, e.g., acorns, burdock roots, pawpaws, persimmons, wild mushrooms
frisée
garlic (peak: September)
goji berries (peak: summer/autumn)
GOOSEBERRIES, CAPE (peak: September–November)
grains, e.g., whole
grapefruit
GRAPES, esp. **green, RED**
greens, e.g., beet, bitter, turnip

guavas (peak: autumn/winter)
heavier dishes
herbs, fresh
horseradish (peak: summer/autumn)
huckleberries (peak: August–September)
jackfruit (October)
kale (peak: November–January)
kiwi (peak: September–December)
kohlrabi (peak: September–November)
kumquats
leeks
lemons, Meyer (peak: October–May)
lentils
lettuces, e.g., Boston, green leaf, red leaf, **Romaine** (peak: summer/autumn)
limequats (peak: summer/autumn)
limes (peak: autumn/winter)
lovage (peak: September–October)
lychees (peak: September–November)
maple syrup
miso, dark
molasses
mushrooms, e.g., **chanterelles** (peak: summer/autumn), chicken of the woods, hedgehog, hen of the woods, lobster, matsutake, **porcini**, shiitake, **wild**
nutmeg
nuts
okra (peak: June–November)
olives (peak: September–January)
onions, e.g., red, Spanish, yellow
oranges
oranges, blood (peak: November–February)
papaya (peak: summer/autumn)
parsley
parsnips (peak: autumn/winter)
passion fruit (peak: November–February)
pawpaws
pears, e.g., Bartlett, Comice, D'Anjou, Seckel (peak: July–October)
pears, Asian (peak: September–November)
peas (peak: April–November)
pecans
peppers
PERSIMMONS (peak: October–January)
pistachios (peak: September)
plums (peak: July–October)
polenta
POMEGRANATES (peak: October–December)
potatoes
PUMPKINS (peak: September–December)
purslane (peak: April–November)
QUINCES (peak: October–December)
quinoa
radicchio (peak: summer/autumn)
rice, wild
roasts
root vegetables, e.g., carrots, parsnips, turnips, esp. fermented, raw, roasted
rutabagas (peak: October–April)
sage
salsify (peak: October–December)
scallops, bay (peak: November–March)
seeds, e.g., pumpkin, sunflower
shallots
slow-cooked dishes
snap peas
snow peas (peaks: spring, autumn)
spices, warming, e.g., black pepper, cayenne, cinnamon, chili powder, cloves, cumin, mustard powder
spinach
SQUASH, WINTER, e.g., acorn, buttercup, butternut, delicata, Hubbard, kabocha (peak: October–December)
stews, e.g., maque choux, succotash
strawberries
stuffings, e.g., chestnut, cornbread, sourdough, wild rice
SWEET POTATOES (peak: October–December)
tangelos (peak: November–January)
tatsoi (peak: autumn/winter)
todok (peak: autumn/winter)
tomatillos (peak: summer/autumn)
tomatoes (peak: September)
truffles, e.g., black, **white**
turnips (peak: autumn/winter)
vegetables, root
vinegar, e.g., balsamic, red wine
WALNUTS (peak: October)
watercress (peaks: spring, autumn)
yacón (tuber; peak: November–December)
yams (peak: November)
yuzu (peak: September–November)
zucchini

Autumn Beers
brown ales
Eisbock

fresh/wet hop beers
harvest ales
Märzen
Oktoberfest beers
pumpkin ales
smoked beers

Autumn Cheeses
Brie
Camembert
Cheddar
goat's milk cheeses
Gruyère
semi-hard cheeses

Autumn cheese accompaniments: apples, bread, chutney, dried fruit, grapes, nuts, pears, pomegranate seeds, walnuts

Autumn Cocktails and Spirits
apple brandy–based cocktails
apple cider–based cocktails
brown spirits, e.g., bourbon, whiskey
chocolate-noted cocktails, e.g., from chocolate-flavored bitters, chocolate liqueur, crème de cacao, Nutella
cinnamon-spiced cocktails
hot buttered rums
maple syrup–sweetened cocktails
nutmeg-spiced cocktails
pepita (pumpkin seed) garnishes, e.g., rims
pumpkin butter or pumpkin puree–flavored cocktails
punches
rum
sangrias
Scotch cocktails
tea-, esp. maple, based cocktails

Autumn Concepts
baked goods, e.g., biscuits, cakes, pies
butter, fruit, e.g., apple, pear
butternut squash soup
pizzas, e.g., with cheese, rosemary, wild mushrooms
salad dressings, e.g., Meyer lemon
soups, esp. warm, e.g., beet, pumpkin
stews
stuffed vegetables, e.g., acorn squash
stuffings

Autumn Desserts
baked or poached fruit, e.g., apples, pears
bread puddings
cakes
galettes, e.g., apple
granitas
ices
pears, roasted
pies, e.g., pecan, pumpkin, squash
puddings
tarts, e.g., apple, pear

Autumn Dressings
apple cider vinegar + maple syrup + mustard

Autumn Flavor Affinities
apples + caramel + Cheddar
apples + caramel + cinnamon
arugula + gorgonzola + pear
avocado + beet + citrus
blue cheese + hazelnuts + pears
blue cheese + pears + salad greens
bourbon + brown sugar + pecans
bourbon + chocolate + pumpkin
cabbage + caraway + sausage
caramel + chocolate + sea salt
(Camembert) cheese + mushrooms + sage
cranberries + orange + walnuts
dates + goat cheese + pistachios
eggplant + olives + red peppers *(e.g., on pasta, pizza)*
escarole + lemon + Parmesan
figs + caramel + cream
figs + honey + strawberries
pears + almonds + sugar

A Trio of Pear Desserts: A Miniature Pear Sorbet, Pear Soufflé, and Pear Tart
—Patrick O'Connell, The Inn at Little Washington (Washington, Virginia)

Banana Bread, Candied Pecan, Coffee Ice Cream
—Jon Shook & Vinny Dotolo, Son of a Gun (Los Angeles)

Chocolate-Hazelnut Buttercream and Banana Jam 12-Layer Cake
—Miro Uskokovic, Gramercy Tavern (New York City), inspired by a Nutella and banana sandwich

Flourless Chocolate Cake with Peanut Butter Mousse, Caramel Corn, and Popcorn Ice Cream
—D'Anthony Foster, The Point (Saranac Lake, New York)

"Pumpkin Pie" Soufflé with Brown Sugar and Grand Marnier Ice Cream
—D'Anthony Foster, The Point (Saranac Lake, New York)

pears + blue cheese + nuts
pears + chocolate + vanilla
pears + Pecorino + walnuts
persimmons + cinnamon + cream + walnuts
persimmons + figs + walnuts
persimmons + hazelnut oil + hazelnuts
sweet potatoes + brown sugar + coconut + vanilla
wild mushrooms + Fontina + rosemary

Autumn Pastas

baked pastas
gnocchi
lasagna
manicotti
ravioli
shell-shaped pastas, e.g., stuffed
squid-ink pastas

Autumn pasta sauces: brown butter sauces, butternut squash–based sauces, cheese-based sauces, cream-based sauces, eggplant-based sauces, lentil-based sauces, meat-based sauces, mushroom-based sauces, red wine–based sauces, roasted vegetable sauces (e.g., cauliflower), walnut-based sauces

Autumn Presentations

pies
pumpkins, stuffed miniature

Autumn Dishes

Beet Fantasia: Three Varieties of Roasted Beets, Beet Mousse, and Citrus Salsa
—Patrick O'Connell, The Inn at Little Washington (Washington, Virginia)

Cabbage Hot Pot: Smoked Cabbage Broth, Cabbage and Kale Ramen Noodles
—Amanda Cohen, Dirt Candy (New York City)

Carotte: Fricassee of Carrot, Taggiasche Olives, Capers, Crunchy Wood Ear Mushrooms, Queen Anne's Lace, and Pink Peppercorn Oil
—Daniel Boulud, Daniel (New York City)

Curry Roasted Cauliflower with Nuts and Seeds, Apricot Yuzu Crème Fraîche
—Loic Leperlier, The Point (Saranac Lake, New York)

Gratin of Fall Roots with Cipollini Onion, Domestic Mushrooms, and Bread Tuile
—Daniel Boulud, Daniel (NYC)

Green Lentil Ragout with Caramelized Onion, Sprouted Lentil Salad
—Daniel Boulud, Daniel (NYC)

Grilled Asparagus, Romesco, Meyer Lemon, Egg, Marcona Almond
—Jon Shook & Vinny Dotolo, Son of a Gun (Los Angeles)

Heirloom Carrot Selection with Black Garlic, Avocado, Sesame, and Ancho Miso Caramel
—Loic Leperlier, The Point (Saranac Lake, New York)

Hubbard Squash Agnolotti with Asgaard Chèvre, Pumpkin Seeds, XO Noble Tonic, and Alba White Truffle
—Loic Leperlier, The Point (Saranac Lake, New York)

Insalata Misticanza with dill, radish, shaved beets, sherry vinaigrette
—Nancy Silverton, Chi Spacca (Los Angeles)

"Open" Ravioli with Roasted Porcini, Caramelized Salsify, Swiss Chard, Tahoon Cress
—Daniel Boulud, Daniel (NYC)

Red Beet Tartare, Horseradish Cream, Cured Egg Yolk, Smoked Eel
—Ludo Lefebvre, Trois Mec (Los Angeles)

Red Kuri Squash Puree with Garlic-Scented "Berkoukes" Semolina, Crispy Shallot, Pioppini Mushroom, and Nasturtium Salad
—Daniel Boulud, Daniel (NYC)

Smoked Cipollini Sformato, Charred Cipollini, Grilled Sylvia's Alaskan Spot Prawn, Prawn Brodo
—Holly Smith, Cafe Juanita (Kirkland, Washington)

Sunseed Farm Winter Squash with Spiced Michigan Maple Brûlée, Savory Granola, Fermented Butter, and Smoky Quince Paste
—James Rigato, Mabel Gray (Hazel Park, Michigan)

Sweet and Spicy Pad Thai with Noodles Made from Butternut Squash, Garnished with Fermented Squash, Pumpkin Dumplings, Tiny Lotus Roots, and Finger Limes, Served Inside a Banana Blossom
—Amanda Cohen, Dirt Candy (New York City)

Young Beets Baked in Seaweed-Salt Crust with Black Cardamom, Sicilian Pistachio, Chive Aïoli, and Horseradish Crème Fraîche
—Daniel Boulud, Daniel (NYC)

Autumn Techniques

baking
braising
glazing
roasting
slow-cooking
stuffing

Autumn Wines

Aglianico
Barbaresco
Barolo
Beaujolais nouveau
Bordeaux, red
Burgundy, red
Cabernet Sauvignon
Champagne
Gewürztraminer
Hermitage
late harvest wines
Madeira
Merlot
Pinot Noir
red wines, esp. fuller-bodied
Rhone wines, red
Rioja
Sauternes
Sherry, PX
sweet dessert wines
Valpolicella, esp. ripasso
Viognier
Zinfandel

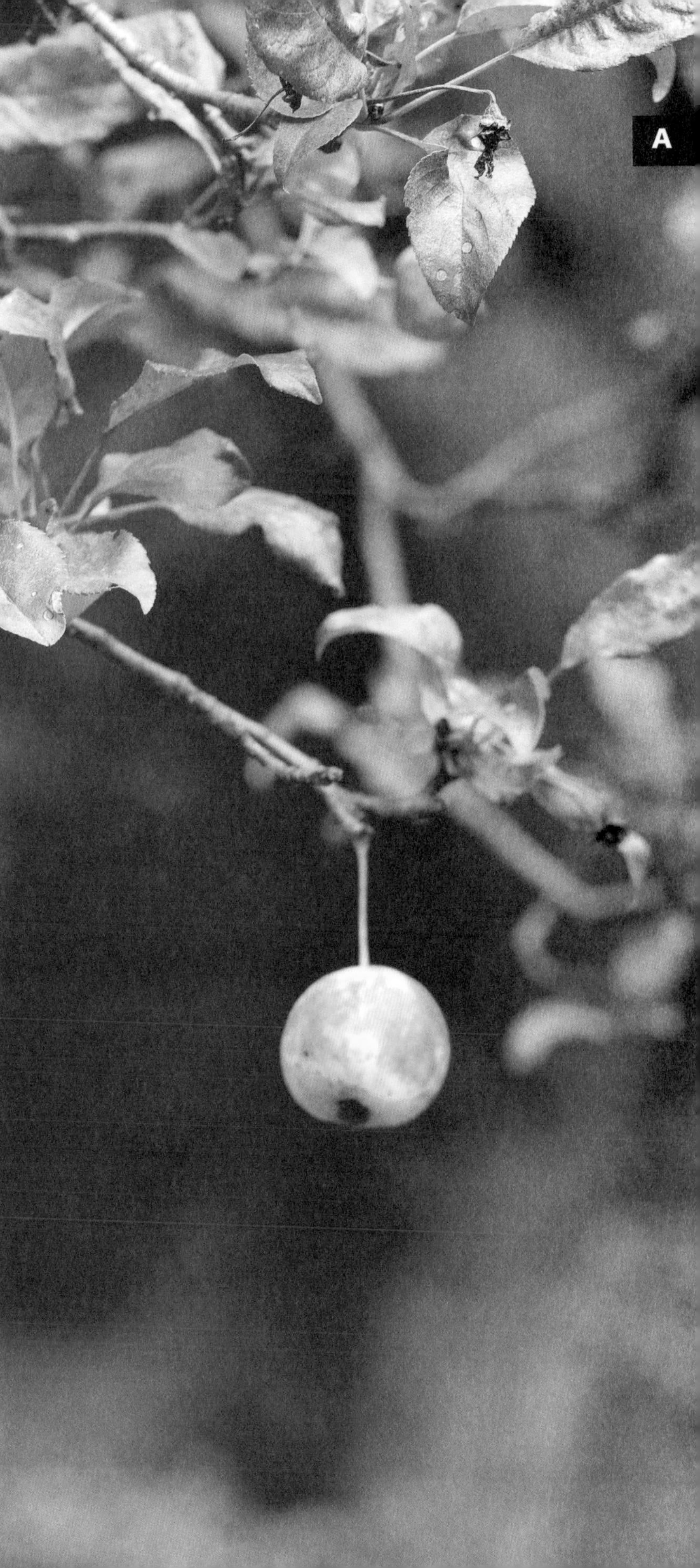

AYURVEDA

Without proper nutrition, medicine is of little use. . . . With proper nutrition, medicine is of little need.

—*CHARAKA SAMHITA* (c. 400–200 BC), one of the oldest and most important Ayurvedic texts

Ancient Indian physicians developed Ayurveda and its approach to eating more than 5,000 years ago.

It's based on the **Five Elements** (from which everything in the universe is said to be created) in order of density: ether (representing pervasiveness), air (vibration), fire (radiance), water (cohesion), and earth (inertia). The three basic Ayurvedic mind/body types are: vata (air + ether, marked by movement), pitta (fire + water, marked by intensity), and kapha (earth + water, marked by strength and endurance). It's possible to balance each of the types through proper eating.

Renewed interest in this ancient system is evidenced through the debut of North America's first Ayurvedic chef certification program at Bhagavat Life, the leading Ayurvedic cooking school in New York City, run by **Prentiss Alter** and his wife **Divya Alter**, NYC chef of Divya's Kitchen and author of *What to Eat for How You Feel*.

Some of the principles of Ayurvedic eating for all the types include eating these six tastes at every meal: sweet, sour, salty, bitter, pungent (which is found in foods such as chiles, garlic, horseradish, mustard, and onions), and astringent (e.g., apples, cranberries, persimmons, spinach, tea).

Point: How can you create a dish and/or a meal around all six tastes?

Counterpoint: Which are the most essential tastes to include in a dish?

Divya Alter

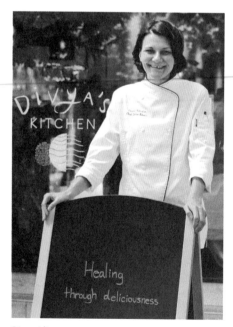

BAGELS AND BIALYS

New York City may not be the origin of the **bagel** (which dates to 1610 Poland, if not earlier), but it's arguably where bagels are being brought to their zenith.

With the opening of Sadelle's, baker and co-owner **Melissa Weller** has created what some believe to be the city's—if not America's—best bagel. It's arguably the freshest, too, as waiters shout, "Hot bagels!" as they circulate throughout the dining room with hot-from-the-oven offerings.

What's there to shout about? Extraordinary flavor and texture, for starters—Weller was inspired by **Nancy Silverton**'s sourdough bagel recipe in her book *Breads from the LaBrea Bakery.*

The flavors, then: everything (caraway seeds + dehydrated garlic + fennel seeds + poppy seeds + salt + sesame seeds), gluten-free everything, pumpernickel everything, pumpernickel raisin, salt and pepper (made with Icelandic sea salt and cracked butcher's pepper).

Other bagel flavors being played with elsewhere include: apple cinnamon, jalapeño, olive, pumpkin raisin, salt and vinegar, sun-dried tomato, and sweet potato.

In addition, the **bialy**—bagel's lighter, flatter cousin with a bit of chopped onion topping its indented center (there's no hole)—is being reinvented, too, by bakeries like the 80-year-old Kossar's, which offers olive, sesame, sun-dried tomato and pesto, and whole wheat onion varieties.

BAKED GOODS

Bakers and chefs are pushing the envelope—being more experimental and embracing mistakes in the kitchen.

Babka can be extraordinary alone (and if you don't agree, you haven't yet tasted **Melissa Weller**'s chocolate babka at Sadelle's in Manhattan). But this Jewish dessert bread, stuffed or swirled with chocolate or cinnamon—or, increasingly, savory takes with fresh herbs—is also being turned into bread pudding, cereal, French toast, and ice cream sandwiches.

Buttermilk **biscuits** work—so why not try switching out the buttermilk for another sweet-and-tangy dairy product, like cottage cheese, kefir, whey, or yogurt?

Challah isn't free from experimentation, either—**Jessamyn Waldman Rodriguez** of Hot Bread Kitchen in New York City creates an egg-free Sephardic challah with caraway, cumin, and sesame seeds. Other bakers have played with versions featuring chocolate chips.

Globalism isn't absent from baked goods, as places like Hot Bread Kitchen celebrate regional specialties among baked goods from all around the world—including Armenian lavash, Moroccan *m'smen,* and Persian *nan-e qandi,* in addition to six dozen other multi-ethnic breads. In turn, you'll find exotic twists on comfort food classics, and even chile peppers incorporated into sweet and spicy turns on baked goods. Popular flavor trends in baked goods include south-of-the-border regional Mexican, Brazilian, and Peruvian as well as Filipino and Southeast Asian.

Demand for **gluten-free** baked goods is pushing bakers to play with nut flours made from chestnuts or hazelnuts (which are often lighter and more flavorful than standard wheat flours), which are especially flavorful in the autumn and winter. **Shauna James Ahern,** better known as the Gluten-Free Girl via her popular website and books, has teamed with her chef-husband **Dan Ahern** to create a line of gluten-free flours.

Milling one's own flour from heirloom and heritage grains via

Half of the stuff that we serve at Milk Bar came from happy accidents and the power of the imaginative "What if?" I taught myself to bake with more of a savory cook's mentality.

—**CHRISTINA TOSI,** 2015 James Beard Foundation Outstanding Pastry Chef, as quoted in the *Washington Post*

Jessamyn Waldman Rodriguez

We are pleased to announce that the grains used in our pasta, bread, and pastry are house-milled and sustainably grown. By stone milling, we harness the flavor of the germ and bran, so not only does our food delight the palate, but it also nourishes the body. Rediscovering grain has brought new energy and inspiration to our work. We are thrilled to be able to share it with you.

—**CLAIRE KOPP MCWILLIAMS,** miller/baker, and **MARC VETRI,** chef/owner, Vetri (Philadelphia)

in-house milling systems can produce baked goods that are more aromatic and flavorful.

Non-wheat flours are rising in popularity, as bakers better understand how to work with alternatives like grain-based barley, buckwheat, polenta, and rye flours and the aforementioned nut flours.

BALANCING, FLAVOR

Joshua Skenes believes that balance "should always be a circle, where you begin with one taste that leads to another, and another, and as they disappear, it repeats itself as a cycle—otherwise, you have corners and [the flavor] is no longer balanced."

What creates "corners"? "The biggest culprits would be acid, salt, sweetness, alcohol—anything that you are left with in your mouth after taking a bite that is a 'hard stop,' which means the dish is *not* balanced," he explains, before adding: "The whole purpose for us is for you *not* to find a corner."

BALKAN CUISINE

The previously war-torn **Balkan** peninsula is inspiring chefs to explore the cuisines of the region—including Albanian, Bosnian, Bulgarian, Croatian, Kosovar, Macedonian, Montenegrin, Ottoman, Romanian, and Serbian—which are marked by seasonal, locally sourced ingredients, vegetable-

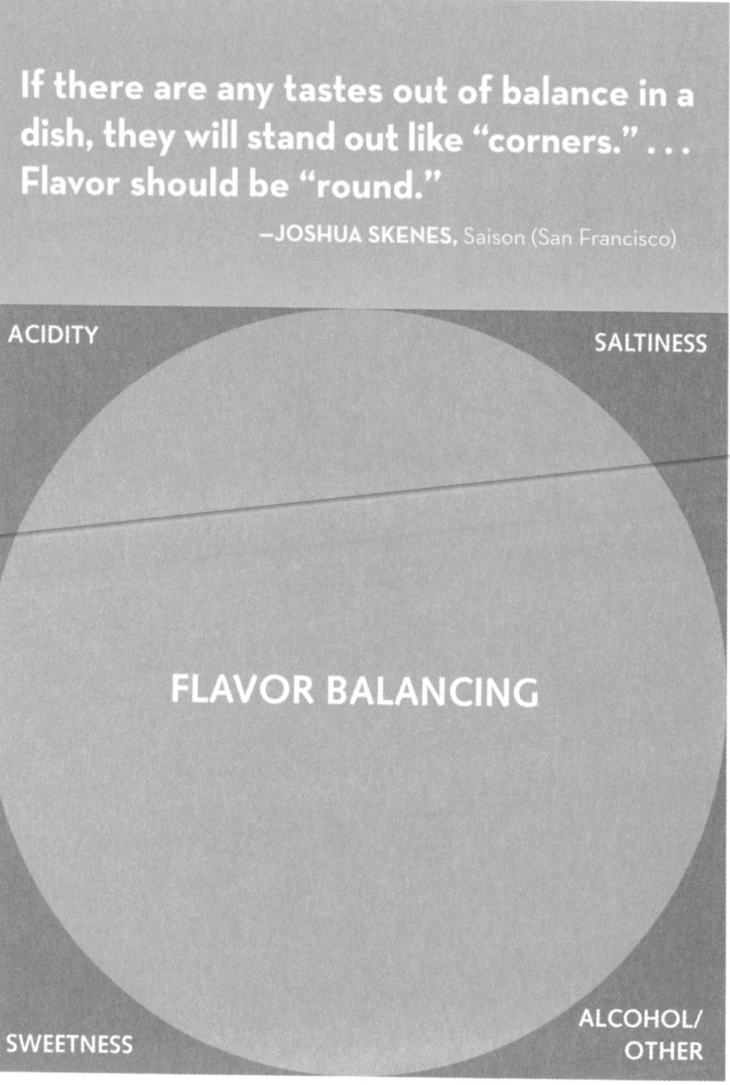
If there are any tastes out of balance in a dish, they will stand out like "corners." . . . Flavor should be "round."
—JOSHUA SKENES, Saison (San Francisco)
ACIDITY
SALTINESS
FLAVOR BALANCING
SWEETNESS
ALCOHOL/
OTHER

driven dishes, and grilled meat. **Ivan Iricanin** and **Richard Sandoval** teamed up to bring the Balkan-inspired restaurant Ambar to Washington, D.C., while **Tim Wiechmann** opened Playska, a new Balkan sandwich shop, in Cambridge in 2015.

Balkan wines are also rising in popularity, with Chicago's Publican Quality Meats hosting a Balkan wine tasting dinner and Chicago's Parachute pouring them by the glass and carafe to accompany its Korean-American cuisine.

BASQUE CULINARY WORLD PRIZE

The **Basque Culinary World Prize** is a new annual award which seeks to recognize chefs around the world whose projects have improved society through gastronomy. Winners receive €100,000 toward "a project or institution of their choice that demonstrates the wider role of gastronomy in society."

More than 200 nominations led to the identification of 110 candidates from 50 countries, and 20 finalists were announced in May 2016. The top 20, reflecting the global reach of the prize, includes chefs from Brazil, Canada, Chile, Colombia, Denmark, France, India, Italy, Mexico, the Netherlands, South Africa, Spain, the U.K., the U.S., and Venezuela. These projects are focused on everything from innovation to education, health, research, sustainability, social entrepreneurship and philanthropy, and the preservation of local cultures.

The inaugural 2016 winner was Venezuela's **María Fernanda Di Giacobbe**, and the 2017 winner was **Leonor Espinosa** of Colombia.

Among the finalists for the Basque Culinary World Prize, as reported on its website, basqueculinaryworldprize.com:

- **Alberto Crisci, U.K.** (2016): Crisci's charity, The Clink, has a series of fine dining restaurants inside four British prisons, in which offenders learn to cook and serve, and can gain vocational qualifications to give them real job opportunities when they leave—all with the aim of reducing rates of reoffending.
- **Ángel León, Spain** (2016): Chef León is renowned for his provocative culinary innovation at his restaurant, Aponiente. Passionate about research, he has been exploring the potential of the oceans as a food source and is documenting valuable knowledge that could preserve exciting new possibilities for future generations.
- **Ann Cooper, U.S.** (2016): The Chef Ann Foundation gives schools the tools and resources to move away from serving highly processed foods to providing fresh, cooked-from-scratch meals, with the aim of contributing towards the reduction of childhood obesity in the United States.
- **Anthony Myint, U.S.** (2017): Chef Myint teamed up with writer **Karen Leibowitz** to create the Perennial restaurant in San Francisco, which aims to make food part of the solution to—versus the cause of—climate change. The duo also works with restaurants to help them eliminate their carbon footprint and encourages progressive agriculture.
- **Dan Giusti, U.S.** (2017): Formerly head chef of Copenhagen's

> **A growing number of chefs have joined the ranks of activists advancing the agenda of changing our food system. . . . Today's food culture has given chefs a platform of influence, including the power, if not the luxury, to innovate. As arbiters of taste, we can help inspire a Third Plate, a new way of eating that puts it all together.**
>
> —**DAN BARBER,** Blue Hill (New York City)

Noma, Giusti seeks to channel the knowledge and experience of professional chefs to transform the way schools serve meals to America's schoolchildren. Through his pilot Connecticut-based Brigaid program, Giusti teaches "real food" along with the pleasures of the table.

- **Daniel Boulud, France/U.S.** (2016): Boulud is the co-director of New York's Citymeals on Wheels, a charity providing healthy meals to elderly people who cannot buy food or cook for themselves. Boulud is also in charge of Chefs Deliver, an initiative in which top chefs cook gourmet meals for the elderly homebound.
- **Daniel Patterson and Roy Choi, U.S.** (2017): High-end chef Patterson teamed up with food-truck legend Choi to found LocoL, which aims to start a "fast-food revolution," beginning in downtown Los Angeles and Oakland, proving that it's possible even in the inner cities to eat better for less.
- **Gabriel Garza, Mexico** (2016): Inspired by working at a local center for the visually impaired, Garza singlehandedly set up Destellos de Sabor, a project that teaches the blind to cook for themselves, giving them independence, self-esteem, and the potential to find future employment.
- **Jessamyn Rodriguez, Canada/U.S.** (2016): The Harlem-based Canadian created a nine-month training program for low-income, immigrant women to become artisanal bakers with Hot Bread Kitchen. Through an employer-driven workforce development and business incubator, it helps women and men professionalize their skills in the culinary arts in order to be able to earn fair wages and achieve financial independence.
- **José Andrés, Spain/U.S.** (2016 and 2017): Following the devastation of Hurricane Katrina in Haiti, Andrés started World Central Kitchen to use the expertise of its chef network to empower locals by providing them with clean cooking stoves and food safety/sanitation training. Additional programs include feeding programs in schools and culinary training for the local hospitality workforce.
- **Joshna Maharaj, India/Canada** (2016): Chef Maharaj works with several hospitals and institutions to help them serve better food to patients. In particular, he rethinks and redesigns all elements of the food chain, from farm to fork, in favor of healthy, fresh, nutritious meals.
- **Kamilla Seidler, Denmark,** and **Michelangelo Cestari, Venezuela** (2016): Seidler and Cestari were chosen by Claus Meyer to take his Melting Pot project to Bolivia where they opened the restaurant Gustu, which also functions as a cookery school. Gustu has put a culinary spotlight on a previously overlooked country, as well as serving to train and empower locals through a wider knowledge and consciousness about their ethnic gastronomy.
- **Leonor Espinosa, Colombia** (2017 winner): Espinosa's Funleo Foundation preserves and promotes ancestral knowledge of indigenous and Afro-Colombian people, and she's also championed the creation of a Comprehensive Gastronomy Centre in Choco as an alternative to drug trafficking.
- **Margot Janse, Holland/South Africa** (2016): Dutch chef Janse runs Isabelo, an initiative that started with a simple gesture—a nutritious muffin given to 70 school children in Franschhoek, South Africa—which has now become a program that produces 1,300 meals a day for local schools.
- **María Fernanda Di Giacobbe, Venezuela** (2016 winner): Maria has built a whole chain of education, entrepreneurship, and economic development around Venezuelan cacao. With Kakao and Cacao de Origen, she supports local producers with the resources they need to improve their product. She also helps women get the necessary training and tools to become chocolate entrepreneurs themselves.

Imagine: What other pressing social problem could be solved through a new food-related initiative?

BEER

U.S. craft beer sales have risen dramatically. Beer is such an important part of the gastronomic world that there's now a brewery located at the Culinary Institute of America's Hyde Park campus.

Chef **Rick Bayless** launched his own Tocayo beer brand in conjunction with Constellation Brands, including a Hominy White Ale made with **coriander + hominy + orange,** and opened the Chicago brewpub Cruz Blanca.

The rising popularity of techniques like curing, fermenting, salting, and smoking provide a challenge for sommeliers, who more frequently turn to craft beers as the perfect pairing.

Brewmasters are thinking more like chefs, creating ingredient-driven beers made from local produce, herbs, and spices, such as at Chicago's Forbidden Root, whose brewmasters told us they turn to ***The Flavor Bible*** for inspiration.

What makes beer beer? What if it didn't have bubbles? Brewmasters are experimenting with bubble-free **still ales** that are high in alcohol and loud in flavor, often further intensified by aging in barrels.

What happens if you pair beer with beer? While the Black and Tan—a beer cocktail made via layering a pale beer (e.g., pale ale) with a dark beer (e.g., stout)—dates back to the late 1800s, the experimentation continues. Brooklyn Brewery's Black and Brooklyn pairs its Brooklyn lager with its seasonal dark lager. While bitter IPAs aren't the best blending candidates, flavored beers and sour beers can work well mixed.

Beer is also being used in cocktails, which might feature American pale ale (as is the case at Chicago's Violet Hour), Hefeweizen foam (as is the case at Boston's Highball Lounge), or Victory Pilsner (as is the case at New York's PDT).

If beer works with beer, what about with other bitter flavors? Craft brewers are adding coffee essence to select darker beers such as porters and stouts, to add roasted nutty notes.

And fruit and fruity hops alike have been adding notes of coconut, mango, and pineapple to beers. . . . What's next?

Imagine: Have you experimented with your own home brew? What flavor combinations would make a great beer?

Even in high-end restaurants, eight to ten percent of sales are beer.

—**GARRETT OLIVER,** brewmaster, Brooklyn Brewery (Brooklyn)

BEST, THE

There is not a good or a bad cuisine, just the one you like the best.

—**FERRAN ADRIÀ,** elBulli (Spain)

While **Ferran Adrià** reminds us that taste is ultimately personal, hard-core food lovers are not about to lose interest in seeking out "the best" in any food category any time soon. As new bars are set for excellence, the world takes notice.

Many of the best chefs keep a close eye on "the best" that is out there—seeking out the best culinary books, TV shows, and films, and being inspired by those chefs they consider to be "the best."

The increasingly high-profile World's 50 Best Restaurants list published by *Restaurant* magazine is not without its critics (including some for its emphasis on male-dominated restaurants, given that the 2016 World's Best Female Chef **Dominique Crenn**'s Atelier Crenn in San Francisco didn't even merit a spot on the top 100 list), but it's become the most prominent ranking of its kind.

Those looking for other takes on the world's best restaurants will find no shortage of other opinions, such as the *Michelin Guide, Zagat Survey,* and *La Liste*—France's Foreign Ministry's ranking of the 1,000 best restaurants in the world that includes entries in 48 countries, with 101 in the United States; the 2015 list was topped by Michelin three-star Restaurant de l'Hotel de Ville in Switzerland, while the highest-ranking U.S. restaurant was Per Se in New York City.

Imagine: If you could become known for creating the best restaurant or dish in any category, what would it be? What are your personal signature dishes that you make best?

BLACK FOODS (SEE ALSO BLUE FOODS AND PURPLE FOODS, AS HUES VARY)

It leaves everything in the dark, but the palate is lit.

—**MASSIMO BOTTURA,** describing at 2009 MadridFusion his all-black Tribute to Thelonious Monk dish inspired by the jazz musician, which he based on meditating and tasting in the dark

beans, black
blackberries
carrots, black
caviar
cherries, black
currants, black
figs, black
garlic, black
grapes, black
lentils, black
licorice
mushrooms, black
Oreos
pasta, squid-ink
plums, black
poppy seeds
quinoa, black
sesame seeds, black
soybeans, black
squid ink and squid ink–dyed foods, e.g., paella, pasta, risotto
tea, black
truffles, black

BLUE FOODS (SEE ALSO BLACK FOODS AND PURPLE FOODS, AS HUES VARY)

blueberries
borage
butterfly pea plants, e.g., whose (dried and powdered) blue flower petals are used to color cocktails, rice, and tea
cheese, blue-veined, e.g., Roquefort, Stilton
cocktails, blue, e.g., made with blue Curaçao
corn, blue
cornflowers
Curaçao, blue
Disco Sour, a cocktail made with butterfly pea flower, which changes from blue to purple when citrus is added
flour, blue corn
mushrooms, bluefoot
potatoes, blue
tortillas, blue corn

BOCUSE D'OR

Since 1987, chefs have competed in the Bocuse d'Or, a biennial global culinary Olympics that brings together dozens of competitors in Lyon, France, and often springboards the careers of participants. But it wasn't until 2015 that an American chef placed among the top three (second place) in the competition. That chef was **Philip Tessier,** executive sous chef of the French Laundry, assisted by commis **Skylar Stover**—and their team was coached by chef **Gavin Kaysen,** a ten-year veteran of the contest.

Gavin Kaysen had previously coached competitor **James Kent,** the former Eleven Madison Park chef de cuisine who went on to become executive chef of the NoMad in Manhattan, Eleven Madison Park's younger sibling. Kaysen and Kent were part of the coaching team for the 2017 Team USA.

In 2017, chef **Mathew Peters** of Per Se and his assistant **Harrison Turone,** representing Team USA at the 2017 Bocuse d'Or and under head coach Tessier, brought home America's first gold medal in the competition for the two required dishes: an interpretation of the Lyonnaise classic *Poulet de Bresse au Ecrevisses* (Bresse chicken stuffed with morel sausage, foie gras, and crawfish), and a first-time challenge of **a 100-percent vegan dish** (California green asparagus with cremini mushrooms, potatoes, and a toasted green almond custard, accented by a vegan Parmesan cheese–like crumble made from almonds and nutritional yeast).

2016 Jury USA chef judges included **James Briscione** (Institute of Culinary Education), **Chris Hastings** (Hot and Hot Fish Club), **Shaun Hergatt** (Juni), **Timothy Hollingsworth** (Otium),

James Kent (left) and Gavin Kaysen (right)

The chef and the dancer share the same ideal: movement and creativity, a quest for the perfect movement and technical excellence in their passion for their art. This is what embodies the spirit of the Bocuse d'Or.

—PAUL BOCUSE, legendary French chef

Gavin Kaysen (Spoon and Stable), **James Kent** (The NoMad), **Gabriel Kreuther** (Gabriel Kreuther), **Barbara Lynch** (Barbara Lynch Gruppo), **Mathew Peters** (Bocuse d'Or Team USA 2017), **Richard Rosendale** (Rosendale Collective), **Bryce Shuman** (Betony), **Robert Sulatycky** (iQKitchen and Team USA 2017 Assistant Coach), and **Philip Tessier** (Head Coach, Team USA 2017).

The **Ment'or BKB Foundation**, founded by chefs **Daniel Boulud, Thomas Keller,** and **Jérôme Bocuse,** evolved out of their efforts to recruit and support the Bocuse d'Or's Team USA, then evolved further in its mission to elevate American cuisine as a whole. The foundation now offers grants to assist young chefs land stages at restaurants around the globe. See mentorbkb.org for more.

BOWLS

Bowls are hot. From Korean **bibimbap** to Hawaiian **poke,** rice-based (including black, brown, jasmine and red) and other grain-based (amaranth, freekah, millet, pearled barley, quinoa) bowls topped with all manner of crunchy raw and cooked vegetables (beets, greens, pickles, sea vegetables), garnishes (egg, raw or cooked fish, nuts, tofu), and highly-flavored sauces (chile oil, garlic, ginger, hot sauce, lemon juice, pickled peppers, ponzu, preserved lemon, sesame oil, soy sauce, vinegar) are enjoying huge popularity.

Dishes

Sorrel Pesto Brown Rice Bowl with Preserved Lemon, Lacto-Fermented Hot Sauce, and a Poached Egg

—Jessica Koslow, Sqirl (Los Angeles)

Imagine: How would you reinvent the bowl?

BREADINGS AND CRUSTS

What do you use besides the traditional bread crumbs and cracker crumbs when you wish to coat ingredients before cooking? Panko breadcrumbs offer enhanced crispiness, and those looking for extra-crunchy crusts are experimenting with double-frying French fries and other foods, which further eliminates the moisture that inhibits crunchiness. But there are lots of other options:

cheese, e.g., Parmesan
Chex cereal, crushed
coconut, flaked
corn chips, crushed
cornflakes, crushed
cornmeal
Cream of Wheat
flax seeds
flour, nut, e.g., almond flour
Grape-Nuts cereal
horseradish
matzoh crumbs
mushrooms, e.g., dried and crushed porcini
noodles, e.g., ground ramen
nuts, crushed, e.g., almonds, hazelnuts, macadamia, peanuts, pecans, pine nuts, walnuts
oats, e.g., rolled
phyllo dough
poha (pressed rice)
potato chips, crushed
potato flakes, mashed
pretzels, crushed
quinoa
rice, e.g., ground Arborio
Rice Krispies, crushed
seeds, e.g., flax seeds
spices, crushed
wasabi

BREAD SERVICE

Guests are embracing whole-grain artisanal **bread offerings** in restaurants.

Who has the best bread service? One candidate is **David Bouley**'s Bouley in New York City, which has featured more than a dozen different breads on its cart, including two gluten-free offerings made of nuts, seeds, and fiber that were among the most popular, even among guests without gluten sensitivity. **Gunnar Gíslason**'s Agern in New York offers an earthenware baking dish filled with warm crusty barley bread with a soft, highly hydrated interior that is paired with whipped butter enhanced with skyr (Iceland's answer to yogurt) and apple cider vinegar powder.

Other notable offerings: The house-baked bread with

Bing Bread at Parachute (Chicago)

Breaded or Crusted Dishes

Corn Flake–Crusted Fish Fillets with Roasted Tomatillo Sauce and Fried Corn

—Rick Bayless, from his recipe contribution to the book *The Breakfast Cereal Gourmet*

Butterflied Shrimp coated in Cream of Wheat

—Floyd Cardoz, in his book *One Spice, Two Spice*

Chocolate-Caramel Tart with Pretzel Crust, Popcorn Ice Cream, and Candied Peanuts

—Colleen Grapes, The Harrison (New York City)

Corn Flake–Crusted French Toast

—Michael Symon, co-host of *The Chew*

carefully paired flavored butters at **Curtis Duffy**'s Grace in Chicago (which features red wine rolls and rosemary focaccia served with Amish cow's milk butter flavored two ways: with sea salt, and herbed) and at **Mark Levy**'s creations at Magdalena at the Ivy Hotel in Baltimore (whose offerings have included miso rolls paired with soy butter, and beet rolls paired with horseradish butter).

Amanda Cohen's Dirt Candy in New York City offers rainbow-colored monkey bread, served in flower pots. And Aquavit's chef **Emma Bengtsson** is the restaurant's former pastry chef who established the restaurant's distinguished bread offerings, including Danish rye and lingonberry bread served with sweet and brown butters, as well as coarse salt.

Regionally inspired breads are served at places like **Vivian Howard**'s Chef & the Farmer in Kinston, North Carolina, which offers Our Daily Bread specials like white Cheddar jalapeño corn bread with salted whipped butter.

Baked potatoes are influencing some of the best bread courses across the country:

- At 2016 James Beard Best Chef: Mid-Atlantic **Aaron Silverman**'s restaurant Rose's Luxury in Washington, D.C., hot potato bread is served with whipped butter, chives, and dried, fried potato skin crumbs that sub for bacon bits in appearance and flavor.
- Chef **John Fraser** at Nix in New York City serves Yukon potato fry bread with broccoli, cheddar cheese, radishes, scallions, and sour cream.
- Chefs **Beverly Kim** and **Johnny Clark** of Parachute in Chicago serve crispy potato, cheddar, and scallion bing bread with sour cream butter.

Imagine: What's the best bread course you can possibly imagine?

BREAKFAST AND BRUNCH

San Francisco pastry chef **William Werner** of Craftsman and Wolves patisserie became a star on Instagram (and earned a 2016 James Beard Foundation Outstanding Pastry Chef nomination) for his Rebel Within green-onion-and-sausage muffin, which features a runny soft-boiled egg inside it.

Right dish, right time: Breakfast is booming. According to OpenTable.com, nearly a third more New York City restaurants offered breakfast in 2016 versus 2013. Some restaurants—like **Jessica Koslow**'s Sqirl in Los Angeles and **Jonathan Brooks**'s Milktooth in Indianapolis—are even serving breakfast all day long.

At Milktooth, dishes like "winter citrus Dutch baby pancake with Meyer lemon curd whipped cream,

The biggest secret in this business is that people like things inside of things. If you cut into something and something oozes out, hallelujah.

—WILLIAM WERNER,
pastry chef, Craftsman and Wolves (San Francisco)

Breakfast at Jon & Vinny's

I don't sit down and rack my brain for dishes. Things come to me. . . . I've had dreams of a dish, woken up, made a note on my phone, and then gone back to it. Sometimes it makes no sense, but sometimes it makes a little bit of sense.

—JONATHAN BROOKS, Milktooth (Indianapolis), as quoted in the *Indianapolis Star*

toasted almonds, powdered sugar, and figs" and "Belgian waffle with salted butter, local honey, and Parmesan" are supplemented by "Coffee" and "Booze" menus.

Brunch—which was first established in American restaurants more than a century ago—is booming, too, though more so in cities than in rural areas, and more so on the coasts than in the middle of the country, according to Google Trends data.

What else is hot at breakfast and brunch time?

Doughnuts! A doughnut bar featuring Los Angeles import Stan's Donuts alongside do-it-yourself toppings (including candy, caramel and chocolate sauces, cereal, chocolate chips, glazes, and sprinkles) marks brunch at La Stanza Ristorante in Chicago.

English breakfast! Hearty plates inspired by the full English (e.g., beans, eggs, mushrooms, sausages, and tomatoes, with toast), reinterpreted with global flavors (e.g., avocados and black beans, with fried bread).

Mimosas! Mimosas and other brunch cocktails are being made tableside, as they do at La Stanza Ristorante in Chicago.

Molletes! New global-inspired brunch offerings include open-faced bean-and-cheese molletes, which we came to discover at **Rick Bayless**'s Frontera Kitchens' O'Hare outpost.

Pizza! Jon Shook and **Vinny Dotolo**'s Jon & Vinny's in Los Angeles features a breakfast pizza with Yukon gold potatoes, eggs, rosemary, olive oil, Parmesan cheese, and red onion. New Orleans's **Susan Spicer** is a fan of breakfast-inspired pizza with Russet potatoes, soft eggs, and chives.

Porridge! The moister "bowl" of the morning hour, boiled-grain porridges—from rice-driven congees to farro- or oat-driven bowls—are featuring all kinds of toppings, such as chili oil, fried garlic, ginger, green onions, and tofu on Asian versions. Given customers' love of risotto (and some chefs' annoyance with the long process of stirring), porridges offer comparable texture at a fraction of the prep time.

Salad! The secret to salads at breakfast is sticking with milder greens (e.g., butter lettuce, romaine, spinach), then topping them with whole grains or crispy potatoes, and possibly finishing with a fried or poached egg.

Sandwiches! Made with biscuits, bagels, English muffins, or sandwich rolls, these are being served open-faced or closed, topped or stuffed with a wide variety of vegetables and spreads more often than the traditional cheeses, eggs, and meats.

Vegetables! Dirt Candy's **Amanda Cohen** offers zucchini pancakes with squash butter, and updates the Bloody Mary with a green-tomato-juice–based Jealous Mary.

Breakfast/Brunch Dishes

Ancient Grain Porridge with Coconut Milk, Blackberry Jam, Pistachios, and Hemp Seeds
—Jonathan Brooks, Milktooth (Indianapolis)

Breakfast Pizza: Yukon Gold Potato, Egg, Rosemary, Olive Oil, Parmesan, and Red Onion
—Jon Shook & Vinny Dotolo, Jon & Vinny's (Los Angeles)

Bread Pudding French Toast with Preserved Apples, Spicebush Syrup, and Whipped Cream
—Katianna Hong, The Charter Oak (St. Helena, California)

Brown Rice Porridge: traditional kokuhu rose brown rice porridge, straus milk, toasted hazelnuts and choice of jam
—Jessica Koslow, Sqirl (Los Angeles)

Croque Monster, a cross between Eggs Benedict and Croque Monsieur
—Sarah Lange, pastry chef, Field Trip (Los Angeles)

French Toast: Brioche Stuffed with Jam & Baked "Pain Purdu" Style served with Crème Fraîche
—Jessica Koslow, Sqirl (Los Angeles)

Green Eggs and Jam: Country bread, creamed spinach, onion jam, fried egg, arugula
—Jessica Koslow, Sqirl (Los Angeles)

Green Huevos & No Ham: Green tortilla, salsa verde, queso fresco, and two tempura-poached eggs
—Amanda Cohen, Dirt Candy (New York City)

Maple-Glazed Pretzels stuffed with Breakfast Sausage
—Sarah Lange, pastry chef, Field Trip (Los Angeles)

Potato & Celeriac Latke with Curried Cauliflower Puree and Onion Marmalade
—Jonathan Brooks, Milktooth (Indianapolis)

Seared Polenta: Spring vegetables cooked in whey, fried egg, greens
—Jessica Koslow, Sqirl (Los Angeles)

Smoked and Grilled Trout, Rye Bread, Fermented Onions, Avocado and Egg Spread
—Katianna Hong, The Charter Oak (St. Helena, California)

Steamed Spare Ribs with Pickled Turnips, Potato Rosti, Eggs Baked in Pork Stock, Our Harissa
—Katianna Hong, The Charter Oak (St. Helena, California)

BREATHE

INSPIRATION: from the Latin *inspiratus*, meaning "to breathe into"

When striving for creative inspiration in the kitchen, don't forget to breathe.

Yes. Seriously.

Jessica Dibb, one of America's leading experts on the practice of breathwork and director of the Inspiration Consciousness School outside Baltimore, reminds us that the first and last thing we do in life is take a breath and let it out. Conscious breathing creates brain coherence and balances our sympathetic and parasympathetic nervous systems. She insists that it can, therefore, significantly enhance creativity.

"Creativity is best supported by embodied presence—a relaxed dynamism in the **body**, an open **heart**, and an awake, quiet, spacious **mind** inquiring into what is, and what is possible," she says. "Even just one conscious breath begins to align all three of these intelligences."

So, how can we keep bringing ourselves back to the present moment and the highest possibility for our creativity in cooking—for clearly perceiving our ingredients and what is possible through them? Dibb recommends:

- **relaxing our bellies** so our diaphragm has the maximum amount of room to expand and take in air;
- **deepening our breath**; and
- **allowing the sensations of our breath to bring our attention to the present moment.**

BURGERS

Americans love **burgers**. Three out of four Americans eat a burger at least once a week, according to Datassential. And the love of burgers is spreading around the globe. Even **Alain Passard**'s Michelin three-star restaurant in France, L'Arpège, has served a veggie burger—one featuring a "steak" made of winter vegetables: celery, horseradish, Jerusalem artichoke, rutabaga, and salsify. The James Beard Foundation's 2013 Outstanding Pastry Chef, **Brooks Headley**, took veggie burgers mainstream at his craveable NYC-based Superiority Burger, one of 20 semifinalists for the 2016 James Beard Foundation Best New Restaurant award and our personal favorite fast-food restaurant.

Among the patty, the bun, and the condiments and toppings, burgers offer a ready flavor platform for creative experimentation. **Daniel Boulud** helped spur the trend for exploring "How high is up?" with his over-the-top DB Burger at db bistro moderne in New York City, which was stuffed with red wine–braised short ribs. More recently portion size has been shrinking, with sliders becoming a staple on many restaurant menus. Your own creative takes on a burger can involve one or more of its three key elements:

- **Patties**: While connoisseurs like their patties crispy on the outside and moist on the inside, there's plenty of room for debate. Mushrooms (especially roasted and chopped or ground) are becoming an increasing percentage of the blend in hamburger patties, reflecting guests' desire to reduce or eliminate meat consumption. Chefs are experimenting like mad with veggie burgers made from vegetables (e.g., **Amanda Cohen**'s Carrot Sliders at Dirt Candy), legumes and grains, including **John Fraser** of Nix, whose black beans + brown rice + oats patty flavored with Dijon mustard and tomato powder won his patty melt third place on *New York*'s list of the best in New York City. Other nonbeef patties are based on fish, chicken, or turkey.

Nix Patty Melt

Brooks Headley

- **Buns**: From egg-rich brioche buns to pretzel buns, focaccia to potato rolls, there's no shortage of bready options to serve a burger between—which didn't stop chefs from frying ramen into "ramen buns" to sandwich around a patty. Gluten-free bun options include eliminating the bun altogether, and serving the patty on top of salad greens, accented by traditional burger toppings.
- **Condiments/toppings**: From tried-and-true to too-much, burgers are being topped with avocado, cheese (American, Cheddar, Muenster, even Parmesan), fried eggs, guacamole, ketchup, lettuce, mayonnaise, mustard, onions (raw or caramelized), pickles, relish, special sauce, sprouts, Sriracha, tomatoes, and truffles.

BURNED FOOD

Who says burning food is a mistake? In this era of live-fire cooking and smoked ingredients, not to mention barbecue culture (with its "burnt ends"), people are discovering a love of **burned and charred foods.** In the 2015 edition of the *Saveur 100*, reflecting the magazine's favorite things to cook and eat, three of the 100 items were "burnt" or "charred" (including burnt citrus salt made from charred citrus zest).

Grano arso, which means "burnt grain" in Italian, originated in the country's Puglia region. And while it was considered *cucina povera* ("cuisine of poverty"), in time many developed a taste for the scorched grains—or for pasta or pizza made with them. Earthy vegetables like Brussels sprouts, cauliflower, onions, and winter squashes pair particularly well with *grano arso*.

Nicholas Stefanelli of Washington, D.C.'s Masseria has turned his burnt-grain pastas into a specialty, with dishes like Orecchiette Grano Arso: Burned Wheat Orecchiette with Mussels, Cherry Tomato, and Basil.

The technique of charring, especially vegetables, is increasing in popularity. While charring vegetables adds a savory depth of flavor to dishes, pastry chefs are also playing with burnt desserts and sauces, as are baristas with ash powder–flecked lattes.

Burnt Dishes

Apple Confit with Charred Lemon Ice Cream
—Jared Bacheller, L'Espalier (Boston)

Burnt Brioche Toast with Ricotta
—Jessica Koslow, Sqirl (Los Angeles)

Charred Carrots with Orange Yogurt, Spicy Raisins, Salt and Butter Pecans, and Capers
—Vivian Howard, Chef & the Farmer (Kinston, North Carolina)

CACIO E PEPE

The craze for this **cheese** (typically Pecorino) + **black pepper** pasta sauce dovetails with guests' love of macaroni and cheese, prompting chefs to play with the combination in dishes spanning doughnuts, ice cream, pizza, popcorn, potatoes, and risotto. Chefs are putting their own spin on it—with the rich and unctuous version at Momofuku Nishi substituting fermented chickpeas for the cheese:

> **Ceci e Pepe: chickpea hozon, black pepper**
>
> —David Chang, Momofuku Nishi (New York City)

CAESAR SALAD

Is the **Caesar salad** the most popular restaurant salad in America? In addition to its seemingly ubiquitous presence on virtually every hotel and steakhouse menu, not to mention at countless other restaurants, what other salad can boast more than *three decades* of its own annual competition? More than two dozen restaurants compete every year in Houston in the categories of Best Classic Caesar, Best Caesar Presentation, Most Creative Caesar, and People's Choice.

Recent winners for Best Creative Caesar include Houston's Bistro Lancaster for its **Hearts of Crisp Romaine "Fries"** (2016), Brennan's of Houston's **Southern Creole Caesar** with collard greens, crispy sweet potatoes, and tasso ham gravy dressing (2015), the San Luis Resort's **Red Chile Tuille Cone stuffed with Caesar Salad with Candied Pumpkin Seeds and Chipotle Pork Belly** (2014), Houston's Kiran's **Indian-inspired chicken Caesar** with cashews and raisins served in crisp Parmesan baskets (2013), and Houston's Ninfa's **BLT Caesar** (2012).

I began reconstructing the dish based on four aromatic elements: mustard, Parmesan, egg yolk, and anchovies. Then I rebuilt the dish using a number of different mustard leaves. You bite the chlorophyll, the Parmesan is crispy, and the anchovies represent the water that the Romans used as a salty stock. That was my first level of evolution for the Caesar salad. Five years later it has become a minimalist salad with mustard leaves. All the elements were inside the salad.

—**MASSIMO BOTTURA,** Osteria Francescana (Italy), on his process behind his signature Caesar Salad in Bloom, as quoted by Niklas Roar on Vice.com

Other Caesar-Inspired Dishes

The Little Beet's Cardini Salad, named in honor of the creator of the Caesar salad, with the dressing's richness provided by pureed chickpeas with chickpea liquid to sub for the usual eggs and cheese

—Franklin Becker, The Little Beet (New York City)

Kale Caesar Salad with Fried Sourdough and Pomegranate

—Jose Garces, Bar Volvér (Philadelphia)

Smoked North Carolina Trout and Kale Salad, with crumbled cornbread and creamy garlic vinaigrette

—Joseph Lenn, J.C. Holdway (Knoxville, Tennessee)

Five-Lettuce Caesar Salad, made with magenta-spashed watermelon radish slices, purplish Castelfranco, Treviso and Tardivo radicchios, bright green Little Gem lettuces, and teal "dinosaur" kale, with a thick dressing heavy on the anchovy paste + Dijon mustard (and without the usual cheese)

—Justin Smillie, Upland (New York City)

Caesar Salad Soup (made with garlic + Parmesan + Romaine) with Bacon Foam

—Noriyuki Sugie, Asiate (New York City)

Chefs across the country enjoy experimenting with a diverse palette of ingredients and iterations:

- *Greens:* Baby Gem lettuce, Boston lettuce, Brussels sprout leaves, collard greens, escarole, iceberg, kale, radicchio, **ROMAINE**
- *Cheese/richness:* aged Gouda, chickpeas (pureed in chickpea liquid), egg yolk, **PARMESAN**
- *"Croutons":* breadcrumbs, chickpeas, cornbread croutons, **CROUTONS**, pumpkin seeds, roasted nuts, sunflower seeds, tempeh croutons
- *Add-ins:* **ANCHOVIES** (umami), avocado (richness), chickpeas (richness), chicken, mushrooms, e.g., shiitakes (umami), pickled or smoked fish (umami), salmon
- *Flavorings:* **GARLIC, LEMON,** mustard, Sriracha, sumac, Thai chiles, **WORCESTERSHIRE SAUCE**
- *Substitutes:* capers (for anchovies), chickpea puree and chickpea water (for egg)
- *Alternative formats:* broiled or grilled salad, ice cream, Popsicles, raw salad, soup, sushi, tacos, tempura
- *Alternative heritage influences:* Creole, Indian, Japanese, Mexican, Southern, Southwestern, Tex-Mex

CARAMEL / CARAMELIZATION

Americans love **caramel.** Indeed, caramel is the third-most-popular dessert flavor on restaurant menus (behind chocolate and vanilla), according to Datassential, and appears on 10 percent more restaurant menus than it did just four years prior.

It's no wonder that the **caramelizing** (i.e., browning the sugar) of sweet produce is increasing in popularity, too. You can caramelize pineapple to enhance its sweetness and deepen its flavor, and caramelize onions to infuse them with welcome complexity. Slowly simmering cow's milk or goat's milk until it caramelizes will result in *dulce de leche* or *cajeta,* respectively.

In the 1970s, caramelized oranges were a popular dessert. Other ingredients that can be caramelized: apples, apricots, bananas, citrus, cow's milk, endive, fennel, figs, ginger, goat's milk, grapefruit, Jerusalem artichokes, leeks, nuts, onions, oranges, parlsey root, parsnips, pears, pecans, pineapple, pumpkin, root vegetables, shallots*, and sugar. (*The savory Caramelized Shallot Tarte Tatin that Per Se alum David Mawhinney served us at Haven's Kitchen in Manhattan was one of the best dishes we tasted in 2015.)

Imagine: What else might you caramelize to delicious effect?

CAULIFLOWER

Cauliflower has become so popular in part because of its versatility, which inspires all the various ways chefs are currently working with it in dishes:

bibimbap
blanched
Buffalo-style, e.g., in lieu of wings
grilled
mashed
pickled
pizza crust
"popcorn"
pulsed, e.g,. into gluten-free "couscous"

Cauliflower and Curry with Green Pea Paneer, Papaya Chutney, and Pappadam
—Amanda Cohen, Dirt Candy (New York City)

Cauliflower Treated Like a Piece of Meat with Mushroom au Jus
—Katianna Hong, The Charter Oak (St. Helena, California)

Fried Cauliflower with Labneh
—Michael Solomonov, Zahav (Philadelphia)

Porridge of Cauliflower and Millet
—Quinn and Karen Hatfield, Odys + Penelope (Los Angeles)

Whole Roasted Cauliflower with Whipped Goat Cheese
—Alon Shaya, Domenica (New Orleans)

pureed, e.g., into "polenta"
"rice," e.g., in curries, stir-fries, sushi
roasted, e.g., carved tableside into "steaks," in honor of its "meaty" flavor
salads
soups
tempura-fried

CELERY AND CELERY ROOT

Chefs are featuring **celery** and especially **celery root** in many more savory and sweet dishes:

Apple Kimchi: Honeycrisp apples in kimchi powder with candied nuts, celery, and creamy yogurt

—James Rigato, Mabel Gray (Detroit)

Celeriac Latkes with Sour Cream and Homemade Applesauce

—Bill Telepan, Oceana (New York City), who grew up eating his Catholic mother's latkes

Celery Cheesecake Roll with Celeriac Ice Cream

—Amanda Cohen, Dirt Candy (New York City)

Celery Root Bundt Cake with Bourbon Frosting

—Christina Tosi, Momofuku Milk Bar (New York City)

CEREAL (SEE ALSO COMMERCIAL FOODS AND NOSTALGIA FOODS)

Necessity is the mother of invention. Even before **Christina Tosi** of Momofuku Milk Bar made her reputation as a pastry chef in part through celebrating her childhood love of breakfast cereal, **Jacques Torres** served chocolate-covered cornflakes at Le Cirque in the 1990s—a move only prompted by his running out of the almonds that he usually used to make the chocolate *petit fours* and rummaging through the Mayfair Hotel's kitchen for a last-minute substitute (see page 50).

Other chefs have been likewise inspired—including **John Park** of Quenelle in Burbank, California, who creates ice cream bars using cereals like Fruity Pebbles and Lucky Charms.

CHAKRAS

Chakras are part of an ancient Indian belief system based on seven key energy centers of the body—each of which is also associated with different foods. For a few examples, see chart.

People who are inherently creative already have a number of energy centers that are open and stimulated, such as the 2nd chakra, which is the center of physical creativity, and the 5th chakra, which is the center of vibrational creativity (such as ideas expressed through the voice or music).

If someone is not creative, it is because there is no clear flow of energy. "Creativity starts in the 2nd chakra, then goes to the throat, and then to the brain," says **Stephen Co,** coauthor with Eric B. Robins, MD, of *Your Hands Can Heal You.* "You can take raw, creative material and send it to the brain to help you make something out of it. Techniques like SuperBrain Yoga and 'turtle breathing' both move the energy up" through the chakras so it can be channeled creatively.

Co also explained that creativity will expand more naturally when all your energy centers are open. His Twin Hearts meditation (see **Love**) activates two of them: the heart and the crown, which Co refers to as the heart of compassion or the spiritual heart. When the heart is open, a person cares about cooking well for the people closest to them—and when their crown is open, they have an even larger scope, and want to help more people, even ones they never meet.

Imagine: How could you use this information on the chakras to comfort or inspire a guest through a dish—or even a seven-course tasting menu?

I focus on the energy going through my chakras and other energy points.

—ERIC RIPERT, Le Bernardin (New York City), describing one of his daily meditations

C

Chakra	Gift (element)	Identity	Having the right to . . .	Concerns	Center of	Foods
7th: Crown	wisdom (thought)	universal	know, transcend	consciousness	universal love	sunshine (vitamin D)
6th: Third Eye	vision (light)	archetypal	see	insight, intuition, imagination	higher will	purple foods, e.g., grapes, plums
5th: Throat	truth (sound)	creative	express, communicate	communication, creativity	higher creativity	blue foods, e.g., blueberries, figs
4th: Heart	love (air)	social	accept, love	relationships, compassion	personal love	green vegetables, e.g., broccoli, spinach
3rd: Solar Plexus	will (fire)	ego	act, self-actualize	power, courage	self-interest	yellow produce, whole grains
2nd: Sacral	passion (water)	emotional	feel	pleasure, sex, creativity	physical creativity	nuts and seeds, orange foods
1st: Root	manifestation (earth)	physical	be, have	safety, survival	action	root vegetables, red foods, e.g., apples

The Third Eye witnesses the internal screen where memory and fantasy, images and archetypes, intuition and imagination, intertwine on endless display. By watching the contents on this screen, we create meaning and bring it to consciousness.

—**ANODEA JUDITH**, PhD, *Wheels of Life*, on the 6th chakra

CHARCUTERIE BOARDS

The commonplace cold cooked meat platters are being joined or replaced by not-so-commonplace cured and preserved ingredients, from seafood (e.g., cured cobia prosciutto, salmon 'nduja, scallop mortadella, seafood sausages) to vegetables. **Nathan Richard** of Kingfish Kitchen & Cocktails in New Orleans offers up a seafood-based Kingfish Charcuterie accented by assorted pickles, mustard, and marmalade. At New York City's Bâtard, **Markus Glocker** serves octopus "pastrami" with braised ham hock, Pommery mustard, and new potatoes.

The vegetarian charcuterie plate at **Graham Dodds**'s Wayward Sons in Dallas features sunchoke pâté, lentil sausage with smoked paprika and roasted pepper, and a three-layer terrine made from ash-dusted chèvre, mushroom duxelles, and pureed butternut squash—all served with sesame-seeded lavash.

CHEFS AND SCIENTISTS

Chef **Dan Barber** of Blue Hill at Stone Barns in New York is actively working with **plant scientists** to create new breeds of plants—including vegetables ranging from purple tomatoes to milder habanero peppers—with the chief driving factor being flavor.

Imagine: What vegetable would you want to team up with a scientist to create?

CHEFS' GATHERINGS

Chefs are establishing **residencies** as a way for visiting chefs to educate and inspire their teams while being showcased in different locales. **Gavin Kaysen** of Minneapolis's Spoon and Stable brought Gramercy Tavern and Untitled chef **Michael Anthony** in from New York City to create a six-course vegetable-focused dinner with his kitchen team. Kaysen, in turn, is a guest chef at **Christine Rivera**'s Galaxy Taco's weekly Takeover Tuesday in San Diego, which has also featured celebrated chefs such as **Nate Appleman** of Chipotle and **Matt Orlando** of Copenhagen's Amass.

New York chef **Heather Carlucci** created the chef-in-residence program in Captiva Island, Florida, for the Robert Rauschenberg Foundation's Rauschenberg Residency program in 2016, working for three months as the acting chef-in-residence while creating the protocol to ensure local, sustainable, and traceable practices.

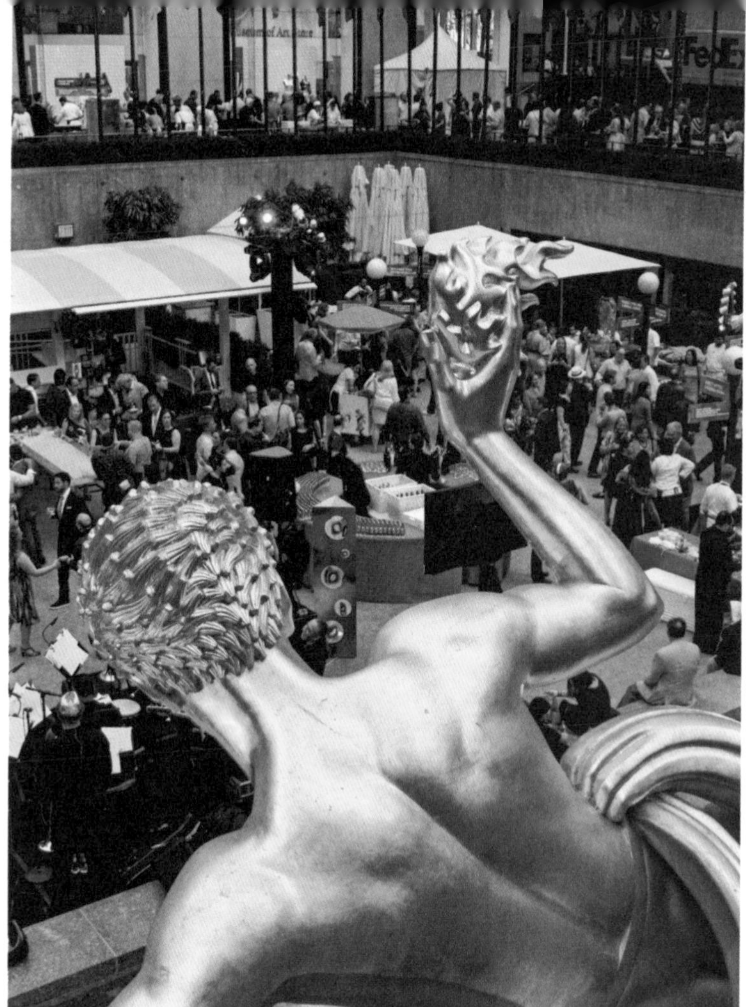

Citymeals' Chefs' Tribute at Rockefeller Center

Conferences

In 2009, we were guests at Spain's **Madrid Fusión**, a conference exploring food, wine, and gastronomy that had been held annually since 2003. While one track had us tasting the best new vintages of Spanish wines, another track led to demonstrations and discussions featuring the likes of **Grant Achatz, Ferran Adrià, Andoni Luis Aduriz, Elena Arzak, Heston Blumenthal, Massimo Bottura, Sebastien Bras, David Chang, Harold McGee, Enrique Olvera,** and **Patricia Quintana.**

Today, the annual conference continues to feature another country as its gastronomic guest, as leading chefs and other culinarians from around the world gather to explore possible future pathways of haute cuisine.

Other conferences gathering chefs globally for the exploration of creative topics include **Cook It Raw** and **StarChefs.**

Charitable Collaborations

Chefs are among the most generous professionals of any kind, so there are countless examples of their collaborating to raise money for charitable causes—which has the added collegial benefit of the sharing of ideas. As just one example, every June, for more than three decades, dozens of America's leading chefs have come together at Manhattan's Rockefeller Center for a Chefs' Tribute to raise money for Citymeals on Wheels, the non-profit organization co-founded by **James Beard** and **Gael Greene,** of which chef **Daniel Boulud** currently serves as co-president with **Bob Grimes.** In 2016, executive director **Beth Shapiro** reported the event raised nearly $1 million to prepare and deliver nutritious meals to New York's homebound elderly, featuring some of the event's founding chefs like **Larry Forgione, Alfred Portale, Wolfgang Puck, Stephan Pyles,** and **Jimmy Schmidt.** America's longest-standing collaborative chef event, the Chefs' Tribute now attracts leading chefs from around the world—including, in 2017, from Croatia, England, Greece, Israel, Italy, Lebanon, and Spain—providing invaluable global inspiration for chef participants as well as hundreds of attendees. Every year, chefs create tasting portions of dishes around a particular theme—from Latin American cuisine to Summer by the Sea, which spurs chefs' creativity.

CHICKPEA WATER

The first time we experienced chickpea liquid (the protein-rich liquid found inside bottles and cans of chickpeas, which is called ***aquafaba***) in a fine-dining setting may have been during chef **Dan Barber**'s 2015 wastED dinner at Blue Hill in New York City. It's since gone on to become popular as a substitute for egg whites, given its ability to whip into a stiff foam and its relatively neutral flavor. It's also being used to create whipped "butter," mayonnaise, meringue, and mousse, and to leaven pancakes and waffles. Granted, it's less stable than egg whites, but vegans are especially interested in its creative possibilities. **David Chang** showcases it in Momofuku Nishi's Ceci e Pepe dish, while **Franklin Becker** uses it in his Caesar-inspired Cardini Salad.

Diane Forley makes exquisite eggless meringues from *aquafaba* in several flavors, including chocolate, maple, orange blossom, and raspberry rose through meringueshop.com.

CHINESE NEW YEAR (AKA LUNAR NEW YEAR)

chicken, e.g., roasted, whole
citrus fruits, e.g., mandarin oranges
dim sum
duck, e.g., roasted, whole
dumplings
fish, e.g., whole
fruit
greens, mustard
noodles, long, e.g., soba
red envelopes (e.g., with treats inside)
rice
rice balls, sweet
rice cakes
scallion pancakes
spring rolls
turnip cakes

Jonathan Wu's holiday menu at Manhattan's Fung Tu included such dishes as red-envelope scallop wontons with mock shark fin, black chicken with goji and walnuts, and black-sesame brownies. Virginia-based chef **Peter Chang** created his Plate of Good Fortune featuring Shredded Tofu Skin with Mala Beef Tenderloin, Sliced Duck, Mustard Sauce, Wok-Fried Asparagus, and Turnip Roll.

CHOCOLATE LAVA CAKE

In 1966, Pillsbury Bake-Off contestant **Ella Rita Helfrich** wowed judges with her oozy-centered Tunnel of Fudge cake, which was baked in the aluminum Bundt pan created in 1950 by **H. David Dahlquist.** Her creation was named first-runner-up, and its popularity among consumers sent sales of Bundt pans soaring.

Since the 1980s, France's **Michel Bras**'s and New York City's **Jean-Georges Vongerichten**'s own versions of a **molten-centered chocolate cake** have taken the rest of the world by storm.

Countless fine-dining chefs created their own versions of what became the most popular dessert of the 1990s, and eventually fast-casual restaurant chains and fast-food outlets followed suit with their own, including **Applebee's** Triple Chocolate Meltdown, **Arby's** Molten Lava Cake, **California Pizza Kitchen**'s Chocolate Molten Lava Cake, and **Chili's** Molten Chocolate Cake.

As Bras hasn't been able to take the creation off its dessert menu, his son, chef **Sébastien Bras**, has played with his own interpretations over the years, including ones inspired by **apricots, blueberries, caramel, coffee, figs**, and other fruits. Sébastien also completely remade the dish in a savory version as "**asparagus** *biscuit tiède coulant*, **tarragon** sorbet, punctuated with a touch of **almond**."

CHRISTMAS

beef, roast
Brussels sprouts
candy canes
chocolates, e.g., chocolate-covered almonds
cinnamon
cookies, Christmas
egg nog
fishes, feast of the seven
gingerbread, e.g., cookies, houses
goose, roast
gratins, e.g., butternut squash, celery root, potato
ham, baked
oysters, raw
pies
plum pudding
potatoes, mashed
trifle
truffles, chocolate bourbon
Yorkshire pudding

CIDER

Sales of **cider** have tripled in recent years in the U.S. and it's increasingly used as an ingredient in tasting menus (due to its mild sweetness and high acidity, which allows it to cut through the richness of butter- and other fat-laden dishes), in cocktails (especially combined with fruit, rum, spices, and other compatible flavors), in savory dishes, and in sweet desserts.

COCKTAILS, SEE DRINKS, ALCOHOLIC

Apple Cider Doughnuts [glazed with a cider reduction, and served with applesauce and barely sweetened whipped cream]
—Karen DeMasco, Hearth (New York City)

Brown Butter–Washed Bourbon with Cider Shrub, Amaro Syrup, Lemon, and Yellow Chartreuse
—Christian Johnston, Tavola's Cicchetti Bar (Charlottesville, Virginia)

Cider Compressed Apples with Smoked Vanilla, Pecan Financier, and Brown Butter Ice Cream
—Noah Carroll, Café Boulud (New York City)

Cider-Glazed Seared Scallops with Cauliflower Puree
—Floyd Cardoz, Paowalla (New York City)

COFFEE

There are increasingly fine distinctions being made about all aspects of food and drink—and **coffee** is no exception. Coffee sommeliers join baristas as a growing group of professionals analyzing the flavors of coffee, using the language of wine (e.g., aroma, body, complexity, terroir) to determine ideal food pairings. The emphasis on flavor is changing brewing techniques, leading to the rise in popularity in cold brewing, and even infusing it with nitrous oxide for a smoother, creamier brew.

Coffee is also being used as an ingredient in cocktails and mocktails. At Manhattan's Maialino, barista **Ryan Clur** flavors tonic water with orange (bitters and a twist), on which he floats a shot of espresso for a caffeine-fueled morning mocktail.

In addition, more chefs are using coffee as an ingredient in a range of sauces as well as savory and sweet dishes. We talked with chef **Hemant Mathur**, of New York City's Haldi and five other Indian restaurants, while he was working on creating a coffee-orange rice dish. Coffee's earthy, bitter flavor pairs well with flavors with a hint or more of sweetness, including carrots and other root vegetables.

COLD ↔ HOT

The juxtaposition of **hot and cold** can prove irresistible. This explains the enduring popularity of hot pie served *à la mode*, which in turn has spurred the current trend of serving other warm desserts and pastries (e.g., churros, waffles) with ice cream.

Josh Hebert of Scottsdale's improvisational restaurant POSH named his informal restaurant Hot Noodles Cold Sake, demonstrating the same principle.

Hot-Cold Dish

"Hot-Cold Egg" of Warm Poached Yolk with Sherry Vinegar–Infused Whipped Cream, Chives, and Canadian Maple Syrup

—Alain Passard, L'Arpège (France)

Imagine: What dishes are typically served hot that might be just as delicious cold? Or vice versa? Which would benefit from a contrasting temperature?

COLOR (SEE ALSO BLACK, BLUE, GREEN, ORANGE, PURPLE, RAINBOW, RED, WHITE, AND YELLOW FOODS)

Perhaps it's no surprise that one of France's greatest chefs credits his passion for color with the development of his uniquely influential cuisine. Even after banishing meat from his menu, **Alain Passard**'s vegetable-driven cuisine managed to retain three Michelin stars.

This passion I have for colors is a strong inspiration, and fifteen years ago I realized that only vegetables, with their colors, could do that.

—**ALAIN PASSARD,** L'Arpège (France)

Our human reaction to color is primal. There is clearly a "language" of color, which can play a role in the creation of dishes. As noted in Stage 1, both **Pizza alla Margherita** [green basil + red tomato sauce + white mozzarella] and **Carpaccio** [red sliced raw beef + white mayonnaise sauce] were inspired by their color schemes.

Researchers at the University of California conducted a study that found young children assigned positive feelings to bright colors and negative feelings to dark ones.

—*Psychology Today*

Emotional Connotations of Colors

- **black**: efficient, sophisticated
- **blue**: dependable, **mental**, *sad*, strong, trustworthy
- **brown**: earthy, reliable, serious
- **green**: *glad*, growth, health, peaceful
- **grey**: balanced, calm, depressed, neutral
- **orange**: cheerful, confident, friendly
- **purple**: creative, imaginative, **spiritual**, wise
- **red**: bold, exciting, *mad*, **physical**, youthful
- **white**: clean, pure, simple
- **yellow**: clear, **emotional**, *happy*, optimistic, warm

Imagine: How could you use the language of color in the creation of your next dish?

COMFORT FOOD

This is obviously individual and personal—tastes differ. But generally speaking, **comforting foods** tend toward the familiar, the homemade, bland-to-sweet in taste, creamy or soft in texture, and/or warm in temperature:

apple cider, esp. warm
bread, esp. warm and served with butter
broths
cakes, e.g., layer
cereal, breakfast
cereal milk
cheese, esp. melted (e.g., cheese dip, grilled cheese sandwich)
childhood favorites
chocolate
classic dishes
cobblers, e.g., fruit
crisps, e.g., fruit
desserts, esp. warm
doughnuts
dumplings
eggs, e.g., deviled
ethnic foods of one's own heritage
hot chocolate
ice cream
macaroni-and-cheese
mashed potatoes
meat loaf
noodles
pasta
pies
pot pies
puddings
roasted foods, e.g., chicken, pot roast
shepherd's pie
slow-cooked foods, e.g., braises, stews
soft-textured foods
soups, esp. classic noodle or rice soups or creamy soups or pureed soups (e.g., split pea)
sweets
treats

Imagine: The next time you're under the weather, think about the foods you crave for a sense of comfort.

COMMERCIAL FOODS (SEE ALSO CEREAL AND NOSTALGIA FOODS)

A number of chefs celebrate big-brand cereals, candies, snacks, and other commercial foods for their nostalgia factor, as Millennials and Post-Millennials fuel the demand for childhood nostalgia foods.

- **Breakfast cereal**: Pastry chef **Christina Tosi** makes ice cream flavored like "cereal milk"—which made it a natural for Kellogg's to approach her to open their Times Square restaurant with a mission of promoting creative new ways to cook with and eat cereal. **Danny Bowien** of Mission Chinese Food has featured Corn Pops and Frosted Flakes at breakfast events.

- **Butterfinger:** Ottawa's **Gezellig** serves a decadent dessert inspired by the candy bar, featuring (dark, milk, and white) chocolate + *dulce de leche* + graham cracker + peanut butter.
- **Cracker Jack:** The sweet + salty flavor profile of this "candy-coated-popcorn-peanuts-and-a-prize" treat lives on at New York City's American Cut in pastry chef **Tara Glick**'s Crackerjack Sundae, which features popcorn ice cream, salted caramel, caramel popcorn, and whipped cream. At Chicago's Swift & Sons, **Meg Galus**'s S&S Cracker Jacks dessert features peanut butter mousse, salted caramel, caramel corn, and popcorn sorbet. Similarly, **Heston Blumenthal** created his Heston from Waitrose Salted Caramel Popcorn Ice Cream by bringing together two of his all-time favorite childhood foods.
- **Fig Newtons: Aaron Silverman** of Rose's Luxury in Washington, D.C., has served Homemade Fig Newton Cookies with orange honey.
- **Pop Tarts:** At Sofra in Cambridge, Massachusetts, pastry chef **Maura Kilpatrick** has served Pistachio Pop Tarts (made with puff pastry).
- **Triscuits:** At New York City's Prune, **Gabrielle Hamilton**'s signature sardine-and-cornichon bar snack sits on a Dijon mustard–smeared Triscuit.
- At the 2017 post-Oscars Governors Ball, Wolfgang Puck Catering executive chef **Eric Klein** even served artisanal chocolate bonbons in "movie-theater flavors," including **Goobers, Red Hots, Sour Patch Kids,** and **York Peppermint Patties.**

Imagine: What—if any!—commercial foods might be worth celebrating in a new dish?

COMPLEMENTARY FOODS

Something is considered ***complementary*** when it supplies that which is wanting in the other.

Imagine: What characteristics does the ingredient you're cooking with have—and lack? What complementary ingredients could fill that lack?

CONSUMER SCHIZOPHRENIA

In my days as a marketing strategy consultant, I loved a colleague's concept of ***consumer schizophrenia***, which referred to the fact that human beings exhibit unpredictable and contradictory behavior. (Witness shopping carts filled with both Diet Coke and Ben & Jerry's!)

Dishes embracing their own schizophrenia, e.g., high/low (caviar beggars' purses), vegan/carnivore (carrot tartare, cauliflower steak), and other dichotomies, can be similarly appealing.

Imagine: How might you create a dish to celebrate two opposite extremes, or the mere idea of them?

COOKBOOKS, TEN

In 2011, *Forbes* magazine's Alex Munipov compiled a list of the **ten best cookbooks** in the world of the past century. While only one opinion, many of the books cited on this list have been cited on other such lists:

Larousse Gastronomique (1938)
Time-Life's *The Good Cook* series (1978–1981)
Japanese Cooking: A Simple Art by Shizuo Tsuji (1980)
On Food and Cooking by Harold McGee (1984)
The Book of Jewish Food by Claudia Roden (1996)
How to Cook Everything by Mark Bittman (1998)
Seductions of Rice by Jeffrey Alford and Naomi Duguid (1998)
How to Cook by Delia Smith (2001)
Jamie's Kitchen by Jamie Oliver (2003)
The Flavor Bible by Karen Page and Andrew Dornenburg (2008)

Imagine: If you could only use **ten cookbooks** for the rest

C

of your life, what would they be? How many dishes could you create using them?

COOLING FOODS (CONTRAST WITH WARMING FOODS)

In addition to their actual temperature, certain foods have an intrinsically **cooling effect** on the body (and "nourishing yin," according to Chinese medicine)—which makes them especially useful in warmer seasons and months, and on unseasonably hot days:

arugula
asparagus
bananas
bitter foods and flavors
*boiling**
broccoli
celery
chilled food and drink
cucumber
eggplant
fruit juices
fruits
greens, dandelion
iced drinks
lettuces, e.g., Romaine
low-temperature cooking
melon, e.g., honeydew
pears
persimmons
*poaching**
salads
seaweed
spinach, cooked
sprouts, alfalfa
squash, summer
*steaming**
strawberries
teas, e.g., chrysanthemum, green, peppermint
tofu
tomatoes
vegetables
water, cold
watercress
watermelon
yogurt

**Traditional Chinese medicine suggests that these techniques help to alter the nature of the food to more yin, which is cooling.*

CREATIVITY, DEFINING

Imagine: Who are the most creative people you know personally? What makes you think of them as creative? How would you characterize each of them? If you posted a sign on your refrigerator reminding you to ask yourself "What would X do?", whose name would you fill in for X to inspire yourself?

CRÈME BRÛLÉE

Even celebrated French pastry chef **Pierre Hermé,** whose *crème brûlée* has induced swoons, has acknowledged that the first time he ever tasted the custard dessert with a caramelized sugar shell was not in Europe but at Le Cirque in New York City.

Owner **Sirio Maccioni** had been inspired by the *crema catalana* he'd tasted in Spain in the 1980s to serve a version at his restaurant once he returned to Manhattan, and Le Cirque pastry chef **Dieter Schorner** decided to serve it in a shallow ceramic dish with a caramelized sugar glaze, winning raves from the *New York Times'* **Mimi Sheraton** and others, which catapulted it into becoming one of the most popular desserts of that decade and beyond.

Crème brûlée continues to inspire new spins, including ones flavored with chai, chocolate, coconut, coffee, maple, pistachio, and pumpkin, and savory versions with corn, foie gras, Parmesan, and roasted garlic.

Its classic flavor affinities of **caramel + cream + vanilla** inspired Hermé himself to create a *crème brûlée*–flavored macaron.

DECEMBER, SEE WINTER

DELICIOUSNESS, COMBATTING POVERTY WITH

Seeking to "**combat poverty with deliciousness**" by helping another country realize its culinary potential, **Claus Meyer**—cofounder of Copenhagen's celebrated Noma restaurant, which was ranked number 1 in the world in 2014—undertook a two-year study to identify countries with high poverty, political stability, low crime, biological diversity, and a cuisine whose ingredients showed room for improvement.

Identifying Bolivia, and then the city of La Paz (where fish are plentiful, as are llama), Meyer created a culinary school and then a restaurant, Gustu, which features strictly local ingredients—such as hundreds of different types of potatoes as well as other tubers, tropical fruits, grains, and herbs.

Imagine: How could the next dish you create combat poverty?

DESSERTS (SEE ALSO ICE CREAM)

In the wake of troubling documentaries, like *Fed Up,* on the evils of sugar, in 2015 for the first time the *Dietary Guidelines for Americans* set a limit for added sugars (i.e., those added to food or drink during processing) in our diets, recommending they comprise less than 10 percent of our caloric intake. Now, **58 percent of Americans seek to limit their sugar consumption**—which outweighs the percentage of those limiting other factors such as calories, carbs, cholesterol, fat, or sodium.

Pastry chef **Emily Luchetti** launched the **#dessertworthy** campaign as a way to remind Americans that desserts should be an occasional treat and not a regular habit.

The use of white sugar is declining, while use of fruit (e.g., very ripe bananas), dried fruit (date paste), and sweet spices (cinnamon, vanilla) rises. Desserts are becoming less sweet, which has an impact on baked goods' moisture and browning.

Growing demand for more healthful dessert options is leading to a rise in the use of **natural ingredients** (e.g., fresh fruit like apples, bananas, pineapple; fresh vegetables like carrots, pumpkin, rhubarb, sweet potatoes, zucchini; mushrooms; whole grains like oats, quinoa); **smaller servings** (and/or miniature dessert options); **sugar substitutes** (e.g., honey, maple syrup); **superfoods** (ancient grains, berries, chia seeds, dark chocolate, not to mention mushrooms and vegetables);

Taeisha Martin's pineapple dessert at Glenmere Mansion (Chester, NY)

Dessert is very artistic. Dessert is sort of an expression of art in a very natural way and in a very sort of decadent way as well.

—DANIEL BOULUD, as quoted by PBS

In France, there's so much tradition that innovation is trickier. In the U.S., there's not as much culinary history, so there's more of a willingness to try stuff from other countries. . . .We're proud of what Dominique Ansel has accomplished in the world of pastry. . . . He single-handedly brought back the conversation about sweets.

—**JACQUES AND HASTY TORRES,** Jacques Torres Chocolate

(above) Dessert at Naha (Chicago)
(top) Petit Fours at Quince (San Francisco)

Dessert Dishes

Banoffee pie with animal cracker pretzel crust, dulce de leche, and brûléed banana

—Bob Blair, Fuel Café (Denver)

Inspirations: banana cream pie → Banoffee pie [English pie: banana + cream + toffee]

Paris-New York, which has the texture of Paris-Brest [i.e., a circle of choux pastry] and the taste of a Snickers bar [soft caramel, milk chocolate, and peanut butter ganache]

—Dominique Ansel (New York City)

Inspirations: Paris-Brest [French pastry typically filled with hazelnut cream] and Snickers bar [his first "meal" after arriving New York]

Eggplant Tiramisu

—Amanda Cohen, Dirt Candy (New York City)

Inspiration: Tiramisu [cocoa + coffee + lady fingers + mascarpone], plus her discovery that juiced eggplant tastes like banana

Praline Chocolate Mousse Cake, Espresso Crema, Chocolate-Dusted Almonds, and Torrone Gelato

—Alex Levin, Osteria Morini (Washington, D.C.)

and **gluten-free** treats (using black bean flour in brownies, or almond flour and whipped egg whites in cupcakes).

Other trends in desserts include incorporating coffee (e.g., espresso) and tea (matcha powder) as ingredients, and drawing on other **bitter and/or smoky flavors** (burnt hay, burnt sugar, toasted marshmallow) and even **spicy/hot flavors** (chiles, Tabasco).

More pastry chefs are incorporating **salt** into desserts, through salted caramel (whose appearance has increased more than 40 percent on restaurant dessert menus in a recent one-year period, and with caramel now the number 3 dessert flavor behind long-time classics chocolate and vanilla), salted brownies, salted pretzels, salted shortbread, and smoked sea salt.

Imagine: The buckle = cake × crumble; the cronut = croissant × doughnut; and the kouign amann = croissant × Palmier. . . . What two baked goods would you want to cross to create a new ultimate pastry or dessert?

DIET

Years past would see **diet** books dominating the bestseller lists (especially in January!), but the idea of diet has shifted significantly over the past decade, with more people looking to eat a healthful diet of more natural and fresh foods rather than counting calories.

Every five years, the U.S. government releases its *Dietary Guidelines for Americans* to help them navigate the winding road to more healthful eating. The *Guidelines* have powerful implications for school lunch programs, and their extensive coverage in the media usually translates into changing consumer preferences.

The 2015 *Guidelines* call for limiting added sugars, certain fats, and protein, while encouraging an emphasis on fruits, vegetables, lean protein, low-fat dairy, and whole grains.

According to the U.S. Centers for Disease Control (CDC) in July 2015, each day only 13 percent of Americans eat the recommended daily allowance of fruit and less than 9 percent eat the recommended daily amount of vegetables. Californians had the highest consumption rate of fresh produce, while Tennesseans and Mississippians had the lowest.

Imagine: How could you add more nutrition and flavor to the next dish you make?

Consider these two statistics: 77 percent of Americans are actively trying to eat healthier—but only 19 percent say they're on a diet.

—*FORTUNE*
reporting on a poll it conducted via SurveyMonkey (May 22, 2015)

DIGESTIFS (SEE ALSO APERITIFS AND DRINKS, ALCOHOLIC)

Digestifs have been increasing in popularity in the United States, along with aperitifs. The rise of Starbucks and coffee consumption has surely played a role in Americans' openness to bitter flavors—notably in the form of Italian *aperitivo* (lower in alcohol, they stimulate the appetite) and *digestivo* (higher in alcohol, they aid digestion), also known as bitters.

Imagine: How could you play with more bitter flavors in the dishes and drinks you create?

DIVERSITY

Alain Ducasse—who was the first chef to earn three Michelin stars for three different restaurants, and currently holds 20 among his 23 restaurants in seven countries—has publicly counted one of the secrets of his success as having a **diverse** team. The chef-restaurateur says he hires for diversity, finding he learns more from having a gender-balanced kitchen team from around the world.

In a country that the U.S. Census predicts will be predominantly multiracial by 2040, it's inevitable that culinary boundaries will only continue to expand.

Imagine: How could you improve your next menu by involving others who represent a diversity of experiences and perspectives?

DOCK TO DISH (SEE ALSO SEAFOOD, SUSTAINABLE)

Andrew got his start cooking professionally at the East Coast Grill in Cambridge, where chef-owner **Chris Schlesinger** has featured the "underappreciated fish of the day with damn good fries" as a way to encourage guests to expand their horizons beyond the usual salmon and tuna.

In 2012, **Sean Barrett** founded the community-based restaurant-supported fish program **Dock to Dish** (docktodish.com) in Montauk, New York, as a way to connect chefs to local fishermen, and to find a home for underappreciated seafood (e.g., the anchovies, dogfish, driver fish, golden tilefish, gurnard, Jonah crabs, mackerel, rockfish, sea robin, sheepshead, shovelnose guitarfish, skate, and squirrelfish that are often caught as the unintentional "bycatch" of fishing for shrimp, salmon, tuna, and other more appreciated seafoods, contributing to high food waste). Using the model of CSAs, CSF (community-supported fishery) customers and restaurants "subscribe" to receive regular seafood deliveries of whatever type of fish are caught that meet DtoD's quality standards—which are so high that they're featured on the menus of some of America's best restaurants, including **Eric Ripert**'s Le Bernardin in Manhattan and **Michael Cimarusti**'s Providence in Los Angeles. Today, Dock to Dish also has operations in Key West, Santa Barbara, and Vancouver.

CSF customers have been inspired by chef subscribers to treat the unfamiliar fish in their CSF deliveries in familiar ways, such as turning them into bouillabaisses, ceviches, croquettes, fish cakes, "fishburgers," rillettes, and tacos.

Imagine: How could you popularize an underappreciated ingredient in your next dish?

DONABE

The traditional Japanese earthenware cookware known as ***donabe*** may be centuries old, but it's experiencing a comeback as other one-pot cooking methods (e.g., slow-cooker cooking) come back into fashion. It's regularly used to make rice and to steam foods as well as to create hot pots, soups, and stews.

Donabe at *Single Thread*

Nagatani-en's 2-cup Kamado-san Donabe Rice Cooker ($140) fits most needs of two people, but there are smaller and larger models available.

For further reference: ***Donabe:** Classic and Modern Japanese Clay Pot Cooking* by Naoko Takei Moore and Kyle Connaughton (Ten Speed Press, 2015)

DOUGHNUTS

Doughnuts are hot—and both classic and inventive flavor pairings are being applied to the flavor platform of doughnuts. James Beard Award–winning chef **Wylie Dufresne** opened Brooklyn-based Du's Donuts in 2017 with flavors such as banana + graham, cinnamon + apple, coffee + malt, grapefruit + chamomile, honey + fennel pollen, peanut butter + yuzu, pomegranate + tahini, and strawberries + cream.

Doughnut Flavors: Beet Stuffed with Ricotta; the Everything (Cream Cheese Glaze topped with Sesame Seeds, Pepitas, Sea Salt and Garlic); the Wayney Wonder (Salted Chocolate with Buttered Pretzel Cookie Crumble)

—The Doughnut Project (New York City)

Doughnut Flavors: Almond Coco Joy; Butterfinger; Green Tea and Ginger; Peanut Butter and Jelly; S'Mores

—Dun-Well Doughnuts (Brooklyn)

All work and no play make for bad doughnuts. We may take our doughnuts seriously, but we believe in fun first. Whether it's playing with food icons from childhood or translating cocktail-inspired flavors to savory and sweet treats: We want your experience of our shop to be as exciting as it is for us.

—**THE DOUGHNUT PROJECT** (New York City)

D

DRAGONFRUIT (AKA PITAYA)

Season: autumn
Flavor: slightly sweet and astringent; juicy, with notes of citrus, flowers, grapes, kiwi, melon, pears, tropical fruit, and/or watermelon; with crunchy seeds akin to kiwi seeds
Volume: quiet
Health benefits: high in antioxidants, fiber, and vitamin C
Native: Central America
Techniques: **raw** (serve chilled)

"ceviche"
citrus, e.g., lemon, lime
coconut
drinks, e.g., cocktails, juices
ginger
margaritas
peach
pickled
pineapple
pork belly
salads, fruit

sauces
seafood, e.g., arctic char
sorbets
stuffed, e.g., with salad
sugar

Dragonfruit Dishes

Dragon Fruit Ceviche
—José Andrés, The Bazaar (Los Angeles)

Fried Quail on a Dragon Fruit Sauce
—José Andrés, China Poblano (Las Vegas)

DREAMS

What harnesses the idea of vision to the creative impulse is the notion that dreams unleash the imagination. And taking this one step further, where the dream addresses some greater good, there is an even stronger tendency to take risks and make the innovative leaps necessary to accomplish its goals. . . . Get yourself out of the way in pursuit of some greater good, in response to a strong pull of mission, and you've liberated the mind.

—DENISE SHEKERJIAN, *Uncommon Genius: How Great Ideas Are Born*, her book based on her interviews with 40 winners of the MacArthur Foundation Fellowship, nicknamed the "genius awards"

DRINKS, ALCOHOLIC (SEE ALSO APERITIFS, DIGESTIFS, AND DRINKS, NONALCOHOLIC)

The **craft cocktail movement** is on the rise, as mixologists leverage classic and cutting-edge flavor combinations into an exciting array of new drinks. There's more of everything—the old and the new, sweet and savory, cold and hot, lighter and heavier—so there's something for virtually everyone interested in alcoholic drinks, of which the following represent just a small sampling:

- The **Bloody Mary** will never go out of style—especially if mixologists keep updating it with new twists, as they're doing throughout the St. Regis luxury hotel group, which offers a signature version of the Bloody Mary at each of its 36 different properties globally. [In Dubai, it's a Golden Mary: gold flakes + yellow tomato juice.] Other independent bars around the globe add interpretive garnishes that are a far cry from the classic celery stalks as stirrers, including octopus tentacles. **Amanda Cohen**'s Bloody Carrie at New York's Dirt Candy features Bloody Mary + grilled carrot juice + mezcal.
- **Brunch cocktails** are evolving beyond just Bloody Marys, with the increasing use of fresh-pressed vegetable and/or fruit juices (besides tomato). Dirt Candy's Mimosa Madness offers a choice of beet, cucumber, and yellow pepper mimosas.
- **Chocolate** is a crowd-pleasing ingredient in everything it touches—cocktails included. Both drier crème de cacao (flavored with cacao beans, it comes in both dark and white versions) and sweeter chocolate liqueurs are playing a role. Peruvian *algarrobina* is a **carob syrup** whose bittersweet tones are reminiscent of chocolate or molasses—it's traditionally combined with **canned milk + cinnamon + eggs + pisco.**
- Echoing the worlds of wine and beer, cocktails are sometimes served in **flights**, especially designed to pair with restaurant tasting menus.
- Mixology is not exempt from the **foraging** trend, which is leading to cocktails featuring ingredients such as black sage, moss, and pine sap. Emily Han's book *Wild Drinks & Cocktails: Handcrafted Squashes, Shrubs, Switchels, Tonics, and Infusions to Mix at Home* chronicles the trend.
- The **global** trend is introducing (or re-introducing) spirits from around the world, such as Brazil's sugarcane spirit ***cachaça***; Bolivia's national spirit *singani*, which is somewhat similar to pisco; and Mexico's ***bacanora, raicilla,*** and **sotol** (lesser-known relatives of

Tempo Dulu (Portland, Maine)

more celebrated agave spirits mezcal and tequila), which can also be served straight or in combination with fruit juices.

- The **green** trend is having mixologists craft eco-friendly cocktails from ingredients that would otherwise be discarded.
- The **health** trend is bringing more fruit, fruit and vegetable juices, and teas (including kombucha, which is fermented tea) into the cocktail world, and requests for more calorie-conscious drinks are prompting bartenders to make more healthful substitutions, such as coconut water for coconut cream in a piña colada.
- In addition to the new category of alcohol-free mocktails, there's been interest in **lower-alcohol cocktails** that eschew higher-proof spirits for lower-alcohol options (e.g., sherry, vermouth).

D

The fact that someone rooted in both fine dining and the French culinary world [i.e., chef Alain Ducasse] is forward-thinking enough to acknowledge that cocktails are a benchmark of quality that any establishment needs is a testament to where cocktail culture has come today.

—**DAVID KAPLAN,** the mixologist behind the NYC and LA cocktail bars Death & Co., Nitecap, and Honeycut, as quoted in the *Wall Street Journal*

Trevin Hutchins on His Cocktail Inspirations

The bartender/beverage manager at Tempo Dulu at the Danforth Inn in Portland and cofounder of the Maine chapter of the U.S. Bartender's Guild, Trevin Hutchins brings a thoughtful culinary sensibility to the creation of his cocktails, along with a showman's flair for presentation.

I love to travel to New York City, and am inspired by many of the great bars there, including the **Dead Rabbit,** and **Death and Company,** which is *really* great; **Eleven Madison Park,** which served the best milk punch I have ever had; and **the NoMad,** which I love. In Las Vegas, at the Mandarin Oriental, they have the **Mandarin Bar** on the 23rd floor—and I don't know if it's a combination of the view and the cocktail, but everything is just right. I also love **Herbs & Rye** in Las Vegas for classic cocktails; they really know what they are doing.

The inspirations for our most popular cocktails are varied:

Jim Thompson

This drink was designed in the basement for our first cocktail menu before the bar was even built. Our Jim Thompson is a silky, light, floral, tea-infused cocktail. It is jasmine-infused Plymouth Gin with rose liqueur and Dolin Blanc vermouth, and finished with rose air.

The name is a natural for this silky cocktail, as Jim Thompson was an American silk designer whose silk was considered the best in the world. He traveled to Hong Kong and Thailand, where he revitalized the silk industry, then disappeared mysteriously while out for a walk in Malaysia. The mystery is still unsolved, but there is a Jim Thompson House museum in Bangkok.

Sake Snow Cone

I wanted to do a frozen slushy-type cocktail. **My goal is not only to layer flavors, but to change the perception of how to enjoy a cocktail.** This one is enjoyed with a spoon instead of a straw. It is a drink whose flavors are inspired by a cocktail called the Amber Dream, which is a martini traditionally made with gin, vermouth, and Yellow Chartreuse. I start with a Laphroaig Scotch mist, and then the drink itself is made with Nigori sake with smoked pineapple leaf, yuzu, and ginger. Then I add salmon caviar and smoked sea salt as garnishes along with mixed micro-flowers (e.g., orchids, marigolds, and mums).

Wayang

This cocktail is named after an Indonesian shadow puppet that is used as an old way of storytelling. [Tempo Dulu has a five-foot-tall bronze puppet on display in its bar.] Marionettes tell Hinduistic or Buddhist stories using the puppets, which are wheeled in and then lit from behind to create shadows, with some plays going on for eight or nine hours.

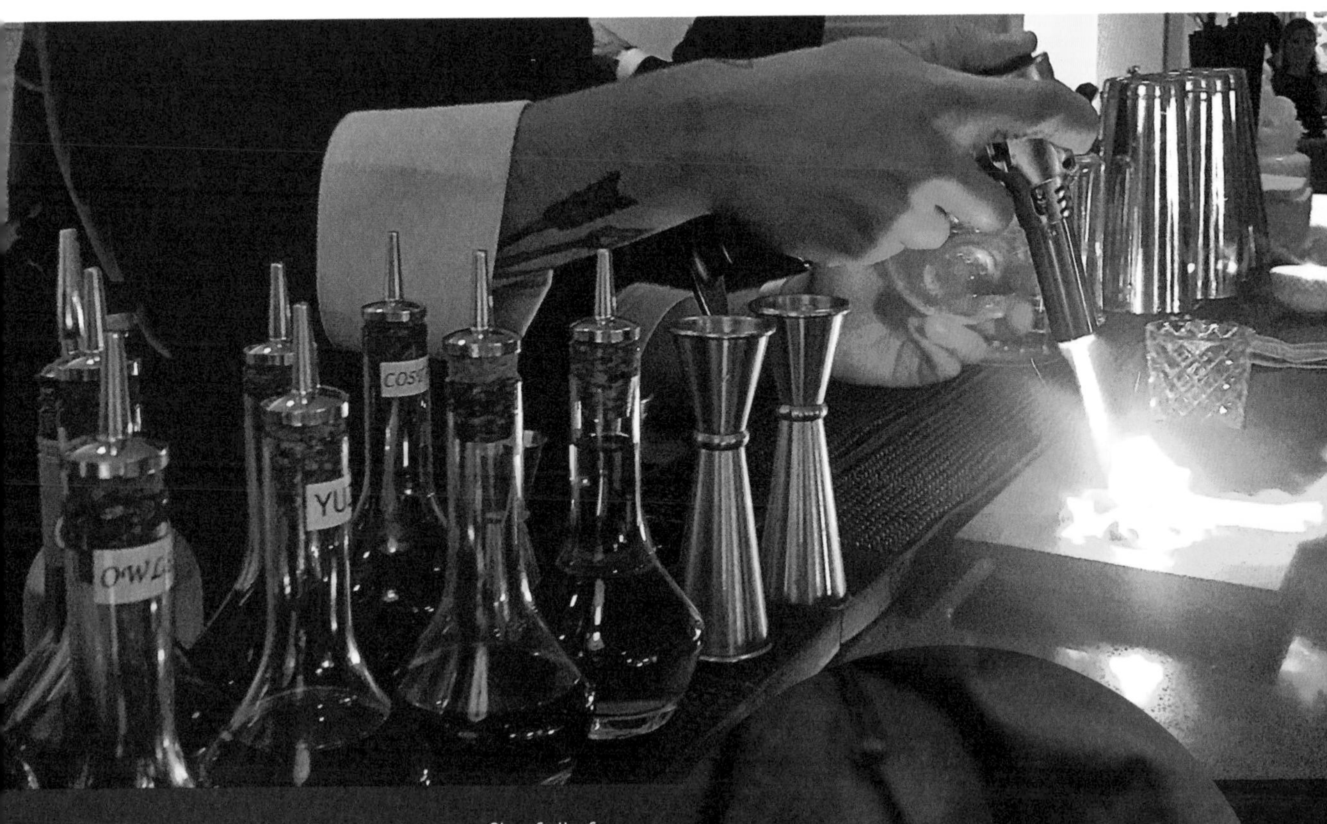

The Wayang has the most Asian profile of all of our cocktails; it drinks like an Indonesian dish. It is made with Double Cross vodka, fresh cilantro, and kaffir lime leaf. In *The Flavor Bible,* which was a huge influence on its creation, lychee is listed with **cilantro + ginger + lime,** but in this case I substituted the mangosteen because it has a similar flavor profile to the lychee. The drink then gets topped with a foam of mangosteen and turmeric. The drink dries your tongue, and then you get the sweetness that refreshes.

Wayang is super-refreshing and one of our most popular cocktails. We had an extern from Thailand who, when she tasted it, said it reminded her of her childhood, when her mom used to feed her mangosteens. That was the best compliment ever.

The Temple

One of my favorite things to do is go to Veranda, which is an Asian market here in Portland, and discover random ingredients like powdered avocado, which pairs well in drinks with fresh lime.

Typically when you muddle with mint, it gets muddled too hard, so it oxidizes and gets bitter. With nitro-muddling, it freezes the mint leaves instantly so when you muddle it turns to glass powder and you get a nice, pure flavor and color. Then sage is added with Tanqueray gin.

The cocktail also gets pandan leaf syrup that is used in Thai desserts, and egg white, and is then shaken. The garnish is dehydrated chartreuse chip. I bought *A Day at elBulli,* in which **Ferran [Adrià]** makes edible clear ravioli, and was inspired by that. I make layers of edible films, then spray on chartreuse and keep layering and then dehydrating it to make a cool edible chip for the garnish. [See page 285.]

It important to dry-shake some cocktails first so they will incorporate the egg white better and give you better bubbles for the cocktail. In egg white cocktails, you really want a silky texture.

Jakarta

[This drink is started by torching a Chinese five-spice mixture, which is then topped with the overturned glass, which is filled with the aromas from the smoke. The rest of this drink is then made separately, and poured into the aromatic glass for the finished drink.] This is my take on the classic Manhattan and Sazerac. The cocktail has Knob Creek rye; Cynar, which is a liqueur distilled from artichokes; Nolan bitters, absinthe, and star anise.

- **Savory** cocktails represent a range of flavor alternatives, from grassy green vegetal notes (incorporating ingredients such as bell peppers) to earthier and even funkier tones (e.g., with beef or chicken stocks, mushroom broths, vegetable broths).
- **Seasonality** drives the ingredients in cocktails as much as it drives those used in cuisine; see also AUTUMN – **Autumn Cocktails; SPRING – Spring Cocktails; SUMMER – Summer Cocktails;** and **WINTER – Winter Cocktails.**
- **Shrubs**—fruit macerated in an acidic liquid, often fruit juice or vinegar—serve as the basis of cocktails (often with bourbon or gin) or mocktails. Some vinegar-based shrubs are termed "drinking vinegars."
- **Spirit alternatives** in cocktails such as beer, Champagne and other sparkling wines, and fortified wines (e.g., port, sherry) have all been entering the mix.
- **Sweet cocktails** are evolving beyond overly sweet appletinis and cosmos, incorporating fresh-pressed juices and artisanal syrups. There are new honey-flavored bourbons, vodkas, and whiskeys on the market whose sweetness is being accented by garnishes like bee pollen.
- **Unusual ingredients** (e.g., edible flowers, spices) abound, and evolve so quickly that to name them is to risk a dated list.
- **Vermouth** is having a revival after a century and a half of being a part of the American cocktail scene. **Dan Barber**'s restaurant Blue Hill is even making its own vermouth.

DRINKS, NON-ALCOHOLIC (AKA MOCKTAILS)

With sales of sugar-laden soft drinks at a low, people haven't lost their need to hydrate—and are increasingly turning to coffee (esp. iced), tea (esp. iced), lemonade (including flavored versions, such as cucumber-thyme, lavender, and strawberry-basil), and other **nonalcoholic drinks** instead.

The Arnold Palmer, a mix of half-iced tea and half-lemonade, is the only drink **Brooks Headley** offers at his six-seat *New York Times* two-star restaurant Superiority Burger.

We've long loved the refreshing *agua frescas* (esp. lime + melon) served at many Mexican restaurants. But with more people seeking lighter, drier (as in less sweet) beverage options that are more healthful as well as more flavorful, there is greater creativity in the realm of housemade non-alcoholic drinks—including both ingredients (e.g., fresh-pressed juices, teas) and techniques (e.g., fermenting).

Singapore chef **André Chiang** of Restaurant André is exploring the use of fermented juices as a nonalcoholic alternative to wine for pairings, emphasizing that the juices don't necessarily have to have a fruity flavor profile, but can run the gamut from acidic to bitter to lactic to smoky with the use of various techniques and ingredients such as fruit, vegetables, herbs, and spices. He'll ferment apples before juicing them, which he combines with pine needles and charcoal.

There is also a burgeoning field of **craft sodas** (many featuring fresh fruit + herbs), many made with farm-to-table ingredients, housemade **shrubs** (acidic liquid, e.g., vinegar + fruit + sugar) and **syrups**, and artisanal **bitters** and **tinctures.**

Many high-end restaurants are regularly offering nonalcoholic beverage pairing options with their tasting menus, including Manhattan's Agern and Atera, and Chicago's Alinea. At **Agern**, nonalcoholic options include shrubs (bitter grapefruit, fennel frond, or plum) as well as "imitations" such as the Bitter Punch (made with **grapefruit + verjus**) and Rory's (**lemon + pine + smoke**). **Atera**'s Cote de Beet mocktail features beets + black currants aged in toasted oak, which is served as a stand-in for a big red wine and reflects the trend toward nonalcoholic "wines" made from ingredients like fermented teas, fruit juices, herbs, and spices.

D

EARTHINESS (CONTRAST WITH FRUITINESS)

achiote
amaranth
beans, dried, e.g., broad
beer, e.g., IPA
beets
burdock root
cheeses, nutty
chocolate, dark
coffee
eggplant
grains, whole, e.g., barley, buckwheat, farro, ryeberries, wheatberries
kasha
legumes, e.g., beans, lentils
maple syrup, esp. dark
miso, esp. dark
mushrooms, e.g., chanterelle, morel, porcini
nuts
onions, roasted
potatoes, baked
pumpkin
rice, brown
risottos
root vegetables, e.g., parsnips, turnips
sesame oil, roasted
spices, brown, e.g., cinnamon, coriander, cumin
sweet potatoes
teas, e.g., pu-erh
truffles
turmeric
wild rice
wines, earthy red, e.g., Pinot Noir with notes of mushrooms (e.g., Burgundy)

EASTER

Date: The Sunday between March 23 and April 25, coinciding with the first Sunday after the full moon following the spring equinox

Traditional celebratory dishes vary around the world, from the Italian Easter pie (which was one of the inspirations behind Chicago's famed stuffed pizza) to Argentina's *torta pascualina,* a spinach and ricotta Easter pie made with whole eggs.

artichokes
asparagus
brunch
cakes
carrots and carrot juice
chocolate and chocolate-flavored cacao liqueur
cocktails made with colorful spirits, e.g., blue curaçao, cacao liqueur
colors, rainbow (e.g., cocktails, dyed eggs)
eggs, hard-boiled and variations (e.g., deviled eggs, egg salad)
ham, e.g., baked
hot cross buns
jelly beans
lamb, spring
marshmallow chicks, yellow
peas, spring
potatoes, new
salads, spring vegetable, e.g., pea shoots
soups, e.g., asparagus
spring vegetables, e.g., asparagus, fava beans, peas

Imagine: Creating an Easter-themed cocktail? Imagine

creating one using carrot juice—or cacao liqueur. Or take your inspiration from the colors of dyed Easter eggs, and turn to blue curaçao. What would you add next?

EATING OUT

Eating out can be one of the greatest sources of inspiration in the kitchen, and as **David Chang** suggests (below), it doesn't have to be fine dining. It can be even more inspiring to taste how the simplest of ingredients are made to taste so irresistible when they are combined just so.

Spice whisperer **Lior Lev Sercarz** of New York City's La Boîte recommends eating out as one of the best ways of developing your palate. "**Eat ethnic food.** Read ethnic cookbooks. Analyze why they put cumin in lamb, or fennel in sausages. . . . Expose yourself to different things, including music. Everything is relevant," he says.

Imagine: Think about the type of restaurants where you eat most often, and resolve to expand your horizons. For example, if you eat mostly from a specific region of the world, track down an acclaimed restaurant that serves a cuisine from a country located on the opposite side of the globe.

When I had dinner at Charlie Trotter's ten years ago, every course came with its own bread. . . . One of the best things I ever tasted was David Chang's Red-Eye Mayonnaise—which was made with instant coffee and Sriracha—with Benton's Country Ham at Momofuku Ssäm Bar. That inspired my country ham fat rolls served with coffee butter.

—**MARK LEVY,** Magdalena at The Ivy Hotel (Baltimore)

EGG SAFETY

Raw or undercooked eggs cause 80 percent of **salmonella enteritis** foodborne illnesses.

Imagine: Rather than put your egg-sensitive guests at risk, what else could you use instead of an egg for the needed function (e.g., adding moisture, binding, leavening) in a particular dish? For example, instead of using one egg to:

- **add moisture:** Use 1/4 cup applesauce, dried fruit (e.g., prune) puree, vegetable puree, or yogurt
- **bind:** Use 1/4 cup avocado (mashed); or 1 tablespoon ground flax seeds plus 3 tablespoons water; or 3 tablespoons nut butter
- **leaven:** Use 1 teaspoon baking soda plus 1 tablespoon apple cider vinegar; or 1/4 cup carbonated water

When I opened [Momofuku] Noodle Bar in 2003, I was coming off a long stretch of eating at either Great NY Noodletown or Oriental Garden. Our ginger scallion sauce is stolen almost entirely from Noodletown. Order the lo mein with ginger and scallions and a side of ginger scallion sauce, and you'll see the genius in that dish. It's the best $4.95 you can spend in New York. I've eaten more meals at Oriental Garden than anywhere else on earth, and their Peking duck was the inspiration for our pork buns, which are the building block of the Momofuku empire. I circle back regularly to those places to remind myself why they've been around for decades: they're doing shit right.

—**DAVID CHANG,** as quoted in *The Last Magazine*

EGGS, DEVILED

Deviled eggs are a nostalgic comfort food that are increasing in popularity on some breakfast and brunch menus, as well as on menus as appetizers and side dishes. Various spins feature a range of ingredients like black truffles, bottarga, lobster, smoked paprika, and uni.

Deviled Egg Dish

Deviled Eggs: Black Truffle Egg, Uni Egg, Trout Roe & Bottarga Egg

—Suprema Provisions (New York City)

EGGS, NONTRADITIONAL

Eggs from animals other than chickens—such as **duck, emu, ostrich, pheasant**, or **quail**—are increasingly available both at high-end restaurants (e.g., Eleven Madison Park, which served our party of four ostrich eggs and truffles) and grocery stores (e.g., some Whole Foods locations). A single ostrich egg is the equivalent of about two dozen chicken eggs.

Chefs in Singapore—as well as chefs around the globe inspired by their enthusiasm—are adding the Chinese cuisine staple of **salted duck egg yolks** to nontraditional dishes, including cookies, croissants, desserts, drinks, ice cream, pastries, pastas, pizzas, and potato chips.

EGG YOLKS, CURED

Have leftover egg yolks after making meringues or cocktails with the whites? **Cure** them in a mixture of salt and sugar (which can alternatively be flavored with other ingredients, from citrus to miso to tamari) until firm, when they can be sliced thinly or Microplaned into flakes.

Or dry the yolks further to harden, before grating the salty, umami-rich cured egg yolks over your choice of dishes, as we've tasted to delicious effect over asparagus at **Dan Barber**'s Blue Hill in New York City. Other possibilities include grains (e.g., congee), greens (bok choy, spinach), legumes (white beans), lettuces (romaine), mushrooms, pastas (bucatini, gnocchi, ravioli), salads, soups, tartares (beef, beet), or other veggies (Brussels sprouts, salsify). In his cookbook *Relae*, chef **Christian Puglisi** grates cured egg yolks over celery root tacos.

Chefs traveling through Italy came to appreciate the salty flavor of bottarga (grated or sliced salted, cured gray mullet fish roe, used to top scrambled eggs or served in a simple bread-and-butter sandwich), leading some to experiment with new ways to get the flavor without using expensive fish roe—such as by **smoking cured egg yolks**, which can be grated atop pasta dishes.

EGO

Creativity and ego cannot go together. If you free yourself from the comparing and jealous mind, your creativity opens up endlessly. Just as water springs from a fountain, creativity springs from every moment. You must not be your own obstacle.

—**JEONG KWAN**, the South Korean Zen Buddhist nun and chef featured on Netflix's *Chef's Table*

Do you ever allow your **ego** to get in the way of your creativity?

Cured Egg Yolk Dishes

Salad of Grilled Lettuce, Cured Egg Yolk, Bottarga, and Sheep's Milk Cheese

or

Wood Fired Smoky NC Chicken Wings with Red Eye Gravy, Charred Scallion, and Cured Egg Yolk

—Sean Brock, Husk (South Carolina)

Lobster Mushroom Carbonara with Smoked Eel and a Grating of Cured Egg Yolk

—Christopher Kostow, The Restaurant at Meadowood (Napa Valley)

ENNEAGRAM

Who are you cooking for? The more deeply you understand your guests, the more deeply you can touch them through *what* you choose to serve them. The **Enneagram** is a tool that helps you understand others on another level.

The widespread personality typing system—which has been taught by as varied a set of groups as the CIA, the Jesuits, and Stanford Business School—characterizes the nine different types of people as having unique lenses through which they see and are motivated to interact with the world.

While the Enneagram is typically used to characterize people, we've experimented with applying the Enneagram to wines (through a lecture we've given over the years at the destination spa **The Lodge at Woodloch** in Hawley, Pennsylvania) and to food (through an interview we gave at the annual **Enneagram Global Summit** on a day devoted to innovative applications), discovering we could extend our understanding of gastronomy through its framework. This chart summarizes the archetypal characterizations of the various types, providing examples that correlate with each of them.

A Type 8 guest may demand to have nothing but a big bottle of Cabernet Sauvignon with their big steak . . . but you can please other guests on a deeper level by getting into their heads and hearts.

For further reference:

Discovering Your Personality Type, by Don Richard Riso and Russ Hudson

The Wisdom of the Enneagram, by Don Richard Riso and Russ Hudson

E

Enneagram Type (and motivation)	Characteristic Attractions	Food and Wine Correlations
Type 1: Reformer (reasoning)	ethics, justice	diets; organic, sustainable, vegetarian, vegan, zero-waste cuisine; Sauternes
Type 2: Helper (giving comfort)	loving and being loved	comfort foods, ethnic foods of one's own heritage; Moscato d'Asti
Type 3: Achiever (excelling)	luxury, high-status, high-performance	caviar, gold leaf, luxury brands (e.g., Dom Pérignon), truffles; Chardonnay
Type 4: Individualist (feeling un-ordinary)	drama, specialness	dark chocolate fondue; special requests (e.g., customizing a dish); Burgundy
Type 5: Investigator (knowing more)	complexity worthy of contemplation	distinctive cheeses, wines; molecular gastronomy; Bordeaux
Type 6: Loyalist (belonging)	"normalcy"	traditional hotel buffet (with something for everyone); house wine
Type 7: Enthusiast (enjoying)	fun, adventure	popcorn; exotic foods; Champagne
Type 8: Challenger (controlling)	dominating	horseradish, wasabi; gamey lamb, dry-aged steak; full-bodied red wines
Type 9: Peacemaker (avoiding conflict)	mediating, neutrality	pasta, potatoes, chicken/seitan; rosé wine

EXPERIENTIAL CUISINE

Chef **Paul Pairet** has described his cuisine as *psycho taste,* in that his dishes are meant to evoke "memory, imagination, experience, and culture." Dinner has become more about the entire experience of stimulating the scenes—or "**experiential cuisine**"—incorporating audio, video, lighting, and scents—in addition to the food and drink, of course. His Ultraviolet, which opened in 2012 and ranked number 42 on the 2016 World's 50 Best Restaurants list, is located in a "secret location" in Shanghai; to dine there, you'll take a special bus to the site that lifts you up to the restaurant in a cage elevator. Each dish is paired with its own song.

> **Tomato Mozza and Again [two "identical" dishes—one savory, one sweet—make guests think twice about flavor expectations]**
>
> —Paul Pairet, Ultraviolet (Shanghai)

Imagine: **Daniel Humm**'s New York menu at Eleven Madison Park started with a savory black-and-white cookie, and ended with a classically sweet black-and-white cookie. What is another dish it might be fun to create in different savory *and* sweet versions?

FARM-TO-TABLE

Farmers are hot—and not only to the chefs who have married them, who include **Kyle Connaughton** (whose wife **Katina Connaughton** runs the farm at Single Thread Farms–Restaurant–Inn in Healdsburg, California), **Tom Douglas** (whose wife **Jackie Cross** runs Prosser Farm in Prosser, Washington), and **Ana Sortun** (whose husband **Chris Kurth** runs Siena Farms in Sudbury, Massachusetts).

Farm/estate–branded items are trending. Farmers even have their own award-winning quarterly magazine: *Modern Farmer,* which was founded in April 2013 and has a popular Instagram account. And the Culinary Institute of America now offers a Conservatory restaurant program allowing students to work in the restaurant and on three farms in Napa Valley.

Independent farmers are responding to chefs' requests for sustainable ingredients such as unique and heirloom varieties of vegetables as well as specialty herbs such as Vietnamese mint—all of which will help chefs to have an edge on their competition.

Likewise, farmers are turning to chefs to help them introduce their produce to customers, and to create specials around the ingredients that nature has produced in great abundance. The support of chefs and restaurants provides more security to farmers, and less food waste.

And those farm interactions are even providing chefs with new inspiration in the kitchen, as San Francisco's **Michael Tusk** discovered at Quince, where he credits his Potatoes and Oysters dish as being inspired through his relationship with **Peter Martinelli**'s Fresh Run Farm in Bolinas, which also supplies Chez Panisse:

> The idea for the dish came about after our team was at Fresh Run for our potato harvest, which was meant for both team building and education regarding organic farming.
>
> When we got out in the field, we noticed the potatoes were covered in a white powder that we discovered was oyster shell "flour," which has several beneficial functions. Peter

Jackie Cross: A lot of these chefs . . . grew up in the city, or grew up in apartments, and they work with produce all the time, but they've never seen a potato grow.

Tom Douglas: It's cool for our chefs to really have an idea of the process.

—**JACKIE CROSS** of Prosser Farm and her chef-husband **TOM DOUGLAS**, as quoted in the *Seattle Times*

told us it is a natural and organically approved treatment for healing and sealing potato seed when it is cut into pieces for planting. Because it is a combination of fine powder and coarser pieces, it acts as both an immediate and also a long-term source of calcium and phosphorus.

With this information in mind, the idea sprang up in the field.

Brian Limoges, Quince's executive sous chef, had been given the assignment to translate what we'd learned into a dish. We wanted to have the feeling of eating a freshly dug potato, skin that could be rubbed off in your hands. We felt the oyster + potato connection was pretty classic, and this is what inspired us to get back to the kitchen. We selected the smallest potatoes and preserved them by cooking them sous vide with oyster juice, olive oil, and brown butter. A brown butter brioche "soil" evoked the soil on the farm that the potatoes were grown in.Oyster harvests take place locally in Marin as well, so that was our other connection. Hog Island Oyster Co. is right down the road, 15 minutes away, so we served

Any chef worth his or her salt should already be cooking farm-to-table.

—RICK BAYLESS, Frontera Grill and Topolobampo (Chicago)

The process of understanding ingredients is not only zeroing in on what they can do for us—such as provide us with great flavor—but also what we can do for them—such as being smart about purchasing them. No one has a harder time than farmers, especially family farmers growing food for people. In 2015, the average farmer operated at a net loss. We can strive to try to keep farmers profitable.

—SPIKE GJERDE, Woodberry Kitchen (Baltimore)

F

the potatoes with a lightly poached oyster, oyster sauce, and oyster leaf for texture.

This year's version will debut in early July and will include salsify and a Kumamoto oyster. Salsify will lend some texture to the dish and will play into the calcium storyline, as its common name is oyster plant.

The dish tells a story and speaks of the connection between why we farm and what we cook.

What we're trying to do is offer new colors of paint to the chef. It's not just about color—it's flavor and texture. It needs to taste good, and if it doesn't, it has no place.

—FARMER LEE JONES, of the Chef's Garden in Ohio, as quoted on NPR's *The Salt*

Imagine: What ingredient would you ask a farmer to supply you with? How would it inspire your creativity?

FATHER'S DAY

Jacques Torres was inspired to create a rum raisin ice cream because it was his father's favorite flavor.

If you're **Marc Forgione**, son of "the godfather of American cuisine" **Larry Forgione**, you can create a **Father's Day** menu based on your father's recipes, as he did on Father's Day 2016 at his Manhattan-based Restaurant Marc Forgione. The menu included miniature mushroom tarts, ladies cabbage, potato chip–encrusted quail, a terrine of American fish garnished with caviar, and strawberry shortcake (via James Beard's recipe made with hard-boiled eggs, which tenderizes the dough).

Otherwise, you can be inspired by the season and your own father's favorites, instead of resorting to the stereotypical alcohol-fueled carnivorous options so ubiquitous during grilling season.

FEAR (SEE ALSO RESISTANCE)

The only real stumbling block is fear of failure. In cooking, you've got to have a what-the-hell attitude.

—JULIA CHILD

FEBRUARY, SEE WINTER

FEMININE MYSTIQUE (SEE ALSO DIVERSITY)

Almost half of the students at the Culinary Institute of America are **women**, up from 21 percent in 1992, and half of all American eateries are currently owned or co-owned by women, according to the National Restaurant Association.

Do women have different sensory abilities from men? In particular, do their palates differ from men's? The November 2014 issue of *PLOS ONE* reported that post-mortem female brains had, on average, 43 percent more cells and almost 50 percent more neurons in their olfactory centers (which is dedicated to smelling and odors) than male brains. No surprise, then, to learn that Yale University researchers found that women also have more taste buds on their tongues.

Imagine: What are the implications to you when cooking for women versus men? What are the implications for women who cook?

For further reference:

Cherry Bombe (cherrybombe .com) publishes a bi-annual magazine, airs weekly radio/ podcast interviews, and hosts an annual New York–based **Jubilee**, all celebrating women and food: "those who grow it, make it, serve it, style it, enjoy, it and everything in between."

Les Dames d'Escoffier (ldei .org) is a by-invitation philanthropic organization of women leaders in the food, fine beverage, and hospitality fields whose local chapters offer educational programs open to the public.

Parabere Forum (parabereforum .com) is an international platform seeking to improve gastronomy with women's vision, and organized recent annual conferences on the themes of entrepreneurship and inspiration.

(top) Lauren DeSteno, Fran Costigan; (middle) Carla Hall, Charleen Badman; (bottom) Irene and Margaret Li, Hillary Sterling

Women Chefs and Restaurateurs (womenchefs.org), to whose national board I was proud to be appointed in 1995 as its first non-chef/restaurateur board member, holds a popular national conference we've spoken at multiple times.

FERMENTATION

We wanted to share our love of great beer, coffee, chocolate, kombucha, charcuterie, pickles. . . . And we realized the connection: They're all fermented in one way or another.

—**KY GUSE,** on launching, with her sister Mel, the Minneapolis fermentation bar GYST, which is an old English word for "yeast"

Through his books, *Wild Fermentation* (2003) and *The Art of Fermentation* (2012), and his own example, **Sandor Katz** helped to inspire the growing trend of seeing fermenting as more than a means of preservation, and more as a means of adding flavor to foods. From apples (cider) to cabbage (kimchi, sauerkraut) to cucumbers (pickles) to grapes (wine) to malted barley (beer) to milk (kefir, yogurt) to soybeans (miso, soy sauce) to tea (kombucha) to wine and cider (vinegar)—what can't you ferment? The list of ingredients chefs are fermenting seems to be growing longer by the day:

- **Ky Guse** and **Mel Guse** ferment yellow or red **beets** into their nonalcoholic drink kvass at Minneapolis's GYST.
- **Rob Weland** of Garrison in Washington, D.C., ferments black **garlic**, which he turns into aioli.
- **Aaron London** ferments his

twice-fried **French fries** at AL's Place in San Francisco.

- **Blaine Wetzel** of Willows Inn on Lummi Island, Washington, adds raw **oysters** to fermenting cabbage brine to change their texture.
- **Will Horowitz,** of New York City's Ducks Eatery and Harry & Ida's, ferments **sourdough miso.**
- **Ed Kenney** ferments **taro** at Honolulu's Mud Hen Water, which celebrates ancient Hawaiian ingredients like sour pa'l'ai, as it's known.
- **Dave Gulino** and **Justin Slojkowski** ferment **tomato sauce** for the Margherita pizza at Bruno in Manhattan.

The James Beard Foundation's 2016 Best New Restaurant semifinalist Baroo is helmed by native Korean chef-owner **Kwang Uh**, whose passion for the fermented foods he grew up eating is such that he made it a central focus of the restaurant. Baroo's offerings include dishes such as *noorook,* which is based on fermented grains accented by toasted sunflower seeds and macadamia nuts in a reduced seaweed broth and that was one of *Los Angeles Times* restaurant critic **Jonathan Gold**'s ten favorite dishes of 2015.

I think we're going back to cooking over wood because it's in our DNA—and because we love it.

—**RICK BAYLESS,** who opened Chicago's Leña Brava in 2016

FIRE

All around the world you'll still find a taste for food made over an **open fire**, via the most ancient and basic form of cooking—from Argentina's *asado* roasting to Japan's *robata*. The popularity of open pits, smokers, and wood-fired grills is seen in **Rick Bayless**'s latest Chicago restaurant, Leña Brava, which features Baja cuisine cooked over a wood fire.

More than just a means of transforming ingredients from raw to cooked, fire is also a means of enhancing flavor. All-wood barbecue is making a comeback after nearing extinction in North Carolina, where gas and electric smokers had become the rage. Chefs are making greater distinctions between the fuel sources they use (including charcoals and woods) and the flavors each impart:

- **Dan Barber** and **Tom Colicchio** are investing in wood-fired grills at their restaurants for the smoky flavors they impart.

- **Andrew Brochu** of Chicago's Roister simmers kettles of ramen broth on an open fire.
- **Josiah Citrin** of Los Angeles's Mélisse opened the more casual restaurant Charcoal, celebrating the flavors imparted by open charcoal flames.
- **Renee Erickson** of Seattle's the Whale Wins roasts vegetables like leeks and onions directly in coals.
- **Norberto Piattoni** of Brooklyn's Mett doesn't even have a stove—instead, all the cooking is done in an open kitchen on a live bed of coals. The Argentine chef trained in open-fire cooking techniques with famed chef **Francis Mallmann**, who runs fire-driven restaurants in Argentina, Uruguay, and Miami's South Beach.

Joshua Skenes has created one of the world's best restaurants around his love of fire, which is rooted in childhood love of camping and open-fire cooking:

> At Saison, we have created our own techniques—like Fire in the Sky, Kiss with a Coal, Over the Embers, and Near the Fire—that are very specific. Fire in the Sky is something that is poached or cooked in its own broth, juices, or fat, and then hung above the fire for roughly three days or so—that is our "dehydrator."
>
> Our pineapple is roasted and basted near the fire and turned for a few hours. We spend a lot of energy on it to create it in a more delicate way.
>
> The benefit is that everything tastes better, because it is made over the fire.

FLAMBÉED DISHES

Fire at the table is hot—as **Grant Achatz** proved by bringing live fire into the dining room at Alinea 2.0 in Chicago. But did it ever really go away in Chicago, whose Greektown restaurants serve countless flaming saganaki dishes every night? People have long loved flambéed dishes:

Baba au Rhum *Flambé* (raisins + rum)
Baked Alaska (while the original recipe, which appeared in the 1896 edition of Fannie Farmer's *Boston Cooking-School Cookbook*, did not contain alcohol, after baking the dish is often flamed with Grand Marnier tableside) (ice cream + meringue)
Bananas Foster (bananas + brown sugar + butter + cinnamon + rum)
Café Brûlot Diabolique (flaming coffee) (brandy + cinnamon + citrus peel + cloves + coffee + sugar)
Cherries Jubilee (cherries + kirsch + lemon)
Crepes Suzette (brandy + caramel + Curaçao + orange)
Mangoes Diablo (mango + tequila)
Peches Louis (peaches + whiskey)
Steak Diane (brandy/Cognac + mustard + shallots + steak)

Imagine: What other dishes could you flambé for guests?

FLOW

F

Being completely involved in an activity for its own sake. The ego falls away. Time flies. Every action, movement, and thought follows inevitably from the previous one, like playing jazz. Your whole being is involved, and you're using your skills to the utmost.

—**MIHALY CSIKSZENTMIHALYI,** author of *Creativity*, defining "flow"

What creative people have in common, according to **Mihaly Csikszentmihalyi,** is that they love what they do—so much so that their engagement causes them to lose track of time and space. This state of **"flow"** has been defined as the "optimal state of consciousness where we feel our best and perform our best." Multiple studies suggest that **being in the flow state can make you five to seven times more creative.**

Research by **Teresa Amabile** of Harvard Business School showed that people are not only more creative in flow, but their creativity is also higher 24 hours after being in a flow state. Another way of putting it: You can train yourself to be more creative by being in flow.

Some of the secrets to achieving flow? Love what you do. Direct your attention to an important problem. Focus on it. Play with it. Let yourself lose track of time. Enjoy the process.

FOOD ALLERGIES, SENSITIVITIES, AND AVERSIONS

One person's food is another person's poison.

Chef-owner **Curtis Duffy** of Grace in Chicago told us that "100 percent" of the restaurant's reservations made special dietary requests, such as those due to allergies or aversions. We assumed he was exaggerating. But Grace's GM/partner **Michael Muser** separately assessed the number at "99 percent."

Chefs must address an allergy-sensitive public: More than 15 million Americans have one or more food allergies—including 9 million (or 4 percent of) adults, and 6 million (or 8 percent of) children. Food allergies are forecast to increase over time, given the 50 percent increase in food allergies among children from 1997 to 2011, and are the cause of more than 200,000 emergency room visits every year. That's one every three minutes.

The so-called Big 8 most common food allergies—which include **eggs, fish,** (cow's) **milk, nuts from trees** (including almonds, Brazil nuts, hazelnuts, pecans, pistachios, walnuts), **peanuts** (groundnuts), **shellfish** (including crab, lobster, mussels, prawns, shrimp), **soybeans,** and **wheat**— account for 90 percent of all allergic reactions in the U.S.

Massachusetts and Rhode Island were the first states to legislate food allergy awareness programs in restaurants, but leading chefs like **José Andrés, Jamie Bissonnette, Stephanie Izard,** and **Ken Oringer** aren't ones to sit back and wait to be asked. They're already creating multiple menus customized for guests who have various food allergies and aversions (e.g., dairy-free, gluten-free). **Mark Buley** and **Bryce Gilmore**'s restaurant Odd Duck in Austin offers different menus every night to guests seeking celiac, dairy-free, gluten-free, shellfish-free, tree nut–free, vegetarian, and vegan options.

Chefs like **Michel Nischan** (and **Franklin Becker**) had their eyes opened when they had kids who were diagnosed with juvenile diabetes. Nischan says that realizing that his son's condition could be treated in part by a change of diet incorporating more fresh vegetables and fruits not only changed the way he cooked at home, but also the way he cooked for his

People are trying to avoid certain ingredients for health reasons. Wouldn't it be awesome if we could rock their week for them?

—**ANA SORTUN,** of Oleana, Sarma, and Sofra (Cambridge, Massachusetts)

Damian Sansonetti on Creating His Own Gluten-Free Pasta and Gnocchi

We make all our pasta by hand, every day [at his restaurant, **Piccolo,** in Portland, Maine]. We get a lot of requests for gluten-free dishes from our customers, and my wife [**Ilma Lopez,** the restaurant's pastry chef] has some gluten sensitivity. . . . We tried some other different things first to make pastas, like gluten-free flour blends, chickpea flour, and fava bean flour [to no avail], or putting xanthan gum into everything. I kept thinking, "There has to be an easier solution." We were shopping at Portland's Veranda Asian Market—which is run by New Yorkers, and where they make an awesome bánh mì for $3.75, by the way—and **looking at all these [gluten-free] rice noodles**, and **I wondered why we couldn't make rice noodles Italian-style?** That led to the idea to take Arborio or carnaroli rice and grind the crap out of it to make flour to make pasta. And the minute you think of it, it seems so obvious, it's like, "Why didn't I think of it before?"

The first few tries weren't great, but we worked it out. To make the gnocchi, we grind the rice fine [e.g., in a coffee grinder] and then sift it through a fine strainer. We bake potatoes on salt [to reduce their moisture], because they take on too much water if they're boiled so you'd have to dry them out, and that's too much work. The baked potatoes should be allowed to cool to room temperature, and then go through the food mill on medium, so you don't overwork the potato. . . . You want [the gnocchi dough to have] just a little bit of tack to it, before rolling it out [into a log], cutting it, then rolling it into balls and making an indentation with your thumb. My grandmother taught me her gnocchi technique, which I use to this day. And another benefit is that the gluten-free gnocchi holds better than our regular gnocchi.

About 30 to 40 percent of our customers ask about gluten-free, vegetarian, and vegan options. . . . Our vegetarian carbonara is made with pureed applewood-smoked Florentine onions, which give it the flavor of smoky bacon. We put it into aioli at night, but we keep extra around for this and other vegetarian dishes and other dishes—like the 75 percent of the dishes on our menu that are predominantly vegetables or starch—when we want that smoky meat-like heft and depth of flavor without meat.

Damian Sansonetti with his pastry chef wife, Ilma Lopez, whose gluten sensitivity inspired his gluten-free gnocchi, and their daughter

When I was the chef at The Point [in Saranac Lake, New York], we had a guest who was deathly allergic to black pepper, including relatives like broccoli. So I had to double-check dishes, because many chefs naturally reach for black pepper. And a number of guests had nut allergies. If we were making an almond cake for dessert, we'd make one without almonds and use the almond arome from Terra Spice in Indiana.

—**MARK LEVY,** Magdalena at The Ivy Hotel (Baltimore)

Every single day we cook and take care of people; we have to figure out how to take care of ourselves, too.

—**GAVIN KAYSEN,** Spoon and Stable (Minneapolis), when first acknowledging his celiac disease to SeriousEats.com's Jacqueline Raposo

restaurant patrons. "If I wouldn't serve dishes to my own family, why would I serve them to my guests?" he reasoned. Realizing that many families with diabetes couldn't afford fresh produce led him to found Wholesome Wave, for which he was awarded the 2016 James Beard Humanitarian of the Year Award.

New restaurants are taking on the challenge. POSH in Scottsdale, Arizona, is a self-described "improvisational cuisine" restaurant offering globally inspired dishes made with local ingredients—all customized to address diners' needs, ranging from mild dislikes to potentially life-threatening allergies. Chef-owner **Joshua Hebert** says the challenge of not having a set menu keeps his staff engaged and turnover low.

Chef **David Kinch** of Los Gatos's Manresa wishes that guests would specify whether their restrictions are based on true allergies or mere aversions, in order to give him and his kitchen team the possibility of rising to the challenge of preparing a disliked ingredient in a manner that might turn around guests' opinions.

Who has food allergies and sensitivities? Here's just a sampling:

Celiac disease: An estimated 20 to 30 percent of the world's population carries the HLA-DQ gene that correlates with a genetic susceptibility to celiac disease, and an estimated 95 percent of celiacs are undiagnosed.

Diabetes: In 2012, more than 29 million Americans (i.e., 9.3 percent of the population) had diabetes—and one out of four of them didn't even know it. An additional 86 million adults—that is, more than one in three adults in the U.S.—have prediabetes, with higher-than-normal blood sugar levels but not high enough to be classified as type 2 diabetes. Approximately 1.25 million American children and adults have type 1 diabetes.

Lactose intolerance: An estimated 75 percent of the world's population is lactose intolerant. In the U.S., an estimated 30 to 50 million people have sensitivities to dairy products.

Nut allergies (to tree nuts): Nearly 2 million Americans have an allergy to tree nuts.

Peanut allergies: An estimated 0.6 to 1.0 percent of the population has peanut allergies, which can vary from mild to severe. The number of children with peanut allergies tripled between 1997 and 2008.

We remember sitting next to dietitian at a dinner party who told us she was taught that some of the least allergenic foods were applesauce, bananas, oats, and rice. However, because *any* food can cause an allergic reaction, it's best to ask your guests in advance about any food allergies, which will allow you to make any necessary adjustments.

Food aversions are common during **pregnancy**—especially for animal proteins such as chicken, fish, and meat, but also for alcohol, coffee and tea, eggs, fatty foods, fried foods, and spicy foods. As **4 percent of the women in America are pregnant at any given time**, that's a not insignificant thing to keep in mind since you might well need to cook for one occasionally.

One might call **vegetarianism** (and **veganism**) an aversion to meat (and dairy, eggs, and other animal products), affecting 5 percent (plus 2 percent) of the U.S. population, in addition to the 46 percent actively seeking to reduce their meat consumption.

Shellfish allergies: An estimated 2.3 percent of the U.S. population has shellfish allergies, or nearly 7 million people.

Imagine: How could you minimize the number of allergens in the next dish you create?

FOOD WASTE (SEE ALSO DOCK TO DISH AND SEAFOOD, SUSTAINABLE)

Every day the U.S. wastes enough food to fill the Rose Bowl, while one in six Americans go hungry.

—**ELIZABETH BENNETT,** founder of Fruitcycle, which handcrafts cinnamon apple chips from imperfect apples

From root-to-leaf and nose-to-tail, chefs are getting creative about using and celebrating every conceivable edible part of their products.

Chef **José Andrés** worked with a team from D.C. Central Kitchen to prepare two seven-foot-wide platters of paella from ingredients destined for landfill, as part of the U.K.–based Feeding the 5,000 event whose mission is to promote awareness of the global problem of **food waste.**

Dan Barber was behind one of 2015's most high-profile food waste initiatives when he closed Blue Hill in Manhattan for the month of March to open **wastED** in its space—a restaurant that featured ingredients that otherwise would have ended up in a garbage dump. Andrew and I had one of our favorite dinners of all time there, which featured veggie burgers made from leftover juice pulp from nearby juice bars on day-old Balthazar buns with pickle butts—a dish Barber teamed with **Danny Meyer** to bring to Shake Shack that summer. **Nicolas Jammet**'s Sweetgreen serves **wastED** salads made from broccoli stalks, cabbage cores, and kale stems flavored with anchovy oil, breadcrumbs, and spiced sunflower seeds, with a percentage of each sold designated for City Harvest.

Chefs participating in **Dan Barber**'s **wastED** initiative included: **Grant Achatz, Dominique Ansel, Joost Bakker, Mario Batali, Philippe Bertineau, April Bloomfield, Danny Bowien, Sean Brock, Marco Canora, Andrew Carmellini, Dominique Crenn, Dale DeGroff, Alain Ducasse, John Fraser, Brooks Headley, Daniel Humm, Dan Kluger, Jessica Koslow, Jim Lahey, Enrique Olvera, Alex Raij, Mads Refslund, Audrey Saunders, Nancy Silverton, Alex Stupak, Bill Telepan,** and **Bill Yosses.** Each created a dish based on ingredients that are commonly discarded.

The increasingly popular best practice of taking steps to reduce America's dismaying 40 percent of food waste is presenting chefs and cooks with the interesting challenge of figuring out how to use every bit of the ingredients that pass through their kitchens, from root to leaf and from nose to tail. This is a great way to save money, and the right thing to do out of respect for the ingredient itself and for the farmer who produced it. For example, using **dehydrating and powdering, charring, fermenting, roasting, smoking,** and other techniques can guarantee that no vegetable need ever be thrown away:

- **Dill stems, scallion greens, tomato skins,** and the like can be dehydrated and powdered, and used as a seasoning.
- **Ginger peelings** can be used to

At Dan Barber's wastED, dessert featured a Milky Oat Ice Cream Sundae (bottom left), while guest mixologist Audrey Saunders's drinks include The Immunity Booster (right) made from Melvin's juice pulp gin and last night's Champagne.

Growing up on a farm, we never wasted anything. We'd put the skin, fat, and bones of the ham into a soup. On the farm, we'd feed the carrot tops to the rabbits, and the whey and vegetable peels to the pigs—and then we'd eat the pig. Here in NYC, we'll send our vegetable peels to D'Artagnan for their "Green Circle" chickens [which are fed a diet of vegetable scraps from commercial restaurant kitchens and farmers' markets that otherwise would have become landfill].

—**DANIEL BOULUD,** Daniel (New York City)

F

flavor ginger broths for use in cocktails, sauces, and soups.

- **Imperfect fruit** can be used in chutneys, jams, jellies, and smoothies.
- **Stale bread** can be used for breadcrumbs, bread puddings, croutons, French toast, strata.
- **Strawberry tops** and **parsley stems** can be used to make pesto, as we learned from Charlotte chef **Chad Barlowe** of Heirloom.
- **Vegetable leaves** (e.g., from broccoli, cauliflower) can be pickled and/or used in salads
- Used **vegetable oil** can be used to fuel vehicles, as it is by Anna's Taqueria truck in Boston.
- **Vegetable peelings** (e.g., beets, carrots, and celery root) can be washed, dried, powdered, and used to flavor dishes and salts.
- **Whey** can be used to add lactic acidity and fermenting.

At his Chefs for Clearwater event to benefit environmental education, **Terrance Brennan** got a steer donated and used various cuts so no part of the animal went to waste. "I braised some and grilled some, and had enough food for 300 guests—all from just one steer. If I were just going to serve a sirloin, rib-eye or filet, I would have had to use 16 steers. So imagine the potential impact if all chefs made just that one paradigm shift of using the whole animal!"

Chefs are also looking to introduce customers to underappreciated fish that represent the 40 percent of commercial fishermen's nets termed "bycatch." Chefs' efforts in decades past transformed underappreciated fish like skate into popular options on top restaurant menus.

The 20 percent or

Trash-to-Treasure Dishes

Bread Salad with orange, roasted vegetables, sunflower seeds, and orange fennel vinaigrette

—Alison Swope, Teaism (Washington, D.C.)

Coconut Milk–Marinated and Panko-Crusted Fried Chard Stems

—Alison Swope, Teaism (Washington, D.C.)

Dumpster Dive Vegetable Salad, made with pistachios blended with damaged storage apples and pears

—Dan Barber, wastED (New York City)

Milky Oat Ice Cream Sundae, made with almond press cake biscuit, fermented cherries, and walnut press candied vegetable pulp

—Dan Barber, wastED (New York City)

Rotation Risotto, made with "second class" grains and seeds, squash seed pulp, pickled peanuts, and spent cheese rinds

—Dan Barber, wastED (New York City)

Stir-Fried Napa Cabbage Butt with housemade gochujang sauce

—Alison Swope, Teaism (Washington, D.C.)

> **We want people to think, "Wow, this is really good. Maybe I should think next time before throwing something away. Or maybe I should get more creative in the kitchen."**
>
> —**MIKE CURTIN,** CEO, D.C. Central Kitchen, as quoted on NPR's *The Salt*

more of produce that goes underappreciated because it's too large, small, or otherwise unusual in appearance prompted the **Ugly Fruits and Veg** campaign to urge consumers to purchase and use this otherwise fresh, nutritious, and delicious produce. Georgetown University students created **MISFIT Juicery**, which presses "ugly" produce into juice. New companies like San Francisco's **Imperfect Produce** deliver such produce to subscribers for 30 to 50 percent off the usual price.

FORAGING AND FIELD-TO-TABLE (SEE ALSO VEGETABLES)

With some of the country's best restaurants leveraging foraging experts like New Jersey's **Tama Matsuoka Wong** (whose ingredients have appeared on the menus of **Daniel Boulud**'s Daniel and **Michael Anthony**'s Gramercy Tavern) and Seattle's **Jeremy Faber** (**Tom Douglas**'s Dahlia Lounge, **Matt Dillon**'s Sitka & Spruce), ingredients foraged from the wild are increasingly making their way into dishes.

Using foraged ingredients allows chefs and guests alike to demonstrate appreciation for the area's bounty and to feel more of a connection to the local terrain.

Eddy Leroux of Restaurant Daniel on Working with a Forager and Foraged Ingredients

A major source of inspiration is working with **Tama Matsuoka Wong**, who forages for Restaurant Daniel [and with whom Leroux co-authored the book ***Foraged Flavor***]. In 2009, she started bringing me foraged ingredients—starting with anise hyssop, which I turned into a shrimp salad for her—and I'm still inspired by the flavors of whatever she brings, from sheep sorrel—which is very acidic but tastes great wilted—to lilac. It's only through trial-and-error that I sometimes learn how to use, and not to use, the ingredients. When making an Asian pear and lilac soup, I found it had to be made *à la minute*, or else the flavor was gone. Other flowers, like honeysuckle, also fade quickly, and have to be made *à la minute*. The inside of cattails taste like cucumber—you can get a ten-inch baton from the bottom of a two-foot cattail, which I've pickled for a new lamb dish. And you can turn brown cattails into cattail flour to use in conjunction with other flours—it tastes like a cross between carob and hay. . . . Working with unfamiliar foraged ingredients is like working with any other unfamiliar ingredients: You really want to get to know your ingredients. You'll look at them carefully, crush them, smell them, and at last taste them—and to learn what works with them and what doesn't. Sometimes my instincts change—there were ingredients she brought me three or four years ago that I didn't like, but now I'm finding I am able to work with. . . . Pawpaws are shaped like mangos, but when you cut them, they taste like cherimoya from South America. I love their stunning flavor, which is complex—like a cross between bananas, mangoes, and dates. . . . There's a shorter season for foraged ingredients, so you have to work quickly so you don't miss the season. And once they're overgrown, their texture isn't ideal, so you want to [get them] younger.

The natural setting of those ingredients is prompting new ways of using them, inspired by the saying, "If it grows together, it goes together."

Examples of foraged ingredients include beach peas, blackcap raspberries, bladderwrack, cape gooseberries, cynamoka berries, devil's club shoots, dune spinach, elderflowers, fennel pollen, fiddlehead ferns, huckleberries, knotweed, landcress, lemon verbena, lichens, licorice fern, licorice root, madrone bark, maple blossoms (e.g., for fritto misto, ice creams), miners lettuce, mosses, nettles, purslane, ramps, rosehips, salmonberry shoots, saskatoon berries, sassafras twigs (e.g., for brines, ice creams), sea beans, sea lettuce, sea vegetables, sorrel, spruce tips (e.g., for flavored oils, syrups, vinegars), wild berries, wild fennel, wild flower honey, wild ginger, wild greens, wild herbs, wild mushrooms (e.g., chanterelles, hedgehog, king boletes, matsutake, morels, porcini), wild onions, wood sorrel, and wood violet.

Foraging is a way of life at the Wickaninnish Inn, a Relais & Châteaux property in Canada whose restaurant the Pointe showcases a number of dishes with ingredients foraged by chefs **Warren Barr** and **David Sider**, who use them to "create a sense of place." The chefs will sometimes showcase the same product harvested during two different years to demonstrate how the products change over time and with the seasons (e.g., serving dried cèpes and cèpe oil made the previous year alongside shaved fresh cèpes).

Gunnar Thompson of Glenmere Mansion on Foraging

My family is Norwegian, and I grew up in Lacrosse, Wisconsin. My grandmother had been a forager, and made her own jams. I'd been **foraging** in Europe for mushrooms and berries. I love to hike, and here at Glenmere [Mansion, in Chester, New York, where he is chef] I've got a great excuse to, because I've found ramps and stinging nettles on the property. Foraging definitely influences my menu choices—wild foods give me focus and create a sense of place wherever I am. When I cooked in Virginia, I'd forage for Southern-style greens, like collards, and golden chanterelles, which have almost an apricot-like aroma and flavor that's wonderful with caramelized onions and pea leaves or watercress in lighter dishes. The French call them *girolles*, and always serve them delicately, often in omelets. When I cooked in California, citrus was local, as were stone fruits—and I learned that pluots were flavor grenades! They're my favorite eating out of hand variety. Having been chef of Erna's Elderberry House in California, I grew to enjoy their interesting tart flavor in jams, syrups, sorbets, and finishing glazes. And our Champagne welcome cocktail always featured elderberry syrup.

Gunnar Thompson

Wild food could probably save the world. It really could.

—JEREMY FABER,
Foraged & Found Edibles
(Seattle)

FOURTH OF JULY (SEE ALSO SUMMER)

baked beans
beer
coleslaw
cornbread
corn on the cob
desserts with sparklers (suggestive of fireworks)
eggs, deviled
grilled dishes
hamburgers and hot dogs, esp. grilled
iced tea
lemonade
pies, e.g., berry
salads, e.g., potato
strawberry shortcake, esp. with blueberries (red + white + blue)
watermelon

FRESHNESS

We only work with vegetables that were harvested that morning. I don't want my vegetables to be refrigerated.

—**ALAIN PASSARD,** L'Arpège (France)

Chefs keep redefining the concept of **freshness.** At Blue Hill at Stone Barns in New York, chef **Dan Barber** serves ingredients that have been picked a few hours or mere minutes before serving.

Imagine: How could you add an uber-fresh touch to your next dish, e.g., herbs snipped into a dish or lemon squeezed on top of it *à la minute*?

FRUIT

Fewer than 13 percent of adults, and fewer than 15 percent of children, meet the government's minimum recommended daily allowance of **fruit.**

A 2016 study by the University of Oxford and the Chinese Academy of Medical Sciences estimated that even a small amount of fresh fruit in the diet can lower the risk of cardiovascular death by 33 percent.

Imagine: How could you deliciously add a serving of fruit to the dish you're making, beyond adding some sliced apples or pears to a salad or a plum salsa to top grilled fish?

FRUITINESS (CONTRAST WITH EARTHINESS)

ales, English
beers, e.g., Weizen/Hefeweizen
berries, e.g., blueberries, raspberries, strawberries
chiles, e.g., habanero
citrus, e.g., grapefruit, lemon, lime, orange, yuzu
fruits, dried, e.g., figs, persimmons, plums
mushrooms, enoki
peppercorns, pink
stone fruits, e.g., cherries, peaches
tomatoes
tree fruit, e.g., apples, pears
tropical fruit, e.g., bananas, papayas, passion fruit
vinegars, e.g., raspberry
wines, e.g., Beaujolais, Gewürztraminer, Pinot Noir (esp. New World), Riesling

FUTURE, THE (SEE ALSO PAST, THE AND PRESENT, THE)

Think about the continuum of a particular ingredient—how it's been used in the past, and how it is currently being used (see examples on pages 346 and 352). Picture a time line going into the future taking that ingredient to its future pinnacle.

Imagine: What will that ingredient look like and taste like in the future, and what will you be able to do with it?

GARLIC

Garlic has for centuries been a beloved source of flavor around the globe—from the Americas to Europe to Africa to the Middle East to Asia. Cooks turn to garlic's pungency as a spice, or even as the star of its own dishes, such as Andalusian *ajo blanco*—a creamy, cold garlic soup made with **bread + garlic + nuts + olive oil + vinegar.**

Garlic scapes are increasing in popularity, and being used everywhere from salad dressings to stir-fries, as consumers get to know this offshoot of the garlic bulb and experiment with grilling and pickling the tender greens.

How to shake up this long-time favorite? Ferment it! Fermented green garlic in the spring offers a more complex garlic note to noodles and potato dishes, while fermented black garlic enhances dips, noodle dishes, pastas, pizzas, risottos, salad dressings, and sauces.

Imagine: What could you do with garlic that you've never done before?

GAZPACHO

Is "gazpacho" a **raw tomato soup,** with particular seasonings? Or could "gazpacho" be a flavor platform for any raw produce to be served as a chilled, refreshing soup? (For the "proper" texture, be sure to remove the skin and seeds of any you use.)

Imagine: What vegetables or fruits other than tomatoes do you think would make a great "gazpacho"?

G

Gazpacho Dishes

Chilled Heirloom Carrot Gazpacho with Buttermilk, Caraway, and Cilantro

—Travis Swikard, Boulud Sud (New York City); photo above

Carrot-Orange Gazpacho

—Wolfgang Puck, Spago (Beverly Hills), who served it as shooters at the Governors Ball

Crab Salad with Chilled Gazpacho Sauce

—Eric Ripert, Le Bernardin (New York City)

Peach Gazpacho with Toasted Almonds

—Daniel Humm, Eleven Madison Park (New York City)

Strawberry Gazpacho (balsamic vinegar + cucumber + garlic + olive oil + tarragon)

—David Kinch, Manresa (Los Gatos)

Sweet Pea Gazpacho

—Joseph Humphrey, Murray Circle at Cavallo Point Lodge (Sausalito, California)

Watermelon Gazpacho with Crab Meat

—Donald Link, Herbsaint (New Orleans)

White Gazpacho (almond milk + breadcrumbs + cucumbers + garlic + pink peppercorns)

—Terrance Brennan, Picholine (New York City)

White Gazpacho with Shishito Peppers, Fluke, and Almonds

—Marcus Samuelsson, Red Rooster (Harlem), served at JBF Chefs & Champagne event

White Gazpacho with Strawberries and Almonds

—Lee Wolen, Boka (Chicago)

GENERATION TO GENERATION: WHO ARE YOU [COOKING FOR]?

It helps to know for whom you're cooking. While more detailed information about your guests' preferences and aversions is infinitely better, it can help to at least keep in mind what age group you're cooking for, and some of the typical considerations of that generational cohort:

- **The Silent Generation** (born 1928–1945): Influenced by the Great Depression, World War II, and the civil rights movement, they prefer simple, traditional foods (e.g., grilled cheese, mashed potatoes, meat loaf, roast turkey, tomato soup).
- **Baby Boomers** (born 1946–1964): Influenced by the civil rights movement, the Vietnam and Russian Cold wars, and space travel, they are the 1970s radicals and 1980s yuppies who like traditional foods—but with an updated twist (e.g., barbecue, Caesar salads, Chinese and Mexican foods). *Fast fact:* Just over a quarter of Baby Boomers have multicultural backgrounds.
- **Generation X** (born 1965–1980): Influenced by Watergate, the energy crisis, and corporate downsizing, they are the first generation to be less financially successful than their parents. Their food preferences tend to include childhood nostalgia foods, flavorful foods, fresh foods, global cuisines (e.g., Japanese and Mediterranean), healthy foods, natural foods, organic foods, and whole foods.
- Generation Y, aka **Millennials** (born 1981–1997): Influenced by digital media, terrorist attacks, and school shootings, they are often children of divorce who grew up with rigid schedules. Their food preferences tend to include **childhood nostalgia foods,** "clockless" eating schedules, delicious foods, flavorful foods, fresh foods, esp. fruits and vegetables; global foods, **healthful foods (e.g., juices, smoothies)**, natural foods, organic foods, restaurant dining, sustainable foods, quality/value offerings (i.e., high quality at affordable prices), whole foods, and wines (esp. among younger women). *Fast facts:* Nearly half of Millennials have multicultural backgrounds. Members of the Millennial generation consumed 42 percent of all wine in 2015, according to the Wine Market Council. One in ten Millennials consider themselves vegan.
- Generation Z, aka **Post-Millennials** (born 1998–2012): Post-Millennials are an even larger group than Millennials, comprising more than a quarter of the U.S. population. Their food preferences tend to include **global foods,** handheld foods, and made-to-order foods. *Fast fact:* Nearly half of Gen Zs have multicultural backgrounds.

Millennials and Post-Millennials currently make up the majority (51 percent) of the U.S. population—so their preferences are particularly influential in shaping the current and future food culture. That means we're likely to experience continuing demand for **foods reminiscent of their childhoods, adventurous global flavors, and healthful foods**. In 2015, for the first time in history, Americans spent more at restaurants than at grocery stores—thanks largely to Millennials, who see restaurant dining as a way of life rather than just for special occasions.

> **When you make something to be enjoyed, the creation is just as much about the person on the receiving end as the one who produced it.**
>
> —**DOMINIQUE ANSEL,** 2014 James Beard Outstanding Pastry Chef

GIRL SCOUT COOKIES

The best cookie I ever tasted was one baked by pastry chef **Jenny McCoy**—author of *Jenny McCoy's Desserts for Every Season* and *Modern Éclairs*—at **Marc Forgione**'s eponymous restaurant in New York City. As the shortbread cookie's **caramel + chocolate + toasted coconut** notes came together on my tongue, I was surprised to find the experience both incredibly delicious and oddly familiar, as it was my first visit to the restaurant. "Samoas!" I finally realized. Only it was the most amazing "Samoa" I'd ever had.

Pastry chef **Cindy Schuman** of Chicago's Sepia found herself stumped during the winter of 2015, when seeking seasonal inspiration for her new dessert menu. Once she realized that Girl Scout cookies were sold during the winter, she took *that* as her inspiration in creating desserts, delighting guests eager to revisit and reimagine their personal favorites, from Thin Mints to Trefoils, as we did during our visit that May 2015 over the James Beard Awards weekend:

- Almond Whiskey Tapioca with Buttercream-Filled Shortbread (inspired by Trefoils)
- Toffee Coconut Cake with Chocolate and Burnt Caramel (inspired by Samoas)
- Torn Chocolate Cake with Oolong Tea Ice Cream, Peppermint, and Chocolate Sauce (inspired by Thin Mints)
- Oatmeal Pavé with Peanut Butter, Chocolate, Oatmeal Ice Cream, and Rum Anglaise (inspired by Tagalongs and Dosidos)

Imagine: What is your favorite Girl Scout cookie? What new dish might it inspire?

GLUTEN-FREE GRAINS

The rise in gluten sensitivity has been accompanied by a rise in interest in gluten-free grains such as **amaranth, buckwheat, millet, quinoa, rice, sorghum,** and **teff,** and pseudograins like **wild rice** (which is actually a grass).

Whole, these are being served as side dishes, and turned into "bowls" (see **Bowls**) and "risottos." Amaranth and sorghum can even be popped like popcorn, and other grains can be puffed to use as textural accents to dishes.

There's also increasing interest in gluten-free flours made from these grains, not to mention gluten-free flours made from coconut, nut, or potato flours.

GRAIN BOWLS, SEE BOWLS

GRAINS, ANCIENT

Increasing interest in **ancient grains**—a term that refers to pre-industrial whole grains such as **einkorn, emmer, millet, quinoa, sorghum,** and **spelt**—led them to be named the number 15 trend for 2016 by the National Restaurant Association. These grains, and so-called pseudograins like **buckwheat** (which is actually a fruit), are often locally sourced from area farmers.

The grains are then used at every time of day in both savory and sweet dishes—from bowls to porridges to "risottos," such as NYC's Bevy chef **Chad Brauze**'s Einkorn Risotto with Morel Cream, Mint, Fava Beans, Asparagus, and Vin Jaune. And they are milled into flours, often in-house (as they do at NYC's Hearth, Philadelphia's Vetri, and even La Jolla's Galaxy Taco, where **Christine Rivera** grinds non-GMO heirloom blue corn from a single trusted farm in Mexico for her acclaimed housemade tortillas), for improved healthfulness and flavor complexity. Flavor is enhanced even further by using the grain in various stages of maturity, from young and green (which can bring out grassy notes) to fully mature (which can bring out a richer character) and even aged (which can bring out greater complexity).

GRAINS, ROLLED

Rolled grains are on a roll. Just as rolling (i.e., flattening with a roller) oats changes their texture and makes them quicker to cook, other grains are being similarly flattened.

I learned about the Indian flattened rice known as ***poha*** while reviewing *Vegetarian India* by **Madhur Jaffrey**. Finding some

G

at **Kalustyan's** in Manhattan, I started playing with it, toasting the poha and soaking it in almond milk, which I sweetened with a drizzle of maple syrup and a sprinkle of toasted almond slivers for a quick and delicious rice pudding.

Rolled grains like rolled barley, rolled rice, rolled rye, and rolled wheat can be used like rolled oats (e.g., in baking), either untoasted (e.g., for porridge or puddings) or lightly toasted for a nuttier flavor and crisper texture (e.g., for granola).

GRAINS, SPROUTED

Grains are being served not only whole, but also sprouted—with different flavor and nutrition implications, making **sprouted grains** a big trend of 2016.

GREEN FOODS

artichokes
asparagus
avocado
broccoli
cabbage
celery
chives
cucumbers
green beans
greens, leafy (e.g., collard, dandelion, mustard, turnip)
herbs, green (e.g., cilantro, mint, parsley)
honeydew melon
kiwi
lentils, green
lettuces
limes
onions, green
pasta, green (e.g., spinach)
peppercorns, green
pesto
scallions
spinach and spinach-hued foods, e.g., pastas
tea, e.g., green, matcha
zucchini

HALLOWEEN (SEE ALSO AUTUMN)

apples, as in the bobbing tradition
candy, e.g., candy corn (orange/yellow/white candy), miniature candy bars
cider, apple
cookies, e.g., pumpkin
doughnuts

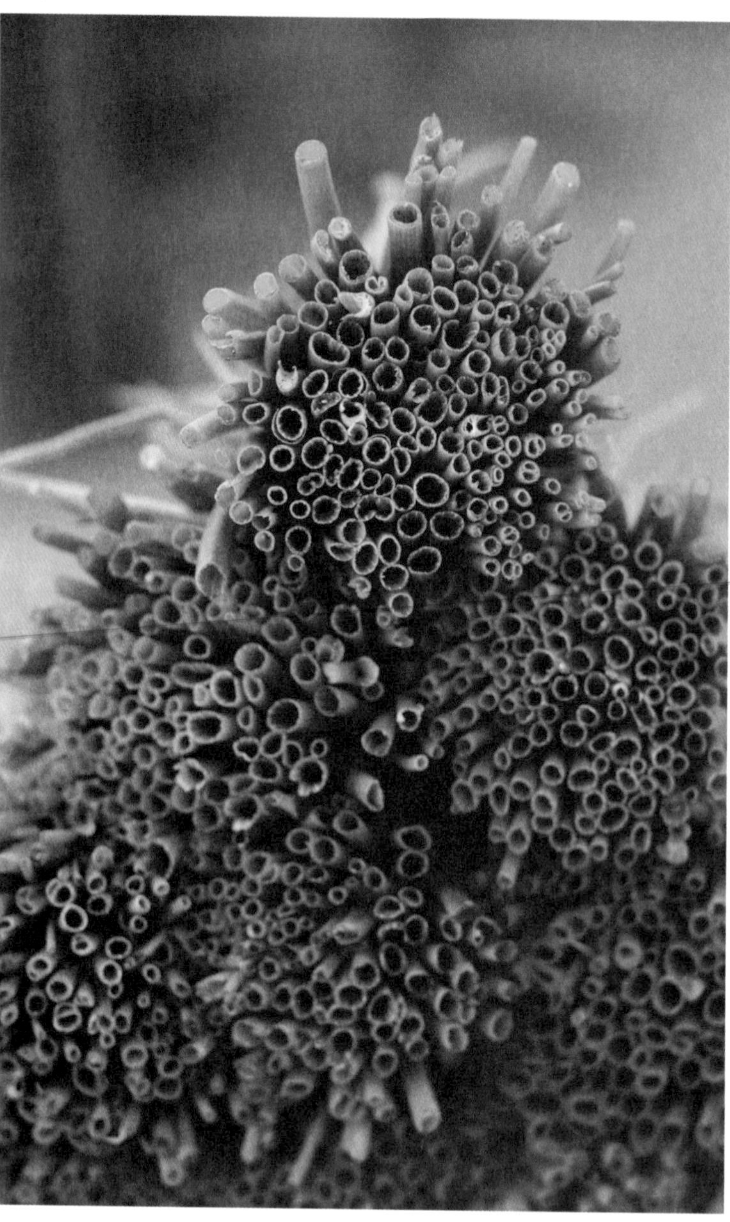

popcorn balls
pumpkin dishes

After making a trip to Transylvania (where he attended a village pig slaughter) to inspire a Dracula-themed dish, chef **Heston Blumenthal** made a blood-red spelt risotto with beet juice and horseradish.

Amanda Cohen served a Pumpkin Ceviche (raw pumpkin + avocado + lime juice + sunflower seeds) at Dirt Candy's Day of the Dead (November 1) dinner.

For his godson's 21st birthday dinner, **Patrick O'Connell**'s tasting menu at the Inn at Little Washington included A Tin of Sin (Royal Osetra Caviar with Sweet Crab and Cucumber Rillette) and a Halloween Pumpkin filled with Pumpkin Risotto and the Season's First White Truffles from Alba.

One of **Phillip Foss**'s Halloween dessert courses at EL Ideas included Pumpkin Ice Cream with Cheesecake, Grapefruit, and Coffee.

HANDHELD FOODS

Multitasking seems to be here to stay, given how much Post-Millennials love **handheld foods**, which include:

arancini, aka rice balls
arepas
burgers/sliders
calzones
cha siu bao, aka Chinese roast pork buns
cookies
corn dogs
doughnuts
empanadas
foods on a stick
French fries
granola bars
gyros
hot dogs
ice cream cones
kati rolls, e.g., Indian street food akin to small burritos
kebabs
knishes
kolaches
Popsicles
salmon cornets
samosas
sandwiches
s'mores
strollers, i.e., Boston wraps
tacos
tamales
turnovers
wraps

HANUKKAH (SEE ALSO WINTER)

brisket
couscous, sweet, e.g., with nuts, raisins
doughnuts, fried, e.g., jelly-filled (aka sufganiyot)
fried foods
latkes, potato—or carrots, celery root, parsnips, zucchini
olive oil
pâté, e.g., chicken liver
rugelach

For Hanukkah at Shaya, **Alon Shaya** has served latkes with toppings far beyond the usual applesauce and sour cream—including caramelized oxtail and onion jam and whipped Bulgarian feta. For dessert, he has topped a pair of sufganiyot with candied satsuma alongside black tahini gelato.

Michael Solomonov's Hanukkah menu at Zahav has featured dishes such as malauch with hummus and green tomato schug, lamb shanks with quince and caramelized mushroom mujadara, and sufganiyot with passionfruit malabi and pistachio sugar.

Even **Danny Meyer**'s beloved Shake Shack was inspired to create a holiday-themed "Concrete" (their uber-thick shakes) inspired by Hanukkah: The Hanukoncrete, featuring vanilla frozen custard mixed with strawberry puree and glazed doughnut chunks.

HEALTH, SEE DIET, LIVING LONG AND WELL, AND NUTRIENT DENSITY

HERITAGE CUISINES

Evolving beyond the moniker *ethnic cuisines*, today, it's all about **heritage cuisines**, or the recognition that various food traditions around the globe are valued expressions of culture. Organizations like UNESCO are looking to preserve their authentic (i.e., traditional) expression through attention to this designation of, say, traditional Mexican cuisine as an

H

Case Study: Acadian Cuisine

Can everything old be made new again? The French colony of Acadia was established on the northern Atlantic seaboard of North America in the 17th century. A century later, many Acadians settled in Louisiana after they were expelled from Canada by the British, where "Acadian" became known as "Cajun." Restaurants across the country reflect a growing interest in potato-and-root-vegetable-laden **Acadian** cuisine and other historical, heritage cuisines.

Duck Fricot with Carrots, Swiss Chard, Dumplings, and Savory

—Jeremie Tomczak, King Bee (New York City)

Ployes, Acadian buckwheat crepes made with finely milled silver-hull buckwheat

—Marc Sheehan, Loyal Nine (Cambridge, Massachusetts)

Poutine Rapee, lamb-stuffed potato dumplings

—Jeremie Tomczak, King Bee (New York City)

Sweet Potato Po' Boy Sandwich made with Roasted Sweet Potato, White Kimchi, Garlic Aioli, and Arugula

—Kevin Nashan, The Peacemaker Lobster & Crab Co. (St. Louis)

important part of the "intangible cultural heritage of humanity."

But so-called *gourmet heritage cuisine* refers to both the growing trend of chefs to bring upscale interpretation to heritage cuisines—such as Chicago's **Rick Bayless** has done for years now with Mexican cuisine—and the further pushing of the envelope being done by other chefs elsewhere, e.g., **Ludo Lefebvre**'s Brown Butter Bean Burrito (**brown butter + pinto beans + preserved lemon + yellow cheese**) at Trois Familia in Los Angeles.

Imagine: How familiar are you with the cuisine of your heritage? How could you bring more awareness and appreciation to that cuisine?

HOMAGE

Imagine: What's the best dish you've ever had in your life? Something cooked by your grandmother, or eaten at a temple of gastronomy? How could you pay **homage** to that dish by creating your own interpretation of it?

HOT CHOCOLATE

Serendipity has been pulling in tourists to New York City for 30 years with the lure of its Frozen **Hot Chocolate.** How do you make hot chocolate *hot* again? New generations of chefs keep discovering the answer. At the turn of the millennium, pastry chefs **Maury Rubin** of City Bakery (the first in Manhattan to popularize extra-rich and extra-thick hot chocolate) and **Jacques Torres** of Jacques Torres Chocolate (who popularized a famously chile-spiked Wicked version) put hot chocolate on the map of New York City—with higher quality, less sweet versions of this childhood favorite aimed at an adult palate—and other chefs followed suit in using melted semisweet chocolate, whole milk, and whipped cream.

Today, **Dominique Ansel** makes marshmallows you can drop into hot chocolate and make blossom, like a flower, and there's greater use of nondairy milks (e.g., almond milk).

HOT HOT HOT

We've become a nation of hotheads. The rising interest in more boldly flavored food led **"ethnic condiments and spices"** to take its place among the 20 hottest trends for 2016, according to the National Restaurant

Woodberry Kitchen's signature hot sauce

Association—with many of those ingredients prized for their ability to add a **hot** punch to dishes. **Aziz Osmani** of Manhattan's Kalustyan's spice store confirmed this trend as behind the retail store's recent doubling in size. More than half of all U.S. households have at least one bottle of **hot sauce**, and more than half of Americans have said they prefer **spicy foods.**

The secret to creating dishes that are delicious as well as hot is to select the ingredient that will provide the dish with the right amount of heat and the right flavor profile. Individual chiles—even of the same variety—vary greatly not only in terms of heat levels, but also in terms of the other flavor notes that come along for the ride, which can range from grassy to fruity to chocolatey, so it's important to always taste before using.

Uses: breakfast (e.g., egg dishes), cocktails/mocktails, desserts, French fries, mayonnaises (e.g., aioli), nuts, salad dressings (e.g., creamy, like ranch; vinaigrettes), sandwich spreads, sauces, snacks (e.g., popcorn)

Drink pairing implications: Alcohol fans the fire created by heat and spices, so lower-alcohol cocktails and wines (e.g., some Rieslings—those with a hint or more of sweetness also help to tame the heat) are the best bet for providing balance.

HUMMUS

What is hummus? While the classic calls for **chickpeas + garlic + lemon juice + olive oil + tahini,** chefs are elevating it to new heights through sharing their time-honored secrets (e.g., "overcooking" the chickpeas with a hint of baking soda to achieve the smoothest possible texture, and using a judicious amount of one of the highest quality tahinis available, e.g., Soom brand) in addition to giving it their own spins.

Some chefs are flavoring classic hummus, taking the experience in new directions, e.g., **garbanzo beans + parsley oil.** Other chefs are substituting other legumes (e.g., black beans, green or red lentils, white beans) for garbanzo beans, and other flavorings for tahini, e.g., **black beans + orange oil.**

ICE CREAM

Of course you can celebrate the tried-and-true: chocolate and vanilla will never go out of style.

Or you can revive interest in an old favorite: **Jacques Torres** always offers rum raisin ice cream, a long-time favorite of his father.

But even Jacques keeps reinventing ice cream, expanding into new flavors through the use of less typical ingredients. His lemon verbena ice cream is made with herbs from his own mother's garden in southern France. His travels through South America led to Peruvian fruits influencing his two newest flavors: cherimoya (which has notes of banana, coconut, and pineapple), and lucuma (a superfood with notes of caramel, maple, and pumpkin).

ICE CREAM SANDWICHES

In New York City in 1899, a pushcart peddler in the Bowery is said to have placed vanilla ice cream between two Graham crackers, creating the first **ice cream sandwich.**

More than a century later, New York chefs are still inspired by the idea. **Dominique Ansel** sandwiches salted caramel ice cream between slices of *kouign amann* pastry. **Francois Payard** fills macarons with coconut-mango and raspberry-pistachio ice creams. **Jacques Torres** is more of a purist, content to perfect his

Kate Jacoby's Churro Ice Cream Sandwich at Philadelphia's V Street

I

vanilla ice cream sandwiched between chocolate chip cookies.

Elsewhere, chefs are just as inspired to cocoon ice cream in pastry packages such as blondies, brioche, brownies, churros, cookies, doughnuts, Graham crackers, macarons, and waffles.

In Atlanta, **Steven Satterfield** serves only one dessert at lunchtime at his restaurant Miller Union: an ice cream sandwich, which has become a signature item. Since opening for lunch in 2010, Miller Union has rotated daily through dozens of seasonal flavors of ice cream, including almond-chocolate ripple, almond toffee, banana nocello, basil, brown butter, brown sugar–oat, brown sugar–pecan, butternut squash, cinnamon gingersnap, cream cheese, dark chocolate–malt, espresso brownie, fennel, maple pecan, Meyer lemon curd, peach, peanut brittle, pecan-bourbon, pumpkin, spiced-almond shortbread, spiced apple butter, strawberry & cream, sweet corn, sweet potato–pecan toffee, vanilla-coconut macaroon, vanilla-lemon shortbread, and yogurt.

IDEA GENERATION

When it comes to ideas, more is better. *Quantity* of ideas stimulates new associations and connections, typically resulting in higher *quality* ideas. When brainstorming ideas, aim to come up with 100—because the first third will usually be obvious, the next third a bit less obvious, and the final third (when you're really pushing the envelope) the most out-of-the-box. Afterward, sort through your ideas to determine the best to actually pursue.

Have an idea? The best are worth their weight in gold. So, write it down. Write it down. Write it down.

Imagine: What was the best idea you ever had? How did it come about? Pay attention the next time you're in similar circumstances.

The important thing to realize is that the conjuring up of the idea is not a deliberate, voluntary act. It is something that happens to us, rather than something we do.

—W. I. B. BEVERIDGE, author, *The Art of Scientific Investigation* (1957)

The best way to have a good idea is to have *a lot* of ideas.

—LINUS PAULING, two-time Nobel Prize winner for Chemistry (1954) and Peace (1962)

Ideas come from space.

—THOMAS EDISON

Dishes

Banana-Rum Ice Cream Sandwich, made with banana bread and garnished with almond toffee
—Cindy Pawlcyn, Cindy's Backstreet Kitchen (St. Helena, California)

Our Southern Butter Pecan Ice Cream Sandwich with Bittersweet Chocolate and Hot Caramel Sauce
—Patrick O'Connell, The Inn at Little Washington (Washington, Virginia)

World's Largest Ice Cream Sandwich: two 8-inch vanilla French macaron shells filled with four types of ice cream: Tahitian vanilla with caramelized bananas, dark rum, caramel, and walnut brittle
—Dominique Ansel, Dominique Ansel Bakery (New York City)

IDEAS, *BIG*

Ideas are like fish. If you want to catch little fish, you can stay in the shallow water. But if you want to catch the big fish, you've got to go deeper.

—DAVID LYNCH

If you're intent on coming up with the biggest ideas you're capable of, you might find inspiration in the best-selling book by award-winning film director **David Lynch.**

Catching the Big Fish: Meditation, Consciousness, and Creativity offers Lynch's insights into the creative process and encourages readers to tap the Unified Field, which he describes as:

> . . . The unity of all the particles and all the forces of creation. This is a field of nothing, but the scientists say that out of this nothing emerges everything that is a thing. This Unified Field is unmanifest yet all manifestation comes from this field.
>
> Ancient Vedic science, the science of consciousness, has always known of this field. Believers say that it is an eternal unbounded ocean of consciousness. And this consciousness has qualities. So this Unified Field, this ocean of consciousness, is a field of unbounded intelligence, unbounded creativity, unbounded happiness, unbounded love, energy and peace.

Too pressed for time to read the book any time soon? Lynch sums things up neatly: "The real story is: **the nature of life is bliss and the individual is cosmic.**" And, of course, you'll find the biggest fish you can imagine in the depths of the ocean of consciousness, which is accessible through meditation.

INEDIBLE → EDIBLE

Increasingly in high-end restaurants, there is a sense of surprise coming from the restaurant magically making the inedible edible.

Flowers once graced only the tabletops, as part of the dining room decor—but now edible flowers (see page 130) have become much more common to finish salads, desserts, and other dishes.

At Chicago's Alinea, chef **Grant Achatz** serves a floating, edible, green apple–flavored helium balloon, while at Mugaritz in Spain, chef **Andoni Luis Aduriz** provides edible cutlery and even displays edible centerpieces.

It is easy to go some place and get inspired by the surface [appearances] or cooking techniques, but it is different to decide to go on a really, really deep dive into understanding. That is what I have taken the time to do. . . . Creativity is great and it is fun to iterate quickly, but at the same time, creativity should come from something that is deeply rooted.

—**KYLE CONNAUGHTON,** Single Thread (Healdsburg, California), referring to his deep appreciation for the philosophy behind Japanese cuisine

INNOVATION

Gastronomy, for me, is not only about cooking techniques or ingredients—it is about innovation. Like music, business, or art, there can be no process in cuisine without an idea.

—FERRAN ADRIÀ

Stay close to everything that makes you glad you are alive.

—**HAFEZ,** Persian poet

Inspiration for us has changed so much over the years. When we first opened, it was the basic rediscovery of all these ingredients—stuff that I had never seen before, growing in our own backyard. With time, as these foodstuffs become as common as a leaf of parsley to us, our inspirations have changed.

—**RENÉ REDZEPI,**
Noma (Copenhagen)

INSPIRATION

Someone who's scared in the kitchen cannot cook better than someone who's inspired to cook for the client.

—**ERIC RIPERT,**
Le Bernardin (New York City)

Eric Ripert says that his **inspiration** never ends. "Because I cultivate it," he explains. "And I cultivate it by making sure I'm not too stressed or too busy." Two of his biggest secrets are meditation and management, and he admits that his team has to support him tremendously.
He adds:

- "For me, **creativity is different than for other cooks and chefs: It is a visual flash that comes to me. I see a picture on an inner screen.** It can be a finished dish, or a dish that is really halfway done.
- "It is all visual, so I need space. I can't be comfortable in a small room or at an office table. In my home, I have a long table, or else I need a window. **I need space for my inner eye to receive, create, and work with those images.** If I am at a desk, I am doomed; it doesn't work.
- "I used to create a lot at night. My wife was puzzled because **I would just sit at the end of my long table with paper and pens and look into space and take notes.** I would work until three or four in the morning, not forcing it. I also would stop after ten minutes if nothing came to me.
- "We have created a room [under the restaurant] that is a source of inspiration: **Our library [which holds hundreds of books] helps us be creative.** It has white boards all around to display old menus, a mood board, and ideas from exotic places, seasonal ingredients, and new ingredients we want to try.
- "When you start to be creative, so many things come up. **You have to stay focused on [one topic]**—and not [multiple topics], because otherwise it becomes an overwhelming avalanche of ideas. After meditating for so many years, I am able to be much more

focused on whatever my topic happens to be."

"Ultimately, creativity is about your surroundings—otherwise, cooking would not be an art," says Ripert. "It is your surroundings and experiences that fuel your creativity."

INVERSIONS, FOOD (SEE ALSO SAVORY ↔ SWEET DISHES)

When Andrew cooked with **Lydia Shire** at Boston's Biba in the early 1990s, Biba's menu featured *vitello tonato*—classically an Italian specialty of Piedmont that consists of chilled sliced veal with a tuna-flavored aioli. Lydia's version, however, featured chilled sliced *tuna* with a *veal*-flavored aioli. I've appreciated **chefs' inversions** of various components in dishes ever since—even and including, at a casual restaurant, a grilled tomato sandwich served with a cup of cheese soup.

Daniel Boulud's db bistro moderne in New York City has served a salad based on the classic combination of **beets + cheese + greens.** However, instead of finding the expected slices of beets amidst salad greens, it was a beet salad with a lettuce coulis and shaved ricotta salata—which essentially turned the lettuce into a salad dressing.

Imagine: The next time you're out for dinner, think about how you might turn one element of a dish into another.

JANUARY, SEE WINTER

JAPANESE CUISINE

Several leading chefs have shared their belief that the most inspirational haute cuisine in the world today is being created in Japan, noting the country's chefs' ability to pay attention to minute details, and through a relatively austere cuisine create extraordinary dishes from simple elements.

Imagine: How would you narrow down the elements of any other cuisine into four key ingredients? How many ways could you combine those ingredients?

Dashi stock, soy sauce, fermented bean paste (miso) and sake are the "big four" of Japanese cooking. One or more of these four substances are used in nearly every Japanese dish.

—SHIZUO TSUJI, *Japanese Cooking: A Simple Art*

JULY, SEE SUMMER

JUNE, SEE SPRING AND SUMMER

KAISEKI

Kaiseki is the Japanese multicourse tasting menu that celebrates not only the season, but a particular day and time. Each course celebrates seasonal ingredients via different cooking techniques.

As chefs increasingly strive to capture the present moment in their dishes, the principles of *kaiseki* can provide inspiration.

The foundation of kaiseki is that the menu is not the same as yesterday or tomorrow. [It focuses] on that day, that moment in nature. We use that structure and philosophy as applied to Sonoma.

—KYLE CONNAUGHTON, Single Thread (Healdsburg, California), as quoted in the *Wall Street Journal*

KENTUCKY DERBY DAY

Will Guidara and chef **Daniel Humm** of New York City's Eleven Madison Park host an annual party in honor of **Kentucky Derby Day,** which for more than 140 years has marked what's been called the Greatest Two Minutes in Sports. EMP's menu includes Champagne and mint juleps, hot browns, and fried chicken and waffles.

At other celebrations both in the South and across the country, certain Southern-inspired drinks and dishes rule:

J K

biscuits, e.g., with butter and ham or jelly
chicken, fried
desserts, bourbon-based
eggs, deviled
grits
iced tea
Kentucky burgoo
Mint Juleps (bourbon + ice + mint + simple syrup)
oysters
pecans, toasted
pies, e.g., Derby, the world's only trademarked pie, its recipe is secret—but its legendary status has inspired other "Kentucky" pies made with bourbon + chocolate + pecans or walnuts
pimento cheese (cheddar + cream cheese + pimentos), served with crackers
truffles, bourbon

KNOW YOURSELF

As a student and practitioner of martial arts (including *judo, ju-jitsu,* and *Baguazhang)* for even longer than he's studied and practiced the culinary arts, Saison's **Joshua Skenes** brings an unusually high level of **self-knowledge** to the kitchen.

"My connection of martial arts and cooking is the honesty [each] gives you," he says. "**You have to self-reflect.**"

Skenes observes that "the proof is in the pudding in martial arts: When you spar with someone, you either get your ass kicked or you win. You can't say you didn't win because you 'didn't feel like it.' Everyone knows. There is a reality to it, and that is the way I look at everything."

What's the equivalent in the kitchen? "There is the reality of, Does this taste good? When you taste crab, you have to ask yourself, Is this the best crab I have ever eaten? If the answer is no, then you need to find a better crab," says Skenes. "As a chef, you have the responsibility to take it as far as you can personally. **You have to live up to your own understanding—and if you don't, you are compromising.**"

Skenes credits both the physical and philosophical aspects of martial arts with changing his life. "I was getting in trouble [when I was 15], taking a break from martial arts and doing drugs. When I was 17, I really looked at everything and did a 180[-degree turnaround]," he remembers. "I got back into martial arts and started eating pescatarian, and mostly plants," a diet he continues to this day, except for the occasional meat that he or someone he knows has hunted.

His own self-knowledge has spurred Skenes to express a unique point of view through his restaurant, along with the discipline to do so at the highest possible level.

Knowing others is intelligence; knowing yourself is true wisdom. Mastering others is strength; mastering yourself is true power.

—**LAO TZU**, *Tao Te Ching*, translated by Stephen Mitchell

KWANZAA (SEE ALSO WINTER)

Dates: December 26–January 1
Colors: black, green, red
Symbols: candleholder, unity cup
Seven guiding principles: unity, self-determination, collective work and responsibility, cooperative economics, purpose, creativity, faith

African cuisine
African-American cuisine
biscuits
black-eyed peas
callaloo
Caribbean cuisine
catfish
cookies, e.g., gingerbread, sugar
corn
cornbread
doro wat
greens, e.g., amaranth, collard
jerked dishes, e.g., chicken
kale
macaroni and cheese
okra, e.g., stewed
peanuts, e.g., roasted
plantains
puddings, e.g., rice, sweet potato
rice, e.g., white
soul food
soups, e.g., peanut

sweet potatoes
tomatillos
yams

Marcus Samuelsson has offered a Kwanzaa menu at his Harlem-based Red Rooster, featuring his take on dishes such as Peanut Soup, Ceebu Jen (Shrimp, Fried Fish, and Jasmine Rice), Yassa Hen (Onion Stew, Tomato, and Collards), and Coconut Rice Pudding.

Topolobampo's dairy-free Tres Leches *cake*

LACTOSE INTOLERANCE

The [almond, coconut, and rice] milks are blended well and then passed through a chinois to make sure there are no chunks from the coconut milk. When using these milks [versus whole, evaporated, and sweetened condensed milks], the mixture is much less sweet. To add sweetness, I added [Perfect Puree] coconut puree, which also boosts the coconut flavor.

—**JENNIFER MELENDREZ**, Topolobampo (Chicago)

Milk and other dairy products are among the most common allergens. Beyond this, an estimated 75 percent of the world's population is **lactose intolerant** (that is, missing sufficient quantities of lactase, the enzyme that breaks down lactose and allows it to be absorbed by the body), leading more chefs to turn away from butter, cheese, cream, and other dairy products in favor of other sources of creaminess and richness.

Jennifer Melendrez served us a decadent yet dairy-free *tres leches* (three milks) cake at Chicago's Topolobampo. She told us it was made from a combination of almond, coconut, and rice milks.

A mixture of half coconut milk and half hemp milk has the heft to foam well for cappuccinos.

Imagine: What could you substitute for dairy products to add creaminess and richness to your next dish?

LARGE-FORMAT DISHES (CONTRAST WITH SMALL PLATES)

Small plates are definitely the trend, but the counter-trend toward **large-format dishes**—whether whole roast fish, or whole suckling pigs—is also notable.

At New York City's Rotisserie Georgette, owner **Georgette Farkas** oversees a menu of Whole Roasts, Fit for a Feast, which include Faroe Island Salmon with Spring Greens Stuffing, Crescent Farm Canard a l'Orange, and Pennsylvania Rabbit with Spring Peas and Tarragon Stuffing.

At the Park Hyatt New York's Bevy, chef **Chad Brauze** has three menu options available "To Share": Whole Grilled Market Fish with Sauce Chermoula and Charred Lemon; a 40-ounce Bone-In Bison Ribeye with Shaved Asparagus and Vinaigrette; and Green Circle Chicken, Stuffed with Bourbon and Rye Berries, with Dressed Lettuces.

LAYERING FLAVORS AND TEXTURES (AND SOUNDS!)

Are you overlooking opportunities to add flavor through your cooking? Deconstruct each element of a dish, and see where you might be able to add more.

Decades ago, a lightbulb went off the day I realized that I didn't have to make rice with water—and that I could substitute vegetable stock for more flavorful rice. That started my thinking about other liquids that would allow me to add more flavor. **Heston Blumenthal** recommends boiling potatoes with garlic cloves and rosemary for added flavor before roasting them.

Why provide only one example of a flavor when five will do? **Joan Roca** at El Celler de Can Roca serves a "milk dessert," featuring multiple components made from sheep's milk, including dulce de leche, ice cream, and mousse, not to mention cotton candy as a stand-in for sheep's wool. (And Roca even manages to layer flavor with *sound*: When diners run their spoons along the rim of this dish, a sheep's bell–like sound is heard.)

LEONARDO DA VINCI

Arguably history's most creative genius, **Leonardo da Vinci** had the ability to look at the world differently than anyone else—something he did as an architect, artist, botanist, engineer, geologist, inventor, mapmaker, mathematician, and musician.

Michael Gelb, author of the bestseller *How to Think Like Leonardo da Vinci* (which has been translated into 24 languages), identified seven principles that characterized da Vinci's behavior and that can enhance your own genius and creativity in the kitchen:

1. **Be curious.** Ask questions.
2. **Think independently.** Seek out different opinions.
3. **Sharpen your senses.** Be mindful. Pay attention. Appreciate beauty.
4. **Embrace uncertainty.** Be confident in the face of the unknown.
5. **Balance logic and imagination.** Use your left brain *and* your right brain.
6. **Balance body and mind.** Cultivate your physical strength and life force (aka *qi*).
7. **Make new connections.** Use mind-mapping to see new patterns.

The painter has the Universe in his mind and hands. . . . Realize that everything connects to everything else.

—LEONARDO DA VINCI

Imagine: Imagine having Leonardo da Vinci over for dinner. What would you make for him?

LIFE CYCLE

Various produce has been popularly used at different points in its **life cycle** in order to achieve different flavors and textures than at their peak of maturity (e.g., green peppers). Dining at **Sarah Grueneberg**'s Monteverde in Chicago was a revelation for her Tortelli Verdi, which showcased winter spinach—which was deliciously sweet—against Parmesan, roasted white miso, Piemontese hazelnuts, ramps, and lemon. Now, new fruits and vegetables and other ingredients are being explored for their own potential when unripe (e.g., green strawberries, which Noma's **René Redzepi** helped to popularize by pickling), especially in the spring months, as a sneak peek suggesting summer's bounty still ahead.

Consider the flavor distinctions between and among ingredients at different points in their life cycles:

- **bell peppers:** green bell peppers (harvested unripe) → yellow/orange bell peppers → red bell peppers (harvested ripe)
- **garlic:** garlic scapes (flower buds) → baby/teenage garlic (harvested young) → garlic bulbs (harvested mature)
- **mangoes:** green mangoes → red mangoes
- **papayas:** green papayas → red papayas

- **parsnips:** spring parsnips (very sweet) ⟶ autumn parsnips (less sweet)
- **plantains:** green plantains (harvested unripe; bland, starchy, firm) ⟶ yellow plantains ⟶ black plantains (sweetest, softest)
- **scallions:** younger scallions ⟶ older spring onions ⟶ mature white onions
- **spinach:** spring spinach (less sweet) ⟶ winter spinach (sweeter)
- **strawberries:** green strawberries (tart) ⟶ red strawberries (tart and sweet)
- **tomatoes:** green tomatoes (harvested unripe) ⟶ red tomatoes (harvested ripe)

Imagine: Consider how an herb, fruit, vegetable, or weed's particular stage of maturity or ripeness affects the subtlety or complexity of its flavor. Imagine something you might be willing to try unripe, or overripe, to discover new possibilities.

Three of the four leading causes of preventable death—heart disease, cancer, and stroke—are diet related. Heavy meat consumption, especially red and processed meat, is associated with increased risks of heart disease, diabetes, and some cancers, while plant-based diets are associated with decreased risks of all three.

—HARVARD'S DEPARTMENT OF NUTRITION CHAIR WALTER WILLETT, AND 700 OTHER HEALTH PROFESSIONALS, in a May 2015 letter endorsing the Dietary Guidelines Advisory Committee's recommendation to reduce consumption of animal-based foods and shift toward a more plant-based diet

LIVING LONG AND WELL (SEE ALSO NUTRIENT DENSITY)

It's a sad comment on the standard American diet (SAD) that the number 1 cause of death in the United States is actually nutritionally controllable diseases.

In 2014, the National Center for Chronic Disease Prevention and Health Promotion reported, **"Seven of the top ten causes of death in 2010 were chronic diseases [such as heart disease, stroke, cancer, diabetes, obesity.** Health risk behaviors that cause chronic diseases include poor nutrition.]. . . . In 2011, more than one-third (36 percent) of adolescents said they ate fruit less than once a day, and 38 percent said they ate vegetables less than once a day. In addition, 38 percent of adults said they ate fruit less than once a day, and 23 percent said they ate vegetables less than once a day." The recommended daily allowance for adults is 2 to 3 cups of vegetables and 1½ to 2 cups of fruits.

The good news is that if a body receives proper nourishment and care through receiving sufficient air, water, nutrients, exercise, sleep, etc., it has the extraordinary ability to heal itself. via homeostasis.

Nutritional science has proven that vegetables and fruits are the most nutritionally dense foods we can eat, filled with nutrients our bodies need to restore or optimize our health and to fight disease.

Imagine: Think of those you love, and imagine creating a dish that could extend their lives. How often would you feed it to them? What ingredients would you choose to include in it?

LOCAL (AND HYPER-LOCAL) SOURCING

In 2007, the Oxford American Dictionary selected ***locavore*** [someone who eats locally grown food] as its word of the year. The concept of sourcing and eating and drinking locally has only increased in the decade since. Seasonality has long been a mantra of leading chefs, but the realization that it is inextricably linked with **eating locally** is comparatively recent—leading to **local sourcing** (e.g., sourcing within a 100-mile radius, versus the 1990s trend of having the best ingredients FedExed in from across the country or around the world—commonplace before the concept of "carbon footprint") and **hyper-local sourcing** (i.e., growing one's own produce in gardens, dedicated plots, farms, or orchards on or near premises,

L

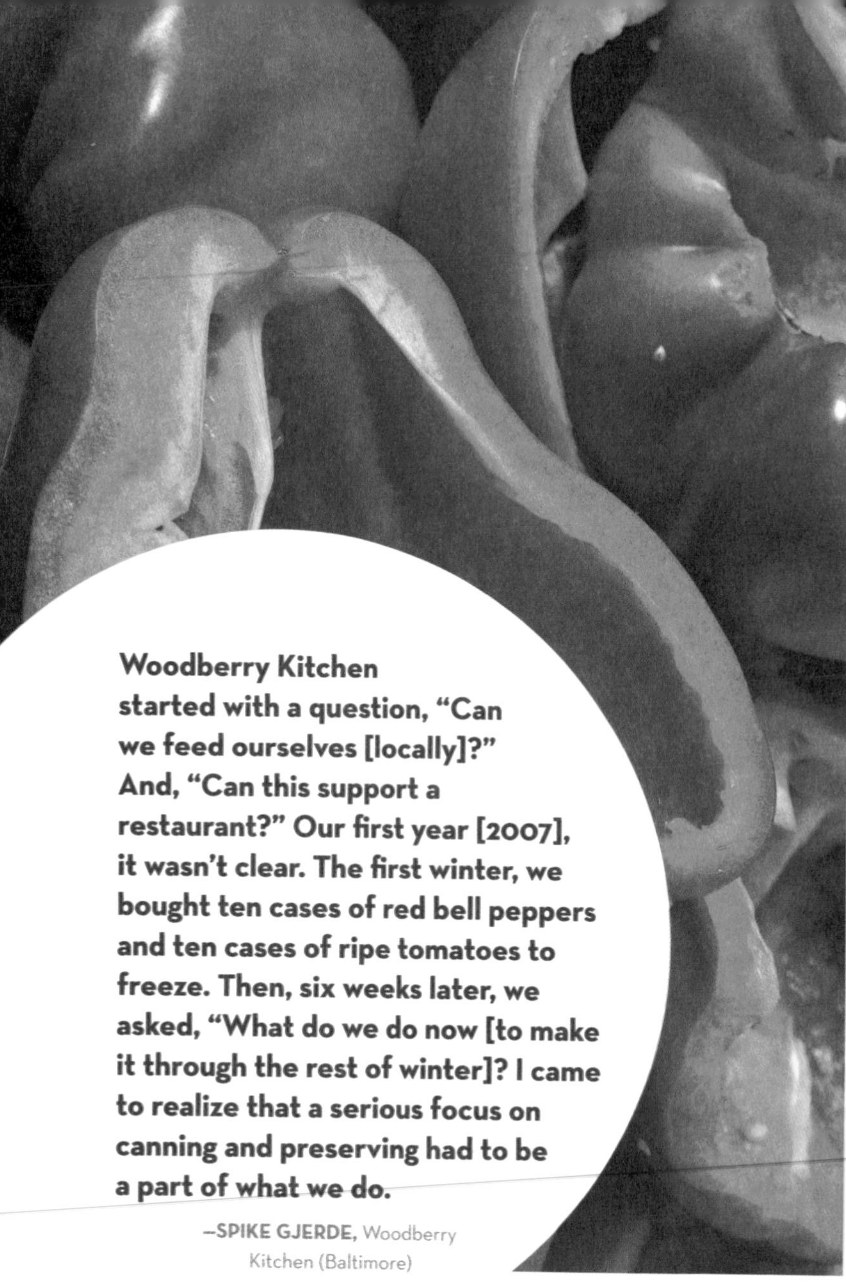

> **Woodberry Kitchen started with a question, "Can we feed ourselves [locally]?" And, "Can this support a restaurant?" Our first year [2007], it wasn't clear. The first winter, we bought ten cases of red bell peppers and ten cases of ripe tomatoes to freeze. Then, six weeks later, we asked, "What do we do now [to make it through the rest of winter]? I came to realize that a serious focus on canning and preserving had to be a part of what we do.**
>
> —**SPIKE GJERDE,** Woodberry Kitchen (Baltimore)

including via rooftop gardens) being two of the top five trends for 2016.

In 2015, **Spike Gjerde** was the first Baltimore chef to win the James Beard Foundation Award for Best Chef: Mid-Atlantic, partly in recognition for his dedicated commitment to **locavorism** through his restaurants Woodberry Kitchen, Parts & Labor, Grand Cru, and Artifact, all of which source locally. Gjerde uses a variety of techniques including canning, fermenting, freezing, and pickling in order to be able to achieve this.

Chefs are increasingly acknowledging the fact that cooking starts with farming and gardening—and are starting restaurant gardens in unprecedented numbers. **Rob Weland** is credited with starting the garden-to-table movement in Washington, D.C., while the chef at Poste. Having since opened his own restaurant, Garrison, he grows basil, heirloom tomatoes, sugar snap peas, and other herbs and vegetables to serve his guests. **Jose Garces**'s 18 restaurants are provided with organic produce from his own 40-acre Luna Farm in Philadelphia. Chicago's **Rick Bayless** has his own rooftop garden serving Frontera Grill and Topolobampo. At L.A.'s Providence, chef **Michael Cimarusti**'s rooftop garden provides the restaurant with basil and other herbs as well as greens, radishes, and other vegetables, and his participation in **Dock to Dish** brings in local seafood (Note: 91 percent of the seafood eaten in America is imported). Chef **Govind Armstrong**'s Post & Beam and Willie Jane in Los Angeles each have on-site gardens. **Tom Colicchio**'s Riverpark menu features produce from its 10,000-square-foot adjacent urban farm.

And chefs are even making the most of patio planters and hanging plants in their restaurants to tap the verdant potential in virtually every imaginable space, as evidenced at **Alex Guarnaschelli**'s Butter in Manhattan.

LOCATION LOCATION LOCATION

Where you cook can and should influence *what* you cook—but don't always follow the conventional wisdom. Here's a look at what chefs are learning while cooking in various locations:

Airlines

Daniel Boulud has done work with Air France to create in-flight dishes such as coconut curry lobster and Moroccan chicken tagine.

Brad Farmerie of New York City's Saxon + Parole has consulted on the menus for JetBlue's premium cross-country Mint service, for which he seasons inflight dishes 20 percent more assertively. In an effort to avoid high-sodium dishes, he turns to herbs and spices as well as umami-rich ingredients.

Danny Meyer's Union Square Hospitality Group is working on in-flight meals inspired by its restaurant concepts for Delta Air Lines.

Alfred Portale of NYC's Gotham Bar and Grill has been working with Singapore Airlines as a member of its International Culinary Panel (which also counts as members France's **Georges Blanc**, Italy's **Carlo Cracco**, Los Angeles's **Suzanne Goin**, China's **Zhu Jun**, India's **Sanjeev Kapoor**, Australia's **Matt Moran**, and Japan's **Yoshihiro Murata**) for more than a decade to create in-flight meals, developing three dozen dishes a year. Portale focuses on moist cooking techniques like braising and confiting for the dishes' ease in reheating, and says he amplifies the flavors used (e.g., salt, acidity, sweetness, heat, spice) because of the very dry air at 35,000 feet, which dries out the taste buds.

American Airlines is tapping chefs like Dallas's **Julian Barsotti**, New York's **Maneet Chauhan**, Hawaii's **Sam Choy**, and the U.K.'s **Mark Sargeant** for help creating its latest in-flight offerings.

Airports

Rick Bayless was told that airport customers wouldn't wait in line for their food, nor would they want very aromatic or spicy foods, when he was reluctantly first considering opening Tortas Fronteras at Chicago's O'Hare Airport. But Bayless insisted on boldly flavored Mexican-inspired food, and found that customers were indeed willing to wait when necessary for what's since become known as having the best airport food in America—our own opinion as well as that of the

I'm working with JetBlue on airline food, and learned that we lose 20 percent of our capacity to taste at the altitude in pressurized cabins. A great dish will underwhelm at that altitude. Necessity is the mother of invention, and we need to create food that fits in a small box that can be heated for 15 minutes at 350 degrees and taste amazing. People want to eat food in the air that's bright, fresh, and light—however, anything too delicate won't work, so soft salads and microgreens are out. I've found the secret isn't using more salt or sugar—it's using umami and acid and heat. I made an insane neon orange carrot, lemongrass, and ginger soup with veg stock and coconut milk with a chili marshmallow that went over really well.

—BRAD FARMERIE, Saxon + Parole (New York City)

Washington Post—and even pre-order via the dedicated app Tortas Frontera O'Hare.

Today, all across America, you can also find restaurants from chefs or restaurateurs like **Cat Cora** (Houston, Salt Lake City, and San Francisco's Cat Cora's Kitchen), **Todd English** (Boston and JFK's Bonfire), **Carla Hall** (Washington National's Page), **Danny Meyer** (JFK's Shake Shack), **Masaharu Morimoto** (LAX's Skewers by Morimoto), **Wolfgang Puck** (Atlanta, Boston, Charlotte, O'Hare, Cincinnati, Denver, Indianapolis, JFK, LAX, Las Vegas, and Seattle-Tacoma's Wolfgang Puck Express; Dallas's The Italian Kitchen), and **Michael Symon** (Pittsburgh's Bar Symon).

At Newark International Airport, a new cadre of chefs have been signed to elevate the level of food, including **Amanda Cohen**, **Alain Ducasse**, **Dan Kluger**, **Marcus Samuelsson**, and **Alex Stupak**.

Cruise Ships

Chefs as diverse as **Guy Fieri** (Guy's Burger Joint, which serves burgers with seasoned fries, chili, spicy onion rings with Carnival), **Thomas Keller** (The Grill with Carnival's Seabourn), **Jamie Oliver** (Jamie's Italian with Royal Caribbean), and **Curtis Stone** (Share with Princess) have been recruited to create new offerings to be available aboard cruise line ships.

Pop-Up Restaurants

With interest in pop-up restaurants growing 8 percent from 2015 to 2016, you'd think it was a new, hot trend. But the truth is that savvy chefs have been plying their wares outside a permanent restaurant setting for decades or longer.

Back in the 1980s, when blackened redfish was all the rage, chef **Paul Prudhomme** essentially sent himself out on the road to do pop-up dinners in New York City and San Francisco, sealing his reputation as one of the country's most famed chefs—one with a perpetual line of prospective guests outside his New Orleans restaurant, K-Paul's.

Today, leading chefs are jetting around the world to introduce their restaurants to discerning audiences abroad, including Alinea's **Grant Achatz**, who took his staff to Madrid and then Miami for one-month stints, **Dominique Ansel**, whose bakery popped up in Tokyo before opening a permanent location there, and **René Redzepi**, who opened pop-ups in Australia and Mexico.

Rising stars are also getting in on the action. While waiting to open her restaurant, Lady of the House, Detroit chef **Kate Williams** has been cooking pop-up dinners around the country, including one we attended at Brooklyn's Traffic and Tide showcasing her #uglyfood advocacy through a captivating menu featuring whey ricotta, smoked mushroom stems, and cheese rind fondue.

Kate Williams

Retail/Restaurant Hybrids

The advent of **Mario Batali**'s Eataly locations in New York (which feature 6 restaurants, 4 counters, and 3 cafes) and beyond have sparked more chefs to create or team up on retail concepts. **Anthony Bourdain**'s Bourdain Market aims to bring global flavors to Manhattan's Pier 57 on the Hudson River, while **José Andrés** has announced plans to team with **Ferran and Albert Adrià** to open an enormous Spanish food hall at 10 Hudson Yards. Urban Outfitters has recruited chefs **Ilan Hall**, **Michael Symon**, and **Marc Vetri** to create in-store restaurants for the retail chain.

The [2016 U.S. Dietary] guidelines have some tremendously important messages, including that overall we should be eating way more fruits and vegetables than we've been eating as a country.

—**CURT ELLIS,** cofounder and CEO of FoodCorps, a national nonprofit that promotes healthy eating in schools

I'm convinced that the only way to really make significant change is in the public school system—it's the place you can reach every child.

—**ALICE WATERS,** Chez Panisse (Berkeley, California), in support of a project to bring edible gardens to schools in California's Orange County

Schools
In October 2012, we were honored to have been invited to join renowned restaurant critic **Gael Greene** for a tour of the White House Kitchen and Kitchen Garden led by then–White House executive pastry chef **Bill Yosses.** Leading students on similar tours of the White House Kitchen Garden led Yosses to understand food as a powerful teaching tool, which he's sharing with teachers via **Kitchen Garden Laboratory,** which teaches science through food and recipes and coaches students on creating rooftop and campus gardens.

Under the leadership of executive chef **Bill Telepan,** who became active more than a decade ago when he saw what his daughter was being served at school and knew he could make improvements, leading chefs across the country are supporting **Wellness in the Schools,** a non-profit that creates healthier environments for children to learn and grow.

Submarines
Derrick Davenport was named Armed Forces Chef of the Year in 2013, and named the American Culinary Federation's USA Chef of the Year in 2015, for which he received $5,000 and a gold medallion.

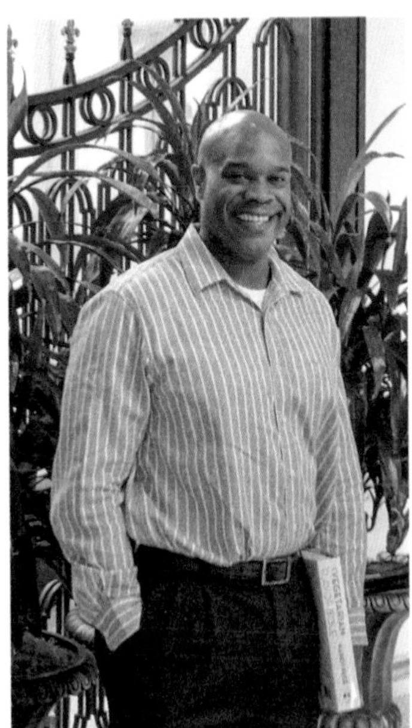

Derrick Davenport

While visiting Paris in the mid-1990s, he'd had a bread epiphany that led him to study bread baking in school. For a while, he was baking on a submarine, including his own bagels, English muffins, hamburger and hot dog buns, and—yes—submarine rolls.

The longest he was out for was 50 days on a submarine—they had 90 days' worth of food on board, but only five days' worth of fresh produce. "On a submarine, the food *is* the morale," he told us. Davenport's making doughnuts for breakfast out of his broom closet–sized kitchen kept his crew's morale high. How did he deal with issues like having the submarine rise unexpectedly while he was baking? Sometimes tongue-in-cheek monikers were in order: "I'd call them 'angle cakes,' he told us, poking fun at some of his cakes' decidedly un-level tops.

White House
See White House State Dinners.

L

Bill Telepan of Oceana on Wellness in the Schools

In the 1970s and 80s, [American] kids' obesity levels were lower than they are now and their grades were higher, ranking among the best in the world. Now, their grades are at their lowest and obesity is the highest. Since 1980, kids' and teens' obesity levels have tripled. One in three are now overweight or obese. Healthy food and more active lifestyles lead to better academic performance.

Even U.S. generals are asking for better diets because kids are too obese to serve [in the armed forces]. **Nutrition affects our national security and our future thinkers and innovators and we are losing out to the rest of the world.**

Why wouldn't we want to invest in our kids? We should invest in our kids now instead of in their healthcare later. Why wouldn't you want to give kids the best food possible? Why should they have to eat the worst food possible? To turn this around, all it takes is someone who cares.

Bill Telepan, as he showcases his mushroom veggie burger at Danny Meyer's Shake Shack, benefiting Wellness in the Schools

The way we went about changing the school menu was by respecting that it was their kitchen. All additional work was done by our staff and not the school staff until we got to know them.

The key to the recipes in the schools was that first I go through a school's procurement book. I did not bring in anything special from the Greenmarket or buy anything extra—it was all what was already available to them. The first thing we eliminated was beef.

I started with a vegetarian chili a dish I knew my daughter liked. This chili is vegan, gluten-free, nut-free, and sugar-free (if you use tomatoes with no added sugar). The chili is tomato paste, onions, peppers, chili powder mix, oregano, cumin, and maybe a few red pepper flakes for some spice. The peppers and the spice do the trick, and we serve it with rice. I have done other riffs on the chili, like Cincinnati-style, but my family wouldn't go for chili over spaghetti. I found the trick was to use elbow macaroni, and it was great.

Working with Kids

With children, you have to keep putting things out and making sure they try it and eventually they will like it. Studies have shown that it takes eight to ten times of trying something for a child to start to eat it regularly.

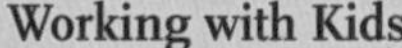

My daughter was a bit of picky eater and it took about 12 times of putting cauliflower on her plate before she tried it and said "This is good." It took a cute bartender to get her to try Brussels sprouts. She now even likes salad with onion on it. So I really worked through her in developing dishes.

Kids like spicy, flavorful foods—they just need exposure. Kids love Italian and Mexican food; they love pesto, chicken, rice and beans.

It is important to make vegetables delicious. If you serve brown, steamed, mushy broccoli, I am not going to eat it, either!

Kids like salads and root vegetables. For salad, it's key to have a good dressing. Kids love sharp flavors. Bitter is hard for them. Kids like to dump a lot of dressing on their salads and they tend to prefer the sweeter ones, like balsamic or honey-mustard, or a cheesy one like Caesar.

Being Creative to Get Kids to Eat Better

It ruins the palate of our nation when kids grow up on processed food. They are missing out on so much. Parents have to be an example as well. You can't be a parent and drink soda. Soda elimination would take away half the problem in a kid's diet.

Take your children's favorite processed food and make it from scratch. Make chicken fingers with good breadcrumbs, and bake (not fry)them. I have even made them without eggs.

Create macaroni and cheese with vegetables in it. Add some cauliflower, and don't hide it. How easy is it to make real macaroni and cheese with milk, flour, butter, and cheese? If something is powdered, there is a problem.

Make something that you normally pull from the freezer—like fresh pizza. Instead of a hamburger, make a chicken burger.

WITS Benefit at Riverpark (September 2016)

I have been involved with Wellness in the Schools for over a decade, and chefs like helping the cause a lot. What is wonderful is that chefs really get behind this because we typically feed the top one percent, and it is a good feeling to give back to those who really need it—like kids.

Rocco [DiSpirito] is someone I engaged with during Hurricane Sandy. For Rocco, this is a natural because he lives in a world about eating well. **Tom Colicchio** is someone who, over the last few years, has gotten into the politics of food. He is fighting the battle to get more money for schools and people on food stamps so they can eat better. He is a natural. **Nancy [Silverton]** is part of No Kid Hungry, and I have done events all over the country with her. She is just a giver and nurturer and her spirit and my spirit match. **Marc Vetri** has his own foundation to feed kids. We have had a lot of dialogue over the years, and have both sent people to talk to foundations.

All these people are fighters, givers, and thought leaders who find the time to do this. They also have staffs to support them to do it. When you have Rocco, Tom, Nancy, and Marc, you have a lot of power to help spread your word.

Rocco DiSpirito, Tom Colicchio, Marc Vetri, Nancy Silverton, Bill Telepan, Dahlia Narvaez, and Riverpark executive chef Andrew Smith in Riverpark's Kitchen

Chefs Give

Chefs give more than [professionals in] any other industry.

We are all citizens of the United States and all have the right to argue about where our tax dollars are going, and to elect the people we think will do what is best not just for our interest but for all.

When someone tells us as chefs that we should stay in the kitchen and not talk politics. . . . Well, you know what? Chefs see all sides of the socioeconomic spectrum. We feed the one percenters, and we work with immigrants and undereducated people. You can't show me anyone who is being touched by so many and such a wide variety of people in one day as a chef.

This profession is wonderful, and I love it. I can find myself instructing a guy from Mexico how to make a salad, at the same time [Emmy Award–winning political talk show host] **John Oliver** is in the restaurant and wants to say hi to me! It is wonderful.

LOUDNESS (CONTRAST WITH QUIETNESS)

Intensity in flavor can be great—or gross, depending on your palate and preferences. These are flavors that demand being the star of their own shows and/or used judiciously:

cheese, e.g., blue, Époisses, limberger
chiles, hot, e.g., Carolina Reaper, ghost pepper, habanero
coffee, dark roast
durian
garlic, raw
ginger, raw
horseradish
kimchi
mustard, hot
rosemary
spirits, high-alcohol
tarragon
vinegar, high-acid
wasabi
wine, sweet, e.g,. Sauternes

LOVE

If you give the ingredients what I call "love," you'll never fail. If you don't have that in your cooking, forget it. You can have all the techniques in the world, but you'll never become a great chef.

—ANDRÉ SOLTNER

The long-time chef of Manhattan's Lutèce, which many considered to be America's best restaurant after first earning four stars from the *New York Times* in 1972, wasn't simply being sentimental.

Love helps open the door to creativity: Experiencing love shifts you from the external to the internal, from the objective to the subjective, from the linear to the nonlinear.

And the internal, subjective, nonlinear field is one of unlimited possibility and creativity.

It's possible to open this flow through a "loving-kindness" meditation. At a number of his 2017 events globally, **Tony Robbins** introduced attendees to author **Stephen Co** and the powerful **Meditation on Twin Hearts**, which is available free at masterstephenco.com/meditation-twin-hearts.

MACARONI + CHEESE

Some version of **macaroni and cheese** has been around since the 14th century, with early versions made from fermented lasagna sheets cut into two-inch squares and tossed with grated cheese (my bet is on Parmesan). But the boxed version of Kraft macaroni and cheese many Americans grew up on originated in 1937—and chefs have been trying to create the ultimate version ever since.

The mac-n-cheese trend grew 21 percent over a recent four-year period, with temples of gastronomy like Virginia's **Inn at Little Washington** and fast-casual restaurants like New York City's **S'MAC** featuring the nostalgic dish on their menus—the former with aged Dutch Gouda and Virginia country ham, served in a Parmesan tuile basket topped with shaved white truffles.

Thomas Keller serves butter-poached Maine lobster with mascarpone-enriched orzo, while **Jean-Georges Vongerichten** serves his wife Marja's recipe, calling for elbow macaroni and three different Cheddars plus Monterey Jack and cream cheese. In Los Angeles at n/naka, **Niki Nakayama** serves hers with uni, blow-torched cheese, and shaved truffles. In Dallas, **Ida Claire** restaurant's pimiento mac-n-cheese is the rage.

Seattle chef **Maria Hines** decided to take the dish to the people by giving them the ultimate mac-n-cheese experience at her **Golden Beetle**, which offers **Build Your Own Mac and Cheese Mondays**. There's a choice of pasta (e.g., elbows, gluten-free penne), creamy béchamel sauce flavors (classic, roasted garlic, spicy harissa), cheese (Gruyère, smoked Gouda, white Cheddar), and meat or vegetable (caramelized cauliflower, kale, roasted Brussel sprouts, crispy Skagit River Ranch bacon), all served with a crispy panko crust.

Fellow Seattle chef **Makini Howell** (Stevie Wonder's former

personal chef) creates a craveable vegan version at her **Plum Bistro.** And lest you think that's an oxymoron and that vegans aren't into mac-n-cheese, I'll point out that Baltimore's 2016 **Vegan Mac 'n' Cheese Smackdown** pulled in more than 1,000 people eager to taste the versions made with cashew cream and vegetable purees.

New York City's first mac-n-cheese food truck, **Mac Truck,** serves BBQ pulled pork mac-n-cheese and buffalo chicken mac-n-cheese, in addition to fried mac-n-cheese bites.

Chicago celebrates the dish with an annual **Mac & Cheese Fest** each fall.

Cheeses: American, Asiago, blue (e.g., gorgonzola), Boursin, Brie, buffalo mozzarella, cacio di Roma, **Cheddar** (one or more types, e.g., aged, extra-sharp, smoked, Vermont, yellow, and/or white), Comté, cottage cheese, cream cheese, fontina, goat (e.g.,chèvre), Gouda (e.g., smoked), Grana Padano, Gruyère, Havarti, Jack, Jarlsberg, mascarpone, Monterey Jack, mozzarella (e.g., smoked), Muenster, Parmesan, Pinconning, provolone, Romano, SarVecchio (Wisconsin-made "Parmesan"), Swiss, Velveeta; three-cheese (e.g., cheddar, Gruyère, Parmesan) or four-cheese (e.g., Cheddar, Monterey Jack, Parmesan, and provolone)

Note: Add cream cheese for meltability; as Parmesan doesn't melt so well, grate on top and broil or torch

Pastas: cavatappi, ditalini, **elbow macaroni,** fusilli, gluten-free, orecchiette, orzo, penne, radiatore, rigatoni, shells, torchio, wagon wheels, ziti

Seasonings: bay leaves, béchamel, beer, chiles (e.g., chipotle, jalapeño, poblano), cilantro, cloves, cream, garlic, horseradish, Mornay sauce, mustard (Dijon, dry), nutmeg, paprika, pepper, pesto, ranch seasoning, shallots, sour cream, soy sauce, Sriracha, Tabasco, thyme, tomato paste, truffle oil, Worcestershire sauce

Add-ins: asparagus, bacon, bell peppers (e.g., roasted), bratwurst, brisket, broccoli, cauliflower, chicken, chiles (jalapeños), collard greens (braised), corn, crab (blue), eggs (fried, poached), ham, kale, lardons, lobster, mushrooms (cremini, morels), onions (caramelized), pancetta, peas, pulled pork, sausage (Andouille, chorizo, lamb, pork), scallops, Serrano ham, short ribs, shrimp, spinach, squash, sun-dried tomatoes, tasso ham, tomatoes, truffles, uni (e.g., macaroni + cheddar + jalapeño + cornbread crumbs)

Garnishes: breadcrumbs (e.g., cornbread, panko, sourdough, esp. toasted); fresh herbs (chopped basil, chives, parsley); fried onions; kale chips; crumbled cornflakes, potato chips or Ritz crackers; grated Parmesan; pork cracklings; green onions/scallions (chopped); toasted walnuts; truffles (black, white)

Vessels: cast-iron skillet, ceramic crock

Formats: deep-fried bites (e.g., fritters); served atop a burger; baked in a loaf pan and sliced; stuffed inside meatloaf; "waffled"

MANIFESTO: INTERNATIONAL AGENDA FOR GREAT COOKING

The 2006 **International Agenda for Great Cooking** declaration put forth by chefs **Ferran Adrià** of elBulli, **Heston Blumenthal** of the Fat Duck, and **Thomas Keller** of the French Laundry and Per Se, in conjunction with writer **Harold McGee**, featured four primary points:

1. Three basic principles guide our cooking: excellence, openness, and integrity
2. Our cooking values tradition, builds on it, and uses it as part of the ongoing evolution of our craft.
3. We embrace innovation—new ingredients, techniques, appliances, information, and ideas—whenever it can make a real contribution to our cooking.
4. We believe that cooking can affect people in profound ways, and that a spirit of collaboration and sharing is essential to true progress in developing this potential.

MANIFESTO: THE NEW NORDIC CUISINE

In 2004, chef **René Redzepi** and his partner **Claus Meyer** convened a symposium in Copenhagen for some of the region's best chefs and other culinary experts to discuss the best approach to nurturing their local food movement. This led to the creation of a ten-point **Manifesto for the New Nordic Cuisine,** which outlined the values, principles, and philosophies of the food revolution they envisioned—which encompassed the ethics, purity, and sustainability embraced by the Nordic culture. The resulting manifesto brought New Nordic Cuisine to the world stage when in 2010 their restaurant Noma was named number 1 on the World's 50 Best Restaurants list.

The aims of The New Nordic Cuisine are:

1. To express the purity, freshness, simplicity and ethics we wish to associate to our region.
2. To reflect the changes of the seasons in the meals we make.
3. To base our cooking on ingredients and produce whose characteristics are particularly in our climates, landscapes and waters.
4. To combine the demand for good taste with modern knowledge of health and well-being.
5. To promote Nordic products and the variety of Nordic producers—and to spread the word about their underlying cultures.
6. To promote animal welfare and a sound production process in our seas, on our farmland and in the wild.
7. To develop potentially new applications of traditional Nordic food products.
8. To combine the best in Nordic cookery and culinary

You don't have to have a restaurant on the World's 50 Best Restaurants list to write your own manifesto. ***David Levi*** *launched his eight-table (plus eight seats at the bar), 100-percent local restaurant Vinland in Portland, Maine, with his own 19-principle manifesto:*

The human is an animal, and animals need food. The decline in the quality of our food began with the Agricultural Revolution, accelerated with the Industrial Revolution, and has now reached a sad and dangerous low. It is time for us to reclaim the dignity, beauty, and sustainability of real food, our birthright, and a blessing to our children. . . .

We are part of a food revolution, which is part of the broader revolution of our time, a revolution in consciousness, politics, and society. . . . We stand in solidarity with the community of life, with indigenous cultures, with true revolutionaries everywhere, guided, in the words of Ernesto Guevara, by a great feeling of love.

Our principles:

1. We are what we eat. We are also what what we eat eats. When we eat healthy beings prepared with love and respect, we are truly nourished.
2. Real food must nourish. If food does not promote physical and soul health, it is not real food.
3. The primary goal of any acceptable food system must be the betterment of the total community. . . .
4. Food should delight. Any acceptable food system must value the aesthetic. . . .
5. Healthy foods taste good. . . . The enjoyment of eating is a cornerstone of a happy life.
6. Genuine creativity does not compromise ethics. . . .

. . . To read more, visit vinland.me/mission.

traditions with impulses from abroad.

9. To combine local self-sufficiency with regional sharing of high-quality products.
10. To join forces with consumer representatives, other cooking craftsmen, agriculture, fishing, food, retail and wholesales industries, researchers, teachers, politicians and authorities on this project for the benefit and advantage of everyone in the Nordic countries.

Imagine: What points would your personal culinary manifesto include?

MARCH, SEE **SPRING** AND **WINTER**

MARDI GRAS

Date: A Tuesday between February 3rd and March 9th (and the day before Ash Wednesday)
What it is: Fat Tuesday in New Orleans

beans, red
beignets
biscuits
black-eyed peas
cocktails, e.g., milk punch, Sazerac
crayfish
grits
gumbo
hush puppies
jambalaya
king cake
rice, dirty
sandwiches, muffuletta
shrimp, e.g., étouffée

At his February 2016 seven-course Mardi Gras Mystique dinner at the James Beard House, New Orleans chef **Daniel Causgrove** of the Grill Room at Windsor Court Hotel served a dessert of Galette des Rois with Ponchatoula Strawberry–Rhubarb Compote and Brown Butter Ice Cream. Chicago chef **Jimmy Bannos** likes to celebrate Mardi Gras every day at Heaven on Seven, where actual Fat Tuesday specials have included fried oysters and bacon with black pepper meunière and duck and

Andouille tamales smothered in mole sauce.

MARIJUANA

James Beard Award–winning pastry chef **Mindy Segal** of Chicago's Hot Chocolate is looking to elevate edibles made with **newly legal marijuana** beyond brownies to new highs. Her experimentation is leading her to pair odor-free cannabis oil with flavors like butterscotch, candied citrus, caramelized white chocolate, dark chocolate, Graham crackers, honey, peanut butter, smoked almonds, toasted oats, toasted pistachios, and toffee bits. While **chocolate is one of pot's most popular flavor pairings**, others include bananas, berries (e.g., strawberries), butter and brown butter, butternut squash, caramel, carrots, cherries, chiles (habanero), coconut, coffee/espresso, dried fruit (apricots), maple syrup, nuts (almonds, cashews, hazelnuts) and nut butters (peanut butter), pumpkin, spices (garam masala, ginger), and vanilla.

While he's not a professional chef, **William Breathes** reviews medical marijuana for Denver's *Westword* and believes there's no better pairing for pot than orange juice, and notes that it can be used to flavor everything from ice cream to salad dressings.

THC, the main active ingredient in marijuana, is fat-soluble, so preparations involving butter, oil, and other fats are common, including pestos and other fat-based sauces (e.g., aioli, mayonnaise).

There is even a Cannabis Cup chef competition encouraging the development of new marijuana-infused dishes, with such edibles estimated to represent as much as half of the estimated $500 billion cannabis industry. Competitors seeking inspiration from books on cooking with cannabis might turn to those by Natural Gourmet Institute alumna **Elise McDonough**, the former *High Times* edible editor, or Culinary Institute of America alumna **Laurie Wolf**, who was called "the Martha Stewart of marijuana edibles" by *The New Yorker*.

MASH-UPS

The Cronut—**Dominique Ansel**'s mash-up of a croissant and a doughnut—is the hottest **mash-up** of the past decade, although other mash-ups abound:

Imagine: Imagine mashing up two (or more) of your favorite foods. What would result?

babka + doughnuts = Doughkas
—Fany Gerson, Dough (New York City)

babka + French toast = Babka French Toast
—Russ & Daughters Cafe (New York City)

bread pudding + French toast = Bread Pudding French Toast with Apple Sauce
—Katianna Hong, Charter Oak (St. Helena, California)

Danish + redeye gravy = Redeye Danish made with ham and coffee gravy
—Eli Kulp, High Street on Hudson (New York City)

oatmeal + soufflé = Oatmeal soufflé, served with maple syrup and currants
—Patrick O'Connell, The Inn at Little Washington (Washington, Virginia)

MAY, SEE SPRING

MEATLESS MONDAY

The Meatless Monday campaign relaunched by **Sid Lerner** in 2003 to encourage Americans to cut their meat consumption by one-seventh by going meat-free on Mondays. On board to lend their support were chefs like **Mario Batali** (Babbo, Del Posto, Lupa), **Susan Feniger** (Border Grill in Las Vegas), **John**

Fraser (Dovetail, Nix), **Mary Sue Milliken** (Border Grill in Las Vegas), **Marcus Samuelsson** (Red Rooster), **Nancy Silverton** (Osteria Mozza), **Ivy Stark** (Dos Caminos), and **Bill Telepan** (Oceana).

Participating restaurants—which also include New York City's Cookshop, db bistro modern, Dell'Anima, Dos Caminos, Pondicheri, Smorgas Chef, and the Meatball Shop; Aspen's Matsuhisa, Baltimore's Woodberry Kitchen, D.C.'s Teaism, and Las Vegas's Otto—pledge to offer meatless entrée options in addition to their regular menu on Mondays.

Participating in Meatless Monday can increase your business, reduce costs, and show the public your commitment to public health and global sustainability.

—MEATLESSMONDAY.COM

MENUS

Who says menus are just for restaurants? Make—and regularly expand—a **menu** of choices for yourself at home, so that when you're hungry but not sure what you're in the mood for, you can scan the list and see what sounds best to you. Track your options, and use them as a shopping list so that you're sure to have the staples on hand to make your favorites.

MENUS, EXPERIMENTAL SECTION OF

A section of the menu at chef **Ted Hopson** and beverage director **Ann-Marie Verdi**'s new Los Angeles restaurant, the Bellwether, is labeled "R&D: works in progress," to signify to customers that these dishes and cocktails are still in the **experimental stage** of the creative process.

On June 30, 2016, the three featured dishes in that section included Crispy Soft Shell Crab, Soba Noodle Salad, Sichimi Togarashi, Soy Marinated Egg; Heirloom Tomato Salad, Greek Salami Vinaigrette, Sorrel, Pita Crumble; and Thyme Is on My Side, House Infused Thyme Tito's Vodka, Elderflower, Lemon, Raspberry.

It serves the same function as a new restaurant's soft opening: a chance to test out as-yet-unperfected ideas on customers adventurous enough to be willing to give them a shot.

MENU STRUCTURE

A classic French menu might include *amuses-bouches*, soup, fish, poultry/meat, cheeses, sorbet, dessert, coffee, *petit fours*, and chocolates.

Since 2002, elBulli only offered a multicourse tasting menu, often consisting of 30 to 35 courses, some no larger than a single bite. The dishes would vary not only by season, but by any particular night, with Adrià vowing to never serve the same menu twice. Dinner there would begin with a ritual introduction to Ferran Adrià in the kitchen. At the table, the menu that unfolded would have consisted of "cocktails" (liquid, semisolid, or solid in form, they could be deconstructed martinis or piña coladas), "snacks," tapas dishes, avant-dishes, desserts, and at the end "morphings."

Examples: a cocktail might be followed by spherical olives, an olive oil spring served in a jewelry box on a bed of salt, mango disks, carrot chips, Parmesan marshmallows, savory Oreos, a popcorn cloud, a golden egg, tempura, melon "caviar," peanut ice cream, mussels with

How you eat is as important as what you eat.

—FERRAN ADRIÀ

a "gargillou" of seaweed, crunchy almonds and tender truffles, mussels with "kikurague," fake "tartufo" of Iberian ham with olive oil, sushi for dessert, and "morphings" e.g., "pink coral," or dark chocolate coated by sour raspberry powder, or "strawberries and pearls."

Today, many restaurant menus tend more toward the unstructured, with groups of guests sharing a variety of small plates. Some chefs like **Tom Colicchio** wish to impose some order on the chaos in order to improve the guest experience, and at certain of his restaurants, the kitchen will send dishes out in an order designed to enhance enjoyment.

MENU TERMS, JAMES BEARD SEMIFINALIST

The *San Francisco Chronicle* reported in May 2016 that "San Francisco–based Quid used its language-analysis software to analyze 292 current restaurant menus from the 2016 James Beard Award semifinalists. The categories included Rising Star Chef, Best New Restaurant, Outstanding Chef, Outstanding Restaurant, and Best Chef in 10 regions."

- The three largest cities represented were **New York** (10 percent), **Chicago** (6 percent), and **San Francisco** (5.3 percent).
- The two most **frequently mentioned descriptors** on menus: **"pickled"** (155 mentions, or more than half the menus) and **"smoked"** (141 mentions).
- **Egg** is becoming one of the most popular animal proteins on menus, ahead of **chicken**—191 vs. 178 mentions.
- The 25 most common ingredient or descriptor words on the James Beard Award semifinalist menus were: 1) **pickled**, 2) **chile**, 3) **smoked**, 4) **strawberry**, 5) **asparagus**, 6) **green garlic**, 7) **herbs**, 8) **cauliflower**, 9) **Pecorino**, 10) **sorrel**, 11) **Wagyu**, 12) **cabbage**, 13) **curry**, 14) **fried**, 15) **ramps**, 16) **sweet potato**, 17) **beef**, 18) **black**, 19) **fermented**, 20) **Gulf**, 21) **halibut**, 22) **kimchi**, 23) **poached**, 24) **rhubarb**, and 25) **sautéed**.

Imagine: If you wanted to create a menu that would help you gain attention for awards consideration, would you incorporate more of the ingredients or techniques mentioned? Or would you avoid them all to set yourself apart as unique?

MILK + COOKIES

Childhood is one of the most frequently cited sources of inspiration by leading chefs. Ever wonder if any of their mothers could have imagined that **milk and cookies** would inspire their restaurant offerings?

Imagine: What would be *your* ultimate take on milk + cookies?

Cereal Milk Ice Cream and Compost Cookies
—Christina Tosi, Milk Bar (New York City)

Chocolate Chip Cookie and Organic Milk Shots [warm cookie in the shape of a shot glass, filled with cold organic milk]
—Dominique Ansel, Dominique Ansel Bakery (New York City)

Chocolate Chip Cookie Dough Soufflé with Milk Ice Cream
—Anne Specker, Kinship (Washington, D.C.)

Gramercy Tavern Cookie Plate with Milk
—Miro Uskokovic, Gramercy Tavern (New York City)

Triple Chocolate Chunk Cookie with Milk
—Miro Uskokovic, Untitled (New York City), above

MILLENNIALS, SEE GENERATION TO GENERATION

MINIMALISM

When we opened Alinea, one of our creative roads was to look at a dish on paper or in front of us and ask, "What else? What else can we do? What else can we add? What can we add to make this better?" Now, I feel like we find ourselves constantly asking, "What can we take away?"

—**GRANT ACHATZ,** Alinea (Chicago), as quoted on Eater.com

Coco Chanel would say, "Before you leave the house, look in the mirror and take one thing off." It's good advice for creating a dish: What ingredient can you take off?

—**JAMES KENT,** The NoMad (New York City)

Imagine: When you're tasting a dish, think about which ingredient is nonessential that you might skip next time.

MISSION (SEE ALSO MANIFESTO ENTRIES)

When we look at a plate of food, we should see the greater ecosystem too. . . . I can see great potential in not dividing knowledge and flavor (just as in art, we should not separate form and content). . . . Food can be political. Food can be about responsibility, sustainability, geography, and culture.

—**RENÉ REDZEPI,** in his cookbook *Noma*

We must protect the sea, the fields, the rivers.

—**ALEX ATALA,** D.O.M. (São Paulo)

We must use food to advance social imperatives.

—**CLAUS MEYER,** co-founder, Noma

Imagine: What is your **mission** when you cook? Don't have one? Think you'd cook (and eat) any differently if you did? What might you choose as your mission?

MONOMANIA

Pizza joints have specialized in celebrating and perfecting a single dish for years. But today when a restaurant focuses on a signature dish or even a signature ingredient, it's "monomania" in action.

There are increasing examples of places singling out for celebration apples, artichokes, Belgian fries, biscuits, casseroles, cereal, churros, clams (e.g., the Clam in New York City), eggs, garlic, grilled cheese (San Francisco's American Grilled Cheese Kitchen), katsu, kolachis, macaroni and cheese (New York City's S'MAC), meatballs, meatloaf, oatmeal, oysters (**Guy Savoy**'s L'Huitrade, Swan Oyster Depot), pelmeni, pho, potatoes, ramen, rice pudding, soufflés, soups, taquitos, tempura, truffles, and more. In an era of greater and greater specialization, it seems an inevitable development.

Imagine: Is there an ingredient or a dish you love enough to make yourself the world's greatest expert at cooking?

MORNING VS. NIGHT

According to a study published in the journal *Thinking & Reasoning* in 2012, those who work better at night can expect inspiration to pop in the morning, while morning people are most creative at night.

M

MOTHER'S DAY (SEE ALSO SPRING)

Date: 2nd Sunday in May

Thirty-two percent of mothers surveyed say having a meal at a restaurant with their loved ones is the best gift they could receive [on Mother's Day]. And their families know it: Mother's Day is the most popular dining-out holiday, followed by Valentine's Day and Father's Day.

—**NATIONAL RESTAURANT ASSOCIATION** (May 9, 2017)

NAME, WHAT'S IN A

Giving context to the dishes you're serving can enhance your guests' appreciation and enjoyment of them.

That's partly why **Rick Bayless**'s team at Chicago's Topolobampo dedicated themselves to analyzing their dishes and naming the categories they fall into on the restaurant's menu. Chef de cuisine **Andres Padilla** told us, "We came up with **vibrant** (e.g., acidic, bright, and tart ceviche), **fresh** (salads, vegetables), **ancient** (pre-Columbian corn-, masa-, and bean-based dishes), **soulful** (chilaquiles, tinga), **bold** (in-your-face spicy dishes, like those we marinate in achiote), **complex** (rich sauces, such as mole negro), **enchanting** (lighter fruit-based desserts), and **luxurious** (indulgent desserts, such as cajeta crepes with plantains). Featuring dishes characterized by their profiles makes the menu more exciting."

Topolobampo's menu is divided into eight categories, based on multiple meetings we held to discuss the major flavor profiles of our food. We were on our phones and using thesauruses to come up with the one word that would capture each major category.

—**ANDRES PADILLA,** Topolobampo (Chicago)

In addition, tasting menus at restaurants across the country and around the globe are also becoming more creatively named. To wit:

The Colours of the Lagoon and of the Countryside [four-course menu]; and **What Is New Is Unforgettable!** [five-course menu]

—Emanuele Scarello, Agli Amici, Michelin two-star restaurant (Italy)

Flora (vegetable-driven) and **Fauna** (meat-driven) [two main tasting menu options]

—Curtis Duffy, Grace (Chicago)

Land and Sea (omnivorous) and **Field and Forest** (vegetarian)

—Gunnar Gíslason, Agern (New York City)

Our Enduring Classics; Our Menu of the Moment; and **The Good Earth** (Our Vegetarian Creations)

—Patrick O'Connell, The Inn at Little Washington (Washington, Virginia)

U.P. (Unlimited Possibilities, an after-hours all-dessert tasting menu) features themes like **American Dreams,** whose featured desserts have names like Eureka!; Carpe Diem; White Picket Fence; Peace; Wall Street; Tech Boom; #GoingViral; and A Wish

—Dominique Ansel, Dominique Ansel Kitchen (New York City)

> **Come forth into the light of things, Let Nature be your teacher.**
>
> —WILLIAM WORDSWORTH

N

NATURE

Nature is an important source of inspiration to many. **Soren Ledet** of Copenhagen's Geranium is one who has spoken of his need to be close to nature. "It makes us relax and feel in harmony with our surroundings," he says. "I am always trying to search for ways to give this connection to our guests here. Our location is urban but you can see the sky, the forests, water as well as the Olympic stadium."

Go for a walk in the sun, somewhere you can be around trees and flowers, if not in the mountains, in a forest, or near the shore. Breathe in the air of the season, of the day.

Imagine: Look. Listen. What is nature telling you?

*We'll never forget finding ourselves in New York's Central Park one rainy day, when the raindrops on the leaves shimmered like diamonds. A few months later, we were in awe when **Dominique Crenn** perfectly captured the beauty of that moment in this dish at San Francisco's Atelier Crenn that was sprinkled with beet "snow" that melted the moment it landed on the leaf-shaped plate, recreating our memories with stunning immediacy, beauty, and flavor.*

> **Ferran Adrià starts with the bounty of nature and then moves on to the bounty of the imagination to do things that have never been done before and that can give us something more from the experience of cooking and eating than we've gotten in the past.**
>
> —**HAROLD McGEE,** author of *On Food and Cooking*

NEUROGASTRONOMY

Neurogastronomy studies the human brain, and the ways in which it might perceive food differently. **Heston Blumenthal** of the Fat Duck plays with a technique—called *encapsulation*—through which a few strategically presented big pops of flavor are more impactful than using a larger quantity throughout an entire dish would have been. This technique allows him to reduce the overall amount of, say, salt or sugar in a dish.

Imagine: What are techniques you could use to encapsulate flavor and reduce the amount of salt, sugar, or other ingredients in your next dish?

NEUROSCIENCE

If **Thomas Keller** is right, then shouldn't chefs use all the tools at their disposal to make their guests happy? What about leading-edge knowledge of **neuroscience** that suggests certain foods trigger reactions in the brain to stimulate positive emotions?

That's what Colombian chef **Juan Manuel Barrientos** strives to do at his ElCielo restaurants in Miami and South America. As he describes his approach on his restaurant's website:

> In ElCielo, we create unique gastronomic experiences that emphasize the senses. We offer a menu that is inspired by ancestral Colombian roots and the study of neurosciences. Our unique menu aims to stimulate the senses through food and gives our patrons a unique sensory journey. We call this food for the soul.
>
> We are artisans and our job is to create a memorable experience for each and every guest that comes to ElCielo.
>
> We scoured Colombia to rescue age-old recipes that have long been a standing tradition in Colombian cuisine. Our job is to find and understand our ancestral roots. We work hand in hand with the indigenous population, farmers, and cooks in Colombia to capture the essence and the magic of our amazing cuisine. We combine these traditions with innovative culinary technology and studies of neuroscience to create a modern cuisine that will resonate with the world.

ElCielo's menu includes courses like Rose Spa (a hand-washing ritual), Chocotherapy, Amazon's Tree of Life, and Rose Petal (which when rubbed on the hands turns into hand lotion, re-centering guests on earth).

Advances in nutritional science let us know that just as some substances are depressants (e.g., alcohol), others serve as mood enhancers that trigger our bodies' "happy hormones" such as serotonin. Dishes that improve brain function and keep blood sugar levels steady can essentially serve as anti-depressants. Given the stresses of air travel, in 2015 London's Gatwick Airport introduced Happy Meals, indicated with smiley-face emojis on the menu and made with mood-enhancing ingredients.

Some foods help the "happy" chemicals —neurotransmitters like **dopamine** and **serotonin**—in our brains to flow. Foods that support dopamine production include **bananas, beets, blueberries, dandelion, eggs, fish, ginkgo biloba, ginseng, nettles, oregano, spirulina**, and **strawberries.** Carbohydrate-rich foods (e.g., **bananas**) as well as **dark chocolate, flax seeds**, and **whey protein** are among those foods said to increase levels of serotonin in the brain.

NEW

The essence of creativity is to be surprised. It's the *newness.*

Imagine: What's new? When was the last time you made a dish you'd never made before? Worked with a new ingredient?

When you acknowledge, as you must, that there is no such thing as perfect food, only the idea of it, then the real purpose of striving toward perfection becomes clear: to make people happy, that is what cooking is all about.

—THOMAS KELLER, *The French Laundry Cookbook*

A new flavor combination? A new technique? How can you incorporate something new into the dish you're making right now?

NEW DISHES

Before we put a new dish on the menu, we ask ourselves: "Is it accessible? Is it true to who we are? Is it our collective voice?"

—**GAVIN KAYSEN,** Spoon and Stable (Minneapolis)

NEW YEAR'S DAY

Date: January 1

black-eyed peas
brunch
fish
greens, braised
Hoppin' John
pork

John Fraser hosts an annual New Year's Day brunch at **Dovetail** in New York City, where in addition to unlimited Champagne he has served truffle arancini canapés, melted leek frittata with Taleggio fondue, and pineapple sticky toffee pudding.

NEW YEAR'S EVE

Date: December 31

Baked Alaska
black-eyed peas
blini
cakes
caviar
Champagne
duck
mushrooms, stuffed
noodles, long
pasta, e.g., fettucine Alfredo
salads, e.g., endive/walnut
soufflés, e.g., Grand Marnier
wines, sparkling (e.g., cava, Moscato d'Asti, prosecco, sake, sekt)

At its New Year's Eve 2016 dinner, **Eleven Madison Park** featured lobster poached with white truffle and a milk-and-custard dessert with bee-pollen ice cream. Meanwhile, its sibling restaurant **the NoMad** served black-truffle tortelloni with celery root and a milk-chocolate ganache with malted ice cream and an orange Creamsicle.

The same night in San Francisco, **MINA Test Kitchen** served Dungeness crab risotto speckled with black truffle, while in Los Angeles, **Providence** served scallop and black truffle mousseline along with uni parfait with osetra caviar.

NOSTALGIA FOODS

Ranch dressing is good on everything.

—**CHRISTINA TOSI,** Milk Bar (New York City)

Since 2015, a restaurant in St. Louis has paid the ultimate compliment to **ranch dressing:** Every dish on **Twisted Ranch**'s menu was created to celebrate the nostalgic favorite. Via flatbreads, lasagnas, salads, sandwiches, and macaroni and cheese, the restaurant lives and breathes its mission: Always Fresh, Always Delicious, and Always Twisted with Ranch.

Not only is ranch a best-selling salad dressing, but as chefs deconstruct and then reconstruct it—including with fresh dill and local buttermilk—it's also an increasingly popular way to add tang and herbaceousness to a variety of dishes:

Queens Comfort restaurant in Astoria, New York, creates wacky interpretations of childhood comfort foods—including Atomic Fire Balls: Deep-Fried Mac-n-Cheese, Sriracha, and Ranch; Disco Tots: Tater Tots, Sawmill Gravy, Cheddar; and Cap'n Crunch Chicken Fingers: Red Chili Bacon Caramel Sauce.

There may be no nostalgic food immune to chefs' reinterpretations:

- **Caitlin Dysart** at 2941 Restaurant in Falls Church, Virginia, was inspired by **baked Alaska** to create Chocolate–Peanut Butter Baked Alaska, featuring a Chocolate Biscuit, Peanut Butter Ice Cream, Caramel Ganache, Pretzel Strudel, Banana, Peanut Feuilletine, and Oranges.
- New York City piano bar Sid Gold's Request Room was inspired by the classic **egg**

N

If you make your own buttermilk, thicken it with sour cream, and add fresh spices and herbs, it's amazing. That's what ranch dressing is to me.

—**SEAN BROCK,** chef of Charleston's Husk, who's sung the praises of ranch dressing as one of the world's great recipes

Crispy Deviled Eggs with Roasted Jalapeño-Ranch Dressing
—John Mooney, Bell, Book & Candle (New York City)

Cucumbers and Cherry Tomatoes with Za'atar and Pickled Ranch Dressing
—Jon Shook and Vinny Dotolo, from a dish served at a James Beard Foundation event in Los Angeles; the duo serve pizza crust dipping sauces with their pizzas at Jon & Vinny's and report that ranch is the most popular

Garlic Fries with Homemade Ranch Dip
—Todd Ginsberg, Fred's Meat & Bread (Atlanta)

Grilled Lamb Kebab with Ranch Labneh
—Todd Ginsberg, Yalla (Atlanta)

cream to create a cocktail made with rum and classic U-Bet chocolate syrup.

- **Heston Blumenthal** was inspired by **Pop Rocks** to create Exploding Chocolate Gateau.
- **Dale Talde** writes in his *Asian-American* cookbook that Hidden Valley **Ranch Seasoning Mix + yogurt** = "Doritos-scented raita."
- Dirt Candy's **Amanda Cohen** was inspired by **Tootsie Rolls** to create Beetsie Rolls from chocolate + beets.

NOVEMBER, SEE AUTUMN AND WINTER

NUTRIENT DENSITY

Nutrient density is a relative measure of the nutrients present in a food per calorie. Foods high in nutrients and low in calories are considered nutrient dense, and most **vegetables, fresh fruits,** and **legumes** fall into this category. Foods low in nutrients and high in calories are considered "empty calories," and oils and sweeteners fall into this category, as do some high-fat cheeses and other dairy products.

Dishes that emphasize more nutrient-dense ingredients make the strongest contribution toward a more healthful diet.

Saison's **Joshua Skenes** says that this reflects the way he eats. "Since I was 19, I have been an omnivore. I only eat wild meat for the most part—meat that either I or a friend has hunted. Otherwise, I stick to sea life and mostly plants," he says, adding, "I stay away from anything processed or commodity goods."

Imagine: How could you reinvent the dish you're cooking by replacing less nutrient-dense

For me, a meal—regardless of where it is—is about taste, nourishment, pleasure, celebration with the people you are with, and feeling decent when you are done. Your body wants real food. It wants nutrient density. It wants some sort of life.

—**JOSHUA SKENES,** Saison (San Francisco)

Dark Green	Most green vegetables (and many herbs and spices)
Green	Most nongreen vegetables, fresh fruit, and legumes
Yellow	Most dried or sweeter fruits, grains, nuts, and seeds
Orange	Most dairy products (e.g., cheese, full-fat milk)
Red	Most oils and sweeteners

ingredients with more nutrient-dense ingredients?

NUTRITION, SEE DIET; LIVING LONG AND WELL; AND NUTRIENT DENSITY

"OCTAPHILOSOPHY"

Singapore chef **André Chiang**, whose Restaurant André was named number 14 of the World's 50 Best Restaurants in 2017, follows what he terms his ***octaphilosophy***—a culinary philosophy incorporating eight factors: 1) salt, 2) texture, 3) memory, 4) purity, 5) terroir, 6) south, 7) artisan, and 8) uniqueness.

Imagine: What would you consider to be the core elements of your own culinary philosophy?

OCTOBER, SEE AUTUMN

OCTOBERFEST

beer
mustard
pork
pretzels
salads, German potato
sauerkraut
sausages
schnitzel
strudel

OMOTENASHI

Omotenashi is the Japanese concept of hospitality where every need of every guest is anticipated.

Many of the basic needs of any human being can be predicted, thanks to Abraham Maslow's famed hierarchy of needs, which have as their base our **physiological** needs (e.g., air, water, food, warmth, rest), followed by **safety/security, love/belonging, esteem** (accomplishment, prestige), and **self-actualization** (achieving one's full creative potential). (See also CHAKRAS, ENNEAGRAM, and GENERATION.)

Imagine: What are the needs of the guest at your table? How can you help to meet more of them through the dining experience?

ORANGE FOODS

apricots
bell peppers, orange
cantaloupe
carrots
cheeses, e.g., American, Cheddar
clementines
guavas
mangoes
nectarines
oranges
papaya
peaches
persimmons
pumpkin
saffron
salmon
squash, e.g., acorn, butternut
sweet potatoes
tangerines

Smoked carrots with jaggery, mint, and peanuts at Parachute (Chicago)

OSCAR NIGHT

A lot of them like comfort food. . . . Perhaps they are nervous.

—**WOLFGANG PUCK,** on catering the Oscars

On the night of the annual Academy Awards, **Wolfgang Puck**'s catering company has catered the **post-Oscars dinner** at the Governors Ball for more than two decades. The menu typically includes new dishes along with long-time guest favorites, like the pot pie with truffles—totaling more than *six dozen* sweet and savory dishes in 2017.

With the 2017 menu (which featured dairy-free, gluten-free, and nut-free options as well as both vegan and vegetarian options), new executive chef and vice president **Eric Klein** brought a fresh take to the proceedings:

The usual **sushi and shellfish station** also boasted Hawaiian poke, all made to order on a custom ice bar.

Passed hors d'oeuvres included lobster corn dogs; spicy tuna tartare on sesame miso cones; sweet pea falafel with hummus and za'atar; and taro root tacos with shrimp, mango, avocado, and chipotle aioli.

Savory bites tapped comfort foods: homemade pretzels with pimento cheese; gold-dusted truffled popcorn; and roasted nuts with rosemary, cayenne, sea salt, and brown sugar.

Passed small plates included a gluten-free vegan gnocchetti with braised mushrooms and cashew cream, and a vegetarian parsnip agnolotti with black winter truffles.

Given the perpetually dieting clientele, it's curious that the menu included more than 50 different **dessert** options—ranging from a gluten-free/nut-free carrot-jalapeño pâte de fruit, to a cherry Pop-Rock Krispy Pop, to an Elderflower Champagne Parfait with Raspberry Espuma.

OSCILLATION

In his best-selling book on peak performance, *The Power of Full Engagement*, author **Tony Schwartz** describes the process of

Emily Luchetti on Taking the Subway

The chief pastry officer of the Cavalier, Marlowe, and Park Tavern (San Francisco) and chair of the James Beard Foundation board of trustees, likes taking the subway.

> The thing I love about the New York subway is the number of people it connects. Everyone is passing like strangers in the night. But if you stand and watch everyone coming and going, they're all coming *from* somewhere and someone, and going *to* somewhere and someone. And they have a whole life inside of them—with dreams, passions, frustrations, successes, and failures. And there's all of this life that's all working all at the same time that you have no idea about. And in a place as big as New York, there's so many little sub-cultures that you can pop to from subway station to subway station, from the Upper West Side to the Lower East Side. And there are all these cultures that you can connect so easily, just by a simple means of transportation. And with food, you're doing the same thing—you're bringing all of these disparate people together to share the same common experience. Food brings people together.

Emily Luchetti

> **It takes something people are familiar with and tweaks it a little bit.**
>
> —LEAH KOENIG, author of *Modern Jewish Cooking*, on her matzoh balls with chopped shallots and jalapeño, as quoted by Bill Daley in *The Chicago Tribune*

oscillation—alternating periods of exertion with periods of rest and recovery—as key to the success of peak performers.

Many chefs have regular preferred outlets for oscillation—**Rick Bayless** does yoga, while **Jean Joho** visits art museums. On her frequent visits to New York City as chairman of the board of the James Beard Foundation, pastry chef **Emily Luchetti** loves to ride the subway, finding it a source of inspiration.

Imagine: What do you do when you disengage from your work that feeds you?

PASSOVER

Date: This weeklong springtime holiday is based on the Hebrew calendar, and starts at sundown on the 15th day of the Hebrew month of Nissan, running through the 22nd day.

Some of the foods served on **Passover** are primarily symbolic: The seder plate features six foods: 1) *maror* and 2) *chazeret* are bitter herbs, e.g., horseradish and romaine, which represent the harshness of slavery; 3) *haroset*, dried fruit + nuts + wine, represents the mortar that held the stones of the pyramid together; 4) *karpas*, a raw vegetable in salt water, represents the slaves' tears; 5) *zeroa*, a meat shank, represents a sacrificed animal; and 6) *beitzah*, a hard-boiled egg, symbolizes mourning.

Other dishes are very traditional, such as:

artichokes
breads, unleavened
brisket, beef
cakes, flourless, e.g., chocolate macaroon, coconut-based, matzoh-based, nut-based
chicken, roasted
chopped liver
gefilte fish

These dishes represent more modern takes with a nod to the originals:

Brisket Braised in Cheroset (Apples + Nuts + Wine)
—Michael Solomonov, Zahav (Philadelphia)

Fragole Caramellate con Zabaglione: Caramelized Strawberries with Zabaglione
—Joyce Goldstein, guest chef, Perbacco (San Francisco)

Matzoh Ball Soup with Truffles, Morels, and Capon Consommé
—Fabio Trabocchi, Fiola (Washington, D.C.)

Matzoh Balls with Chopped Shallots and Jalapeño
—Leah Koenig, author, *Modern Jewish Cooking*

Matzoh Covered in Chocolate Ganache and Sprinkled with Fleur de Sel
—Daniel Boulud, Épicerie (New York City)

Matzoh Toffee Buttercrunch
—Magnolia Bakery (New York City)

Moroccan-Style Lamb or Vegetable Tagine with Matzoh Crepes
—Susan Feniger, Street (Los Angeles)

My Not Kosher Shallot and Thyme Matzoh
—Wolfgang Puck and Barbara Lazaroff, Spago (Beverly Hills)

Pan di Spagna alle Nocciole: Passover Hazelnut Sponge Cake
—Joyce Goldstein, guest chef, Perbacco (San Francisco)

kugel
lamb
latkes
leeks
macaroons
matzoh brei, e.g., for breakfast
meringues
salads, e.g., asparagus
soups, e.g., chicken, matzoh ball
tzimmes
wine, kosher for Passover

Finding my inspiration always means going backwards in time. I ask myself: What do I really like? What do I want to eat? And how do I make it into something classic?

—**EMMA BENGTSSON,** Aquavit (New York City), in the *Village Voice*

Emma Bengtsson

I often go back in time in search of flavors that made me feel special and try to re-create them in an original way. Other times I have dreams, wake up in the middle of the night, write an idea, and in the morning turn it into something great, and sometimes not!

—**SOREN LEDET,** Geranium (Copenhagen), in conversation with Geeta Bansal, *OC Weekly*

The secret to creativity on Passover is understanding the traditions that can't be touched (which may vary by family or by table), and using a bit of ingenuity to add a twist to others.

Think about the "flavor chords" that make Passover Passover, e.g., dried fruit (e.g., dates, figs, raisins) [+ fresh fruit (apples, pears)] + nuts (almonds, walnuts) [+ sugar] + wine.

And consider the "flavor platforms" that allow you an opportunity for emboldening flavors, such as brisket (e.g., serving spice-rubbed brisket), flourless cake, matzoh ball soup, or short ribs.

PAST, THE (SEE ALSO FUTURE, THE AND PRESENT, THE)

The past can offer up endless inspiration for a new dish—whether our collective past told through history, spice routes, folk pathways, classic dishes, migration, and cultural adaptations, or our individual memories of dishes that we were fed or even cooked ourselves throughout our childhoods.

The Restaurant at Meadowood's **Christopher Kostow** writes in his cookbook, *A New Napa Cuisine*, "I'm a product of the American Midwest, and my food memories are based on the ethnic foods—Thai, Chinese, Mexican, German—found there," adding, "**Food memories are my greatest single source of inspiration when creating a new dish**, and more often than not, they serve as my starting point."

Imagine: What are your strongest memories of your favorite things to eat as a child?

PERFECT MEAL, THE

There are 11 requirements for **an ideal meal**, according to Marinetti, who nearly a century ago presaged many aspects of the experimental gastronomy of this era:

1. Originality and harmony in the table setting (crystal, china, décor), extending to

Absolute originality in the food . . . the abolition of the knife and fork . . . the creation of simultaneous and changing canapés which contain ten, twenty flavors to be tasted in a few seconds.

—FILIPPO TOMMASO MARINETTI,
describing "the perfect meal" in *The Futurist Cookbook* (1932)

the flavors and colors of the foods.

2. Absolute originality in the food.
3. The invention of appetizing food sculptures, whose original harmony of form and color feeds the eyes and excites the imagination before it tempts the lips.
4. The abolition of the knife and fork for eating food sculptures, which can give prelabial tactile pleasure.
5. The use of the art of perfumes to enhance tasting. (Every dish must be preceded by a perfume which will be driven from the table with the help of electric fans.)
6. The use of music, limited to the intervals between courses so as not to distract the sensitivity of the tongue and palate but to help annul the last taste enjoyed by re-establishing gustatory virginity.
7. The abolition of speech-making and politics at the table.
8. The use, in prescribed doses, of poetry and music as surprise ingredients to accentuate the flavors of a given dish with their sensual intensity.
9. The rapid presentation, between courses, under the eyes and nostrils of the guests, of some dishes they will eat and others they will not, to increase their curiosity, surprise, and imagination.
10. The creation of simultaneous and changing canapés which contain ten, twenty flavors to be tasted in a few seconds. In Futurist cooking these canapés have by analogy the same amplifying function that images have in literature. A given taste of something can sum up an entire area of life, the history of an amorous passion, or an entire voyage to the Far East.
11. A battery of scientific instruments in the kitchen: ozonizers to give liquids and foods the perfume of ozone; ultra-violet ray lamps (since many foods when irradiated with ultra-violet rays acquire active properties, become more assimilable, preventing rickets in young children, etc.); electrolyzers to decompose juices and extracts, etc. in such a way as to obtain from a known product a new product with new properties; colloidal mills to pulverize flours, dried fruits, drugs, etc.; atmospheric and vacuum stills, centrifugal autoclaves, dialyzers. The use of these appliances will have to be scientific, avoiding the typical error of cooking foods under steam pressure, which provokes the destruction of active substances (vitamins, etc.) because of the high temperatures. Chemical indicators will take into account the acidity and alkalinity of these sauces and serve to correct possible errors: too little salt, too much vinegar, too much pepper, or too much sugar.

Source: *The Futurist Cookbook* by Filippo Tommaso Marinetti (1932)

PERSPECTIVE

PERSPECTIVE: point of view, especially as one regards something

Sometimes a problem can be solved by changing your **perspective.** So, change where you are in *time* (e.g., sleep on it!) and/or *space:* Turn around. Take a walk around the block. Try standing on your head.

P

See tradition from a distance.

—MASSIMO BOTTURA, Osteria Francescana (Italy)

Imagine: Think about a classic dish. How do you perceive the dish? Now, imagine the same dish from a different perspective: How would someone close to you perceive that same dish? How do you imagine someone of a different gender, age, country, dietary preference, etc. would perceive the same dish? What insights does this give you about the dish?

PESTO

What is "pesto"? The classic Italian sauce (or paste) is based on **basil + garlic [+ lemon juice] + olive oil + Parmesan + pine nuts.**

Today, however, it's often being deconstructed and reconstructed—for example:

basil = green herb/greens ⟶ arugula, beet greens, broccoli, broccoli rabe, carrot tops, chervil, chives, cilantro, collard greens, dandelion greens, fennel tops, kale, mint, mustard greens, parsley (leaves and stems), peas, radish tops, sage, scallions, sorrel, spinach, strawberry tops, tarragon, watercress

garlic = pungent allium ⟶ garlic scapes, ramps

olive oil = oil/fat ⟶ canola oil, grapeseed oil, peanut oil, walnut oil

Parmesan = hard (aged) cheese ⟶ aged Asiago, Gouda, Grana Padano, Manchego, Pecorino

pine nuts = nuttiness ⟶ almonds, macadamias, peanuts, pecans, pistachios, pumpkin seeds, sesame seeds, sunflower seeds, walnuts

Imagine: How would you use the basic idea of a "pesto" to make one that reflects a new flavor combination?

Pesto Variations

beet greens + garlic + oil + cheese + pistachios
—Amanda Cohen, Dirt Candy (New York City)

collard greens + garlic + oil + cheese + peanuts
—Joe Sparatta and Lee Gregory, Southbound (Richmond, Virginia)

mint/parsley + garlic + olive oil + Parmesan + breadcrumbs
—Massimo Bottura, Osteria Francescana (Modena, Italy)

PIES

The enduring and rising popularity of pies is evidenced by the fact that when Bouley alum **Bill Yosses** left his position as pastry chef at

the White House, it was to open Perfect Pie in New York City.

And while **apple, Key lime,** and **pecan** are America's most popular pie flavors (with **pumpkin** joining them during the holiday season), the less usual savory flavor combinations of Yosses's pies sound perfect indeed, whether it is his **chicken pot pie with truffles,** or his vegan **turmeric tofu and vegetable pie in millet crust.**

Bud Royer's Royers Roundtop Café in Round Top, Texas, has served more than a half-million pies since its opening nearly three decades ago, with classics like pecan and pumpkin pie being joined by newer flavors like Texas

Apple Crumb with Rosemary Caramel
—Cheryl Perry and Felipa Lopez, Pie Corps (Brooklyn)

Banana Cream Pie with Chocolate Shavings
—Elisabeth Prueitt and Chad Robertson, Tartine Bakery (San Francisco)

Beef Cheek and Stout Pie with Stilton Pastry
—Daniel Doherty, Duck & Waffle (London and New York City)

Blackberry Blood Orange Tart: Blackberry Almond Frangipane, Blackberry Jam, Honey-Rosemary Poached Blood Oranges, Vanilla Sable Tart Shell
—Dominique Ansel, Dominique Ansel Bakery (New York City)

Blueberry Pie (for two): Cookie Crust, Bourbon, and Lemon Thyme Ice Cream
—Scott Cioe, Bevy (New York City), see photos at left

Caramel Pumpkin Pie
—Brian Noyes, Red Truck Bakery (Warrenton, Virginia)

Pot Pie, inspired by his grandmother's use of torn chicken + chicken broth + dill + potato dumplings
—Michael Anthony, in his cookbook *V is for Vegetables*

Salted Caramel Apple Pie
—Emily and Melissa Elsen, Four & Twenty Blackbirds (Brooklyn)

Trash (chocolate + pecan) and white chocolate macadamia nut.

Both on Pi(e) Day (March 14th) and throughout the year, creative bakers look to shake up the elements of a pie in different ways:

- **Crusts,** e.g., cereal crumbs (cornflake, crisped rice, granola), cookie crumbs (Oreos, vanilla wafers) or cookie dough (oatmeal shortbread), gingersnap crumbs, graham cracker crumbs, ice cream cone crumbs, pastry, pretzel crumbs, shortbread
- **Fillings,** e.g., savory (green tomatoes) or sweet (banana cream, berries, Boston cream, chocolate cream, coconut cream, custard, pumpkin, sweet potato, vanilla custard)
- **Toppings,** e.g., chocolate shavings, nuts (pecans, walnuts), streusel, whipped cream

PILLSBURY BAKE-OFF

Who needs more incentive than a $1 million grand prize to try to whip up a new dish using at least two of a sponsor's specified products, yet no more than seven total ingredients? Indeed, as keynote speakers at the 2010 **Pillsbury Bake-Off,** we learned that a number of finalists and semifinalists swore by *The Flavor Bible* for their new recipe creation ideation for this beloved mother of all bake-offs, which has attracted tens of thousands of entries and awarded millions in prizes since its founding in 1949.

The recipe has to taste good, but creative use of sponsor products also helps. . . . To me, the cachet of the Bake-Off is that an "everyday" home cook—who isn't a movie star, a corporate pirate, a reality-show survivor, or even a celebrity chef—can use a little creativity and walk away with a million dollars.

—**VALERIE PHILLIPS,** *Deseret News,* who has covered seven-plus Bake-offs

P

$1 Million Winners and Their Dishes

2014: Peanutty Pie Crust Clusters by Beth Royals
2013: Loaded Potato Pinwheels by Glori Spriggs
2012: Pumpkin Ravioli with Salted Caramel Whipped Cream by Christina Verrelli
2010: Mini Ice Cream Cookie Cups by Sue Compton

My "O My Ganache" Cherry Macaroon Torte got me into the finals. I love the individual flavors of cherries and coconut, but a two-ingredient recipe would not fly. My torte was born out of looking up these ingredients to see what I might add to the mix as a connecting idea. Create from what you love. Of course, chocolate is a top ten love. Almonds also came into play as a connecting taste and texture. Texture is the forgotten flavor in my rules of creating. . . . My Cheesey Chorizo Breakfast Pizza got me into the semifinals. . . . I used *The Flavor Bible* to look at all the potential combos and especially regional favorites.

—DENNIS DEEL of Wooster, Ohio, multiple-time Pillsbury Bake-Off finalist or semifinalist

She nailed it as far as all the things we were looking for. She put her own twist on something.

—ALICE CURRAH, *PBS Parents* columnist and author, and Pillsbury Bake-Off judge, on 2013 winner Glori Spriggs

2008: Double Delight Peanut Butter Cookies by Carolyn Gurtz
2006: Baked Chicken and Spinach Stuffing by Anna Ginsberg
2004: Oats 'n Honey Granola Pie by Suzanne Conrad
2002: Chicken Florentine Panini by Denise Joanne Yenni
2000: Cream Cheese Brownie Pie by Roberta Sonefeld
1949: The first competition, which had a prize of $50,000, and first winning dish: No-Knead Water-Rising Twists by Theodora Smafield

PLACE (SEE ALSO ALTITUDE; LOCAL; AND TIME)

Uniqueness of time and place is the essence of almost every fine dining experience that I know of in traditional Japanese cooking and other forms of serious cooking.

—MICHAEL ANTHONY, Gramercy Tavern and Untitled (New York City)

A great meal, and the great dishes that comprise it, reflect a specific **place** and time.

Imagine: What is the essence of the **place** where the meal you're planning is happening?

PLATFORMS, FLAVOR

If you like a mixture such as broccoli rabe, toasted almonds, and manchego cheese with pasta, chances are it'll be great on pizza, too.

—ANNIE SOMERVILLE, Greens (San Francisco)

Every dish needs a **platform** on which to hang its flavor—such as a starch (e.g., bread, frittatas, grains, noodles, pasta, pizza dough, rice, tortillas, etc.), a vegetable (eggplant in eggplant Parmesan, peppers in stuffed peppers), an animal protein (eggs, meat, poultry, seafood) or a plant-based protein (legumes, seitan, tempeh, tofu), and/or a format (bowl, omelet, pizza, salad, sandwich, soup, stew, taco).

One's choice of a platform will often drive other decisions, given regional implications (e.g., using fish sauce vs. soy sauce to season rice).

Once you learn to deconstruct dishes into their flavor platforms and flavor chords, you can apply those chords to other platforms. (See Playing with Chords on pages 80–82.)

PLATING

We have heard so often that the way our food is organized on the plate looks like a landscape, which is true, but the plating happens quite naturally because our first inspiration is always from where we get the food, when we are out on a shoreline or in the forest. It's almost not deliberate.

—**RENÉ REDZEPI,** Noma (Copenhagen)

The website TheArtOfPlating.com has amassed more than 500,000 followers of its Instagram feed (@theartofplating), sharing photos of plated food at restaurants. Celebrating gastronomy as a form of high art is The Art of Plating's focus, according to editor **Maria Nguyen**, whose staff has assessed the Ten Essential Plating Cookbooks:

1. *The Fat Duck Cookbook*
2. *Benu*
3. *Coi: Stories and Recipes*
4. *El Celler de Can Roca*
5. *Octaphilosophy: The Eight Elements of Restaurant André*
6. *The NoMad Cookbook*
7. *D.O.M.: Rediscovering Brazilian Ingredients*
8. *Mexico from the Inside Out*
9. *Relae: A Book of Ideas*
10. *Central*

PLAY

Without the playing with fantasy, no creative work has ever yet come to birth. The debt we owe to the play of imagination is incalculable.

—**CARL JUNG**

All work and no **play** makes a cook uncreative.

As Jung also attested, "The creation of something new is not accomplished by the intellect but by the play instinct acting from inner necessity. **The creative mind plays with the objects it loves.**"

POETRY

Named the 2016 World's Best Female Chef, **Dominique Crenn** of San Francisco's Atelier Crenn puts **poetry** on a plate. The restaurant has no menus—she merely presents guests with the original poem that inspired the meal.

Vinland's **David Levi**, who has studied, taught, and written **poetry**—including on floor-to-ceiling chalkboards in his restaurant's restrooms—won't cook with ingredients that aren't local to Portland, Maine. Still, he doesn't see cooking 100 percent local as a restriction any more than he thinks of writing a sonnet as a restriction. "I think of it as form," he says. "And every form allows for its own possibilities—which don't exist in the absence of it."

Levi believes the reason some see it that way is because it's uncommon. "People wouldn't ask an Italian restaurant why they weren't using miso, and they wouldn't ask a Japanese restaurant why they aren't using miso," he argues, saying he finds

P

David Levi

Vinland's form "liberating," because it allows him to do whatever he wishes within it, taking inspiration from Italy or Japan or anywhere else. "Our '100 percent local' form sparks tremendous creativity," he says. As does New Formalism in poetry.

POPCORN / POPPED GRAINS

People have been **popping corn** for ages, but chefs are getting more creative about popping a greater variety of grains (including **amaranth**, **quinoa**, and **sorghum**), which are being used for texture and flavor in dishes, ranging from salads to hot entrées to desserts.

At the 2017 post-Oscars Governors Ball, Wolfgang Puck Catering's executive chef **Eric Klein** served a cold passed small plate of chopped salad with shaved carrots, feta, Dijon-Champagne vinaigrette, and popped sorghum.

POP-UP RESTAURANTS, SEE LOCATION LOCATION LOCATION

POUTINE

Who'd have thought that the humble Canadian dish **poutine**—cheese curds over French fries, smothered with gravy—could inspire high-end chefs across America to riff on it, such as with locally sourced cheese curds? Local chefs' versions have proven so popular that a 2017 *Seattle Times* headline declared, "Poutine Is the New Nachos."

Curried Fries: Homemade Fries with Fresh Paneer and Curry

—Amanda Cohen, Dirt Candy (New York City), created as an ode to the Toronto native's Canadian roots

Poutine o' the Sea: Thick clam chowder poured over open-faced littleneck clams and fries, with bacon bits

—The White Swan Public House (Seattle)

Poutine with Pimento Cheese and Bacon Gravy

—Witness Bar (Seattle)

PRESENT, THE (SEE ALSO FUTURE, THE AND PAST, THE)

Be in the moment. Use all your senses.

Imagine: What do you desire to eat? How do you desire to feel—*right now?*

PRESENTATION

It is likely not even conscious the extent to which we eat with our eyes. But every sighted person does.

We can avoid the misperception that a dish is common by its uncommon **presentation**—for example, serving a soup not in a bowl with a spoon, but in a shot glass accented by a tempura-ed vegetable whose flavor echoes that of the soup (as they do at **Patrick O'Connell**'s Inn at Little Washington in Virginia) or serving crudités not on a platter but in a bowl molded from ice (as they do at **Andrew Carmellini**'s Little Park in New York City). While the classic white plate will never go out of style (or will it?), chefs are having fun presenting their creations on alternative surfaces, ranging from slate to manmade materials to an iPad.

Michael Tusk of San Francisco's Quince playfully

> **It's really about filling ourselves with interesting knowledge that's within our trade. With the right team, you're able to take all of these lessons and bring them into the now, the moment we are standing in, so something new happens. It's difficult, though, to see the synergies between something in the past and something in the now.**
>
> —**RENÉ REDZEPI,** Noma (Copenhagen)

Kyle Connaughton of Single Thread in Healdsburg, California, contrasts the Western approach with the Eastern philosophy he learned while cooking in Japan: "There are important guiding principles behind Japanese arts, including plating aesthetics, called *ten-chi-jin,* which means heaven [*ten,* often represented by the tallest element on a plate], earth [*chi,* which is suggestive of the horizon, or where the ocean meets the shore], and human [*jin,* which is the focal point on the plate]. The way I arrange a dish will have elements of this aesthetic, as will the way [Kyle's wife and the restaurant's farmer] Katina puts together a flower arrangement, so that there is interconnectivity between both in the dining room."

In Western philosophy, there is a fairly limited number of rules guiding presentation, such as putting an odd number of things on a plate and providing negative space.

—**KYLE CONNAUGHTON,** Single Thread (Healdsburg, California), who credits his time cooking in Japan with developing his aesthetic sensibility

presents a dish called A Dog in Search of Gold—porcini-dusted white truffle fritter with salt-roasted celeriac and roasted porcini mushroom, accented by a chestnut puree and roasted chestnut—on an actual iPad (albeit one covered with plexiglass and served in a custom wooden box) playing a video of the moment a truffle dog first uncovers a truffle during a hunt.

Example:

Crusty Gamba on a White Plate Shaped and Decorated with Algae to Resemble the Sand and the Small Rocks of a Seabed

—Joan Roca, El Celler de Can Roca (Spain)

P

PRESENTATION, ANTI-

"This is it? This looks like a pile of shit."

—IGNACIO MATTOS, Estela (New York City), caricaturing some customers' impressions of his dishes' presentation

Ignacio Mattos is a chef whose presentation style sometimes gets no respect—even as his dishes' bold and complex flavors and textures get mad respect at his restaurant Estela, which ranked number 44 on the 2016 World's Best Restaurants list.

We were puzzled by the seeming over-simplicity of Mattos's winter endive salad [in which whole endive leaves sit like little canoes atop toasted walnuts and crumbled cheese]—until we tasted and interacted with it, getting to know the dish (and, wordlessly, the chef's intention that we scoop the latter into the open crevice of the former) as we simultaneously learned something about our preconceptions and prejudices. To our amazement, that "simple" salad stayed with us as one of our most memorable dishes of the year—without a single pyrotechnic trick in sight.

PRIORITIZATION

What is most important to you as a cook? Your cuisine is the sum of all the decisions you make. Where would you rank the **importance** of local vs. quality, for example?

Imagine: Consider every factor you believe to be important to good cooking—e.g., abundance, aroma, balance, flavor, freshness, harmony, healthfulness, quality, regionality, ripeness, seasonality, variety—and rank them in order of importance to you.

PROBLEM-SOLVING (SEE ALSO FOOD WASTE; SEAFOOD, SUSTAINABLE; AND SUSTAINABILITY / SUSTAINABLE CUISINE)

Creativity is called for when contemplating solutions to the **problems** facing us—and especially so the larger those problems are.

We live in a world that is from one perspective perfect and limitless, and from another wrought with challenges, some of which might be considered "acts of God" (e.g., droughts) and others entirely man-made (e.g., pollution, overfishing, unsustainable levels of meat consumption).

With regard to the former, co-hosts of PBS's *Growing a Greener World,* chef **Nathan Lyon** and his partner **Sarah Forman,** were spurred by California's drought to teach people ways to reduce water waste in the kitchen—including by cooking with vegetables and fruits that require less water to grow (which the website **waterfootprint.org** tracks), by using cooking techniques that require less water (e.g., favoring grilling over boiling), and by re-using water (e.g., cooking water and/or ice, on plants).

PROTEIN

The average American adult requires just 50 to 60 grams of **protein** a day, which can easily be provided by a plant-based (i.e., vegetarian or vegan) diet. However, the average American typically consumes 70 to 100 grams of protein a day, primarily from animal-based sources (e.g., meats, poultry, seafood)—a level of overconsumption that correlates with a higher risk of diseases such as heart disease, Alzheimer's disease, and certain cancers, as well as other health problems (e.g., higher blood cholesterol levels, plus higher risks of atherosclerosis, osteoporosis, and kidney stones).

Menus of Change, a joint project of the Culinary Institute of America and Harvard T. H. Chan School of Public Health's Department of Nutrition, helps chefs and cooks reduce the level of animal protein in meals through the "protein flip." This approach encourages chefs to substitute plant or other animal proteins with a smaller environmental footprint than red meat. The California-based Mushroom Council is working with the James Beard Foundation's **Blended Burger Project** to promote the blending of mushrooms into dishes such as burgers, meatballs, and tacos as more sustainable, nutritious, and flavorful.

PURE FOOD

Europeans already consider artificial ingredients (whether artificial colorants, GMO foods, or meat from animals raised on antibiotics) to be verboten, and Americans are starting to follow suit. Chefs surveyed by the National Restaurant Association deemed "**natural ingredients/ minimally processed food**" as the fifth biggest trend for 2016.

PURPLE FOODS (SEE ALSO BLACK FOODS AND BLUE FOODS, AS HUES VARY)

Pastry chef **Dominique Ansel** set out on a quest to find a taste for the color **purple**—which led him to create his Purple Tart, combining blackberries, Concord grapes, and plums. Their commonality is color, which then led him to discover and celebrate their flavor commonalities as well.

asparagus
blackberries
butterfly pea plants, whose (dried and powdered) bluish-purple flower petals are used to color cocktails, rice, and tea
cabbage
carrots
cauliflower
corn, purple
Disco Sour, a cocktail made with butterfly pea flower, which changes from blue to purple when citrus is added
eggplant
endive
grapes, purple, e.g., Concord
olives
peppers
plums
potatoes, purple
rice, purple
wheat, purple
wine, red

QUALITY

Quality is about the product, and the variables we can control to make something taste its best.

—**JOSHUA SKENES,** Saison (San Francisco)

Quality and flavor are the two most important things, "because ultimately [we are in] the pleasure business, and you have to bring people some sort of joy," explains Saison's **Joshua Skenes.** "**In the kitchen, it is about the product.** We obsess about finding the product, and that is the hard part. **Our purpose is to find the best that is in existence.** We even employ fishermen and we are buying a boat for them. . . . [Ours] brings all our fish fresh from the ocean with no middleman."

"We think about everything involved in the process," Skenes adds. "**We want to get the best product at the right time** when it is truly ready. **Everything has a sweet spot.** We handle it in a certain way, begin the cooking process at a certain time, and get the timing all right. **Then, we get it into someone's mouth where it actually means something.**"

QUIETNESS (CONTRAST WITH LOUDNESS)

Some flavors shout—these are some that whisper:

bean sprouts
bread
cauliflower
crackers
flour
grains, e.g., farro, quinoa
noodles
oats
pasta
potatoes, mashed
rice
tofu
vanilla
water

RAINBOW FOODS

Be a rainbow in someone else's cloud.

—MAYA ANGELOU

Rainbows keep inspiring creations that showcase a spectrum of colors.

Baker **Scot Rossillo** of the Bagel Store in the Williamsburg section of Brooklyn had a viral hit with his blue-green-orange-purple-yellow-hued **Rainbow Bagels,** which he'd been making for two decades, but trended as New Yorkers embraced their inner rainbows.

Amanda Cohen launched Dirt Candy's new larger Allen Street location with **rainbow-colored monkey bread,** featuring conjoined balls of dough baked in a flower pot, along with a **rainbow-hued vegetable ice cream salad** that was as easy on the eye as it was on the palate.

At the end of 2015, **Dominique Ansel** created a **Rainbow Mille-Feuille,** which alternated puff pastry with layers of blueberry, clementine, lemon, mint, and raspberry pastry creams.

Not to be outdone in the realm of circular rainbow pastries, Moe's Doughs Donut Shop in Brooklyn launched its own **Rainbow Donut** in 2016.

For years now at Virginia's Inn at Little Washington, breakfast has included **a rainbow-colored flight of fresh-squeezed juices.**

Imagine: What rainbow-hued foods or drinks or flights would you actually find it fun to taste? Want to turn that fantasy into your next dish?

RAMADAN

Dates: A 30-day period falling between June and August, the Muslim holiday of Ramadan takes place during the ninth month of the Islamic calendar.

beans, broad
breads, e.g., pita
cheeses
couscous
custards, fruit
dal
dates
dumplings
fasting, sunrise to sunset
fattoush
fritters, e.g., paneer, vegetables
fruit, fresh
hummus
Indian cuisine
Indonesian cuisine
jackfruit
Lebanese cuisine
meats, halal
Middle Eastern cuisines
milk
North African cuisines
Pakistani cuisine
rice-based dishes, e.g., biryani
Rooh Afza (carrot + coriander + mint + orange + pineapple + rose petals + spinach)
salads, e.g., fattoush, tabbouleh
soups, e.g., harira, lentil, tomato, vegetable
stews, e.g., bean
stuffed vegetables, e.g., eggplant, peppers, tomatoes, vine leaves, zucchini
sweets
tabbouleh
tea, mint
Turkish cuisine
vegetables, fresh
yogurt
zucchini, *e.g., stuffed*

RATIOS

The more we know about cooking, the less we believe in recipes.

There are simply too many variables to be able to expect to follow a recipe to the letter in order to end up with a great

In Washington, D.C., even during slavery time, some of the diplomats would send their cooks to French cooking schools, and that would create a lot of good cooking around Washington. My aunt had cooked in Washington, and came back and lived three towns away. I used to go and visit her, and her kitchen smelled divine. She was a great cook. I didn't cook at her house, but I just tasted her food and noted what she was doing. She had a dime on the table all the time for her baking soda, and a nickel for her cream of tartar. I think that was pretty common, using a dime and a nickel [to measure out the soda and tartar in a 2:1 ratio to make one's own baking powder].

—**EDNA LEWIS**, the late chef called the Julia Child of the South by *The Washington Post*, as quoted in our book *Becoming a Chef* (1995)

Chefs also express different preferences for acidity, such as in their preferred ratio of oil to vinegar in a simple vinaigrette (perhaps ranging from 3:1 to 5:1).

—*BECOMING A CHEF* (1995)

dish. Having a developed palate, good judgment, and seasoning know-how is far more important.

However, we are big believers in **rules of thumb**, the kind of guidelines that can get you in the ballpark to achieve whatever you want to achieve, whether mixing up a cocktail or getting dinner on the table quickly. Through our research for *Becoming a Chef*, we realized how long chefs have been using these rules of thumb, or ratios. With the increasing importance of legumes and grains at the center of the plate with vegetables, it's helpful to keep in mind rules of thumb for cooking them—even if the exact thickness of your pot and the tightness of your lid differ from ours and call for slightly different ratios. For example:

Ingredient	Ratio of Ingredient to Cooking Liquid
Amaranth	1:3
Barley	1:3
Barley, pearled	1:2½ to 1:3½
Beans, Anasazi	1:3
Buckwheat	1:2 to 1:3
Bulgur	1:1½ (finer) to 1:2½ (coarser)
Cornmeal	1:3 (firm, to grill or sauté) to 1:5 or 1:6 (soft, creamy cornmeal or polenta)
Couscous	1:1 to 1:2
Farro	1:2 to 1:3
Lentils, black	1:2¼
Lentils, brown	1:3
Lentils, French	1:2½
Lentils, green	1:2½
Lentils, red	1:2
Quinoa	1:1½ to 1:2
Rice, Arborio	1:3 to 1:3½
Rice, basmati	1:1½
Rice, black	1:2
Rice, brown	1:2
Rice, jasmine	1:1½
Rice, sticky	1:1⅓
Rice, sushi	1:1½
Wild rice	1:3 to 1:4

In the world of cocktails, you can make a virtually endless number of dynamite drinks by applying Pegu Club owner **Audrey Saunders**'s magic formula below. Simply fill in the blanks with your favorites.

R

Sour cocktails: 2 ounces base liquor + ¾ ounce sour + ¾ ounce sweet

—Audrey Saunders, mixologist and owner, Pegu Club (New York City), on the "secret recipe" behind her famed sour cocktails

For example:

base liquor: rum, tequila, vodka, whiskey

+ **sour**: lemon juice, lime juice, grapefruit juice

+ **sweet**: simple syrup, fruit juice, honey, maple syrup

These are common ways of shaking things up (so common, you'll recognize their names!), but you can use them to inspire your own combinations:

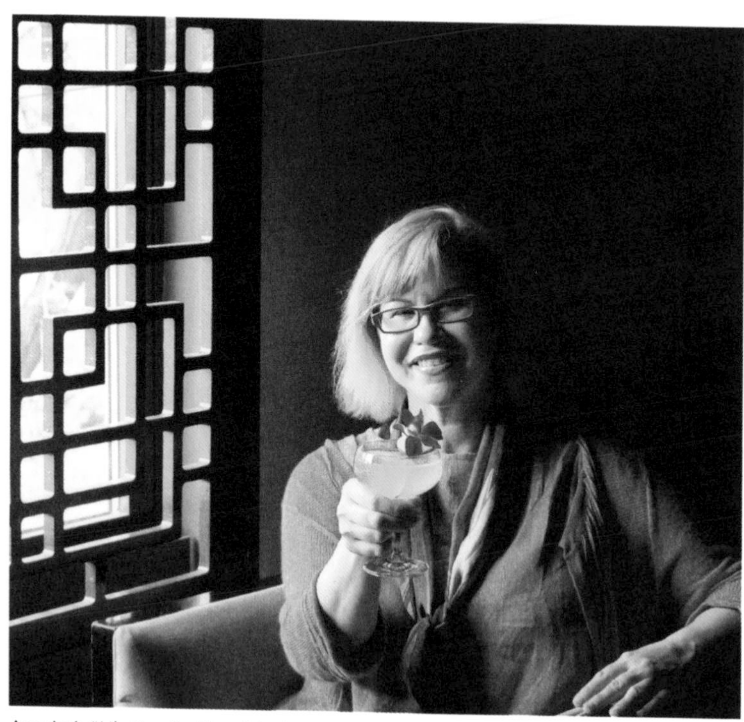

America's "Libation Goddess," Audrey Saunders, at the Pegu Club (New York City)

Base Liquor	Sour	Sweet	Other	Cocktail
rum	+ lime juice	+ simple syrup		= daiquiri
rum	+ lime juice	+ simple syrup	+ club soda + mint	= mojito
tequila	+ lime juice	+ simple syrup	+ orange liqueur	= margarita
vodka	+ lime juice	+ triple sec + cranberry juice	+ orange twist	= cosmopolitan
vodka	+ lime juice	+ triple sec		= kamikaze
whiskey	+ lemon juice	+ simple syrup + maraschino cherry + orange wheel half		= whiskey sour

Likewise, New York City mixologist **Colin Asare-Appiah**, who also serves as the senior portfolio brand ambassador for Bacardi, has shared his simple ratio for a balanced punch: "One of sour, two of sweet, three of strong, four of weak."

See also: *Ratio* by Michael Ruhlman

RED FOODS

apples
beans, cranberry
beets, beet juice, and beet-hued foods, e.g., pastas
bell peppers, red
blood oranges
cabbage, red
cayenne and cayenne-hued foods, e.g., pasta
chard, red
cherries
chiles, red
cranberries
grapefruit, pink
guava
nasturtiums
onions, red
paprika and paprika-hued foods, e.g., pasta
pastas, e.g., colored with cayenne or paprika

Marc Aumont's buttermilk + rhubarb + strawberry dessert

pomegranates
potatoes, red
radicchio
radishes
raspberries
rhubarb
strawberries
tomatoes
watermelon
wine, red

REFRESHING

When a food or drink is described as **refreshing**, what factors play a role in that determination? In one study, participants named **temperature, sweetness, smoothness, juiciness, wetness,** and **color** as among the key factors. (Some of our own favorite refreshers include raspberry lemonade and watermelon salad with feta.)

Imagine: How could you use this information to create a new dish or drink that's likely to be found to be refreshing?

REINVENTING THE WHEEL

You don't have to do it.

Imagine: How can you simply give an old dish a new, useful, and/or fascinating spin?

RESISTANCE (CONTRAST WITH FLOW)

One of my *very* favorite books of all time, *The War of Art*, tells it like it is: The *only* thing that gets in the way of our creativity is **Resistance.**

Resistance is, of course, author Steven Pressfield's umbrella concept encompassing every single aspect of fear and doubt and self-sabotage that keeps us from creating. The more we love what we're attempting to create, the more Resistance we'll encounter.

The most important part of being creative is this: Do the work. As Pressfield tells us: "Nothing else matters except sitting down every day and trying."

> **Most of us have two lives: The life we live, and the unlived life within us. Between the two stands Resistance.**
>
> —**STEVEN PRESSFIELD,** novelist, in his nonfiction bestseller *The War of Art*

R

ROSH HASHANAH (SEE ALSO **AUTUMN**)

Dates: The Jewish New Year takes place in September or October, correlating with the Hebrew calendar dates of 1 and 2 Tishrei, and marks the beginning of the High Holy Days, a ten-day period that concludes with Yom Kippur.

APPLES
beans, e.g., string
beets
brisket
carrots
challah bread, sweetened with honey
chard, Swiss
chicken, baked
dates
fish
fruit
gefilte fish
gourds, e.g., **pumpkin, squash**
greens, e.g., spinach, Swiss chard
heads, e.g., cabbage, fish, garlic, sheep
HONEY
kugel
latkes
leeks
peas, black-eyed
pomegranates
soup, chicken
spinach

ST. PATRICK'S DAY

Date: March 17
What it is: A day when everyone is Irish

beer, e.g., green, Guinness, Irish
boiled dinner, e.g., cabbage, corned beef, potatoes
breads, e.g., Irish brown, Irish soda
cabbage
champ, i.e., mashed potatoes with scallions
cheeses, e.g., Cashel Blue, Cheddar, farmhouse, goat, and/or Irish
corned beef
green foods
lamb, spring
potatoes
salmon, smoked Irish
soup, e.g., colcannon, potato-leek
shepherd's pie
stew, e.g., beef, Irish, lamb
trout, smoked
whiskey, Irish

> **The wildly inventive Sam Mason of OddFellows Ice Cream Company has created three flavors spiked with Irish whiskeys just in time for St. Patrick's Day: burned marshmallow; Dead Rabbit Irish coffee, based on a recipe from the lower Manhattan bar; and a 14-year-old single-malt ice cream with sherry caramel syrup.**
>
> —**FLORENCE FABRICANT,** *New York Times*

SALT-BAKED AND SAND-BAKED DISHES

Salt-baked dishes have been around for more than 2,000 years, since the ancient Chinese perfected the technique as a means of retaining moisture and cooking evenly when roasting chicken and fish. They're still readily found on contemporary restaurant menus, and applied to seafood (e.g., salmon), poultry, and vegetables (beets, carrots, celery root, parsnips, potatoes, and other root vegetables) alike. Salt-baked dishes by chefs like **Alain Passard** at L'Arpège in Paris and **Gunnar Gíslason** at Agern are presented and cracked open at guests' tables, as in:

> **Salt and Ash Baked Beet Root, with horseradish and huckleberries**
>
> —Gunnar Gíslason, Agern (New York City)

But a newer twist being seen at upscale restaurants is using sand as a medium for **sand-baked** dishes—from bread (e.g., brown bread) to vegetables (beans) to seafood (clams, snapper) and poultry (chicken). Ingredients are wrapped in foil, plastic, and cloth in order to protect them from the sand and to seal in aroma and flavor.

Other contemporary chefs are experimenting with taking

things a step deeper by cooking in the earth—via open pits or earth ovens, another ancient technique.

SAVORY ↔ SWEET DISHES (SEE ALSO INVERSIONS, FOOD)

Chefs are creating **savory versions of traditionally sweet dishes—and vice versa**—making it a top trend.

Take a food that is typically served sweet, and imagine a savory version of it. Examples:

- **babka:** anchovies + fennel + olives, from Thierry Marx of Michelin two-star Cordeillan-Bages in Paulliac
- **bread pudding:** cheese + mushroom +/or seasonal vegetables
- **chocolate sauce:** mole made with dark chocolate + nuts + seeds
- **Dutch baby pancakes:** cheese + herbs; crème fraîche + lox + onions
- **French toast:** garlic + herbs + Parmesan
- **ice cream:** Daniel Boulud's foie gras ice cream; Morimoto's sea urchin ice cream
- **kugelhopf:** Gabriel Kreuther's savory version, served with chive + fromage blanc
- **panna cotta:** flavored with beets, cauliflower, corn, parsnips, peas
- **tarte Tatin:** flavored with caramelized red onions, shallots, or tomatoes
- **waffles:** chicken-n-waffles; potato waffles with smoked salmon + crème fraîche; Floyd Cardoz's dosa waffle with pineapple + sweet jaggery syrup
- **yogurt:** Blue Hill's, flavored with beets, butternut squash, carrots, parsnip, sweet potato, tomato

Take a food that is typically served savory, and imagine a sweet version of it—which is essentially how chocolate fondue came about. Examples:

- **burgers:** Hubert Keller's Cream Cheese Cake Burger with caramelized pineapple sandwiched between a split Krispy Kreme doughnut; and his Nutella Mousse Burger with a chocolate-nut patty, kiwi instead of pickles, and strawberries instead of tomatoes
- **carrot** cake
- chocolate **onion** cake: Amanda Cohen's version at Dirt Candy
- **eggplant** tiramisu: Amanda Cohen's version at Dirt Candy
- **pizza:** berries + chocolate + ricotta; fresh fruit + mascarpone; Nutella + nuts
- **red bean** ice cream: à la Japanese restaurants
- sweet **corn** ice cream: Claudia Fleming's version at Gramercy Tavern
- **vegetable** ice cream: Amanda Cohen's version at Dirt Candy
- **zucchini** bread

Mark Miller

SCALE

During a conversation with Coyote Café founding chef **Mark Miller** about creativity, he made an argument for CIA alum **Steve Ells** as being one of the most creative chefs in America. As former sous chef to **Jeremiah Tower** and currently the founder, CEO, and chairman of Chipotle Mexican Grill, Ells had an imaginative vision of serving "Food with Integrity" to millions—and pioneered new territory in the world of fast food by being the first national chain to serve free-range pork and source naturally raised meats through Chipotle's 2,000 locations.

S

Jacques Torres sings the praises of his friend **Eric Lecoq,** a fellow native of France, master pastry chef, and baker with an unusual gift for producing quality as well as quantity. "His croissant factory makes 50,000 croissants an hour. He has a mind for it," says Torres. "Eric started off in his garage, and still has his first rolling pin and cutter. Today, he is the number-one croissant maker in the U.S. and supplies Ritz-Carlton hotels all across the country."

Imagine: Creative ideas can be grand as well as great. How big could you make your idea?

SEAFOOD, SUSTAINABLE (SEE ALSO DOCK TO DISH)

Our oceans are in crisis: Roughly 90 percent of global fish stocks are fully or overexploited, and around 90 percent of large fish are gone. The culprit? Overfishing.

Intersecting the trends to reduce food waste and to promote **sustainable seafood** (which the National Restaurant Association named one of the top ten trends of 2016) is *bycatch*—the term given to marine life (including endangered species) such as dolphins, porpoises, seabirds, sea turtles, seals, sharks, tortoises, whales, and less-popular fish species (e.g., anchovies, dogfish, rockfish, skate, squirrelfish, tautog) that are unintentionally caught in commercial fishers' nets targeting other species. Bycatch conservatively amounts to more than 40 percent of the total catch, on average. Some forward-looking chefs and environmental advocates encourage offering those less-popular fish species on restaurant menus to reduce food waste, rather than simply tossing their carcasses overboard, which is common practice for those not used as fish bait.

Monterey Bay Aquarium opened in 1984, and in the wake of the 1990s' sustainable seafood movement's growth, in 1999 created **SeafoodWatch.org,** the consumer guide to sustainable seafood choices that are fished or farmed in ways that have less impact on the environment—with green **Best Choices** (e.g., Alaskan king crab); yellow Good Alternatives (wild sea scallops), and red Avoid (bluefin tuna) given as the July through December 2017 recommendations. There's also a free **Seafood Watch app** available with up-to-date recommendations.

Chef **Eric Ripert** is among sustainable seafood's leading advocates, and he's unwilling to serve any seafood at New York City's Le Bernardin that isn't eco-friendly (e.g., no Chilean sea bass or swordfish). Across the country in Los Angeles, Dock-to-Dish advocate **Michael Cimarusti** (an avid fisherman) runs the seafood-centered tasting menu restaurant Providence; the more casual "seafood shack" Connie and Ted's; and Cape Seafood and Provisions—all of which sell Monterey Bay Aquarium–approved fish.

When D.C.–based chef **Barton Seaver** ran Hook, he showcased more than 70 different fish species on the restaurant's menu in a single year. Today, Seaver leads the Sustainable Seafood and Health Initiative at the Center for Health and the Global Environment at the Harvard T.H. Chan School of Public Health and writes books about seafood sustainability.

> **If we can create a better world by conserving our resources today, and changing our habits today, I want to be a part of that in any way that I can. . . . When people are informed about what is at stake, they are actually excited and supportive.**
>
> —**ERIC RIPERT,** Le Bernardin (New York City)

For further reference:
Fish Forever by Paul Johnson
For Cod and Country by Barton Seaver
Good Fish by Becky Selengut
Monterey Bay Aquarium's Seafood Watch: seafoodwatch.org

Imagine being served a plate of sushi. But this plate also holds all the animals that were killed for your serving of sushi. The plate might have to be five feet across.

—JONATHAN SAFRAN FOER, in *Eating Animals*, defining the concept and scale of seafood "bycatch"

SEASONALITY / SEASONS (SEE ALSO AUTUMN, SPRING, SUMMER, AND WINTER)

Seasonal = Local: The too-often unsung truth of cooking **seasonally** is that it also demands cooking **locally**—that is, when the ingredients available to you are at their seasonal peak. The availability of any particular season's ingredients can vary by many weeks, even months, in different parts of the country. And seasonality often doesn't fit into the nice, neat categories we try to put ingredients into as we struggle to memorize when particular ingredients will be available—some are available in more than just a single season.

There is still wisdom to be found in thinking generally about the seasons—that is, SPRING, SUMMER, AUTUMN, and WINTER—and developing a sense of the "rules of thumb" of what works best when. As you gain experience as a cook, you can benefit from making increasingly finer distinctions about seasonality, and you may find yourself drawn to the distinctions that have been made by the Chinese seasonal calendar, which divides the year into 24 seasons—or even the Japanese seasonal calendar, which subdivides the year into 72 micro-seasons.

Regardless of where you draw the line, cooking in step with what's in season ensures that you'll be using ingredients when they are at their peak, which means maximum flavor at the minimum price, with the lowest carbon footprint.

Imagine: What is a quintessentially seasonal and local dish you could make *today*, based on the ingredients available at your closest farmers' market?

SEASONS, 72 JAPANESE

In Japan, you don't choose the vegetables and fruits you eat. Rather, they choose you—through the seasons in which they present themselves.

The Japanese word ***kisetsukan*** refers to the celebration of food at its "peak of the season" (or *shun*, pronounced "shoon"). Seasonal festivals are a way of life in Japan, which finds a way to celebrate everything from planting to harvesting.

In addition to the observation of the four major seasons, the Japanese ancient calendar emulates the Chinese practice of dividing the year into 24 two-week mini-seasons (known as *sekki*)—and then goes further in dividing the seasons into 72 distinct five-day farming cycles referred to as micro-seasons (*shichijuuni-ko*).

For further reference:

The free app **72 Seasons** celebrates each of the five-day micro-seasons with beauty and grace, providing inspiration for each period.

Novelist **Liza Dalby**, the first non-Japanese ever to have trained as a geisha and who consulted on the film *Memoirs of a Geisha*, is the author of ***East Wind Melts the Ice: A Memoir Through the Seasons***, which celebrates the 72 microseasons as she experienced them in her garden, at her table, and through her life in Northern California.

SEA VEGETABLES (AKA SEA GREENS, SEA LETTUCES, AND SEAWEED)

Chefs have looked far beyond the dark green paper-like **nori** typically used to make Japanese maki rolls and other sushi to experiment with a whole new range of seaweeds—including **arame, dulce, hiziki, kombu,** and **wakame**—which are becoming more widely known as sea greens, sea lettuces, and sea vegetables, and in contexts far beyond their traditional uses in Japanese cuisine.

Part of the drive behind their popularity has been their recognition as powerful sources of the umami flavor. Chefs at mainstream fine-dining restaurants now find the seaweed-driven broth *dashi* to be as or even more important than traditional stocks in their kitchens. In addition to its flavor, seaweed is also prized for its nutritional value (with certain types containing as much as 40 percent protein), sustainability, and versatility.

In 2016, the appearance of seaweed on fine-dining menus shot up by more than 10 percent, according to industry tracker Datassential MenuTrends. Maine is America's leading state in the harvest of seaweed, where the most popular local type is **rockweed**. Others include **sugar kelp** (which can flavor butter and serve as a gluten-free sub for pasta) and **Irish moss** (which can thicken creamy desserts like custards, flans, and mousses).

Sea vegetables are also being dried and powdered and used as high-flavor, low-sodium salt substitutes. Vegans and vegetarians haven't been the only ones to rejoice at the discovery that the seaweed **dulse**, when fried (and especially when smoked), tastes uncannily bacon-like. Chef **Eric Tucker** of San Francisco's Millennium first tipped us off that dried and powdered **sea lettuce** is an "umami bomb" that tastes just like black truffles.

For further reference:

Superfood Seagreens: A Guide to Cooking with Power-Packed Seaweed by Barton Seaver

SENSES, SEE SMELL AND SOUND

SEPTEMBER, SEE SUMMER AND AUTUMN

SHOWER

Need inspiration? Take a shower. *Fast Company* reported a 2014 study revealing that **72 percent of people experience new ideas in the shower**. An additional 14 percent of respondents said they took showers simply to generate new ideas.

SHRUBS (SEE ALSO DRINKS, ALCOHOLIC AND DRINKS, NON-ALCOHOLIC)

Shrubs are slowly fermented macerated fruits that have been mixed with vinegar (e.g., apple cider, balsamic, Champagne, red wine) so that they're virtually equal parts fruit, sugar, and vinegar. They are increasingly used for beverages, from cocktails (e.g., blended with spirits) to nonalcoholic drinks (blended with bubbly water). Some of the most popular fruits used include blueberries, cherries, peaches, pears, plums, and strawberries, and the good news is that it's a great way to use up less-than-perfect fruit that is ripe and sweet.

SLEEP

Besides being the greatest creative aphrodisiac, sleep also affects our every waking moment, dictates our social rhythm, and even mediates our negative moods. Be as religious and disciplined about your sleep as you are about your work.

—**MARIA POPOVA,** BrainPickings.org, whose free weekly newsletter is many creative professionals' Sunday morning must-read

SLIDERS, SEE BURGERS

SMALL PLATES (CONTRAST WITH LARGE-FORMAT DISHES)

The trend toward **small-sized share plates** is more often providing multiple guests with a single bite, versus the experience of eating an entire entrée-sized plate of food. This is leading chefs to season food differently, amping up the flavor to make an impression with that single bite. They're also turning away from white dinner plates and toward more unusual serving dishes, including small crocks, ramekins, and even Mason jars.

A number of **Tom Colicchio**'s restaurants in Manhattan have been working to add method to the madness of small plates by serving them in courses in order to enhance the flavor experience.

SMASHING

When did **smashing** get to be such a big thing in cooking? While we've long been enjoying smashed green plantains, we're seeing more smashed vegetables on menus—from **Brooks Headley**'s smashed cucumber salad at Superiority Burger in Manhattan to **Jeremy Fox**'s swoon-worthy smashed potato salad at Rustic Canyon in Los Angeles. Chefs tell us it adds an appealing rustic texture to the vegetables that is not only more pleasing to the palate, but better for soaking up dressings and sauces.

SMELL (SEE ALSO SMOKED FOODS)

We know that an estimated 80 to 95 percent or more of flavor is actually due to **aroma**.

But how else can chefs be inspired by the sense of smell?

Many perfumes were historically created from ingredients like fruits (e.g., mandarins), peppers, and spices (e.g., cardamom, vanilla)—a subcategory of perfumes which the French term *les parfums gourmands,* or "culinary scents," exemplified by fragrances like Chanel's Egoiste (coriander + mandarin + vanilla) and Tom Ford's Tobacco Vanille (cocoa + dried fruit + tonka bean + vanilla).

In collaboration with **Chandler Burr**, one of the world's most noted fragrance experts, **Jean-Georges Vongerichten** has created multicourse tasting menus based on perfumes created by Hermès and Thierry Mugler as delicious exercises in translating the sense of smell into that of taste.

The aroma of garlic can get you excited to eat a dish. If we're serving table 96 a dish, I want table 25 to be able to smell it and get excited. . . . We also use a cloche [cover] to hold in the tagine spices, and release it at the table toward the guest's face so that they can enjoy the aroma of cinnamon and turmeric and ras el hanout. That helps to make the experience memorable.

—**TRAVIS SWIKARD,** Boulud Sud (New York City)

S

SMOKED FOODS

Where there's **smoke**, there's fire. Or so our taste buds would have us believe. Smoky foods remind of us of heat and warmth, no matter what their actual temperature.

The flavor of smoke reminds us of the primal flame-grilling of the summertime, and our needs to be blanketed with warmth in the winter—which explains why smoked flavors are experiencing unprecedented popularity year-round now. We can't get enough of them—in foods as well as drinks.

Ingredients already smoked: canned chipotles in adobo sauce, mezcal, Scotch, smoked meats (e.g., bacon), smoked paprika, smoked salt, smoked teas (e.g., lapsang souchong)

Techniques: charring, low-temperature grilling, smoking via hand-held smoking guns

Ingredients being charred and/or smoked: cheese (e.g., firm), eggs (hard-boiled), ice cubes, flours, fruits (lemons, peaches), meats (bacon, ham, sausage), nuts (pecans, pistachios, walnuts), oils (canola, olive), seafood (oysters, shellfish), teas, tofu, vegetables(asparagus, bell peppers, carrots, onions, peas, potatoes, tomatoes, zucchini)

Dishes being smoked: ice creams (imagine smoked vanilla ice cream on a s'mores dessert; risottos, salad dressings, salads (e.g., potato salad)

Woods being used for smoking: alder (quieter, sweet), apple (fruity, quieter, sweet), cherry (fruity, quieter, sweet), hickory (louder), maple (quieter, sweet), peach (fruity, quieter, sweet), whiskey barrel chips (complex)

Imagine: What new ways can you introduce the aroma and taste of smoke in a dish? How would smoking change the texture and experience of tasting an ingredient?

I love smoked flavors, and will use ingredients like smoked roe, smoked fish, and smoked yogurt to add a roasted/umami-like flavor.

—**JAMES KENT,** The NoMad (New York City)

My childhood influences me. I grew up on a farm in Alsace, smoking bacon and ham and eating a lot of smoked foods. So [before it was a trend] of course I found a way to bring smoke to the table [using a smoking gun and placing it under a clear glass cloche] at The Modern. Bringing the sense of smell alive at the table changes the experience. It's a reminder of what's in the dish. Your goal shouldn't be to create a theme park experience—but to offer a little surprise and trigger something nice. If it's too theatrical, it's too much.

—**GABRIEL KREUTHER,** Gabriel Kreuther (New York City)

S'MORES

One of the most enduring flavor combinations of childhood Scouting days is that of **chocolate + Graham crackers + marshmallows,** more affectionately known as **s'mores.**

Rick Bayless featured a s'mores-inspired dessert at the White House when he served as guest chef at the Obama administration's second state dinner in May 2010 (see page 404).

More recently, **Dominique Ansel** turned down the temperature of the toasted campfire favorite to create his frozen s'mores, where a chocolate cookie cube was encased in blow-torched marshmallow after being filled with frozen custard—with the whole concoction served on its own applewood smoked tree branch.

Their popularity led to the opening of a Dominique Ansel S'Mores Pop Up in Tokyo, from January 2 to February 14, 2016, selling not only frozen s'mores but s'mores cereal along with chocolate-covered caramel marshmallows.

Wolfgang Puck Catering's executive chef **Eric Klein** even served an Oreo Cookie S'More Dome at the 2017 post-Oscars Governors Ball.

We're huge fans of the three-layer S'Mores Pie [graham cracker crust, chocolate ganache, and housemade marshmallow] that **Marc Jacksina**'s staff toasts to order with a blowtorch at Earl's Grocery in Charlotte, North Carolina.

Chefs and mixologists have created savory and sweet dishes and even cocktails (made easier by the release of marshmallow-flavored vodkas) inspired by the classic flavor combination in particular, and marshmallows in general. (They have paired marshmallow with apples, beets, bourbon, butterscotch, chocolate, grapefruit, pecans, root vegetables, rum, schnapps, strawberries, and winter squashes.)

Striking a chord of nostalgia before a bite has even been taken is like good foreplay before sex.

—PHILLIP FOSS,
EL Ideas (Chicago)

S'Mores Pie at Earl's Grocery (Charlotte, North Carolina)

Imagine: In honor of **August 10**—which is **National S'Mores Day**—can you envision a new version of s'mores you'd be excited to taste?

SOCIAL CONSCIOUSNESS

I take kids out of jail and teach them to play with knives and fire—and make the community better.

—**CHAD HOUSER,** cofounder, Café Momentum (Dallas)

Does food taste better if it is socially conscious? Given the increasing popularity of chef-driven businesses and nonprofits with a social conscience, the answer appears to be yes.

In 2011, then-**Parigi** restaurant co-owners **Janice Provost** and **Chad Houser** founded the nonprofit **Café Momentum**, which trains and employs at-risk teens. Its mission is to "transform young lives by equipping our community's most at-risk youth with life skills, education, and employment opportunities to help them achieve their full potential." After catering numerous four-course dinners at pop-up locations, Café Momentum moved into an 85-seat permanent location in downtown Dallas in 2014. In addition to their culinary and hospitality training, participants receive instruction in anger management, art, and financial literacy.

Imagine: How can the next dish you create have the greatest possible positive impact beyond a sensory one?

Giving your time and talent to a cause you believe in makes you feel amazing.

—**JANICE PROVOST,** cofounder, Café Momentum (Dallas)

Janice Provost

Now [Roy Choi] and fellow chef Daniel Patterson are changing the world with their ambitious startup, LocoL, whose goal is to bring healthy food, at an affordable price, to underserved inner-city neighborhoods across America while employing residents of those neighborhoods—basically, replacing traditional fast food with a more positive, socially responsible institution.

—**ANTHONY BOURDAIN,** writing in *Time* magazine about Roy Choi's being named to the 2016 *Time*'s 100 Most Influential People list

SODIUM

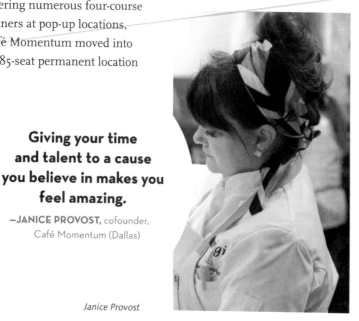

We use very little salt here.

—**JOSHUA SKENES,** Saison (San Francisco)

The *Dietary Guidelines for Americans* suggest that consumers cut their **sodium** intake by 33 percent, and encourage restaurants and food manufacturers alike to reduce the amount of salt in foods.

At Saison, **Joshua Skenes** uses housemade Saison Sauce, which he describes as "an elixir made from grilled grains, seaweeds, and little fish that are in season. We use all the byproduct from our sea life in the sauce. We use what is local and seasonal, like silverfish or herring, which is the best because it has such an incredible flavor."

Proposing an analogy for those who haven't had the enormous pleasure of tasting firsthand this smoky-noted, umami-rich sauce (which is so potent it requires just a drop or two to enhance flavor), Skenes muses, "It is almost like a combination of white soy sauce and grilled fish sauce mixed with dashi."

Imagine: Consider all the ways you can enhance the flavor of your next dish without using salt.

SOLID VS. LIQUID

Serendipity's frozen hot chocolate has been a signature attraction for tourists to New York City for decades. It's basically an extra-cold milkshake, but the clever name is both media and guest bait.

There's a trend toward flavorful ice cubes in cocktails, with mixologists freezing fruit or vegetable juices that become part of the drink.

Dehydrating vinegars into vinegar powders allows chefs to add acidity to dishes without adding moisture. Kalustyan's in New York City carries a number of versions, including apple cider vinegar powder, malt vinegar powder, and red wine vinegar powder.

Toasting (for about 5 hours in a 300-degree oven) vs. melting sugar to caramelize it lets it take on caramel flavors while retaining solidity.

Imagine: How can you turn a liquid into a solid? How can you turn a solid into a liquid?

SOUND (SEE ALSO **X FACTOR**)

The expanding field of flavor science continues to prove that which many chefs have long known intuitively—we taste not only with our tongues (and noses and mouths), but with our eyes and ears.

Tablecloths are coming back as a way to soften the tabletop clinking and clanking marked by serving food and drink on bare tables, which can distract from the food itself. Restaurant designers like **David Rockwell** have noted clients' increasing knowledge of acoustics and sensitivity to a restaurant's "soundscape" as part of the design process.

Chefs like **Phillip Foss** of Chicago's Michelin-starred EL Ideas have taken this a step further by pairing dishes with specific pieces of music:

> Emotion follows after music. You'll hear a song or taste a dish and remember where you were when you'd heard that song or tasted that dish before—and you'll either love it or hate it. Offering a music course is great, because music is an art form near and dear to many, and we can have fun with it. During 1980s Week here, we play Madonna's "Like a Virgin" while serving little spheres filled with cherry juice to explode in your mouth. The same week, we also serve a "**cocaine**" course [really, an edible powder made of dehydrated coconut and lime] that's served on a mirror with a razor blade and a straw.

Philip Foss tasting "cocaine"

Our study confirmed that in an environment of loud noise, our sense of taste is compromised. Interestingly, this was specific to sweet and umami tastes, with sweet taste inhibited, as others have shown largely through affective testing, and umami taste significantly enhanced. . . . Thus, the multisensory properties of the environment we consume our food within can alter our perception of the foods we eat.

—**KIMBERLY S. YAN** and **ROBIN DANDO** of Cornell University, in the *Journal of Experimental Psychology* (2015)

S

During another themed dinner, we explain the line "What are the yams?" in Kendrick Lamar's rap [which symbolize a declaration of individualism], and serve tempura-battered yams and maitake mushrooms with a whole calf that's been smoked and shredded and served with a mustard barbecue sauce while the rap "King Kunta" plays.

SPACE (SEE ALSO ALTITUDE AND TIME)

Imagine: Think about the physical properties (e.g., the three-dimensional position and direction) of the next dish you create. How might you represent them in a new way?

SPICES (SEE ALSO HOT HOT HOT)

Why reach for one spice over another? Tradition? Flavor? Health?

The recipes for classic dishes call for a time-tested selection of spices. But with an increasing emphasis on health considerations, are there other spices that would work just as well while providing greater benefits?

Lior Lev Sercarz of La Boîte, the Manhattan-based spice store that creates blends in conjunction with leading chefs like New York City's **Eric Ripert** and Boston's **Ana Sortun**, leads regular classes on the authentic sourcing as well as toasting, grinding, and blending of spices.

Imagine: What spice(s) could you reach for to season your next dish that might benefit the dish (or the guest you're serving it to) beyond flavor alone?

Some of these ingredients help digestion, and they have amazing flavors.

—**STEVEN REDZIKOWSKI,** chef-owner, Brider (Denver), who uses ginger in cold-pressed juices and fried rice, as quoted in *Nation's Restaurant News*

Your kitchen's spice rack may also hold some secret weapons against conditions such as inflammation, heart disease, cancer, and more. . . . So instead of flavoring your food with salt and butter, which can contribute to high blood pressure and heart disease, consider using the following spices: turmeric . . . coriander . . . paprika . . . cumin . . . cinnamon . . . ground ginger.

—HARVARD HEALTH LETTER

SPIRALIZING

More chefs are **spiralizing**—i.e., using a spiralizer designed for this purpose, or simply a mandoline or knife—produce (e.g., apples, beets, carrots, celery root, cucumbers, squash, sweet potatoes, zucchini) into ribbons or "noodles," at once enhancing a dish's nutrient density and flavor while eliminating a typical source of gluten (i.e., grain-based noodles or pasta).

Raw Sugar Pumpkin Salad: Spiralized raw sugar pumpkin with brown butter, grated Bianca Sardo, pickled red jalapeño, fried almonds, dates, and chives

—Michael Scelfo, Alden & Harlow (Cambridge, Massachusetts), see photo above

For further reference:

Inspiralized: Turn Vegetables into Healthy, Creative, Satisfying Meals by Ali Maffucci

SPRING

Weather: typically cool/warm
Needs: staying cool, releasing energy

Spring Ingredients
(See Seasonal Ingredients Key on page 249.)
aprium (peak: May–June)
artichokes (peaks: autumn; **spring**)
artichokes, Jerusalem (peaks: autumn; spring)
arugula (peak: spring/summer)
ASPARAGUS, e.g., green, purple, white (peak: April)
avocados (peak: spring/summer)
bamboo shoots (peak: spring/summer)
beans, fava (peak: April–June)
beets
blackberries (peak: spring/summer)
blueberries (peak: spring/summer)
borage
BOYSENBERRIES (peak: May–June)
cauliflower (peak: March)
celery root (peak: August–June)
chard, Swiss
cheeses, spring, e.g., Brillat-Savarin, Chabichou, chèvre, **fresh**
cherimoya (peak: December–June)
cherries
chervil
chicory
chive blooms
chives, esp. garlic
cilantro (peak: spring/summer)
cucumbers (peak: spring/summer)
currants (peak: March–July)

S

dill (peak: spring/summer)
eggplant, e.g., Chinese, common, Japanese (peak: April–November)
eggs
endive, e.g., Belgian, curly
escarole
fennel, esp. baby
fennel pollen (peak: spring/summer)
FIDDLEHEAD FERNS (peak: March–June)
flowers, edible, e.g., marigolds, nasturtiums, violas
foraged ingredients, e.g., chickweed, dandelion, lovage, mâche, miner's lettuce, purslane, etc.
FRESHNESS, i.e., ingredients that are raw or only lightly cooked
garlic, e.g., **green** (peak: March), **spring**
garlic root
garlic scapes
ginger (peak: winter/spring)
GOOSEBERRIES (peak: March–May)
greens, e.g., collard, dandelion (peak: May–June), fava (peak: January–May), lolla rossa, mizuna, mustard, radish, red oak, salad, spring, wild
herbs, e.g., flowering, fresh
jicama (peak: winter/spring)
kumquats (peak: November–July)
lamb, spring
lavender
leeks
lemons
lemons, Meyer
lettuces, e.g., lamb's (aka mâche), leaf, oak leaf, romaine, spring
lighter dishes
limes, key
LOGANBERRIES (peak: March–April)
LOQUATS (peak: April–June)
LYCHEES (peak: May–June)
mâche
mangoes (peak: spring/summer)
micro-grains, e.g., barley, buckwheat, oat, wheat
microgreens, e.g., amaranth, borage, bull's blood, dandelion, red ribbon sorrel, thyme
mint
miso, light
mushrooms, e.g., chanterelles, **MORELS** (peak: April–June), shiitake
nettles (peak: spring/summer)
noodles, e.g., somen
okra (peak: spring/summer)
ONIONS, e.g., **SPRING**, **VIDALIA** (peak: April–June)
oranges, e.g., **blood** (peak: winter/spring), **Cara Cara** (peak: December–April), **mandarin** (peak: winter/spring), navel (peak: March)
oysters
pastas, e.g., with spring vegetables, e.g., peas, primavera
peas, e.g., **English** (peak: May–July), **snow** (peak: April–November), **sugar snap** (peak: April–November), **sweet**
plumcots (peak: spring/summer)
pea shoots
potatoes, e.g., **fingerling**, **new**
radishes
RAMPS (peak: March–June)
RHUBARB (peak: April)
scallions
shoots, e.g., garlic, pea (peak: winter/spring)
snow peas (peaks: spring; autumn)
sorrel (peak: May)
soufflés
soups, lighter, e.g., spring vegetable, e.g., nettle, spring pea
spinach
sprouts, e.g., daikon
squash, summer, e.g., zucchini
strawberries (peak: spring/summer)
STRAWBERRIES, WILD (peak: April–June)
sugar snap peas (peak: spring)
tea, green, esp. early
tomatillos (peak: spring/summer)
tomatoes, e.g., heirloom and other specialty
wakame (peak: winter/spring)
watercress (peak: spring/summer)

watermelon (peak: spring/summer)
zucchini, e.g., baby
zucchini blossoms

Spring Beers
amber ales, American
bock beer
doppelbock
farmhouse ales
Maibock, a bock beer intended to be drunk in May
Saison
stouts, dry
wheat ales and beers

Spring Cheeses
blue cheeses, milder, e.g., Beenleigh
Brie
Camembert
Cheddar
chèvre
cream cheese
goat's milk cheese, fresh
Gruyère
sheep's milk cheese, fresh
younger cheeses
Spring cheese accompaniments: bread, crackers, radishes, strawberries

Spring Cocktails and Spirits
cider-based cocktails
classic cocktails, e.g., gin and tonic, Manhattan, Sazarec
cocktails with pickled vegetables
cucumber-driven cocktails
edible flowers, e.g., borage flowers, jasmine blossoms
ginger beer–based cocktails
lighter-bodied cocktails
margaritas, e.g., sorrel-flavored
mint-driven cocktails
Moscow mule, lighter versions of, e.g., garden mule or raspberry mule
sparkling wine–based cocktails
tea-based cocktails (esp. from spring-harvested teas)
vegetable juice–based (e.g., parsnips, peas) cocktails
white spirits, e.g., gin, vodka

Spring Concepts
frittatas
gumbos
moussaka
omelets
pancakes, e.g., blueberry
pastas, e.g., with artichokes, asparagus, mushrooms, primavera, and/or spring peas
pizzas, e.g.., with arugula, chèvre, new potatoes, spring onions
ragouts, e.g., vegetable
risottos, e.g., asparagus
salads, e.g., artichoke, arugula, asparagus, fava bean, spinach, spring vegetable, sprouts, watercress
salads, e.g., warm
sautés
stir-fries
tempura

Spring Desserts
cobblers, fruit, e.g., rhubarb, strawberry
semifreddos, e.g., strawberry
shortcakes, strawberry
tarts, e.g., rhubarb, strawberry

Brooks Cherries al Forno: Perugian almond tart and dried cherry brittle
—Dahlia Narvaez, Pizzeria Mozza (Los Angeles)

Butterscotch Budino: Maldon sea salt and rosemary pine nut cookies
—Dahlia Narvaez, Pizzeria Mozza (Los Angeles)

Fried Strawberry Pies with Strawberry Ice Cream
—Dolester Miles, Highlands Bar and Grill (Birmingham)

Pavlova: Olive Oil Chantilly, Rhubarb Jam, and Almond Sandie
—Scott Cioe, Bevy at the Park Hyatt (New York City)

Sorbets: Prickly Pear Mezcal, Rhubarb Champagne, Grapefruit Angostura
—Scott Cioe, Bevy at the Park Hyatt (New York City)

Strawberries 'n' Cream: Elderflower, Pickled Strawberries, Vanilla Bean Semifreddo
—Scott Cioe, Bevy at the Park Hyatt (New York City)

Tortino di Burrata: Burrata Cheese Cake, Harry's Berry & Rhubarb Salad, Rhubarb Sorbet
—Lidia Bastianich and Fortunato Nicotra, Felidia (New York City)

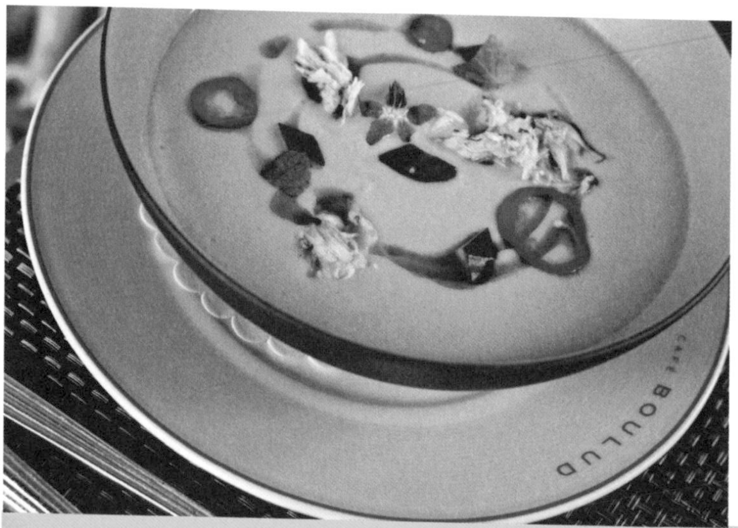

Spring Dressings

delicate, light sauces
Green Goddess dressing
vinaigrettes

Spring Flavor Affinities

artichoke + butter + garlic + lemon + parsley
artichoke + Parmesan + pine nuts
arugula + olive oil + spring garlic
asparagus + bulgur + lemon

Spring Dishes

A Crispy Potato Napoleon with Wild Morels and Local Asparagus on Spinach Parsley Risotto
—Patrick O'Connell, The Inn at Little Washington (Washington, Virginia)

A Shot of Local Asparagus Soup with Tempura Asparagus
—Patrick O'Connell, The Inn at Little Washington (Washington, Virginia)

Asparagus, Oyster Sauce, Cured Egg, Nasturtium, Elephant Garlic
—Beverly Kim and Johnny Clark, Parachute (Chicago)

Asperges d'Avignon: French white asparagus with Comté cheese foam and Oregon state morels
—David Bouley, Bouley (New York City)

Blackened Catfish with celery root, ramp & corn fritters, basil mayonnaise, herb salad
—Spike Gjerde, Woodberry Kitchen (Baltimore)

Broccoli: Smoke, Meyer Lemon, Miner's Lettuce
—Curtis Duffy, Grace (Chicago)

Cat Tail Hearts and Flowers
—Iliana Regan, Elizabeth (Chicago)

Chawanmushi: Warm, Local Duck Egg "Tea Cup" Custard with Ginger-Scented Asian Tea
—Patrick O'Connell, The Inn at Little Washington (Washington, Virginia)

Chocolate: coconut, finger lime, basil
—Curtis Duffy, Grace (Chicago)

Corn Soup, Sweet Garlic Flan, Cracked Blue Crab, Roasted Sunchokes, and Argan Oil
—Carrie Nahabedian, Naha (Chicago)

Cucumber Avocado Soup: Peekytoe Crab, Red Pickled Fresno Chili, and Mint
—Aaron Bludorn, Café Boulud (New York City), see photo above

English Pear: rhubarb, burrata, apple mint
—Curtis Duffy, Grace (Chicago)

Five-Hour Smoked Lamb with Plantain Dumplings, Peas, Fava Beans, and Caribbean Curry
—J.J. Johnson, Minton's (Harlem)

Gilfeather Rutabaga with Ginger Labnue, Tesa, and Chive Blossoms
—Charleen Badman, FnB (Scottsdale, Arizona)

Halloumi with Stewed Strawberries, Pickled Chilies, and Carob Molasses
—Alon Shaya, Shaya (New Orleans)

Insalata Primavera: Spring Salad, Fava Beans, Fagiolini, Asparagus, Prosciutto
—Lidia Bastianich and Fortunato Nicotra, Felidia (New York City)

asparagus + butter + chanterelles + chervil + parsley + shallots
asparagus + chervil + cream + morels + shallots
asparagus + cream + lemon + morels
asparagus + garlic + ginger + sesame
asparagus + goat cheese + lemon
asparagus + leeks + morels + pasta
asparagus + lemon juice + olive oil + Parmesan
asparagus + mayonnaise + tarragon
asparagus + ricotta + spring onions
broad beans + bacon + onions
broccoli + anchovies + lemon zest + parsley
broccoli + garlic + parsley
carrots + chervil + cream
carrots + cumin + garlic + orange
carrots + red onions + thyme
cauliflower + pine nuts + raisins
chives + garlic + morels + olive oil + parsley
cinnamon + orange + rhubarb
fava beans + butter + mint
fava beans + butter + savory
green garlic + brine + chili pepper flakes
new potatoes + dill
ramps + olive oil + red wine vinegar
rhubarb + cloves + orange + vanilla

Lobster: Butter-Poached with Nettles, Fiddleheads & Shellfish Bisque
—Daniel Humm and James Kent, The NoMad (New York City)

Morel: ramp, potato, chive
—Curtis Duffy, Grace (Chicago)

Mushroom: Tarte with Ricotta, Quail Egg & Salsa Verde
—Daniel Humm and James Kent, The NoMad (New York City)

Organic Carnaroli Risotto and "Porcelet de Lait," Baby Artichokes, Spinach, and Preserved Black Truffle
—Carrie Nahabedian, Naha (Chicago)

Ravioli Ripieni con Cacia e Pere: Pear & Pecorino Filled Ravioli, Aged Pecorino, Crushed Black Pepper
—Lidia Bastianich and Fortunato Nicotra, Felidia (New York City)

Red Carrot Tartare with Root Chips and Duck Egg Gribiche
—Charleen Badman, FnB (Scottsdale, Arizona)

Smoked Carrots, Jaggery, Peanuts, Mint
—Beverly Kim and Johnny Clark, Parachute (Chicago)

Snow Pea: Chiffonade with Pancetta, Pecorino & Mint
—Daniel Humm and James Kent, The NoMad (New York City)

Spaghetti with Garlic Scapes, Almonds & Basil
—Daniel Humm and James Kent, The NoMad (New York City)

Spring Beet Falafel with Dill and Sina's Special Sauce
—Charleen Badman, FnB (Scottsdale, Arizona)

Spring Vegetable Salad with beets, celery root, ramps, parsnip, radish, miso, benne, herbs
—Spike Gjerde, Woodberry Kitchen (Baltimore)

Tilghman Island Crab Cake with potato pavé, Boh battered ramps, young lettuce, cocktail and tartar sauces
—Spike Gjerde, Woodberry Kitchen (Baltimore)

Watermelon Radish with green strawberry, cashew, fennel
—Curtis Duffy, Grace (Chicago)

Yukon Potato Gnocchi, Locally Raised Shrimp, Sungold Tomatoes and Eggplant, Garlic Chive and Dandelion, Vine-Ripe Tomato "Juice," EVOO and Goats Milk Butter
—Carrie Nahabedian, Naha (Chicago)

rhubarb + ginger + strawberries
rhubarb + lemon + vanilla
spring peas + green garlic + lettuce
strawberries + lemon + sugar
sugar snap peas + mint + pecorino

Spring Pastas

angel hair
cavatelli
farfalle
fusilli
gnocchi
linguine
penne
ravioli
reginetti
rigatoni
spaghetti
Spring pasta sauces: herb-based sauces, pesto, primavera

Spring Presentations

soufflés

Spring Techniques

boiling
pan-roasting
steaming
stove-top cooking

Spring Wines

Barbera
Beaujolais
Cabernet Franc
Chardonnay, unoaked
Chenin Blanc
Gewürztraminer
Greek wines
Grüner Veltliner
Moscato d'Asti
Muscadet
Riesling
Rosé
Sauvignon Blanc
Torrontés
Txakolina
Vouvray

STEAKS

The idea of **"steaks"** has evolved from slabs of animal meat (e.g., beef or tuna) into an array of other offerings, which include cauliflower, eggplant, mushrooms (e.g., portobello), squash (butternut), and tofu. The plant-based slab serves as a platform for other flavors and techniques (grilling, marinating, rubbing).

Imagine: What else could you turn into a "steak"?

Cauliflower "steak"

STORY

Eating an egg is not the same thing as eating an egg that has a story behind it. We like to eat stories.

—**ANDONI LUIS ADURIZ,** Mugaritz (Spain)

Every dish has a **story**—whether told as a short story, a play, a poem, a song, or something else altogether. When you share a dish's story with guests at your restaurant or in your home (such as how you grew the ingredients in your home garden, or the restaurant you visited on vacation that inspired it), it enhances the experience and helps to create a memory.

A tasting menu has the power to tell an even deeper story, as **Kyle Connaughton** of Single Thread in Healdsburg, California, reminded us:

> Here [at Single Thread], the menu is based on the kaiseki menu, but not kaiseki cuisine. There is an order and a structure to the menu. . . . Within that, there is infinite creativity that can happen.
>
> Everyone here understands the architecture of the menu. The sum of the parts arrive somewhere having a diversity of flavors and techniques. We are mindful of the physiology of the guest and of how much fat, carb, sugar, and protein [we serve]. We want you to arrive at a place where you are satiated but not destroyed and rolling out, and you feel you got great value and did not overindulge.
>
> It is not about just having dishes become heavier and heavier. We have a constant that runs through our dishes. There is a constant umami that is more of an expression of our personal cooking.
>
> By the way, this applies to any type of menu, and not just fine dining: You have certain boxes and a narrative. You have a formula. People

Cuisine is a story . . . When we prepare a dish, we bring so much to it, including the entire human aspect involved: the farmer, the fisherman, and the market gardener. So it's something interesting because from all of these factors we are telling a story.

—**ALAIN PASSARD,** L'Arpège (France)

S

hear "formula" and think, "I don't want to be formulaic," but having a structure allows you to step back and be very creative within the system. . . . It informs the narrative from start to finish.

It is no different than if you are writing a screenplay or a novel: If you understand the plot and how it is going to unfold, and where the plot twist is, then you can step back and tinker with the individual acts.

People think creativity is this wide-open-sky thing involving big thinking—but you need to know where everything is going to fit. If you look at a large painting, it can seem like one static image, but if you look closely, you will see many different things that all come together.

By the way, I enthusiastically recommend **Robert McKee**'s famed 30-hour **Story** seminar, which had been recommended to me by novelist **Steven Pressfield** (*The Legend of Bagger Vance, Gates of Fire*) and which I found does exactly what McKee claims it will: elevate storytelling "from an intellectual exercise to an emotional one, transforming the craft into an art form."

Imagine: How would you tell the story of your dish, or your menu—its protagonists, its challenges, its triumphs?

STRESS

Stress is the cause of 95 percent of illness and diseases. And the stresses professional chefs are under are well-known, as spotlighted by *Hi, Anxiety* author **Kat Kinsman** through her launching of ChefsWithIssues.com.

And it's next-to-impossible to be creative when you're stressed out.

Stress can exacerbate the anxiety or depression caused by chemical imbalances, as noted by *Top Chef Masters* winner **Chris Cosentino** in a ChefsFeed video about his own struggles. However, anxiety due primarily or exclusively to stress can be modified.

So, train your mind and body to better handle stress if you cook professionally, recommends author **Stephen Co**, who offers the following recommendations:

1. Meditate. If you meditate, you have already established a pattern of stillness, so you are at a better starting point when stress hits. People don't realize that when they are stressed—especially when someone is screaming in their face—it is hard to visualize calm.

2. Practice your breathing. Breathwork is very, very important because you can do it simultaneously as you are dealing with a crisis. You can't "visualize" to try to fix the problem in a situation when someone is screaming. Move your breathing from your chest to your belly. Breathe rhythmically and slowly: Expand your belly as you inhale, hold your breath, and exhale while compressing your belly, then hold the exhale. You can do a count of 6 (inhale), 3 (hold), 6 (exhale), 3 (hold); or 7-1-7-1.

3. When stress hits, use your breathing techniques. Most people under stress hyperventilate—there is no pause. So if you're too stressed to count, at least be aware enough to pause: Inhale, pause, exhale, pause.

4. After a stressful event, energetically disconnect from it. That way, you can start fresh. People don't always realize that the thoughts and emotions that were created

> **Cooking for a living—which may mean being a line or pastry cook or even a chef—is one of the most grueling lines of work in America, according to CareerCast.**
>
> —**DANIELA GALARZA,** Eater.com (April 14, 2015)

at the time of crisis are so real they can continue to affect you. But if you cut away from them energetically, there is a sense of closure. Imagine your flat hand as a knife, and move it like a karate chop while thinking about what stressed you out, and say, "I disconnect" while making that motion. Just by doing that, most people feel so much better.

STUFF YOU CAN STUFF

Stuffing is a way to add layers of flavor and texture to a dish See also STUFFINGS below.

artichokes
bell peppers, roasted
cabbage
chiles, e.g., jalapeños, poblanos
dates
eggplant
eggs, hard-boiled
grape leaves
mushrooms
pastas, e.g., cannelloni, manicotti, shells
peppers, hot, e.g., piquillo
pizza, Chicago-style
potatoes, e.g., baked, skins
poultry, e.g., chicken, quail, goose, turkey
pumpkins, mini
raspberries
sandwiches, e.g., po' boys
squash, summer and winter
strawberries
tomatoes
zucchini
zucchini blossoms

Imagine: What else can you stuff, that might not typically be stuffed—and what could you stuff it with, to add a new dimension to your dish?

STUFFINGS

BREAD, e.g., cubed
brioche
cauliflower
chestnuts
cornbread, crumbed
couscous
fruits, dried, e.g., raisins
grains, e.g., barley, quinoa
mushrooms
nuts, e.g., almonds, cashews, chestnuts, pecans, walnuts
oysters
quinoa
rice, e.g., sticky, wild
sausage
seeds, e.g., pumpkin
wild rice

SUMMER

Weather: typically hot
Needs: staying cool, releasing energy

Summer Ingredients

(See Seasonal Ingredients Key on page 249.)

amaranth
anise hyssop
apples
APRICOTS (peak: June)
arugula (peak: spring/summer)
avocados (peak: spring/summer)
bamboo shoots (peak: spring/summer)
BASIL, e.g., **Italian, lemon, opal** (peak: summer)
beans, e.g., cranberry, **FAVA,** French, **green,** lima, long, Romano, shelling, wax
BEANS, GREEN (peak: June–September)
bell peppers, e.g., red or yellow (peak: summer/autumn)
berries (peak: spring/summer)
blackberries (peak: spring/summer)
BLUEBERRIES (peak: July)
blueberries, wild
boiled dishes
bok choy (peak: summer/autumn)
boysenberries (peak: June)
broccoli
burdock (peak: June–October)
cactus pads, aka nopales (peak: May–October)
callaloo
carrots and **carrot tops**
cauliflower
celery (peak: summer/autumn)
chard (peak: summer/autumn)

chayote (peak: May–October)
cheeses, summer, e.g., Fourme d'Ambert, mascarpone, mozzarella, ricotta, soft cheeses
cherries, e.g., sour, sweet
chervil
chickpeas, fresh
chiles (peak: June–October)
chilled dishes and beverages
Chinese okra (peak: May–October)
chives
cilantro (peak: spring/summer)
clams, e.g., cherrystone, littleneck, razor
CORN (peak: July–August)
CUCUMBERS (peak: August)
currants, black
dill (peak: spring/summer)
dragon fruit (peak: summer/autumn)
edamame
EGGPLANT, e.g., **Chinese, common, Japanese** (peak: June–October)
elderberries and elderflower
escarole (peak: summer/autumn)
fennel
fennel pollen (peak: spring/summer)
FIGS, e.g., **Black Mission** (peak: July–October)
flowers, edible, e.g., anise hyssop, borage, nasturtiums, oxalis blooms, violas
FRESHNESS
GARLIC (peak: August)
goji berries (peak: summer/autumn)
grapes, e.g., **CHAMPAGNE** (peak: June–September), **CONCORD** (peak: August–September), **green** (peak: summer/autumn)
greens, e.g., baby, beet, leafy, mizuna, young
grilled dishes
guavas (peak: summer/autumn)
HERBS, cooling, e.g., basil, cilantro, dill, fennel, licorice, marjoram, mint
horseradish (peak: summer/autumn)
huckleberries
ICE CREAM
ices and granitas
jackfruit
kohlrabi (peak: summer/autumn)
lamb's quarter
lavender
leeks
lemongrass
lemons
lettuce, e.g., Bibb, Boston, green leaf, **iceberg,** lamb's, lolla rossa, red leaf, **Romaine**
limequats (peak: July–November)
limes (peak: June)
loquats
lychees
mamey sapote (peak: July–October)
mangoes (peak: July–October)
MELONS, e.g., **CANTALOUPE** (peak: August)
microgreens, e.g., basil, beet, cress, radish
mint, e.g., chocolate, pineapple
miso, light
mushrooms, e.g., chanterelles (peak: July–January), chicken of the woods, hedgehog, **lobster** (peak: July–October), **porcini** (peak: June–October)
NECTARINES (peak: May–October)
nettles, e.g., stinging (peak: spring/summer)
noodles, e.g., chilled, somen
okra (peak: April–September)
olives, green
onions, e.g., red (peak: July), Spanish, Vidalia (peak: April–June), **Walla Walla** (peak: June–August)
onions, green
onions, petite
ORANGES, VALENCIA (peak: June–September)
papalo
papayas (peak: summer/autumn)
parsley
passion fruit (peak: July–February)
PEACHES (peak: May–October)
pears, e.g., Bartlett, Bosc (peak: June–March), D'Anjou (peak: September–July)
peas, English (peak: May–July)
peas, snow (peak: April–November), **sugar snap** (peak: April–November)
peppers
picnics
plumcots (peak: May–July)
plums (peak: August)
pluots (peak: May–September)
popcorn shoots
POTATOES, e.g., **new** (peak: summer)
puddings, summer
purslane
radicchio (peak: May–January)
radishes
RASPBERRIES (peak: June–August)
raw foods (e.g., salads)
rhubarb (peak: March–September)

SALADS, e.g., **fruit, green, pasta**
salsas, fresh
sauces, raw, e.g., pestos, tomato (chopped)
savory, summer
scallions
scallops, sea
sea beans
SHALLOTS (peak: May–July)
shiso, e.g., green, red
slaws
sorbets
sorrel
soups, chilled, e.g., fruit, gazpacho
soups, summer vegetable, e.g., corn, tomato
spices, cooking, e.g., peppercorns, white; turmeric
spinach
sprouts, daikon (peak: spring/ summer)
SQUASH, SUMMER, e.g., pattypan, Peter Pan, sunshine, striped ball, yellow, zephyr, zucchini (peak: June–October)
steamed dishes
stone fruits, e.g., nectarines, peaches, plums
strawberries (peak: spring/ summer)
summer rolls, e.g., Vietnamese
tarragon
tatsoi
thyme
TOMATILLOS (peak: August)
TOMATOES, e.g., **cherry, currant, grape, specialty, yellow**
turnips, petite
vegetables, green leafy
vinegar, e.g., balsamic
watercress
WATERMELON (peak: spring/ summer)
ZUCCHINI
ZUCCHINI BLOSSOMS (peak: June–July)

Summer Beers
cream ales, American
fruit beers
Hefeweizen
India Pale Ales (IPAs)
Kölsch
lambic beers, e.g., Framboise
Pilseners
stouts, American
summer ales

Summer Cheeses
blue cheeses, milder
burrata
fresh cheeses
goat's milk cheeses, e.g., Cheddar, chèvre, feta
mozzarella
Quadrello di Bufala, i.e., water buffalo milk cheese
Reblochon
ricotta
Saint-Marcellin
sheep's milk cheeses, young
softer cheeses
Summer cheese accompaniments: basil, bread, melon, olives, peaches, tomatoes

Summer Cocktails/ Mocktails and Spirits
agua frescas
batidas, Brazilian tropical-fruit cocktails
Bellini (white peach juice + Prosecco)
Caipirinha
Campari spritzer
Cosmopolitans
Cuba Libre cocktails
daiquiris
fruitinis and other fruit- or fruit juice–based cocktails
gin and tonic
ginger ale–based cocktails
iced drinks
lemonades, spiked
lime rickeys, cherry or raspberry
Long Island iced tea
margaritas, esp. frozen
martini, cucumber
mint julep
mojitos, e.g., basil
Negroni slushes
Pimm's Cup
piña colada
punches, e.g., Planter's
sangrias
spritzes, e.g., Aperol + orange (slice) + prosecco + soda water
white spirits

Summer Concepts
buffets, cold and room temperature
fritto misto, e.g.,. artichokes,

asparagus, green beans, parsley, zucchini
grilled dishes
noodles, e.g., served chilled
pastas with raw sauces, e.g,. chopped tomatoes, pestos
picnics
pizzas, e.g., with fresh basil, mozzarella, tomatoes
ratatouille
roulades
***salads**, e.g., chilled, green, green bean, pasta, summer fruit, tomato*
sandwiches, e.g,. open-faced
slaws, e.g., cole
*soups, e.g., carrot, **chilled**, corn, cucumber, fresh, gazpacho, light, raw, tomato, watercress*
tarts, e.g., plum, tomato

Summer Desserts

crisps, fruit, e.g., berries, peaches, plums
crostatas, summer fruit
fools
frozen and semi-frozen desserts, e.g., semi-freddos
granitas, e.g., grape, melon
grilled fruit, e.g., peaches
ice creams and gelatos
ice cream sandwiches
ice cream sundaes, e.g., hot fudge, strawberry
ices, e.g., grape, melon
macerated fresh fruit
semi-freddos
shortcakes, e.g., strawberry
sorbets, e.g., grape, melon
tarts, summer fruit, e.g., berry, peach

Summer Dressings

anchovies + lemon + olive oil
basil + garlic + lemon + olive oil + scallions + thyme
basil + lemon juice
chives + mayonnaise + parsley + sour cream + tarragon + watercress [Green Goddess]
citrus vinaigrettes
cucumber + dill + lemon juice + onion
dill + olive oil + red onion + white wine vinegar

Summer Flavor Affinities

apricots + almonds + Cronut
apricots + cardamom + cherries
apricots + honey + yogurt
blackberries + rose water + watermelon
blackberries + rose water + yogurt
blueberries + cinnamon + maple syrup + peaches + ricotta
blue cheese + figs + walnuts
cherries + cardamom + orange + pistachios
chiles + corn + squash blossoms
cucumbers + chives + cream + dill + onion
eggplant + sausage + tomato
figs + goat cheese + pecans
figs + mascarpone + pine nuts
peaches + Champagne + raspberries
peaches + orange + mascarpone cheese
plums + cloves + orange
raspberries + lemon + orange
tomatoes + basil + mozzarella
tomatoes + feta + watermelon
zucchini + mozzarella + scallions

Grilled Corncake with Peaches, Blueberries, Peach Sorbet, Corn Husk Cream, and Popcorn
—Hattie McDaniels, Vida (Indianapolis)

Local Peach Tarte Tatin with Chestnut Honey & Cinnamon Ice Cream
—Mark Levy, Magdalena at The Ivy Hotel (Baltimore)

Peach Tartufo Bianco with Peaches, Blackberries & Soy Yogurt
—Mark Ladner, Del Posto (New York City)

Raspberry & Chocolate Cornetto with Almonds, Candied Bread & Coffee
—Mark Ladner, Del Posto (New York City)

Vegetable Ice Cream Salad with Walnut Cake Croutons
—Amanda Cohen, Dirt Candy (New York City)

TIP: If an ingredient goes with orange, it will likely go with similarly flavored blood oranges, clementines, Grand Marnier, mandarins, orange juice, orange zest, orange Muscat wine, orange tea, tangerines, triple sec, etc.—and possibly with other citrus fruit.

Summer Dishes

A Melange of Our Garden's Summer Squash with House-Made Lemon Ricotta
—Patrick O'Connell, The Inn at Little Washington (Washington, Virginia)

Avocado Toast: JJ's Avocados, Hot Pickled Carrot, Green Garlic Crème Fraîche, Wood Sorrel, Za'atar
—Jessica Koslow, Sqirl (Los Angeles)

Canapes of Tomato Coulis: Tomato snow, cucumber gelee, pickled radish, Robiolina di buffalo
—David Bouley, Bouley (New York City)

Charred Avocado, Rhubarb, Ember Oil, Mayo
—Katianna Hong, The Charter Oak (St. Helena, California)

Charred, Foraged Wild Mushrooms with Slow-Suffered Tree Nut Ragu, Sour Apple Citronette & Sage in Flower
—Mark Ladner, Del Posto (New York City)

Chilled Plum Soup, Marinated Beets, Walnuts, and Shiitake Mushrooms
—Michael Anthony, Gramercy Tavern (New York City)

Corn & Mascarpone Agnolotti, Brown Butter, Confit Cherry Tomato & Parmesan
—Travis Lett, Gjelina (Venice, California)

Crispy Purple Potato, Pickled Mustard Seed, Dill, Fresno & Lemon
—Travis Lett, Gjelina (Venice, California)

Fresh Scungilli Pasta Shells with Green Bean Pesto & Whipped Pinenut Butter
—Mark Ladner, Del Posto (New York City)

Grapefruits Grilled Over the Fire, Rosemary Sugar
—Katianna Hong, The Charter Oak (St. Helena, California)

Grilled Avocado with Tomatillo, Poblano, Cotija Cheese & Cilantro Stems
—Aaron Silverman, Rose's Luxury (Washington, D.C.)

Grilled Peach, Burrata, Arugula, Radicchio & Prosciutto
—Travis Lett, Gjelina (Venice, California)

Heirloom Tomato, Avocado & Black Olive "Panzanella" with Goat Cheese Bonbon
—Mark Levy, Magdalena at The Ivy Hotel (Baltimore)

Insalata Estiva Della Terra with Robiolina, Sweet Pea Puree & Citronette
—Mark Ladner, Del Posto (New York City)

Kudzu Crisp: Lagres aligote, Australian summer black truffle
—David Bouley, Bouley (New York City)

Lemon and Honey Poached Japanese Eggplant with Baba Ghanoush
—Patrick O'Connell, The Inn at Little Washington (Washington, Virginia)

Lobster Mushroom "Steak" with Charred Onions, Red Wine Reduction, and Silver Queen Corn Salsa
—Patrick O'Connell, The Inn at Little Washington (Washington, Virginia)

Our Roasted Chioggia Beets with Belgian Endive and Bleu Cheese Ice Cream
—Patrick O'Connell, The Inn at Little Washington (Washington, Virginia)

Pappardelle with Rabbit and Peach
—Marc Vetri, Vetri (Philadelphia)

Parsley-Crusted Jamison Farms Lamb Loin "Cassoulet" with Summer Vegetables
—Patrick O'Connell, The Inn at Little Washington (Washington, Virginia)

Pistachio Fettucine with Artichokes
—Marc Vetri, Vetri (Philadelphia)

Salad of Roasted Poblano Peppers with Quince, Pickled Hearts of Palm & Crottin de Chavignol
—Mark Levy, Magdalena at The Ivy Hotel (Baltimore)

Spiced Candied Eggplant, Smoked Maitake & Quail Egg "Bric" with Espelette Yogurt
—Mark Levy, Magdalena at The Ivy Hotel (Baltimore)

Watermelon Salad with Heirloom Cherry Tomatoes, Persian Cucumber, Almond Cheese, Toasted Pistachios, and Balsamic Gastrique
—Tal Ronnen and Scot Jones, Crossroads (Los Angeles)

Summer Pastas
angel hair
bucatini
corkscrew pasta
linguine
orecchiette
pasta salads
spaghettini
Summer pasta sauces: broccoli rabe + goat cheese; cherry tomato sauce; chili flakes + garlic + olive oil; fresh herb-based sauces; fresh tomato sauces; fresh vegetable sauces; pesto; seafood preparations (e.g., clams, scallops, shrimp); white wine–based sauces

Summer Presentations
compostable plates and flatware
crudités, served in carved or molded ice bowls
picnics
roadside stand–style baskets

Summer Techniques
chilling
freezing
marinating
***outdoor cooking**, e.g., barbecuing, **grilling**, live-fire cooking*
quick cooking
sautéing
serving raw
steaming

Summer Wines
Albarino
Arneis
Beaujolais
Cava
Chablis
Chenin Blanc
Dolcetto
Falanghina
Fiano
Greek wines
Grüner Veltliner
Lambrusco
lighter-bodied wines
Loire wines
lower-alcohol wines
Pinot Grigio/Pinot Gris
Prosecco
Riesling
Rosé
Sancerre
Sauvignon Blanc
Torrontés
Txakoli
Vinho Verde
Vouvray
white, esp. light-bodied, unoaked

SUPER BOWL

Leading chefs have cooked for the annual **Taste of the NFL** event over Super Bowl weekend for more than a dozen years, bringing creativity to the event's usual "guy food" fare (e.g., burgers, chili, heroes, nachos, pizza, wings)—while raising more than $25 million for hunger relief.

While watching the big game, shareable, interactive snacks are sure to please. Chef **Michael Mina** suggests cheese fondue with an assortment of bread and grilled vegetables for dipping, and cookies or other handheld sweets for dessert.

This time of year [Super Bowl season] is all about football. And football is all about cheap beer and wings. . . . I was living in Bermuda when I got the idea to cut off the tip of a chicken wing and fill the center with blue cheese mousse. These were sliced and fried before tossing in Buffalo hot sauce, which we serve like lollipops on candied celery with hot sauce and a shot of PBR [Pabst Blue Ribbon beer]. It's a very painstaking preparation, but people especially love it during football season playoffs because it's a way for people to connect with what's on their plates. It's never just about the food on the plate—it's about the way it's delivered, and having a sense of humor can help.

—**PHILLIP FOSS,** EL Ideas (Chicago)

Sample dishes from leading chefs, and the teams they represented:

Manchego Cheese with Quince Preserve and Candied Almonds

—Justin Aprahamian, Sanford (Milwaukee), for the Green Bay Packers

BBQ Texas Red Fish with Pickled Onion Salad and Smoked Chile Adobo Sauce

—Robert Del Grande, RDG and Bar Annie (Houston), for the Houston Texans

Corn Fried Soft Shell Crab with Smoked Gouda Grits and Cherry Tomato Relish

—Nancy Longo, Pierpoint Restaurant (Baltimore), for the Baltimore Ravens

Tomales Bay Oyster Stew, Nueske's Bacon "Shards," Smoked Fingerling Potatoes, and Buttermilk "Bandaged" Cheddar Cracker Biscuit

—Carrie Nahabedian, Naha (Chicago), for the Chicago Bears

Andouille Bacon and Green Tomato Crudo, Fresno Strawberry Gelee, Pickled Shallot, Masa Crème Fraîche, Pepita Brittle

—Deb Paquette, Etch (Nashville), for the Tennessee Titans

Fried Oysters with Artichoke Bread Pudding

—Susan Spicer, Bayona (New Orleans), for the New Orleans Saints

Rum Glazed Pork Belly & Cuban Black Bean Stew

—Allen Susser, Burger Bar by Chef Allen (Miami), for the Miami Saints

SURPRISE

Unpredictability is a fundamental part of a meal that lasts 150 minutes. . . . [You] have to tickle [your diners'] intellect, imagination, sense of humor, and memory, and, of course, test their capacity for surprise, play with their expectations, and give them the exact opposite.

—**ANDONI LUIS ADURIZ,** Mugaritz (San Sebastian, Spain)

SUSTAINABILITY / SUSTAINABLE CUISINE (SEE ALSO SEAFOOD, SUSTAINABLE)

Environmental **sustainability** in food was cited as the number 6 trend for 2016 by the National Restaurant Association—but a recent poll of professional chefs predicted it to be the trend that will grow the most over the next ten years.

Chef **Christian Puglisi** and co-owner **Kim Rossen**'s Relae in Copenhagen has the distinction of being the only certified organic restaurant (with its own organic farm, no less) to hold a Michelin star. In Spain, **Eneko Atxa**'s restaurant, Azurmendi, is made with environmentally friendly materials, and also recycles its own waste. The restaurant also harvests rainfall, cooling itself through the use of geothermal energy.

Both restaurants have been honored as the world's most sustainable restaurants through the World's 50 Best Restaurants award.

Environmentally minded chefs and managers around the globe are taking steps to make sure they're part of the solution, and not the problem, through:

- collaborating with farmers
- cooking with perennial crops, which assist in reducing topsoil erosion and carbon emissions
- cutting energy consumption
- donating unused food (which is required by law in France)
- recycling restaurant waste to feed fish that will end up on their menu, as they do at San Francisco's Perennial
- saving water, especially in drought-hit states like California, where Big Sur's Sierra Mar clears dishes of leftovers with compressed air instead of water before putting them into dishwashers (which use as much as two-thirds of the water in restaurants), saving an estimated hundreds of thousands of gallons of water per year

TASTING MENUS

The secret to a **tasting menu?** Pick a star: the food, or the wine. The other should be secondary to the menu's primary focus, and support its flavors.

How many courses? Some tasting menus in New York City top 20 courses. At elBulli **Ferran Adrià** famously served 30 to 35 courses—some of only a single bite.

But success is about quality, not quantity, as Eleven Madison Park aimed to prove by halving its 14-course tasting menu to seven larger courses. The tasting menu format serves as a creative spur for many chefs, with the goal being to have guests trust the chef enough to put themselves into his or her hands, and for the restaurant to deliver a profound experience that leaves a lasting impression.

T

Dessert-only tasting menus? Why not? For the past decade, pastry chef **Chika Tillman**'s 15-seat ChikaLicious has had a wait for its $16 three-course dessert prix fixe (with optional tea or wine pairings).

In 2012, the no-reservations salon at **Thomas Keller**'s Per Se in Manhattan started offering its own five-course dessert prix-fixe menu, as did **Dominique Crenn**'s Atelier Crenn in San Francisco. Since then, pastry chef **Dominique Ansel** opened U.P. ("Unlimited Possibilities"), a tasting menu concept above his New York bakery offering dessert courses paired with cocktails.

Imagine: **Mario Batali**'s Babbo is the first restaurant we ever visited offering a pasta tasting menu. What course do *you* love so much that you might consider creating a tasting menu around it?

TEAM

At El Celler de Can Roca in Spain, which was ranked the world's number 1 restaurant in 2015, the synergistic magic is the result of a **team** of three gifted **Roca brothers**—chef **Joan**, pâtissier **Jordi**, and sommelier **Josep**—who together create a self-described "modern freestyle" experience that is a wine lover's fantasy.

Imagine: Who would *your* ideal teammates be for your next culinary creation?

Innovation is not just coming up with a new flavor. It is also finding a way at looking at a problem and figuring out what to do about it in the future.

—**JACQUES TORRES,** Jacques Torres Chocolate (New York City)

TECHNIQUES

When you apply different **techniques** to the same ingredient, you create different flavors. Think about an egg—and the differences in flavor and texture that result from baking, frying, hard-boiling, poaching, scrambling, or soft-boiling it. One of our favorite ways to cook eggs at home is by steaming them via a stovetop milk steamer typically used to make cappuccino.

We learned from **Jacques Torres**'s wife and partner, chocolatier **Hasty Torres**, that her husband's mechanical mind is an important spur to his creativity with confections. "He will take a machine that has nothing to with chocolate and find a way to use it," she told us.

Jacques explained, "Usually to grind chocolate you would use two rollers made of granite, but that doesn't get it fine enough. We bought a refiner, which is a stainless-steel roller that can be used for cosmetics (e.g., lipstick). It grinds [a substance] down into a super-soft paste. This machine is perfect for getting the finest possible texture and mouthfeel."

Hasty agreed: "The grind is so soft you can't feel any texture on your tongue. Jacques will also use it to grind nuts fine to make nut butters or pralines, or pistachios for marzipan."

Imagine: What's a new technique you can apply to an ingredient you use regularly?

TEMPERATURE

Temperature's critical role in the enjoyment of flavor is being acknowledged not only in food but in drink.

Gabriel Kreuther's namesake restaurant in New York City serves iced tea in the summertime with ice cubes made from iced tea, so as not to dilute the beverage. And "sidecars" are experiencing renewed popularity as cocktails are more frequently served with an accompanying chilled carafe of the drink to ensure its optimal temperature and enjoyment.

On our first visit to the Inn at Little Washington, **Patrick O'Connell**'s team sent up afternoon tea to our room with the teapot nestled in a tea cozy to ensure that our tea stayed hot.

Imagine: What change could you make that would help to maintain the temperature and/or flavor of a cold or hot beverage or dish?

TERROIR

Terroir refers to the natural environment in which a wine or other foodstuff is produced, which includes such factors as climate, soil composition, and terrain, as well as to the resulting characteristic flavor imparted to that wine or food. (In our book *The Food Lover's Guide to Wine,* we characterize the "three Gs" that affect the flavor of any wine: the **grape** from which it's made, the **guy or gal** who made it and his/her decisions, as well as the **ground** in which it's grown and climate, weather, etc.—which when they get out of hand are known as "acts of **God.**" Terroir is most closely related to the third.)

Inspired by the world of wine, chef **Yannick Alléno** of Terroir Parisien–Maison de la Mutualité in Paris has been focusing on an exploration of the effects of terroir on fermented vegetable extractions. Foreseeing a renaissance in the art of sauce-making, he believes chefs can use vegetable extractions and fermentation to create increasingly flavorful and complex sauces. Alléno sees **FERMENTATION** as the key to "unlocking the essence of the terroir."

TEXTURE

As we know from Stage 2, **texture** is part of mouthfeel. Understanding the connection between taste and mouthfeel can enhance your creativity, as **Joshua Skenes** explains:

> Savoriness, sweetness, and fat all play a role in creating a subtle mouthfeel that is more enjoyable to me sometimes, rather than a hard contrast of **textures.** For our beet dish [which has the texture of filet mignon, after the beets are hung above the fire for three days], when you cut into it, the texture begins on the fork and knife. . . . That is a pleasurable experience to some degree. You put it in your mouth and get the chewiness, then the concentrated flavor of the grill and fire, and then the fat kicks in and you go into the [flavor balancing] cycle [see page 256].

Texture begins on the fork and knife; it does not start in your mouth.

—JOSHUA SKENES, Saison (San Francisco)

THANKSGIVING

Once the biggest day for eating at home, **Thanksgiving** dinner is changing. More than 10 percent of Americans dined out on the fourth Thursday in November in 2015, more than double the rate of 40 years ago, according to the National Restaurant Association. In New York City, Thanksgiving Day has evolved into the second-busiest day of the year for restaurant dining—right behind Valentine's Day. Even more (18 million) turned to takeout for all or part of the meal they enjoyed at home. So home cooks and restaurant chefs alike are finding themselves looking for new ideas this time of year.

Most diners still seek a traditional Thanksgiving dinner—roast turkey, stuffing (e.g., cornbread or sourdough), gravy, soup (butternut squash, mushroom), vegetable side dishes (mashed potatoes, candied sweet potatoes, green bean casserole, Brussels sprouts, chestnut puree, creamed onions), cranberry relish, rolls (Parker House), pies (especially pumpkin) and other desserts (Indian pudding, poached pears in red wine, pumpkin cheesecake), etc. But dietary restrictions and preferences have put new emphasis on gluten-free, vegetarian, vegan, and other options. And self-respecting home cooks and restaurant chefs alike welcome new spins on old standbys:

Dishes

Turkey confit sweet potato fritters

—José Andrés, America Eats Tavern (MacLean, Virginia)

Turkey-and-stuffing dumplings with a cranberry dipping sauce

—Marian and Hannah Cheng, Mimi Cheng's Dumplings (New York City)

Celery-flavored croissant stuffed with turkey, gravy, and cranberries

—Christina Tosi, Milk Bar (New York City)

Cabernet-Rosemary Seitan with Celeriac Puree, Wild Mushrooms, Crispy Onions, and Porcini Reduction

—Joy Pierson and Bart Potenza, Candle 79 (New York City)

Acorn Squash Bisque with Crispy Bacon and Kale, Topped with Whipped Crème Fraîche

—Sherry Yard, Tuck Room Tavern (Westwood, California)

Turkey: brined, deep-fried, smoked

Alternative entrées: cauliflower steak with lentils and spinach; pumpkin gnocchi with toasted pepitas; winter squash tortellini

Stuffing: brioche stuffing; New England–style stuffing (e.g., with oysters); sticky rice with scallions and shiitakes; wild mushroom bread pudding

Gravy: smoked gravy; wild mushroom and roasted garlic gravy

Vegetable side dishes: crudités; mashed potatoes made with Red Bliss or Yukon Golds; maple parsnips; sweet potatoes with a savory twist (e.g., horseradish)

Desserts: apple fig pie; chocolate pecan pie; ginger cake; pecan praline pie; sweet potato flan

THEATER, DINNER AS

Theatricality is experiencing a rebirth in some restaurants—but in others, it never went away. A theater major in college, Patrick O'Connell brings a whimsical sense of the theatrical to dinner at the **Inn at Little Washington** in Virginia. (The experience even comes with popcorn—with shaved truffles over it, of course!—not to mention a mooing cow named Faira who serves as the restaurant's cheese cart and is "introduced" to guests before dessert.) At Ron Zimmerman's famed restaurant, the **Herbfarm** in Woodinville, Washington, the curtain onto the kitchen opens and closes as part of the one-seating-a-night dinner show.

We visited **Eleven Madison Park** for dinner after the staff was trained to perform a card trick at the table—an incarnation we personally loved. At the sibling restaurant the **NoMad**, there's a weekly magic show featuring gifted magician Dan White in the **Library**—truffle popcorn included.

TIME (SEE ALSO PLACE)

Uniqueness of time and place is the essence of almost every fine dining experience that I know of in traditional Japanese cooking and other forms of serious cooking.

—MICHAEL ANTHONY, Gramercy Tavern and Untitled (New York City)

A great meal, and the great dishes that comprise it, reflect a specific **time** and place.

Imagine: What is the essence of the **time** when the meal you're planning will be happening (i.e., special significance, year, season, month, day of the week, time of day, etc.)?

TIME = AN INGREDIENT

Whereas certain dishes (e.g., long-simmered braises) are often better the day after cooking (or even the day after that, once their flavors have been allowed to concentrate), other foods are meant to be consumed immediately (e.g., fresh-baked madeleines, which lose their magic in minutes). At **Dominique Ansel**'s Kitchen, where **time is an ingredient,** 70 percent of the dishes are made *à la minute*—that is, when they are ordered. Exceptions include his macarons, which he believes must be refrigerated at least overnight in order for the flavors and textures to moisten and meld.

At San Francisco's Saison, **Joshua Skenes** aims to minimize the amount of time the ingredients he serves have been out of the water or the dirt. He describes his ongoing pursuit of reducing the gap of time between products' leaving the ocean or the earth to arriving in his guests' mouths to "zero" as his "life pursuit," explaining:

> Our farm is 45 minutes away. We have the process of picking a radish down to a science: It is picked that morning, it gets misted with the dirt left on, and it is left whole so that all the flavor transfers as much as possible. Then, we only process it when we need it.
>
> Still, it is never the same as picking it out of the ground and eating it. In the same way, you can't replace picking a sea urchin underwater, opening it, rinsing it in seawater, and eating it [immediately]. It is impossible and it is a hard truth.
>
> There are moments in time when there is something that has this incredible taste that exists. . . . How do you capture all that in one place? My next aim is to shorten the gap to zero. You have to reduce all the commercial elements as much as possible.

To respect time as a supreme ingredient is a battle of breaking habits and changing perceptions. . . . When you treat time as an ingredient, it changes everything.

—DOMINIQUE ANSEL, *Dominique Ansel: The Secret Recipes*

TIME, PASSAGE OF (SEE ALSO AGING)

Andoni Luis Aduriz is inspired by abstract notions. In his *Mugaritz* cookbook, the chef shares the example of a dish he serves featuring Camellia leaves with their vegetal layer washed away (as those leaves appear in nature at a certain moment in autumn) that he connects to the **passage of time,** and the melancholy of its passing.

Similarly, **Massimo Bottura** of Italy's Osteria Francescana offers a signature dish of Five Ages of Parmigiano Reggiano, which provides a sense of the aging process within a single dish, with differences highlighted via texture and temperature.

T

TIME TRAVEL

Giving yourself a reference point in time to inspire your next dish or menu will challenge your creativity—and **the flavors can take you to another place and time.**

Rick Bayless's Mexico 1491 menu at Topolobampo in Chicago celebrated pre-Colombian cuisine, serving dishes such as pineapple ceviche and frog leg tamales.

Grant Achatz's French Laundry 1996 menu at Chicago's Next returned to Achatz's alma mater.

Imagine: What is a moment in time to which you'd wish to return? How could you go there through food?

TOP CHEF

My observant editor, **Mike Szczerban**, and I had an exchange during this book's creation about the fact that the popularity of the TV show ***Top Chef***, which debuted in 2006, reflects part of the thesis of this book: that culinary success is increasingly about creativity, rather than the execution of someone else's recipes. (Correspondingly, it's been gratifying to see so many of the show's winners and runners-up—including **Nina Compton, Carla Hall, Hung Huynh, Stephanie Izard, Dale Levitski, Hosea Rosenberg,** and **Michael Voltaggio**—name either *The Flavor Bible* or *Culinary Artistry* as their favorite book for inspiration in the kitchen.)

Competition can stir creativity. As an exercise, think of the types of challenges that chefs are given on the show—such as making a classic dish without its main ingredient, creating a dish showcasing a trio of flavors (e.g., chicken + onion + potato), and limiting available kitchen tools.

Imagine: How could you use competition, even if it's just against yourself, to break yourself out of your creative box?

TOURISTS

Food tourism is on the rise. **Tourists** want to experience local specialties, and an estimated 35 million people have traveled just for a culinary experience (guilty!), with most vacation travelers willing to scrimp elsewhere to be able to splurge on great food. Nearly half of all travelers surveyed would prefer to spend on food than on hotel, airfare, or entertainment.

Imagine: What other region or country would you most like to visit? What could you do to take yourself on a virtual trip there through food?

TRAINING

Don't be myopic about where to learn more that will make you a more creative cook—there are lots of options beyond cooking school. Consider taking a wine course, a bartending course, even a perfumery course.

Imagine: Flip through a continuing education course catalog. Is there anything you might study that *wouldn't* make you a better cook?

TRAVEL AS INSPIRATION

After chef **Diego Muñoz** helped Peru's Astrid y Gastón win a place on the World's 50 Best Restaurants list, he resigned in order to **travel around the world** to find inspiration for his own restaurant.

Imagine: Take a virtual trip around the world when you're trying to figure out what to do with a new ingredient: Imagine what a local in Western Europe, Eastern Europe, Scandinavia, Asia, Australia, Latin America, or elsewhere would do with that ingredient.

TWO-IN-ONE TECHNIQUES AND TOOLS

Corinne Trang, the author of *Essentials of Asian Cuisine*, taught us her brilliant one-step steam-fry technique for dumplings (where dumplings are placed at the bottom of a pan containing both water and oil, so as soon as the water evaporates while the dumplings steam, they then automatically fry in the oil that remains), which led us to make them much more regularly.

On the lookout for other **two-in-one techniques**, we remember reading about **Daniel Patterson**'s poach-scramble technique, whereby he drops a beaten egg into boiling water and cooks it, covered, for 20 seconds before straining—resulting in an uber-creamy (and uber-fast) scrambled egg, made without added fat.

We've used our cappuccino steamer nozzle not only to foam milk but also to steam scrambled eggs, adding cheese and scallions for the moistest scrambled eggs imaginable. Listening to NPR, I first learned that some actually use their woks as mini-smokers, too.

Imagine: Could you combine two cooking techniques in one, as a timesaver, flavor enhancer, and/or for other benefits? Can you think of another use for a tool already in your kitchen?

UNIVERSE, THE

Your eyes are the eyes of the universe. Your heart is the heart of the universe. Your body is the body of the universe. When you move, the universe stirs. . . . The universe has waited eons to awaken in you. It continues to evolve through you, right here and right now. As you sow seeds of creativity in the flowering garden of the world, realize that, frail creature that you are, you also soar as a god.

—**ROBERT PENG,** world-renowned qigong master, *The Master Key: Qigong Secrets for Wisdom, Love, and Vitality*

UNPLUG

The greater our distractions, the lesser our creativity. So, at least from time to time, remember to **unplug**—from phone calls, texts, email, social media. Give yourself the opportunity to focus without distractions in order to enhance your creativity.

VALENTINE'S DAY (SEE ALSO RED FOODS AND WINTER)

Date: February 14

aphrodisiacs, e.g., artichokes, asparagus, avocadoes, bananas, coffee, figs, honey, oysters
cake, e.g., red velvet
caviar
Champagne, e.g., rosé
chocolate
cookies, e.g., heart-shaped
flowers, edible
hearts, e.g., artichoke, of palm
lobster
oysters, raw
passion fruit
red foods, e.g., bell peppers, cherries, chiles, raspberries, strawberries
truffles
wine, e.g., red, rosé

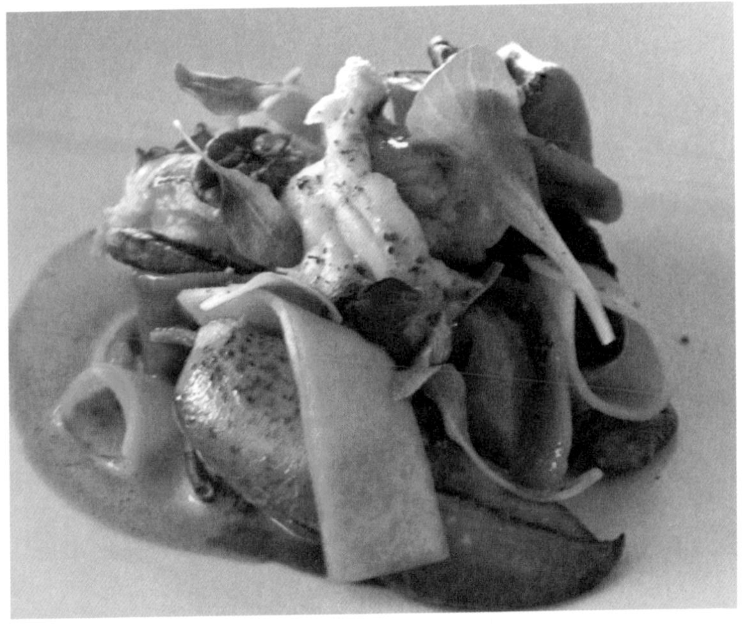

U V

VEGETABLE-CENTRIC / VEGETARIAN / VEGAN FOOD

In an expectation-thwarting move, during [spring and summer] Noma will become a fully vegetarian restaurant.

—**JEFF GORDINIER,** *New York Times* (September 16, 2015), on René Redzepi's globally celebrated restaurant

When he announced his decision to focus on a tasting of **vegetables**—The Grands Crus du Potager—as his signature menu at L'Arpège in Paris, chef **Alain Passard** described it as "the natural progression of my thinking over 30 years as a chef."

Our idea of healthful eating has been evolving over the years as well, away from fad dieting to feeling good about what we put in our bodies every single day. The nutritional science is clear that vegetables are the best foods we can put in our bodies not only to maintain and enhance our health but also to actively fight diseases. Environmentalists argue that minimizing meat consumption is best for the planet. Chefs have proclaimed vegetables' primacy as the foremost bearer of flavor in dishes. All of this is leading vegetables to take their place in the center of our plates.

With 54 percent of Americans seeking to reduce (47 percent) or eliminate (5 percent vegetarians plus 2 percent vegans) meat from their diets, it is now the mainstream majority that is seeking out and supporting the explosion of vegetable-centric dishes on menus, from fast-casual to fine dining. The latter segment is seeing an increasing number of vegetarian and even vegan tasting menus at restaurants including **Daniel, Eleven Madison Park,** the **Inn at Little Washington**, and **Per Se**, catering not only to vegetarians and vegans, but to this 54 percent majority seeking more meatless options.

What's in a Name?

Fewer people may be using the labels **vegetarian** (i.e., those who abstain from eating meat, poultry, and seafood) and **vegan** (i.e., vegetarians who also eschew eggs, dairy products, and other animal-derived products such as gelatin and honey) because of the terms' focus on what these diets don't include, favoring **plant-based**, to emphasize the abundant bounty of plants they do celebrate, including vegetables, fruits, legumes, grains, mushrooms, nuts, seeds, and more.

Two of America's best plant-based restaurants—Vedge in Philadelphia, whose co-owners, chef **Rich Landau** and pastry chef **Kate Jacoby**, have been nominated for James Beard Foundation awards, and Crossroads in Los Angeles, where co-chefs **Tal Ronnen** and **Scot Jones** man the stoves—eschew the vegan moniker, given that many if not most of the always-packed restaurants' clientele do not count themselves as vegan.

Tal Ronnen of Crossroads has developed vegan proxies for the "mother sauces" of modern gastronomy, with cashew cream (a blend of cashews + water) an invaluable substitute for heavy cream.

After discovering as a teenager that a vegan diet could control his asthma, chef **Chad Sarno** has worked to realize the flavor potential of plant-based cuisine, and currently serves as vice president of culinary wellness at Rouxbe culinary school, which offers the leading online plant-based cooking program. **Fran Costigan**, the author of *Vegan Chocolate* who has been rightly called the Queen of Vegan Desserts by many (including us), is Rouxbe's director of vegan baking and

As an intelligent, evolved society, I think it's inevitable that we will move toward a plant-based lifestyle.

—**MATTHEW KENNEY,** Plant Food and Wine (Los Angeles)

pastry, and advises egg and dairy substitutes in vegan baking.

At Brooklyn's Semilla, **José Ramírez-Ruiz** and **Pamela Yung** describe their cuisine as a "vegetable-forward tasting menu" that allows vegetables to shine, with any seafood or meat strictly as part of the supporting cast.

More vegetables from around the globe are being explored as the inspiration for a wider range of dishes than ever before, as both common and uncommon vegetables are being given new consideration. **Foraging** (see FORAGING) is becoming more commonplace, with some restaurateurs such as **Daniel Boulud** employing their own foragers—Daniel's chef de cuisine **Eddy Leroux** works with forager **Tama Matsuoka Wong** to bring in unusual products, and even coauthored the book *Foraged Flavor* with her. Louisiana's **John Folse** included recipes for foraged cattail pollen pancakes and fresh thistle salad in his latest cookbook, *Can You Dig It*.

The cooking of plant-based ingredients is expanding, including through a variety of techniques and dishes formerly reserved for animal proteins:

Treating Plants Like Meat

brining
bourguignon, e.g., beet, celery root
burgers, e.g., portobellos, veggie
carpaccio, e.g., beet, carrot, eggplant, king oyster mushroom, persimmon, root vegetables, winter squash, zucchini
charring
cheesesteaks, e.g., seitan (à la Philadelphia's Blackbird Pizza's version made with rosemary and garlic seared seitan, grilled onions and green peppers, and vegan whiz, served on an artisan hoagie roll)
confit, e.g., bell pepper, carrots, garlic, mushrooms, onions, shallots, squash, tomatoes
fondue, e.g., rutabaga (à la Rich Landau's version at Philadelphia's Vedge)
dry-rubbing
grilling
marinating
meatballs, e.g., legumes, mushrooms
porterhouse, e.g., cabbage (à la

V

Terrance Brennan

Bourguignon is typically garnished with button mushrooms, pearl onions, and lardons. My vegetarian version is made with celery root in a red wine sauce made from roasted vegetable stock that is dark, dark, dark and full of umami. I roast the celery root whole, and cut off a wedge to puree because I love pureed celery root, then add the red wine sauce. I will also cut some of the celery root in the shape of lardons, which we will smoke so they taste like bacon before poaching in red wine sauce to take on the color. . . . For the vegetarian "ramen," I had to figure out how to infuse fattiness so that it is not simply brothy. So I added white miso and cooked pureed cashews that get emulsified right before serving to give it that richness of texture.

—**TERRANCE BRENNAN,** Roundhouse (Beacon, New York)

Marc Forgione's version at NYC's American Cut)
roasting, e.g., beets (à la John Fraser's version at NYC's Narcissa)
searing
shawarma, e.g., seitan (marinated in black pepper + chili powder + coriander + cumin + garlic + marjoram + olive oil + onion + oregano + rosemary + thyme) or trumpet mushroom (à la Rich Landau's version at Philadelphia's V Street)
smoking, e.g., cabbage, carrots (think lox), cheese (e.g., Gouda, mozzarella), corn, eggplant, nuts, olives, potatoes, tempeh, tofu, tomatoes
steaks, e.g., beet, cabbage, cauliflower, winter squash
stewing
tartare, e.g., beet, carrot
torchon, e.g., mushroom (à la Eric Ziebold's version at DC's Kinship)
Wellington, e.g., carrot (à la John Fraser's version at New York City's Narcissa)
wood-roasting, e.g., asparagus

Dishes

Celery Root with the Flavors of Beef Bourguignon
—Terrance Brennan, Roundhouse (Beacon, New York)

Shoyu Tofu Mushroom Ramen with vegetable broth, rice noodles, soft tofu, Japanese mushrooms, asparagus, eggplant, kabocha squash, edamame, and chili oil
—Takashi Yagihashi, Slurping Turtle (Chicago)

Vegetable "Ramen" ("Kohlramen," made from spiralized kohlrabi), with miso eggplant "belly," umami broth, pickled stems, and cashew "cheese" (vegan and gluten-free)
—Terrance Brennan, Roundhouse (Beacon, New York)

Imagine: Chef **Todd Gray** of Equinox in Washington, D.C., started the Vegan Smackdown Challenge to create vegan versions of recipes from prominent chefs such as **José Andrés, Todd**

English, and **Carla Hall.** How would you go about creating a meatless, eggless and dairy-free version of a classic dish?

WAFFLES

Every time we hear the title of **Dan Shumski**'s book, ***Will It Waffle?***, we smile. The actual book has borne out its value, containing amusing inspiration for filling a waffle iron with virtually anything other than waffle batter (from mac-n-cheese to scallion pancake batter to cookie dough).

In addition to serving them as a breakfast and brunch staple, some chefs are using waffles in savory dishes like chicken and waffles (which White House chef **Cristeta Comerford** even served as hors d'oeuvres) or waffle sandwiches.

Chicken and Waffles: Fried "Chicken," Waffles, and Warm Maple Hot Sauce
—Tal Ronnen and Scot Jones, Crossroads (Los Angeles)

Fried Chicken, Waffles + Honey
—Ashley Christensen, Beasley's and Poole's Diner (Raleigh, North Carolina)

Buttermilk-Fried Sweetbreads with White Corn Waffles, Rhode Island Maple Syrup, and Smoked Pecan Gravy
—hors d'oeuvres at Rhode Island chefs' dinner at the James Beard House in New York City

Chicken Liver Pâté with Rosemary Waffles, Pickled Elderberries, Pecans, and Bourbon Barrel-Aged Maple Syrup
—Kristin Butterworth, Lautrec (Farmington, Pennsylvania)

WALDORF ASTORIA

The reputed home of culinary inventions ranging from the Waldorf salad to Eggs Benedict to red velvet cake (see page 58), the **Waldorf Astoria** hotel chain seeks to make lightning strike again and again by inaugurating in 2014 an annual culinary competition, Taste of Waldorf Astoria, to come up with the hotel's next iconic dish—by pairing its chefs from five locations around the globe with five James Beard Foundation Rising Star finalists.

The 2015 winner was Celery Risotto alla Waldorf, courtesy of the team of chef **Heinz Beck** of Waldorf Astoria Rome Cavalieri's Michelin three-star La Pergola and Rising Star chef **David Posey** of Chicago. The dish substitutes finely chopped celery root for the usual Arborio rice and echoes the flavors of the Waldorf salad with apples, hazelnuts, Parmesan cheese, and black truffles.

The 2016 winner was the Jing Roll, courtesy of the team of chef **Benoit Chargy** of Waldorf Astoria Beijing and Rising Star chef **Erik Bruner-Yang** of Toki Underground in Washington, D.C. The Jing Roll features Chinese napa cabbage wrapped around minced Wagyu beef with black mushrooms and Chinese chili peppers, hoisin sauce, local salted duck eggs, okra, and sweet purple potatoes. The 2017 competition challenged chefs to create an "unforgettable 'Fifth Hour' concoction comprised of one cocktail, one mocktail, and two paired bites." The 2017 winner was the team of chef **Michael Zachman** of Waldorf Astoria Park City and Rising Star chef **Alex Bois** of Lost Bread Co. in Philadelphia. The winning entry was Beet-Cured Steelhead Trout (Rye & Shine Prosecco Cocktail) and Spicy Togarashi Prawn (Ginger Yuzu Asian Pear Mo(ck)jito).

Winning dishes are added to the menu at 25 Waldorf Astoria restaurants around the world.

WARMING FOODS (CONTRAST WITH COOLING FOODS)

In addition to their actual temperature, certain foods have a warming effect on the body ("nourishing yang," according to Chinese medicine)—which makes them especially useful in colder seasons and months, and on unseasonably cold days. In addition, they're beneficial in dishes for health-conscious and weight-conscious guests, as studies indicate correlations between capsaicin and both heart health and weight control, and between spicy foods and

W

boosting metabolism and burning calories.

baking
broccoli rabe
broiling
cardamom
cayenne
chile peppers
chives
cinnamon
cloves
coffee
cumin
garlic
ginger
grilling
hot foods
nutmeg
nuts, e.g., peanuts, walnuts
oats
oil, toasted sesame
onions
parsnips
pepper, black
pine nuts
quinoa
rice, basmati
root vegetables, e.g., carrots, potatoes
rosemary
rutabagas
sautéing
scallions
seeds, e.g., mustard, sesame
soups
squash, winter
stir-frying
sugar, refined
teas
turmeric
vinegar
wasabi
wine

WAYS TO EXPEDITE CREATIVITY

Set a clear intention. As author **Deepak Chopra** has noted, "The act of creation is reducible to one ingredient: intention."

Use your resources. **Stephen R. Covey**, author of *The 7 Habits of Highly Effective People,* reminded me in a telephone interview that each of us has four gifts—self-awareness, creative imagination, independent will, and conscience—which "give us the ultimate human freedom: the power to choose, to respond, to change."

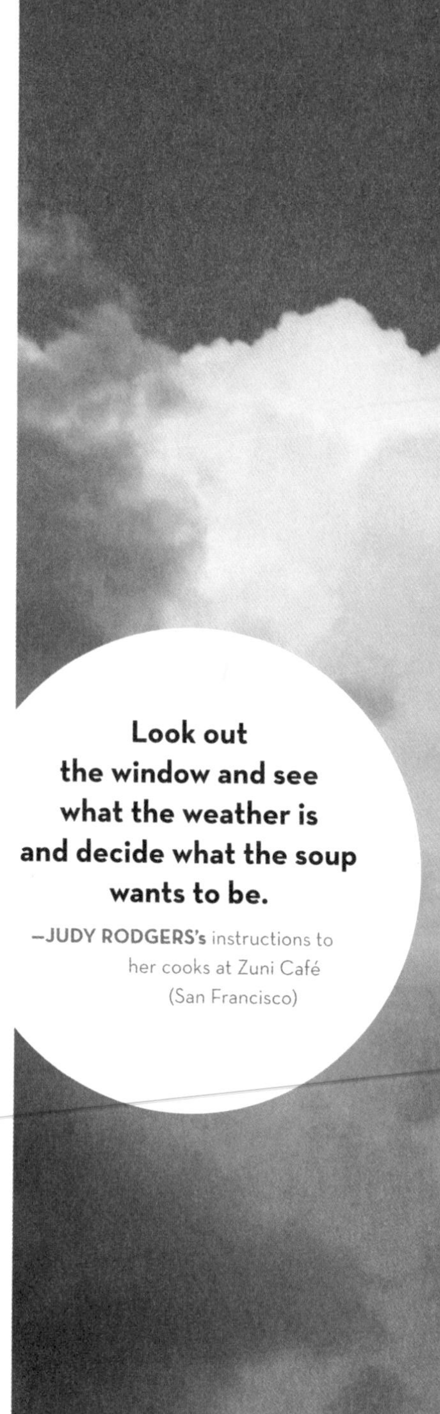

Look out the window and see what the weather is and decide what the soup wants to be.

—**JUDY RODGERS's** instructions to her cooks at Zuni Café (San Francisco)

WEATHER (SEE ALSO SEASONALITY / SEASONS AND TIME)

With global warming and greater **weather** unpredictability in general, you can't always anticipate an unseasonably warm day in January or an unseasonably cold night in July. So in addition to paying attention to the season, you'll want to pay attention to the day's weather. Guests will appreciate COOLING FOODS on warm to hot days, and WARMING FOODS on cool to cold days.

WEDDINGS

Wedding traditions vary around the globe, but you don't have to be native to a particular country to

take inspiration from its symbolic food choices:
almonds, candied (Greece, with the bitter almonds and sweet candies representing a marriage's lows and highs)
cake, multi-tiered layer
Champagne
clams (Japan)
consommé (Germany)
croquembouche (France)
flowers, edible
fruitcake (England)
gingko nuts (China)
honey (India)
marzipan (Iraq)
roe, herring (Japan)
whiskey cake (Ireland)
white foods

WHAT?

What can we do that no one else can? This is the fundamental question, the beating heart of my work. . . . I wonder what we are gathering and squeezing from our life experiences that we can point to as our own, that we can set before a guest knowing the dish could have only been found here.

—CHRISTOPHER KOSTOW, *A New Napa Cuisine*

WHEN?, SEE AUTUMN, SPRING, SUMMER, TIME, AND WINTER

WHERE?, SEE ALTITUDE, LOCAL [AND HYPER-LOCAL] SOURCING, AND PLACE

WHEY

The popularity of Greek yogurt has led to an overabundance of a byproduct of that process: **whey.**

Traditionally, whey is used to make ricotta or to feed pigs—as they do with the whey from Parmigiano Reggiano, whereby the pigs are then turned into prosciutto di Parma.

Producers like Chobani can't simply dump acid whey, because its toxicity to nature causes environmental problems, so they

Christopher Kostow

W

actually pay farmers to take it off their hands.

Creative chefs and mixologists are discovering new uses for whey—which is mostly water, plus lactose [milk sugar] and some minerals—including as a replacement for water in beignets, mashed potatoes, pancakes, and yeast breads, or as an ingredient in concoctions ranging from caramel sauces to cocktails. At **Spike Gjerde**'s Woodberry Kitchen in Baltimore, whey is featured in the Dirty Rhubarb cocktail with **gin + lemon juice + rhubarb syrup.** At **Gunnar Gíslason**'s Agern in Manhattan, a creamy mocktail features **whey + lemon thyme + verjus.**

WHITE FOODS

almond milk
almonds, peeled
bell peppers, white
bread, white
carrots, white
cauliflower
cheese, e.g., feta, white cheddar
chocolate, white
coconut
cream
flour, white
garlic, white
kefir
lychees
milk
mushrooms, white
onions, white
parsnips
rice, white
scallions, white part of
sour cream
sugar: powdered, white
tofu
yogurt

Lychees are in season right now, so I'll take lychees and all kinds of white vegetables—maybe white bell peppers, white carrots, white onions, the white part of scallions, fresh garlic—and add some almond milk, and make a beautiful gazpacho that looks great. It's completely blonde. It's got a lot of the same characteristics as a gazpacho but it's a little bit rich, a little bit acidic and definitely creamy.

—**JAMIE BISSONNETTE,** Coppa and Toro (Boston), as quoted in the *Wall Street Journal*

White dishes as celebrated at Gabriel Kreuther (New York City), Parachute (Chicago), and Empellón (New York City)

WHITE HOUSE STATE DINNERS

Imagine the creative challenges facing **White House Chef Cristeta Comerford** (2005–present), **pastry chefs Bill Yosses** (2007–2014), and **Susan Morrison** (2015–present) as they created menus in honor of heads of state. The Obamas hosted visiting dignitaries from India, Mexico, China, Germany, South Korea, the United Kingdom, France, Japan, China, Canada, and five Nordic countries.

Simply imitating their guests' countries' native dishes could be a recipe for failure—while offering a nod to them while reinterpreting ideas through their own lens, using American ingredients, seems respectful and even conversation-provoking.

Generally, American beef is the most frequently served entrée at the White House. The only dinner to offer an option was the dinner hosted for **India,** which offered both a meat-based entrée and a vegetarian entrée. Indeed, that entire menu was primarily vegetarian, out of respect for the vegetarian diet of then-Prime Minister Manmohan Singh.

HIGHLIGHTS OF STATE DINNERS, 2009–2016

Five Nordic Countries (2016)

At the May 13, 2016, State Dinner in honor of the President of Finland and the Prime Ministers of Norway, Sweden, Denmark, and Iceland and their spouses, canapés included a Chicken and Waffles hors d'oeuvre along with Venison Tartare with Truffle Vinaigrette (as a more readily available substitute for more traditional Nordic reindeer) and Baby Radish with Vermont Butter and Maldon Salt, which was served on foraged wood from the White House backyard.

At dessert time, which featured a Caramel Almond Mille-Feuille with Vanilla Bean Chantilly and Lingonberry Cream, edible fishing boats (made of chocolate and gum paste) flying the flags of the United States and the five countries being honored were placed on each table, surrounded by *petit fours* such as elderberry custard tarts, ginger-gooseberry cookies, raspberry kringle, and red currant chocolates.

> **In reading, I realized that waffles are such a big thing in the Nordic countries. So we're doing chicken and waffles [as a canapé], which is an American thing.**
>
> —WHITE HOUSE CHEF CRISTETA COMERFORD, on the challenges of creating a multi-course menu in May 2016 for heads of state from Finland, Norway, Sweden, Denmark, and Iceland, as quoted in the *Washington Post*

Canada (2016)

The March 2016 State Dinner found chef **Cristeta Comerford** serving Justin Trudeau and his wife, and other assembled guests, a spin on the Canadian dish poutine (french fries + cheese curds + gravy): a one-bite canapé of a fried potato wafer topped with cheese curds and bits of smoked duck, with a red-wine gravy. Pastry chef **Susan Morrison** capped off dinner with Maple Pecan Cake with Cocoa Nib Wafer and Butterscotch Swirl Ice Cream, which was accompanied by a 2013 Chateau Chantal Ice Wine.

China (2015)

In conjunction with guest chef **Anita Lo:**

State Dinner
In Honor of
His Excellency Xi Jinping,
the President of the People's Republic of China, Madame Peng Liyuan
The White House
September 25, 2015

Inspired by Autumn: The China State Dinner menu is inspired by the harvest of the late summer and fall. Chef **Cris**

Comerford and Chef **Susie Morrison**, in collaboration with chef **Anita Lo,** created original dishes that highlight American cuisine with nuances of Chinese flavors. The courses begin with a consommé of locally grown mushrooms, hinted with black truffle and Shaoxing Wine. It is finished with slivers of squashes from the White House Kitchen Garden, crisped squash seeds, and drizzled pumpkinseed oil. The Fish Course pairs a Butter Poached Maine Lobster with traditional rice noodle rolls embedded with morsels of spinach, shiitake mushroom, and leeks. It is then gingerly coated with the lobster reduction and dotted with tomalley butter. The Main Course showcases a Grilled Cannon of Colorado Lamb garnished with garlic fried milk, a surprisingly crunchy variation of a savory panna cotta dipped in a light tempura, then fried into a crispy perfection. This is complemented with a crisped sauté of baby broccoli from a local farmer's market. The Dessert Course is made up of layers of lightly buttered artisanal bread accented with a delicate egg custard, including a Meyer lemon curd and lychee sorbet. Meyer lemons are thought to have originated in China and were introduced in the U.S. in the early 1900s. "A Stroll Through the Garden" is a dessert display that is a tribute to the beauty of gardens—composed of a handmade chocolate pavilion and bridge, pulled sugar roses and white lotus flowers that symbolize good fortune. A selection of miniature pastries—including pumpkin mooncakes, peanut sesame bars, mango kiwi cups, maple chocolates, and apple cider tarts—celebrates Chinese and American cuisine by fusing traditional Chinese ingredients sourced from New Hampshire, Maryland, California, and Virginia.

—The White House State Dinner program

Dinner Menu

Wild Mushroom Soup with Black Truffle

Shaoxing Wine

Butter Poached Maine Lobster with Spinach, Shiitake and Leek Rice Noodle Rolls

Penner-Ash Viognier "Oregon" 2014

Grilled Cannon of Colorado Lamb with Garlic Fried Milk and Baby Broccoli

Pride Mountain Merlot "Vintner Select" 2012

Poppyseed Bread and Butter Pudding
with Meyer Lemon Curd Lychee Sorbet

Schramsberg Cremant Demi-Sec 2011

Japan (2015)

In conjunction with guest chef **Masaharu Morimoto:**

Toro Tartare and Caesar Sashimi Salad

Smoked Salmon—Grilled Chicken—Koji

The First Course is a nod to the classic American Caesar Salad with a Japanese twist, literally. The salad is wrapped in a clear acetate and tied with a Mizuhiki cord emulating a gift to be opened.

—WHITE HOUSE STATE DINNER PROGRAM

France (2014)

The State Dinner celebrates the best of American cuisine. This event highlights the talents of our Nation's cheese artisans, as well as the bountiful produce grown by farmers across our country.

—WHITE HOUSE STATE DINNER PROGRAM

United Kingdom (2012)

A Winter Harvest Dinner: The United Kingdom State Dinner takes its inspiration from the Kitchen Garden's late winter harvest and some early spring greens, which chefs harvested the day before the dinner.

—WHITE HOUSE STATE DINNER PROGRAM

The menu's first course—Crisped Halibut with Potato Crust, Shaved Brussels Sprouts, Applewood Smoked Bacon—was served on a bed of braised baby kale fresh from the White House garden.

Anita Lo on Her Inspirations

[The White House] emailed me, and I wondered, "Is this for real?" So I Googled the name of the person who'd emailed me and saw it was legit. I had limited time to come up with 12 items that were Chinese-American and good for a banquet, as I was traveling from India to Mexico to Washington, D.C.—it was crazy. But I had always wanted to do it. [To create the menu,] I pulled in all kinds of influences, some from decades ago. At Union Pacific, **Rocco di Spirito** made a mushroom soup with oloroso sherry that I loved. At Annisa [her restaurant in New York City], I had a mushroom soup on the menu without black truffle, but the one we made for this dinner was fancier, with black truffles and different kinds of wild mushrooms, accented by acorn jelly—which is traditional to Korea, where I studied—and acorn squash and a bit of pumpkin seed and pumpkin seed oil on top.

I came up with a version of [the poached lobster] in the early 1990s at Mirezi, very loosely based on a dish we did at Chanterelle, which was a pasta sheet with stuff in it and lobster with a curried lobster sauce, like a cannoli. I used chow fun noodles—those thick, fresh rice noodles that are a dim sum classic—and added spinach, leeks, and shiitakes with oyster sauce. I added Maine lobster, lobster tomalley, and roe.

Anita Lo

At Mirezi, we did used to fry big squares of garlic milk, but [the cannon of lamb] was a very different take on that. I'd first read about fried milk in a cookbook by a Chinese chef. It's set with cornstarch, and I use a bit of gelatin so that it melts. Chinese broccoli—gai lun—classic, sautéed with garlic. The loin had chiles and lime and more garlic.

The inspiration for [the bread pudding] originally came out of staff meal. It's a Chinese thing: You can never throw anything away, especially food, and I was trying to come up with a way of using leftover bread from Amy's Bread. I ended up making a custard bread pudding, and it turned out really well. We used to make little goat cheese quiches as canapés at Bouley with a custard filling, so I based the custard on that. I just love Meyer lemon and lemon curd—and I decided that these were basically Chinese because these [Meyer] lemons were brought over from China by Mr. [Frank Nicholas] Meyer. And I added the poppy seeds, because [of the classic pairing] **poppy seeds + lemon.**

Imagine: Imagine being the White House chef—or guest chef—with the guests of honor from a country of your choice. What would you serve to pay tribute to them?

W

South Korea (2011)

Tonight's menu highlights the best of local produce combined with Korean flavors and traditions. . . . The second course, an Early Fall Harvest Salad, includes red and green lettuces grown in the White House Kitchen Garden which are wrapped in daikon sheets and served with masago rice pearl crispies and a sesame vinaigrette as a nod to Korean traditions.

—WHITE HOUSE STATE DINNER PROGRAM

Germany (2011)

The meal is completed with a delicious dessert, an apple strudel. The apples are from Maryland, the raisins from California and the topfen, a Farmer's Cheese, is from Vermont. The apple and topfen combination is a twist on a traditional German recipe for strudel and will be served with schlag, an unsweetened whipped cream.

—WHITE HOUSE STATE DINNER PROGRAM

China (2011)

At the request of the Chinese Delegation, the White House has arranged a "quintessentially American" evening, complete with a menu, décor, and entertainment that reflect some of the nation's most recognizable offerings.

—WHITE HOUSE STATE DINNER PROGRAM

The menu included a pear, goat cheese, and walnut salad; Maine lobster; lemon sorbet; dry-aged rib-eye steak with buttermilk crisp onions, double-stuffed potatoes, and creamed spinach; and old-fashioned apple pie with vanilla ice cream.

Mexico (2010)

For the Obama administration's second state dinner, the White House has once again turned the cooking over to a guest chef. **Rick Bayless** has been asked to prepare the elegantly balanced, many layered Mexican food for which he has become famous at the dinner on May 19 that will honor President Felipe Calderon of Mexico.

—MARIAN BURROS, *New York Times*

In conjunction with guest chef **Rick Bayless:**

Dinner Menu

Jicama with Oranges, Grapefruit, and Pineapple

Citrus Vinaigrette

Ulises Valdez Chardonnay 2007 "Russian River"

Herb Green Ceviche of Hawaiian Opah

Sesame-Cilantro Cracker

Oregon Wagyu Beef in Oaxacan Black Mole

Black Bean Tamalon and Grilled Green Beans

Herrera Cabernet Sauvignon 2006 "Selección Rebecca"

Chocolate-Cajeta Tart
Toasted Homemade Marshmallows
Graham Cracker Crumble and Goat Cheese Ice Cream
Mumm Napa "Carlos Santana Brut" N/V

India (2009)

Mrs. Obama worked with Guest Chef **Marcus Samuelsson** and White House Executive Chef Cristeta Comerford and her team to create a menu that reflects the best of American cuisine, continues this White House's commitment to serving fresh, sustainable and regional food, and honors the culinary excellence and flavors that are present in Indian cuisine. Herbs and lettuces are harvested from the White House Kitchen Garden.

—WHITE HOUSE STATE DINNER PROGRAM

Dinner Menu
Potato and Eggplant Salad
White House Arugula
With Onion Seed Vinaigrette
2008 Sauvignon Blanc, Modus Operandi, Napa Valley, California

Red Lentil Soup with Fresh Cheese
2006 Riesling, Brooks "Ara," Wilamette Valley, Oregon

Roasted Potato Dumplings
With Tomato Chutney
Chick Peas and Okra
or
Green Curry Prawns
Caramelized Salsify
With Smoked Collard Greens
and
Coconut Aged Basmati
2007 Granache, Beckmen Vineyards, Santa Ynez, California

Pumpkin Pie Tart
Pear Tatin
Whipped Cream and Caramel Sauce
Sparkling Chardonnay, Thibaut Janisson Brut, Monticello, Virginia

Petit Fours and Coffee
Cashew Brittle
Pecan Pralines
Passion Fruit and Vanilla Gelees
Chocolate-Dipped Fruit

The meal was accompanied by both American and Indian breads (e.g., cornbread, naan)—so that guests could literally "break bread" together, according to guest chef **Marcus Samuelsson.**

WHO? (SEE ALSO ENNEAGRAM AND GENERATION TO GENERATION)

Who determines what we grow, cook, and eat?

Imagine: Who *should* determine what we grow, cook, and eat?

We decide what we want, and then we demand that the land produce it—when in fact, it should really work the other way around. Instead of consumers dictating what farmers grow, we should listen to the soil.

—DAN BARBER, Blue Hill at Stone Barns (Pocantico Hills, New York)

WHY?

Why do we eat what we eat?

Why *should* we eat what we eat?

Why bother to create a new dish? Because **Jean Anthelme Brillat-Savarin** had it right:

The discovery of a new dish confers more happiness on humanity than the discovery of a new star.

W

WINTER

Weather: typically cold
Needs: staying warm, storing energy

Winter Ingredients

(See Seasonal Ingredient key on page 249.)

allspice
apples
artichokes, Jerusalem (peak: autumn/winter)
baked dishes
bananas
beans, e.g., dried, pinto, white
BEETS
braised dishes
broccoli (peak: February)
Brussels sprouts (peak: December)
buckwheat
butter
cabbage, e.g., green, red, savoy
cardoni (peak: October–April)
cardoons (peak: autumn/winter)
casseroles
cauliflower (peak: autumn/winter)
celery
celery root (peak: August–June)
chayote
CHEESES, esp. winter, e.g., **bold cheeses**, Comté, Reblochon, Vacherin Mont d'Or
cherimoya (peak: winter/spring)
chestnuts (peak: autumn/winter)
chickpeas
chicories
chocolate
cinnamon
citron (peak: November–January)
citrus
CLEMENTINES (peak: November–March)
coconut

cranberries (peak: autumn/winter)
cream
daikon (peak: autumn/winter)
dates (peak: December)
endive, Belgian
escarole
fennel (peak: autumn/winter)
flour, heavier, e.g., buckwheat
frisée
ginger (peak: November–June)
grains, heavy
grapefruit (peak: February)
gratins
GREENS, BITTER, e.g., dandelion (peak: January–May), mustard, turnip, **winter**
guavas (peak: September–March)
hearty foods
herbs, dried
hot chocolate
hot dishes
jicama (peak: winter/spring)
kale
kasha
kiwi (peak: autumn/winter)
kohlrabi (peak: November–April)
kumquats (peak: winter/spring)
leeks
legumes
lemons (peak: January)
lemons, Meyer (peak: October–May)
lemons, preserved
lentils (peak: autumn/winter)
limes (peak: autumn/winter)
mâche
maple syrup
melon, winter
miso, dark
mushrooms, e.g., matsutake, wild
nettles (peak: January–July)
noodles, soba, esp. served hot
nutmeg
nuts
oils, nut, e.g., **walnut**
onions, e.g., pearl, Spanish
ORANGES
oranges, blood (peak: winter/spring)
oranges, Cara Cara (peak: winter/spring)
oranges, mandarin (peak: January)
ORANGES, SEVILLE, i.e., **sour**
parsley root
parsnips
passion fruit (peak: July–February)
pastas, e.g., gnocchi
pears, e.g., **Bartlett, Bosc, Comice, D'Anjou, Seckel**
pineapple
plantains
pomelos (peak: November–April)
potatoes, esp. baked
pressure-cooked dishes
radicchio
radishes, e.g., black (peak: winter/spring)
ragoûts
roasts and roasted dishes

root vegetables, e.g., carrots, celery root, parsnips, rutabagas, sweet potatoes, turnips
rosemary
rutabagas (peak: October–April)
sage
salsify (peak: autumn/winter)
sauces, creamy
savory, winter
scallops, bay (peak: November–March)
shallots
shoots, pea (peak: January–May)
SLOW-COOKED DISHES
soups, e.g., hot, root vegetable, winter squash
spices, warming
squash, winter, e.g., acorn, buttercup, butternut, delicata
stews
sweet potatoes (peak: December)
TANGERINES (peak: December–February)
taro
tatsoi (peak: autumn/winter)
todok
truffles, e.g., black
turmeric
turnips (peak: December)
ugli fruit (peak: winter/spring)
vinegar, e.g., sherry
wakame (peak: winter/spring)
walnuts
water chestnuts (peak: February)
wines, e.g., full-bodied, red, sparkling, sweet
YAMS (peak: December)

Winter Beers

barleywine
Christmas ales
holiday ales
lambic beers, Belgian-style
old ales, English
porters, e.g., Baltic, fuller-bodied
stouts, e.g., American, Guinness, Imperial
Scotch-style ales
winter lagers

Winter Cheeses

aged cheeses
blue, e.g., Roquefort
Brie
Camembert
Cheddar, e.g., aged
Cheshire
cream cheese
firmer cheeses
Gouda
richer cheeses
Roquefort
Stilton
Taleggio
Vacherin Mont d'Or
Winter cheese accompaniments: apples, bread, chutney, dried fruit, grapes, nuts, pears, walnuts

Winter Cocktails and Spirits

Caipairinha
Champagne cocktails
Chartreuse cocktails
coffee drinks
egg nog
hot buttered rum
hot chocolate + amaro (Italian)
hot chocolate + green Chartreuse (French)
hot toddies
Irish coffee
margaritas
mulled ciders and wines
punches
sparkling wine–based cocktails
winter warmers made from hot chocolate, coffee, tea, or soup (e.g., borscht)

Winter Concepts

baked dishes, e.g., beans, eggs, pastas
baked goods, e.g., cakes, cookies, tarts
baked pastas, e.g., lasagna
black bean soup
braised dishes, e.g., short ribs, winter greens
bread pudding
candied citrus zest
carrot-parsnip soup
casseroles, e.g., eggplant parmesan, macaroni and cheese
cassoulet
chili
chowders, e.g., winter vegetable
citrus fruit salads
compotes, e.g., winter fruit (e.g., apple)
confits
cookies
crepes, e.g., buckwheat
fondue, e.g., cheese, chocolate
gratins
grits, e.g., cheese
hot chocolate
lentil soup, e.g., with winter vegetables
marmalades, e.g., bitter orange
omelets and scrambles
onion soup, e.g., with cheese and croutons
pancakes
pastas, e.g., baked (e.g., lasagna)
pizzas, e.g., eggplant, thicker-crust
polenta, e.g., creamy
potatoes, e.g., baked, stuffed
pot pies, e.g., winter vegetable

puddings, e.g., bread, chocolate, plum
risottos, e.g., winter squash with winter greens
roasted produce, e.g., mushrooms, pears, squash
roasts
root vegetable salad
salads, warm, e.g., cabbage
salads, winter, e.g., beet, celery, chicory, fattoush, kale, root vegetable, winter squash (e.g., acorn)
salads, winter fruit, e.g., citrus fruit, Waldorf (apple + walnuts)
shepherd's pie—or veg gardener's pie
soufflés
soups, e.g., pureed single-vegetable (e.g., cauliflower), bean, lentil
stews
stroganoff with buttered noodles
tagines
terrines
winter vegetable soup
winter vegetable stew with chickpeas

Winter Desserts
bread puddings
cakes
cheesecakes
cookies
pies
puddings
tarts

Apple: Sorbet with Bay Leaf, Crème Brûlée, and Hibiscus
—Daniel Humm, Eleven Madison Park (New York City)

Banana Cake with Hazelnut Brittle and Concord Grapes
—Miro Uskokovic, Untitled (New York City)

Bomboloni Doughnuts served with Lemon Ricotta, Dark Chocolate, and Bay Leaf
—Francis Joven, Marea (New York City)

Carrot Meringue Pie
—Amanda Cohen, Dirt Candy (New York City)

Champagne Sabayon with candied rose petals, almond cake
—Terrance Brennan, Roundhouse (Beacon, New York)

Pineapple "Pappardelle" with passion fruit, lime pudding, cilantro, coconut crumb, and sorbet
—Terrance Brennan, Roundhouse (Beacon, New York)

Salted Caramel Semifreddo with Chocolate, Banana, Pomegranate, and Almonds
—Francis Joven, Marea (New York City)

Sticky Toffee Cake with Pears and Chai
—Miro Uskokovic, Untitled (New York City)

Sweet Potato: Cheesecake with Honey and Chestnut
—Daniel Humm, Eleven Madison Park (New York City)

Winter Dressings
blue cheese–based dressings
buttermilk-based dressings
cheese-based dressings
citrus vinaigrettes
creamy dressings
dashi + oil + soy sauce dressing
hot dressings, e.g., hot bacon on wilted spinach salad
mayonnaise-based dressings
Meyer lemon–based dressings
shallot vinaigrettes

Winter Flavor Affinities
acorn squash + Parmesan + thyme
apples + blue cheese + pecans
apples + Brussels sprouts + walnut oil
apples + celery + walnuts
apples + walnuts + winter greens
banana + pineapple + rum
barley + mushrooms + onions
beets + beet greens + citrus
beets + blue cheese + orange + red onion + walnuts
beets + dill + goat cheese + nuts (e.g., hazelnuts, walnuts)
beets + orange + quinoa
beets + goat cheese + orange
black truffles + chanterelles + Pecorino
blood oranges + fennel + olive oil + radicchio
blue cheese + dates + walnuts
broccoli + anchovy + garlic
brown butter + capers + cauliflower + mustard
Brussels sprouts + fat (e.g., butter, olive oil) + garlic
carrots + almonds + dukkah
chicory + balsamic vinegar + Parmesan cheese

chicory + citrus juice + pecans + ricotta
dates + Parmesan cheese + salad greens
dried apricots + cardamom + dark chocolate + pistachios
endives + gorgonzola + walnuts
endives + croutons + lardons + mustard + olive oil + poached egg
fennel + orange + walnuts + watercress
grapefruit + mint + pomegranate molasses
grapes + maple syrup + orange
kale + mustard + potatoes
kale + onions + parsnips
kiwi + pineapple + winter basil
lentils + tomato sauce + winter vegetables
mascarpone + pears + Pecorino + pepper (black)
mushrooms + ricotta + walnuts
oranges + red onions + watercress
Parmesan + porcini + rosemary + sage + white wine
parsnips + balsamic vinegar + brown sugar + rosemary
pears + balsamic vinegar + Pecorino Romano cheese + salad greens
pears + gorgonzola cheese + red wine
potatoes + cheese + winter greens (e.g., as a casserole)

Winter Dishes

Beet: Pickled with Yogurt and Nasturtium
—Daniel Humm, Eleven Madison Park (New York City)

Beetroot Tartare with Horseradish Cream
—Alain Passard's signature dish at L'Arpège (France)

Black Dirt Carrot Steak served with Squash Rings, Smoked Apple, and Bordelaise
—Dan Barber, Blue Hill (New York City)

Butternut Squash Tortelloni with Brown Butter, Sage, and Apple
—Sarah Gruenberg, Monteverde (Chicago)

Cauliflower Soup with Crisp Cauliflower Scented with North African *Dukka* Spices, Afghani Saffron, Crème Fraiche, and Chives
—Carrie Nahabedian, Naha (Chicago)

Cheddar: Savory Black-and-White Cookie with Apple
—Daniel Humm, Eleven Madison Park (New York City)

Chestnut Agnolloti with foraged mushrooms, treviso, black truffles, and apple broth
—Terrance Brennan, Roundhouse (Beacon, New York)

Hepworth Farms Cauliflower Variations, with cured egg yolk bottarga, Parmesan, lemon, and pistachio
—Terrance Brennan, Roundhouse (Beacon, New York)

Lacquered Aged Moulard Duck Breast, Preserved Cherries, Beluga Lentils, and Caramelized

Belgian Endive, Balsam Fir, Candied Honeybell Orange, and Mandarin Napoleon Liqueur
—Carrie Nahabedian, Naha (Chicago)

Mushroom: Sabayon with Chive Oil, Smoked with Everything Bagel Crumble, Pickles, and Cucumber Caviar
—Daniel Humm, Eleven Madison Park (New York City)

Pansotti with Taleggio, Red Kuri Squash, Swiss Chard, and Hazelnuts
—Lauren DeSteno, Marea (New York City)

Roasted Carrots with Smoked Quark
—Eric Ziebold, Kinship (Washington, D.C.)

Squash: Roasted with Cranberries, Pumpkin Seeds, and Sourdough
—Daniel Humm, Eleven Madison Park (New York City)

Squash Soup with Porcini Mushrooms, Chestnuts, and Farro
—Abram Bissell, The Modern (New York City)

Winter Fruits and Vegetables, featuring Celery Root, Lady Apples, Pickled Potato, and Mushroom
—Dan Barber, Blue Hill (New York City)

Winter Vegetable Pot Pie, with Butternut Squash, Parsnip, Turnip, Carrot, Parsnip Cream, Rosemary, and Whole Wheat Top
—Spike Gjerde, Woodberry Kitchen (Baltimore)

prunes + Armagnac +/or chocolate
root vegetables + honey + sherry vinegar

Winter Pastas
agnolotti
baked pasta
bow-tie pasta
fettucine
gemelle
gnocchi , e.g., sweet potato
lasagna
pappardelle
penne
rigatoni
stuffed pastas
tagliatelle

Winter pasta sauces: Alfredo sauce, alla vodka sauce (cream + tomato + vodka), brown-butter sauces, cacio e pepe (cheese + black pepper), carbonara sauces, cheese-based sauces, cream-based sauces, egg-enriched sauces, meat-based sauces, mushroom-based sauces, red wine–based sauces, roasted tomato sauce, roasted-vegetable sauces, truffle-enriched sauces

Winter Presentations
baked dishes
casseroles
roasts
soups
stews

Winter Techniques
baking
braising
caramelizing
glazing
roasting
simmering
slow-cooking
stewing

Winter Wines
Amarone
Bordeaux, red
Burgundy, red
Brunello di Montalcino
Cabernet Sauvignon
Cahors
Champagne
Chardonnay, oaked
Côte-Rôtie
fuller-bodied wines
Gewürztraminer
Grenache
higher-alcohol wines
Madeira
Malbec
Marsanne/Roussanne
port
red wines
Rhône wines
Rioja
Sauternes
Shiraz/Syrah
sparkling wines
sweet wines
Viognier
Zinfandel

X FACTOR

Going back as far as my memory can take me, I see a kitchen in my vision of my mother, my aunts, my cousins, and I visualize a specific dish for each of them.

—JACQUES PÉPIN

A sensory experience should appeal to *all* the senses, as suggested by the X Factor in the Flavor Equation (page 83).

Kyle Connaughton of Healdsburg's Single Thread explains the influence of cooking at the Fat Duck:

> **Heston [Blumenthal]** was obsessed with the multisensory aspects of dining. He was always talking about sound, sight, hearing, touch, context, memory, and nostalgia, which were all fascinating to him. We put them into dishes quite literally. Sound of the Sea was a dish you ate while listening to an iPod [playing the sound of breaking waves, which Blumenthal believed to enhance the flavor of the sashimi with edible tapioca "sand"].
>
> We use directional speakers above every table [at Single Thread]. Every single table is in its own sound environment. We create a curtain of sound around each table. You feel the energy of other people but don't hear their conversation. I worked with sound engineers on how the sound is projected and absorbed.
>
> During dinner service last night, the lights changed seven times. The lights slowly come up and down throughout the restaurant on the walls, tables, and flowers. I want the environment to change while you are sitting here for three-and-half-hours. It is done gradually while set to an atomic clock so it knows when sunset is that day and begins its program based on the sunset. At the end of the night, the lights come up a little to give people more energy.

As adults, new memories are not only created through the experience of eating, but past memories are also invariably present and shaping both the experiences we have and the new memories we are creating.

Our experiences and memories are affected by input from all of our senses—not only taste and smell and touch (texture), but also sight (shapes, presentation, dining room design and lighting) and sound (ambient noise, music). These all affect our perception and memory of flavor.

Like Jacques Pépin's, our own memories of dishes from childhood are often imbued with love, the ultimate aspect of the X Factor.

Dining is often about memories of food, the sensory experience, and how you will remember it.

—**JOAN ROCA,** El Celler de Can Roca (Spain)

How do we season with sound? With light? With elements of emotions?

—**GRANT ACHATZ,** Alinea (Chicago)

Jacques Pépin on Making a Dish Your Own

The X Factor is a part of everything you cook—intentionally or not.

When you create a recipe, you can do anything. For me, I start with an idea. I go to the market, and you have infinite freedom there. You take A and B and you put them together, then you add a structure, and perhaps this and that. . . . By the time [the recipe] is finished, I have a typewritten page, and the minute I give it to someone, it becomes a total reversal: From the freedom I had to start with when I could do anything, it is now totally structured so that you have to do this, this, and that.

At least on that philosophical level, writing down a recipe is *destroying* the recipe [as the exact set of circumstances under which the recipe was created—e.g., the ingredients, the temperature of the oven, the weather, the humidity—will never be repeated]. The whole idea [of creating a dish] is the knowledge of food, compensation [for the actual state of ingredients you find yourself with], and adjustment [to their characteristics].

[Pépin advises that people follow a recipe exactly the first time they make it. By the third or fourth time, they should improve the recipe. They could start to massage it to their aesthetic and sense of taste. A year and a half later, they won't know where it came from, because it becomes their recipe. Pépin feels it's gratifying to him when people do this with his recipes.]

A recipe is like sheet music. When you hear someone playing "Moonlight Serenade," and then you hear it played by someone else, it will sound very different because of the speed and tempo and other factors. If you give the same recipe to ten different people, you will have ten different dishes. This is the paradox.

[As a cooking instructor,] I would ask fifteen students to cook a salad, a boiled potato, and a roast chicken, and would always tell them, "You want to blow my mind? You want to be different? Please don't." No matter what, I will have fifteen different chickens—with three practically perfect, three undercooked, three cold, three burned, and three whatever, but they are going to be different. So you actually don't have to torture yourself to be different. If you cook with your gut, you are different. You cannot be the same as others.

Jacques Pépin

Great cooking favors the prepared hands.

—JACQUES PÉPIN, on Mastery

Cooking is the art of adjustment."

—JACQUES PÉPIN, on Alchemy

I would advise people to cook for the right reason: for love.

—JACQUES PÉPIN, on Creativity

YELLOW FOODS

apples, golden
bananas
beets, golden
bell peppers, yellow
butter
corn
grapefruit
lemons
pineapple
rutabagas
saffron-dyed foods, e.g., pasta doughs
squash, yellow
star fruit
tomatoes, yellow
turnips
watermelon, yellow

"YES, AND . . . "

The first rule of improv is to never knock what came before you. The best way to do this is to take what is as a given, and to build on it by saying, "**Yes, and . . .** " before adding your own contribution.

The second rule of improv is that it's not about you. It's about the group. Trust the group to come up with something that is greater than any individual could have created on their own.

The third rule of improv is to go with the flow. Trust your first impulse, and go with it.

Keeping an improvisational stance in the kitchen will help you to keep your ego at bay, and to remain open to whatever arises, turning it into something that serves you.

YIN / YANG = BALANCE

The ancient Chinese concept of ***yin/yang*** is about life stemming from a perfect balance. According to this theory, everything—including colors, foods, human behaviors, seasons, shapes, and times of day—can be placed somewhere on the yin or yang scale. Traditional Chinese medicine believes that health is achieved through the harmony of yin and yang.

Yin = receptive | cool, negative, inactivity, midnight, black (see COOLING FOODS)
Yang = creative | hot, positive, activity, noon, white (see WARMING FOOD)
Yin / Yang = duality (of complements and opposites)
Circle (containing Yin and Yang) = unity

Yin	**Yang**
Earth	Heaven
Feminine	Masculine
Winter	Summer
Rest	Work
Water	Fire
Moist	Dry
Light	Heavy
Left	Right
Empty	Full
Dark	Light
Inside	Outside
Cooling	Warming
Boiling	Deep-Frying
Poaching	Grilling
Steaming	Stir-Frying

Imagine: How can you balance your next dish through incorporating its dominant feature(s)' opposite(s)?

Heston [Blumenthal, of England's Fat Duck] and I were two sides of the same coin when we worked together. He was wildly inquisitive with wild ideas, while I was trained to instill order. He'd have incredible ideas, and then I would go off and create that in order of importance. He was about freedom and not structuring a menu in a certain way, while my experience in Japan was one of having things nicely compartmentalized. The two of us hit our best stride together when we could get things into a narrative.

—KYLE CONNAUGHTON,
Single Thread (Healdsburg, California)

YOGA

While visiting the **Culinary Institute of America**, we learned that the school offers yoga classes to students on its Greystone campus, which have been increasing in popularity in the wake of mentions of meditation and the like in programs like Netflix's ***Chef's Table.*** We happened upon a class being offered by wine professor and private yoga instructor **Christie Dufault**, who explained how the practice enhances creativity:

"Yoga helps to reduce stress, increase mental focus, and taste on a deeper, more profound level," the acclaimed former sommelier of Gary Danko and Quince told us. "Some forms are more physical and others more spiritual, but yoga enhances the sensory acuity, awareness, and mindfulness required of being a culinarian—especially in the pressure-cooker environment of a kitchen."

Rick Bayless has been doing yoga [including Ashtanga, Anusura, Hatha, *and* Vinyasa *yoga] for more than two decades. He travels with a yoga mat, and tipped us off to using the YogaGlo app while traveling.*

Pratyahara **can be described as the withdrawal of the senses or the internal focusing of the outward sense receptors. . . . *ShanMukhi mudra* [a seated pose with thumbs in the ears, while fingers cover the eyes, nose, and mouth] closes off the [outer] senses.**

—SARAH GIRARD, our favorite yoga instructor in New York City, on the best yoga pose to open the inner senses and creativity

Y

APPENDIX

James Beard Foundation Award Winners for Outstanding Chef

YEAR	OUTSTANDING CHEF
2017	Michael Solomonov, Zahav (Philadelphia) *Other nominees: Gabrielle Hamilton, Prune (New York City); David Kinch, Manresa (Los Gatos, California); Christopher Kostow, The Restaurant at Meadowood (St. Helena, California); Donald Link, Herbsaint (New Orleans)*
2016	Suzanne Goin, Lucques (Los Angeles) *Other nominees: Sean Brock, Husk (Nashville); Donald Link, Herbsaint (New Orleans); Michael Solomonov, Zahav (Philadelphia); Michael Tusk, Quince (San Francisco)*
2015	Michael Anthony, Gramercy Tavern (New York City) *Other nominees: Sean Brock, Husk (Charleston); Suzanne Goin, Lucques (Los Angeles); Donald Link, Herbsaint (New Orleans); Marc Vetri, Vetri (Philadelphia)*
2014	Nancy Silverton, Pizzeria Mozza (Los Angeles) *Other nominees: Michael Anthony, Gramercy Tavern (New York City); Sean Brock, McCrady's (Charleston); Suzanne Goin, Lucques (Los Angeles); David Kinch, Manresa (Los Gatos, California); Marc Vetri, Vetri (Philadelphia)*
2013	Tie: David Chang, Momofuku Noodle Bar (New York City) *and* Paul Kahan, Blackbird (Chicago) *Other nominees: Sean Brock, McCrady's (Charleston); Gary Danko, Restaurant Gary Danko (San Francisco); Suzanne Goin, Lucques (West Hollywood); Nancy Silverton, Pizzeria Mozza (Los Angeles)*
2012	Daniel Humm, Eleven Madison Park (New York City) *Other nominees: David Chang, Momofuku Ssäm Bar (New York City); Gary Danko, Restaurant Gary Danko (San Francisco); Paul Kahan, Blackbird (Chicago); Donald Link, Herbsaint (New Orleans); Nancy Silverton, Pizzeria Mozza (Los Angeles)*
2011	José Andrés, minibar (Washington, D.C.)
2010	Tom Colicchio, Craft (New York City)
2009	Dan Barber, Blue Hill (New York City)
2008	Grant Achatz, Alinea (Chicago)
2007	Michel Richard, Michel Richard Citronelle (Washington, D.C.)
2006	Alfred Portale, Gotham Bar & Grill (New York City)
2005	Mario Batali, Babbo (New York City)
2004	Judy Rodgers, Zuni Café (San Francisco)
2003	Eric Ripert, Le Bernardin (New York City)
2002	Lidia Bastianich, Felidia Ristorante (New York City)
2001	Patrick O'Connell, The Inn at Little Washington (Washington, Virginia)
2000	David Bouley, Danube (New York City)
1999	Charlie Trotter, Charlie Trotter's (Chicago)
1998	Wolfgang Puck, Spago Beverly Hills (Beverly Hills) *(tie)* Jean-Georges Vongerichten, Jean Georges (New York City)
1997	Thomas Keller, The French Laundry (Yountville, California)
1996	Jeremiah Tower, Stars (San Francisco)
1995	Rick Bayless, Frontera Grill / Topolobampo (Chicago)
1994	Daniel Boulud, Daniel (New York City)
1993	Larry Forgione, An American Place (New York City)
1992	Alice Waters, Chez Panisse (Berkeley)
1991	Wolfgang Puck, Spago (Los Angeles)

James Beard Foundation Award Winners for Outstanding Pastry Chef

YEAR	OUTSTANDING PASTRY CHEF
2017	Ghaya Oliveira, Daniel (New York City)
2016	Dahlia Narvaez, Osteria Mozza (Los Angeles)
2015	Christina Tosi, Momofuku (New York City)
2014	Dominique Ansel, Dominique Ansel Bakery (New York City)
2013	Brooks Headley, Del Posto (New York City)
2012	Mindy Segal, Mindy's HotChocolate (Chicago)
2011	Angela Pinkerton, Eleven Madison Park (New York City)
2010	Nicole Plue, Redd (Yountville, California)
2009	Gina DePalma, Babbo (New York City)
2008	Chad Robertson and Elisabeth Prueitt, Tartine Bakery (San Francisco)
2007	Michael Laiskonis, Le Bernardin (New York City)
2006	Johnny Iuzzini, Jean Georges (New York City)

2005 Karen DeMasco, Craft (New York City)

2004 Emily Luchetti, Farallon (San Francisco)

2003 Ben and Karen Barker, Magnolia Grill (Durham)

2002 Sherry Yard, Spago (Los Angeles)

2001 Gale Gand, Tru (Chicago)

2000 Claudia Fleming, Gramercy Tavern (New York City)

1999 Marcel Desaulniers, The Trellis (Williamsburg, Virginia)

1998 Stephen Durfee, The French Laundry (Yountville, California)

1997 Richard Leach, Park Avenue Café (New York City)

1996 Sarabeth Levine, Sarabeth's (New York City)

1995 Francois Payard, Daniel (New York City)

1994 Jacques Torres, Le Cirque (New York City)

1993 Lindsey Shere, Chez Panisse (Berkeley)

1992 Albert Kumin, Vie de Frances International Pastry Arts Center (Elmsford, New York)

1991 Nancy Silverton, Campanile (Los Angeles)

James Beard Foundation Award Winners for Outstanding Baker

YEAR	OUTSTANDING BAKER
2017	Mark Furstenberg, Bread Furst (Washington, D.C.)
2016	Joanne Chang, Flour Bakery + Cafe (Boston)
2015	Jim Lahey, Sullivan Street Bakery (New York City)

James Beard Foundation Award Winners for Rising Star Chef

This award is given to "a chef age 30 or younger who displays an impressive talent and who is likely to make a significant impact on the industry in years to come."

YEAR	RISING STAR CHEF
2017	Zachary Engel, Shaya (New Orleans)
2016	Daniela Soto-Innes, Cosme (New York City)
2015	Jessica Largey, Manresa (Los Gatos, California)
2014	Jimmy Bannos, The Purple Pig (Chicago) *and* Blaine Wetzel, The Willows Inn (Lummi Island, Washington)
2013	Danny Bowien, Mission Chinese Food (San Francisco)
2012	Christina Tosi, Momofuku Milk Bar (New York City)
2011	Gabriel Rucker, Le Pigeon (Portland, Oregon)
2010	Timothy Hollingsworth, The French Laundry (Yountville, California)
2009	Nate Appleman, A16 (San Francisco)
2008	Gavin Kaysen, Café Boulud (New York City)
2007	David Chang, Momofuku Noodle Bar (New York City)
2006	Corey Lee, French Laundry (Yountville, California) ⟶ Benu, San Francisco
2005	Christopher Lee, Striped Bass (Philadelphia)
2004	Allison Vines-Rushing, Jack's Luxury Oyster Bar (New York City)
2003	Grant Achatz, Trio (Evanston, Illinois)
2002	Jean François Bruel, DB Bistro Moderne (New York City)
2001	Galen Zamarra, Bouley Bakery (New York City)
2000	Andrew Carmellini, Café Boulud (New York City)
1999	Marcus Samuelsson, Aquavit (New York City)
1998	Keith Luce, Spruce (Aspen)
1997	Michael Mina, Aqua (San Francisco)
1996	Douglas Rodriguez, Patria (New York City)
1995	Traci Des Jardins, Rubicon (San Francisco)
1994	Sarah Stegner, The Ritz-Carlton (Chicago)
1993	Bobby Flay, Mesa Grill (New York City)
1992	Debra Ponzek, Montrachet (New York City)
1991	Todd English, Olives (Cambridge, Massachusetts)

Restaurant magazine's World's 50 Best Restaurants and Their Chefs—2017

(Note: American restaurants and chefs are in **bold**.)

RESTAURANT (LOCATION) / CHEF

1. **Eleven Madison Park (New York City) Daniel Humm**
2. Osteria Francescana (Modena, Italy) Massimo Bottura
3. El Celler de Can Roca (Girona, Spain) Joan Roca
4. Mirazur (Menton, France) Mauro Colagreco

5. Central (Lima)
Virgilio Martínez Véliz

6. Asador Etxebarri (Axpe, Spain)
Victor Arguinzoniz

7. Gaggan (Bangkok)
Gaggan Anand

8. Maido (Lima)
Mitsuharu Tsumura

9. Mugaritz (Errenteria, Spain)
Andoni Luis Aduriz

10. Steirereck (Vienna)
Heinz Reitbauer

11. **Blue Hill at Stone Barns (Pocantico Hills, New York)**
Dan Barber

12. L'Arpège (Paris)
Alain Passard

13. Alain Ducasse au Plaza Athénée (Paris)
Alain Ducasse / Romain Meder

14. Restaurant André (Singapore)
André Chiang

15. Piazzo Duomo (Alba, Italy)
Enrico Crippa

16. D.O.M. (São Paulo)
Alex Atala

17. **Le Bernardin (New York City)**
Eric Ripert

18. Narisawa (Tokyo)
Yoshihiro Narisawa

19. Geranium (Copenhagen)
Rasmus Kofoed

20. Pujol (Mexico City)
Enrique Olvera

21. **Alinea (Chicago)**
Grant Achatz

22. Quintonil (Mexico City)
Jorge Vallejo

23. White Rabbit (Moscow)
Vladimir Mukhin and Victor Khripachev

24. Amber (Hong Kong)
Richard Ekkebus and Maxime Gilbert

25. Tickets (Barcelona)
Albert Adrià

26. The Clove Club (London)
Isaac McHale

27. The Ledbury (London)
Brett Graham

28. Nahm (Bangkok)
David Thompson

29. Le Calandre (Padua, Italy)
Massimiliano Alajmo

30. Arzak (San Sebastián, Spain)
Juan Mari & Elena Arzak

31. Alléno Paris au Pavillion Ledoyen (Paris)
Yannick Alléno

32. Attica (Melbourne)
Ben Shewry

33. Astrid y Gastón (Lima)
Diego Muñoz and Gastón Acurio

34. De Librije (Zwolle, Netherlands)
Jonnie Boer

35. Septime (Paris)
Bertrand Grébaut

36. Dinner by Heston Blumenthal (London)
Heston Blumenthal

37. **Saison (San Francisco)**
Joshua Skenes

38. Azurmendi (Larrabetzu, Spain)
Eneko Atxa

39. Relae (Copenhagen)
Christian Puglisi

40. **Cosme (New York City)**
Enrique Olvera and Daniela Soto-Innes

41. Ultraviolet by Paul Pairet (Shanghai)
Paul Pairet

42. Boragó (Santiago, Chile)
Rodolfo Guzmán

43. Reale (Castel di Sangro, Italy)
Niko Romito

44. Brae (Birregurra, Australia)
Dan Hunter

45. Den (Tokyo)
Zaiyu Hasegawa

46. L'Astrance (Paris)
Pascal Barbot

47. Vendôme (Cologne, Germany)
Joachim Wissler

48. Restaurant Tim Raue (Berlin)
Tim Raue

49. Tegui (Buenos Aires, Argentina)
Germán Martitegui

50. Hof van Cleve (Kruishoutem, Belgium)
Peter Goossens with Floris Van Der Veken

Additional U.S. restaurants on the 2017 Top 100

58. Momofuku Ko (New York City)
David Chang

66. Estela (New York City)
Ignacio Mattus

67. Benu (San Francisco)
Corey Lee

68. The French Laundry (Yountville, California)
Thomas Keller

82. Chef's Table at Brooklyn Fare (New York City)
César Ramirez

83. Atelier Crenn (San Francisco)
Dominique Crenn

84. The Restaurant at Meadowood (St. Helena, California)
Christopher Kostow

87. Per Se (New York City)
Thomas Keller

90. Manresa (Los Gatos, California)
David Kinch

CHEFS AND OTHER CULINARY EXPERTS MENTIONED IN *KITCHEN CREATIVITY*

(Starred names are chefs interviewed by the author.)

Grant Achatz is chef/owner of Alinea in Chicago, which was named number 21 on the 2017 World's 50 Best Restaurants list. He was named 2008 Outstanding Chef by the James Beard Foundation. | alinearestaurant.com

Albert Adrià is the chef/owner of Tickets in Barcelona, which was named number 25 on the 2017 World's 50 Best Restaurants list, and he is the former pastry chef of Spain's elBulli. | ticketsbar.es

Ferran Adrià was the chef/owner of elBulli in Spain, which was named number 1 on the World's 50 Best Restaurants list in 2002 and 2006–2009. | elbulli.com

Andoni Luis Aduriz is the chef/owner of Mugaritz in San Sebastien, Spain, which was named number 9 on the 2017 World's 50 Best Restaurants list. | mugaritz.com

*__José Andrés__ is the founding chef/owner of ThinkFoodGroup, based in Washington, D.C., whose more than two dozen restaurants include the Bazaar, Beefsteak, China Chilcano, Jaleo, minibar by José Andrés, Oyamel, and Zaytinya. He was named 2011 Outstanding Chef by the James Beard Foundation, and one of *Time*'s "100 Most Influential People" of 2012. | joseandres.com | thinkfoodgroup.com

Dominique Ansel is the chef/owner of Dominique Ansel Bakery in New York, London, and Tokyo, and was named the 2014 Outstanding Pastry Chef by the James Beard Foundation. He is the author of *Dominique Ansel: The Secret Recipes*. | dominiqueansel.com

*__Michael Anthony__ is the executive chef of Gramercy Tavern and Untitled in New York City. He was named the 2015 Outstanding Chef by the James Beard Foundation, which also named him 2012 Best Chef: New York City. He is the author of *The Gramercy Tavern Cookbook* and *V Is for Vegetables*. | gramercytavern.com

Alex Atala is the chef/owner of D.O.M. in Sao Paulo, Brazil, which was named number 16 on the 2017 World's 50 Best Restaurants list. | domrestaurante.com.br

*__Marc Aumont__ is the pastry chef at Gabriel Kreuther and Kreuther Handcrafted Chocolate in New York City. He previously served as pastry chef at the Modern, Compass, and Bouley Bakery. | gabrielkreuther.com | kreutherchocolate.com

*__Damon Baehrel__ is the chef/owner of Damon Baehrel restaurant in Earlton, New York, which was cited by *The New Yorker* as the most exclusive restaurant in America. The 10-year waiting list to experience its five-hour menu was the subject of an answer on Jeopardy. He is the author of *Native Harvest: The Inspirational Cuisine of Damon Baehrel*. | damonbaehrel.com

*__Dan Barber__ is the chef/owner of Blue Hill in New York City and Blue Hill at Stone Barns in Pocantico Hills, New York, which was named number 11 on the 2017 World's 50 Best Restaurants list. He was named 2009 Outstanding Chef by the James Beard Foundation, which named Blue Hill at Stone Barns the 2015 Outstanding Restaurant. He is the author of *The Third Plate: Field Notes from the Future of Food*. | bluehillfarm.com

Lidia Bastianich is the chef/owner of Felidia in New York City. She was named the 2002 Outstanding Chef by the James Beard Foundation. | felidia-nyc.com

*__Christopher Bates, M.S.__, is the chef/owner of FLX Wienery in Dundee and FLX Table in Geneva, and co-founder of Element Winery in Arkport, all in the Finger Lakes region of New York. He was named a 2016 *Food & Wine* Sommelier of the Year. | flxtable.com | flxwienery.com | elementwinery.com

*__Rick Bayless__ is the chef/owner of Frontera Grill and Topolobampo, both based in Chicago. He was named 1991 Best Chef: Midwest and 1995 Outstanding Chef by the James Beard Foundation, which also honored as Outstanding Restaurant both Frontera Grill (2007) and Topolobampo (2017). He is the host of PBS's *Mexico: One Plate at a Time*, and author of several cookbooks including *Authentic Mexican*. | rickbayless.com

Emma Bengtsson is the chef at the Michelin two-star Aquavit in New York City, where she previously served as the restaurant's executive pastry chef. | aquavit.org

*__Rick Billings__ is the director of research and development and pastry chef at José Andrés's ThinkFoodGroup, based in Washington, D.C. | thinkfoodgroup.com

April Bloomfield is the chef/owner of the Spotted Pig in New York City. She was named 2014 Best Chef: New York City by the James Beard Foundation. | thespottedpig.com

*__Aaron Bludorn__ is the executive chef of Café Boulud in New York City, where he worked his way up through the ranks. He previously cooked with chef Douglas Keane at Sonoma's Michelin-starred Cyrus restaurant. | cafeboulud.com/nyc

Heston Blumenthal is the chef/owner of several restaurants, including the Fat Duck and Dinner by Heston Blumenthal in England. The latter was ranked number 36 on the 2017 World's 50 Best Restaurants list. | thefatduck.co.uk | dinnerbyheston.com

Massimo Bottura is the chef/owner of Osteria Francescana in Italy, which was named number 1 on the 2016 World's 50 Best Restaurants list. | osteriafrancescana.it

David Bouley has been the chef/owner of multiple restaurants in New York City including Bouley, which he closed in 2017. Bouley was named the 2000 Outstanding Chef by the James Beard Foundation, while his eponymous restaurant was named Outstanding Restaurant in 1991. | davidbouley.com

***Daniel Boulud** is the chef/owner of the Dinex Group based in New York City, whose restaurants globally include Bar Boulud, Boulud Sud, Café Boulud, Daniel, and DB Bistro Moderne. His James Beard Foundation honors include 1994 Outstanding Chef, 2006 Outstanding Restaurateur, 2009 Outstanding Service, and 2010 Outstanding Restaurant. | danielboulud.com

Michel Bras and his son **Sébastian Bras** are the chefs/owners of the Michelin three-star restaurant Bras in Laguiole, France. | bras.fr

***Terrance Brennan** is the chef of Roundhouse in Beacon, New York. He previously served as chef/owner of Picholine in New York City, which earned four stars from New York, three stars from the *New York Times*, and two Michelin stars. | terrancebrennan.com | roundhousebeacon.com

Sean Brock is the chef/owner of Husk and McCrady's in Charleston, South Carolina. He was named 2010 Best Chef: Southeast by the James Beard Foundation. | huskrestaurant.com

Jonathan Brooks is the chef of Milktooth in Indianapolis. He was named a semifinalist for Best Chef: Great Lakes by the James Beard Foundation in 2016 and 2017. | milktoothindy.com

***Jean François Bruel** is the executive chef of Daniel in New York City, which was named number 8 on the World's 50 Best Restaurants list during his tenure. | danielboulud.com

David Chang is the chef/owner of several restaurants globally, including Momofuku Ko in New York City, which was ranked number 58 on the World's 50 Best Restaurants list. | momofuku.com

Roy Choi is the co-chef/co-owner of LocoL in Los Angeles and Oakland, California. LocoL was named Restaurant of the Year by Pulitzer Prize–winning restaurant critic Jonathan Gold of the *Los Angeles Times*. | welocol.com

***Amanda Cohen** is the chef/owner of Dirt Candy in New York City, the first vegetarian restaurant in 17 years to receive a two-star review from the *New York Times*, and of Thyme at Newark Airport in New Jersey. She was the first vegetarian chef to compete on *Iron Chef America* and her cookbook, *Dirt Candy*, is the first graphic novel cookbook to be published in North America. | dirtcandy.com

Tom Colicchio is the chef/owner of multiple restaurants including Craft and Riverpark in New York City. He was named 2010 Outstanding Chef by the James Beard Foundation. | craftedhospitality.com

***Kyle Connaughton** is the chef/owner (with his wife, farmer Katina Connaughton) of Single Thread in Healdsburg, California, which was the first restaurant in history to earn a four-star rating from the *San Francisco Chronicle* upon its opening. | singlethreadfarms.com

Dominique Crenn is the chef/owner of the Michelin two-star Atelier Crenn in San Francisco, which was named number 83 on the 2017 World's Best Restaurants list, which also named her the 2016 World's Best Female Chef. Crenn was named a finalist for 2017 Best Chef: West by the James Beard Foundation. | ateliercrenn.com

***Derrick Davenport** was named the Armed Forces Chef of the Year in 2013, and as senior chief and executive chef of the U.S. Navy, he went on to be named Chef of the Year by the American Culinary Federation in 2015.

***Vinny Dotolo** is the co-chef/co-owner (with Jon Shook) of Animal (which was nominated for 2009 Best New Restaurant by the James Beard Foundation), Son of a Gun, and Jon & Vinny's, and co-owner of Petit Trois, Trois Familia, and Trois Mec, all in Los Angeles. The duo was named 2016 Best Chef: West by the James Beard Foundation. | animalrestaurant.com | jonandvinnys.com

Alain Ducasse is the chef/owner of Alain Ducasse au Plaza Athénée in Paris, which was named the number 13 World's Best Restaurant in 2017. | alain-ducasse.com

***Curtis Duffy** is the chef/owner of Grace in Chicago, which was awarded three Michelin stars and four stars from the *Chicago Tribune*, which declared it the city's number-two best restaurant in 2017. Duffy was named 2016 Best Chef: Great Lakes by the James Beard Foundation. His life is the subject of the documentary film *For Grace* by Kevin Pang and Mark Helenowski. | grace-restaurant.com

Jeremy Faber is the proprietor of Foraged & Found Edibles in Seattle. | foragedandfoundedibles.com

*__Brad Farmerie__ is the executive chef/owner of Saxon + Parole in New York City and Moscow. He served as chef/partner, with the design team AvroKO, of Public, which won two James Beard Foundation awards and a Michelin star. After winning a 2009 *Iron Chef America* battle, Farmerie created the inflight menu for JetBlue's Mint experience. | saxonandparole.com

*__Phillip Foss__ is the chef/owner of EL Ideas in Chicago, which he self-describes as "the most unlikely of Michelin-starred restaurants" yet indeed holds a Michelin star. The *Chicago Tribune* awarded Foss's "mad-genius cooking" three stars, and Eater.com declared "No chef in America cooks dinner quite like Phillip Foss." | elideas.com

*__D'Anthony Foster__ is the pastry chef of the Point in Saranac Lake, New York. He previously held positions at the Relais & Chateaux–affiliated properties Hotel Fauchere in Milford, Pennsylvania, and the Inn at Dos Brisos in Texas. | thepointsaranac.com

*__Jeremy Fox__ is the executive chef at Rustic Canyon in Santa Monica, California. He was previously the executive chef at Ubuntu in Napa, where he earned a Michelin star. He has been nominated several times as Best Chef: West by the James Beard Foundation, including in 2017, and is the author of *On Vegetables*. | rusticcanyonwinebar.com

*__Meg Galus__ is the executive pastry chef of Boka, Momotaro, and Swift & Sons in Chicago. She was a finalist for the 2016 Outstanding Pastry Chef award from the James Beard Foundation. | bokachicago.com

*__Ruben Garcia__ is the culinary creative director of ThinkFoodGroup, based in Washington, D.C., where he serves on chef José Andrés's team for creative projects including television programming and cookbooks. He previously spent five years working with Ferran and Albert Adrià at elBulli in Spain. | thinkfoodgroup.com

Gunnar Gíslason is the chef of Agern in New York City, which earned three stars from the *New York Times*. He is the author of *North: The New Nordic Cuisine of Iceland*. | agernrestaurant.com

*__Spike Gjerde__ is a local-food advocate and chef/owner of Woodberry Kitchen (named one of the Best Restaurants in America via the Eater.com 38, 2015–2017), Artifact Coffee, Bird in Hand, and Parts & Labor, all in Baltimore, and A Rake's Progress in Washington, D.C. In 2015, Gjerde became the first and only Baltimore chef to be named Best Chef: Mid-Atlantic by the James Beard Foundation. | woodberrykitchen.com

*__Della Gossett__ is the pastry chef of Spago in Beverly Hills. She previously spent a decade as pastry chef of Chicago's Charlie Trotter's, and also completed stints in Spain with Ferran Adria and master confectioner Ramon Morato. After earning a B.A. in arts education and painting at the University of Illinois/Champaign-Urbana, she worked in pastry for six years at Trio in Evanston, Illinois. | wolfgangpuck.com/dining/spago

Sarah Grueneberg is the chef/owner of Monteverde in Chicago. She was named 2017 Best Chef: Great Lakes by the James Beard Foundation, after her first nomination. | chefsarahjayne.com | monteverdechicago.com

Will Guidara is the partner (of chef Daniel Humm) in Eleven Madison Park in New York City, which was ranked number 1 on the 2017 World's 50 Best Restaurants list. | elevenmadisonpark.com

*__Karen Hatfield__ is the pastry chef and co-owner (with Quinn Hatfield) of Odys + Penelope and Sycamore Kitchen in Los Angeles. She honed her skills under Sherry Yard at Spago, where she also met her husband, Quinn, and at Café Boulud, Gramercy Tavern, and Jean Georges. The couple's previous restaurant, Hatfield's, was named a best new restaurant by *Bon Appétit* and won a perfect four-star review from the *Los Angeles* magazine. | odysandpenelope.com

*__Quinn Hatfield__ is the chef and co-owner (with Karen Hatfield) of Odys + Penelope and Sycamore Kitchen in Los Angeles. He previously cooked at Spago, where he also met his wife, Karen, and in New York at Bouley, Jean Georges, and Union Pacific. The couple's previous restaurant, Hatfield's, was named one of the top 10 restaurants of the decade by the Los Angeles Zagat Survey. | odysandpenelope.com

Brooks Headley is the chef/owner of Superiority Burger in New York City, which was named a semifinalist for 2016 Best New Restaurant by the James Beard Foundation. While the executive pastry chef at Del Posto, he was named 2013 Outstanding Pastry Chef by the James Beard Foundation. | superiorityburger.com

John Hong is the chef de cuisine of the Restaurant at Meadowood in St. Helena, California, which was ranked number 84 on the 2017 World's 50 Best Restaurants list. | therestaurantatmeadowood.com

*__Katianna Hong__ is the executive chef of the Charter Oak in St. Helena, California, and was previously chef de cuisine at the Restaurant at Meadowood in St. Helena, California—the only female chef de cuisine of a U.S. Michelin three-star restaurant. | thecharteroak.com

Chad Houser is the chef of Café Momentum in Dallas. | cafemomentum.org

Daniel Humm is the executive chef/partner (with Will Guidara) of Eleven Madison Park in New York City, which was ranked number 1 on the 2017 World's 50 Best Restaurants list. | elevenmadisonpark.com

*__Trevin Hutchins__ is the drink designer and beverage manager at Tempo Dulu at the Danforth Inn in Portland, Maine, and of Natalie's at the

Camden Harbour Inn in Camden, Maine. | tempodulu.restaurant | camdenharbourinn.com

*__Stephanie Izard__ is the chef/owner of Girl & the Goat in Chicago. She was the first female winner of *Top Chef* (season 4), and was named the 2013 Best Chef: Great Lakes by the James Beard Foundation. | girlandthegoat.com

Kate Jacoby is the pastry chef and co-owner (with Rich Landau) of Vedge and V Street in Philadelphia. | vedgerestaurant.com | vstreetfood.com

*__Scot Jones__ is the executive chef of Crossroads in Los Angeles. He was previously the executive chef at Vegiterranean in Akron, Ohio, a vegan restaurant concept conceived by musician Chrissie Hynde (The Pretenders) and Chef Tal Ronnen. | crossroadskitchen.com

*__Cameron Karger__ is the general manager of the Point resort in Saranac Lake, New York. He previously served as a manager of the Inn at Dos Brisas in Washington, Texas, where he launched an in-house cheesemaking program, and assistant winemaker for Mark Aubert. | thepointsaranac.com

*__Gavin Kaysen__ is the executive chef/owner of Spoon and Stable in Minneapolis and Bellecour in Wayzata, Minneapolis. He previously served as executive chef and director of culinary operations at Café Boulud in New York City, Palm Beach, and Toronto. | spoonandstable.com

Thomas Keller is the chef/owner of the French Laundry in Yountville, California (which was named number 1 on the World's 50 Best list in 2003 and 2004), and Per Se in New York City. He was named 1997 Outstanding Chef by the James Beard Foundation. | thomaskeller.com

*__Matthew Kenney__ is the chef/owner of Plant Food and Wine in Los Angeles. | matthewkenneycuisine.com

*__James Kent__ was the executive chef at Eleven Madison Park who was named opening chef de cuisine of the NoMad in New York City, which was named to the World's 50 Best Restaurants list during his tenure. | elevenmadisonpark.com | thenomadhotel.com/dining

Beverly Kim and **Johnny Clark** are co-chefs/owners of Parachute in Chicago. They were named finalists for 2017 Best Chef: Great Lakes by the James Beard Foundation. | parachuterestaurant.com

David Kinch is the chef/owner of Manresa in Los Gatos, California. He was named a finalist for 2017 Outstanding Chef by the James Beard Foundation. | manresarestaurant.com

Eric Klein is the executive chef, vice president, and partner at Wolfgang Puck Catering based in Beverly Hills, and the former chef of Spago in Las Vegas. | summer.wolfgangpuck.com

Jessica Koslow is the chef/owner of Sqirl in Los Angeles, and the author of *Everything I Want to Eat: Sqirl and the New California Cooking.* | sqirlla.com

Christopher Kostow is the executive chef of the Restaurant at Meadowood in St. Helena, California, which was ranked number 84 on the 2017 World's 50 Best Restaurants list. He was named 2013 Best Chef: West by the James Beard Foundation, which also named him a finalist for 2017 Outstanding Chef. | therestaurantatmeadowood.com

*__Gabriel Kreuther__ is the chef/owner of Gabriel Kreuther in New York City, which earned three stars from the *New York Times* and was named one of the 10 best new restaurants in the world for 2016 by the *Robb Report* and one of America's 10 Best Restaurants by *The Daily Meal.* He was named the 2009 Best Chef: New York by the James Beard Foundation while executive chef of the Modern at the Museum of Modern Art. | gknyc.com

*__Chris Kurth__ is the farmer/owner of Siena Farms in Sudbury and Concord, Massachusetts, which provides more than 100 varieties of vegetables to his wife chef Ana Sortun's Cambridge restaurants and beyond. | sienafarms.com

Jeong Kwan is a Zen Buddhist nun based in the Chunjinam Hermitage at the Baegyangsa temple in South Korea, and was featured on the first episode of season 3 of the Netflix series *Chef's Table.*

Rich Landau is the chef and co-owner (with Kate Jacoby) of Vedge and V Street in Philadelphia. He was named a finalist several times for Best Chef: Mid-Atlantic by the James Beard Foundation, including in 2017. | vedgerestaurant.com | vstreetfood.com

*__Jessica Largey__ is the chef/partner at Simone in Los Angeles. She was previously chef at Manresa in Los Gatos, California, which was named number 90 on the World's Best Restaurants list in 2017.

Soren Ledet is the restaurant manager and co-owner (with chef Rasmus Kofoed) of Geranium in Copenhagen. | geranium.dk

Corey Lee is the chef/owner of Benu and Monsieur Benjamin, and chef/partner of In Situ in San Francisco. Benu was ranked number 67 on the World's 50 Best Restaurants list. Lee was named 2017 Best Chef: West by the James Beard Foundation. | benusf.com

Ludo Lefebvre is the chef/partner (with Vinny Dotolo and Jon Shook) in Trois Mec and Petit Trois in Los Angeles, and has been described by the *Los Angeles Times'* Jonathan Gold as "probably the buzziest chef in a city filled with buzzy chefs, the telegenic inventor of the pop-up restaurant." | troismec.com | petittrois.com

*__Loic Leperlier__ is the executive chef of the Point in Saranac Lake, New York. He previously served as chef de cuisine at the Relais & Chateaux–affiliated property Hotel Fauchere in Milford, Pennsylvania. | thepointsaranac.com

*__Eddy Leroux__ is the chef de cuisine of Daniel in New York City. He is the coauthor with Tama Matsuoka Wong of *Foraged Flavor: Finding Fabulous Ingredients in Your Backyard or Farmers' Market.* | danielnyc.com

*__David Levi__ is the chef/owner of Vinland in Portland, Maine, the self-described "first restaurant in the United States to serve 100 percent local, organic food," which London's *Financial Times* characterized as "a serious star." | vinland.me

*__Mark Levy__ is the executive chef of Magdalena at the Ivy Hotel in Baltimore, and previously held the same position at the Point in Saranac Lake, New York. | theivybaltimore.com | magdalenarestaurant.com

*__Anita Lo__ is the founding chef/owner of Annisa in New York City, which earned three stars from the *New York Times* before closing in 2017. She was named a finalist multiple times for Best Chef: New York City by the James Beard Foundation, including in 2017.

*__Michael Lomonaco__ is the chef/owner of Porter House Bar and Grill in New York City. | porterhousenyc.com

*__Chris Long__ is the co-chef (with Shelby Stevens) of Natalie's at the Camden Harbour Inn in Camden, Maine. An alum of the kitchen at Chicago's Charlie Trotter's, he was named the 2013 Maine Lobster Chef of the Year. | camdenharbourinn.com | nataliesrestaurant.com

*__Emily Luchetti__ is the pastry chef of the Cavalier, Marlowe, and Park Tavern in San Francisco. She was named 2004 Outstanding Pastry Chef by the James Beard Foundation, which elected her chairman of its board of trustees in 2012. | emilyluchetti.com | thecavaliersf.com | marlowesf.com

Barbara Lynch is the chef/owner of Menton in Boston. She was named 2003 Best Chef: Northeast and 2014 Outstanding Restaurateur by the James Beard Foundation, only the second woman to be so honored with the latter. | barbaralynch.com

*__Taiesha Martin__ is the executive pastry chef of Glenmere Mansion in Chester, New York. An alumna of Johnson & Wales, she previously worked in the kitchens of Aureole, David Burke Townhouse, Fleur de Sel, and Toqueville, and cooked at the James Beard House in 2014. | glenmeremansion.com

Ignacio Mattos is the chef/owner of Estela in New York City, which was ranked number 44 on the 2016 World's 50 Best Restaurants list. Mattos was named a finalist for 2017 Best Chef: New York City by the James Beard Foundation. | estelanyc.com

Jacques Maximin is the long-time chef of Le Chantecler at the Hotel Negresco in Nice, France, and a restaurant consultant. | jacquesmaximin.com

Claus Meyer is the founding owner of Noma in Copenhagen, which was number 1 on the World's 50 Best Restaurants list in 2010, 2011, 2012, and 2014. | meyersmad.dk/om-meyers/claus-meyer

Danny Meyer is the owner of Shake Shack and the Union Square Hospitality Group, headquartered in New York City. | shakeshack.com | ushgnyc.com

*__Mark Miller__ is the founding chef/owner of Coyote Café in Santa Fe, where he was named 1993 Best Chef: Southwest by the James Beard Foundation. | coyotecafe.com

*__Isa Chandra Moskowitz__ is the chef/owner of Modern Love in Omaha and Brooklyn, whose bestselling books include *Veganomicon* and *Isa Does It.* | modernloveomaha.com | modernlovebrooklyn.com

*__Carrie Nahabedian__ is the chef/owner of Naha and Brindille in Chicago. She was named 2008 Best Chef: Great Lakes and a semifinalist for 2017 Outstanding Chef by the James Beard Foundation. | naha-chicago.com | brindille-chicago.com

Dahlia Narvaez is the executive pastry chef of Osteria Mozza and Pizzeria Mozza in Los Angeles. She was named 2016 Outstanding Pastry Chef by the James Beard Foundation. | osteriamozza.com | pizzeriamozza.com

Michel Nischan is the founder of Wholesome Wave, and was named 2015 Humanitarian of the Year by the James Beard Foundation. | chefnischan.com

*__Patrick O'Connell__ is the chef/owner of the Inn at Little Washington in Washington, Virginia. He was named 2001 Outstanding Chef by the James Beard Foundation, which named the Inn at Little Washington the 1993 Outstanding Restaurant. He is the author of *The Inn at Little Washington Cookbook, Patrick O'Connell's Refined American Cuisine*, and *The Inn at Little Washington: A Magnificent Obsession.* | theinnatlittlewashington.com

*__Ghaya Oliveira__ is the executive pastry chef of Daniel in New York City. She was named 2017 Outstanding Pastry Chef by the James Beard Foundation. A native of Tunisia, she trained as a ballerina and is a former stock trader. | danielnyc.com

Paul Pairet is the chef/owner of Ultraviolet in Shanghai. It was named number 41 on the 2017 World's 50 Best Restaurants list. | paulpairet.com

*__Andres Padilla__ is the chef de cuisine of Topolobampo in Chicago, which was named the 2017 Outstanding Restaurant by the James Beard Foundation. | rickbayless.com/restaurants/topolobampo

Alain Passard is the chef/owner of Arpège in Paris, which is number 12 on the 2017 World's 50 Best Restaurants list and has held three Michelin stars for more than two decades. | alain-passard.com

Daniel Patterson is the founding chef of Coi in San Francisco and LocoL in Oakland and Los Angeles. He was named 2014 Best Chef: California by the James Beard Foundation, and

LocoL was named 2017 Restaurant of the Year by Pulitzer Prize–winning restaurant critic Jonathan Gold of the *Los Angeles Times*. | dpgrp.co

*__Jacques Pépin__ is the author of many culinary books, including *Heart and Soul in the Kitchen*, *New Complete Techniques*, and *A Grandfather's Lessons: In the Kitchen with Shorey*. He is the host of *Heart and Soul* on KQED/PBS. | ww2.kqed.org/jpepinheart

Janice Provost is the executive chef/owner of Parigi and the cofounder of Café Momentum in Dallas. | parigidallas.com

Wolfgang Puck is the chef/owner of Spago in Beverly Hills. He was named the 1991 and 1998 Outstanding Chef by the James Beard Foundation. | wolfgangpuck.com

*__Joe Raffa__ is the executive chef of José Andrés's ThinkFoodGroup, based in Washington, D.C. | thinkfoodgroup.com

René Redzepi is the chef/owner of Noma in Copenhagen, which was ranked number 1 on the World's 50 Best Restaurants list in 2010, 2011, 2012, and 2014. | noma.dk

*__Eric Ripert__ is the chef/owner of Le Bernardin in New York City, which was number 17 on the 2017 World's 50 Best Restaurants list. He was named 2003 Outstanding Chef by the James Beard Foundation, which also named Le Bernardin the 1998 Outstanding Restaurant. | le-bernardin.com

Joël Robuchon is the chef/owner of several acclaimed restaurants globally, and was named Chef of the Century by the *Gault-Millau* guide in 1989. | joel-robuchon.com

Joan Roca is a chef/owner of El Celler de Can Roca in Catalonia, Spain, which was twice ranked number 1 on the World's 50 Best list, which ranked it number 3 in 2017. | cellarcanroca.com

*__Tal Ronnen__ is the founder and chef/owner of Crossroads in Los Angeles. He is the author of the *New York Times* bestseller *The Conscious Cook* as well as the *Crossroads* cookbook. | crossroadskitchen.com

*__Marcus Samuelsson__ is the chef/owner of Red Rooster, Ginny's Supper Club, and Streetbird in Harlem, New York, and other restaurants in Sweden, Finland, Norway, Bermuda, and London. He was named 1999 Rising Star Chef and 2003 Best Chef: New York City by the James Beard Foundation, which also honored his books *The Soul of a New Cuisine* and *Yes, Chef*. | marcussamuelsson.com

*__Damian Sansonetti__ is the chef/owner of Piccolo in Portland, Maine, where his wife, Ilma Lopez, is the pastry chef. Previously, he was the chef de cuisine at Daniel Boulud's Bar Boulud in New York City. | piccolomaine.com

*__Audrey Saunders__ is a legendary mixologist and the owner of the Pegu Club in New York City, whose opening has been credited with kick-starting the cocktail renaissance. | peguclub.com

*__Michael Scelfo__ is the chef/owner of Alden & Harlow, Waypoint, and Longfellow in Cambridge, Massachusetts. Scelfo was named 2017 Best Chef/General Excellence by *Boston* magazine, which also named Alden & Harlow Boston's Best Restaurant of 2016 in the category of General Excellence. | aldenharlow.com

*__Lior Lev Sercarz__ is the owner of La Boîte in New York City. He was previously part of the kitchen team as sous chef at Daniel Boulud's Restaurant Daniel. Sercarz is the author of *The Art of Blending* and *The Spice Companion*. | laboiteny.com

Alon Shaya is the chef/owner of Domenica and Shaya in New Orleans. He was named the 2015 Best Chef: South by the James Beard Foundation. | shayarestaurant.com

*__Jon Shook__ is the co-chef/co-owner (with Vinny Dotolo) of Animal (which was nominated for 2009 Best New Restaurant by the James Beard Foundation), Son of a Gun, Jon & Vinny's, Petit Trois, Trois Familia, and Trois Mec in Los Angeles. The duo was named 2016 Best Chef: West by the James Beard Foundation.| animalrestaurant.com | jonandvinnys.com

*__Nancy Silverton__ is the chef/owner of Osteria Mozza, Pizzeria Mozza, and Chi Spacca in Los Angeles. She was named 1991 Outstanding Pastry Chef and 2014 Outstanding Chef by the James Beard Foundation, which named her previous restaurant, Campanile, 2001 Outstanding Restaurant. Her cookbooks include the *Mozza Cookbook*, *Mozza at Home*, and *Nancy Silverton's Breads from the La Brea Bakery*. | la.pizzeriamozza.com | osteriamozza.com

*__Joshua Skenes__ is the chef/co-owner (with wine director Mark Bright) of Saison in San Francisco, which was named number 37 on the 2017 World's 50 Best Restaurants list. He has been named a semifinalist multiple times for Best Chef: West by the James Beard Foundation. A Relais & Chateaux property, Saison holds four stars from the *San Francisco Chronicle*. | saisonsf.com

Michael Solomonov is the chef/owner of Zahav in Philadelphia. He was named 2017 Outstanding Chef by the James Beard Foundation, which also named his 2016 cookbook, *Zahav*, Cookbook of the Year. | zahavrestaurant.com

André Soltner is the founding chef/owner of Lutèce in New York City, which held four stars from the *New York Times* for decades. He received the 1993 Lifetime Achievement Award from the James Beard Foundation.

*__Annie Somerville__ is the executive chef of Greens in San Francisco, where she trained under founding chef Deborah Madison before being named to her position in 1985. She is also author of the books *Everyday Greens* and *Field of Greens*. | greensrestaurant.com

*__Ana Sortun__ is the chef/owner of Oleana, Sarma, and Sofra in Cambridge, Massachusetts. She was named the 2005 Best Chef: Northeast by the James Beard Foundation, which has also named her a semifinalist for its Outstanding Chef award multiple times. | oleanarestaurant.com

*__Susan Spicer__ is the chef/owner of Bayona and Mondo in New Orleans. She was named the 1993 Best Chef: Southeast by the James Beard Foundation. | bayona.com | mondoneworleans.com

*__Shelby Stevens__ is the co-chef (with Chris Long) of Natalie's at the Camden Harbour Inn in Camden, Maine. She is an alum of the kitchens at San Francisco's Coi and Manhattan's Restaurant Daniel. | camdenharbourinn.com | nataliesrestaurant.com

*__Vikram Sunderam__ is the executive chef of two Rasika restaurants and the Indian street-food restaurant Bindaas in Washington, D.C. He was named the 2014 Best Chef: Mid-Atlantic by the James Beard Foundation. Sunderam is the coauthor of the 2017 cookbook *Rasika: Flavors of India*. | rasikarestaurant.com

*__Travis Swikard__ is the executive chef of Boulud Sud in New York City. He started with Daniel Boulud's Dinex Group as part of Gavin Kaysen's team at Café Boulud before being named executive sous chef at Boulud Sud. | bouludsud.com

*__Bill Telepan__ is the chef of Oceana in New York City, and also serves as executive chef of Wellness in the Schools based in New York City. | oceanarestaurant.com | wellnessintheschools.org

*__Gunnar Thompson__ is the executive chef of Glenmere Mansion in Chester, New York. He formerly served as executive chef of Erna's Elderberry House at Chateau de Sureau in Yosemite, California, where he was designated a Relais & Chateaux "Grand Chef." He previously cooked at La Pyramide in Vienne, France. | glenmeremansion.com

*__Hasty Torres__ is a chocolatier who created and owned Madame Chocolat in Beverly Hills. She teamed up with Jacques Torres to serve as opening chef of his 8,000-square-foot chocolate factory and boutique in SoHo at Jacques Torres Chocolate, based in New York City. | mrchocolate.com

*__Jacques Torres__ is the chocolatier/owner of Jacques Torres Chocolate, based in New York City. He won the 1994 Outstanding Pastry Chef award from the James Beard Foundation, in recognition of his term as executive pastry chef at Le Cirque. In 2016, he was named a French Chevalier of the Legion of Honor, the highest decoration in France, at the French Consulate in New York City. | mrchocolate.com

Christina Tosi is the pastry chef/owner of Momofuku Milk Bar in New York City. She won the 2012 Rising Star Chef and the 2015 Outstanding Pastry Chef awards from the James Beard Foundation. | milkbarstore.com

*__Michael Tusk__ is the chef/owner of Quince in San Francisco, a Relais & Chateaux property that holds four stars from the *San Francisco Chronicle*. He was named the 2011 Best Chef: Pacific by the James Beard Foundation, which also named Quince a 2017 finalist for Outstanding Restaurant. | quincerestaurant.com

*__Norman Van Aken__ is the chef/owner of 1921 by Norman Van Aken in Florida. He was named the 1997 Best Chef: Southeast by the James Beard Foundation. | 1921nva.com

*__Michael Voltaggio__ is the chef/owner of ink, ink.sack, and ink.well in Los Angeles. He won season 6 of TV's *Top Chef*, and is the coauthor (with chef Bryan Voltaggio) of the cookbook *VOLT ink: Recipes, Stories, Brothers*. | mvink.com

Melissa Weller is the baker/partner in Sadelle's in New York City. She was named a 2016 semifinalist for Outstanding Baker by the James Beard Foundation. | sadelles.com

William Werner is the pastry chef/owner of Craftsman and Wolves in San Francisco. He was named a finalist for 2016 Outstanding Pastry Chef by the James Beard Foundation. | craftsman-wolves.com

Blaine Wetzel is the head chef of Willows Inn on Lummi Island, Washington, where he was named 2015 Best Chef: Northwest by the James Beard Foundation. Wetzel is the author of *Sea and Smoke: Flavors from the Untamed Pacific Northwest*. | willows-inn.com

*__Lee Wolen__ is the chef of Boka in Chicago, which earned four stars from *Chicago* magazine, three stars from the *Chicago Tribune*, and a Michelin star. He was named 2014 Chef of the Year by the *Chicago Tribune* and Eater.com, and has been nominated multiple times for Best Chef: Great Lakes by the James Beard Foundation, including in 2016 and 2017. | bokachicago.com

Sherry Yard serves as chief operating officer of Tuck Hospitality Group—Restaurant Division of iPic Entertainment, where she leads culinary innovation for restaurants including the Tuck Room Tavern in New York City. | thehelmsbakery.com

ACKNOWLEDGMENTS

Gratitude opens the door to . . . the power, the wisdom, the creativity of the universe.

—DEEPAK CHOPRA

Our hearts overflow with gratitude to some of the most extraordinary people we know across the universe who contributed their power, their wisdom, and their creativity to the creation of this book, including:

- The "dream team" at Little, Brown and Hachette Book Group for their efforts on behalf of *Kitchen Creativity*, especially my very creative, food-loving executive editor, **Mike Szczerban** (for such wide-ranging conversations, for coming up with just the right words at just the right moments, and for riding into town on his white horse at the 11th hour to save the day more than once!), as well as senior production editor **Ben Allen**; Little, Brown publisher **Reagan Arthur**; marketing director **Pamela Brown**, proofreader **Robin Charney**, senior production manager **Lisa Ferris**, editorial assistant **Nicky Guerreiro**, cover designer **Lucy Kim**, publicity manager **Zea Moscone**, Hachette CEO **Michael Pietsch**, copyeditor **Deri Reed**, proofreader **Audrey Sussman**, and marketing manager **Lauren Velasquez**. Thanks, too, to **Ashley Prine**, creative director of Tandem Books, for her ebullient interior design.

- All of the chefs and other experts you've met in these pages whose work has inspired us, and especially those who made time to speak with us personally and to be photographed—and/or who opened their beautiful restaurants and/or homes to us to photograph their exquisite dishes and drinks and lives, including: José Andrés and everyone at ThinkFoodGroup; Rob Arthur, Mark Levy, Emmanuel West, and everyone at Magdalena and the Ivy Hotel; Damon Baehrel; Dan Barber, Philippe Gouze, Irene Hamburger, and everyone at Blue Hill and Blue Hill at Stone Barns (especially for the honor of inviting us to speak about our work over family meal); Rick and Deann Bayless and everyone at Frontera Grill, Topolobampo, and Lena Brava; Daniel Boulud, Carly DeFilippo, and everyone at the Dinex Group; Chad Brauze, Scott Cioe, Greg Mosko, and everyone at Bevy and Nomi at the Park Hyatt; Raymond Brunyanszki and everyone at the Camden Harbour Inn and the Danforth Inn; Joanne Chang and Flour Bakery; Dan DeSimone, Alan Stenberg, and everyone at Glenmere Mansion; Curtis Duffy, Michael Muser and everyone at Grace; the James Beard House; Cameron Karger, Joe Maiurano, Jake Kipping, and everyone at the Point; Thomas Keller and everyone at the Thomas Keller Restaurant Group; Christopher Kostow, Martina Kostow, Katianna Hong, and everyone at the Charter Oak; Gabriel Kreuther, Eben Dorros, Joe Anthony, Marc Aumont, and everyone at Gabriel Kreuther; Corey Lee, Jasmine Peterlin, and In Situ; Danny Meyer, Michael Anthony, and everyone at the Union Square Hospitality Group and Shake Shack; Patrick O'Connell, Rachel Hayden, and everyone at the Inn at Little Washington; Michael Scelfo and everyone at Alden and Harlow; Michael Tusk and everyone at Quince; and members of other chefs' teams who eased every step of the way, including Laiko Bahrs, Heather Freeman, Kristine Keefer, Chloe Mata, and Martha Tiller.

- Our family, friends, colleagues, and even strangers, for their kindnesses, large and small—including Rosario Acquista, Patricia Andrés, Carrie Bachman, Melanie Baker, Melissa Balmain, Steve Beckta, Bill Bratton, Priscilla Bright, Brian Burry, Susan Bulkeley Butler, Heather Carlucci, Belinda Chang, Howard Childs, Stephen Co, Fran Costigan, Mihaly Csikszentmihalyi, Julia D'Amico, Blake Davis, Julia Davis, Susan Davis, Caroline Day, Laura Day, Samson Day, Sheri de Borchgrave, Susan Dey, Jessica Dibb, Deborah Domanski, Jill Eikenberry, Georgette Farkas, Bill FitzPatrick, Ashley Garrett, Michael Gelb, Richard Giles of Lucky Dog Farm, Sarah Girard, Diane Goldner, Gael Greene, Howard Greynolds, Glenn Hall, Glen Hansard, Sarah Hirshan, Russ Hudson, Marketa Irglova, Alan Jones, Erica Kane, Scott Barry Kaufman, BFF extraordinaire Rikki Klieman, Lisa Klinck-Shea, Matt Lambert of the Musket Room, Barbara Lazaroff, Dongmei Liu, Leonard Lopate, Tess Masters, Karen McCoy, Yana Morgan, Jeanne Nicastri, Jody Oberfelder, Heidi Olson, Kelley Olson, Scott Olson, Robert Peng, Cynthia Penney, Jeff Penney, Emilie Perrier, Joy Pierson, Bart Potenza, Steven Pressfield, Mike Randleman, Judith Regan, Jasper Riehm, Juergen Riehm, Lara Riggio, Stuart Rockefeller, Cheryl Rogowski, Troy Rohne, Anthony Rudolf, Amy Scherber, Stephen Schiff, Beth Shapiro, S&SO Produce Farms, Dana Sachs Stoddard, Katherine Sieh Takata, Mike Tucker, Jane Umanoff, Mark Varsano (of our favorite chocolatier in New York City, Varsano's, which also makes a *great* caramel apple!), Valerie Vigoda, Earl Weiner, Steve Wilson, and Karen's supportive friends and colleagues through the Council of 100 at Northwestern University, Les Dames d'Escoffier, and the New York Women's Forum and International Women's Forum.

Say the word and you'll be free . . .
Have you heard the word is LOVE?

—**JOHN LENNON AND PAUL MCCARTNEY,** "The Word"

- For one of the most inspirational afternoons of our lives, let alone of our study of creativity: librarian DJ Hoek at Northwestern University, which holds one of the world's most important collections of Beatles manuscripts. Karen, a lifelong Beatles fan, knew that even the "World's Greatest Rock 'n' Roll Band" got its start as a cover band, performing other musicians' work. The privilege of holding in our hands Paul McCartney's and John Lennon's actual handwritten lyrics, jotted in ink or markers on pages of notebook paper or the backs of envelopes, prompted an unforgettable moment of clarity: **Creativity stems from the inspirations and imaginations and initiatives of *real people in the midst of living everyday lives.***

- And, finally, each other—for taking the leap as newlyweds to sign our first joint book contract on August 25, 1992, in the hope that something good might come of it, and for being the other's favorite co-creator and collaborator over the past 25 years...and still.

LOVE,
Karen Page and **Andrew Dornenburg**
August 2017

The greater your capacity for sincere appreciation, the deeper the connection to your heart, where intuition and unlimited inspiration and possibilities reside.

—**HEARTMATH INSTITUTE**

ABOUT THE AUTHOR AND THE PHOTOGRAPHER

Author **Karen Page** and photographer **Andrew Dornenburg** have been described as "perhaps the most influential and important of all food writers working today" (KLAV Radio), having created "many definitive guides" (*Wall Street Journal*) and "some of the most important books on cooking" (*Good Food*, KCRW/NPR), "making their mark with books that bring us inside the craft and life of America's chefs and their restaurants" (*The Splendid Table*, NPR).

Drawing on a shared passion for food, as well as previous careers as a creativity and strategy consultant to Fortune 500 companies (Page) and as a restaurant chef (Dornenburg), the duo's thought-provoking books are often fueled by creative pursuits outside the kitchen, from Harvard Business School's famed creativity course to a dance company's advisory board. Their books have been translated into multiple languages and received citations as sources of information and/or inspiration in numerous scholarly, fiction, nonfiction, and other creative works globally.

Former *Washington Post* wine columnists who have run six marathons between them, the married couple lives in New York City.

@KarenAndAndrew | Twitter
/KarenAndAndrew | Facebook
@theflavorbible | Instagram
KarenAndAndrew.com